THE PROPHECIES OF

DANIEL AND THE REVELATION

THE PROPHECIES OF

DANIEL

and the

REVELATION

BY

URIAH SMITH

REVISED AND NEWLY ILLUSTRATED

PACIFIC PRESS PUBLISHING ASSOCIATION

MOUNTAIN VIEW, CALIFORNIA

PORTLAND, OREGON CRISTOBAL, CANAL ZONE OMAHA, NEBRASKA

BROOKFIELD, ILLINOIS (FOREIGN LANGUAGE PUBLICATIONS)

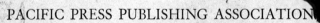

First printing, 1944, 6,000
Second printing, 1945, 9,000
Third printing, 1945, 10,000
Fourth printing, 1946, 5,000

PACIFIC PRESS PUB. ASSN.
PRINTED IN U·S·A

FOREWORD

IN OFFERING this book to the public, the publishers believe they are doing a great service to its readers.

The volume is devoted largely to tracing the story of God's marvelous dealing with nations and with notable men in fulfillment of the great prophecies of the Bible in the past, but more particularly to the unrolling of the prophetic scroll as seen in the stirring events of the throbbing present, and of those impending in the immediate and ominous future. Such events are of the greatest personal significance to every man and woman.

No one can afford to live in a time like ours without acquainting himself with the vital issues it has pleased God to open to our understanding in this fast moving age. Such issues are freighted with eternal consequences to every soul.

The author of this book lived and wrote a generation ago, and in the literary and polemic style of those times. His interpretation of prophecy, however, and the doctrines of truth he established through intensive study of the Scriptures, have borne the test of time and of diligent scrutiny by Bible students. Indeed, they have borne the test so well that they are the more worthy of being perpetuated in a revised edition, and in the new setting of our own times, which it is our great pleasure to offer in this present attractive form.

No effort has been spared by the editors to simplify and clarify the presentation of truth in the fluent and appealing diction of the writer, to verify all historical and exegetical sources drawn upon by the author, and in notable instances to fortify the teaching by new evidence not available at the time of the original writing. They have sought also to bring to bear upon prophetic interpretation the additional weight of significance so obviously discernible in political, social, and religious developments pressing upon our attention in these culminating days of the gospel era.

Thoughtful and open-minded consideration of these vital themes by every candid reader is earnestly invited.

THE PUBLISHERS

T. K. MARTIN, ARTIST

THE LIGHTED WAY

Like beacon lights, the prophecies of the Holy Word illuminate the rugged path to the heavenly land.

CONTENTS

THE PROPHECIES OF DANIEL

THE PROPHECIES OF THE REVELATION

REFERENCES

LIST OF ILLUSTRATIONS

DANIEL

THE REVELATION

THE LIGHT OF GOD'S WORD

O'er all the moral world, where, otherwise,
No light would come, or through its midnight gloom
No cheering ray appear, to dissipate
The darkness, God has set a guiding star—
A luminary bright—whose rays divine
Should pierce the night—the deep'ning shades dispel,
Which o'er the earth in sullen silence brood.
Nay, more, a ray of God's own brightness, sent
Direct to man from off His radiant throne;
That those who gladly should the light receive,
And follow where it led, should here enjoy
A glorious foretaste of the bliss of Heaven.

It is God's Holy Word, immutable,
Through life's bewildering maze alone can guide
The wandering traveler to eternal rest.
Without it, man were lost—lost in the deep,
Dark labyrinth of dread uncertainty—
Where doubts distract, and fearful thoughts arise—
With nought his steps to lead, save the dim lamp
Of human reason, whose misguiding flame
Would serve to make the gloom still more profound,
The darkness deeper, and more keenly felt.
But 'twas not God's design to leave man thus,
In error's devious paths, to grope his way;
So, through His Sacred Word, His will revealed,
And pointed out the narrow path, that bright
And brighter shines, e'en to the perfect day.

(From the poem "The Warning Voice of Time and Prophecy," by Uriah Smith.)

THE RESPONSE OF HISTORY TO THE PROPHECY OF DANIEL

 T. K. MARTIN, ARTIST

UNVEILING THE FUTURE

Only in Bible prophecy can a true revelation of the future be found.

INTRODUCTION

THAT the book of Daniel was written by the person whose name it bears, there is no reason to doubt. Ezekiel, who was contemporary with Daniel, bears testimony, through the Spirit of prophecy, to his piety and uprightness, ranking him in this respect with Noah and Job: "If I send a pestilence into that land, and pour out My fury upon it in blood, to cut off from it man and beast; though Noah, Daniel, and Job were in it, as I live, saith the Lord God, they shall deliver neither son nor daughter; they shall but deliver their own souls by their righteousness." Ezekiel 14: 19, 20. His wisdom, also, even at that early day, had become proverbial, as appears from the same writer. To the prince of Tyrus he was directed by the Lord to say, "Behold, thou art wiser than Daniel; there is no secret that they can hide from thee." Ezekiel 28: 3. But above all, our Lord recognized him as a prophet of God, and bade His disciples understand the predictions given through him for the benefit of His church: "When ye therefore shall see the abomination of desolation, spoken of by Daniel the prophet, stand in the holy place (whoso readeth, let him understand), then let them which be in Judea flee into the mountains." Matthew 24: 15, 16.

Though we have a more minute account of his early life than is recorded of that of any other prophet, yet his birth and lineage are left in complete obscurity, except that he was of the royal line, probably of the house of David, which had at this time become very numerous. He first appears as one of the noble captives of Judah, in the first year of Nebuchadnezzar, king of Babylon, at the beginning of the seventy years' captivity, 606 B. C. Jeremiah and Habakkuk were yet uttering their prophecies. Ezekiel began soon after, and a little later, Obadiah; but all these finished their work years before the close of the long and brilliant career of Daniel. Three prophets only succeeded him, Haggai and Zechariah, who exercised the prophetic office for a brief period contemporaneously, 520-518 B. C., and Malachi, the last of the Old Testament prophets, who flourished a little season about 397 B. C.

During the seventy years' captivity of the Jews, 606-536 B. C., predicted by Jeremiah (Jeremiah 25: 11), Daniel resided at the court of Babylon, most of the time prime minister of that monarchy. His life affords a most impressive lesson of the importance and advantage of maintaining from earliest youth strict integrity toward God, and furnishes a notable instance of a man's maintaining eminent piety, and faithfully discharging all the duties that pertain to the service of God, while at the same time engaging in the most stirring activities, and bearing the weightiest cares and responsibilities that can devolve upon men in this earthly life.

What a rebuke is his course to many at the present day, who, having not a hundredth part of the cares to absorb their time and engross their attention that he had, yet plead as an excuse for their almost utter neglect of Christian duties, that they have no time for them. What will the God of Daniel say to such, when He comes to reward His servants impartially, according to their improvement or neglect of the opportunities offered them?

But it is not alone nor chiefly his connection with the Chaldean monarchy, the glory of kingdoms, that perpetuates the memory of Daniel, and covers his name with honor. From the height of its glory he saw that kingdom decline, and pass into other hands. Its period of greatest prosperity was embraced within the limits of the lifetime of one man. So brief was its supremacy, so transient its glory. But Daniel was intrusted with more enduring honors. While beloved and honored by the princes and potentates of Babylon, he enjoyed an infinitely higher exaltation in being beloved and honored by God and His holy angels, and admitted to a knowledge of the counsels of the Most High.

His prophecy is, in many respects, the most remarkable of any in the sacred record. It is the most comprehensive. It was the first prophecy giving a consecutive history of the world from that time to the end. It located the most of its predictions within well-defined prophetic periods, though reaching many centuries into the future. It gave the first definite chronological prophecy of the coming of the Messiah. It marked the time of this event so definitely that the Jews forbid any attempt to interpret its numbers, since that prophecy shows them to be without excuse in rejecting Christ; and so accurately had its minute and literal predictions been fulfilled down to the time of Porphyry, A. D. 250, that he declared (the only loophole he could devise for his hard-pressed skepticism) that the predictions were not written in the age of Babylon, but after the events themselves had occurred. This evasion, however, is not now available; for every succeeding century has borne additional evidence to the truthfulness of the prophecy, and we are just now, in our own day, approaching the climax of its fulfillment.

The personal history of Daniel reaches to a date a few years subsequent to the subversion of the Babylonian kingdom by the Medes and Persians. He is supposed to have died at Shushan, or Susa, in Persia, about the year 530 B. C., aged nearly ninety-four years; his age being the probable reason why he did not return to Judea with other Hebrew captives, under the proclamation of Cyrus (Ezra 1: 1), 536 B. C., which marked the close of the seventy years' captivity.

BROWN BROTHERS

THE GLORY OF BABYLON

The greatest of ancient cities was Babylon, with its great wall, hanging gardens, and lofty temples.

CHAPTER I

A CAPTIVE IN BABYLON'S ROYAL COURT

VERSE 1 In the third year of the reign of Jehoiakim king of Judah came Nebuchadnezzar king of Babylon unto Jerusalem, and besieged it. 2 And the Lord gave Jehoiakim king of Judah into his hand, with part of the vessels of the house of God: which he carried into the land of Shinar to the house of his god; and he brought the vessels into the treasure house of his god.

WITH a directness characteristic of the sacred writers, Daniel enters at once upon his subject. He begins his book in a simple historical style. The first six chapters, with the exception of the prophecy of chapter 2, are narrative in content. With chapter 7 we reach the prophetical part of the book.

Siege of Jerusalem.—Like one conscious of uttering only well-known truth, he proceeds at once to state a variety of particulars by which his accuracy could be tested. The overthrow of Jerusalem recorded here was predicted by Jeremiah, and was accomplished in 606 B. C.* (Jeremiah 25: 8-11.) Jeremiah places this captivity in the fourth year of Jehoiakim, Daniel in the third. This seeming discrepancy is explained by the fact that Nebuchadnezzar set out on his expedition near the close of the third year of Jehoiakim, from which point Daniel reckons. But the king did not accomplish the subjugation of Jerusalem until about the ninth month of the year following, from which year Jeremiah reckons. Jehoiakim, though bound for the purpose of being taken to Babylon, humbled himself and was permitted to remain as ruler in Jerusalem, tributary to the king of Babylon.

* The date 606 B. C. is widely supported by Ussher, Hales', and other chronologists, but more recent research by archeologists favors the date 605. This apparently more accurate date, however, in no way affects the calculation of prophetic periods presented by the author, for it should be remembered that the Jews and other ancients counted both the first and last years of a period.—*Editors.*

This was the first time Jerusalem was taken by Nebuchadnezzar. Twice subsequently the city revolted, but was recaptured by the same king, and more severely dealt with each succeeding time. The second overthrow was during the time of Jehoiachin, son of Jehoiakim, when all the sacred vessels were either taken or destroyed, and the best of the inhabitants were led with the king into captivity. The third was under Zedekiah, when the city endured a formidable siege. During its continuance for a year and a half, the inhabitants of the city suffered all the horrors of extreme famine. At length the garrison and the king attempted to escape from the city, but they were captured by the Chaldeans. The sons of the king were slain before his face. His eyes were put out, and he was taken to Babylon. Thus was fulfilled the prediction of Ezekiel that he should be carried to Babylon, and die there, yet he should not see the place. (Ezekiel 12: 13.) The city and temple were at this time utterly destroyed, and the entire population of the country, with the exception of a few husbandmen, were carried captive to Babylon, in 586 B. C.

Such was God's passing testimony against sin—not that the Chaldeans were the favorites of Heaven, but that God made use of them to punish the iniquities of His people. Had the Israelites been faithful to God, and kept His Sabbath, Jerusalem would have stood forever. (Jeremiah 17: 24-27.) But they departed from Him, and He abandoned them. They profaned the sacred vessels by bringing idols into the temple; therefore God allowed these vessels to be further profaned by letting them go as trophies to heathen shrines abroad.

Hebrew Captives in Babylon.—During these days of trouble and distress upon Jerusalem, Daniel and his companions were nourished and instructed in the palace of the king of Babylon. Though captives in a strange land, they were doubtless in some respects much more favorably situated than they could have been in their native country.

VERSE 3 And the king spake unto Ashpenaz the master of his eunuchs, that he should bring certain of the children of Israel, and of the king's seed, and of the princes; 4 children in whom was no blemish, but well favored, and skillful in all wisdom, and cunning in knowledge, and understanding science, and such as had ability in them to stand in the king's palace, and whom they might teach the learning and the tongue of the Chaldeans. 5 And the king appointed them a daily provision of the king's meat, and of the wine which he drank: so nourishing them three years, that at the end thereof they might stand before the king.

Here is recorded the probable fulfillment of the judgments predicted by the prophet Isaiah to King Hezekiah more than a hundred years before. When this king had vaingloriously shown to the messengers of the king of Babylon all the treasures and holy things of his palace and kingdom, Hezekiah was told that all these good things would be carried as trophies to the city of Babylon, and that even his own children, his descendants, would be taken away and be eunuchs in the palace of the king there. (2 Kings 20: 14-18.)

The word "children" as applied to these captives is not to be confined to the sense to which it is limited at the present time. It included youth also. We learn from the record that these children were already "skillful in all wisdom, and cunning in knowledge, and understanding science, and . . . had ability in them to stand in the king's palace." In other words, they had acquired a good degree of education, and their physical and mental powers were so far developed that a skillful reader of human nature could form an accurate estimate of their capabilities. They are supposed to have been about eighteen or twenty years of age.

In the treatment which these Hebrew captives received, we see an instance of the wise policy and the liberality of the rising king, Nebuchadnezzar. Instead of choosing means for the gratification of low and base desires, as too many kings of later times have done, he chose young men to be educated in all matters pertaining to the kingdom, that he might have efficient help in administering its affairs. He appointed them daily provision of his own food and drink. Instead of the coarse fare which some would have thought good enough for captives, he offered them his own royal viands. For the space of three years

 R. M. ELDRIDGE, ARTIST

DANIEL TAKEN CAPTIVE

The youthful Daniel and his companions were taken as captives from their Palestinian home to far-away Babylon.

they had all the advantages the kingdom afforded. Though captives, they were royal children, and were treated as such by the humane king of the Chaldeans.

VERSE 6 Now among these were of the children of Judah, Daniel, Hananiah, Mishael, and Azariah: 7 unto whom the prince of the eunuchs gave names: for he gave unto Daniel the name of Belteshazzar; and to Hananiah, of Shadrach; and to Mishael, of Meshach; and to Azariah, of Abednego.

Daniel and His Companions Renamed.—This change of names was probably made on account of the signification of the words. In the Hebrew, Daniel signified, "judge for God;" Hananiah, "gift of the Lord;" Mishael, "who is what God is;" and Azariah, "whom Jehovah helps." Since these names had some reference to the true God and signified some connection with His worship, they were changed to names which had definitions linking them to the heathen divinities and worship of the Chaldeans. Thus Belteshazzar, the name given to Daniel, signified "prince of Bel;" Shadrach, "servant of Sin" (the moon god); Meshach, "who is what Aku is" (Aku being the Sumerian equivalent of Sin, the name of the moon god); and Abednego, "servant of Nebo."

VERSE 8 But Daniel purposed in his heart that he would not defile himself with the portion of the king's meat, nor with the wine which he drank: therefore he requested of the prince of the eunuchs that he might not defile himself. 9 Now God had brought Daniel into favor and tender love with the prince of the eunuchs. 10 And the prince of the eunuchs said unto Daniel, I fear my lord the king, who hath appointed your meat and your drink: for why should he see your faces worse liking than the children which are of your sort? Then shall ye make me endanger my head to the king. 11 Then said Daniel to Melzar, whom the prince of the eunuchs had set over Daniel, Hananiah, Mishael, and Azariah, 12 Prove thy servants, I beseech thee, ten days; and let them give us pulse to eat, and water to drink. 13 Then let our countenances be looked upon before thee, and the countenance of the children that eat of the portion of the king's meat: and as thou seest, deal with thy servants. 14 So he consented to them in this matter, and proved them ten days. 15 And at the end of ten days their countenances appeared fairer and fatter in flesh than all the children which did eat the portion of the king's meat. 16 Thus Melzar took away the portion of their meat, and the wine that they should drink; and gave them pulse.

In this record Nebuchadnezzar appears wonderfully free from bigotry. It seems that he took no means to compel his royal captives to change their religion. Provided they had some religion, he seemed to be satisfied, whether it was the religion he professed or not. Although their names had been changed to signify some connection with heathen worship, this may have been more to avoid the use of Jewish names by the Chaldeans than to indicate any change of sentiment or practice on the part of those to whom these names were given.

Daniel's Diet.—Daniel purposed not to defile himself with the king's food or with his wine. Daniel had other reasons for this course than simply the effect of such a diet upon his physical system, though he would derive great advantage in this respect from the fare he proposed to adopt. It was frequently the case that food used by the kings and princes of heathen nations, who were often the high priests of their religion, was first offered in sacrifice to idols, and the wine they used, poured out as a libation before their gods. Again, some of the flesh food used by the Chaldeans was pronounced unclean by the Jewish law. On either of these grounds Daniel could not, consistently with his religion, partake of these articles. Hence he respectfully requested the proper officer that from conscientious scruples he might not be obliged to defile himself.

The prince of the eunuchs feared to grant Daniel's request, since the king himself had appointed the food for Daniel and his companions. This shows the great personal interest the king took in these captives. It appears that his sincere object was to secure in them the best mental and physical development that could be attained. How different is this from the bigotry and tyranny which usually hold supreme control over the hearts of those who are clothed with absolute power. In the character of Nebuchadnezzar we shall find many things worthy of our highest admiration.

It is interesting to note what was included in Daniel's request for his diet. The Hebrew word זֵרֹעִים, *zeroim*, here translated "pulse," is built on the same root as the word "seed" in the record of creation, where it mentions "every herb *seeding seed*," and again, the "fruit of a tree *seeding seed*." Genesis 1: 29. This makes it clear enough that Daniel's request included grains, legumes, and fruits. Then, too, if we understand Genesis 9: 3 correctly, the "green herb" itself must have been included in the diet requested. In other words, the menu for which Daniel asked and which he received was made up of cereals, legumes, fruits, nuts, and vegetables—a vegetarian diet of good variety, together with the universal drink for man and beast, clear water.

The *Cambridge Bible* has this note on *zeroim:* "vegetable food in general; there is no reason for restricting the Hebrew word used to leguminous fruits, such as beans and peas, which is what the term 'pulse' properly denotes."

Gesenius gives this definition: "Seed-herbs, greens, vegetables, *i.e.*, vegetable food, such as was eaten in a half fast, opposed to meats and the more delicate kinds of food."

A ten days' trial of this diet resulting favorably, Daniel and his companions were permitted to continue it during the whole course of their training for the duties of the palace.

VERSE 17 As for these four children, God gave them knowledge and skill in all learning and wisdom: and Daniel had understanding in all visions and dreams. 18 Now at the end of the days that the king had said he should bring them in, then the prince of the eunuchs brought them in before Nebuchadnezzar. 19 And the king communed with them; and among them all was found none like Daniel, Hananiah, Mishael, and Azariah: therefore stood they before the king. 20 And in all matters of wisdom and understanding, that the king inquired of them, he found them ten times better than all the magicians and astrologers that were in all his realm. 21 And Daniel continued even unto the first year of king Cyrus.

After Three Years' Study.—To Daniel alone seems to have been committed an understanding in visions and dreams. But the Lord's dealing with Daniel in this respect does not prove his companions any less accepted in His sight. By their preservation in the midst of the fiery furnace they had equally good evidence of the divine favor. Daniel probably had some

STANDARD PUBLISHING CO.

STANDING FOR PRINCIPLE

With profound reverence for his God, Daniel purposed in his heart not to defile himself with the king's meat.

natural qualifications that peculiarly fitted him for this special work.

The same personal interest in these individuals heretofore manifested by the king, he still continued to maintain. At the end of the three years, he called them to a personal interview. He must know for himself how they had fared, and to what proficiency they had attained. This interview also shows the king to have been a man well versed in all the arts and sciences of the Chaldeans, else he would not have been qualified to examine others in them. Recognizing merit wherever he saw it without respect to religion or nationality, he acknowledged them to be ten times superior to any in his own land.

It is added that Daniel "continued even unto the first year of King Cyrus."

T. K. MARTIN, ARTIST

THE COURSE OF EMPIRES

With unerring accuracy, the pen of prophecy has traced the course of history down to our day.

CHAPTER II

THE KING DREAMS OF WORLD EMPIRES

VERSE 1 And in the second year of the reign of Nebuchadnezzar Nebuchadnezzar dreamed dreams, wherewith his spirit was troubled, and his sleep brake from him.

DANIEL was carried into captivity in the first year of Nebuchadnezzar. For three years he was placed under instructors, during which time he would not of course be reckoned among the wise men of the kingdom, nor take part in public affairs. Yet in the second year of Nebuchadnezzar, the transactions recorded in this chapter took place. How, then, could Daniel be brought in to interpret the king's dream in his second year? The explanation lies in the fact that Nebuchadnezzar reigned for two years conjointly with his father, Nabopolassar. From this point the Jews reckoned, while the Chaldeans reckoned from the time he began to reign alone on the death of his father. Hence, the year here mentioned was the second year of his reign according to the Chaldean reckoning, but the fourth according to the Jewish.[1] It thus appears that the next year after Daniel had completed his preparation to participate in the affairs of the Chaldean empire, the providence of God brought him into sudden and remarkable prominence throughout the kingdom.

VERSE 2 Then the king commanded to call the magicians, and the astrologers, and the sorcerers, and the Chaldeans, for to show the king his dreams. So they came and stood before the king.

The King's Wise Men Fail Him.—The magicians practiced magic, using the term in its bad sense; that is, they employed all the superstitious rites and ceremonies of fortunetellers, and

[1] See Adam Clarke, *Commentary on the Old Testament*, Vol. IV, pp. 564, 567, notes on Daniel 1: 1; 2: 1; Thomas Newton, *Dissertations on the Prophecies*, Vol. I, p. 231; Albert Barnes, *Notes on Daniel*, pp. 111, 112, comment on Daniel 2: 1.

casters of nativities, and the like. Astrologers were men who pretended to foretell events by the study of the stars. The science, or the superstition, of astrology was extensively cultivated by the Eastern nations of antiquity. Sorcerers were such as pretended to hold communication with the dead. In this sense, we believe, the word "sorcerer" is always used in the Scriptures. The Chaldeans here mentioned were a sect of philosophers similar to the magicians and astrologers, who made natural science and divinations their study. All these sects or professions abounded in Babylon. The result desired by each was the same—the explaining of mysteries and the foretelling of events—the principal difference between them being the means by which they sought to accomplish their object. The king's difficulty lay equally within the province of each to explain; hence he summoned them all. With the king it was an important matter. He was greatly troubled, and therefore concentrated upon the solution of his perplexity the wisdom of his realm.

VERSE 3 And the king said unto them, I have dreamed a dream, and my spirit was troubled to know the dream. 4 Then spake the Chaldeans to the king in Syriac, O king, live forever: tell thy servants the dream, and we will show the interpretation.

In whatever else the ancient magicians and astrologers may have been efficient, they seem to have been thoroughly schooled in the art of drawing out sufficient information to form a basis for some shrewd calculation, or of framing their answers in such an ambiguous manner that they would be applicable whichever way the events turned. In the present case, true to their cunning instincts, they called upon the king to make known to them his dream. If they could get full information respecting this, they could easily agree on some interpretation which would not endanger their reputation. They addressed themselves to the king in Syriac, a dialect of the Chaldean language which was used by the educated and cultured classes. From this point to the end of Daniel 7, the record continues in Chaldaic, the language spoken by the king.

VERSE 5 The king answered and said to the Chaldeans, The thing is gone from me: if ye will not make known unto me the dream, with the interpretation thereof, ye shall be cut in pieces, and your houses shall be made a dunghill. 6 But if ye show the dream, and the interpretation thereof, ye shall receive of me gifts and rewards and great honor: therefore show me the dream, and the interpretation thereof. 7 They answered again and said, Let the king tell his servants the dream, and we will show the interpretation of it. 8 The king answered and said, I know of certainty that ye would gain the time, because ye see the thing is gone from me. 9 But if ye will not make known unto me the dream, there is but one decree for you: for ye have prepared lying and corrupt words to speak before me, till the time be changed: therefore tell me the dream, and I shall know that ye can show me the interpretation thereof. 10 The Chaldeans answered before the king, and said, There is not a man upon the earth that can show the king's matter: therefore there is no king, lord, nor ruler, that asked such things at any magician, or astrologer, or Chaldean. 11 And it is a rare thing that the king requireth, and there is none other that can show it before the king, except the gods, whose dwelling is not with flesh. 12 For this cause the king was angry and very furious, and commanded to destroy all the wise men of Babylon. 13 And the decree went forth that the wise men should be slain; and they sought Daniel and his fellows to be slain.

These verses contain the record of the desperate struggle between the wise men and the king. The former sought some avenue of escape, since they were caught on their own ground. The king was determined that they should make known his dream, which was no more than should be expected from their profession.

Some have severely censured Nebuchadnezzar in this matter, as acting the part of a heartless, unreasonable tyrant. But what did these magicians profess to be able to do?—To reveal hidden things, to foretell events, to make known mysteries entirely beyond human foresight and penetration, and to do this by the aid of supernatural agencies. There was therefore nothing unjust in Nebuchadnezzar's demand that they should make known his dream. When they declared that none but the gods whose dwelling was not with flesh could make known the king's matter, it was a tacit acknowledgment that they had no communication with these gods, and knew nothing beyond what human wisdom and discernment could reveal. "For this cause the king was angry and very furious."

He saw that he and all his people were being made the victims of deception. While we cannot justify the extreme measures to which he resorted, dooming them to death, and their houses to destruction, we cannot but feel a hearty sympathy with him in his condemnation of a class of miserable impostors. The king would be no party to dishonesty or deception.

VERSE 14 Then Daniel answered with counsel and wisdom to Arioch the captain of the king's guard, which was gone forth to slay the wise men of Babylon: 15 he answered and said to Arioch the king's captain, Why is the decree so hasty from the king? Then Arioch made the thing known to Daniel. 16 Then Daniel went in, and desired of the king that he would give him time, and that he would show the king the interpretation. 17 Then Daniel went to his house, and made the thing known to Hananiah, Mishael, and Azariah, his companions: 18 that they would desire mercies of the God of heaven concerning this secret; that Daniel and his fellows should not perish with the rest of the wise men of Babylon.

Daniel to the Rescue.—In this narrative we see the providence of God working in several remarkable particulars. It was providential that the dream of the king should leave such a powerful impression upon his mind as to raise him to the greatest height of anxiety, and yet the thing itself be held from his recollection. This led to the complete exposure of the false system of the magicians and other pagan teachers. When put to the test to make known the dream, they were unable to do what they professed was entirely within their power.

It was remarkable that Daniel and his companions, so lately pronounced by the king ten times better than all his magicians and astrologers, should not have been consulted in this matter. But there was a providence in this. Just as the dream was held from the king, so he was unaccountably restrained from appealing to Daniel for a solution of the mystery. Had he called on Daniel at the first to make known the matter, the magicians would not have been brought to the test. But God would give the heathen systems of the Chal deans the first chance. He would let them try and ignominiously fail, and then confess their utter incompetency, even under the penalty of death, that they might be the better prepared to acknowledge His intervention when He should finally manifest His power in behalf of His captive servants, and for the honor of His name.

It appears that the first intimation Daniel had of the matter was the presence of the executioners, come for his arrest. His own life being thus at stake, he was led to seek the Lord with all his heart until He should work for the deliverance of His servants. Daniel gained his request of the king for time to consider the matter—a privilege which probably none of the magicians could have obtained, as the king had already accused them of preparing false and corrupt words, and of seeking to gain time for this very purpose. Daniel at once went to his three companions, and asked them to unite with him in desiring mercy of the God of heaven concerning this secret. He could have prayed alone, and doubtless would have been heard. But then, as now, in the union of God's people there is prevailing power. The promise of the accomplishment of that which is asked, is to the two or three who shall agree concerning it. (Matthew 18: 19, 20.)

VERSE 19 Then was the secret revealed unto Daniel in a night vision. Then Daniel blessed the God of heaven. 20 Daniel answered and said, Blessed be the name of God forever and ever: for wisdom and might are His: 21 and He changeth the times and the seasons: He removeth kings, and setteth up kings: He giveth wisdom unto the wise, and knowledge to them that know understanding: 22 He revealeth the deep and secret things: He knoweth what is in the darkness, and the light dwelleth with Him. 23 I thank Thee, and praise Thee, O Thou God of my fathers, who hast given me wisdom and might, and hast made known unto me now what we desired of Thee: for Thou hast now made known unto us the king's matter.

Whether or not the answer came while Daniel and his companions were yet offering up their petitions, we are not informed. It was in a night vision that God revealed Himself in their behalf. The words "night vision" mean anything that is seen, whether through dreams or visions.

Daniel immediately offered up praise to God for His gracious dealing with them, and while his prayer is not preserved, his responsive thanksgiving is fully recorded. God is

© AUTOTYPE FINE ART CO.

THE HEBREW YOUTH IN PRAYER

Both in emergencies and in normal times, Daniel sought his God in prayer, and the Lord never failed him.

honored by our praise to Him for the things He has done for us, as well as by our petitions to Him for help. Let Daniel's course be our example in this respect. Let no mercy from the hand of God fail of its due return of thanksgiving and praise. In the days of Christ's ministry on earth, did He not cleanse ten lepers, and only one returned to give Him thanks? "But where," asks Christ sorrowfully, "are the nine?" Luke 17: 17.

Daniel had the utmost confidence in what had been shown him. He did not first go to the king to see if what had been revealed to him was indeed the king's dream, but he immediately praised God for having answered his prayer.

Although the matter was revealed to Daniel, he did not take honor to himself as though it were by his prayers alone that the answer had been obtained; but he immediately associated his companions with him, and acknowledged it to be as much an answer to their prayers as it was to his own. It was, said he, "what *we* desired of Thee," and Thou hast made it "known unto *us*."

VERSE 24 Therefore Daniel went in unto Arioch, whom the king had ordained to destroy the wise men of Babylon: he went and said thus unto him: Destroy not the wise men of Babylon: bring me in before the king, and I will show unto the king the interpretation.

Daniel's first plea was for the wise men of Babylon. Destroy them not, for the king's secret is revealed, he implored. True, it was through no merit of theirs or their heathen systems of divination that this revelation was made. They were worthy of as much condemnation as before. But their own confession of utter impotence in the matter was humiliation enough for them, and Daniel was anxious that they should so far partake of the benefits shown him as to have their lives spared. They were saved because there was a man of God among them. Thus it ever is. For the sake of Paul and Silas, all the prisoners with them were loosed. (Acts 16: 26.) For the sake of Paul, the lives of all that sailed with him were saved. (Acts 27: 24.) How often the wicked are benefited by the presence of the righteous! Well would it be if they would remember the obligations under which they are thus placed.

What saves the world today? For whose sake is it still spared?—For the sake of the few righteous persons who are yet left. Remove these, and how long would the wicked be suffered to run their guilty career?—No longer than the antediluvians were suffered after Noah had entered the ark, or the Sodomites after Lot had departed from their polluted and polluting presence. If only ten righteous persons could have been found in Sodom, the multitude of its wicked inhabitants would for their sakes have been spared. Yet the wicked will despise, ridicule, and oppress the very ones on whose account it is that they are still permitted the enjoyment of life and all its blessings.

VERSE 25 Then Arioch brought in Daniel before the king in haste, and said thus unto him, I have found a man of the captives of Judah, that will make known unto the king the interpretation.

It is ever a characteristic of ministers and courtiers to ingratiate themselves with their sovereign. So here Arioch represented that he had found a man who could make known the desired interpretation, as if with great disinterestedness in behalf of the king he had been searching for some one to solve his difficulty, and had at last found him. In order to see through this deception of his chief executioner, the king had but to remember, as he probably did, his interview with Daniel, and Daniel's promise, if time could be granted, to show the interpretation of the dream. (Verse 16.)

VERSE 26 The king answered and said to Daniel, whose name was Belteshazzar, Art thou able to make known unto me the dream which I have seen, and the interpretation thereof? 27 Daniel answered in the presence of the king, and said, The secret which the king hath demanded cannot the wise men, the astrologers, the magicians, the soothsayers, show unto the king; 28 but there is a God in heaven that revealeth secrets, and maketh known to the king Nebuchadnezzar what shall be in the latter days. Thy dream, and the visions of thy head upon thy bed, are these.

"Art thou able to make known unto me the dream?" was the king's salutation to Daniel as he came into the royal presence. Notwithstanding his previous acquaintance with this Hebrew, the king seemed to question his ability, so young and inexperienced, to make known a matter in which the aged and venerable magicians and soothsayers had utterly failed. Daniel declared plainly that the wise men, the astrologers, the soothsayers, and the magicians could not make known this secret. It was beyond their power. Therefore the king should not be angry with them, nor put confidence in their vain superstitions. The prophet proceeded to make known the true God, who rules in heaven, and is the only revealer of secrets. He it is, said Daniel, who "maketh known to the king Nebuchadnezzar what shall be in the latter days."

VERSE 29 As for thee, O king, thy thoughts came into thy mind upon thy bed, what should come to pass hereafter: and He that revealeth secrets maketh known to thee what shall come to pass. 30 But as for me, this secret is not revealed to me for any wisdom that I have more than any living, but for their sakes that shall make known the interpretation to the king, and that thou mightest know the thoughts of thy heart.

Here is brought out another of the commendable traits of Nebuchadnezzar's character. Unlike some rulers, who fill up the present with folly and debauchery without regard to the future, the king thought forward upon the days to come, with an anxious desire to know with what events they should be filled. It was partly for this reason that God gave him this dream, which we must regard as a token of divine favor to the king. Yet God would not work for the king independently of His own people. Though He gave the dream to the king, He sent the interpretation through one of His acknowledged servants.

Daniel first disclaimed all credit for the interpretation, and then he sought to modify the king's natural feelings of pride in being thus noticed by the God of heaven. He informed him that although the dream had been given to him, it was not for his sake alone that the interpretation was sent, but also for their sakes through whom it should be given. Ah! God had some servants there, and it was for them that He was working. They were of more value in His sight than the mightiest kings and potentates of earth.

How comprehensive was the work of God in this instance! By this one act of revealing the king's dream to Daniel, He made known to the king the things he desired, He saved His servants who trusted in Him, He brought conspicuously before the Chaldean nation the knowledge of Him who knows the end from the beginning, He poured contempt on the false systems of the soothsayers and magicians, and He honored His own name and exalted His servants in their eyes.

Daniel Relates the Dream.—After making it clear to the king that the purpose of the "God in heaven" in giving him the dream, was to reveal "what shall be in the latter days," Daniel related the dream itself.

VERSE 31 Thou, O king, sawest, and behold a great image. This great image, whose brightness was excellent, stood before thee; and the form thereof was terrible. 32 This image's head was of fine gold, his breast and his arms of silver, his belly and his thighs of brass, 33 his legs of iron, his feet part of iron and part of clay. 34 Thou sawest till that a stone was cut out without hands, which smote the image upon his feet that were of iron and clay, and brake them to pieces. 35 Then was the iron, the clay, the brass, the silver, and the gold, broken to pieces together, and became like the chaff of the summer threshingfloors; and the wind carried them away, that no place was found for them: and the stone that smote the image became a great mountain, and filled the whole earth.

Nebuchadnezzar, a worshiper of the gods of the Chaldean religion, was an idolater. An image was an object which would at once command his attention and respect. Moreover, earthly kingdoms, which, as we shall hereafter see, were represented by this image, were objects of esteem and value in his eyes.

But how admirably adapted was this representation to convey a great and needful truth to the mind of Nebuchadnezzar. Besides delineating the progress of events through the whole course of time for the benefit of His people, God would show Nebuchadnezzar the utter emptiness and worthlessness of earthly pomp and glory. How could this be more impressively done than by an image whose head was of gold? Below this head was a body composed of inferior metals descending in value until they reached their basest form in the feet and toes of iron mingled with miry clay. The whole was then dashed to pieces, and made like the empty chaff. It was finally blown away where no place could be found for it, after which something durable and of heavenly worth occupied its place. So would God show to the children of men that earthly kingdoms are to pass away, and earthly greatness and glory, like a gaudy bubble, will break and vanish. In the place so long usurped by these, the kingdom of God shall be set up and have no end, while all who have an interest in that kingdom shall rest under the shadow of its peaceful wings forever and ever. But this is anticipating.

VERSE 36 This is the dream; and we will tell the interpretation thereof before the king. 37 Thou, O king, art a king of kings: for the God of heaven hath given thee a kingdom, power, and strength, and glory. 38 And wheresoever the children of men dwell, the beasts of the field and the fowls of the heaven hath He given into thine hand, and hath made thee ruler over them all. Thou art this head of gold.

Daniel Interprets the Dream.—Now opens one of the most comprehensive of the histories of world empire. Eight short verses of the inspired record tell the whole story, yet that story embraces the history of this world's pomp and power. A few moments will suffice to commit it to memory, yet the period which it covers, beginning more than twenty-five centuries ago, reaches from that far-distant point past the rise and fall of kingdoms, past the setting up and overthrow of empires, past cycles and ages, past our own day, to the eternal state. It is so comprehensive that it embraces all this, yet it is so minute that it gives us the great outlines of earthly kingdoms from that time to this. Human wisdom never devised so brief a record that embraced so much. Human language never set forth in so few words such a great volume of historical truth. The finger of God is here. Let us heed the lesson well.

With what interest and astonishment must the king have listened as he was informed by the prophet that his kingdom was the golden head of the magnificent image. Daniel in-

 R. M. ELDRIDGE, ARTIST

"THOU ART THIS HEAD OF GOLD"

Fearlessly Daniel revealed to Nebuchadnezzar that the head of gold is a symbol of great Babylon.

formed the king that the God of heaven had given him his kingdom, and made him ruler over all. This would restrain him from the pride of thinking that he had attained his position by his own power and wisdom, and would enlist the gratitude of his heart toward the true God.

The kingdom of Babylon, which finally developed into the nation represented by the golden head of the great historic image, was founded by Nimrod, the great-grandson of Noah, more than two thousand years before Christ. "Cush begat Nimrod: he began to be a mighty one in the earth. He was a mighty hunter before the Lord: wherefore it is said, Even as Nimrod the mighty hunter before the Lord. And the beginning of his kingdom was Babel ["Babylon," margin], and Erech, and Accad, and Calneh, in the land of Shinar." Genesis 10: 8-10. It appears that Nimrod also founded the city of Nineveh, which afterward became the capital of Assyria. (See marginal reading of Genesis 10: 11.)

Fulfillment of the Dream.—The Babylonian Empire rose to power under the general who also became king, Nabopolassar. When he died in 604 B. C. his son Nebuchadnezzar became king. As R. Campbell Thompson declares: "Events had already shown that Nebuchadrezzar was a vigorous and brilliant commander, and physically as well as mentally a strong man, fully worthy of succeeding his father. He was to become the greatest man of his time in the Near East, as a soldier, a statesman, and an architect. Had his successors been of such a stamp instead of callow boys or *dilettanti* without redeeming vigor, the Persians would have found Babylonia a harder problem. 'All the nations,' says Jeremiah (Jeremiah 27: 7, R. V.), 'shall serve him, and his son, and his son's son, until the time of his own land come.' "[2]

Jerusalem was taken by Nebuchadnezzar in the first year of his reign, and the third year of Jehoiakim, king of Judah (Daniel 1: 1), 606 B. C. Nebuchadnezzar reigned two years

[2] *The Cambridge Ancient History*, Vol. III, p. 212. By permission of the Macmillan Company, publishers in the United States.

conjointly with his father, Nabopolassar. From this point the Jews computed his reign, but the Chaldeans from the date of his sole reign, 604 B. C., as stated above. Respecting the successors of Nebuchadnezzar, the authority just quoted adds:

"Nebuchadnezzar died about August-September, 562 B. C., and was succeeded by his son Amel-Marduk (562-560 B. C.), whom Jeremiah calls Evil-Merodach. He was given little time to prove his worth; the two years of his brief reign are merely enough to show that political conditions were again hostile to the royal house." [3]

The later Babylonian rulers, weak in power, could not equal the reign of Nebuchadnezzar. Cyrus, king of Persia, besieged Babylon, and took it by stratagem.

The character of the Babylonian Empire is indicated by the head of gold. It was the golden kingdom of a golden age. Babylon, its metropolis, towered to a height never reached by any of its successors. Situated in the garden of the East; laid out in a perfect square said to be sixty miles in circumference, fifteen miles on each side; surrounded by a wall estimated to have been two hundred to three hundred feet high and eighty-seven feet thick, with a moat, or ditch, around this, of equal cubic capacity with the wall itself; divided into squares by its many streets, each one hundred and fifty feet in width, crossing at right angles, every one of them straight and level; its two hundred and twenty-five square miles of enclosed surface laid out in luxuriant pleasure grounds and gardens, interspersed with magnificent dwellings—this city, with its sixty miles of moat, its sixty miles of outer wall, its thirty miles of river wall through its center, its gates of solid brass, its hanging gardens rising terrace above terrace till they equaled in height the walls themselves, its temple of Belus three miles in circumference, its two royal palaces, one three and a half and the other eight miles in circumference, with its subterranean tunnel under the River Euphrates connecting these two

---

[3] *Ibid.*, p. 217.

palaces, its perfect arrangement for convenience, ornament, and defense, and its unlimited resources—this city, containing in itself many things which were themselves wonders of the world, was itself another and still mightier wonder. There, with the whole earth prostrate at her feet, a queen in peerless grandeur, drawing from the pen of inspiration itself this glowing title, "The glory of kingdoms, the beauty of the Chaldees' excellency," stood this city, fit capital of that kingdom which was represented by the golden head of this great historic image.

Such was Babylon, with Nebuchadnezzȧr in the prime of life, bold, vigorous, and accomplished, seated upon its throne, when Daniel entered within its walls to serve as a captive in its gorgeous palaces for seventy years. There the children of the Lord, oppressed more than cheered by the glory and prosperity of the land of their captivity, hung their harps on the willows by the Euphrates, and wept when they remembered Zion.

There began the captive state of the church in a still broader sense; for ever since that time the people of God have been in subjection to earthly powers, and more or less oppressed by them. So they will be until all earthly powers shall finally yield to Him whose right it is to reign. And lo, that day of deliverance draws on apace!

Into another city, not only Daniel, but all the children of God, from least to greatest, from lowest to highest, are soon to enter. It is a city not merely sixty miles in circumference, but fifteen hundred miles; a city whose walls are not brick and bitumen, but precious stones and jasper; whose streets are not the stone-paved streets of Babylon, smooth and beautiful as they were, but transparent gold; whose river is not the Euphrates, but the river of life; whose music is not the sighs and laments of broken-hearted captives, but the thrilling pæans of victory over death and the grave, which ransomed multitudes shall raise; whose light is not the intermittent light of earth, but the unceasing and ineffable glory of God and the

Lamb. To this city they shall come, not as captives entering a foreign land, but as exiles returning to their father's house; not as to a place where such chilling words as "bondage," "servitude," and "oppression," shall weigh down their spirits, but to one where the sweet words, "home," "freedom," "peace," "purity," "unutterable bliss," and "unending life," shall thrill their souls with delight forever and ever. Yea, our mouths shall be filled with laughter, and our tongue with singing, when the Lord shall turn again the captivity of Zion. (Psalm 126: 1, 2; Revelation 21: 1-27.)

VERSE 39 And after thee shall arise another kingdom inferior to thee, and another third kingdom of brass, which shall bear rule over all the earth.

Nebuchadnezzar reigned forty-three years, and was succeeded by the following rulers: His son, Evil-Merodach, two years; Neriglissar, his son-in-law, four years; Laborosoarchod, Neriglissar's son, nine months, which, being less than one year, is not counted in the canon of Ptolemy; and lastly, Nabonidus, whose son, Belshazzar, grandson of Nebuchadnezzar, was associated with him on the throne.

"The proof of this association is contained in the cylinders of Nabonadius [Nabonidus] found at Mugheir, where the protection of the gods is asked for Nabu-nadid and his son Bel-shar-uzur, who are coupled together in a way that implies the cosovereignty of the latter. (*British Museum Series*, Vol. I. pl. 68, no. 1.) The date of the association was at the latest 540 B. C., Nabonadius's fifteenth year, since the third year of Belshazzar is mentioned in Daniel 8: 1. If Belshazzar was (as I have supposed) a son of a daughter of Nebuchadnezzar married to Nabonadius after he became king, he could not be more than fourteen in his father's fifteenth year."[4]

The Fall of Babylon.—In the first year of Neriglissar, only two years after the death of Nebuchadnezzar, broke out that fatal war between the Babylonians and the Medes, which re-

[4] George Rawlinson, *The Seven Great Monarchies of the Ancient Eastern World*, Vol. II, p. 610, Note 202.

sulted in the overthrow of the Babylonian kingdom. Cyaxares, king of the Medes, who is called "Darius" in Daniel 5: 31, summoned to his aid his nephew Cyrus of the Persian line. The war was prosecuted with uninterrupted success by the Medes and Persians, until in the eighteenth year of Nabonidus (the third year of his son Belshazzar), Cyrus laid siege to Babylon, the only city in all the East which then held out against him. The Babylonians gathered within their seemingly impregnable walls, with provision on hand for twenty years, and land within the limits of their broad city sufficient to furnish food for the inhabitants and garrison for an indefinite period. They scoffed at Cyrus from their lofty walls, and derided his seemingly useless efforts to bring them into subjection. According to all human calculation, they had good ground for their feelings of security. Never, weighed in the balance of earthly probability, could that city be taken with the means of warfare then known. Hence they breathed as freely and slept as soundly as though no foe were waiting and watching around their beleaguered walls. But God had decreed that the proud and wicked city should come down from her throne of glory. And when He speaks, what mortal arm can defeat His word?

In their feeling of security lay the source of their danger. Cyrus resolved to accomplish by stratagem what he could not effect by force. Learning of the approach of an annual festival in which the whole city would be given up to mirth and revelry, he fixed upon that day as the time to carry his purpose into execution.

There was no entrance for him into that city unless he could find it where the River Euphrates entered and emerged, as it passed under the walls. He resolved to make the channel of the river his highway into the stronghold of his enemy. To do this, the water must be turned aside from its channel through the city. For this purpose, on the evening of the feast day above referred to, he detailed one body of soldiers to turn the river at a given hour into a large artificial lake a short

BABYLON'S CRUCIAL HOUR

Cyrus the Persian, with his army, entered the golden city through unbarred gates.

distance above the city; another to take their station at the point where the river entered the city; and a third to take a position fifteen miles below, where the river emerged from the city. The two latter bodies were instructed to enter the channel as soon as they found the river fordable, and in the darkness of the night explore their way beneath the walls, and press on to the palace of the king where they were to surprise and kill the guards, and capture or slay the king. When the water was turned into the lake, the river soon became shallow enough to ford, and the soldiers followed its channel into the heart of the city of Babylon.[5]

But all this would have been in vain, had not the whole city given itself over on that eventful night to the most abandoned carelessness and presumption, a state of things upon which Cyrus calculated largely for the carrying out of his purpose. On each side of the river through the entire length of the city were walls of great height, and of equal thickness with the outer walls. In these walls were huge gates of brass, which, when closed and guarded, debarred all entrance from the river bed to any of the streets that crossed the river. Had the gates been closed at this time, the soldiers of Cyrus might have marched into the city along the river bed, and then marched out again, for all that they would have been able to accomplish toward the subjugation of the place.

But in the drunken revelry of that fatal night, these river gates were left open, as had been foretold by the prophet Isaiah years before in these words: "Thus saith the Lord to His anointed, to Cyrus, whose right hand I have holden, to subdue nations before him; and I will loose the loins of kings, to open before him the two-leaved gates; and the gates shall not be shut." Isaiah 45: 1. The entrance of the Persian soldiers was not perceived. Many a cheek would have paled with terror, had the sudden going down of the river been noticed, and its

---

[5] See Herodotus, pp. 67-71; George Rawlinson, *The Seven Great Monarchies of the Ancient Eastern World*, Vol. II, pp. 254-259; Humphrey Prideaux, *The Old and New Testament Connected in the History of the Jews*, Vol. I, pp. 136, 137.

fearful import understood. Many a tongue would have spread wild alarm through the city, had the dark forms of armed foes been seen stealthily treading their way to the citadel of their supposed security. But no one noticed the sudden subsidence of the waters of the river; no one saw the entrance of the Persian warriors; no one took care that the river gates should be closed and guarded; no one cared for aught but to see how deeply and recklessly he could plunge into the wild debauch. That night's dissipation cost the Babylonians their kingdom and their freedom. They went into their brutish revelry subjects of the king of Babylon; they awoke from it slaves to the king of Persia.

The soldiers of Cyrus first made known their presence in the city by falling upon the royal guards in the vestibule of the palace of the king. Belshazzar soon became aware of the cause of the disturbance, and died fighting for his life. This feast of Belshazzar is described in the fifth chapter of Daniel, and the scene closes with the simple record, "In that night was Belshazzar the king of the Chaldeans slain. And Darius the Median took the kingdom, being about threescore and two years old."

The historian Prideaux says: "Darius the Mede, that is, Cyaxares, the uncle of Cyrus, took the kingdom; for Cyrus allowed him the title of all his conquests as long as he lived."[6]

Thus the first empire, symbolized by the head of gold of the great image, came to an ignoble end. It would naturally be supposed that the conqueror, becoming possessed of so noble a city as Babylon, far surpassing anything else in the world, would have taken it as the seat of his empire, and maintained it in its splendor. But God had said that that city should become a heap, and the habitation of the beasts of the desert; that its houses should be full of doleful creatures; that the wild beasts of the islands should cry in its desolate dwellings, and dragons in its pleasant palaces. (Isaiah 13: 19-22.) It must

---

[6] Humphrey Prideaux, *The Old and New Testament Connected in the History of the Jews*, Vol. I, p. 137.

first be deserted. Cyrus established a second capital at Susa, a celebrated city in the province of Elam, east from Babylon, on the banks of the River Choaspes, a branch of the Tigris. This was probably done in the first year of his sole reign.

The pride of the Babylonians being particularly provoked by this act, in the fifth year of Darius Hystaspes, 517 B. C., they rose in rebellion and brought upon themselves again the whole strength of the Persian Empire. The city was once more taken by stratagem. Darius took away the brazen gates of the city, and beat down the walls from two hundred cubits to fifty cubits. This was the beginning of its destruction. By this act, it was left exposed to the ravages of every hostile band. Xerxes, on his return from Greece, plundered the temple of Belus of its immense wealth, and then laid the lofty structure in ruins. Alexander the Great endeavored to rebuild it, but after employing ten thousand men two months to clear away the rubbish, he died from excessive drunkenness and debauchery, and the work was suspended. In the year 294 B. C., Seleucus Nicator built the city of New Babylon in the neighborhood of the old city, and took much of the material and many of the inhabitants of the old city, to build up and people the new. Now almost exhausted of inhabitants, neglect and decay were telling fearfully upon the ancient capital. The violence of Parthian princes hastened its ruin. About the end of the fourth century, it was used by the Persian kings as an enclosure for wild beasts. At the end of the twelfth century, according to a celebrated traveler, the few remaining ruins of Nebuchadnezzar's palace were so full of serpents and venomous reptiles that they could not be closely inspected without great danger. And today scarcely enough even of the ruins is left to mark the spot where once stood the largest, richest, and proudest city of the ancient world.

Thus the ruin of great Babylon shows us how accurately God fulfills His word, and makes the doubts of skepticism appear like willful blindness.

"After thee shall arise another kingdom inferior to thee."

W. KAULBACH, ARTIST

THE NAVAL BATTLE OF SALAMIS

One of the most noted battles between the Greeks and the Persians was fought at Salamis in 480 B. C.

The use of the word "kingdom" here, shows that kingdoms, and not particular kings, are represented by the different parts of this image. Hence when it was said to Nebuchadnezzar, "Thou art this head of gold," although the personal pronoun was used, the kingdom not the king himself was meant.

Medo-Persian Kingdom.—The succeeding kingdom, Medo-Persia, answered to the breast and arms of silver of the great image. It was to be inferior to the preceding kingdom. In what respect inferior? Not in power, for it conquered Babylon. Not in extent, for Cyrus subdued all the East from the Ægean Sea to the River Indus, and thus erected a more extensive empire. But it was inferior in wealth, luxury, and magnificence.

Viewed from a Scriptural standpoint, the principal event under the Babylonian Empire was the captivity of the children of Israel; under the Medo-Persian kingdom it was the restoration of Israel to their own land. At the taking of Babylon Cyrus, as an act of courtesy, assigned the first place in the kingdom to his uncle, Darius, in 538 B. C. But two years afterward Darius died, leaving Cyrus sole monarch of the empire. In this year, which closed Israel's seventy years of captivity, Cyrus issued his famous decree for the return of the Jews and the rebuilding of their temple. This was the first installment of the great decree for the restoration and building again of Jerusalem (Ezra 6: 14), which was completed in the seventh year of the reign of Artaxerxes, 457 B. C., a date of much importance, as will hereafter be shown.

After a reign of seven years, Cyrus left the kingdom to his son Cambyses, who reigned seven years and five months, to 522 B. C. Ten monarchs reigned between this time and the year 336 B. C. The year 335 B. C. is set down as the first of Darius Codomannus, the last of the line of the old Persian kings. This man, according to Prideaux, was of noble stature, of goodly person, of the greatest personal valor, and of a mild and generous disposition. It was his ill fortune to have to contend with one who was an agent in the fulfillment of prophecy, and no qualifications, natural or acquired, could make him successful in the unequal contest. Scarcely was he warm upon the throne, ere he found his formidable enemy, Alexander, at the head of the Greek soldiers, preparing to dismount him from it.

The cause and the particulars of the contest between the Greeks and the Persians we leave to histories especially devoted to such matters. Suffice it to say that the deciding point was reached on the field of Arbela in 331 B. C., where the Grecians, though only one to twenty in number as compared with the Persians, won a decisive victory. Alexander became absolute lord of the Persian Empire to an extent never attained by any of its own kings.

Grecian Empire.—"Another third kingdom of brass . . . shall bear rule over all the earth," the prophet had said. Few and brief are the inspired words which involved in their fulfillment a succession in world rulership. In the ever-changing political kaleidoscope, Grecia came into the field of vision, to be for a time the all-absorbing object of attention, as the third of what are called the universal empires of the earth.

After the battle which decided the fate of the empire, Darius endeavored to rally the shattered remnants of his army, and make a stand for his kingdom and his rights. But he could not gather out of all the host of his recently so numerous and well-appointed army a force with which he deemed it prudent to hazard another engagement with the victorious Grecians. Alexander pursued him on the wings of the wind. Time after time Darius barely eluded the grasp of his swiftly following foe. At length three traitors, Bessus, Nabarzanes, and Barsaentes, seized the unfortunate prince, shut him up in a close cart, and fled with him as their prisoner toward Bactria. It was their purpose, if Alexander pursued them, to purchase their own safety by delivering up their king. Hereupon Alexander, learning of the dangerous position of Darius in the hands of the traitors, immediately put himself with the lightest part of his army upon a forced pursuit. After several days' hard march, he came up with the traitors. They urged Darius to mount on horseback for a more speedy flight. Upon his refusing to do this, they gave him several mortal wounds, and left him dying in the cart, while they mounted their steeds and rode away.

When Alexander arrived, he beheld only the lifeless form of the Persian king, who but a few months before was seated upon the throne of universal empire. Disaster, overthrow, and desertion had come suddenly upon Darius. His kingdom had been conquered, his treasure seized, and his family reduced to captivity. Now, brutally slain by the hand of traitors, he lay a bloody corpse in a rude cart. The sight of the melancholy spectacle drew tears from the eyes of even Alexander, familiar though he was with all the horrible vicissitudes and bloody scenes of war. Throwing his cloak over the body, he commanded that it be conveyed to the ladies of the Persian royal family who were captives at Susa, and furnished from his own treasury the necessary means for a royal funeral.

When Darius died, Alexander saw the field cleared of his last formidable foe. Thenceforward he could spend his time in his own manner, now in the enjoyment of rest and pleasure, and again in the prosecution of some minor conquest. He entered upon a pompous campaign into India, because, according to Grecian fable, Bacchus and Hercules, two sons of Jupiter, whose son he also claimed to be, had done the same. With contemptible arrogance, he claimed for himself divine honors. He gave up conquered cities, freely and unprovoked, to the mercy of his bloodthirsty and licentious soldiery. He often murdered his friends and favorites in his drunken frenzies. He encouraged such excessive drinking among his followers that on one occasion twenty of them died as the result of their carousal. At length, having sat through one long drinking spree, he was immediately invited to another, when, after drinking to each of the twenty guests present, he twice drank, says history, incredible as it may seem, the full

Herculean cup containing six of our quarts. He was seized with a violent fever, of which he died eleven days later, June 13, 323 B. C., while yet he stood only at the threshold of mature life, in the thirty-second year of his age.

VERSE 40 And the fourth kingdom shall be strong as iron: forasmuch as iron breaketh in pieces and subdueth all things: and as iron that breaketh all these, shall it break in pieces and bruise.

Iron Monarchy of Rome.—Thus far in the application of this prophecy there is a general agreement among expositors. That Babylon, Medo-Persia, and Greece are represented respectively by the head of gold, the breast and arms of silver, and the sides of brass, is acknowledged by all. But with as little ground for a diversity of views, there is strangely a difference of opinion as to what kingdom is symbolized by the fourth division of the great image—the legs of iron. What kingdom succeeded Greece in the empire of the world, for the legs of iron denote the fourth kingdom in the series? The testimony of history is full and explicit on this point. One kingdom did this, and one only, and that was Rome. It conquered Grecia; it subdued all things; like iron, it broke in pieces and bruised.

Says Bishop Newton: "The four different metals must signify four different nations: and as the gold signified the Babylonians, and the silver the Persians, and the brass the Macedonians; so the iron cannot signify the Macedonians again, but must necessarily denote some other nation: and we will venture to say that there is not a nation upon earth, to which this description is applicable, but the Romans."[7]

Gibbon, following the symbolic imagery of Daniel, thus describes this empire:

"The arms of the Republic, sometimes vanquished in battle, always victorious in war, advanced with rapid steps to the Euphrates, the Danube, the Rhine, and the ocean; and the images of gold, or silver, or brass, that might serve to represent

---

[7] Thomas Newton, *Dissertations on the Prophecies*, Vol. I, p. 240.

the nations and their kings, were successively broken by the iron monarchy of Rome."[8]

At the opening of the Christian Era, this empire took in the whole south of Europe, France, England, the greater part of the Netherlands, Switzerland, and the south of Germany, Hungary, Turkey, and Greece, not to speak of its possessions in Asia and Africa. Well therefore may Gibbon say of it:

"The empire of the Romans filled the world, and when that empire fell into the hands of a single person, the world became a safe and dreary prison for his enemies. . . . To resist was fatal, and it was impossible to fly."[9]

It will be noticed that at first the kingdom is described unqualifiedly as strong as iron. This was the period of its strength, during which it has been likened to a mighty colossus bestriding the nations, conquering everything, and giving laws to the world. But this was not to continue.

VERSE 41 And whereas thou sawest the feet and toes, part of potters' clay, and part of iron, the kingdom shall be divided; but there shall be in it of the strength of the iron, forasmuch as thou sawest the iron mixed with miry clay. 42 And as the toes of the feet were part of iron, and part of clay, so the kingdom shall be partly strong, and partly broken.

Rome Divided.—The element of weakness symbolized by the clay, pertained to the feet as well as to the toes. Rome, before its division into ten kingdoms, lost that iron vigor which it possessed to a superlative degree during the first centuries of its career. Luxury, with its accompanying effeminacy and degeneracy, the destroyer of nations as well as of individuals, began to corrode and weaken its iron sinews, and thus prepared the way for its disintegration into ten kingdoms.

The iron legs of the image terminate in feet and toes. To the toes, of which there were of course ten, our attention is called by the explicit mention of them in the prophecy. The

---

[8] Edward Gibbon, *The Decline and Fall of the Roman Empire*, Vol. III, general observations following chap. 38, p. 634. There are many editions of Gibbon's work beside the one used in the preparation of this book. For the student who has a different edition, the chapter is included in all references to facilitate the finding of the quotations.

[9] *Ibid.*, Vol. I, chap. 3, pp. 99, 100.

ADOLPH HIRSCHL, ARTIST

ROME SACKED BY THE VANDALS

The great "iron empire" of Rome crumbled under the violent attacks of invading hordes from the north.

kingdom represented by that part of the image to which the toes belonged, was finally divided into ten parts. The question therefore naturally arises, Do the ten toes of the image represent the ten final divisions of the Roman Empire? We answer, Yes.

The image of Daniel 2 is exactly parallel with the four beasts in the vision of Daniel 7. The fourth beast represents the same kingdom as do the iron legs of the image. The ten horns of the beast correspond naturally to the ten toes of the image. These horns are plainly declared to be ten kings which should arise. They are as much independent kingdoms as are the beasts themselves, for the beasts are spoken of in precisely the same manner—as "four kings, which shall arise." Daniel 7: 17. They do not denote a line of successive kings, but kings or kingdoms which existed contemporaneously, for three of them were plucked up by the little horn. The ten horns, beyond controversy, represent the ten kingdoms into which Rome was divided.

We have seen that in Daniel's interpretation of the image he uses the words "king" and "kingdom" interchangeably, the former denoting the same as the latter. In verse 44 he says that "in the days of these kings shall the God of heaven set up a kingdom." This shows that at the time the kingdom of God is set up, there will exist a plurality of kings. It cannot refer to the four preceding kingdoms; for it would be absurd to use such language in reference to a line of successive kings, since it would be in the days of the last king only, not in the days of any of the preceding, that the kingdom of God would be set up.

The Ten Kingdoms.—Here, then, is a division presented; and what have we in the symbol to indicate it?—Nothing but the toes of the image. Unless they do, we are left utterly in the dark on the nature and extent of the division which the prophecy shows did exist. To suppose this would be to cast a serious imputation upon the prophecy itself. We are therefore held to the conclusion that the ten toes of the image denote the ten parts into which the Roman Empire was divided.

This division was accomplished between A. D. 351 and 476. The era of this dissolution thus covered a hundred and twenty-five years, from about the middle of the fourth century to the last quarter of the fifth. No historians of whom we are aware, place the beginning of this work of the dismemberment of the Roman Empire earlier than A. D. 351, and there is general agreement in assigning its close in A. D. 476. Concerning the intermediate dates, that is, the precise time from which each of the ten kingdoms that arose on the ruins of the Roman Empire is to be dated, there is some difference of views among historians. Nor does this seem strange, when we consider that there was an era of great confusion, that the map of the Roman Empire during that time underwent many sudden and violent changes, and that the paths of hostile nations charging upon its territory crossed and recrossed each other in a labyrinth of confusion. But all historians agree in this, that out of the territory of Western Rome, ten separate kingdoms were ultimately established, and we may safely assign them to the time between the dates above named; namely, A. D. 351 and 476.

The ten nations which were most instrumental in breaking up the Roman Empire, and which at some time in their history held respectively portions of Roman territory as separate and independent kingdoms, may be enumerated (without respect to the time of their establishment) as follows: Huns, Ostrogoths, Visigoths, Franks, Vandals, Suevi, Burgundians, Heruli, Anglo-Saxons, and Lombards. * The connection between these and some of the modern nations of Europe, is still traceable in the names, as England, Burgundy, Lombardy, France, etc.

But it may be asked, Why not suppose the two legs to denote division as well as the toes? Would it not be as inconsistent to say that the toes denote division and the legs do not, as to say that the legs denote division and the toes do not? We answer that the prophecy itself must govern our conclu-

---

* In harmony with seven leading commentators, the author includes the Huns as one of the ten kingdoms. Others, however, with historical precedent, name the Alamanni, or Germans, instead of the Huns.—*Editors.*

sions in this matter; for though it says nothing of division in connection with the legs, it does introduce the subject of division as we come to the feet and toes. The record says, "Whereas thou sawest the feet and toes, part of potters' clay and part of iron, the kingdom shall be divided." No division could take place, or at least none is said to have taken place, until the weakening element of the clay is introduced; and we do not find this until we come to the feet and toes. But we are not to understand that the clay denotes one division and the iron the other; for after the long-existing unity of the kingdom was broken, no one of the fragments was as strong as the original iron, but all were in a state of weakness denoted by the mixture of iron and clay.

The conclusion is inevitable, therefore, that the prophet has here stated the cause for the effect. The introduction of the weakness of the clay element, as we come to the feet, resulted in the division of the kingdom into ten parts, as represented by the ten toes; and this result, or division, is more than intimated in the sudden mention of a plurality of contemporaneous kings. Therefore, while we find no evidence that the legs denote division, but serious objections against such a view, we do find good reason for supposing that the toes denote division, as here claimed.

Furthermore, each of the four monarchies had its own particular territory, which was the kingdom proper, and where we are to look for the chief events in its history shadowed forth by the symbol. We are not, therefore, to look for the divisions of the Roman Empire in the territory formerly occupied by Babylon, or Persia, or Grecia, but in the territory proper of the Roman kingdom, which was finally known as the Western Empire. Rome conquered the world, but the kingdom of Rome proper lay west of Grecia. That is what was represented by the legs of iron. There, then, we look for the ten kingdoms, and there we find them. We are not obliged to mutilate or deform the symbol to make it a fit and accurate representation of historical events.

VERSE 43 And whereas thou sawest iron mixed with miry clay, they shall mingle themselves with the seed of men: but they shall not cleave one to another, even as iron is not mixed with clay.

Rome the Last Universal Empire.—With Rome fell the last of the world's universal empires. Heretofore it was possible for one nation, rising superior to its neighbors in prowess, bravery, and the science of war, to consolidate them into one vast empire. But when Rome fell, such possibilities forever passed away. The iron was mixed with the clay, and lost the power of cohesion. No man or combination of men can again consolidate the fragments. This point is so well set forth by another that we quote his words:

"From this, its divided state, the first strength of the empire departed—but not as that of the others had done. No other kingdom was to succeed it, as it had the three which went before it. It was to continue, in this tenfold division, until the kingdom of the stone smote it, upon its feet; broke them in pieces, and scattered them as the wind does 'the chaff of the summer threshing-floor!' Yet, through all this time, a portion of its strength was to remain. And so the prophet says, 'And as the toes of the feet were part of iron, and part of clay, so the kingdom shall be partly strong, and partly broken.' Verse 42. . . . Time and again men have dreamed of rearing on these dominions *one* mighty kingdom. Charlemagne tried it. Charles V tried it. Louis XIV tried it. Napoleon tried it. But neither succeeded. A single verse of prophecy was stronger than all their hosts. . . . '*Partly strong*, and *partly broken*,' was the prophetic description. And such, too, has been the historic fact concerning them. . . . Ten kingdoms were formed out of it; and 'broken,' as then it was, it still continues—i.e., '*partly* broken.' . . . It is 'partly strong'—i.e., it retains, even in its broken state, enough of its iron strength to resist all attempts to mold its parts together. '*This shall not be*,' says the word of God. '*This has not been*,' replies the book of history.

"But then, men may say, 'Another plan remains. If force cannot avail, diplomacy and reasons of state may—we will try them.' And so the prophecy foreshadows this when it says, 'They shall mingle themselves with the seed of men'—i.e., marriages shall be formed, in hope thus to consolidate their power, and, in the end, to unite these divided kingdoms into one.

"And shall this device succeed?—No. The prophet answers: 'They shall not cleave one to another, even as iron is not mixed with clay.' And the history of Europe, is but a running commentary on the exact fulfillment of these words. From the time of Canute until the present age, it has been the policy of the reigning monarchs, the beaten path which they have trodden, in order to reach a mightier scepter and a wider sway. . . . Napoleon . . . sought to reach by alliance what he could not gain by force, i.e., to build up *one* mighty, consolidated empire. And did he succeed?—Nay. The very power with which he was allied, proved his destruction, in the troops of Blucher, on the field of Waterloo! The iron would not mingle with clay."[10]

But Napoleon was not the last to try the experiment. Numerous European wars followed the efforts of the Little Corporal. To avert future conflicts, benevolent rulers resorted to the expedient of intermarriage to ensure peace, until by the opening of the twentieth century it was asserted that every ranking hereditary ruler of Europe was related to the British royal family. World War I showed the futility of these attempts.

Out of the horrors of that titanic struggle was born an ideal expressed by President Woodrow Wilson, who exclaimed, "The world has been made safe for democracy!" With the conviction that a war had been fought which would end war came the announced inherent rights of minorities, and the principles of self-determination, ensured by a world league of nations which would restrain dictators and punish aggressors.

Yet under the very shadow of the League of Nations' palace arose leaders who would destroy world peace and shatter

---

[10] William Newton, *Lectures on the First Two Visions of the Book of Daniel*, pp. 34-36.

R. M. ELDRIDGE, ARTIST

"THE KINGDOM SHALL BE DIVIDED"

Thus the prophetic word foretold the breaking up of the mighty Roman Empire.

the ideal of world union, while preaching a new social revolution. They vainly promised the triumph of culture and a union born of racial superiority ensuring the "partly strong" and "partly broken" nations of Europe "a thousand years of tranquillity."

Out of the welter of confusion, the wreck of nations, the destruction of institutions, the sacrifice of treasure resultant from centuries of frugality, through eyes grief-dimmed by the loss of the flower of its young manhood, the ravishment of its womanhood, the slaughter of infancy and age, through clouds of smoking human blood a distraught world looks anxiously for its signs of surcease. Will the elusive mirage of world peace based upon a trust in European solidarity, the result of wishful thinking, again cause men to forget the counsel of the word of God, "They shall not cleave one to another"?

Alliances may come, and it may appear that the iron and miry clay of the feet and toes of the great image have finally fused, but God said, "They shall not cleave one to another." It may seem that old animosities have disappeared and that the "ten kings" have gone the way of all the earth, but "the Scripture cannot be broken." John 10: 35.

We conclude with a word by William Newton: "And yet if, as the result of these alliances, or of other causes, that number is sometimes disturbed, it need not surprise us. It is, indeed, just what the prophecy seems to call for. The iron was 'mixed with the clay.' For a season, in the image, you might not distinguish between them. But they would not remain so. 'They *shall not cleave* one to another.' The nature of the substances forbids them to do so in the one case; the word of prophecy in the other. Yet there was to be the attempt to mingle—nay, more, there was an approach at mingling in both cases. But it was to be abortive. And how marked the emphasis with which history affirms this declaration of the word of God!"[11]

---

[11] *Ibid.*, p. 36.

VERSE 44 And in the days of these kings shall the God of heaven set up a kingdom, which shall never be destroyed: and the kingdom shall not be left to other people, but it shall break in pieces and consume all these kingdoms, and it shall stand forever. 45 Forasmuch as thou sawest that the stone was cut out of the mountain without hands, and that it brake in pieces the iron, the brass, the clay, the silver, and the gold; the great God hath made known to the king what shall come to pass hereafter: and the dream is certain, and the interpretation thereof sure.

The God of Heaven to Set Up a Kingdom.—We here reach the climax of this stupendous prophecy. When Time in his onward flight shall bring us to the sublime scene here predicted, we shall have reached the end of human history. The kingdom of God! Grand provision for a new and glorious dispensation, in which His people shall find a happy terminus of this world's sad, degenerate, and changing career. Transporting change for all the righteous, from gloom to glory, from strife to peace, from a sinful to a holy world, from death to life, from tyranny and oppression to the happy freedom and blessed privileges of a heavenly kingdom! Glorious transition, from weakness to strength, from the changing and decaying to the immutable and eternal!

But when is this kingdom to be established? May we hope for an answer to an inquiry of such momentous concern to our race? These are the very questions on which the word of God does not leave us in ignorance, and herein is seen the surpassing value of this heavenly boon.

The Bible plainly declares that the kingdom of God was still future at the time of our Lord's last Passover. (Matthew 26: 29.) Christ did not set up the kingdom before His ascension. (Acts 1: 6.) It states further that flesh and blood cannot inherit the kingdom of God. (1 Corinthians 15: 50.) It is a matter of promise to the apostles, and to all those who love God. (James 2: 5.) It is promised in the future to the little flock. (Luke 12: 32.) Through much tribulation the saints are to enter the coming kingdom. (Acts 14: 22.) It is to be set up when Christ shall judge the living and the dead. (2 Timothy 4: 1.) This is to be when He shall come in

His glory with all His holy angels. (Matthew 25: 31-34.)

We do not say that the exact time is revealed (we emphasize the fact that it is not) in this prophecy of Daniel 2 or in any other prophecy; but so near an approximation is given that the generation which is to see the establishment of this kingdom may mark its approach unerringly, and make that preparation which will entitle the children of God to share in all its glories.

Time has fully developed this great image in all its parts. Most accurately does it represent the important political events it was designed to symbolize. It has stood complete for more than fourteen centuries. It waits to be smitten upon the feet by the stone cut out of the mountain without hand, that is, the kingdom of Christ. This is to be accomplished when the Lord shall be revealed in flaming fire, "taking vengeance on them that know not God, and that obey not the gospel of our Lord Jesus Christ." 2 Thessalonians 1: 8. (See also Psalm 2: 8, 9.) In the days of these kings the God of heaven is to set up a kingdom. We have been in the days of these kings for many centuries, and we are still in their days. So far as this prophecy is concerned, the very next event is the setting up of God's everlasting kingdom. Other prophecies and innumerable signs show unmistakably that the coming of Christ is near at hand.

The early Christian church interpreted the prophecies of Daniel 2, 7, and 8 as we do now. Hippolytus, who lived A. D. 160-236, and is thought to have been a disciple of Irenæus, one of the four greatest theologians of his age, says in his exposition of Daniel 2 and Daniel 7:

"The golden head of the image and the lioness denoted the Babylonians; the shoulders and arms of silver, and the bear, represented the Persians and Medes; the belly and thighs of brass, and the leopard, meant the Greeks, who held the sovereignty from Alexander's time; the legs of iron, and the beast dreadful and terrible, expressed the Romans, who hold the sovereignty at present; the toes of the feet which were part clay and part iron, and the ten horns, were emblems of the

© R. & H. PUB. ASSN.

T. K. MARTIN, ARTIST

"A STONE SMOTE THE IMAGE UPON HIS FEET"

The last act in the drama of world events will be the establishment of Christ's kingdom in the earth.

kingdoms that are yet to rise; the other little horn that grows up among them meant the Antichrist in their midst; the stone that smites the earth and brings judgment upon the world was Christ."[12]

"Speak with me, O blessed Daniel. Give me full assurance, I beseech thee. Thou dost prophesy concerning the lioness in Babylon; for thou wast a captive there. Thou hast unfolded the future regarding the bear; for thou wast still in the world, and didst see the things come to pass. Then thou speakest to me of the leopard; and whence canst thou know this, for thou art already gone to thy rest? Who instructed thee to announce these things, but He who formed thee in (from) thy mother's womb? That is God, thou sayest. Thou hast spoken indeed, and that not falsely. The leopard has arisen; the he-goat is come; he hath smitten the ram; he hath broken his horns in pieces; he hath stamped upon him with his feet. He has been exalted by his fall; (the) four horns have come up from under that one. Rejoice, blessed Daniel! thou hast not been in error: all these things have come to pass.

"After this again thou hast told me of the beast dreadful and terrible. 'It had iron teeth and claws of brass: it devoured and brake in pieces, and stamped the residue with the feet of it.' Already the iron rules; already it subdues and breaks all in pieces; already it brings all the unwilling into subjection; already we see these things ourselves. Now we glorify God, being instructed by thee."[13]

The part of the prophecy that had been fulfilled at that time was clear to the early Christians. They saw also that there would develop ten kingdoms out of the Roman Empire, and that the Antichrist would appear among them. They looked forward with hope to the grand consummation, when the second coming of Christ would bring an end to all earthly kingdoms, and the kingdom of righteousness would be set up.

---

[12] Hippolytus, "Treatise on Christ and Antichrist," *Ante-Nicene Fathers*, Vol. V, p. 210, par. 28.

[13] *Ibid.*, pars. 32, 33.

The coming kingdom! This ought to be the all-absorbing topic with the present generation. Reader, are you ready for the issue? He who enters this kingdom shall dwell in it not merely for such a lifetime as men live in this present state. He shall not see it degenerate, or be overthrown by a succeeding and more powerful kingdom. No, he enters it to participate in all its privileges and blessings, and to share its glories forever, for this kingdom is not to "be left to other people."

Again we ask you, Are you ready? The terms of heirship are most liberal: "If ye be Christ's, then are ye Abraham's seed, and heirs according to the promise." Galatians 3: 29. Are you on terms of friendship with Christ, the coming King? Do you love His character? Are you trying to walk humbly in His footsteps, and obey His teachings? If not, read your fate in the cases of those in the parable, of whom it was said, "But those Mine enemies, which would not that I should reign over them, bring hither, and slay them before Me." Luke 19: 27. There is to be no rival kingdom where you can find an asylum if you remain an enemy to this, for God's kingdom is to occupy all the territory ever possessed by any and all of the kingdoms of this world, past or present. It is to fill the whole earth. Happy they to whom the rightful Sovereign, the all-conquering King, at last can say, "Come, ye blessed of My Father, inherit the kingdom prepared for you from the foundation of the world." Matthew 25: 34.

VERSE 46 Then the king Nebuchadnezzar fell upon his face, and worshiped Daniel, and commanded that they should offer an oblation and sweet odors unto him. 47 The king answered unto Daniel, and said, Of a truth it is, that your God is a God of gods, and a Lord of kings, and a revealer of secrets, seeing thou couldest reveal this secret. 48 Then the king made Daniel a great man, and gave him many great gifts, and made him ruler over the whole province of Babylon, and chief of the governors over all the wise men of Babylon. 49 Then Daniel requested of the king, and he set Shadrach, Meshach, and Abednego, over the affairs of the province of Babylon: but Daniel sat in the gate of the king.

We must return to the palace of Nebuchadnezzar, and to Daniel, as he stands in the presence of the king. He has made known to the monarch the dream and its interpretation, while the courtiers and the baffled soothsayers and astrologers waited in silent awe and wonder.

Nebuchadnezzar Exalts Daniel.—In fulfillment of his promise of rewards the king made Daniel a great man. There are two things which in this life are specially supposed to make a man great, and both these Daniel received from the king: A man is considered great if he is a man of wealth; and we read that the king gave him many and great gifts. If in conjunction with riches a man has power, certainly in popular estimation he is considered a great man; and power was bestowed upon Daniel in abundant measure. He was made ruler over the province of Babylon, and chief of the governors over all the wise men of Babylon. Thus speedily and abundantly did Daniel begin to be rewarded for his fidelity to his own conscience and the requirements of God.

Daniel did not become bewildered or intoxicated by his signal victory and his wonderful advancement. He first remembered the three who were companions with him in anxiety respecting the king's matter. As they had helped him with their prayers, he determined that they should share his honors. At his request they were placed over the affairs of Babylon, while Daniel himself sat in the gate of the king. The gate was the place where councils were held and where matters of chief moment were considered. The record is a simple declaration that Daniel became chief counselor to the king.

A TEST OF FAITH

The Hebrew youth in the fiery furnace were saved by the power of God.

CHAPTER III

INTEGRITY TESTED BY FIRE

VERSE 1 Nebuchadnezzar the king made an image of gold, whose height was threescore cubits, and the breadth thereof six cubits: he set it up in the plain of Dura, in the province of Babylon.

WE MAY well believe that this image had some reference to the dream of the king as described in the previous chapter. In that dream the head was of gold, representing Nebuchadnezzar's kingdom. That was succeeded by metals of inferior quality, denoting a succession of kingdoms. Nebuchadnezzar was doubtless gratified that his kingdom should be represented by the gold; but that it should ever be succeeded by another kingdom was not so pleasing. Therefore, instead of having simply the head of his image of gold, he made it all of gold, to denote that his kingdom should not give way to another kingdom, but be perpetual.

VERSE 2 Then Nebuchadnezzar the king sent to gather together the princes, the governors, and the captains, the judges, the treasurers, the counselors, the sheriffs, and all the rulers of the provinces, to come to the dedication of the image which Nebuchadnezzar the king had set up. 3 Then the princes, the governors, and captains, the judges, the treasurers, the counselors, the sheriffs, and all the rulers of the provinces, were gathered together unto the dedication of the image that Nebuchadnezzar the king had set up; and they stood before the image that Nebuchadnezzar had set up. 4 Then an herald cried aloud, To you it is commanded, O people, nations, and languages, 5 that at what time ye hear the sound of the cornet, flute, harp, sackbut, psaltery, dulcimer, and all kinds of musick, ye fall down and worship the golden image that Nebuchadnezzar the king hath set up: 6 and whoso falleth not down and worshipeth shall the same hour be cast into the midst of a burning fiery furnace. 7 Therefore at that time, when all the people heard the sound of the cornet, flute, harp, sackbut, psaltery, and all kinds of musick, all the people, the nations, and the languages, fell down and worshiped the golden image that Nebuchadnezzar the king had set up.

Dedication of the Image.—The dedication of this image was made a great occasion, for the chief men of the kingdom were called together. To such pains and expense will men go in sustaining idolatrous and heathen systems of worship. Alas, that those who have the true religion should be so far outdone in these respects by the upholders of the false and counterfeit! The worship was accompanied with music; and whoever failed to participate therein was threatened with being thrown into a fiery furnace. Such are ever the strongest motives to impel men in any direction—pleasure on the one hand, pain on the other.

VERSE 8 Wherefore at that time certain Chaldeans came near, and accused the Jews. 9 They spake and said to the king Nebuchadnezzar, O king, live forever. 10 Thou, O king, hast made a decree, that every man that shall hear the sound of the cornet, flute, harp, sackbut, psaltery, and dulcimer, and all kinds of musick, shall fall down and worship the golden image: 11 and whoso falleth not down and worshipeth, that he should be cast into the midst of a burning fiery furnace. 12 There are certain Jews whom thou hast set over the affairs of the province of Babylon, Shadrach, Meshach, and Abednego; these men, O king, have not regarded thee: they serve not thy gods, nor worship the golden image which thou hast set up.

Three Hebrews Under Trial.—The Chaldeans who accused the Jews were probably the sect of philosophers who went by that name, and who were still smarting under their failure to interpret the king's dream of Daniel 2. They were eager to seize upon any pretext to accuse the Jews before the king, and either disgrace or destroy them. They worked upon the king's prejudice by strong insinuations of their ingratitude. Thou hast set them over the affairs of Babylon, and yet they have disregarded thee, they said. Where Daniel was upon this occasion, is not known. He was probably absent on some business of the empire. But why should Shadrach, Meshach, and Abednego, since they knew they could not worship the image, be present on the occasion? Was it not because they were willing to comply with the king's requirements as far as they could without compromising their religious principles? The king required them to be present. With this requirement they could comply, and they did. He required them to worship the image. This their religion forbade, and this they therefore refused to do.

VERSE 13 Then Nebuchadnezzar in his rage and fury commanded to bring Shadrach, Meshach, and Abednego. Then they brought these men before the king. 14 Nebuchadnezzar spake and said unto them, Is it true, O Shadrach, Meshach, and Abednego, do not ye serve my gods, nor worship the golden image which I have set up? 15 Now if ye be ready that at what time ye hear the sound of the cornet, flute, harp, sackbut, psaltery, and dulcimer, and all kinds of musick, ye fall down and worship the image which I have made; well: but if ye worship not, ye shall be cast the same hour into the midst of a burning fiery furnace; and who is that God that shall deliver you out of my hands? 16 Shadrach, Meshach, and Abednego, answered and said to the king, O Nebuchadnezzar, we are not careful to answer thee in this matter. 17 If it be so, our God whom we serve is able to deliver us from the burning fiery furnace, and He will deliver us out of thine hand, O king. 18 But if not, be it known unto thee, O king, that we will not serve thy gods, nor worship the golden image which thou hast set up.

The forbearance of the king is shown in his granting Shadrach, Meshach, and Abednego another trial after their first failure to comply with his requirements. Doubtless the matter was thoroughly understood. They could not plead ignorance. They knew what the king wanted, and their failure to fulfill his command was an intentional and deliberate refusal to obey him. With most kings this would have been enough to seal their fate. But no, said Nebuchadnezzar, I will overlook this offense if upon a second trial they comply with the law. But they informed the king that he need not trouble himself to repeat the test.

Their answer was both honest and decisive. "We are not careful," said they, "to answer thee in this matter." That is, you need not grant us the favor of another trial; our minds are made up. We can answer as well now as at any future time; and our answer is, We will not serve thy gods, nor worship the golden image which thou hast set up. Our God can deliver if He so desires; but if not, we shall not complain. We know His will, and we shall render Him unconditional obedience.

VERSE 19 Then was Nebuchadnezzar full of fury, and the form of his visage was changed against Shadrach, Meshach, and Abednego: therefore he spake, and commanded that they should heat the furnace one seven times more than it was wont to be heated. 20 And he commanded the most mighty men that were in his army to bind Shadrach, Meshach, and Abed-nego, and to cast them into the burning fiery furnace. 21 Then these men were bound in their coats, their hosen, and their hats, and their other garments, and were cast into the midst of the burning fiery furnace. 22 Therefore because the king's commandment was urgent, and the furnace exceeding hot, the flame of the fire slew those men that took up Shadrach, Meshach, and Abednego. 23 And these three men, Shadrach, Meshach, and Abed-nego, fell down bound into the midst of the burning fiery furnace. 24 Then Nebuchadnezzar the king was astonied and rose up in haste, and spake, and said unto his counselors, Did not we cast three men bound into the midst of the fire? They answered and said unto the king, True, O king. 25 He answered and said, Lo, I see four men loose, walking in the midst of the fire, and they have no hurt; and the form of the fourth is like the Son of God.

Nebuchadnezzar was not entirely free from the faults and follies into which an absolute monarch so easily runs. Intoxicated with unlimited power, he could not brook disobedience or contradiction. Let his expressed authority be resisted on however good grounds, and he exhibits the weakness common to our fallen humanity under like circumstances, and flies into a passion of rage. Ruler of the world, he was not equal to that still harder task of ruling his own spirit. Even the form of his visage was changed. Instead of the calm, dignified, self-possessed ruler that he should have appeared, he betrayed himself in look and act as the slave of ungovernable passion.

Cast Into the Fiery Furnace.—The furnace was heated seven times hotter than usual; in other words, to its utmost capacity. The king overreached himself in this for even if the super-heated furnace had the expected effect upon the ones he cast into it, the victims would only have been destroyed the sooner. The king would have gained nothing by his fury. But seeing they were delivered from it, much was gained on the part of the cause of God and His truth; for the more intense the heat, the greater and more impressive the miracle when the young men were delivered from it.

Every circumstance revealed the direct power of God. The Hebrews were bound in all their garments, but came out with not even the smell of fire upon them. The mightiest men in the army were chosen to cast them in, but the fire burned them before they came in contact with it. But upon the Hebrews it had no effect, although they were in the very midst of its flames. It is evident that the fire was under the control of some supernatural intelligence, for while it consumed the cords with which they were bound, so that they were free to walk about in the midst of the fire, it did not even singe their garments. They did not spring out of the fire as soon as free, but remained in it; for the king had put them into the furnace, and it was his place to call them out. Then, too, the form of the fourth was with them, and in His presence they could be content and joyful, as well in the furnace of fire as in the delights and luxuries of the palace. Let us in all our trials, afflictions, persecutions, and straitened places, but have the "form of the fourth" with us, and it is enough.

The King Gets a New Vision.—The king said, "The form of the fourth is like the Son of God." This language is by some supposed to refer to Christ. A more literal rendering, according to the Revised Version, and other good authorities, is "like a son of the gods," that is, He had the appearance of a divine being. Though this was doubtless Nebuchadnezzar's accustomed way of speaking of the gods he worshiped (see comments on Daniel 4: 18), it does not at all prevent its referring to Christ, inasmuch as the word אֱלָהִין *elahin*, used here in its Chaldean form, although in the plural number, is regularly translated "God" throughout the Old Testament.

What a scathing rebuke upon the king for his folly and madness was the deliverance of these worthies from the fiery furnace! A higher power than any on earth had vindicated those who stood firm against idolatry, and poured contempt on the worship and requirements of the king. None of the gods of the heathen ever had wrought such deliverance as that, nor were they able to do so.

VERSE 26 Then Nebuchadnezzar came near to the mouth of the burning fiery furnace, and spake, and said, Shadrach, Meshach, and Abednego, ye servants of the most high God, come forth, and come hither. Then Shadrach, Meshach, and Abednego, came forth of the midst of the fire.

27 And the princes, governors, and captains, and the king's counselors, being gathered together, saw these men, upon whose bodies the fire had no power, nor was an hair of their head singed, neither were their coats changed, nor the smell of fire had passed on them. 28 Then Nebuchadnezzar spake, and said, Blessed be the God of Shadrach, Meshach, and Abednego, who hath sent His angel, and delivered His servants that trusted in Him, and have changed the king's word, and yielded their bodies, that they might not serve nor worship any god, except their own God. 29 Therefore I make a decree, That every people, nation, and language, which speak anything amiss against the God of Shadrach, Meshach, and Abednego, shall be cut in pieces, and their houses shall be made a dunghill: because there is no other God that can deliver after this sort. 30 Then the king promoted Shadrach, Meshach, and Abednego, in the province of Babylon.

When bidden, these three men came forth from the furnace. Then the princes, governors, and king's counselors, through whose advice, or at least concurrence, they had been cast into the furnace (for the king said to them, "Did not *we* cast three men bound into the midst of the fire?" Verse 24), were gathered together to look upon these men, and have tangible proof of their miraculous preservation. The worship of the great image was forgotten. The interest of this vast concourse of people was concentrated upon these three remarkable men. How the knowledge of this deliverance would be spread abroad throughout the empire, as the people should return to their respective provinces! What a notable instance in which God caused the wrath of man to praise Him!

The King Acknowledges the True God.—Then the king blessed the God of Shadrach, Meshach, and Abednego, and made a decree that none should speak against Him. This the Chaldeans had undoubtedly done. In those days, each nation had its god or gods, for there were "gods many, and lords many." The victory of one nation over another was supposed to be won because the gods of the conquered nation were not able to deliver it from the conquerors. The Jews had been wholly subjugated by the Babylonians, who had no doubt spoken disparagingly or contemptuously of the God of the Jews. This the king now prohibited; for he plainly understood that his success against the Hebrews was the result of their sins and not of any lack of power on the part of their God. In what a conspicuous and exalted light this placed the God of the Hebrews in comparison with the gods of the nations! It was an acknowledgment that He held men amenable to some high standard of moral character, and that He did not regard with indifference their actions in reference to it. Nebuchadnezzar did right in publicly exalting the God of heaven above all other gods. But he had no more right, either civil or moral, to attempt to force his subjects to similar confession and reverence, and to threaten men's lives for not worshiping the true God, than he had to threaten death to all who refused to worship the golden image. God never compels the conscience.

Three Hebrews Promoted.—The king promoted the young captives, that is, he restored to them the offices which they held before the charges of disobedience and treason were brought against them. At the end of verse 30 the Septuagint, the Greek version of the Old Testament, adds to the Hebrew text: "He advanced them to be governors over all the Jews that were in his kingdom." It is not probable that he insisted on any further worship of his image.

R. M. ELDRIDGE, ARTIST

NEBUCHADNEZZAR'S PRIDE

With pride, Nebuchadnezzar exclaimed: "Is not this great Babylon, that I have built . . . by the might of my power, and for the honor of my majesty?" Daniel 4: 30.

CHAPTER IV

THE MOST HIGH RULETH

VERSE 1 Nebuchadnezzar the king, unto all people, nations, and languages, that dwell in all the earth: Peace be multiplied unto you. 2 I thought it good to show the signs and wonders that the high God hath wrought toward me. 3 How great are His signs! and how mighty are His wonders! His kingdom is an everlasting kingdom, and His dominion is from generation to generation.

THIS chapter, says Adam Clarke, "is a regular decree, and is one of the most ancient on record; and no doubt was copied from the state papers of Babylon. Daniel has preserved it in the original language." [1]

The King Magnifies the True God.—This decree of Nebuchadnezzar was promulgated in the usual way. He wished to make known, not to a few men only, but to all peoples, and nations, God's wonderful dealings with him. People are ever ready to tell what God has done for them in the way of benefits and blessings. We ought to be no less ready to tell what God has done for us in the way of humiliation and chastisements. Nebuchadnezzar set us a good example in this respect, as we shall see from the subsequent parts of this chapter. He frankly confessed the vanity and pride of his heart, and freely told the methods God used to humble him. With a genuine spirit of repentance and humiliation, he thought it good to show these things, that the sovereignty of God might be extolled and His name adored. Nebuchadnezzar no longer claimed immutability for his own kingdom, but made a full surrender to God, acknowledging His kingdom alone to be everlasting, and His dominion from generation to generation.

VERSE 4 I Nebuchadnezzar was at rest in mine house, and flourishing in my palace: 5 I saw a dream which made me afraid, and the thoughts upon my bed and the visions of my head troubled me. 6 Therefore made I a decree to bring in all the wise men of Babylon before me, that they might

[1] Adam Clarke, *Commentary on the Old Testament*, Vol. IV, p. 582, note on Daniel 4: 1.

make known unto me the interpretation of the dream. 7 Then came in the magicians, the astrologers, the Chaldeans, and the soothsayers: and I told the dream before them; but they did not make known unto me the interpretation thereof. 8 But at the last Daniel came in before me, whose name was Belteshazzar, according to the name of my god, and in whom is the spirit of the holy gods: and before him I told the dream, saying, 9 O Belteshazzar, master of the magicians, because I know that the spirit of the holy gods is in thee, and no secret troubleth thee, tell me the visions of my dream that I have seen, and the interpretation thereof. 10 Thus were the visions of mine head in my bed: I saw, and behold, a tree in the midst of the earth, and the height thereof was great. 11 The tree grew, and was strong, and the height thereof reached unto heaven, and the sight thereof to the end of all the earth: 12 the leaves thereof were fair, and the fruit thereof much, and in it was meat for all: the beasts of the field had shadow under it, and the fowls of the heaven dwelt in the boughs thereof, and all flesh was fed of it. 13 I saw in the visions of my head upon my bed, and, behold, a watcher and an holy one came down from heaven; 14 he cried aloud, and said thus, Hew down the tree, and cut off his branches, shake off his leaves, and scatter his fruit: let the beasts get away from under it, and the fowls from his branches: 15 nevertheless leave the stump of his roots in the earth, even with a band of iron and brass, in the tender grass of the field; and let it be wet with the dew of heaven, and let his portion be with the beasts in the grass of the earth: 16 let his heart be changed from man's, and let a beast's heart be given unto him; and let seven times pass over him. 17 This matter is by the decree of the watchers, and the demand by the word of the holy ones: to the intent that the living may know that the Most High ruleth in the kingdom of men, and giveth it to whomsoever He will, and setteth up over it the basest of men. 18 This dream I king Nebuchadnezzar have seen. Now thou, O Belteshazzar, declare the interpretation thereof, forasmuch as all the wise men of my kingdom are not able to make known unto me the interpretation: but thou art able; for the spirit of the holy gods is in thee.

This part of the narrative opens with Nebuchadnezzar as a victor over his foes. He had accomplished successfully all his military enterprises. He had subdued Assyria, Phœnicia, Judea, Egypt, and Arabia. These great conquests probably betrayed him into vanity and self-confidence. At this very time, when he felt most secure, when it was most unlikely that anything would occur to disturb his self-complacent tranquillity—at this time God chose to trouble him with fears and forebodings.

The King Troubled by Another Dream.—But what could strike fear to the heart of such a monarch as Nebuchadnezzar? He had been a warrior from his youth. He had often faced the perils of battle, the terrors of slaughter and carnage, and in the midst of such scenes he had been unmoved. What could make him afraid now? No foe threatened, no hostile cloud was visible! His own thoughts and visions were used to teach him what nothing else could—a salutary lesson of dependence and humility. He who had terrified others, but whom no others could terrify, was made a terror to himself.

A still greater humiliation than that narrated in the second chapter was brought upon the magicians. At that time they boasted that if they only knew the dream they could make known the interpretation. Upon this occasion Nebuchadnezzar distinctly remembered the dream and related it to them, but his magicians ignominiously failed him again. They could not make known the interpretation, and once again the king turned to the prophet of God.

The reign of Nebuchadnezzar is symbolized by a tree in the midst of the earth. Babylon, the city where Nebuchadnezzar reigned, was approximately in the center of the then-known world. The tree reached unto heaven, and the leaves thereof were fair. Its external glory and splendor were great. Its fruit was abundant, and it had food for all. The beasts of the field had shadow under it, and the fowls of heaven dwelt in its branches. What could more plainly and forcibly represent the fact that Nebuchadnezzar ruled his kingdom in such a way as to afford the fullest protection, support, and prosperity to all his subjects? When the order was given that this tree should be cut down, it was commanded that the stump should be left in the earth. It was to be protected with a band of iron and brass, that it might not decay, but that the source of future growth and greatness might be left.

The day is coming when the wicked shall be cut down, and no hope will be left them. No mercy will be mingled with their punishment. They shall be destroyed both root and branch.

"Let *seven times* pass over him," was the decree. This

simple expression is evidently to be understood literally. But how long a period is denoted by the words "seven times"? This may be determined by ascertaining how long Nebuchadnezzar, in fulfillment of this prediction, was driven out to have his dwelling with the beasts of the field. This, Josephus informs us, was seven years.[2] A "time," here, then, denotes one year.

What an interest the holy ones, or angels, take in human affairs! They see, as mortals never can, how unseemly a thing is pride in the human heart. As ministers of God they cheerfully execute His decrees for the correction of evil. Man must know that he is not the architect of his own fortune, for there is One who ruleth in the kingdom of men on whom his dependence should be humbly placed. A man may be a successful monarch, but he should not pride himself upon that; for unless the Lord had permitted him to rule, he would never have reached this position of honor.

Nebuchadnezzar acknowledged the supremacy of the true God over the heathen oracles. He appealed to Daniel to solve the mystery. "Thou art able," he said; "for the spirit of the holy gods is in thee."

As remarked on Daniel 3: 25, Nebuchadnezzar here again used his accustomed way of mentioning "gods" in the plural, though the Septuagint renders the phrase "the Holy Spirit of God is in thee."

VERSE 19 Then Daniel, whose name was Belteshazzar, was astonied for one hour, and his thoughts troubled him. The king spake, and said, Belteshazzar, let not the dream, or the interpretation thereof, trouble thee. Belteshazzar answered and said, My lord, the dream be to them that hate thee, and the interpretation thereof to thine enemies. 20 The tree that thou sawest, which grew, and was strong, whose height reached unto the heaven, and the sight thereof to all the earth; 21 whose leaves were fair, and the fruit thereof much, and in it was meat for all; under which the beasts of the field dwelt, and upon whose branches the fowls of the heaven had their habitation: 22 it is thou, O king, that art grown and become strong: for thy greatness is grown, and reacheth unto heaven, and thy dominion to the end of the

---

[2] See Flavius Josephus, "Antiquities of the Jews," book 10, chap. 10, sec. 6, *Works of Flavius Josephus*, p. 316.

earth. 23 And whereas the king saw a watcher and an holy one coming down from heaven, and saying, Hew the tree down, and destroy it; yet leave the stump of the roots thereof in the earth, even with a band of iron and brass, in the tender grass of the field; and let it be wet with the dew of heaven, and let his portion be with the beasts of the field, till seven times pass over him; 24 this is the interpretation, O king, and this is the decree of the Most High, which is come upon my lord the king: 25 that they shall drive thee from men, and thy dwelling shall be with the beasts of the field, and they shall make thee to eat grass as oxen, and they shall wet thee with the dew of heaven, and seven times shall pass over thee, till thou know that the Most High ruleth in the kingdom of men, and giveth it to whomsoever He will. 26 And whereas they commanded to leave the stump of the tree roots; thy kingdom shall be sure unto thee, after that thou shalt have known that the Heavens do rule. 27 Wherefore, O king, let my counsel be acceptable unto thee, and break off thy sins by righteousness, and thine iniquities by showing mercy to the poor; if it may be a lengthening of thy tranquillity.

The hesitation of Daniel, who sat astonished for one hour, did not arise from any difficulty he had in interpreting the dream, but from the delicate matter of making known its meaning to the king. Daniel had received favor from the king —nothing but favor, so far as we know—and it was hard for him to be the bearer of so terrible a threatening of judgment against him as was involved in this dream. The prophet was troubled to determine in what way he could best make it known. It seems the king had anticipated something of this kind, for he assured the prophet by telling him not to let the dream or the interpretation trouble him. It was as if he had said, Do not hesitate to make it known, whatever bearing it may have upon me.

Daniel Interprets the Dream.—Thus assured, Daniel spoke with forceful and delicate language: "The dream be to them that hate thee, and the interpretation thereof to thine enemies." A calamity is set forth in this dream, which Daniel wished might come upon the king's enemies rather than upon him.

Nebuchadnezzar had given a minute statement of his dream, and as soon as Daniel informed him that the dream applied to him, it was evident that the king had pronounced his own sentence. The interpretation which follows is so plain that it needs no explanation. The threatened judgments were conditional. They were to teach the king "that the Heavens do rule," the word "heavens" here being put for God, the ruler of the heavens. Hence Daniel took occasion to give the king counsel in view of the threatened judgment. But he did not denounce him in a harsh and censorious spirit. Kindness and persuasion were the weapons he chose to wield: "Let my counsel be acceptable unto thee." In like manner the apostle Paul beseeches men to suffer the word of exhortation. (Hebrews 13: 22.) If the king would break off his sins "by righteousness," and his iniquities "by showing mercy to the poor," it might result in a lengthening of his tranquillity, or, as the margin reads, "An healing of thine error." By repentance he might even have averted the judgment the Lord designed to bring upon him.

Verse 28 All this came upon the king Nebuchadnezzar. 29 At the end of twelve months he walked in the palace of the kingdom of Babylon. 30 The king spake, and said, Is not this great Babylon, that I have built for the house of the kingdom by the might of my power, and for the honor of my majesty? 31 While the word was in the king's mouth, there fell a voice from heaven, saying, O king Nebuchadnezzar, to thee it is spoken: The kingdom is departed from thee. 32 And they shall drive thee from men, and thy dwelling shall be with the beasts of the field: they shall make thee to eat grass as oxen, and seven times shall pass over thee, until thou know that the Most High ruleth in the kingdom of men, and giveth it to whomsoever He will. 33 The same hour was the thing fulfilled upon Nebuchadnezzar: and he was driven from men, and did eat grass as oxen, and his body was wet with the dew of heaven, till his hairs were grown like eagles' feathers, and his nails like birds' claws.

The King's Self-exaltation and Humiliation.—Nebuchadnezzar failed to profit by the warning he had received, yet God bore with him twelve months longer before the blow fell. All that time he cherished pride in his heart, and at length it reached a climax beyond which God could not suffer it to pass. The king was walking in the palace, and as he looked forth upon the splendors of that wonder of the world, great Babylon, the beauty of kingdoms, he forgot the source of all his strength and greatness, and exclaimed, "Is not this great Babylon, that *I* have built?" Archeologists have found the ruins of that ancient city, which Sir Frederic Kenyon describes in the following sentences:

"These confirmed the generally wrecked character of the site, but also revealed much as to its plan, architecture, and ornamentation. The buildings found were almost wholly the work of Nebuchadnezzar, who rebuilt the previous city most extensively, his own enormous palace ('this great Babylon that I have built for the house of the kingdom by the might of my power and for the honor of my majesty') being the most conspicuous building of all." [3]

The time had come for Nebuchadnezzar's humiliation. A voice from heaven again announced the threatened judgment, and divine providence proceeded immediately to execute it. His reason departed. No longer the pomp and glory of his great city charmed him. God with a touch of His finger took away his capability to appreciate and enjoy it. He forsook the dwellings of men, and sought a home and companionship among the beasts of the field.

VERSE 34 And at the end of the days I Nebuchadnezzar lifted up mine eyes unto heaven, and mine understanding returned unto me, and I blessed the Most High, and I praised and honored Him that liveth forever, whose dominion is an everlasting dominion, and His kingdom is from generation to generation: 35 and all the inhabitants of the earth are reputed as nothing: and He doeth according to His will in the army of heaven, and among the inhabitants of the earth: and none can stay His hand, or say unto Him, What doest thou? 36 At the same time my reason returned unto me; and for the glory of my kingdom, mine honor and brightness returned unto me; and my counselors and my lords sought unto me; and I was established in my kingdom, and excellent majesty was added unto me. 37 Now I Nebuchadnezzar praise and extol and honor the King of heaven, all whose works are truth, and His ways judgment: and those that walk in pride He is able to abase.

Nebuchadnezzar Extols the "King of Heaven."—At the end of seven years God removed the hand of affliction, and the reason and understanding of the king returned to him. His first act was to bless the Most High. On this Matthew Henry makes the following appropriate remark: "Those may justly be reck-

[3] Sir Frederic Kenyon, *The Bible and Archæology*, p. 126.

oned void of understanding that do not bless and praise God; nor do men ever rightly use their reason till they begin to be religious, nor live as men till they live to the glory of God."[4]

His honor and brightness returned to him, his counselors sought him, and he was once more established in the kingdom. The promise was that his kingdom should be sure to him. (Verse 26.) During his insanity, his son Evil-Merodach is said to have reigned as regent in his stead. Daniel's interpretation of the dream was doubtless well understood in the palace, and was probably more or less the subject of conversation. Hence the return of Nebuchadnezzar to his kingdom must have been anticipated, with interest. Why he was permitted to make his home in the open field in so forlorn a condition instead of being comfortably cared for by the attendants of the palace, we are not informed.

The affliction had its designed effect. The lesson of humility was learned. The king did not forget it with returning prosperity. He was ready to acknowledge that the Most High rules in the kingdom of men, and gives it to whomsoever he will. He sent forth through all his realm a royal proclamation containing an acknowledgment of his pride, and a manifesto of praise and adoration to the King of heaven.

This is the last Scripture record we have of Nebuchadnezzar. This decree is dated 563 B. C., in the Authorized Version, says Adam Clarke,[5] one year before Nebuchadnezzar's death, though some place the date of this decree seventeen years before his death. There is no record that the king ever lapsed again into idolatry. We may therefore conclude that he died a believer in the God of Israel.

Thus closed the life of this remarkable man. With all the temptations incident to his exalted position as king, may we not suppose that God saw in him honesty of heart, integrity, and purity of purpose, which he could use to the glory of His name? Hence His wonderful dealings with him, all of which

---

[4] Matthew Henry, *Commentary*, Vol. II, p. 965, note on Daniel 4: 34-37.

[5] Adam Clarke, *Commentary on the Old Testament*, Vol. IV, p. 585, note on Daniel 4: 37.

seem to have been designed to wean him from his false religion, and attach him to the service of the true God. We have his dream of the great image, containing a valuable lesson for the people of all coming generations. We remember his experience with Shadrach, Meshach, and Abednego in their refusal to worship his golden image, wherein he was again led to an acknowledgment of the supremacy of the true God. Finally, we have the wonderful incidents recorded in this chapter, showing the unceasing efforts of the Lord to bring Nebuchadnezzar to a full acknowledgment of the Creator. May we not hope that the most illustrious king of Babylon, the head of gold, may at last have part in that kingdom before which all earthly kingdoms shall become as chaff and the glory of which shall never fade?

THE FALL OF BABYLON

The Persian armies, having gained entrance to the city, soon brought an end to all resistance. Great Babylon had fallen.

CHAPTER V

THE HANDWRITING ON THE WALL

VERSE 1 Belshazzar the king made a great feast to a thousand of his lords, and drank wine before the thousand.

THIS chapter describes the closing scenes of the Babylonian Empire, the transition from the gold to the silver of the great image of Daniel 2, and from the lion to the bear of Daniel's vision in chapter 7. This feast is supposed by some to have been an appointed annual festival in honor of one of the heathen deities. Cyrus, who was then besieging Babylon, learned of the celebration, and laid his plans for the overthrow of the city. Our translation reads that Belshazzar, having invited a thousand of his lords, "drank . . . before the thousand." Some translate it "drank . . . *against* the thousand," showing that in addition to whatever other weaknesses he may have had, he was also a heavy drinker.

VERSE 2 Belshazzar, whiles he tasted the wine, commanded to bring the golden and silver vessels which his father Nebuchadnezzar had taken out of the temple which was in Jerusalem; that the king, and his princes, his wives, and his concubines, might drink therein. 3 Then they brought the golden vessels that were taken out of the temple of the house of God which was at Jerusalem; and the king, and his princes, his wives, and his concubines, drank in them. 4 They drank wine, and praised the gods of gold, and of silver, of brass, of iron, of wood, and of stone.

That this festival had some reference to former victories over the Jews may be inferred from the fact that when the king began to be heated with his wine, he called for the sacred vessels which had been taken from Jerusalem. He would most likely use them to celebrate the victory by which they were obtained. Probably no other king had carried his impiety to such length as this. And while they drank wine from vessels dedicated to the true God, they praised their gods of gold, silver, brass, iron, wood, and stone. Perhaps, as we have noted in the comments on Daniel 3: 29, they celebrated the superior power of their gods over the God of the Jews, from whose vessels they now drank to their heathen deities.

VERSE 5 In the same hour came forth fingers of a man's hand, and wrote over against the candlestick upon the plaister of the wall of the king's palace: and the king saw the part of the hand that wrote. 6 Then the king's countenance was changed, and his thoughts troubled him, so that the joints of his loins were loosed, and his knees smote one against another. 7 The king cried aloud to bring in the astrologers, the Chaldeans, and the soothsayers. And the king spake, and said to the wise men of Babylon, Whosoever shall read this writing, and show me the interpretation thereof, shall be clothed with scarlet, and have a chain of gold about his neck, and shall be the third ruler in the kingdom. 8 Then came in all the king's wise men: but they could not read the writing, nor make known to the king the interpretation thereof. 9 Then was king Belshazzar greatly troubled, and his countenance was changed in him, and his lords were astonied.

Handwriting on the Wall.—No flashes of supernatural light, no deafening peals of thunder, announced the interference of God in their impious revelries. A hand silently appeared, tracing mystic characters upon the wall. It wrote over against the candlestick. Terror seized the king, for his conscience accused him. Although he could not read the writing, he knew it was no message of peace and blessing that was traced in glittering characters upon his palace wall. The description the prophet gives of the effect of the king's fear cannot be excelled in any particular. The king's countenance was changed, his heart failed him, pain seized upon him, and so violent was his trembling that his knees smote one against another. He forgot his boasting and revelry. He forgot his dignity. And he cried aloud for his astrologers and soothsayers to solve the meaning of the mysterious inscription.

VERSE 10 Now the queen by reason of the words of the king and his lords came into the banquet house: and the queen spake and said, O king, live forever: let not thy thoughts trouble thee, nor let thy countenance be changed: 11 there is a man in thy kingdom, in whom is the spirit of the holy gods; and in the days of thy father light and understanding and wisdom, like the wisdom of the gods, was found in him; whom the king Nebuchadnezzar thy father, the king, I say, thy father, made master of the magicians, astrologers, Chaldeans, and soothsayers; 12 forasmuch as an excellent spirit, and knowledge, and understanding, interpreting of dreams, and showing of hard sentences, and dissolving of doubts, were found in the same Daniel, whom the king named Belteshazzar: now let Daniel be called, and he will show the interpretation. 13 Then was Daniel brought in before the king. And the king spake and said unto Daniel, Art thou that Daniel, which art of the children of the captivity of Judah, whom the king my father brought out of Jewry? 14 I have even heard of thee, that the spirit of the gods is in thee, and that light and understanding and excellent wisdom is found in thee. 15 And now the wise men, the astrologers, have been brought in before me, that they should read this writing, and make known unto me the interpretation thereof: but they could not show the interpretation of the thing: 16 and I have heard of thee, that thou canst make interpretations, and dissolve doubts: now if thou canst read the writing, and make known to me the interpretation thereof, thou shalt be clothed with scarlet, and have a chain of gold about thy neck, and shalt be the third ruler in the kingdom.

It appears from the circumstance here narrated, that Daniel as a prophet of God had been lost sight of at the court and palace. This was doubtless because he had been absent at Shushan, in the province of Elam, whither he had gone on the business of the kingdom. (Daniel 8: 1, 2, 27.) Probably the invasion of the country by the Persian army compelled him to return to Babylon at this time. The queen, who made known to the king that there was such a person to whom appeal could be made for knowledge in supernatural things, is supposed to have been the queen mother, the daughter of Nebuchadnezzar. She must have remembered the wonderful counsel Daniel had given in her father's reign.

Nebuchadnezzar is here called Belshazzar's father, according to the then common custom of calling any paternal ancestor father, and any male descendant son. Nebuchadnezzar was in reality his grandfather. When Daniel came in, the king inquired if the prophet were of the children of the captivity of Judah. Thus it seems to have been ordered that, while the princes were holding impious revelry in honor of their false gods, a servant of the true God, one whom they were holding in captivity, was called in to pronounce the merited judgment upon their wicked course.

VERSE 17 Then Daniel answered and said before the king, Let thy gifts be to thyself, and give thy rewards to another; yet I will read the writing

THE HANDWRITING ON THE WALL

The fall of Babylon, unexpected by King Belshazzar, came in confirmation of sacred prophecy.

unto the king, and make known to him the interpretation. 18 O thou king,
the most high God gave Nebuchadnezzar thy father a kingdom, and majesty, and glory, and honor: 19 and for the majesty that He gave him, all
people, nations, and languages, trembled and feared before him: whom he would he slew; and whom he would he kept alive; and whom he would he set up; and whom he would he put down. 20 But when his heart was lifted
up, and his mind hardened in pride, he was deposed from his kingly throne, and they took his glory from him: 21 and he was driven from the sons of
men; and his heart was made like the beasts, and his dwelling was with the wild asses: they fed him with grass like oxen, and his body was wet with the dew of heaven; till he knew that the most high God ruled in the kingdom of men, and that he appointeth over it whomsoever he will. 22 And thou
his son, O Belshazzar, hast not humbled thine heart, though thou knewest
all this; 23 but hast lifted up thyself against the Lord of heaven; and they have brought the vessels of His house before thee, and thou, and thy lords, thy wives, and thy concubines, have drunk wine in them; and thou hast praised the gods of silver, and gold, of brass, iron, wood, and stone, which see not, nor hear, nor know: and the God in whose hand thy breath is, and whose are all thy ways, hast thou not glorified: 24 then was the part of the hand
sent from Him; and this writing was written.

Daniel Rebukes Belshazzar.—Daniel first disclaimed the idea of being influenced by such motives as governed the soothsayers and astrologers. He said, "Let thy rewards be to another." He wished it distinctly understood that he did not enter upon the work of interpreting this matter on account of the offer of gifts and rewards. He then rehearsed the experience of the king's grandfather, Nebuchadnezzar, as set forth in the preceding chapter. He told Belshazzar that though he knew all this, yet he had not humbled his heart, but had lifted up himself against the God of heaven. He had even carried his impiety so far as to profane God's sacred vessels, praising the senseless gods of men's invention, and refusing to glorify God in whose hand his breath was. For this reason, Daniel told him, the hand had been sent forth from the God whom he had daringly and insultingly challenged, to trace those characters of fearful, though hidden import. He then proceeded to explain the writing.

VERSE 25 And this is the writing that was written, MENE, MENE,
TEKEL, UPHARSIN. 26 This is the interpretation of the thing: MENE;
God hath numbered thy kingdom, and finished it. 27 TEKEL; Thou art

BABYLON AS IT APPEARS TODAY
The great city Babylon, once the pride of its rulers, and of the ancient world, now lies humbled in the dust of centuries.

weighed in the balances, and art found wanting. 28 PERES; Thy kingdom is divided, and given to the Medes and Persians. 29 Then commanded Belshazzar, and they clothed Daniel with scarlet, and put a chain of gold about his neck, and made a proclamation concerning him, that he should be the third ruler in the kingdom.

Daniel Interprets the Writing.—In this inscription each word stands for a short sentence. *Mene*, "numbered;" *Tekel*, "weighed;" *Upharsin*, from the root *peres*, "divided." God, whom thou hast defied, has thy kingdom in His own hands, and has numbered its days and finished its course just at the time thou thoughtest it at the height of its prosperity. Thou, who hast lifted up thy heart in pride as the great one of the earth, art weighed, and found lighter than vanity. Thy kingdom, which thou didst dream was to stand forever, is divided between the foes already waiting at thy gates.

Notwithstanding this terrible denunciation, Belshazzar did not forget his promise, but invested Daniel at once with the scarlet robe and chain of gold, and proclaimed him third ruler in the kingdom. This Daniel accepted, probably with a view to being better prepared to look after the interests of his people during the transition to the succeeding kingdom.

VERSE 30 In that night was Belshazzar the king of the Chaldeans slain.
31 And Darius the Median took the kingdom, being about threescore and two years old.

The scene here so briefly mentioned is described in remarks on Daniel 2: 39. While Belshazzar was indulging in his presumptuous revelry, while the angel's hand was tracing the doom of the empire on the walls of the palace, while Daniel was making known the fearful import of the heavenly writing, the Persian soldiery, through the emptied channel of the Euphrates, had made their way into the heart of the city, and were speeding forward with drawn swords to the palace of the king. Scarcely can it be said that they surprised him, for God had just forewarned him of his doom. But they found him and slew him, and in that hour the empire of Babylon ceased to be.

> "That night they slew him on his father's throne,
> The deed unnoticed and the hand unknown:
> Crownless and scepterless Belshazzar lay,
> A robe of purple round a form of clay."[1]

---

[1] Edwin Arnold, "The Feast of Belshazzar," *Poetical Works*, p. 170.

© AUTOTYPE FINE ART CO.

DANIEL IN PRAYER

Unafraid of the royal decree and with unswerving loyalty, Daniel prayed daily to his God.

CHAPTER VI

DANIEL IN THE LIONS' DEN

VERSE 1 It pleased Darius to set over the kingdom an hundred and twenty princes, which should be over the whole kingdom; 2 and over these three presidents; of whom Daniel was first: that the princes might give accounts unto them, and the king should have no damage. 3 Then this Daniel was preferred above the presidents and princes, because an excellent spirit was in him; and the king thought to set him over the whole realm. 4 Then the presidents and princes sought to find occasion against Daniel concerning the kingdom; but they could find none occasion nor fault; forasmuch as he was faithful, neither was there any error or fault found in him. 5 Then said these men, We shall not find any occasion against this Daniel, except we find it against him concerning the law of his God.

BABYLON was taken by the Persians, and Darius the Median was placed upon the throne in 538 B. C. When Darius died two years later, Cyrus took the throne. Somewhere, therefore, between these two dates the event occurred which is narrated in this chapter.

Daniel was an active leader in the kingdom of Babylon at the height of its glory. From that time until the Medes and Persians took the throne of universal empire, he was at least a resident of the capital city, acquainted with all the affairs of the kingdom. Yet he gave us no consecutive account of events that occurred during his long connection with these kingdoms. He touched upon only an event here and there which would inspire faith, hope, and courage in the hearts of the people of God in every age, and lead them to be steadfast in their adherence to the right. The event narrated in this chapter is alluded to in Hebrews 11, where we read of those who through faith "stopped the mouths of lions."

Daniel Prime Minister in Medo-Persia.—Darius set over the kingdom one hundred twenty princes, there being at that time, as is supposed, one hundred twenty provinces in the empire, each one having its prince, or governor. By the victories of Cambyses and Darius Hystaspes, it was afterward enlarged to one hundred twenty-seven provinces. (Esther 1: 1.) Over these princes were set three presidents, and of these Daniel was chief. Daniel was doubtless advanced to this high position because of the excellent spirit and fidelity manifest in his work.

As a great man in the empire of Babylon, Daniel might have been regarded an enemy by Darius, and have been banished or otherwise put out of the way. Or as a captive from a nation then in ruins, he might have been despised and set at naught. But to the credit of Darius be it said, Daniel was preferred over all the others, because the discerning king saw in him an excellent spirit. The king thought to set him over the whole realm.

Then was the envy of the other rulers raised against him, and they set about to destroy him. As related to the kingdom, Daniel's conduct was perfect. He was faithful and true. They could find no ground for complaint against him on that score. They then said they could find no occasion to accuse him, except as concerning the law of his God. So let it be with us. A person can have no better recommendation.

VERSE 6 Then these presidents and princes assembled together to the king, and said thus unto him, King Darius, live forever. 7 All the presidents of the kingdom, the governors, and the princes, the counselors, and the captains, have consulted together to establish a royal statute, and to make a firm decree, that whosoever shall ask a petition of any God or man for thirty days, save of thee, O king, he shall be cast into the den of lions. 8 Now, O king, establish the decree, and sign the writing, that it be not changed, according to the law of the Medes and Persians, which altereth not. 9 Wherefore king Darius signed the writing and the decree. 10 Now when Daniel knew that the writing was signed, he went into his house; and his windows being open in his chamber toward Jerusalem, he kneeled upon his knees three times a day, and prayed, and gave thanks before his God, as he did aforetime.

Plot Against Daniel.—Mark the course these persons took to accomplish their nefarious purposes. They came together to the king—came tumultuously, says the margin. They came as if some urgent matter had suddenly sprung up, and they had come to present it before him. They claimed that all were agreed. This was false, for Daniel, the chief of them all, was of course not consulted in the matter.

The decree they presented was designed to increase honor and respect for the royal will. No prayer or petition, they declared, was to be addressed to any man or god, save the king, for thirty days. By this flattering approach the princes hid their evil design against Daniel. The king signed the decree, and it became an unalterable law of the Medes and Persians.

Mark the subtlety of these men—the length to which they went to accomplish the ruin of the good. If they had made the decree read that no petition should be asked of the God of the Hebrews, which was the real design of the matter, the king would at once have divined their object, and the decree would not have been signed. But they gave it a general application, and were willing to ignore and heap insult upon their own religion, and all the multitude of their gods, in order to ruin the object of their hatred.

Daniel realized that a conspiracy was formed against him, but he took no means to thwart it. He simply committed himself to God, and left the issue to His providence. He did not leave the capital on pretended business, or perform his devotions with more than ordinary secrecy. When he knew the writing was signed, he knelt in his chamber three times a day, as was his usual custom, with his face turned toward his beloved Jerusalem, and offered his prayers and supplications to God.

VERSE 11 Then these men assembled, and found Daniel praying and making supplication before his God. 12 Then they came near, and spake before the king concerning the king's decree: Hast thou not signed a decree, that every man that shall ask a petition of any God or man within thirty days, save of thee, O king, shall be cast into the den of lions? The king answered and said, The thing is true, according to the law of the Medes and Persians, which altereth not. 13 Then answered they and said before the king, That Daniel, which is of the children of the captivity of Judah, regardeth not thee, O king, nor the decree that thou hast signed, but maketh his petition three times a day. 14 Then the king, when he heard these words, was sore displeased with himself, and set his heart on Daniel to deliver him: and he labored till the going down of the sun to deliver him. 15 Then these

BRITTON RIVIERE, ARTIST

GOD HONORS FIDELITY

Daniel was safer in the lions' den with God's protection than he would have been in the courts of Babylon without it.

men assembled unto the king, and said unto the king, Know, O king, that the law of the Medes and Persians is, That no decree nor statute which the king establisheth may be changed. 16 Then the king commanded, and they brought Daniel, and cast him into the den of lions. Now the king spake and said unto Daniel, Thy God, whom thou servest continually, He will deliver thee. 17 And a stone was brought, and laid upon the mouth of the den; and the king sealed it with his own signet, and with the signet of his lords, that the purpose might not be changed concerning Daniel.

Daniel Cast Into the Lions' Den.—After the trap was set, it only remained for these men to watch their victim that they might ensnare him. So they again came together, this time at the residence of Daniel, as though some important business called them suddenly to consult the chief of the presidents; and lo, they found him, just as they intended and hoped, praying to his God. So far their scheme worked well. They were not long in going to the king with the matter.

Receiving an acknowledgment from the monarch that the decree was in force, they were ready to inform him against Daniel. In an attempt to excite the prejudices of the king they said, "That Daniel, which is of the children of the captivity of Judah, regardeth not thee, O king, nor the decree that thou hast signed." Yes, they complained, that poor captive, who is entirely dependent on you for all that he enjoys, so far from being grateful and appreciating your favors, regards you not, nor pays any attention to your decree. Then the king saw the trap that had been prepared for him as well as for Daniel, and he labored until the going down of the sun to deliver him, probably by personal efforts with the conspirators to cause them to relent, or by arguments and endeavors to procure the repeal of the law. But the law was sustained; and Daniel, the venerable, the grave, the upright, and the faultless servant of the kingdom, was thrown into the den of lions.

VERSE 18 Then the king went to his palace, and passed the night fasting; neither were instruments of musick brought before him: and his sleep went from him. 19 Then the king arose very early in the morning, and went in haste unto the den of lions. 20 And when he came to the den, he cried with a lamentable voice unto Daniel: and the king spake and said to Daniel, O Daniel, servant of the living God, is thy God, whom thou servest

continually, able to deliver thee from the lions? 21 Then said Daniel unto
the king, O king, live forever. 22 My God hath sent His angel, and hath
shut the lions' mouths, that they have not hurt me: forasmuch as before Him
innocency was found in me; and also before thee, O king, have I done no
hurt. 23 Then was the king exceeding glad for him, and commanded that
they should take Daniel up out of the den. So Daniel was taken up out of the
den, and no manner of hurt was found upon him, because he believed in his
God. 24 And the king commanded, and they brought those men which had
accused Daniel, and they cast them into the den of lions, them, their children,
and their wives; and the lions had the mastery of them, and brake all their
bones in pieces or ever they came at the bottom of the den.

Daniel Delivered.—The course of the king after Daniel had been cast into the den of lions attests his genuine interest in the prophet's behalf, and the severe condemnation he felt for his own course in the matter. At dawn he repaired to the den of hungry and ravenous beasts. Daniel was alive, and his response to the monarch's salutation was no reproach for his having yielded to his evil counselors. In terms of respect and honor he said, "O king, live forever." Afterward he reminded the king, in a manner which he must have keenly felt, but to which he could take no exception, that before him he had done no wrong. Because of his innocency, God, whom he served continually, had sent His angel and had shut the lions' mouths.

Here, then, stood Daniel, preserved by a power higher than any power of earth. His cause was vindicated, his innocency declared. "No manner of hurt was found upon him, because he believed in his God." Faith did it. A miracle had been wrought. Why, then, were Daniel's accusers brought and cast in? They probably attributed the preservation of Daniel, not to any miracle in his behalf, but to the fact that the lions chanced at that time not to be hungry. The king may have said, "In that case they will no more attack you than him, so we will test the matter by putting you in." The lions were hungry enough when not restrained by divine intervention, and these men were torn to pieces before they reached the bottom of the den. Thus was Daniel doubly vindicated, and the words of Solomon were strikingly fulfilled: "The righteous is delivered out of trouble, and the wicked cometh in his stead." Proverbs 11: 8.

VERSE 25 Then king Darius wrote unto all people, nations, and languages, that dwell in all the earth: Peace be multiplied unto you. 26 I make a decree, That in every dominion of my kingdom men tremble and fear before the God of Daniel: for He is the living God, and steadfast forever, and His kingdom that which shall not be destroyed, and His dominion shall be even unto the end. 27 He delivereth and rescueth, and He worketh signs and wonders in heaven and in earth, who hath delivered Daniel from the power of the lions. 28 So this Daniel prospered in the reign of Darius, and in the reign of Cyrus the Persian.

Daniel Prospered.—Daniel's deliverance resulted in another proclamation's being sent out through the empire in favor of the true God, the God of Israel. All men were commanded to fear and tremble before Him. The plot which Daniel's enemies had designed to prove his ruin, resulted only in his advancement. In this case, and in the experience of the three Hebrews in the fiery furnace, the approval of God is placed on two great lines of duty—the refusal to yield to any known sin, and the refusal to omit any known duty. From these instances the people of God in all ages may derive encouragement.

The decree of the king sets forth the character of the true God: He is the Creator; all others are without life in themselves. He is steadfast forever; all others are helpless and unavailing. He has a kingdom; for He made and governs all. His kingdom shall not be destroyed; all others come to an end. His dominion is without end; no human power can prevail against it. He delivers those who are in bondage. He rescues His servants from their enemies when they call upon Him for help. He works wonders in the heavens and signs upon the earth. And to complete all, He has delivered Daniel, giving before our eyes the fullest proof of His power and goodness in rescuing His servant from the power of the lions. How excellent a eulogy of the great God and His faithful servant!

Thus closes the historical part of the book of Daniel.

 FRANKLIN BOOTH, ARTIST

FOUR SYMBOLIC BEASTS

In Daniel's vision of the four beasts are portrayed the characteristics of four universal kingdoms.

CHAPTER VII

THE STRUGGLE FOR WORLD DOMINION

VERSE 1 In the first year of Belshazzar king of Babylon Daniel had a dream and visions of his head upon his bed: then he wrote the dream, and told the sum of the matters.

THIS is the same Belshazzar mentioned in Daniel 5. Chronologically, this chapter precedes the fifth chapter; but chronology is here disregarded in order that the historical part of the book may stand by itself.

VERSE 2 Daniel spake and said, I saw in my vision by night, and, behold, the four winds of the heaven strove upon the great sea. 3 And four great beasts came up from the sea, diverse one from another.

Daniel Relates His Own Vision.—All Scripture language is to be taken literally, unless there exists some good reason for regarding it as figurative. All that is figurative is to be interpreted by that which is literal. That the language here used is symbolic, is evident from verse 17, which reads, "These great beasts, which are four, are four kings which shall arise out of the earth." That kingdoms are intended, and not merely individual kings, is clear from the word, "But the saints of the Most High shall take the kingdom." In explaining verse 23, the angel said, "The fourth beast shall be the fourth kingdom upon the earth." These beasts are therefore symbols of four great kingdoms. The circumstances under which they arose, as represented in the prophecy, are also stated in symbolic language. The symbols introduced are the four winds, the sea, four great beasts, ten horns, and another horn which had eyes and a mouth and which rose up in war against God and His people. We have now to inquire what they denote.

In symbolic language winds represent strife, political commotion, and war, as we read from the prophet Jeremiah:

"Thus saith the Lord of hosts, Behold, evil shall go forth from nation to nation, and a great whirlwind shall be raised up from the coasts of the earth. And the slain of the Lord shall be at that day from one end of the earth even unto the other end of the earth." Jeremiah 25: 32, 33. The prophet speaks of a controversy which the Lord is to have with all nations. The strife and commotion which produces all this destruction is called "a great whirlwind."

That winds denote strife and war is evident in the vision itself. As the result of the blowing of the winds, kingdoms arise and fall through political strife.

Seas, or waters, when used as a Bible symbol, represent peoples, and nations, and tongues. Said the angel to the prophet John, "The waters which thou sawest . . . are peoples, and multitudes, and nations, and tongues." Revelation 17: 15.

The definition of the symbol of the four beasts is given to Daniel before the close of the vision: "These great beasts, which are four, are four kings which shall arise out of the earth." Verse 17. With this explanation of the symbols, the field of the vision is definitely opened before us.

Since these beasts denote four kings, or kingdoms, we inquire, Where shall we begin and what four empires are represented? These beasts arise consecutively, for they are enumerated from the first to the fourth. The last one is in existence when all earthly scenes are brought to an end by the final judgment. From the time of Daniel to the end of this world's history, there were to be but four universal kingdoms, as we learned from Nebuchadnezzar's dream of the great image in Daniel 2, interpreted by the prophet sixty-five years before. Daniel was still living under the kingdom denoted by the head of gold.

The first beast of this vision must therefore denote the same kingdom as the head of gold of the great image, namely, Babylon. The other beasts no doubt represent the succeeding kingdoms portrayed by that image. But if this vision covers essentially the same period of history as the image of Daniel 2, the query may arise, Why is it given? Why was not that first vision sufficient? We answer, The history of world empires is passed over again and again in order that additional characteristics may be brought out, and additional facts and features may be presented. It is thus that we have "line upon line" according to the Scriptures. In chapter 2, only the political aspects of world dominion are portrayed. Here earthly governments are introduced in their relationship to God's truth and God's people. Their true character is shown by symbols of wild and ravenous beasts.

VERSE 4 The first was like a lion, and had eagle's wings: I beheld till the wings thereof were plucked, and it was lifted up from the earth, and made stand upon the feet as a man, and a man's heart was given to it.

The Lion.—In the vision of Daniel 7, the first beast seen by the prophet was a lion. For the use of the lion as a symbol, read Jeremiah 4: 7; 50: 17, 43, 44. The lion as first seen in the vision before us had eagle's wings. The symbolic use of wings is impressively described in Habakkuk 1: 6-8, where it is said that the Chaldeans should "fly as the eagle that hasteth to eat."

From these symbols we may easily deduce that Babylon was a kingdom of great strength, and that under Nebuchadnezzar its conquests were extended with great rapidity. But there came a time when the wings were plucked. It no longer rushed upon its prey like an eagle. The boldness and spirit of the lion were gone. A man's heart—weak, timorous, and faint—took the place of a lion's strength. Such was the case with the nation during the closing years of its history, when it had become enfeebled and effeminate through wealth and luxury.

VERSE 5 And behold another beast, a second, like to a bear, and it raised up itself on one side, and it had three ribs in the mouth of it between the teeth of it: and they said thus unto it, Arise, devour much flesh.

The Bear.—As in the image of Daniel 2, so in this series of symbols a marked deterioration is noticed as we descend from one kingdom to another. The silver of the breast and arms is inferior to the gold of the head. The bear is inferior to the lion. Medo-Persia fell short of Babylon in wealth, magnificence, and brilliance. The bear raised itself up on one side. The kingdom was composed of two nationalities, the Medes and the Persians. The same fact is represented by the two horns of the ram in Daniel 8. Of these horns it is said that the higher came up last, and of the bear that it raised itself up on one side. This was fulfilled by the Persian division of the kingdom, for although it came up last, it attained the higher eminence, becoming a dominant influence in the nation. (See comments on Daniel 8: 3.) The three ribs doubtless signify the three provinces of Babylon, Lydia, and Egypt, which were especially oppressed by Medo-Persia. The command, "Arise, devour much flesh," would naturally refer to the stimulus given to the Medes and Persians by the overthrow of these provinces. The character of the power is well represented by a bear. The Medes and Persians were cruel and rapacious, robbers and spoilers of the people. This Medo-Persian kingdom continued from the overthrow of Babylon by Cyrus to the battle of Arbela in 331 B. C., a period of 207 years.

VERSE 6 After this I beheld, and lo another, like a leopard, which had upon the back of it four wings of a fowl; the beast had also four heads; and dominion was given to it.

The Leopard.—The third kingdom, Grecia, is here represented by the symbol of a leopard. If wings upon the lion signified rapidity of conquest, they would signify the same here. The leopard itself is a swift-footed beast, but this was not sufficient to represent the career of the nation here symbolized. It must have wings in addition. Two wings, the number the lion had, were not sufficient; the leopard must have four. This would denote unprecedented celerity of movement, which we find to be a historical fact in the Grecian kingdom. The conquests of Grecia under Alexander had no parallel in ancient times for suddenness and rapidity. His military achievements are summarized by W. W. Tarn:

"He was a master in the combination of various arms; he taught the world the advantages of campaigning in winter, the value of pressing pursuit to the utmost, and the principle of 'march divided, fight united.' He marched usually in two divisions, one conducting the impediments and his own [division] traveling light; his speed of movement was extraordinary. It is said that he attributed his military success to 'never putting anything off.' . . . The enormous distances traversed in unknown country imply a very high degree of organizing ability; in ten years he had only two serious breakdowns. . . . Had a lesser man attempted what he achieved, and failed, we should have heard enough of the hopeless military difficulties of the undertaking." [1]

"The beast had also four heads." The Grecian Empire maintained its unity but little longer than the lifetime of Alexander. After his brilliant career ended in a fever induced by a drunken debauch, the empire was divided among his four leading generals. Cassander had Macedonia and Greece in the west; Lysimachus had Thrace and the parts of Asia on the Hellespont and the Bosphorus in the north; Ptolemy had Egypt, Lydia, Arabia, Palestine, and Cœle-Syria in the south; and Seleucus had Syria and all the rest of Alexander's dominions in the east. By the year 301 B. C., with the death of Antigonus, the division of the kingdom of Alexander into four parts was completed by his generals. [2] These divisions were denoted by the four heads of the leopard.

Thus accurately were the words of the prophet fulfilled. As Alexander left no available successor, why did not the huge empire break up into countless petty fragments? Why into just four parts, and no more?—For reasons that the prophecy foresaw and foretold. The leopard had four heads, the rough goat four horns, the kingdom was to have four divisions; and thus it was. (See more fully in comments on Daniel 8.)

---

[1] *The Cambridge Ancient History*, Vol. VI, pp. 425, 426. By permission of the Macmillan Company, publishers in the United States.

[2] *Ibid.*, pp. 461-504.

VERSE 7 After this I saw in the night visions, and behold a fourth beast, dreadful and terrible, and strong exceedingly; and it had great iron teeth: it devoured and brake in pieces, and stamped the residue with the feet of it: and it was diverse from all the beasts that were before it; and it had ten horns.

A Dreadful Beast.—Inspiration finds no beast in nature to symbolize the power here illustrated. No addition of hoofs, heads, horns, wings, scales, teeth, or nails to any beast found in nature will answer. This power is diverse from all the others, and the symbol is wholly different from anything found in the animal kingdom.

The foundation for a volume is laid in verse 7, but for lack of space we are compelled to treat it briefly here. This beast corresponds to the fourth division of the great image—the legs of iron. In the comment on Daniel 2: 40 are given some reasons for believing this power to be Rome. The same reasons are applicable to the present prophecy. How accurately Rome answered to the iron portion of the image! How accurately it answers to the beast before us! In the dread and terror which it inspired, and in its great strength, it answered admirably to the prophetic description. The world had never seen its equal. It devoured as with iron teeth, and broke in pieces all that stood in its way. It ground the nations into the dust beneath its brazen feet. It had ten horns, which are explained in verse 24 to be ten kings, or kingdoms, which should arise out of this empire. As already noticed in comments on Daniel 2, Rome was divided into ten kingdoms. These divisions have ever since been spoken of as the ten kingdoms of the Roman Empire.

VERSE 8 I considered the horns, and, behold, there came up among them another little horn, before whom there were three of the first horns plucked up by the roots: and, behold, in this horn were eyes like the eyes of man, and a mouth speaking great things.

Daniel considered the horns. A strange movement appeared among them. Another horn, at first little, but afterward more stout than its fellows, thrust itself up. It was not content quietly to find a place of its own, and fill it; it must thrust aside some of the others, and usurp their places. Three kingdoms were thus plucked up.

A Little Horn Among the Ten.—This little horn, as we shall have occasion to notice more fully hereafter, was the papacy. The three horns plucked up by the roots represented the Heruli, the Ostrogoths, and the Vandals. The reason for their removal was their opposition to the teachings and claims of the papal hierarchy.

"In this horn were eyes like the eyes of man, and a mouth speaking great things"—fit emblems of the shrewdness, penetration, and arrogant claims of an apostate religious organization.

VERSE 9 I beheld till the thrones were cast down, and the Ancient of days did sit, whose garment was white as snow, and the hair of His head like the pure wool: His throne was like the fiery flame, and His wheels as burning fire. 10 A fiery stream issued and came forth from before Him: thousand thousands ministered unto Him, and ten thousand times ten thousand stood before Him: the judgment was set, and the books were opened.

A Judgment Scene.—A sublimer description of a more awe-inspiring scene is not to be found in the word of God. Not the grand and lofty imagery alone could arrest our attention; the nature of the scene itself demands most serious consideration. The judgment is here brought to view. Whenever the judgment is mentioned, it ought to take an irresistible hold upon every mind, for all have a deep concern in its eternal issues.

By an unfortunate translation in verse 9, a wrong idea is almost sure to be conveyed. The phrase "cast down" is from a Chaldee word רְמִי, *remi*, which may properly be rendered "hurled by violence," as is plainly the case where it is used to describe the casting of the three Hebrews into the fiery furnace, and of casting Daniel into the den of lions. But another equally correct translation is "to set or place in order," as in the placing of the judgment seats mentioned here, as also a like setting or placing in Revelation 4: 2, in which the Greek bears out the same meaning. The Revised Version in Daniel 7: 9 reads properly, "thrones were placed," as Gesenius defines

 T. K. MARTIN, ARTIST

THE GREAT JUDGMENT DAY

None will be excused from the final judgment. "We shall all stand before the judgment seat of Christ." Romans 14: 10.

the root *remah*, with reference to Daniel 7: 9 as an example.

The "Ancient of days," God the Father, presides at the judgment. Mark the description of His person. Those who believe in the impersonality of God are obliged to admit that He is here described as a personal being, but they console themselves by saying that it is the only description of the kind in the Bible. We do not admit this latter assertion; but granting that it were true, is not one description of this kind as fatal to their theory as though it were repeated a score of times? The thousand thousands who minister unto Him, and the ten thousand times ten thousand who stand before Him, are not sinners arraigned before the judgment seat, but heavenly intelligences who wait before Him, attendant on His will. John saw the same heavenly attendants before the throne of God, and he describes the majestic scene in these words: "I beheld, and I heard the voice of many angels round about the throne and the beasts and the elders: and the number of them was ten thousand times ten thousand, and thousands of thousands." Revelation 5: 11. A fuller understanding of these verses involves an understanding of the sanctuary services.

The closing up of the ministration of Christ, our great High Priest, in the heavenly sanctuary, is the work of judgment here introduced. It is an investigative judgment. The books are opened, and the cases of all come up for examination before that great tribunal, that it may be decided beforehand who are to receive eternal life when the Lord shall come to confer it upon His people. It will appear from the testimony of Daniel 8: 14 that this solemn work is even now going on in the sanctuary above.

VERSE 11 I beheld then because of the voice of the great words which the horn spake: I beheld even till the beast was slain, and his body destroyed, and given to the burning flame. 12 As concerning the rest of the beasts, they had their dominion taken away: yet their lives were prolonged for a season and time.

End of the Fourth Beast.—There are those who believe in a thousand years' reign of righteousness over all the world before the coming of Christ. There are others who believe in probation after the Lord comes, during which the immortal righteous still proclaim the gospel to mortal sinners, and lead them into the way of salvation. Neither of these theories can be substantiated from the Bible, as we shall see.

The fourth terrible beast continues without change of character, and the little horn continues to utter its blasphemies, holding its millions of votaries in the bonds of blind superstition, until the beast is given to the burning flame. This is not its conversion, but its destruction. (See 2 Thessalonians 2: 8.)

The life of the fourth beast is not prolonged after its dominion is gone, as were the lives of the preceding beasts. Their dominion was taken away, but their lives were prolonged for a season. The territory and subjects of the Babylonian kingdom still existed, though made subject to the Persians. So with the Persian kingdom in respect to Greece, and Greece in respect to Rome. But what succeeds the fourth kingdom? No government or state in which mortals have any part, follows it. Its career ends in the lake of fire, and it has no existence beyond. The lion was merged into the bear, the bear into the leopard, the leopard into the fourth beast. But the fourth beast is not merged into another beast. It is to be cast into a lake of fire.

VERSE 13 I saw in the night visions, and, behold, one like the Son of man came with the clouds of heaven, and came to the Ancient of days, and they brought Him near before Him. 14 And there was given Him dominion, and glory, and a kingdom, that all people, nations, and languages, should serve Him: His dominion is an everlasting dominion, which shall not pass away, and His kingdom that which shall not be destroyed.

The Son of Man Receives His Kingdom.—The scene here described is not the second coming of Christ to this earth, for the Ancient of days is not on this earth, and the coming here spoken of is to the Ancient of days. There, in the presence of the Father, dominion, and glory, and a kingdom are given to the Son of man. Christ receives His kingdom before His return to this earth. (See Luke 19: 10-12.) Therefore, this is a scene which takes place in heaven, and is closely connected with that brought to view in verses 9 and 10. Christ receives His kingdom at the close of His priestly work in the sanctuary. The people and nations that shall serve Him are the redeemed (Revelation 21: 24), not the wicked nations of the earth, for these are destroyed at the second advent of Christ by the brightness of His coming. (Psalm 2: 9; 2 Thessalonians 2: 8.) Out of all nations, tribes, and kindreds of the earth will come those who serve God with joy and gladness. They shall inherit the kingdom of our Lord.

VERSE 15 I Daniel was grieved in my spirit in the midst of my body, and the visions of my head troubled me. 16 I came near unto one of them that stood by, and asked him the truth of all this. So he told me, and made me know the interpretation of the things. 17 These great beasts, which are four, are four kings, which shall arise out of the earth. 18 But the saints of the Most High shall take the kingdom, and possess the kingdom forever, even forever and ever.

Vision Interpreted to Daniel.—We should be no less concerned than was Daniel to understand the truth of these things. We have the assurance that when we inquire with sincerity of heart, we shall find the Lord as ready now as in the days of the prophet to lead to a correct understanding of these important truths. The beasts and the kingdoms which they represent, have already been explained. We have followed the prophet through the course of events, even to the destruction of the fourth beast, the final overthrow of all earthly governments. Then the scene changes, for we read, "The saints . . . shall take the kingdom." Verse 18. The saints! despised, reproached, persecuted, cast out; looked upon as the least likely of all men ever to realize their hopes—these shall take the kingdom, and possess it forever. The usurpation and misrule of the wicked shall come to an end. The inheritance forfeited because of sin shall be redeemed. Peace and righteousness shall reign eternally over all the fair expanse of the earth made new.

VERSE 19 Then I would know the truth of the fourth beast, which was diverse from all the others, exceeding dreadful, whose teeth were of iron, and his nails of brass; which devoured, brake in pieces, and stamped the residue with his feet; 20 and of the ten horns that were in his head, and of the other which came up, and before whom three fell; even of that horn that had eyes, and a mouth that spake very great things, whose look was more stout than his fellows.

Truth of the Fourth Beast.—Of the first three beasts in this vision, Daniel had a clear understanding. But he was astonished at the fourth beast, because of its unnatural and dreadful character. It was of this beast and its ten horns, more particularly of the little horn which came up last, "whose look was more stout than his fellows," that he desired further information. The lion is a production of nature, but it must have the addition of two wings to represent the kingdom of Babylon. The bear we also find in nature, but as a symbol of Medo-Persia an unnatural ferocity must be denoted by the three ribs in its mouth. So the leopard is a beast of nature, yet fitly to represent Grecia, four wings and three more heads must be added. But nature furnishes no symbol which can fitly illustrate the fourth kingdom. The vision therefore introduces a beast the likeness of which was never before seen, a beast dreadful and terrible, with nails of brass, and teeth of iron, so cruel, rapacious, and fierce that from mere love of oppression it devoured, and broke in pieces, and trampled its victims beneath its feet.

Astounding as all this was to the prophet, there was something still more remarkable that gripped his attention. A little horn came up, and, true to the nature of the beast from which it sprang, thrust aside three of its fellows. Lo, the horn had eyes, not the uncultivated eyes of a brute, but the keen, shrewd, intelligent eyes of a man. Stranger yet, it had a mouth, and with that mouth it uttered proud sayings, and put forth preposterous and arrogant claims. No wonder the prophet made special inquiry respecting this monster, so unearthly in its instincts, so fiendish in its works and ways. In the following verses some specifications are given respecting the little horn, which enable the student of prophecy to make an application of this symbol without danger of mistake.

VERSE 21 I beheld, and the same horn made war with the saints, and prevailed against them; 22 until the Ancient of days came, and judgment was given to the saints of the Most High; and the time came that the saints possessed the kingdom.

Little Horn to Make War With the Saints.—The amazing wrath of this little horn against the saints particularly attracted the attention of Daniel. The rise of the ten horns, or the division of Rome into ten kingdoms, between A. D. 351 and 476, has already been noticed in comments on Daniel 2: 41.

As these horns denote kingdoms, the little horn must denote a kingdom also, yet not of the same nature, because it was *diverse* from the others. They were political kingdoms. Now we have but to inquire if, since A. D. 476, any kingdom has risen among the ten divisions of the Roman Empire which was diverse from them all; and if so, what one? The answer is, Yes, the spiritual kingdom of the papacy. It answers to the symbol in every particular, as we shall see as we proceed.

Daniel beheld this power making war upon the saints. Has such a war been waged by the papacy? Millions of martyrs answer, Yes. Witness the cruel persecutions of the Waldenses, the Albigenses, and Protestants in general, by the papal power.

In verse 22 three consecutive events seem to be brought to view. Looking onward from the time when the little horn was in the height of its power to the full end of the long contest between the saints and Satan with all his agents, Daniel notes three prominent events that stand as mileposts along the way:

The coming of the Ancient of days, that is, the position which Jehovah takes in the opening of the judgment scene described in verses 9, 10.

The judgment that is given to the saints, that is, the time when the saints sit with Christ in judgment a thousand years, following the first resurrection (Revelation 20: 1-4), apportioning to the wicked the punishment due for their sins. The martyrs will then sit in judgment upon the great persecuting power, which, in the days of their trial, hunted them like the

 R. M. ELDRIDGE, ARTIST

THE GREAT AND TERRIBLE BEAST

Among the horns of the fourth beast there came up a horn which blasphemed God.

beasts of the desert, and poured out their blood like water.

The time that the saints possess the kingdom, that is, the time of their entrance upon the possession of the new earth. Then the last vestige of the curse of sin, and of sinners, root and branch, will have been wiped away, and the territory so long misruled by the wicked powers of earth, the enemies of God's people, will be given to the righteous, to be possessed by them forever and ever. (1 Corinthians 6: 2, 3; Matthew 25: 34.)

VERSE 23 Thus he said, The fourth beast shall be the fourth kingdom upon earth, which shall be diverse from all kingdoms, and shall devour the whole earth, and shall tread it down, and break it in pieces. 24 And the ten horns out of this kingdom are ten kings that shall arise: and another shall rise after them; and he shall be diverse from the first, and he shall subdue three kings. 25 And he shall speak great words against the Most High, and shall wear out the saints of the Most High, and think to change times and laws: and they shall be given into his hand until a time and times and the dividing of time. 26 But the judgment shall sit, and they shall take away his dominion, to consume and to destroy it unto the end.

Rise and Work of the Little Horn.—Perhaps enough has already been said respecting the fourth beast (Rome) and the ten horns, or ten kingdoms, which arose out of this power. The little horn now more particularly demands attention. As stated in comments on verse 8, we find the fulfillment of the prophecy concerning this horn in the rise and work of the papacy. It is a matter of both interest and importance, therefore, to inquire into the causes which resulted in the development of this arrogant power.

The first pastors or bishops of Rome enjoyed a respect proportionate to the rank of the city in which they resided. For the first few centuries of the Christian Era, Rome was the largest, richest, and most powerful city in the world. It was the seat of empire, the capital of the nations. "All the inhabitants of the earth belong to her," said Julian; and Claudian declared her to be "the fountain of laws." "If Rome is the queen of cities, why should not her pastor be the king of bishops?" was the reasoning these Roman pastors put forth. "Why should not the Roman Church be the mother of Christendom? Why should not all nations be her children, and her authority their sovereign law? It was easy," says D'Aubigné, from whom we quote these words, "for the ambitious heart of man to reason thus. Ambitious Rome did so."[3]

The bishops in the different parts of the Roman Empire felt a pleasure in yielding to the bishop of Rome some of that honor which that city received from the nations of the earth. There was originally no dependence implied in the honor thus paid. "But," continues D'Aubigné, "usurped power increases like an avalanche. Admonitions, at first simply fraternal, soon became absolute commands in the mouth of the pontiff. . . . The Western bishops favored this encroachment of the Roman pastors, either from jealousy of the Eastern bishops, or because they preferred submitting to the supremacy of a pope rather than to the dominion of a temporal power."[4] Such were the influences clustering around the bishop of Rome, and thus was everything tending toward his speedy elevation to the spiritual dominance of Christendom.

Challenge of Arianism.—But the fourth century was destined to witness an obstacle thrown across the path of this ambitious dream. The prophecy had declared that the power represented by the little horn would "subdue three kings." In the rise and development of Arianism early in the fourth century and the challenge it presented to papal supremacy, we find the causes leading to the plucking up of three of the kingdoms of Western Rome by the papal power.

Arius, parish priest of the ancient and influential church of Alexandria, promulgated his doctrine to the world, occasioning so fierce a controversy in the Christian church that a general council was called at Nicæa, by the emperor Constantine in A. D. 325, to consider and rule upon its teaching. Arius maintained "that the Son was totally and essentially distinct from the Father; that He was the first and noblest of those be-

---

[3] Jean Henri Merle d'Aubigné, *History of the Reformation of the Sixteenth Century,* Vol. I, p. 8.

[4] *Ibid.,* p. 9.

ings whom the Father had created out of nothing, the instrument by whose subordinate operation the Almighty Father formed the universe, and therefore inferior to the Father, both in nature and dignity." This opinion was condemned by the council, which decreed that Christ was of one and the same substance with the Father. Hereupon Arius was banished to Illyria, and his followers were compelled to give their assent to the creed composed on that occasion.[5]

The controversy itself, however, was not to be disposed of in this summary manner. For ages it continued to agitate the Christian world, the Arians everywhere becoming the bitter enemies of the pope and of the Roman Catholic Church. It was evident that the spread of Arianism would check the onward march of Catholicism, and that the possession of Italy and its renowned capital by a people of the Arian persuasion would be fatal to the supremacy of a Catholic bishop. The prophecy, however, had declared that this horn symbolizing the papacy would rise to supreme power, and that in reaching this position it would subdue three kings.

Little Horn Overthrows Three Arian Powers.—Some difference of opinion has existed in regard to the particular powers which were overthrown by the papacy in its rise to power. In this connection the remarks of Albert Barnes seem pertinent: "In the confusion that existed on the breaking up of the Roman Empire, and the imperfect accounts of the transactions which occurred in the rise of the papal power, it would not be wonderful if it should be difficult to find events *distinctly* recorded that would be in all respects an accurate and absolute fulfillment of the vision. Yet it is possible to make out the fulfillment of this with a good degree of certainty in the history of the papacy."[6]

Joseph Mede supposes the three kingdoms plucked up to have been the Greeks, the Lombards, and the Franks; and Sir

---

[5] See John L. Mosheim, *An Ecclesiastical History, Ancient and Modern*, Vol. I, p. 412; Arthur P. Stanley, *Lectures on the History of the Eastern Church*, pp. 239, 240.

[6] Albert Barnes, *Notes on Daniel*, p. 324, comment on Daniel 7: 25.

Isaac Newton supposes they were the exarchate of Ravenna, the Lombards, and the senate and dukedom of Rome. Thomas Newton[7] states serious objections to both these suppositions. The Franks could not have been one of these kingdoms, for they were never plucked up. The Lombards could not have been one, for they were never made subject to the popes. Says Albert Barnes further, "I do not find, indeed, that the kingdom of the Lombards was, as is commonly stated, among the number of the temporal sovereignties that became subject to the authority of the popes."[8] The senate and dukedom of Rome could not have been one, for as such they never constituted one of the ten kingdoms, three of which were to be plucked up before the little horn.

But we apprehend that the chief difficulty in the application made by these eminent commentators lay in the fact that they supposed that the prophecy respecting the exaltation of the papacy had not been fulfilled, and could not have been, until the pope became a temporal prince. Therefore they sought to find an accomplishment of the prophecy in the events which led to the pope's temporal sovereignty. But evidently the prophecy of verses 24, 25, refers, not to his civil power, but to his power to domineer over the minds and consciences of men. The papacy reached this position, A. D. 538, as will hereafter appear.

The word "before" used in verses 8 and 20 represents the Chaldee קֳדָם, *qadam*, with the root meaning "front." Combined with *min*, meaning "from," as it is in these two verses, Davidson translates it "from the presence of," and Gesenius says it is equivalent to the Hebrew לִפְנֵי, *lipna*, meaning "in the presence of." It therefore has here the meaning "before" in the sense of "place," as it does in the same phrase in verse 10, where it is properly translated in the Authorized Version "*from before* Him." We have, then, in verse 8 the picture of the

[7] Thomas Newton, *Dissertations on the Prophecies*, Vol. I, pp. 275, 276.

[8] Albert Barnes, *Notes on Daniel*, p. 327, comment on Daniel 7: 25.

little horn pressing in among the ten and forcibly plucking up three horns *from before* it. In verse 20, it is declared that the three horns "*fell*" from before it, as if overcome by it. In verse 24, we read that another king, representing the little horn, "shall *subdue* three kings [horns]," evidently by acts of force. While the word *qadam* is also used in the sense of time, as in the word "before" in verse 7, there can scarcely be a doubt that it is used in the sense of place in the three verses cited above. With this interpretation Edward Elliott clearly agrees. (See page 128.)

The position is here confidently taken that the three powers, or horns, plucked up by the roots were the Heruli, the Vandals, and the Ostrogoths; and this position rests upon reliable historical data. Odoacer, the leader of the Heruli, was the first of the barbarians who reigned over the Romans. He took the throne of Italy, A. D. 476. Of his religious belief Gibbon says: "Like the rest of the barbarians he had been instructed in the Arian heresy; but he revered the monastic and episcopal characters; and the silence of the Catholics attests the toleration which they enjoyed."[9]

The same author says: "The Ostrogoths, the Burgundians, the Suevi, and the Vandals, who had listened to the eloquence of the Latin clergy, preferred the more intelligible lessons of their domestic teachers; and Arianism was adopted as the national faith of the warlike converts who were seated on the ruins of the Western Empire. This irreconcilable difference of religion was a perpetual source of jealousy and hatred; and the reproach of *barbarian* was embittered by the more odious epithet of *heretic*. The heroes of the north, who had submitted with some reluctance to believe that all their ancestors were in hell, were astonished and exasperated to learn that they themselves had only changed the mode of their eternal condemnation."[10]

---

[9] Edward Gibbon, *The Decline and Fall of the Roman Empire*, Vol. III, chap. 36, pp. 515, 516.

[10] *Ibid.*, chap. 37, p. 547.

The Arian doctrine had a marked influence on the church at that time, as will be observed in the following paragraphs: "The whole of the vast Gothic population which descended on the Roman Empire, so far as it was Christian at all, held to the faith of the Alexandrian heretic. Our first Teutonic version of the Scriptures was by an Arian missionary, Ulfilas. The first conqueror of Rome, Alaric, the first conqueror of Africa, Genseric, were Arians. Theodoric the Great, king of Italy, and hero of the 'Nibelungenlied,' was an Arian. The vacant place in his massive tomb at Ravenna is a witness of the vengeance which the Orthodox took on his memory, when on their triumph they tore down the porphyry vase in which his Arian subjects had enshrined his ashes."[11]

Ranke states: "But she [the church] fell, as was inevitable, into many embarrassments, and found herself in an entirely altered condition. A pagan people took possession of Britain; Arian kings seized the greater part of the remaining West; while the Lombards, long attached to Arianism, and as neighbors most dangerous and hostile, established a powerful sovereignty before the very gates of Rome. The Roman bishops, meanwhile, beset on all sides, exerted themselves, with all the prudence and pertinacity which have remained their peculiar attributes, to regain the mastery—at least in their patriarchal diocese."[12]

Machiavelli says: "Nearly all the wars which the northern barbarians carried on in Italy, it may be here remarked, were occasioned by the pontiffs; and the hordes with which the country was inundated, were generally called in by them."[13]

The relation which these Arian kings sustained to the pope is shown in the following testimony from Mosheim in his church history:

"On the other hand, it is certain, from a variety of the most authentic records, that both the emperors and the nations in

---

[11] Arthur P. Stanley, *Lectures on the History of the Eastern Church*, p. 151.

[12] Leopold Ranke, *History of the Popes*, Vol. I, p. 9.

[13] Niccolo Machiavelli, *History of Florence*, p. 14.

general were far from being disposed to bear with patience the yoke of servitude which the see of Rome was arrogantly imposing upon the Christian church. The Gothic princes set bounds to the power of the bishop of Rome in Italy, permitted none to be raised to the pontificate without their approbation, and reserved to themselves the right of judging concerning the legality of every new election."[14]

An instance in proof of this statement occurs in the history of Odoacer, the first Arian king above mentioned.[15] When, on the death of Pope Simplicius, A. D. 483, the clergy and people had assembled for the election of a new pope, suddenly Basilius, lieutenant of King Odoacer, appeared in the assembly, expressed his surprise that any such work as appointing a successor to the deceased pope should be undertaken without him, in the name of the king declared all that had been done null and void, and ordered the election to be begun anew.

Meanwhile, Zeno, the emperor of the East, and friend of the pope, was anxious to drive Odoacer out of Italy, a movement which he soon had the satisfaction of seeing accomplished without trouble to himself. Theodoric had come to the throne of the Ostrogothic kingdom in Mœsia and Pannonia. Being on friendly terms with Zeno, he wrote him, stating that it was impossible for him to restrain his Goths within the impoverished province of Pannonia, and asking his permission to lead them to some more favorable region which they might conquer and possess. Zeno gave him permission to march against Odoacer and take possession of Italy. Accordingly, after a five years' war, the Herulian kingdom in Italy was overthrown, Odoacer was treacherously slain, and Theodoric established his Ostrogoths in the Italian peninsula. As already stated, he was an Arian, and the law of Odoacer subjecting the election of the pope to the approval of the king, was still retained.

---

[14] John L. Mosheim, *An Ecclesiastical History, Ancient and Modern*, Vol. I, pp. 113, 114.

[15] See Archibald Bower, *The History of the Popes*, Vol. I, p. 257.

The following incident will show how completely the papacy was in subjection to his power. The Catholics in the East having begun a persecution against the Arians, A. D. 523, Theodoric summoned Pope John into his presence and thus addressed him: " 'If the emperor [Justin, the predecessor of Justinian] therefore does not think fit to revoke the edict which he has lately issued against those of my persuasion [that is, the Arians], it is my firm resolution to issue the like edict against those of his [that is, the Catholics]; and to see it everywhere executed with the same rigor. Those who do not profess the faith of Nice, are heretics to him, and those who do are heretics to me. Whatever can excuse or justify his severity to the former, will excuse and justify mine to the latter. But the emperor,' continued the king, 'has none about him who dare freely and openly speak what they think, or to whom he would hearken if they did. But the *great veneration which he professes for your See*, leaves no room to doubt but he would hearken to you. I will therefore have you to repair forthwith to Constantinople, and there to remonstrate, both in my name and your own, against the violent measures in which that court has so rashly engaged. It is in your power to divert the emperor from them; and till you have, nay, till the Catholics [this name Theodoric applies to the Arians] are restored to the free exercise of their religion, and to all the churches from which they have been driven, you must not think of returning to Italy.' "[16]

The pope who was thus peremptorily ordered by the Arian emperor not to set his foot again upon Italian soil until he had carried out the will of the king, certainly could not hope for much advancement toward any kind of supremacy until that power was taken out of the way.

The feelings of the papal party toward Theodoric may be accurately estimated, according to a quotation already given, by the vengeance which they took on his memory. They tore from his tomb the vase in which his Arian subjects had en-

---

[16] *Ibid.*, Vol. I, p. 325.

shrined his ashes. These feelings are put into language by Baronius, who inveighs "against Theodoric as a cruel barbarian, as a barbarous tyrant, as an impious Arian."[17]

While the Catholics were thus feeling the restraining power of an Arian king in Italy, they were suffering a violent persecution from the Arian Vandals in Africa.[18] Elliott says: "The Vandal kings were not only Arians, but persecutors of the Catholics; in Sardinia and Corsica under the Roman Episcopate, we may presume, as well as in Africa."[19]

Such was the position of affairs, when, A. D. 533, Justinian entered upon his Vandal and Gothic wars. Wishing to obtain the influence of the pope and the Catholic party, he issued that memorable decree which was to constitute the pope the head of all the churches, and from the carrying out of which, A. D. 538, the period of papal supremacy is to be dated. And whoever will read the history of the African campaign, 533-534, and the Italian campaign, 534-538, will notice that the Catholics everywhere hailed as deliverers the army of Belisarius, the general of Justinian.

But no decree of this nature could be carried into effect until the Arian horns which stood in its way were overthrown. A turn came, however, in the tide of affairs, for in the military campaign in Africa and Italy the victorious legions of Belisarius dealt a crushing blow to Arianism, so much so that its final supporters were vanquished.

Procopius relates that the African war was undertaken by Justinian for the relief of the Christians (Catholics) in that quarter, and that when he expressed his intention in this respect, the prefect of the palace came very near dissuading him from his purpose. But a dream appeared to him in which he was bidden "not to shrink from the execution of his design;

[17] *Ibid.*, p. 328.

[18] See Edward Gibbon, *The Decline and Fall of the Roman Empire*, Vol. III, chap. 37, pp. 548-552.

[19] Edward B. Elliott, *Horæ Apocalypticæ*, Vol. III, p. 139, Note 3.

for by assisting the Christians he would overthrow the power of the Vandals."[20]

Mosheim declares: "It is true, the Greeks who had received the decrees of the Council of Nice [that is, from the Catholics], persecuted and oppressed the Arians wherever their influence and authority could reach; but the Nicenians, in their turn, were not less rigorously treated by their adversaries [the Arians], particularly in Africa and Italy, where they felt, in a very severe manner, the weight of the Arian power, and the bitterness of their resentment. The triumphs of Arianism were, however, transitory; and its prosperous days were entirely eclipsed when the Vandals were driven out of Africa, and the Goths out of Italy, by the arms of Justinian."[21]

Elliott summarizes: "I might cite *three* that were eradicated from before the pope out of the list first given, viz., the *Heruli* under Odoacer, the *Vandals*, and the *Ostrogoths*."[22]

From the historical testimony above cited, we think it clearly established that the three horns plucked up were the powers named: the Heruli, A. D. 493, the Vandals, in 534, and the Ostrogoths finally in 553, though effective opposition by the latter to the decree of Justinian ceased when they were driven from Rome by Belisarius in 538,[23] as stated on page 127.

Little Horn to "Speak Great Words Against the Most High."—This prophecy, too, has been unhappily fulfilled in the history of the pontiffs. They have sought, or at least have permitted to be applied to them, titles which would be hyperbolical and blasphemous if applied to an angel of God.

Lucius Ferraris, in his *Prompta Bibliotheca* which the *Catholic Encyclopedia* refers to as "a veritable encyclopedia of religious knowledge" and "a precious mine of information," declares, in its article on the pope, that "the pope is of so great dignity and so exalted that he is not a mere man, but as it

---

[20] Theodoret and Evagrius, *A History of the Church*, p. 399.

[21] John L. Mosheim, *An Ecclesiastical History, Ancient and Modern*, Vol. I, pp. 142, 143.

[22] Edward B. Elliott, *Horæ Apocalypticæ*, Vol. III, p. 139, Note 1.

[23] See *Student's Gibbon*, pp. 309-319.

were God, and the vicar of God. . . . The pope is of such lofty and supreme dignity that, properly speaking, he has not been established in any rank of dignity, but rather has been placed upon the very summit of all ranks of dignities. . . . The pope is called most holy because he is rightfully presumed to be such. . . .

"The pope alone is deservedly called by the name 'most holy,' because he alone is the vicar of Christ, who is the fountain and source and fullness of all holiness. . . . 'He is likewise the divine monarch and supreme emperor, and king of kings.' . . . Hence the pope is crowned with a triple crown, as king of heaven and of earth and of the lower regions. . . . Moreover the superiority and the power of the Roman Pontiff by no means pertain only to heavenly things, to earthly things, and to things under the earth, but are even over angels, than whom he is greater. . . . So that if it were possible that the angels might err in the faith, or might think contrary to the faith, they could be judged and excommunicated by the pope. . . . For he is of so great dignity and power that he forms one and the same tribunal with Christ. . . .

"The pope is as it were God on earth, sole sovereign of the faithful of Christ, chief king of kings, having plenitude of power, to whom has been intrusted by the omnipotent God direction not only of the earthly but also of the heavenly kingdom. . . . The pope is of so great authority and power that he can modify, explain, or interpret even divine laws."[24]

Christopher Marcellus, at the fourth session of the fifth Lateran Council in an oration to the Pope, exclaimed: "Thou art the shepherd, thou art the physician, thou art the director, thou art the husbandman; finally, thou art another God on earth."[25]

Again, Adam Clarke says on verse 25: " 'He shall speak as if he were God.' So St. Jerome quotes from Symmachus. To

---

[24] Translated from Lucius Ferraris, *Prompta Bibliotheca*, art. "Papa," II, Vol. VI, pp. 26-29.

[25] P. Joannis Harduin, *Acta Conciliorum*, Vol. IX, p. 1651.

none can this apply so well or so fully as to the popes of Rome. They have assumed infallibility, which belongs only to God. They profess to forgive sins, which belongs only to God. They profess to open and shut heaven, which belongs only to God. They profess to be higher than all the kings of the earth, which belongs only to God. And they go *beyond* God in pretending to loose whole nations from their oath of allegiance to their kings, when such kings do not please them. And they go *against* God when they give indulgences for sin. This is the worst of all blasphemies."[26]

Little Horn to "Wear Out the Saints of the Most High."—It requires but little historical investigation to prove that Rome, both in the times of antiquity and during the Dark Ages, carried forward a work of destruction against the church of God. Abundant evidences can be given showing that prior to and following the great work of the Reformation, wars, crusades, massacres, inquisitions, and persecutions of all kinds were the methods adopted to compel all to submit to the Roman yoke.

The story of medieval persecution is a frightful one, and we dread to dwell upon its detail. Yet for a proper understanding of this passage it is necessary that we recall some of the happenings of these unhappy times. Albert Barnes, in his comment on this passage, remarks:

"Can anyone doubt that this is true of the papacy? The Inquisition, the 'persecutions of the Waldenses;' the ravages of the Duke of Alva; the fires of Smithfield; the tortures at Goa—indeed, the whole history of the papacy may be appealed to in proof that this is applicable to that power. If anything *could* have 'worn out the saints of the Most High'—could have cut them off from the earth so that evangelical religion would have become extinct, it would have been the persecutions of the papal power. In the year 1208, a crusade was proclaimed by Pope Innocent III against the Waldenses and Albigenses, in which a million of men perished. From the beginning of the

---

[26] Adam Clarke, *Commentary on the Old Testament*, Vol. IV, p. 596, note on Daniel 7: 25.

order of the Jesuits, in the year 1540, to 1580, nine hundred thousand were destroyed. One hundred and fifty thousand perished by the Inquisition in thirty years. In the Low Countries fifty thousand persons were hanged, beheaded, burned, and buried alive, for the crime of heresy, within the space of thirty-eight years from the edict of Charles V against the Protestants, to the peace of Chateau Cambreses in 1559. Eighteen thousand suffered by the hand of the executioner in the space of five years and a half during the administration of the Duke of Alva. Indeed, the slightest acquaintance with the history of the papacy will convince any one that what is here said of 'making war with the saints' (verse 21), and 'wearing out the saints of the Most High' (verse 25), is strictly applicable to that power, and will accurately describe its history."[27]

These facts are confirmed by the testimony of W. E. H. Lecky. He declares:

"That the Church of Rome has shed more innocent blood than any other institution that has ever existed among mankind, will be questioned by no Protestant who has a complete knowledge of history. The memorials, indeed, of many of her persecutions are now so scanty that it is impossible to form a complete conception of the multitude of her victims, and it is quite certain that no powers of imagination can adequately realize their sufferings. . . . These atrocities were not perpetrated in the brief paroxysms of a reign of terror, or by the hands of obscure sectaries, but were inflicted by a triumphant church, with every circumstance of solemnity and deliberation."[28]

It makes no difference that in numerous instances the victims were turned over to the civil authorities. It was the church that made the decision upon the question of heresy, and it then passed the offenders over to the secular court. But in those days the secular power was but the tool in the

---

[27] Albert Barnes, *Notes on Daniel*, p. 328, comment on Daniel 7: 25.

[28] William E. H. Lecky, *History of the Rise and Influence of the Spirit of Rationalism in Europe*, Vol. II, pp. 35, 37.

"HE . . . SHALL WEAR OUT THE SAINTS"

As a result of ruthless persecutions against religious minorities, millions of godly men and women lost their lives for their faith.

hands of the church. It was under its control and did its bidding. When the church delivered its prisoners to the executioners to be destroyed, with fiendish mockery it made use of the following formula: "And we do leave and deliver thee to the secular arm, and to the power of the secular court; but at the same time do most earnestly beseech that court so to moderate its sentence as not to touch thy blood, or to put thy life in any danger."[29] Then, as intended, the unfortunate victims of popish hate were immediately executed.

The testimony of Lepicier is to the point in this connection: "The civil power can only punish the crime of unbelief in the manner and to the extent that the crime is judicially made known to it by ecclesiastical persons, skilled in the doctrine of the faith. But the church taking cognizance by herself of the crime of unbelief, can by herself decree the sentence of death, yet not execute it; but she hands over the execution of it to the secular arm."[30]

The false claims of some Catholics that their church has never killed dissenters, have been flatly denied by one of their own standard writers, Cardinal Bellarmine, who was born in Tuscany in 1542, and who, after his death in 1621, came very near being placed in the calendar of saints on account of his great services in behalf of the church. This man, on one occasion, under the spur of controversy, betrayed himself into an admission of the real facts in the case. Luther having said that the church (meaning the true church) never burned heretics, Bellarmine, understanding it of the Roman Catholic Church, made answer: "This argument proves not the sentiment, but the ignorance or impudence of Luther; for as *almost an infinite number* were either burned or otherwise put to death, Luther either did not know it, and was therefore ignorant; or if he knew it, he is convicted of impudence and falsehood—for that

---

[29] Michael Geddes, "A View of the Court of Inquisition in Portugal," *Miscellaneous Tracts*, Vol. I, p. 408. See also Philip Limborch, *The History of the Inquisition*, Vol. II, p. 289.

[30] Alexius M. Lepicier, *The Stability and Progress of Dogma*, p. 195.

heretics were often burned *by the church*, may be proved by adducing a few from many examples."[31]

Alfred Baudrillart, rector of the Catholic Institute of Paris, when referring to the attitude of the church toward heresy, remarks:

"When confronted by heresy, she does not content herself with persuasion; arguments of an intellectual and moral order appear to her insufficient, and she has recourse to force, to corporal punishment, to torture. She creates tribunals like those of the Inquisition, she calls the laws of state to her aid, if necessary she encourages a crusade, or a religious war, and all her 'horror of blood' practically culminates into urging the secular power to shed it, which proceeding is almost more odious—for it is less frank—than shedding it herself.

"Especially did she act thus in the sixteenth century with regard to Protestants. Not content to reform morally, to teach by example, to convert people by eloquent and holy missionaries, she lit in Italy, in the Low Countries, and above all in Spain, the funeral piles of the Inquisition. In France under Francis I and Henri II, in England under Mary Tudor, she tortured the heretics, while both in France and Germany, during the second half of the sixteenth, and the first half of the seventeenth centuries, if she did not actually begin, at any rate she encouraged and actively aided the religious wars."[32]

In a letter of Pope Martin V (A. D. 1417-1431), are the following instructions to the King of Poland:

" 'Know that the interest of the Holy See, and those of your crown, make it a duty to exterminate the Hussites. Remember that these impious persons dare proclaim principles of equality; they maintain that all Christians are brethren, and that God has not given to privileged men the right of ruling the nations; they hold that Christ came on earth to abolish slavery; they call the people to liberty, that is, to the annihilation of kings

[31] John Dowling, *The History of Romanism*, p. 547.

[32] Alfred Baudrillart, *The Catholic Church, the Renaissance, and Protestantism*, pp. 182, 183.

and priests! Whilst there is still time, then, turn your forces against Bohemia; burn, massacre, make deserts everywhere, for nothing could be more agreeable to God, or more useful to the cause of kings, than the extermination of the Hussites.' "[33]

All this was in harmony with the teaching of the church. Heresy was not to be tolerated, but to be destroyed.

Pagan Rome persecuted the Christian church relentlessly. It is estimated that *three million* Christians perished in the first three centuries of the Christian Era. Yet it is said that the primitive Christians prayed for the continuance of imperial Rome, for they knew that when this form of government should cease, another far worse persecuting power would arise, which would literally "wear out the saints of the Most High," as this prophecy declares. Pagan Rome could slay the infants, but spare the mothers; but papal Rome slew both the mothers and infants together. No age, no sex, no condition in life, was exempt from her relentless rage.

Little Horn to "Think to Change Times and Laws."—What laws and whose? Not the laws of other earthly governments; for it was nothing marvelous or strange for one power to change the laws of another, whenever it could bring such power under its dominion. Not human laws of any kind; for the little horn had power to change these so far as its jurisdiction extended; but the times and laws in question were such as this power should only *think* to change, but not be able to change. They are the laws of the same Being to whom the saints belong who are worn out by this power, namely, the laws of the Most High. And has the papacy attempted this?—Yes, even this.

It has added the second commandment of the Decalogue to the first, making them one, and divided the tenth into two, making the ninth forbid the coveting of a neighbor's wife, and the tenth that of a neighbor's property—thus making up the

[33] L. M. de Cormenin, *The Public and Private History of the Popes of Rome*, Vol. II, pp. 116, 117.

THE TEN COMMANDMENTS

(*Exodus 20: 3-17*)

I

Thou shalt have no other gods before Me.

II

Thou shalt not make unto thee any graven image, or any likeness of any thing that is in heaven above, or that is in the earth beneath, or that is in the water under the earth: thou shalt not bow down thyself to them, nor serve them: for I the Lord thy God am a jealous God, visiting the iniquity of the fathers upon the children unto the third and fourth generation of them that hate Me; and showing mercy unto thousands of them that love Me, and keep My commandments.

III

Thou shalt not take the name of the Lord thy God in vain; for the Lord will not hold him guiltless that taketh His name in vain.

IV

Remember the Sabbath day, to keep it holy. Six days shalt thou labor, and do all thy work: but the seventh day is the Sabbath of the Lord thy God: in it thou shalt not do any work, thou, nor thy son, nor thy daughter, thy manservant, nor thy maidservant, nor thy cattle, nor thy stranger that is within thy gates: for in six days the Lord made heaven and earth, the sea, and all that in them is, and rested the seventh day: wherefore the Lord blessed the Sabbath day, and hallowed it.

V

Honor thy father and thy mother: that thy days may be long upon the land which the Lord thy God giveth thee.

VI

Thou shalt not kill.

VII

Thou shalt not commit adultery.

VIII

Thou shalt not steal.

IX

Thou shalt not bear false witness against thy neighbor.

X

Thou shalt not covet thy neighbor's house, thou shalt not covet thy neighbor's wife, nor his manservant, nor his maidservant, nor his ox, nor his ass, nor anything that is thy neighbor's.

THE TEN COMMANDMENTS

*As Abbreviated in Vernacular Roman Catholic Catechisms**

"He shall think himself able to change times and laws."
Daniel 7: 25, Douay Version.

I

I am the Lord thy God. Thou shalt not have strange gods before Me.

II

Thou shalt not take the name of the Lord thy God in vain.

III

Remember thou keep holy the Sabbath day.

IV

Honor thy father and thy mother.

V

Thou shalt not kill.

VI

Thou shalt not commit adultery.

VII

Thou shalt not steal.

VIII

Thou shalt not bear false witness against thy neighbor.

IX

Thou shalt not covet thy neighbor's wife.

X

Thou shalt not covet thy neighbor's goods.

---

* Such as Keenan's and Geiermann's in English. The two vernacular catechisms here quoted and many more like them, bear the imprimatur of bishops of the Church and are used for teaching the laity.

full number ten. While the full wording of the second commandment is retained in the Roman Catholic Bible and in the *Roman Catechism* authorized by the Council of Trent, painstaking explanation is made that in the case of images and likenesses of any kind except that of God Himself, their making and use are not forbidden by the commandment when employed only to venerate the virtues of the saints and not to worship them as gods, which latter is expressly forbidden in the commandment. The same principle is applied also to ashes, bones, and other relics of saints, and to representations of angels.

As to the fourth commandment, numbered as the third in their arrangement, the catechism of highest authority in the Roman Catholic Church retains the commandment entire, and urges punctilious observance of the Sabbath in the personal life and in public worship as a sacred privilege and duty. Nevertheless the position is taken that the particular *day* on which the Sabbath is to be observed, was connected with the ceremonial ordinances of the Jews, and was with them done away in Christ. Reasons are then given why the Sabbath should be observed on the first day of the week commonly called Sunday.

In support of the foregoing brief statement on the changing of "times and laws" by the papacy, we draw evidence from the catechism of highest authority in the Roman Catholic Church, cited hereafter. According to *The Catholic Encyclopedia*, "the authority of this catechism is higher than that of any other, but is, of course, not on a level with that of the canons and decrees of a council."[34]

Before making quotations, it should be first stated that in the polity of the Roman Catholic Church, the canons and decrees of an ecumenical church council are both official and supreme. Outstanding among such ecumenical church councils is the Council of Trent, held at Trent, Italy, from 1545 to

---

[34] *Catholic Encyclopedia*, art., "Doctrine, Christian," Vol. V, p. 79.

1563. Since that council, called to counteract the spreading influence of the Protestant Reformation, dealt so widely with the doctrines and usages of the church, it officially decreed the following: "The holy synod commands all bishops . . . [to explain the sacraments] according to the form to be prescribed by the holy synod for all the sacraments *in a catechism*, which bishops will take care to have faithfully translated into the vulgar tongue, and expounded to the people by the parish priests."[35]

In pursuance of this command, a catechism was composed in Latin for the Roman Catholic Church by St. Charles Borromeo and other theologians, in 1566, and published in Rome by the Vatican Congregation for Propagation of the Faith, under the title *Catechismus Romanus ex decreto Sacrosancti Concilii Tridentini, jussu S. Pii V Pontificis Maximi editus*, in other words, *Roman Catechism according to the decree of the Sacred Council of Trent, published by order of St. Pius V, Pontifex Maximus.*"

This book was translated into English by "Very Rev. J. Donovan, D. D. . . . Domestic Prelate to His Holiness Gregory XVI," etc., and published in Dublin with a preface dated June 10, 1829. The title of this book reads, *Catechism According to the Decree of the Council of Trent, edited by the command of our Most Illustrious Lord Pius the Fifth.*

From the fifth edition of this *Roman Catechism* published in Rome in 1796, we quote the following from Donovan's English Translation, in regard to the fourth (Catholic third) commandment:

"It pleased the church of God, that the religious celebration of the Sabbath day should be transferred to 'the Lord's day' [meaning Sunday]; for as on that day light first shone on the world; so by the resurrection of our Redeemer on that day, who opened to us the gate to life eternal, our life was recalled out of darkness into light; whence also the Apostles would have it named 'the Lord's day.' We also observe in the

---

[35] J. Donovan, quoting from "Council of Trent, Sess. xxiv, c. vii, on Reformation," *Catechism of the Council of Trent*, p. 4.

Sacred Scriptures that this day was held sacred because on that day the creation of the world commenced, and the Holy Ghost was given to the apostles."[36]

Here is the declaration of the papacy that the Roman Catholic Church changed the time for observing the Sabbath from the seventh day according to the decalogue to the first day of the week, which it here erroneously calls "the Lord's day." (See comment on Revelation 1: 10.) It will be observed that the apostles are here charged with making the change from the seventh day to the first, but without any proof whatsoever from the Scriptures, because there is no such proof. All the reasons for the change given in this declaration, are purely of human and ecclesiastical invention.

The foregoing testimony is sufficient to show how the papacy has thought to change times and laws. How later Roman Catholic catechisms for instruction of "the faithful" come out boldly in declaring that the church changed the day, and even taunt Protestants with acceptance and observance of the change, will be found in our comment on the mark of the beast in Revelation 13, pages 608-612.

Before leaving this matter of the change of the Sabbath, it will be enlightening to observe other reasons given by the papacy for the change than the false one that it was made by the apostles. In the same *Roman Catechism* referred to above, is an attempt to explain how the Sabbath commandment differs from the others in the decalogue:

"That difference, then, appears certain, that the other precepts of the decalogue belong to the natural law, and are perpetual and unalterable, whence is it that, although the law of Moses has been abrogated, yet the Christian people observe all the commandments which are contained in the two tables, not because Moses so commanded, but because they agree with the law of nature, by the force of which men are impelled to their observance; whereas this commandment,

---

[36] *Catechism of the Council of Trent*, p. 347.

touching the sanctification of the Sabbath, if considered as to the time appointed [for its observance], is not fixed and unalterable, but susceptible of change, nor does it belong to the moral but ceremonial law, neither is it a principle of the natural law, for we are taught or formed by nature to give external worship to God on that rather than on any other day; but from the time the people of Israel were liberated from the bondage of Pharaoh, they observed the Sabbath day. . . .

"But the time when the observance of the Sabbath was to be removed, is that same time when the other Hebrew rites and ceremonies were to be abrogated, namely, at the death of Christ; for as those ceremonies are, as it were, images that shadowed forth the light and the truth (Hebrews x,1), it was, therefore, necessary that they should be removed at the coming of the light and truth, which is Jesus Christ."[37]

The reader needs only to be reminded that the ten-commandment law was written with God's finger on tables of stone, while the ceremonial laws were written by Moses in a book. More than this, the decalogue was written *before* the ceremonial laws were given to Moses. Shall we charge God with mixing in one ceremonial commandment with the nine of the moral law, and leave it to a presumptuous ecclesiastical body to make the correction? The reason also for the observance of the seventh-day Sabbath, as given in the commandment itself, is that the Creator Himself rested on that day, and set it apart as a memorial of His work of creation, but with no intimation whatever of its being "a shadow of things to come" in Christ, to whom all ceremonial ordinances pointed forward.

One more quotation from the *Roman Catechism* is worth noticing:

"The Apostles, therefore, resolved to consecrate the first day of the seven to divine worship, which they called 'the Lord's day;' for St. John, in his Apocalypse, makes mention of 'the Lord's day' (Apocalypse i,10); and the Apostle orders

[37] *Ibid.*, pp. 342, 343.

collections to be made 'on the first day of the week' (1 Corinthians xvi,2), which is, as St. Chrysostom interprets, the Lord's day; to give us to understand, that even then the Lord's day was kept holy in the church."[38]

In addition to falsely charging the apostles with changing the day of the Sabbath, it is here represented that the business reckoning of one's accounts on the first day of the week is a reason for its observance as the Sabbath contrary to God's unchangeable law.

This quotation also reveals the fact that the practices and interpretations of the Fathers, such as "St. Chrysostom," here mentioned, are relied on rather than the Scriptures themselves for proof that the Sabbath of God's law was changed to Sunday.

One more observation is appropriate here, especially for Protestant clergy and laymen to consider. In this *Roman Catechism*, composed by order of Pope Pius V about the middle of the sixteenth century, is contained virtually every argument used by Protestants in our day to support the change of the Sabbath from the seventh to the first day of the week. Note these:

They assume without proof that the seventh-day Sabbath was part of the ceremonial law (though embodied in the very heart of the moral law written by the finger of God), and therefore done away in Christ.

They boldly claim that the apostles ordained that the first day of the week be observed in place of the seventh, citing John's use of the term "Lord's day" in Revelation 1: 10, despite the fact that the only day God ever set apart as holy and claimed as His own by resting on it Himself was the seventh day of the fourth commandment.

They claim that the Sabbath law of rest "agrees with the law of nature" requiring cessation of labor and a period for meditation and worship, but assert that the *time* of its observ-

---

[38] *Ibid.*, pp. 343, 344.

ance is "susceptible of change," since, according to their argument, it does not "belong to the moral but ceremonial law," and was therefore changed by the apostles, by the Fathers, and by the church to the first day of the week.

The arguments they use for such change are that light first shone on the world on the first day of the week, the resurrection of Christ took place on that day, the Holy Spirit descended on the apostles on the same day of the week, Paul admonished Christians to reckon their business accounts and lay aside a portion for the Lord on the first day of the week—all of human invention and without Scriptural authority as reasons for such a change. The only reasons given by the Creator and Lord of the Sabbath, are that He created the world in six days, rested on the seventh, and set apart that day for holy use on the same permanent and unalterable basis as He created all other things on the other days of creation week.

Protestants may not be aware that in defense of the Sunday sabbath they are using the Roman Catholic arguments contained in the *Catechism of the Council of Trent* published in the sixteenth century, but every one of them mentioned above is found in that work. Our appeal to every Protestant is to break away fully from the papacy, and hold to the Bible and the Bible only in his belief and practice.

"*A Time and Times and the Dividing of Time.*"—The pronoun "they" in the sentence containing this phrase embraces the saints, the times, and the laws just mentioned. How long a time were they to be given into the hands of this power? A time, as we have seen from Daniel 4: 23, is one year; two times, the least that could be denoted by the plural, two years, and the dividing of time, or half a time, half a year. The word "dividing" in the phrase "dividing of time" is translated from the Chaldee word פְּלַג, *pelag*, which Gesenius defines as "a half," and refers to Daniel 7: 25 as an example. The Septuagint translates it "half." We thus have three years and a half for the continuance of this power. The Chaldee word for "time" in the text before us, is עִדָּן, *iddan*, which

Gesenius defines thus: "*Time.* Spec. in prophetic language for a *year.* Daniel 7: 25, עַד־עִדָּן וְעִדָּנִין וּפְלַג עִדָּן *for a year, also* two *years and half a year; i.e.,* for three years and a half; comp. Jos. B.J.I.I.I."

We must now consider that we are in the midst of symbolic prophecy; hence in this measurement the time is not literal, but symbolic. The inquiry then arises, How long a period is denoted by the three years and a half of prophetic time? The principle given us in the Bible is, that when a day is used in symbolic prophecy, it stands for a year. (Ezekiel 4: 6; Numbers 14: 34.) Under the Hebrew word for day, יוֹם, *yom,* Gesenius has this remark on its plural: "Sometimes יָמִים [*yamim*] marks a definite space of *time;* viz., *a year;* as also Syr. and Chald. עִדָּן [*iddan*] denotes both *time* and *year;* and as in English several words signifying time, weight, measure, are likewise used to denote certain specified times, weights, and measures."

Bible students have recognized this principle through the ages. The following quotations reveal the agreement of various authorities on this point. Joachim, abbot of Calabria, one of the great ecclesiastical figures of the twelfth century, applied the year-day principle to the 1260-year period. "The woman, clothed with the sun, who signifies the church, remained hidden in the wilderness from the face of the serpent, a day without doubt being accepted for a year and a thousand two hundred and sixty days for the same number of years." [39]

"Three times and an half; that is, for 1260 solar years, reckoning a time for a calendar year of 360 days, and a day for a solar year. After which 'the judgment is to sit, and they shall take away his dominion,' not at once, but by degrees, to consume, and to destroy it unto the end." [40]

The Bible year, which must be used as the basis of reckoning, contained three hundred and sixty days. (See comments on Revelation 11: 3.) Three years and a half contained

[39] Joachim of Floris, *Concordantia,* book 2, chap. 16, p. 12b.
[40] Sir Isaac Newton, *Observations Upon the Prophecies of Daniel,* pp. 127, 128.

twelve hundred and sixty days. As each day stands for a year, we have twelve hundred and sixty years for the continuation of the supremacy of this horn. Did the papacy possess dominion that length of time? The answer again is, Yes. The edict of the emperor Justinian, dated A. D. 533, made the bishop of Rome the head of all the churches. But this edict could not go into effect until the Arian Ostrogoths, the last of the three horns that were plucked up to make room for the papacy, were driven from Rome; and this was not accomplished, as already shown, until A. D. 538. (See p. 127.) The edict would have been of no effect had this latter event not been accomplished; hence from this latter year we are to reckon, as this was the earliest point where the saints were in reality in the hands of this power. From this point did the papacy hold supremacy for twelve hundred and sixty years?—Exactly. For 538 + 1260 = 1798; and in the year 1798, Berthier, with a French army, entered Rome, proclaimed a republic, took the pope prisoner, and inflicted a deadly wound upon the papacy. Though it has never since enjoyed all the privileges and immunities which it possessed before, we are seeing a gradual restoration of its former strength.

The Judgment Shall Sit.—After describing the terrible career of the little horn, and stating that the saints should be given into his hand for 1260 years, bringing us down to 1798, verse 26 declares: "But the judgment shall sit, and they shall take away his dominion, to consume and to destroy it unto the end." In verse 10 of the same chapter we have substantially the same expression regarding the judgment: "The judgment was set." It would seem consistent to suppose that the same judgment is referred to in both instances. But the sublime scene described in verse 10 is the opening of the investigative judgment in the sanctuary in heaven, as will appear in remarks on Daniel 8: 14 and 9: 25-27. The opening of this judgment scene is located by the prophecy at the close of the great prophetic period of 2300 years, which terminated in 1844. (See comments on Daniel 9: 25-27.)

Four years after this, in 1848, the great revolution which shook so many thrones in Europe, also drove the pope from his dominions. His restoration shortly after was through the force of foreign bayonets, by which alone he was upheld until his final loss of temporal power in 1870. The overthrow of the papacy in 1798 marked the conclusion of the prophetic period of 1260 years, and constituted the "deadly wound," prophesied in Revelation 13: 3 to come upon this power; but this deadly wound was to be "healed."

Deadly Wound to Be Healed.—In 1800 another pope was elected, his palace and his temporal dominion over the Papal States were restored, and, as George Croly, noted British commentator, says, every prerogative except that of a systematic persecutor was again his, for the "deadly wound" was beginning to be healed.

How could that "deadly wound" be healed, and the specifications of Daniel 7: 26, "They shall take away his dominion, to consume and to destroy it unto the end," be realized? How are we to explain this apparent paradox? Whatever the exegetical difficulties may be, the fact remains that in the history of the papacy these two specifications are being seen.

In 1844 the judgment began its work in the heavenly sanctuary. (Verse 10.) In verse 11 we are told that because of "the great words which the horn spake . . . the beast was slain." December 8, 1854, the dogma of the Immaculate Conception was decreed by the pope. In 1870 the armies of Victor Emmanuel took away the temporal power of the pope, the very year that the Twentieth Ecumenical Council decreed the infallibility of the pope when speaking *ex cathedra*, that is, when as shepherd and teacher of all Christians he defines a doctrine concerning faith or morals. But despite the increasing honors heaped upon the office of the bishop of Rome by the clergy, the pope's temporal power was wholly taken away. Thereafter the popes shut themselves up as prisoners in the Vatican at Rome until the signing of the concordat with

Italy, in 1929, which restored "his dominion" over the Vatican City, a small section of the city of Rome.

VERSE 27 And the kingdom and dominion, and the greatness of the kingdom under the whole heaven, shall be given to the people of the saints of the Most High, whose kingdom is an everlasting kingdom, and all dominions shall serve and obey him. 28 Hitherto is the end of the matter. As for me Daniel, my cogitations much troubled me, and my countenance changed in me: but I kept the matter in my heart.

After beholding the dark and desolate picture of papal oppression of the church, the prophet is permitted once more to turn his eyes upon the glorious period of the saints' rest, when they shall have the kingdom, free from all oppressive powers, in everlasting possession. How could the children of God keep heart in this present evil world, amid the misrule and oppression of the governments of earth, and the abominations that are done in the land, if they could not look forward to the kingdom of God and the return of their Lord, with full assurance that the promises concerning them both shall certainly be fulfilled, and that speedily?

T. K. MARTIN, ARTIST

THE RAM AND THE HE-GOAT

The vision recorded in the eighth chapter of Daniel depicts two great world powers in mortal combat.

CHAPTER VIII

THE WORLD ARRAIGNED BEFORE THE COURT OF HEAVEN

"WE NOW come once more," says Adam Clarke, "to the Hebrew, the Chaldee part of the book being finished. As the Chaldeans had a particular interest both in the history and the prophecies from chapter 2: 4 to the end of chapter 7, the whole is written in Chaldee; but as the prophecies which remain concern times posterior to the Chaldean monarchy, and principally relate to the church and people of God generally, they are written in the Hebrew language, this being the tongue in which God chose to reveal all His counsels given under the Old Testament relative to the New."[1]

VERSE 1 In the third year of the reign of king Belshazzar a vision appeared unto me, even unto me Daniel, after that which appeared unto me at the first.

One prominent characteristic of the sacred writings which should forever shield them from the charge of being works of fiction, is the frankness and freedom with which the writers state all the circumstances connected with events which they record. Here verse 1 states the time when this vision was given to Daniel. The first year of Belshazzar was 540 B. C. His third year, in which this vision was given, would consequently be 538. Since Daniel was probably about twenty years of age when he was carried to Babylon in the first year of Nebuchadnezzar in 606 B. C., he was at this time about eighty-eight years of age. The vision he refers to as the one which appeared unto him at the first, is doubtless the vision of the seventh chapter, which he had in the first year of Belshazzar's reign.

[1] Adam Clarke, *Commentary on the Old Testament*, Vol. IV, p. 598, note on Daniel 8: 1.

VERSE 2 And I saw in a vision; and it came to pass, when I saw, that I was at Shushan in the palace, which is in the province of Elam; and I saw in a vision, and I was by the river of Ulai.

As verse 1 states the time when the vision was given, this verse gives the place where the prophet received the revelation. Shushan was the metropolis of the province of Elam, which was then in the hands of the Babylonians, and the king of Babylon had a royal palace there. Daniel as minister of state employed in the king's business, was in that place. Abradates, viceroy of Shushan, gave his allegiance to Cyrus, and the province was joined to the Medes and Persians; so that, according to the prophecy of Isaiah 21: 2, Elam went up with the Medes to besiege Babylon. Under the Medes and Persians, Elam regained its liberties, of which it had been deprived by the Babylonians, according to the prophecy of Jeremiah 49: 39.

VERSE 3 Then I lifted up mine eyes, and saw, and, behold, there stood before the river a ram which had two horns: and the two horns were high; but one was higher than the other, and the higher came up last. 4 I saw the ram pushing westward, and northward, and southward; so that no beasts might stand before him, neither was there any that could deliver out of his hand; but he did according to his will, and became great.

Kingdoms of Media and Persia.—In verse 20 an interpretation of this symbol is given in plain language: "The ram which thou sawest having two horns are the kings of Media and Persia." We have only therefore to consider how well the power answers to the symbol in question. The two horns represented the two nationalities of which the empire was composed. The higher came up last. This symbolized Persia, which at first was simply an ally of the Medes, but later came to be the leading division of the empire. The directions in which the ram pushed denote the directions in which the Medes and Persians carried their conquests. No earthly powers could stand before them as they marched toward the exalted position to which the providence of God had summoned them. So successful were their conquests that in the days of Ahasuerus (Esther 1: 1) the Medo-Persian kingdom, consisting of one hundred twenty-seven provinces, extended from India to Ethiopia, the boundaries of the then-known world.

VERSE 5 And as I was considering, behold, an he-goat came from the west on the face of the whole earth, and touched not the ground: and the goat had a notable horn between his eyes. 6 And he came to the ram that had two horns, which I had seen standing before the river, and ran unto him in the fury of his power. 7 And I saw him come close unto the ram, and he was moved with choler against him, and smote the ram, and brake his two horns: and there was no power in the ram to stand before him, but he cast him down to the ground, and stamped upon him: and there was none that could deliver the ram out of his hand.

Kingdom of Grecia.—"As I was considering," said the prophet. Here is an example for every lover of truth and all who have any regard for spiritual things. When Moses saw the burning bush, he said, "I will now turn aside, and see this great sight." How few are willing at the present time to turn aside from their pursuit of business or pleasure to consider the important themes which God seeks to bring to their attention.

The symbol here introduced is explained to Daniel by the angel. "The rough goat is the king [or kingdom] of Grecia." Verse 21. Concerning the fitness of this symbol to represent the Grecian, or Macedonian, people, Thomas Newton observes that the Macedonians, "about two hundred years before Daniel, were denominated *Ægeadæ*, or the *goat's people*." He explains the origin of the name as recounted by heathen authors: "Caranus, their first king, going with a great multitude of Greeks to seek new habitations in Macedonia, was commanded by the oracle to take the goats for his guides to empire: and afterwards seeing a herd of goats flying from a violent storm, he followed them to Edessa, and there fixed the seat of his empire, made the goats his ensigns or standards, and called the city *Ægeæ*, or the *goat's town*, and the people *Ægeadæ*, or the *goat's people*. . . . The city of Ægeæ, or Ægæ, was the usual burying place of the Macedonian kings.

It is also very remarkable that Alexander's son by Roxana was named *Alexander Ægus*, or the *son of the goat;* and some of Alexander's successors are represented in their coins with goat's horns."[2]

The "goat came from the west on the face of the whole earth." That is, Greece lay west of Persia and attacked from that direction. The Greek army swept everything on the face of the earth before it.

The goat "touched not the ground." Such was the marvelous celerity of his movements that he seemed to fly from point to point with the swiftness of the wind. The same characteristic of speed is indicated by the four wings of the leopard in the vision of Daniel 7, representing the same nation.

Alexander the "Notable Horn."—The notable horn between his eyes is explained in verse 21 to be the first king of the Macedonian Empire. This king was Alexander the Great.

A concise account of the overthrow of the Persian Empire by Alexander is given in verses 6 and 7. The battles between the Greeks and the Persians are said to have been exceedingly fierce. Some of the scenes recorded in history vividly bring to mind the figure used in the prophecy—a ram standing before the river, and the goat running toward him in "the fury of his power." Alexander first vanquished the generals of Darius at the River Granicus in Phrygia. He next attacked and routed Darius at the passes of Issus in Cilicia, and afterward defeated him on the plains of Arbela in Syria. This latter battle occurred in 331 B. C., and marked the fall of the Persian Empire. By this event Alexander became master of the whole country. Concerning verse 6—"He [the goat] came to the ram that had two horns, which I had seen standing before the river, and ran unto him in the fury of his power"—Thomas Newton says: "One can hardly read these words without having some image of Darius's army standing and guarding the River Granicus, and of Alexander on the other side with his forces plunging in,

[2] Thomas Newton, *Dissertations on the Prophecies*, Vol. I, pp. 303, 304.

swimming across the stream, and rushing on the enemy with all the fire and fury that can be imagined."[3]

Ptolemy begins the reign of Alexander in 332 B. C. but it was not until the battle of Arbela the year following that Alexander became "absolute lord of that empire in the utmost extent in which it was ever possessed by any of the Persian kings."[4]

On the eve of this battle, Darius sent ten of his chief relatives to sue for peace. When they had presented their conditions to Alexander, he is said to have replied, "Heaven cannot support two suns, nor the earth two masters."[5]

The language of verse 7 sets forth the completeness of the subjection of Medo-Persia to Alexander. The two horns were broken, and the ram was cast to the ground and stamped upon. Persia was subdued, the country ravaged, its armies cut to pieces and scattered, and its cities plundered. The royal city of Persepolis, the capital of the Persian Empire—even in its ruins one of the wonders of the world to the present day—was sacked and burned. Thus the ram had no power to stand before the goat, and there was none that could deliver him out of his hand.

VERSE 8 Therefore the he-goat waxed very great: and when he was strong, the great horn was broken; and for it came up four notable ones toward the four winds of heaven.

Great Horn Broken.—The conqueror is greater than the conquered. The ram, Medo-Persia, became "great;" the goat, Greece, became "very great." "When he was strong, the great horn was broken." Human foresight and speculation would have said, When he becomes weak, his kingdom torn by rebellion, or weakened by luxury, then the horn will be broken, and the kingdom shattered. But Daniel saw it broken in the prime of its strength, at the height of its power, when

---

[3] *Ibid.*, p. 306.

[4] Humphrey Prideaux, *The Old and New Testament Connected in the History of the Jews*, Vol. I, p. 378.

[5] Walter Fogg, *One Thousand Sayings of History*, p. 210.

 R. M. ELDRIDGE, ARTIST

THE LITTLE HORN DEVELOPED

After destroying the Persian ram, the Grecian goat's notable horn was broken. Out of one of its four divisions arose the powerful "little horn."

every beholder would have exclaimed, Surely, the kingdom is established, and nothing can overthrow it. Thus it is often with the wicked. The horn of their strength is broken when they think they stand most firm. The Scripture says, "Let him that thinketh he standeth take heed lest he fall." 1 Corinthians 10: 12.

Four Notable Horns Come Up.—After Alexander's death there arose much contention among his followers respecting the succession. After a seven days' contest, it was agreed that his natural brother, Philip Aridæus, should be declared king. By him, and by Alexander's infant sons, Alexander Ægus and Hercules, the name and show of the Macedonian Empire were for a time sustained. But the boys were soon murdered, and the family of Alexander became extinct. Then the chief commanders of the army, who had gone into different parts of the empire as governors of the provinces, assumed the title of king. They at once began warring against one another to such a degree that within a few years after Alexander's death, the number was reduced to *four*—the exact number specified in the prophecy.

Four notable horns were to come up toward the four winds of heaven in place of the great horn that was broken. These were Cassander, who had Greece and the neighboring countries; Lysimachus, who had Asia Minor; Seleucus, who had Syria and Babylon, and from whom came the line of kings known as the "Seleucidæ," so famous in history; and Ptolemy, son of Lagus, who had Egypt, and from whom sprang the "Lagidæ." These held dominion toward the four winds of heaven. Cassander had the western parts, Lysimachus the northern regions, Seleucus the eastern countries, and Ptolemy the southern portion of the empire. These four horns may therefore be named Macedonia, Thrace (which then included Asia Minor, and those parts lying on the Hellespont and the Bosphorus), Syria, and Egypt.

VERSE 9 And out of one of them came forth a little horn, which waxed exceeding great, toward the south, and toward the east, and toward the

pleasant land. 10 And it waxed great, even to the host of heaven; and it cast
down some of the host and of the stars to the ground, and stamped upon
them. 11 Yea, he magnified himself even to the prince of the host, and by
him the daily sacrifice was taken away, and the place of his sanctuary was
cast down. 12 And an host was given him against the daily sacrifice by
reason of transgression, and it cast down the truth to the ground; and it
practiced, and prospered.

A Little Horn Comes Forth.—A third power is here introduced into the prophecy. In the explanation given to Daniel by the angel this symbol is not described as definitely as are Medo-Persia and Greece.

There are two common interpretations of the symbol which need be noticed in these brief comments. The first is that the "little horn" denotes the Syrian king, Antiochus Epiphanes. The second is that it denotes the Roman power. It is an easy matter to test these two positions.

Does the Little Horn Denote Antiochus?—If Antiochus Epiphanes does not fulfill the specifications of the prophecy, the application cannot be made to him. The little horn came out of one of the four horns of the goat. It was therefore a power existing distinct from any of the other horns of the goat. Was Antiochus such a power?

Who was Antiochus? From the time that Seleucus made himself king over the Syrian portion of Alexander's empire, thus constituting the Syrian horn of the goat, until that country was conquered by the Romans, twenty-six kings ruled in succession over that territory. The eighth of these was Antiochus Epiphanes. Antiochus, then, was simply one of the twenty-six kings who constituted the Syrian horn of the goat. He was, therefore, for the time being, that horn. Hence he could not at the same time be a separate and independent power, or another and remarkable horn, as was the little horn.

If it were proper to apply the little horn to any one of these twenty-six Syrian kings, it should certainly be applied to the most powerful and illustrious of them all; but Antiochus Epiphanes was not by any means the most powerful king of the Syrian line. Although he took the name Epiphanes, that is,

"The Illustrious," he was illustrious only in name. Nothing, says Prideaux, on the authority of Polybius, Livy, and Diodorus Siculus, could be more alien to his true character; because of his vile and extravagant folly, some thought him a fool and changed his name from Epiphanes, "The Illustrious," to Epimanes, "The Madman."[6]

Antiochus the Great, the father of Epiphanes, being defeated in a war with the Romans, was able to procure peace only by the payment of a prodigious sum of money and the surrender of a part of his territory. As a pledge that he would faithfully adhere to the terms of the treaty, he was obliged to give hostages, among whom was Epiphanes, his son, who was carried to Rome. The Romans ever afterward maintained this ascendancy.

The little horn of the goat was to wax exceeding great; but Antiochus Epiphanes did not become exceeding great. On the contrary, he did not enlarge his dominion, except by some temporary conquests in Egypt. These he immediately relinquished when the Romans took the part of Ptolemy and *commanded* him to desist from his designs on that territory. The rage of his disappointed ambition he vented upon the unoffending Jews.

The little horn, in comparison with the powers that preceded it, was exceeding great. Persia is simply called great, though it consisted of a hundred twenty-seven provinces. (Esther 1: 1.) Grecia, being more extensive still, is called very great. Now the little horn, which waxed *exceeding* great, must surpass them both. How absurd, then, to apply this to Antiochus, who was obliged to abandon Egypt at the dictation of the Romans. It cannot take long for anyone to decide the question which was the greater power—the one which evacuated Egypt, or the one which commanded that evacuation.

The little horn was to stand up against the Prince of princes, which expression refers, beyond controversy, to Jesus

[6] See Humphrey Prideaux, *The Old and New Testament Connected in the History of the Jews*, Vol. II, pp. 106, 107.

Christ. (Daniel 9: 25; Acts 3: 15; Revelation 1: 5.) But Antiochus died one hundred sixty-four years before our Lord was born. The prophecy cannot therefore apply to him, for he does not fulfill the specifications in a single particular. The question may then be asked, Why has anyone ever tried to apply it to him? We answer, Roman Catholics take that view to avoid the application of the prophecy to themselves; and many Protestants follow them, apparently in order to oppose the doctrine that the second advent of Christ is now at hand.

The Little Horn Denotes Rome.—It has been an easy matter to show that the little horn does not denote Antiochus Epiphanes. It will be as easy to show that it does denote Rome.

The field of vision here is substantially the same as that covered by Nebuchadnezzar's image of Daniel 2, and the vision of Daniel 7. In both these prophetic delineations we have found that the power which succeeded Grecia as the fourth great power was Rome. The only natural inference would be that the little horn, the power which in this vision succeeds Grecia as an "exceeding great" kingdom, is also Rome.

The little horn comes forth from one of the horns of the goat. How, it may be asked, can that be true of Rome? Earthly governments are not introduced into prophecy until they become in some way connected with the people of God. Rome became connected with the Jews, the people of God at that time, by the famous Jewish League in 161 B. C.[7] But seven years before this, that is, in 168 B. C., Rome had conquered Macedonia, and made that country a part of its empire. Rome is therefore introduced into prophecy just as, from the overthrow of the Macedonian horn of the goat, it is going forth to new conquests in other directions. It appeared to the prophet as coming forth from one of the horns of the goat.

---

[7] See 1 Maccabees 8; Flavius Josephus, "Antiquities of the Jews," book 12, chap. 10, sec. 6, *The Works of Flavius Josephus*, p. 374; Humphrey Prideaux, *The Old and New Testament Connected in the History of the Jews*, Vol. II, p. 166.

The little horn waxed great toward the south. This was true of Rome. Egypt was made a province of the Roman Empire in 30 B. C., and continued such for some centuries.

The little horn waxed great toward the east. This also was true of Rome. She conquered Syria in 65 B. C., and made it a province.

The little horn waxed great toward the pleasant land. So did Rome. Judea is called "the pleasant land" in many scriptures. The Romans made it a province of their empire in 63 B. C., and eventually destroyed the city and the temple, and scattered the Jews throughout the earth.

The little horn "waxed great, even to [against, margin] the host of heaven; and it cast down some of the host and of the stars to the ground." Rome did this also. In this expression two figures are introduced, "the host" and "the stars." When used in a symbolic sense concerning events taking place on earth, these figures refer almost always to the people of God and their leaders. In verse 13 of this chapter we read that both the sanctuary and the host will be trodden under foot. Here undoubtedly reference is made to God's people and the place of their worship. The stars would naturally represent the leaders of the work of God. This thought is further indicated in one of the applications of Revelation 12: 4 where we read that the great red dragon, a symbol of Rome, cast down a third part of the stars to the ground.

The little horn "magnified himself even to the Prince of the host." Rome alone did this. In the interpretation (verse 25) the little horn is said to "stand up against the Prince of princes." This is clearly an allusion to the crucifixion of our Lord under the jurisdiction of the Romans.

Rome in Two Aspects.—By the little horn "the daily sacrifice was taken away." This little horn symbolizes Rome in its entire history, including its two phases, pagan and papal. These two phases are elsewhere spoken of as the "daily" (*sacrifice* is a supplied word) and the "transgression of desolation;" the daily (desolation) evidently signifying the pagan

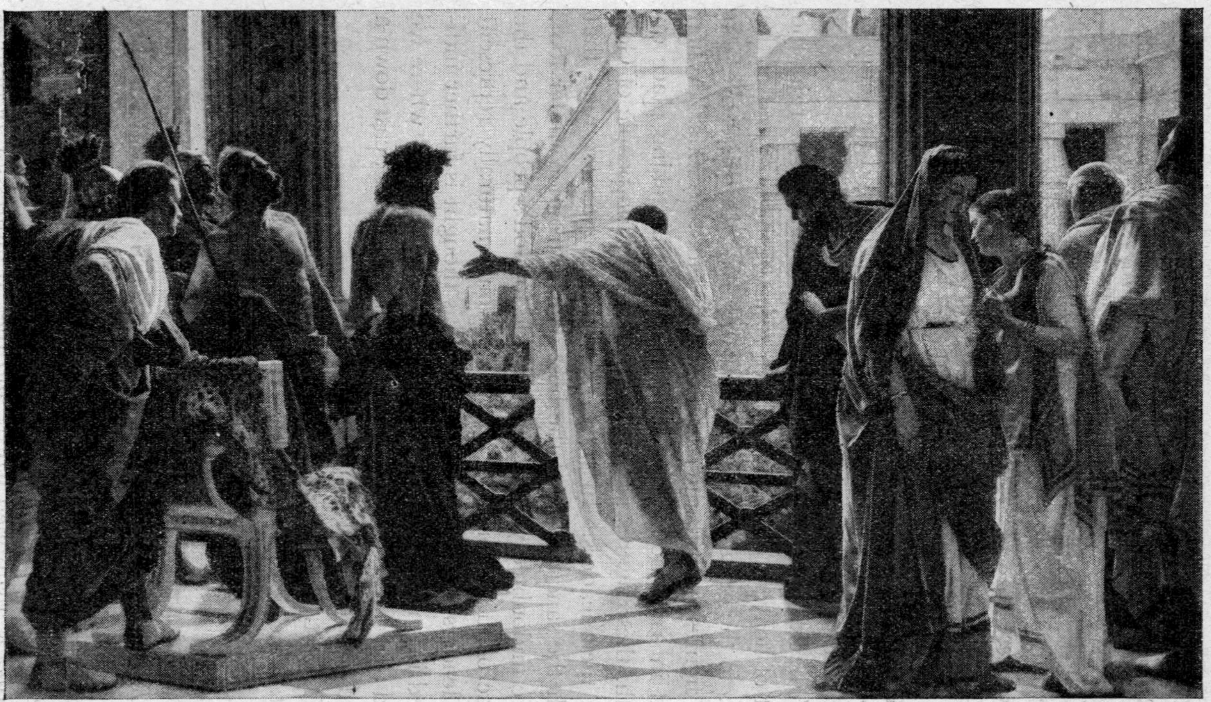

ANTONIO CISERI, ARTIST

"BEHOLD THE MAN!"

By the shameful trial and crucifixion of Christ, the "little horn" power stood "up against the Prince of princes."

form, and the transgression of desolation, the papal. (See comments on verse 13.) In the actions ascribed to this power, sometimes one form is spoken of, sometimes the other. "By him [the papal form] the daily [the pagan form] was taken away." Pagan Rome was remodeled into papal Rome. "The place of his sanctuary," or worship, the city of Rome, was cast down. The seat of government was removed by Constantine to Constantinople, A. D. 330. This same transaction is brought to view in Revelation 13: 2, where it is said that the dragon, pagan Rome, gave to the beast, papal Rome, his seat, the city of Rome.

A "host was given him [the little horn] against the daily." The barbarians that subverted the Roman Empire in the changes, attritions, and transformations of those times, became converts to the Catholic faith, and the instruments of the dethronement of their former religion. Though conquering Rome politically, they were themselves vanquished religiously by the theology of Rome, and became the perpetuators of the same empire in another phase. This was brought about by reason of "transgression;" that is, by the working of the mystery of iniquity. The papacy may be called a system of iniquity because it has done its evil work under the pretense of the pure and undefiled religion. Of this false religious system, Paul wrote in the first century to the Thessalonians, "The mystery of iniquity doth already work." 2 Thessalonians 2: 7.

The little horn "cast down the truth to the ground, and practiced and prospered." This describes in few words the work and career of the papacy. The truth is by it hideously caricatured, loaded with traditions, turned into mummery and superstition, cast down and obscured.

Of this ecclesiastical power it is declared that it has "practiced"—practiced its deceptions on the people, practiced its schemes of cunning to carry out its own ends and aggrandize its own power.

Likewise it has "prospered." It has made war upon the saints, and prevailed against them. It has well-nigh run its allotted career, and is soon to be broken without hand, to be given to the burning flame, and to perish in the consuming glories of the second appearing of our Lord.

Rome meets all the specifications of the prophecy. No other power does meet them. Hence Rome, and no other, is the power in question. The inspired descriptions given in the word of God of the character of this system are fully met, and the prophecies concerning it have been most strikingly and accurately fulfilled in history.

VERSE 13 Then I heard one saint speaking, and another saint said unto that certain saint which spake, How long shall be the vision concerning the daily sacrifice, and the transgression of desolation, to give both the sanctuary and the host to be trodden under foot? 14 And he said unto me, Unto two thousand and three hundred days; then shall the sanctuary be cleansed.

The Time in the Prophecy.—These two verses of Daniel 8 close the vision proper. They introduce the one remaining point which of all others would naturally be of most absorbing interest to the prophet and to the church, namely, the length of time the desolating powers previously brought to view were to continue. *How long* shall they continue their course of oppression against God's people? If time had been given, Daniel might have asked this question himself, but God ever anticipates our desires, and sometimes answers them before we ask.

Two celestial beings converse upon this subject. This is an important matter which the church should understand well. Daniel heard one saint speaking. What this saint said, we are not informed. But another saint asked an important question: "How long shall be the vision?" Both the question and the answer are placed upon record, which is prima facie evidence that this is a matter the church should understand. This view is further confirmed by the fact that the answer was addressed to Daniel, as the one whom it chiefly concerned, and for whose information it was given.

The 2300 Days.—The angel declared, "Unto two thousand and three hundred days; then shall the sanctuary be cleansed."

The question may be raised, Why does the Vatican edition of the Septuagint (LXX) render this number "twenty-four hundred days"? On this point S. P. Tregelles writes:

"Some writers on prophecy have, in their explanations or interpretations of this vision, adopted the reading 'two thousand and *four* hundred days;' and in vindication of it, they have referred to the common printed copies of the LXX version. In this book, however, the translation of Theodotion has been long substituted for the real LXX: and further, although 'two thousand *four* hundred' is found in the common printed Greek copies, that is merely an erratum made in printing the Vatican edition of 1586, which has been habitually perpetuated. I looked (in 1845) at the passage in *the* Vatican MS., which the Roman editions professedly followed, and it reads exactly the same as the Hebrew text ["twenty-three hundred days"]; so also does the *real* LXX of Daniel. (So too Cardinal Mai's edition from the Vatican MS. which appeared in 1857)."[8]

Further substantiating the veracity of the twenty-three-hundred-day period, we quote the following:

"The edition of the Greek Bible which is commonly used, is printed, as you will find it stated in Prideaux and Horne, not after that of the 70, but after that of Theodotion, made about the end of the second century. There are three principal standard editions of the Septuagint Bible, all containing the version of Daniel by Theodotion; viz., the Complutensian, published in 1514; the Aldine, 1518; and the Vatican, 1587, from which the last English editions of the 70 have been chiefly taken; to these three we may add a fourth, being that of the Alexandrian text, published between 1707 and 1720. Besides these, there is one called the Chisian, 1772, which contains the Greek text both of Theodotion and of the 70. Of all these six copies the Vatican alone reads 2400, all the rest agreeing with the Hebrew and our English Bibles. Moreover, the manuscript itself, in the Vatican, from which the edition

[8] S. P. Tregelles, *Remarks on the Prophetic Visions in the Book of Daniel*, p. 89, footnote.

was printed, has 2300, and not 2400, and therefore it is indisputable that the number 2400 is nothing but a misprint."[9]

These quotations show clearly that no confidence whatever can be placed in this rendering of the Vatican edition of the Septuagint.

What Is the Daily?—We have proof in verse 13 that "sacrifice" is the wrong word to be supplied in connection with the word "daily." If the taking away of the daily sacrifice of the Jewish service is here meant, as some suppose (which sacrifice was at a certain point of time taken away), there would be no propriety in the question, *How long* shall be the vision concerning it? This question evidently implies that those agents or events to which the vision relates occupy a series of years. Continuance of time is the central idea. The whole time of the vision is filled by what is here called the "daily" and the "transgression of desolation." Hence the daily cannot be the daily sacrifice of the Jews, for when the time came for it to be taken away, that action occupied but an instant of time, when the veil of the temple was rent in twain at the crucifixion of Christ. It must denote something which extends over a period of years.

The word here rendered "daily" occurs in the Old Testament one hundred and two times, according to the Hebrew concordance. In the great majority of instances it is rendered "continual" or "continually." The idea of sacrifice is not attached to the word at all. Nor is there any word in the text which signifies sacrifice. That is a supplied word, the translators putting in that word which their understanding of the text seemed to demand. They evidently entertained an erroneous view, the sacrifices of the Jews not being referred to at all. But it appears to be more in accordance with both the construction and the context to suppose that the word "daily" refers to a desolating power, like the "transgression of desolation," with which it is connected. Then we have two

[9] *Dialogues on Prophecy*, Vol. I, pp. 326, 327.

desolating powers, which for a long period oppress, or desolate, the church. Literally, the text may be rendered, "How long shall be the vision [concerning] the continuance and the transgression of desolation?"—the word "desolation" being related to both "continuance" and "transgression," as though it were expressed in full thus: "The continuance of desolation and the transgression of desolation."

Two Desolating Powers.—By the "continuance of desolation," or the perpetual desolation, we understand that paganism, through all its history, is meant. When we consider the long ages through which paganism had been the chief agency of Satan's opposition to the work of God in the earth, the propriety of the term "continuance" or "perpetual," as applied to it, becomes apparent. We likewise understand that "the transgression of desolation" means the papacy. The phrase describing this latter power is stronger than that used to describe paganism. It is the transgression (or rebellion, as the word also means) of desolation; as if under this period of the history of the church the desolating power had rebelled against all restraint previously imposed upon it.

From a religious point of view, the world has presented these two strong phases of opposition against the Lord's work in the earth. Hence, although three earthly governments are introduced in the prophecy as oppressors of the church, they are here ranged under two heads: "the daily" and the "transgression of desolation." Medo-Persia was pagan; Grecia was pagan; Rome in its first phase was pagan. These were all embraced in the "daily." Then comes the papal form, the "transgression of desolation," a marvel of craft and cunning, an incarnation of cruelty. No wonder the cry has gone up from suffering martyrs from age to age, "How long, O Lord, how long?" No wonder the Lord, in order that hope might not wholly die out of the hearts of His downtrodden, waiting people, has shown them the future events of the world's history. All these persecuting powers shall meet an utter and everlasting destruction. For the redeemed there are unfading glories beyond the suffering and sorrow of this present life.

The Lord's eye is upon His people. The furnace will be heated no hotter than is necessary to consume the dross. It is through much tribulation that we are to enter the kingdom. The word "tribulation" is from *tribulum*, a threshing sledge. Blow after blow must be laid upon us, until all the wheat is beaten free from the chaff, and we are made fit for the heavenly garner. But not a kernel of wheat will be lost.

Says the Lord to His people, "Ye are the light of the world," "the salt of the earth." In His eyes there is nothing else on the earth of consequence or importance. Hence the peculiar question here asked, "How long . . . the vision concerning the daily and the transgression of desolation?" Concerning what?—the glory of earthly kingdoms? the skill of renowned warriors? the fame of mighty conquerors? the greatness of human empire?—No, but concerning the sanctuary and the host, the people and the worship of the Most High. How long shall they be trodden underfoot? Here is where all heaven's interest and sympathy are enlisted.

He who touches the people of God, touches not mere mortals, weak and helpless, but Omnipotence. He opens an account which must be settled in the judgment of heaven. Soon all these accounts will be adjusted and the iron heel of oppression will be crushed. A people will be brought out of the furnace of affliction prepared to shine as the stars forever and ever. Every child of God is an object of interest to heavenly beings, one whom God loves and for whom He is preparing a crown with immortality hereafter. Reader, are you one of the number?

There is no information in this chapter concerning the 2300 days, introduced for the first time in verse 14. It is necessary, therefore, to pass this period of time for the present. Let the reader be assured, however, that we are not left in any uncertainty concerning those days. The declaration respecting them is part of a revelation which is given for the instruction of the people of God, and is to be understood. The 2300 days are mentioned in the midst of a prophecy which the angel Gabriel was commanded to make Daniel understand. Gabriel carried out this instruction, as will be found in the study of the next chapter.

What Is the Sanctuary?—Connected with the 2300 days is another subject of equal importance which now presents itself for consideration, namely, the sanctuary. With this is connected the subject of its cleansing. An examination of this matter will reveal the importance of having an understanding of the beginning and the end of the 2300 days, that we may know when the great event called "the cleansing of the sanctuary" is to take place. All the inhabitants of the earth, as will appear in due time, have a personal interest in that solemn work.

Several views have been held as to what the sanctuary is, such as the earth, the land of Canaan, the church, and the sanctuary in heaven, the "true tabernacle, which the Lord pitched, and not man," which is "in the heavens," and of which the Jewish tabernacle was a type, pattern, or figure. (Hebrews 8: 1, 2; 9: 23, 24.) Which of these conflicting views is correct, must be decided by the Scriptures. Fortunately the testimony is neither meager nor ambiguous.

It Cannot Be the Earth.—The word "sanctuary" occurs in the Old and New Testaments one hundred forty-four times. From the definitions of lexicographers, and its use in the Bible, we learn that it is used to signify a holy or sacred place, a dwelling place for the Most High. If the earth is the sanctuary, it must answer to this definition. But what single characteristic pertaining to this earth will satisfy the meaning of the term? The earth is neither a holy nor a sacred place, nor is it a dwelling place for the Most High. It has no mark of distinction from other worlds, except as being a revolted planet, marred by sin, scarred and withered by the curse of transgression. Moreover, it is nowhere in all the Scriptures called the sanctuary. Only one text can be produced in favor of this view, and that by an unreasonable application: "The glory of

Lebanon shall come unto thee, the fir tree, the pine tree, and the box together, to beautify the place of My sanctuary; and I will make the place of My feet glorious." Isaiah 60: 13. This language undoubtedly refers to the new earth; but even that is not called the sanctuary, but only the "place" of the sanctuary, even as it is called "the place" of the Lord's feet. This is an expression which probably denotes the continual presence of God with His people, as it was revealed to John when it was said, "Behold, the tabernacle of God is with men, and He will dwell with them, and they shall be His people, and God Himself shall be with them, and be their God." Revelation 21: 3. All that can be said of the earth, therefore, is that when renewed it will be the place where the sanctuary of God will be located. It cannot present any claim to being the sanctuary at the present time, or the sanctuary of Daniel's prophecy.

It Cannot Be the Land of Canaan.—So far as we may be governed by the definition of the word "Canaan," it can present no better claim than the earth to that distinction. If we inquire where in the Bible it is called the sanctuary, a few texts are brought forward which are supposed by some to furnish the requisite testimony. The first of these is Exodus 15: 17. Moses, in his song of triumph and praise to God after the passage of the Red Sea, exclaimed: "Thou shalt bring them in, and plant them in the mountain of Thine inheritance, in the place, O Lord, which Thou hast made for Thee to dwell in, in the sanctuary, O Lord, which Thy hands have established." Moses here speaks in anticipation. His language is a prediction of what God would do for His people. Let us see how it was accomplished.

We turn to David, who records as a matter of history what Moses uttered as a matter of prophecy. (Psalm 78: 53, 54.) The subject of the psalmist is the deliverance of Israel from Egyptian servitude, and their establishment in the Promised Land. He says: "He [God] led them on safely, so that they feared not: but the sea overwhelmed their enemies. And He brought them to the border of His sanctuary, even to this mountain, which His right hand had purchased." The "mountain" here mentioned by David is the same as the "mountain of Thine inheritance" spoken of by Moses, in which the people were to be planted. This mountain David calls, not the sanctuary, but only the *border* of the sanctuary. What, then, was the sanctuary? Verse 69 of the same psalm informs us: "He *built* His sanctuary like high palaces, like the earth which He hath established forever." The same distinction between the sanctuary and the land is pointed out in the prayer of the good king Jehoshaphat: "Art not Thou our God, who didst drive out the inhabitants of this land before Thy people Israel, and gavest it to the seed of Abraham Thy friend forever? And they dwelt therein, and have built Thee a sanctuary therein for Thy name." 2 Chronicles 20: 7, 8.

Taken alone, Exodus 15: 17 is used by some as an inference that the mountain was the sanctuary; but when we take in connection with it the language of David, which is a record of the fulfillment of Moses' prediction, and an inspired commentary upon his language, such an idea cannot be entertained. David plainly says that the mountain was simply the "border" of the sanctuary, and that in that border, or land, the sanctuary was "built" like high palaces, reference being made to the beautiful temple of the Jews, the center and symbol of all their worship. But whoever will read carefully Exodus 15: 17 will see that not even an inference is necessary that Moses by the word "sanctuary" means the mountain of inheritance, much less the whole land of Palestine. In the freedom of poetic license, he employs elliptical expressions, and passes rapidly from one idea or object to another. First, the inheritance engages his attention, and he speaks of it; then the fact that the Lord was to dwell there, then the place He was to provide for His dwelling there, namely, the sanctuary which He would cause to be built. David thus associates Mount Zion and Judah together in Psalm 78: 68, because Zion was in Judah.

The three texts, Exodus 15: 17; Psalm 78: 54, 69, are the ones chiefly relied on to prove that the land of Canaan is the

THE TWO SANCTUARIES

The services of the earthly tabernacle typified those of the heavenly sanctuary.

sanctuary. But, singularly enough, the two latter, in plain language, clear away the ambiguity of the first, and thereby disprove the claim that is based on it.

Respecting the earth or the land of Canaan as being the sanctuary, we offer one thought more. If either constitutes the sanctuary, it should not only be somewhere described as such, but the same idea should be carried through to the end, and the purification of the earth or of Palestine should be called the cleansing of the sanctuary. The earth is indeed defiled, and it is to be purified by fire; but fire, as we shall see, is not the agent which is used in the cleansing of the sanctuary. This purification of the earth, or any part of it, is nowhere in the Bible called the cleansing of the sanctuary.

It Cannot Be the Church.—The solitary text adduced to support the idea that the church is the sanctuary is Psalm 114: 1, 2: "When Israel went out of Egypt, the house of Jacob from a people of strange language; Judah was His sanctuary, and Israel His dominion." If we take this text in its most literal sense, it would prove that the sanctuary was confined to one of the twelve tribes. This would mean that a part of the church only, not the whole, constitutes the sanctuary. Why Judah is called the sanctuary in the text quoted, need not be a matter of perplexity when we remember that God chose Jerusalem, which was in Judah, as the place of His sanctuary. "But chose," says David, "the tribe of Judah, the Mount Zion which He loved. And He built His sanctuary like high palaces, like the earth which He hath established forever." Psalm 78: 68, 69. This clearly shows the connection which existed between Judah and the sanctuary. That tribe itself was not the sanctuary, but it is once spoken of as such when Israel came forth from Egypt, because God purposed that in the midst of the territory of that tribe His sanctuary should be located.

If it could be shown that the church is anywhere called the sanctuary, it would be of no consequence to our present purpose, which is to determine what constitutes the sanctuary of Daniel 8: 13, 14; for the church is there spoken of as something distinct: "To give *both* the sanctuary and the host to be trodden underfoot." That by the term "host" the people of God is here meant, none will dispute; the sanctuary is therefore something different from the church.

The Sanctuary Is the Temple in Heaven.—There now remains but one claim to be examined, namely, that the sanctuary mentioned in the text is identical with the one in Hebrews 8: 1, 2, which is called the "true tabernacle, which the Lord pitched, and not man," to which is expressly given the name of "the sanctuary," and which is located in "the heavens." Of this sanctuary there existed in ancient times a pattern, type, or figure, first in the tabernacle built by Moses, and afterward in the temple at Jerusalem.

Let us put ourselves in the place of Daniel, and view the subject from his standpoint. What would he understand by the term "sanctuary"? At the mention of that word, his mind would inevitably turn to the sanctuary of his people; and certainly he well knew where that was. His mind did turn to Jerusalem, the city of his fathers, which was then in ruins, and to their "beautiful house," which, as Isaiah laments, was burned with fire. (Isaiah 64: 11.) Accordingly, with his face turned toward the place of their once-venerated temple, as was his custom, Daniel prayed God to cause His face to shine upon His sanctuary, which was at that time desolate. By the word "sanctuary" he evidently understood the temple at Jerusalem.

On this point, the Scripture bears testimony which is most explicit: "Then verily the first covenant had also ordinances of divine service, and a worldly sanctuary." Hebrews 9: 1. What was the sanctuary of the first covenant? The answer follows: "For there was a tabernacle made; the first [or first apartment], wherein was the candlestick, and the table, and the shewbread; which is called the sanctuary [holy place," A. R. V.]. And after the second veil, the tabernacle which is called the Holiest of all; which had the golden censer, and the ark of the covenant overlaid round about with gold, wherein was the golden pot that had manna, and Aaron's rod that budded, and the tables of the covenant; and over it the cherubims of glory shadowing the mercyseat; of which we cannot now speak particularly." Hebrews 9: 2-5.

There is no mistaking what is described here. It is the tabernacle erected by Moses according to the direction of the Lord (which was afterward merged into the temple at Jerusalem), with a holy and a most holy place, and various articles of service. A full description of this building, as well as the sacred articles of furniture and their uses, will be found in Exodus 25 and onward. If the reader is not familiar with this subject, he is urged to turn and read the description of this building. Plainly, this was the sanctuary of the first covenant, and we wish the reader carefully to mark the logical value of this declaration. By telling us what constituted the sanctuary, the book of Hebrews sets us on the right track of inquiry. It gives us a basis on which to work. We have before us a distinct and plainly defined object, minutely described by Moses, and declared in Hebrews to be the sanctuary during the time of the first covenant, which reached to the days of Christ.

But the language in Hebrews has greater significance even than this. It annihilates the claims put forth that the earth, the land of Canaan, or the church, is the sanctuary. The arguments which would prove any of these to be the sanctuary at any time, would prove it to be such under ancient Israel. If Canaan was at any time the sanctuary, it was such when Israel was planted in it. If the church was ever the sanctuary, it was such when Israel was led forth from Egypt. If the earth was ever the sanctuary, it was such during the same period. But was any of these the sanctuary during that time? The answer must be negative, for the writers of the books of Exodus and Hebrews tell us in detail that not the earth, not Canaan, not the church, but the tabernacle built by Moses, replaced by the temple later, constituted the sanctuary of Old Testament times.

The Earthly Sanctuary.—This building answers in every respect to the definition of the term, and to the use for which the sanctuary was designed. It was the earthly dwelling place of God. "Let them make Me a sanctuary," said He to Moses, "that I may dwell among them." Exodus 25: 8. In this tabernacle, which they erected according to His instructions, He manifested His presence. It was a holy, or sacred place—"the holy sanctuary." Leviticus 16: 33. In the word of God it is repeatedly called the sanctuary. Of the more than one hundred thirty instances in which the word is used in the Old Testament, it refers in almost every case to this building.

The tabernacle was at first constructed in such a manner as to be adapted to the conditions under which the children of Israel lived at that time. They were entering upon their forty years' wandering in the wilderness when this building was set up in their midst as the habitation of God and the center of their religious worship. Journeying was a necessity, and the tabernacle had to be moved from place to place. This was made possible because the sides were composed of upright boards, and the covering consisted of curtains of linen and dyed skins. Therefore, it could be readily taken down, conveniently transported, and easily erected at each successive stage of their journey. After Israel entered the Promised Land, this temporary structure gave place in time to the magnificent temple of Solomon. In this more permanent form the sanctuary existed, except during the time it lay in ruins in Daniel's day, until its final destruction by the Romans, A. D. 70.

This is the only sanctuary connected with the earth concerning which the Bible gives us any instruction or history any record. But is there nowhere any other? This one was the sanctuary of the first covenant, and with that covenant it came to an end. Is there no sanctuary which pertains to the second, or new, covenant? There must be, otherwise the analogy would be lacking between these covenants. In such a case the first covenant would have a system of worship, which, though minutely described, would be unintelligible, and the second covenant would have a system of worship which would be indefinite and obscure. The writer of Hebrews virtually asserts that the new covenant, in force since the death of Christ, the testator, has a sanctuary; for when, in contrasting the two covenants, as he does in Hebrews 9: 1, he says that the first covenant "had *also* ordinances of divine service, and a worldly sanctuary." This is the same as saying that the new covenant has likewise its services and its sanctuary. Furthermore, verse 8 of this chapter speaks of the worldly sanctuary as the *first* tabernacle. If that was the first, there must be a second; and as the first tabernacle existed as long as the first covenant was in force, when that covenant came to an end, the second tabernacle must have taken the place of the first, and must be the sanctuary of the new covenant. There can be no evading this conclusion.

The Heavenly Sanctuary.—Where, then, shall we look for the sanctuary of the new covenant? The use of the word "also" in Hebrews 9: 1 intimates that this sanctuary had been spoken of before. We turn back to the beginning of the previous chapter, and find a summing up of the foregoing arguments as follows: "Now of the things which we have spoken this is the sum: We have such an high priest, who is set on the right hand of the throne of the Majesty in the heavens; a minister of the sanctuary, and of the true tabernacle, which the Lord pitched, and not man." Can there be any doubt that we have in this text the sanctuary of the new covenant? A plain allusion is here made to the sanctuary of the first covenant. That was pitched by man, erected by Moses; but this was pitched by the Lord, not by man. That was the place where the earthly priests performed their ministry; but this is the place where Christ, the High Priest of the new covenant, performs His ministry. That was on earth; this is in heaven. That was therefore very properly called a "worldly sanctuary;" this is a "heavenly" one.

This view is further sustained by the fact that the sanctuary built by Moses was not an original structure, but was built after a pattern. The great original existed somewhere else, and what Moses constructed was but a type, or model.

Note the directions the Lord gave him on this point: "According to all that I show thee, after the pattern of the tabernacle, and the pattern of all the instruments thereof, even so shall ye make it." Exodus 25: 9. "Look that thou make them after their pattern which was showed thee in the mount." Verse 40. (For further clarification of this point, see Exodus 26: 30; 27: 8; Acts 7: 44.)

Now of what was the earthly sanctuary a type, or figure? —Of the sanctuary of the new covenant, the "true tabernacle, which the Lord pitched and not man." The relation which the first covenant sustains to the second is that of type to antitype. Its sacrifices were types of the greater sacrifice of the new covenant. Its priests were types of our Lord in His more perfect priesthood. Their ministry was performed unto the example and shadow of the ministry of our High Priest above. The sanctuary where they ministered was a type, or figure, of the true sanctuary in heaven, where our Lord performs His ministry.

All these facts are plainly stated in Hebrews. "If He [Christ] were on earth, He should not be a priest, seeing that there are priests that offer gifts according to the law: who serve unto the example and shadow of heavenly things, as Moses was admonished of God when he was about to make the tabernacle: for, See, saith He, that thou make all things according to the pattern showed to thee in the mount." Hebrews 8: 4, 5. This testimony shows that the ministry of the earthly priests was a shadow of Christ's priesthood. The evidence is the direction which God gave to Moses to make the tabernacle according to the pattern showed him in the mount. This clearly identifies the pattern showed to Moses with the sanctuary, or true tabernacle, in heaven, where our Lord ministers, as mentioned in Hebrews 8: 2.

The Scripture further says: "The Holy Ghost this signifying, that the way into the holiest of all was not yet made manifest, while as the first tabernacle was yet standing;

which was a *figure* for the time then present."* Hebrews 9: 8, 9. While the first tabernacle stood, and the first covenant was in force, the ministration of the more perfect tabernacle was not, of course, carried forward. But when Christ came, a high priest of good things to come, when the first tabernacle had served its purpose and the first covenant had ceased, then Christ, raised to the throne of the Majesty in the heavens as a minister of the true sanctuary, entered by His own blood (verse 12) "into the holy place," that is, the heavenly sanctuary.

Therefore, the first tabernacle was a figure for the time then present. If any further testimony is needed, the writer of Hebrews speaks in verse 23 of the earthly tabernacle, with its apartments and instruments, as "patterns" of things in the heavens; and in verse 24, he calls the holy places made with hands, that is, the earthly tabernacles and temples of ancient Israel, "figures" of the true, that is, of the tabernacle in heaven.

This view is still further corroborated by the testimony of John. Among the things which he was permitted to behold in heaven were seven lamps of fire burning before the throne (Revelation 4: 5), an altar of incense, and a golden censer (Revelation 8: 3), and the ark of God's testament (Revelation 11: 19). All of this was seen in connection with

* The Greek original of what is here translated "holiest of all" is the same as that rendered "sanctuary" in Hebrews 8: 2; 9: 1. It should therefore be translated "sanctuary" in Hebrews 9: 8 also. The same original phrase is used, too, in verses 12, 24, 25, and is more fittingly translated "sanctuary" than "holy place," so as to convey its true meaning more clearly. In Hebrews 10: 19 the original of "holiest" is the same as that in all the verses cited above, and should therefore be also translated "sanctuary." This gives a simple, accurate, uniform, and easily understood rendering of the same original phrase in all these passages. Moreover, the reference of the phrase is obviously and uniformly to the heavenly sanctuary in all these citations, with the exception of Hebrews 9: 1, 25, which refer to the earthly. The original phrases cited above have of course the usual variations for number and case common to all languages. The nominative form is τά ἅγια, *ta hagia*, plural in all instances here cited except in 9: 1, where it is τὸ ἅγιον, *to hagion*, singular. In Hebrews 9: 2 the word "sanctuary" plainly applies to the first apartment only, and would be better translated "holy place" as suggested in the margin of the Authorized Version, while the phrase "holiest of all" in verse 3, naming the second apartment, is a true translation of a different original regularly used to designate that apartment in distinction from the first and from the entire sanctuary. "Holiest of all" or "holiest" is not therefore a true translation in either Hebrews 9: 8 or 10: 19.—*Editors.*

a "temple" in heaven. (Revelation 11: 19; 15: 8.) These objects every Bible reader must at once recognize as the furniture of the sanctuary. They owed their existence to the sanctuary, and were confined to it, to be employed in the ministration connected therewith. Even as they would not have existed without the sanctuary, so wherever we find them, we may know that there is the sanctuary. Hence the fact that John saw these things in heaven after the ascension of Christ, is proof that there is a sanctuary in heaven, and that he was permitted to behold it.

However reluctant a person may have been to acknowledge that there is a sanctuary in heaven, the testimony that has been presented is certainly sufficient to prove this fact. The Bible says that the tabernacle of Moses was the sanctuary of the first covenant. Moses says that God showed him in the mount a pattern, according to which he was to make this tabernacle. The book of Hebrews testifies again that Moses did make it according to the pattern, and that the pattern was the true tabernacle in heaven, which the Lord pitched, and not man; and that of this heavenly sanctuary the tabernacle erected with hands was a true figure, or representation. Finally, to corroborate the statement of the Scriptures that this sanctuary is in heaven, John bears testimony as an eyewitness that he beheld it there. What further testimony could be required?

As far as the question of what constitutes the sanctuary is concerned, we now have the sanctuary before us in one harmonious whole. The sanctuary of the Bible—mark it well—consists, first, of the typical tabernacle established by the Hebrews in the exodus from Egypt, which was the sanctuary of the first covenant. Secondly, it consists of the true tabernacle in heaven, of which the former was a type, or figure, which is the sanctuary of the new covenant. These are inseparably related as type and antitype. From the antitype we go back to the type, and from the type we are carried forward naturally and inevitably to the antitype.

Thus we see how a sanctuary service has been provided from the Exodus to the end of probation.

We have said that Daniel would at once understand by the word "sanctuary" the sanctuary of his people at Jerusalem; so would anyone at the time of its existence. But does the declaration of Daniel 8: 14 have reference to that sanctuary? That depends upon the time to which it applies. All the declarations respecting the sanctuary which apply during the time of ancient Israel, have respect of course to the sanctuary of that time. All those declarations which apply under the Christian Era must have reference to the sanctuary of that era. If the 2300 days, at the termination of which the sanctuary is to be cleansed, ended before Christ, the sanctuary to be cleansed was the sanctuary of that time. If they reach over into the Christian Era, the sanctuary to which reference is made is the sanctuary of this era—the new-covenant sanctuary in heaven. This is a point which can be determined only by a further argument on the 2300 days. This will be found in remarks on Daniel 9: 24, where the subject of time is resumed and explained.

The Cleansing of the Sanctuary.—What we have thus far said respecting the sanctuary has been only incidental to the main question in the prophecy. That question has respect to its cleansing. "Unto two thousand and three hundred days; then shall the sanctuary be cleansed." But it was necessary first to determine what constituted the sanctuary, before we could understandingly examine the question of its cleansing. For this we are now prepared.

After learning what constitutes the sanctuary, the question of its cleansing and how it is accomplished, is soon decided. It has been noticed that whatever constitutes the sanctuary of the Bible must have some service connected with it which is called its cleansing. There is such a service connected with the institution which we have shown to be the sanctuary, and which, in reference to both the earthly building and the heavenly temple, is called its cleansing.

Does the reader object to the idea of there being anything in heaven which needs to be cleansed? The book of Hebrews plainly affirms the cleansing of both the earthly and the heavenly sanctuary: "Almost all things are by the law purged with blood; and without shedding of blood is no remission. It was therefore necessary that the patterns of things in the heavens should be purified [Greek, καθαρίζεσθαι, *katharizesthai*, cleansed] with these; but the *heavenly things themselves* [*cleansed*] with better sacrifices than these." Hebrews 9: 22, 23. In the light of foregoing arguments, this may be paraphrased thus: "It was therefore necessary that the tabernacle erected by Moses, with its sacred vessels, which were patterns of the true sanctuary in heaven, should be cleansed with the blood of calves and goats; but the heavenly things themselves, the sanctuary of the Christian Era, the true tabernacle, which the Lord pitched, and not man, must be cleansed with better sacrifices, even with the blood of Christ."

We now inquire, What is the nature of this cleansing, and how is it to be done? According to the language just quoted, it is accomplished by means of blood. The cleansing is not, therefore, a cleansing from physical uncleanness or impurity, for blood is not the agent used in such a work. This consideration should satisfy the objector's mind in regard to the cleansing of the heavenly things. The fact that heavenly things are to be cleansed, does not prove that there is any physical impurity in heaven, for that is not the kind of cleansing referred to in the Scriptures. The reason assigned why this cleansing is performed with blood, is that without the shedding of blood there is no *remission*, no forgiveness of sin.

The Cleansing Is From Sin.—Remission of sin, then, and the putting away of sin, is the work to be done. The cleansing, therefore, is not physical cleansing, but a cleansing from sin. But how did sin come to be connected with the sanctuary, either the earthly or the heavenly, that it should need to be cleansed? This question is answered by the ministration connected with the type, to which we now turn.

The closing chapters of Exodus give us an account of the construction of the earthly sanctuary, and the arrangement of the service connected therewith. Leviticus opens with an account of the ministration which was there to be performed. All that it is our purpose to notice here is one particular branch of the service. The person who had committed sin brought his offering, a live animal, to the door of the tabernacle. Upon the head of this victim he placed his hand for a moment, and, as we may reasonably infer, confessed over it his sin. By this expressive act he signified that he had sinned, and was worthy of death, but that in his stead he consecrated his victim, and transferred his guilt to it. With his own hand (and what must have been his emotions!) he then took the life of the animal. The law demanded the life of the transgressor for his disobedience. The life is in the blood. (Leviticus 17: 11, 14.) Hence without the shedding of blood, there is no remission; but with the shedding of blood remission is possible, for the demand of life by the law is thus satisfied. The blood of the victim, representative of a forfeited life, and the vehicle of its guilt, was then taken by the priest and ministered before the Lord.

By his confession, by the slaying of the victim, and by the ministry of the priest, the sin of the individual was transferred from himself to the sanctuary. Victim after victim was thus offered by the people. Day by day the work went forward, and thus the sanctuary became the receptacle of the sins of the congregation. But this was not the final disposition of these sins. The accumulated guilt was removed by a special service for the cleansing of the sanctuary. This service, in the type, occupied one day in the year, the tenth day of the seventh month, which was called the Day of Atonement. On this day, while all Israel refrained from work and afflicted their souls, the priest brought two goats, and presented them before the Lord at the door of the tabernacle. On these goats he cast lots, one lot for the Lord, and the other lot for the scapegoat. The one upon which the Lord's lot fell was then slain, and his blood

 T. K. MARTIN, ARTIST

THE DAY OF ATONEMENT

In the earthly sanctuary the high priest atoned for his people once a year. They anxiously awaited his reappearance.

carried by the priest into the most holy place of the sanctuary, and sprinkled upon the mercy seat. This was the only day on which he was permitted to enter that apartment. Coming forth, he was then to "lay both his hands upon the head of the live goat, and confess over him all the iniquities of the children of Israel, and all their transgressions in all their sins, putting them upon the head of the goat." Leviticus 16: 21. He was then to send the goat away by the hand of a fit man into a land not inhabited, a land of separation, or forgetfulness, the goat never again to appear in the camp of Israel, and the sins of the people to be remembered against them no more.

This service was for the purpose of cleansing the people from their sins, and also for cleansing the sanctuary, its furniture, and its sacred vessels from the sins of the people. (Leviticus 16: 16, 30, 33.) By this process, sin was entirely removed. Of course this was only in figure, for all that work was typical.

The reader to whom these views are new will perhaps be ready here to inquire with some astonishment, What could this strange work possibly be designed to typify, and what was it designed to prefigure in our day? We answer, A similar work in the ministration of Christ, as the Scriptures clearly teach. After the statement in Hebrews 8: 2 that Christ is the minister of the true tabernacle, the sanctuary in heaven, it is declared in verse 5 that the priests on earth served "unto the example and shadow of heavenly things." In other words, the work of the earthly priests was a shadow, a type of the ministration of Christ above.

Ministration in Figure and in Fact.—These typical priests ministered in both apartments of the earthly tabernacle, and Christ ministers in both apartments of the heavenly temple. That temple in heaven has two apartments, or it was not correctly represented by the earthly sanctuary. Our Lord officiates in both apartments, or the service of the priest on earth was not a correct shadow of His work. It is stated plainly in Hebrews 9: 21-24 that both the tabernacle and all the vessels in the ministry were "patterns of things in the heavens."

Therefore the service performed by Christ in the heavenly temple corresponds to that performed by the priests in both apartments of the earthly building. But the work in the second apartment, or most holy place, was a special work to close the yearly round of service and cleanse the sanctuary. Hence Christ's ministration in the second apartment of the heavenly sanctuary must be a work of like nature, and constitutes the close of His work as our great High Priest, and the cleansing of that sanctuary.

As through the typical sacrifices of old the sins of the people were transferred in figure by the priests to the earthly sanctuary, where those priests ministered; so ever since Christ ascended to be our intercessor in the presence of His Father, the sins of all those who sincerely seek pardon through Him are transferred in fact to the heavenly sanctuary, where He ministers. Whether Christ ministers for us in the heavenly holy places with His own blood literally, or only by virtue of its merits, we need not stop to inquire. Suffice it to say that His blood has been shed, and through that blood remission of sins is obtained in fact, which was obtained only in figure through the blood of the calves and goats of the former ministration. But those typical sacrifices had real virtue in the respect that they signified faith in a real sacrifice to come. Thus those who employed them have an equal interest in the work of Christ with those who in our era come to Him by faith through the ordinances of the gospel.

The continual transfer of sins to the heavenly sanctuary makes its cleansing necessary on the same ground that a like work was required in the earthly sanctuary. An important distinction between the two ministrations must here be noticed. In the earthly tabernacle, a complete round of service was accomplished every year. On every day of the year except one, the ministration went forward in the first apartment. One day's work in the most holy completed the yearly round. The work then began again in the holy place, and went forward until another Day of Atonement completed the year's work. And so on, year by year. A succession of priests performed this round of service in the earthly sanctuary. But our divine Lord "ever liveth to make intercession" for us. Hebrews 7: 25. Hence the work of the heavenly sanctuary, instead of being a yearly work, is performed once for all. Instead of being repeated year by year, one grand cycle is allotted to it, in which it is carried forward and finished forever.

One year's round of service in the earthly sanctuary represented the entire work of the sanctuary above. In the type, the cleansing of the sanctuary was the brief closing work of the year's service. In the antitype, the cleansing of the sanctuary must be the closing work of Christ, our great High Priest, in the tabernacle in heaven. In the type, to cleanse the sanctuary, the high priest entered into the most holy place to minister in the presence of God before the ark of His testament. In the antitype, when the time comes for the cleansing of the true sanctuary, our High Priest, in like manner, enters into the most holy place once for all to make a final end of His intercessory work in behalf of mankind.

Reader, do you now see the importance of this subject? Do you begin to perceive what an object of interest for all the world is the sanctuary of God? Do you see that the whole plan of salvation centers here, and that when it is done, probation is ended, and the cases of the saved and lost are eternally decided? Do you see that the cleansing of the sanctuary is a brief and special work by which the great plan of salvation is forever finished? Do you see that if it can be ascertained when the work of cleansing begins we shall know when salvation's last mighty hour has come, when that most solemn announcement of the prophetic word is due to the world—"Fear God, and give glory to Him; for the hour of His judgment is come"? Revelation 14: 7. This is exactly what the prophecy is designed to show; it is to make known the commencement of this momentous work. "Unto two thousand and three hundred days; then shall the sanctuary be cleansed." The heavenly sanctuary is the one in which the decision of all cases is to be

CHRIST, OUR HIGH PRIEST

"We have such an High Priest, who is set on the right hand of the throne of the Majesty in the heavens." Hebrews 8: 1.

rendered. The progress of the work there should be the special concern of mankind. If people understood the bearing of these subjects on their eternal interests, they would give them their most careful and prayerful study.

VERSE 15 And it came to pass, when I, even I Daniel, had seen the vision, and sought for the meaning, then, behold, there stood before me as the appearance of a man. 16 And I heard a man's voice between the banks of Ulai, which called, and said, Gabriel, make this man to understand the vision.

We now enter upon the interpretation of the vision. We have already mentioned Daniel's longing to understand these things. He sought for the meaning. Immediately there stood before the prophet one who had the appearance of a man. Daniel heard a man's voice, that is, the voice of an angel as of a man speaking. The commandment was given to make this man Daniel understand the vision. It was addressed to Gabriel, a name that signifies "the strength of God," or "man of God." He continues his instruction to Daniel in chapter 9. Centuries later this same angel was commissioned to announce the birth of John the Baptist to his father Zacharias, and that of the Messiah to the virgin Mary. (Luke 1: 26.) To Zacharias, he introduced himself with these words: "I am Gabriel, that stand in the presence of God." Luke 1: 19. From this it appears that Gabriel was here addressed by one still higher in rank, who had power to command and control his work. This one was probably no other than the Archangel, Michael, or Christ.

VERSE 17 So he came near where I stood: and when he came, I was afraid, and fell upon my face: but he said unto me, Understand, O son of man: for at the time of the end shall be the vision. 18 Now as he was speaking with me, I was in a deep sleep on my face toward the ground: but he touched me, and set me upright. 19 And he said, Behold, I will make thee know what shall be in the last end of the indignation: for at the time appointed the end shall be.

It was not for the purpose of worship that Daniel fell before the angel, for it is forbidden to worship angels. (See Revelation 19: 10; 22: 8, 9.) Daniel seems to have been completely overcome by the majesty of the heavenly messenger.

He prostrated himself with his face to the ground. The angel laid his hand upon him to give him assurance (how many times have mortals been told by heavenly beings to "fear not"!), and from this helpless and prostrate condition set him upright.

With a general statement that at the time appointed the end shall be, and that he will make him to know "what shall be in the last end of the indignation," the angel enters upon an interpretation of the vision. "The indignation" must be understood to cover a period of time. What period of time? God told His people Israel that He would pour upon them His indignation for their wickedness; and thus He gave directions concerning the "profane wicked prince of Israel:" "Remove the diadem, and take off the crown. . . . I will overturn, overturn, overturn, it: and it shall be no more, until He come whose right it is; and I will give it Him." Ezekiel 21: 25-27,31.

Here is the period of God's indignation against His covenant people, the period during which the sanctuary and host are to be trodden underfoot. The diadem was removed, and the crown taken off, when Israel was subjected to the kingdom of Babylon. It was overturned by the Medes and Persians, again by the Grecians, again by the Romans, corresponding to the three times the word is repeated by the prophet. The Jews, having rejected Christ, were soon scattered abroad over the face of the earth. Spiritual Israel has taken the place of the literal seed; but they are in subjection to earthly powers, and will be until the throne of David is again set up—until He who is its rightful heir, the Messiah, the Prince of peace, shall come. Then the indignation will have ceased. The events that shall take place in the end of this period are now to be made known to Daniel by the angel.

VERSE 20 The ram which thou sawest having two horns are the kings of Media and Persia. 21 And the rough goat is the king of Grecia: and the great horn that is between his eyes is the first king. 22 Now that being broken, whereas four stood up for it, four kingdoms shall stand up out of the nation, but not in his power.

The Vision Interpreted.—As the disciples said to the Lord, so may we here say of the angel who spoke to Daniel, "Lo, now speakest thou plainly, and speakest no proverb." This explanation of the vision is in language plain to be understood. (See comments on verses 3-8.) The distinguishing feature of the Persian Empire, the union of the two nationalities which composed it, is represented by the two horns of the ram. Grecia attained its greatest glory as a unit under the leadership of Alexander the Great, a general as famous as the world has ever seen. This part of her history is represented by the first phase of the goat, during which time the one notable horn symbolized Alexander the Great. Upon his death, the kingdom fell into fragments, but soon consolidated into four grand divisions. These were represented by the second phase of the goat, when it had four horns which came up in the place of the first, which had been broken. These divisions did not stand in his power. None of them possessed the strength of the original kingdom. These great waymarks of history on which the historian has written volumes, the inspired penman here gives us in sharp outline, with a few strokes of the pen.

VERSE 23 And in the latter time of their kingdom, when the transgressors are come to the full, a king of fierce countenance, and understanding dark sentences, shall stand up. 24 And his power shall be mighty, but not by his own power: and he shall destroy wonderfully, and shall prosper, and practice, and shall destroy the mighty and the holy people. 25 And through his policy also he shall cause craft to prosper in his hand; and he shall magnify himself in his heart, and by peace shall destroy many: he shall also stand up against the Prince of princes; but he shall be broken without hand.

This power succeeds to the four divisions of the goat kingdom in the latter time of their kingdom, that is, toward the termination of their career. It is of course the same as the little horn of verse 9 and onward. Apply it to Rome, as set forth in remarks on verse 9, and all is harmonious and clear.

"*A King of Fierce Countenance.*"—In predicting punishment to come upon the Jews from this same power, Moses calls it "a *nation* of fierce countenance." Deuteronomy 28: 49, 50.

No people made a more formidable appearance in warlike array than the Romans.

As to "understanding dark sentences," Moses says in the scripture before mentioned, "Whose tongue thou [the Jews] shalt not understand." This could not be said of the Babylonians, Persians, or Greeks, in reference to the Jews; for the Chaldean and Greek languages were used to some extent in Palestine. This was not the case, however, with the Latin.

When do the transgressors "come to the full"? All along, the connection between God's people and their oppressors is kept in view. It was on account of the transgressions of His people that they were sold into captivity. Their continuance in sin brought more and more severe punishment. At no time were the Jews as a nation more corrupt morally than at the time they came under the jurisdiction of the Romans.

Papal Rome "Mighty, but Not by His Own Power."—The success of the Romans was owing largely to the aid of their allies, and divisions among their enemies, of which they were ever ready to take advantage. Papal Rome also was mighty by means of the secular powers over which she exercised spiritual control.

"He shall destroy wonderfully." The Lord told the Jews by the prophet Ezekiel that He would deliver them to men who were "skillful to destroy" (Ezekiel 21: 31); and the slaughter of eleven hundred thousand Jews at the destruction of Jerusalem by the Roman army, was a terrible confirmation of the prophet's words. Rome in its second, or papal, phase was responsible for the death of millions of martyrs.

"Through his policy also he shall cause craft to prosper in his hand." Rome has been distinguished above all other powers for a policy of craft, by means of which it brought the nations under its control. This is true of both pagan and papal Rome. Thus by peace it destroyed many.

Finally, in the person of one of its governors, Rome stood up against the Prince of princes, by giving sentence of death against Jesus Christ. "But he shall be broken without hands."

This parallels the prophecy of Daniel 2: 34, where the stone "cut out without hands" destroys all earthly powers.

VERSE 26 And the vision of the evening and the morning which was told is true: wherefore shut thou up the vision; for it shall be for many days. 27 And I Daniel fainted, and was sick certain days; afterward I rose up, and did the king's business; and I was astonished at the vision, but none understood it.

"The vision of the evening and the morning" refers to the period of 2300 days. In view of the long period of oppression, and the calamities which were to come upon his people, Daniel fainted and was sick certain days. He was astonished at the vision, but did not understand it. Why did not Gabriel at this time fully carry out his instructions, and cause Daniel to understand the vision? Undoubtedly because Daniel had received all that he could then bear. Further instruction is therefore deferred to a future time.

"AND IT CAME TO PASS"

The prophecy of the ninth chapter of Daniel foretold with unerring accuracy the exact year of Christ's death on Calvary.

CHAPTER IX

A PROPHETIC YARDSTICK SPANS THE CENTURIES

Verse 1 In the first year of Darius the son of Ahasuerus, of the seed of the Medes, which was made king over the realm of the Chaldeans; 2 in the first year of his reign I Daniel understood by books the number of the years, whereof the word of the Lord came to Jeremiah the prophet, that He would accomplish seventy years in the desolations of Jerusalem.

THE VISION recorded in the preceding chapter was given in the third year of Belshazzar, 538 B. C. The events narrated in this chapter occurred in the first year of Darius. Since Belshazzar was the last ruler of Babylon and Darius the first ruler of Medo-Persia, probably less than one year elapsed between the events of these two chapters.

Seventy Years of Captivity.—Although Daniel, as prime minister of the foremost kingdom on the earth, was cumbered with cares and burdens, he did not let this deprive him of the privilege of studying into things of higher moment—the purposes of God revealed to His prophets. He understood by books, that is, the writings of Jeremiah, that God would accomplish seventy years in the captivity of His people. This prediction is found in Jeremiah 25: 12; 29: 10. The knowledge of it, and the use that was made of it, shows that Jeremiah was early regarded as a divinely inspired prophet; otherwise his writings would not have been so soon collected, and so extensively copied. Though for a time contemporary with him, Daniel had a copy of his works which he carried with him in his captivity. Though he was so great a prophet himself, he was not above studying carefully what God might reveal to others of His servants.

The seventy years of captivity must not be confused with the seventy weeks that follow. Dating the period of the seventy years of captivity from 606 B. C., Daniel understood that they were now drawing to their close, and that God had even begun the fulfillment of the prophecy by overthrowing the kingdom of Babylon.

VERSE 3 And I set my face unto the Lord God, to seek by prayer and supplications, with fasting, and sackcloth, and ashes.

Because God has promised, we are not released from the responsibility of beseeching Him for the fulfillment of His word. Daniel might have reasoned in this manner: God has promised to release His people at the end of the seventy years, and He will accomplish this promise; I need not therefore concern myself at all in the matter. Daniel did not thus reason; but as the time drew near for the accomplishment of the word of the Lord, he set himself to seek the Lord with all his heart.

How earnestly he engaged in the work, even with fasting, and sackcloth, and ashes! This was probably the year when Daniel was cast into the lions' den. The reader will recall that the decree approved by the king had forbidden all his subjects to ask any petition of any god except the king, on pain of death. But regardless of the decree, Daniel prayed this prayer three times a day with his windows open toward Jerusalem.

VERSE 4 And I prayed unto the Lord my God, and made my confession, and said, O Lord, the great and dreadful God, keeping the covenant and mercy to them that love Him, and to them that keep His commandments.

Daniel's Remarkable Prayer.—We here have the opening of Daniel's wonderful prayer, a prayer expressing such humiliation and contrition of heart that one must be without feeling who can read it unmoved. He begins by acknowledging the faithfulness of God, who never fails in any of His engagements with His followers. It was not from any lack on God's part in defending and upholding them, that the Jews were then in captivity, but only on account of their sins.

VERSE 5 We have sinned, and have committed iniquity, and have done wickedly, and have rebelled, even by departing from Thy precepts and from Thy judgments: 6 neither have we hearkened unto Thy servants the prophets, which spake in Thy name to our kings, our princes, and our fathers, and to all the people of the land. 7 O Lord, righteousness belongeth unto Thee, but unto us confusion of faces, as at this day; to the men of Judah, and to the inhabitants of Jerusalem, and unto all Israel, that are near, and that are far off, through all the countries whither Thou hast driven them, because of their trespass that they have trespassed against Thee. 8 O Lord, to us belongeth confusion of face, to our kings, to our princes, and to our fathers, because we have sinned against Thee. 9 To the Lord our God belong mercies and forgivenesses, though we have rebelled against Him; 10 neither have we obeyed the voice of the Lord our God, to walk in His laws, which He set before us by His servants the prophets. 11 Yea, all Israel have transgressed Thy law, even by departing, that they might not obey Thy voice; therefore the curse is poured upon us, and the oath that is written in the law of Moses the servant of God, because we have sinned against Him. 12 And He hath confirmed His words, which He spake against us, and against our judges that judged us, by bringing upon us a great evil: for under the whole heaven hath not been done as hath been done upon Jerusalem. 13 As it is written in the law of Moses, all this evil is come upon us: yet made we not our prayer before the Lord our God, that we might turn from our iniquities, and understand Thy truth. 14 Therefore hath the Lord watched upon the evil, and brought it upon us: for the Lord our God is righteous in all His works which He doeth: for we obeyed not His voice.

To this point Daniel's prayer is employed in making a full and heartbroken confession of sin. He vindicates fully the course of the Lord, acknowledging the sins of his people to be the cause of all their calamities, as God had threatened them by the prophet Moses. He does not discriminate in favor of himself. No self-righteousness appears in his petition. Although he had suffered long for others' sins, enduring seventy years of captivity for the wrongs of his people, he lived a godly life, and received signal honors and blessings from the Lord. He brings no accusations against anyone, pleads no sympathy for himself as a victim of others' wrongs, but classes himself with the rest, saying, *We* have sinned, and unto *us* belongs confusion of face. He acknowledges that they had not heeded the lessons God designed to teach them by their afflictions.

VERSE 15 And now, O Lord our God, that hast brought Thy people forth out of the land of Egypt with a mighty hand, and hast gotten Thee renown, as at this day; we have sinned, we have done wickedly. 16 O Lord, according to all Thy righteousness, I beseech Thee, let Thine anger and Thy fury be turned away from Thy city Jerusalem, Thy holy mountain:

because for our sins, and for the iniquities of our fathers, Jerusalem and Thy people are become a reproach to all that are about us. 17 Now therefore, O our God, hear the prayer of Thy servant, and his supplications, and cause Thy face to shine upon Thy sanctuary that is desolate, for the Lord's sake. 18 O my God, incline Thine ear, and hear; open Thine eyes, and behold our desolations, and the city which is called by Thy name: for we do not present our supplications before Thee for our righteousnesses, but for Thy great mercies. 19 O Lord, hear; O Lord, forgive; O Lord, hearken and do; defer not, for Thine own sake, O my God: for Thy city and Thy people are called by Thy name.

The prophet now pleads the honor of the Lord's name as a reason why he desires his petition to be granted. He refers to the fact of the deliverance of Israel from Egypt, and the great renown that had accrued to the Lord's name for all His wonderful works manifested among them. All this would be lost, should He now abandon them to perish. Moses used the same argument in pleading for Israel. (Numbers 14.) Not that God is moved with motives of ambition and vainglory; but when His people are jealous for the honor of His name, when they evince their love for Him by pleading with Him to work, not for their own personal benefit, but for His own glory, that His name may not be reproached and blasphemed among the heathen, this is acceptable with Him. Daniel then intercedes for the city of Jerusalem, called by God's name, and His holy mountain, for which He has had such love, and beseeches Him, for His mercies' sake, to let His anger be turned away. Finally, his mind centers upon the holy sanctuary, God's own dwelling place upon this earth, and he pleads that its desolations may be repaired.

Daniel understood the seventy years of captivity to be near their termination. From his allusion to the sanctuary, it is evident that he so far misunderstood the important vision given him in Daniel 8 as to suppose that the 2300 days expired at the same time. This misapprehension was at once corrected when the angel came to give him further instruction in answer to his prayer.

Verse 20 And whiles I was speaking, and praying, and confessing my sin and the sin of my people Israel, and presenting my supplication before the Lord my God for the holy mountain of my God; 21 yea, whiles I was speaking in prayer, even the man Gabriel, whom I had seen in the vision at the beginning, being caused to fly swiftly, touched me about the time of the evening oblation.

Daniel's Prayer Is Answered.—We here have the result of Daniel's supplication. He is suddenly interrupted by a heavenly messenger. The angel Gabriel, appearing again as he had before in the form of a man, whom Daniel had seen in the vision at the beginning, touched him. An important question is at this point to be determined, namely, Has the vision of Daniel 8 ever been explained, and can it ever be understood? To what vision does Daniel refer by the expression, "the vision at the beginning"? It will be conceded by all that it is a vision of which we have some previous record, and that in that vision we shall find some mention of Gabriel. We must go back beyond this ninth chapter, for all that we have in this chapter previous to this appearance of Gabriel, is simply a record of Daniel's prayer. Looking back, then, through previous chapters, we find mention of only three visions given to Daniel. The interpretation of the dream of Nebuchadnezzar was given in a night vision. (Daniel 2: 19.) But there is no record of any angelic agency in the matter. The vision of Daniel 7 was explained to Daniel by "one of them that stood by," probably an angel; but we have no information as to what angel, nor is there anything in that vision which needed further explanation. The vision of Daniel 8 gives some particulars which show this to be the vision referred to. Gabriel is there introduced by name. He was commanded to make Daniel understand the vision. Daniel had said that he did not understand it, showing that Gabriel, at the conclusion of Daniel 8, had not completed his mission. There is no place in all the Bible where this instruction is continued, if it is not in Daniel 9. If therefore the vision of Daniel 8 is not the one referred to, we have no record that Gabriel ever complied fully with the instructions given him, or that that vision has ever been explained. The instruction which the angel now gives to Daniel, as we shall see from the following verses, does exactly complete what was lacking in Daniel 8. These considerations prove beyond a doubt the connection between Daniel 8 and 9, and this conclusion will be still further strengthened by a consideration of the angel's instructions.

VERSE 22 And he informed me, and talked with me, and said, O Daniel, I am now come forth to give thee skill and understanding. 23 At the beginning of thy supplications the commandment came forth, and I am come to show thee; for thou art greatly beloved: therefore understand the matter, and consider the vision.

Gabriel's Mission.—The manner in which Gabriel introduces himself on this occasion shows that he has come to complete some unfinished mission. This can be nothing less than to carry out the instruction to make this man "understand the vision," as recorded in Daniel 8. He says, "I am now come forth to give thee skill and understanding." As the charge still rested upon him to make Daniel understand, and as he had explained to Daniel in chapter 8 all that he could then bear, and yet he did not understand the vision, he now comes to resume his work and complete his mission. As soon as Daniel began his fervent supplication, the commandment came forth; for Gabriel received instruction to visit Daniel, and impart to him the requisite information.

From the time it takes to read Daniel's prayer down to the point at which Gabriel made his appearance upon the scene, the reader can judge of the speed with which this messenger was dispatched from the court of heaven to this servant of God. No wonder that Daniel says he was caused to fly swiftly, or that Ezekiel compares the movements of these celestial beings to a flash of lightning. (Ezekiel 1: 14.)

"Understand the matter," he says to Daniel. What matter? Evidently that which he did not before understand, as stated in the last verse of Daniel 8. "Consider the vision." What vision? Not the interpretation of Nebuchadnezzar's image, nor the vision of Daniel 7, for there was no difficulty with either of these; but the vision of Daniel 8, in reference to which his mind was filled with astonishment and lack of understanding. "I am come to show thee," also said the angel.

Daniel had no difficulty in understanding what the angel told him about the ram, the he-goat, and the little horn, symbolizing the kingdoms of Medo-Persia, Greece, and Rome. Nor was he mistaken in regard to the ending of the seventy years' captivity. But the burden of his petition was in respect to the repairing of the desolations of the sanctuary, which lay in ruins. He had undoubtedly drawn the conclusion that the time when the end of the seventy years' captivity came was the time for the fulfillment of what the angel had said in regard to the cleansing of the sanctuary at the end of the 2300 days. Now he must be set right. This explains why at this particular time, so soon after the previous vision, instruction was sent to him.

The seventy years of captivity were drawing to their close. Daniel was acting upon a misunderstanding. He must not be suffered longer to remain ignorant of the true import of the former vision. "I am now come forth to give thee skill and understanding," said the angel. How could the connection between the former visit of the angel and this one be more distinctly shown than by such words at such a time from such a person?

Daniel Greatly Beloved.—One expression seems worthy of notice before we leave verse 23. It is the declaration of the angel to Daniel, "For thou art greatly beloved." The angel brought this declaration direct from the courts of heaven. It expressed the state of feeling that existed there in regard to Daniel.

Think of celestial beings, the highest in the universe,—the Father, the Son, the holy angels,—having such esteem for a mortal man here upon earth as to authorize an angel to bear the message to him that he is greatly beloved! This is one of the highest pinnacles of glory to which mortals can attain. Abraham reached another, when it could be said of him that he was the "friend of God;" and Enoch another, when it could

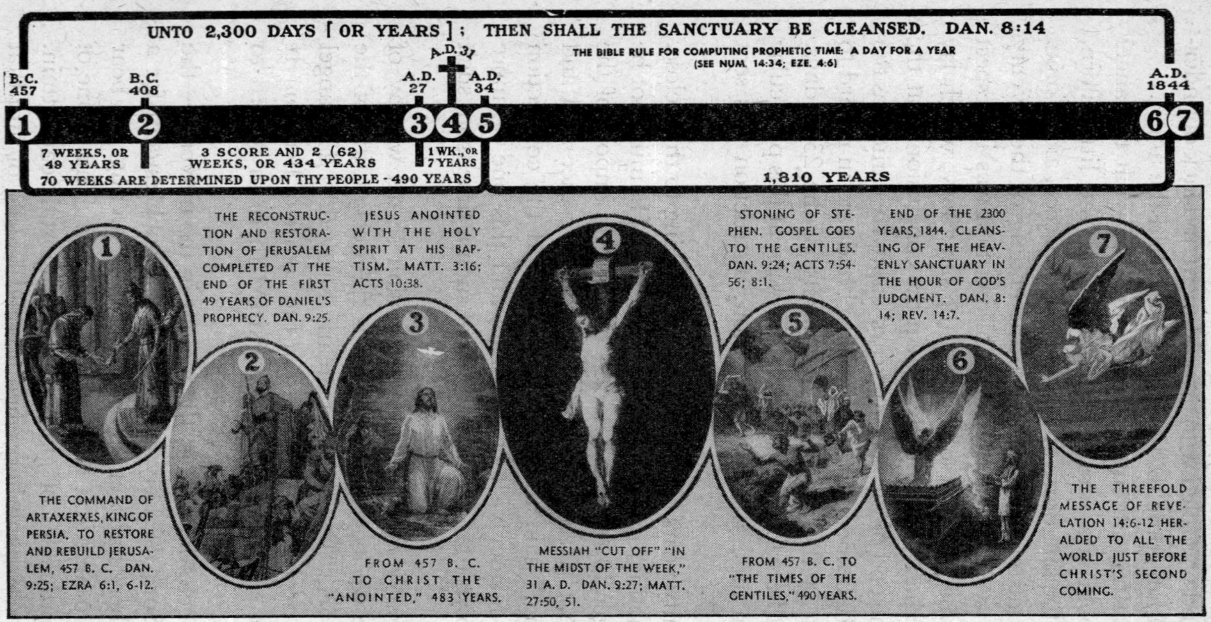
UNTO 2,300 DAYS [OR YEARS]; THEN SHALL THE SANCTUARY BE CLEANSED. DAN. 8:14
THE BIBLE RULE FOR COMPUTING PROPHETIC TIME: A DAY FOR A YEAR (SEE NUM. 14:34; EZE. 4:6)
B.C. 457
B.C. 408
A.D. 27
A.D. 31
A.D. 34
A.D. 1844
1
2
3
4
5
6
7
7 WEEKS, OR 49 YEARS
3 SCORE AND 2 (62) WEEKS, OR 434 YEARS
1 WK., OR 7 YEARS
70 WEEKS ARE DETERMINED UPON THY PEOPLE - 490 YEARS
1,810 YEARS
THE COMMAND OF ARTAXERXES, KING OF PERSIA, TO RESTORE AND REBUILD JERUSALEM, 457 B. C. DAN. 9:25; EZRA 6:1, 6-12.
THE RECONSTRUCTION AND RESTORATION OF JERUSALEM COMPLETED AT THE END OF THE FIRST 49 YEARS OF DANIEL'S PROPHECY. DAN. 9:25.
JESUS ANOINTED WITH THE HOLY SPIRIT AT HIS BAPTISM. MATT. 3:16; ACTS 10:38.
FROM 457 B. C. TO CHRIST THE "ANOINTED," 483 YEARS.
MESSIAH "CUT OFF" "IN THE MIDST OF THE WEEK," 31 A. D. DAN. 9:27; MATT. 27:50, 51.
STONING OF STEPHEN. GOSPEL GOES TO THE GENTILES. DAN. 9:24; ACTS 7:54-56; 8:1.
FROM 457 B. C. TO "THE TIMES OF THE GENTILES," 490 YEARS.
END OF THE 2300 YEARS, 1844. CLEANSING OF THE HEAVENLY SANCTUARY IN THE HOUR OF GOD'S JUDGMENT. DAN. 8:14; REV. 14:7.
THE THREEFOLD MESSAGE OF REVELATION 14:6-12 HERALDED TO ALL THE WORLD JUST BEFORE CHRIST'S SECOND COMING.

THE 2300 DAYS

This great span of years, the longest prophetic period in the Bible, was to reach, according to Daniel's prophecy, "from the going forth of the commandment to restore and to build Jerusalem," to the time for the cleansing of the sanctuary. The command to rebuild Jerusalem was given in 457 B. C. Seventy weeks (490 years) were cut off for the Jews, and it was at the end of that period, in A. D. 34, that the gospel began to be preached to the Gentiles. From the beginning of the period to Messiah the Prince was to be sixty-nine weeks (483 years). Precisely at the time foretold, in the autumn of A. D. 27, Jesus was baptized in the Jordan River by John the Baptist; and being anointed by the Holy Spirit, He began His public ministry. "In the midst of the week" (three and one half years later) Messiah was cut off. The entire period of 2300 years reached from 457 B. C. to A. D. 1844, at

be said of him that he "walked with God." Can we arrive at any such attainments? God is no respecter of persons; but He is a respecter of character. If in virtue and godliness we could equal these eminent men, we could move the divine love to equal depths. We, too, could be greatly beloved—could be friends of God, and could walk with Him. We must be in our generation what they were in theirs.

There is a figure used in reference to the last church which denotes the closest union with God: "If any man hear My voice, and open the door, I will come in to him, and will sup with him, and he with Me." Revelation 3: 20. To sup with the Lord denotes an intimacy equal to being greatly beloved by Him, walking with Him, or being His friend. How desirable a position! Alas for the evils of our nature, which cut us off from this communion! O for grace to overcome these, that we may enjoy this spiritual union here, and finally enter the glories of His presence at the marriage supper of the Lamb!

VERSE 24 Seventy weeks are determined upon thy people and upon thy holy city, to finish the transgression, and to make an end of sins, and to make reconciliation for iniquity, and to bring in everlasting righteousness, and to seal up the vision and prophecy, and to anoint the most holy.

Seventy Weeks.—These are the first words the angel uttered to Daniel in imparting to him that instruction which he came to give. Why did he thus abruptly introduce a period of time? We must again refer to the vision of Daniel 8. We have seen that Daniel, at the close of that chapter, says that he did not understand the vision. Some parts of that vision were at the time clearly explained. It could not have been these parts which he did not understand. We therefore inquire what it was that Daniel did not understand, or what part of the vision was left unexplained.

In that vision four prominent things are brought to view: the ram, the he-goat, the little horn, and the period of 2300 days. The symbols of the ram, the he-goat, and the little horn were explained, but nothing was said respecting the period of time. This must therefore have been the point that he did not understand. The other parts of the vision were of no avail while the application of this period of 2300 days was left in obscurity.

Says the learned Dr. Hales, in commenting upon the seventy weeks, "This chronological prophecy . . . was evidently designed to explain the foregoing vision, especially in its chronological part of the 2300 days."[1]

If this view of the subject is correct, we should naturally expect the angel to begin with the point which had been omitted, namely, the time. This we find to be true in fact. After citing Daniel's attention to the former vision in the most direct and emphatic manner, and assuring him that he had now come forth to give him understanding, he begins with the very point there omitted: "Seventy weeks are determined upon thy people and upon thy holy city."

Cut Off From the 2300 Days.—But how does this language show any connection with the 2300 days, or throw any light upon that period? We answer: The language cannot be intelligently referred to anything else. The word here rendered "determined" signifies "cut off," and no other period is given in the vision here referred to from which the seventy weeks could be cut off, except the 2300 days. How direct and natural, then, is the connection. "Seventy weeks are cut off." Cut off from what?—The 2300 days, most assuredly.

The word "determined" in this clause is a translation of the Hebrew נֶחְתַּךְ, *nechtak*, based on a primitive root defined by Strong as meaning "to *cut* off, (i.e., fig.) to *decree*—determine" (the latter by implication). The Authorized Version employs the remoter definition by implication, "determine," as in the text before us. The Revised Version uses the second definition, and makes it read, "seventy weeks are *decreed* [i.e., allotted] upon thy people." Taking the basic and simpler definition, we have "seventy weeks are *cut off* for thy people."

---

[1] William Hales, *A New Analysis of Chronology*, Vol. II, p. 517.

If cut off, it must be from some whole larger than itself—in this case from the twenty-three hundred years of the prophecy heretofore discussed. It may be added that Gesenius gives the same definition as Strong: "*to cut off*, . . . *to divide*, and so *to determine*, *to decree*." He then refers to Daniel 9: 24, and translates the phrase, "are decreed upon thy people." Davidson also gives exactly the same definition, and refers likewise to Daniel 9: 24 as an example.

Why, then, it may be asked, did our translators render the word "determined," when it so obviously means "cut off"? The answer is, They doubtless overlooked the connection between the eighth and ninth chapters, and considering it improper to render it "cut off," when nothing was given from which the seventy weeks could be cut off, they gave the word its figurative instead of its literal meaning. But, as we have seen, the definition and context require the literal meaning, and render any other inadmissible.

Seventy weeks, then, or 490 days of the 2300, were allotted to Jerusalem and the Jews. The events which were to be consummated within that period are briefly stated. The transgression was to be finished, that is, the Jewish people were to fill up the cup of their iniquity, which they did in the rejection and crucifixion of Christ. An end of sins, or of sin offerings,* was to be made. This took place when the great offering was made on Calvary. Reconciliation for iniquity was to be provided. This was accomplished by the sacrificial death of the Son of God. Everlasting righteousness was to be brought in, the righteousness which our Lord manifested in His sinless life. The vision and the prophecy were to be sealed, or made sure.

---

* The Hebrew word, חַטָּאת, *chattath*, translated "sins" in Daniel 9: 24, denotes either *sin* or *sin offering*. Leviticus 4: 3 is an example of its use in both senses in the same verse: "Let him bring for his *sin* . . . a young bullock . . . for his *sin offering*," the same Hebrew word being used in both instances. This is a common usage through the Levitical books including Leviticus 16 and elsewhere in the Old Testament. It can therefore clearly be used in the sense of sin offerings in Daniel 9: 24, for an end of sin offerings was actually made at the cross.—*Editors.*

By the events which were to occur in the seventy weeks, the prophecy is tested. By this the application of the whole vision is determined. If the events of this period are accurately fulfilled, the prophecy is of God, and will all be accomplished. If these seventy weeks are fulfilled as weeks of years, then the 2300 days, of which these are a part, are so many years.

Day for a Year in Prophecy.—As we enter upon the study of the seventy weeks, or 490 days, it will be well to remind ourselves of the fact that in Scripture prophecy a day represents a year. On page 144 we have already submitted evidence of the acceptance of the year-day principle; however, for the benefit of the reader, we present two further quotations as follows:

"In the same way it was opened up to Daniel in what way the last reviling would be after the sanctuary shall have been cleansed and the vision shall have been fulfilled; and this after 2300 days from the hour of the going forth of the commandment, . . . according to the predicted number by resolving a day into a year, according to the unfolding made to Ezekiel."[2]

"It is a singular fact that the great mass of interpreters in the English and American world have, for many years, been wont to understand the *days* designated in Daniel and in the Apocalypse, as the representatives or symbols of *years*. I have found it difficult to trace the origin of this general, I might say almost universal, custom."[3]

The year-day principle numbers among its supporters such names as Augustine, Tichonius, Primasius, Andreas, the Venerable Bede, Ambrosius, Ansbertus, Berengaud, and Bruno Astensis, besides the leading modern expositors.[4] But what is more conclusive than all else is the fact that the prophecies have actually been fulfilled on this principle—a demonstration of its correctness from which there is no appeal. This will be found in the prophecy of the seventy weeks throughout, and

---

[2] Nicholas von Cusa, *Conjectures of Cardinal Nicholas von Cusa Concerning the Last Days*, p. 934.

[3] Moses Stuart, *Hints on the Interpretation of Prophecy*, p. 74.

[4] See Edward B. Elliott, *Horæ Apocalypticæ*, Vol. III, p. 234, notes 2-6.

all the prophetic periods of Daniel 7 and 12, and Revelation 9, 12, and 13.

Thus the events of the seventy weeks, calculated in this rational way, furnish a key to the whole vision.

"*To Anoint the Most Holy.*"—According to the prophecy the "most holy" was to be anointed. The Hebrew phrase קֹדֶשׁ קָדָשִׁים, *qodesh qadashim*, here translated "most holy," is a term used freely through the Levitical books to characterize *things* and *places*, but is nowhere applied to *persons*, unless by exception in this verse. While it is used in the Old Testament and its Greek equivalent in the New, to distinguish the most holy place in the tabernacle, it is by no means confined to this use. It is employed also to characterize many articles connected with the holy service of the sanctuary, such as the brazen altar, the table, the candlestick, the incense, the unleavened bread, the sin offering, the trespass offering, every devoted thing, and the like, but never to *persons* connected with that service. (See Exodus 29: 37; 30: 10, 29, 36; Leviticus 6: 17, 29; 7: 1; 27: 28.)

On the other hand, in the case of *anointing* for service, the term is applied to the tabernacle itself, as well as to all its vessels. (Exodus 30: 26-29.) In Daniel 9: 24, a case of *anointing* is specified in the prophecy. Consistent with the uses of "most holy" pointed out above, there is every reason to believe that in this verse the anointing of the heavenly tabernacle is predicted. The tabernacle was anointed for the typical service; and true to pattern, it is most appropriate that the heavenly tabernacle should be anointed for the antitypical, or real, service as our High Priest enters upon His gracious work of ministering in behalf of sinners.

In the examination of the sanctuary in comments on Daniel 8: 14, we saw that a time came when the earthly sanctuary gave place to the heavenly, and the priestly ministration was transferred from the one to the other. Before the ministration in the earthly sanctuary began, the tabernacle and all the holy vessels were to be anointed. (Exodus 40: 9,

ARTAXERXES SIGNED THE DECREE

Artaxerxes, king of Persia, granted to Nehemiah and his people permission to return and rebuild Jerusalem.

10.) The last event of the seventy weeks here brought to view, therefore, is the anointing of the heavenly tabernacle for the opening of the ministration there.

VERSE 25 Know therefore and understand, that from the going forth of the commandment to restore and to build Jerusalem unto the Messiah the Prince shall be seven weeks, and threescore and two weeks: the street shall be built again, and the wall, even in troublous times. 26 And after threescore and two weeks shall Messiah be cut off, but not for Himself: and the people of the prince that shall come shall destroy the city and the sanctuary; and the end thereof shall be with a flood, and unto the end of the war desolations are determined. 27 And He shall confirm the covenant with many for one week: and in the midst of the week He shall cause the sacrifice and the oblation to cease, and for the overspreading of abominations He shall make it desolate, even until the consummation, and that determined shall be poured upon the desolate.

Seventy Weeks Subdivided.—The angel now relates to Daniel the event which is to mark the beginning of the seventy weeks. They were to date from the going forth of the commandment to restore and build Jerusalem. Not only is the event given which determines the time of the commencement of this period, but also those events which take place at its close. Thus a double test is provided by which to try the application of this prophecy. But more than this, the period of seventy weeks is divided into three grand divisions. One of these is again divided, and the intermediate events are given which were to mark the termination of each one of these divisions. If we can find a date which will harmonize with all these events, we have beyond a doubt the true application, for none but that which is correct could meet and fulfill so many conditions.

Let the reader now take in at one view the points of harmony to be made, that he may be the better prepared to guard against a false application. We are to find at the beginning of the period a commandment going forth to restore and build Jerusalem. To this work of restoration seven weeks are allotted. As we reach the end of this first division, seven weeks from the beginning, we are to find Jerusalem restored in its material aspect, the work of building the street and the wall fully accomplished. From this point sixty-two weeks are measured off. As we reach the termination of this division, sixty-nine weeks from the beginning, we are to see the manifestation of Messiah the Prince before the world. One week more is given us, completing the seventy. In the midst of this week the Messiah is to be cut off, and to cause the sacrifice and oblation to cease. At the expiration of that period which was allotted to the Jews as the time during which they were to be the special people of God, we naturally look for the going forth of the blessing and work of God to other people.

Beginning of the Seventy Weeks.—We now inquire for the initial date which will harmonize with all these particulars. The command respecting Jerusalem was to include more than mere building. There was to be restoration. By this we must understand all the forms and regulations of civil, political, and judicial society. When did such a command go forth? At the time these words were spoken to Daniel, Jerusalem lay in utter desolation, and had thus been lying for many years. The restoration pointed to in the future must be its restoration from this desolation. We then inquire, When and how was Jerusalem restored after the seventy years' captivity?

There are four events which can be taken as answering to the commandment to restore and build Jerusalem. These are:

1. The decree of Cyrus for the rebuilding of the house of God, 536 B. C. (Ezra 1: 1-4.)

2. The decree of Darius for the prosecution of that work which had been hindered, 519 B. C. (Ezra 6: 1-12.)

3. The decree of Artaxerxes to Ezra, 457 B. C.* (Ezra 7.)

4. The commission to Nehemiah from the same king in his twentieth year, 444 B. C. (Nehemiah 2.)

Dating from the first two of these decrees, the seventy prophetic weeks, or 490 literal years, would fall many years

* The years of Artaxerxes' reign are among the most easily established dates of history. The Canon of Ptolemy, with its list of kings and astronomical observations, the Greek Olympiads, and allusions in Greek history to Persian affairs all combine to place the seventh year of Artaxerxes at 457 B. C. beyond successful controversion. See Sir Isaac Newton, *Observations Upon the Prophecies of Daniel*, pp. 154-157.—*Editors.*

short of reaching even to the Christian Era. Besides this, these decrees had reference principally to the restoration of the temple and the temple worship of the Jews, not to the restoration of their civil state and polity, all of which must be included in the expression, "To *restore* and to build Jerusalem."

These two decrees made a beginning of the work. They were preliminary to what was afterward accomplished. But of themselves they were altogether insufficient to meet the requirements of the prophecy, both in their dates and in their nature. Thus falling short, they cannot be brought into the discussion as marking the point from which the seventy weeks are to begin. The only question now lies between the decrees which were granted to Ezra and to Nehemiah respectively.

The facts between which we are to decide here are briefly these: In 457 B. C., a decree was granted to Ezra by the Persian emperor Artaxerxes Longimanus to go up to Jerusalem with as many of his people as were minded to go with him. The commission granted him an unlimited amount of treasure, to beautify the house of God, to procure offerings for its service, and to do whatever else might seem good to him. It empowered him to ordain laws, set magistrates and judges, and execute punishment even unto death; in other words, to restore the Jewish state, civil and ecclesiastical, according to the law of God and the ancient customs of that people. Inspiration has seen fit to preserve this decree; and a full and accurate copy of it is given in Ezra 7. This decree is recorded not in Hebrew, like the rest of the book of Ezra, but in the official Chaldaic, or Eastern Aramaic. Thus we are referred to the original document by virtue of which Ezra was authorized to restore and build Jerusalem.

Thirteen years after this, in the twentieth year of the same king, 444 B. C., Nehemiah sought and obtained permission to go up to Jerusalem. (Nehemiah 2.) Permission was granted him, but we have no evidence that it was anything more than oral. It pertained to him individually, since nothing was said about others going up with him. The king asked him how long a journey he wished to make, and when he would return. He received letters to the governors beyond the river to help him on his way to Judea, and an order to the keeper of the king's forest for timber.

When he arrived at Jerusalem, he found rulers and priests, nobles and people, already engaged in the work of building Jerusalem. (Nehemiah 2: 16.) They were, of course, acting under the decree given to Ezra thirteen years before. Finally, after arriving at Jerusalem, Nehemiah finished in fifty-two days the work he came to accomplish. (Nehemiah 6: 15.)

Now which of these commissions, Ezra's or Nehemiah's, constitutes the decree for the restoration of Jerusalem, from which the seventy weeks are to be dated? It hardly seems that there can be any question on this point.

Reckoning from the commission to Nehemiah, 444 B. C., the dates throughout are entirely disarranged; for from that point the troublesome times which were to attend the building of the street and wall did not last seven weeks, or forty-nine years. If we reckon from that date, the sixty-nine weeks, or 483 years, which were to extend to the Messiah the Prince would bring us to A. D. 40; but Jesus was baptized of John in Jordan, and the voice of the Father was heard from heaven declaring Him His Son, A. D. 27, thirteen years before.[5] According to this calculation, the midst of the last or seventieth week, which is marked by the crucifixion, is placed in A. D. 44, but the crucifixion took place in A. D. 31, thirteen years previous. And lastly, the seventy weeks, or 490 years, dating from the twentieth year of Artaxerxes, would extend to A. D. 47, with absolutely nothing to mark their termination. Hence if that be the year, and the grant to Nehemiah the event, from which to reckon, the prophecy has proved a failure. As it is, it only proves that theory to be a failure which dates the seventy weeks from Nehemiah's commission in the twentieth year of Artaxerxes.

---

[5] See S. Bliss, *Analysis of Sacred Chronology*, pp. 180, 182; Karl Wieseler, *A Chronological Synopsis of the Four Gospels*, pp. 164-247.

It is thus evident that the decree granted to Ezra in the seventh year of Artaxerxes, 457 B. C., is the point from which to date the seventy weeks. That was the going forth of the decree in the sense of the prophecy. The two previous decrees were preparatory and preliminary to this. Indeed they are regarded by Ezra as parts of it, the three being taken as one great whole. For in Ezra 6: 14 we read: "They builded, and finished it, according to the commandment of the God of Israel, and according to the commandment of Cyrus, and Darius, and Artaxerxes king of Persia." It will be noticed that the decrees of these three kings are spoken of as one,—"*the* commandment [margin, "decree," singular number] of Cyrus, and Darius, and Artaxerxes," showing that they are all reckoned as a unit, the different decrees being but the successive steps by which the work was accomplished. This decree could not be said to have "gone forth" as intended by the prophecy, until the last permission which the prophecy required was embodied in the decree, and clothed with the authority of the empire. This point was reached in the grant given to Ezra, but not before. Here the decree assumed the proportions and covered the ground demanded by the prophecy, and from this point its "going forth" must be dated.

Harmony of the Subdivisions.—Will these dates harmonize if we reckon from the decree to Ezra? Let us see. Our starting-point then is 457 B. C. Forty-nine years were allotted to the building of the city and the wall. On this point, Prideaux says: "In the fifteenth year of Darius Nothus ended the first seven weeks of the seventy weeks of Daniel's prophecy. For then the restoration of the church and state of the Jews in Jerusalem and Judea was fully finished, in that last act of reformation, which is recorded in the thirteenth chapter of Nehemiah, from the twenty-third verse to the end of the chapter, *just forty-nine* years after it had been first begun by Ezra in the seventh year of Artaxerxes Longimanus."[6] This was 408 B. C.

---

[6] Humphrey Prideaux, *The Old and New Testament Connected in the History of the Jews,* Vol. I, p. 322.

CHARLES COPELAND. ARTIST

REBUILDING JERUSALEM'S WALLS

Under great difficulties, the ruined walls of Jerusalem were rebuilt.

So far we find harmony. Let us apply the measuring rod of the prophecy still further. Sixty-nine weeks, or 483 years, were to extend to Messiah the Prince. Dating from 457 B. C., they end in A. D. 27. What event then occurred?* Luke thus informs us: "Now when all the people were baptized, it came to pass, that Jesus also being baptized, and praying, the heaven was opened, and the Holy Ghost descended in a bodily shape like a dove upon Him, and a voice came from heaven, which said, Thou art My beloved Son; in Thee I am well pleased." Luke 3: 21, 22. After this, Jesus came "preaching the gospel of the kingdom of God, and saying, *The time* is fulfilled." Mark 1: 14, 15. *The* time here mentioned must have been some specific, definite, and predicted period; but no prophetic period can be found terminating then except the sixty-nine weeks of the prophecy of Daniel, which were to extend to Messiah the Prince. The Messiah had now come, and with His own lips He announced the termination of that period which was to be marked by His manifestation.†

---

* There is abundance of authority for A. D. 27 as the date of Christ's baptism. See S. Bliss, *Sacred Chronology*, p. 180; *New International Encyclopedia*, art. "Jesus Christ;" Karl Wieseler, *Chronological Synopsis of the Four Gospels*, pp. 164-247.

† Luke declared that Jesus "began to be about thirty years of age" at the time of His baptism (Luke 3: 23); and almost immediately after this He entered upon His ministry. How, then, could His ministry begin in A. D. 27, and He still be of the age named by Luke? The answer to this question is found in the fact that Christ was born between three and four years before the beginning of the Christian Era, that is, before the year called A. D. 1. The mistake of dating the Christian Era somewhat over three years this side of the birth of Christ, instead of dating it from the year of His birth, as it was designed to be, arose on this wise. One of the most important of ancient eras was reckoned from the building of the city of Rome—*ab urbe condita*—expressed by the abbreviation A. U. C., or more briefly, U. C. In the year which is now numbered A. D. 532, Dionysius Exiguus, a Scythian by birth, and a Roman abbot, who flourished in the reign of Justinian, invented the Christian Era. According to the best evidence at his command, he placed the birth of Christ U. C. 753. But Christ was born before the death of Herod; and it was afterward ascertained on the clearest evidence that the death of Herod occurred in April, U. C. 750. Allowing a few months for the events recorded in Christ's life before the time of Herod's death, his birth is carried back to the latter part of U. C. 749, a little more than three years before A. D. 1. Christ was therefore thirty years of age in A. D. 27. "The Vulgar [common] era began to prevail in the West about the time of Charles Martel and Pope Gregory II, A. D. 730; but was not sanctioned by any public Acts or Rescripts till the first German Synod, in the time of Carolomannus, Duke of the Franks, which, in the preface, was said to be assembled '*Anno ab incarnatione Dom.* 742, 11 Calendas Maii.' But it was not established till the time of Pope Eugenius IV, A. D. 1431, who ordered this era to be used in the public Registers: according to Mariana, and others."—*William Hales, "A New Analysis of Chronology," Vol. I, p. 84.* (See also Samuel J. Andrews, *Life of Our Lord Upon the Earth*, pp. 29,

Here, again, is indisputable harmony. But further, the Messiah was to confirm the covenant with many for one week. This would be the last week of the seventy, or the last seven years of the 490. In the midst of the week, the prophecy informs us, He should cause the sacrifice and oblation to cease. These Jewish ordinances, pointing to the death of Christ, could cease only at the cross. There they did virtually come to an end when the veil of the temple was rent at the crucifixion of Christ, though the outward observance was kept up until the destruction of Jerusalem, A. D. 70. After threescore and two weeks, according to the record, the Messiah was to be cut off. It is the same as if it had read: After threescore and two weeks, in the midst of the seventieth week, shall Messiah be cut off, and cause the sacrifice and oblation to cease. Now, as the word *midst* here means middle, the crucifixion is definitely located in the middle of the seventieth week.

Date of the Crucifixion.—It now becomes an important point to determine in what year the crucifixion took place. It is not to be questioned that our Saviour attended every Passover that occurred during His public ministry, and we have mention of only four such occasions previous to His crucifixion. These are found in the following passages: John 2: 13; 5: 1; 6: 4; 13: 1. At the last-mentioned Passover He was crucified. From facts already established, let us then see where this would locate the crucifixion. As He began His ministry in the autumn of A. D. 27, His first Passover would occur the following

30.) The Christian Era had become so well established before the mistake above referred to was discovered, that no change in the reckoning has been attempted. It makes no material difference, as it does not interfere at all with the calculation of dates. If the era began with the actual year of Christ's birth, the number of years B. C. in any case would be four years less, and the years A. D. four years more. To illustrate: If we have a period of twenty years, one half before and the other half in the Christian Era, we say that it began 10 B. C. and ended A. D. 10. But if we place the era back to the real point of Christ's birth there would be no change of either terminus of the period, but we should then say that it began 6 B. C. and ended A. D. 14; that is, four years would be taken from the figures B. C. and added to those of A. D. Some have so far misapprehended this subject as to claim that the current year should have four years added to it, to denote the real year of the Christian Era. This would be true, if the reckoning began from the actual date of Christ's birth. But this is not the case, the starting point being between three and four years later.—*Editors.*

spring, A. D. 28; His second, A. D. 29; His third, A. D. 30; and His fourth and last, A. D. 31. This gives us three years and a half for His public ministry, and corresponds exactly to the prophecy that He would be cut off in the midst, or middle, of the seventieth week. As that week of years began in the autumn of A. D. 27, the middle of the week would occur three and one half years later, in the spring of 31, when the crucifixion took place. Dr. Hales quotes Eusebius, A. D. 300, as saying: "It is recorded in history that the whole time of our Saviour's teaching and working miracles was three years and a half, which is the half of a week [of years]. This, John the evangelist will represent to those who critically attend to his Gospel."[7]

Of the unnatural darkness which occurred at the crucifixion, Hales thus speaks: "Hence it appears that the darkness which 'overspread the whole land of Judea' at the time of our Lord's crucifixion was preternatural, 'from the sixth until the ninth hour,' or from noon till three in the afternoon, in its *duration*, and also in its *time*, about full moon, when the moon could not possibly eclipse the sun. The time it happened, and the fact itself, are recorded in a curious and valuable passage of a respectable Roman Consul, Aurelius Cassiodorus Senator, about A. D. 514. 'In the consulate of Tiberius Cæsar Aug. V and Ælius Sejanus (U. C. 784, A. D. 31), our Lord Jesus Christ suffered, on the 8th of the Calends of April (25th of March), when there happened such an eclipse of the sun as was never before nor since.'

"In this year, and in this day; agree also the Council of Cæsarea, A. D. 196 or 198, the Alexandrian Chronicle, Maximus Monachus, Nicephorus Constantinus, Cedrenus; and in this year, but on different days, concur Eusebius and Epiphanius, followed by Kepler, Bucher, Patinus, and Petavius, some reckoning it the 10th of the Calends of April, others the 13th." (See comments on Daniel 11: 22.)[8]

---

[7] William Hales, *A New Analysis of Chronology*, Vol. I, p. 94.

[8] *Ibid.*, pp. 69, 70.

C. MENTE. AFTER WILLIAM HOLE. ARTIST

THE ANOINTING OF THE MESSIAH

It was at His baptism that Christ was anointed by God for His Messianic mission. The time was fulfilled.

Here, then, are thirteen creditable authorities who locate the crucifixion of Christ in the spring of A. D. 31. We may therefore set this down as a fixed date. This being in the middle of the last week, we have simply to reckon backward three and a half years to find where sixty-nine of the weeks ended, and forward from that point three and a half years to find the termination of the whole seventy weeks. Thus going back three and a half years from the crucifixion in the spring of A. D. 31, we come to the autumn of A. D. 27, when, as we have seen, the sixty-nine weeks ended, and Christ began His public ministry. Going forward from the crucifixion three and a half years, we are brought to the autumn of A. D. 34, as the grand terminating point of the whole period of the seventy weeks. This date is marked by the martyrdom of Stephen, the formal rejection of the gospel of Christ by the Jewish Sanhedrin in the persecution of His disciples, and the turning of the apostles to the Gentiles. These are the events which one would expect to take place when that specified period cut off for the Jews and allotted to them as a peculiar people, should fully expire.

From the facts above set forth, we see that, reckoning the seventy weeks from the decree given to Ezra in the seventh year of Artaxerxes, 457 B. C., there is perfect harmony throughout. The important and definite events of the manifestation of the Messiah at His baptism, the commencement of His public ministry, the crucifixion, and the rejection of the Jews and the preaching of the gospel to the Gentiles, with the proclamation of the new covenant—all come in in their exact place, sealing the prophecy and making it sure.

End of the 2300 Days.—With the seventy weeks we are now through; but there remains a longer period, and other important events are to be considered. The seventy weeks are but the first 490 years of the 2300-year period. Take 490 from 2300, and there remains 1810. The 490, as we have seen, ended in the autumn of A. D. 34. If to this date we now add the remaining 1810 years, we shall have the termination of the

FREDERICK SHIELDS, ARTIST

"WE TURN TO THE GENTILES"

Upon the rejection of the gospel by the Jews, the apostles turned to the Gentiles, who gladly received them.

whole period. So to A. D. 34, autumn, add 1810, and we have the autumn of A. D. 1844. Thus speedily and surely do we find the termination of the 2300 days, when once the seventy weeks have been located.

Why in 1844?—The query may here arise how the days can be extended to the autumn of 1844 if they began in 457 B. C., as it requires only 1843 years, in addition to the 457, to make the whole number 2300. Attention to one fact will clear this point of all difficulty: It takes 457 *full* years before Christ, and 1843 *full* years after, to make 2300; so that if the period began with the very *first* day of 457, it would not terminate till the very *last* day of 1843. Now it will be evident to all that if any part of the year 457 had passed away before the 2300 days began, just so much of the year 1844 must pass away before they would end. We therefore inquire, From what point in the year 457 are we to begin to reckon? From the fact that the first forty-nine years were allotted to the *building* of the street and wall, we learn that the period is to be dated, not from the starting of Ezra from Babylon, but from the actual beginning of the work at Jerusalem. This beginning could hardly be earlier than the seventh month (autumn) of 457, as he did not arrive at Jerusalem until the fifth month of that year. (Ezra 7: 9.) The whole period would therefore extend to the seventh month, autumn, Jewish time, of 1844.

The momentous declaration made by the angel to Daniel, "Unto two thousand and three hundred days: then shall the sanctuary be cleansed," is now explained. In our search for the meaning of the sanctuary and its cleansing, and the application of the time, we have found not only that this subject can be easily understood, but lo, the event is even now in process of accomplishment. Here we pause a brief moment to reflect upon the solemn position into which we are brought.

We have seen that the sanctuary of the Christian Era is the tabernacle of God in heaven, the house not made with hands, where our Lord ministers in behalf of penitent sinners, the place where between the great God and His Son Jesus

Christ the "counsel of peace" prevails in the work of salvation for perishing men. (Zechariah 6: 13; Psalm 85: 10.) We have seen that the cleansing of the sanctuary consists in the removing of the sins from it, and is the closing act of the ministration performed in it; that the work of salvation now centers in the heavenly sanctuary; and that when the sanctuary is cleansed, the work is done. Then the great plan of salvation devised at the fall of man is brought to its final termination. Mercy no longer pleads, and the great voice is heard from the throne in the temple in heaven, saying, "It is done." Revelation 16: 17. What then? All the righteous have the gift of everlasting life; all the wicked are doomed to everlasting death. Beyond that point, no decision can be changed, no reward can be lost, and no destiny of despair can be averted.

The Solemn Judgment Hour.—We have seen (and this is what brings the solemnities of the judgment to our own door) that that long prophetic period which was to mark the beginning of this final work in the heavenly sanctuary, has met its termination. In 1844 the days ended. Since that time the final work for man's salvation has been going forward. This work involves an examination of every man's character, for it consists in the remission of the sins of those who shall be found worthy to have them remitted, and determines who among the dead shall be raised. It also decides who among the living shall be changed at the coming of the Lord, and who of both dead and living shall be left to have their part in the fearful scenes of the second death. All can see that such a decision as this must be rendered before the Lord appears.

Every man's destiny is to be determined by the deeds done in the body, and each one is to be rewarded according to his works. (2 Corinthians 5: 10; Revelation 22: 12.) In the books of record kept by the heavenly scribes above, every man's deeds will be found recorded. (Revelation 20: 12.) In the closing sanctuary work these records are examined, and decisions are rendered in accordance with the findings. (Daniel 7: 9, 10.) It would be natural to suppose that the work would begin with the first members of the human race, that their cases would be first examined, and decision rendered, and so on with all the dead, generation by generation, in chronological succession, until we reach the last generation—the generation of the living, with whose cases the work would close.

When the cases of all the dead have been examined, and when the cases of the living have been reached, no man can know. But since the year 1844 this solemn work has been going forward. Light from the types, and the very nature of the work, forbid that it should be of long continuance. In his sublime views of heavenly scenes, John saw millions of attendants and assistants engaged with our Lord in His priestly work. (Revelation 5.) Thus the ministration goes forward. It ceases not, it delays not, and it must soon be forever finished.

Here we stand then, with the last, the greatest, and the most solemn crisis in the history of our race immediately impending. The plan of salvation is about finished. The last precious years of probation are almost ended. The Lord is about to come to save those who are ready and waiting, and to cut asunder the careless and unbelieving. The world—alas! What shall we say of it? Deceived with error, crazed with cares and business, delirious with pleasure, and paralyzed with vice, the inhabitants have not a moment to spare for listening to solemn truth, nor a thought to bestow upon their eternal interests. Let the people of God, with eternity in view, be careful to escape the corruption that is in the world through lust, and prepare to pass the searching test when their cases shall come up for examination at the great tribunal above. Let them be diligent in warning sinners of the wrath to come, and in pointing them to a loving Saviour who intercedes in their behalf.

To the careful attention of every student of prophecy we commend the subject of the sanctuary and its service. In the sanctuary is seen the ark of God's testament, containing His

FORREST C. CROOKS, ARTIST

CHRIST OUR ADVOCATE

In the books of heaven there are accurate records of every life. Mercy and justice will both be

holy law. This suggests a reform in our obedience to that great standard of morality. The opening of this heavenly temple, or the beginning of the service in its second apartment, marks the commencement of the sounding of the seventh angel. (Revelation 11: 15, 19.) The work performed therein is the foundation of the third angel's message of Revelation 14,—the last message of mercy to a perishing world. This subject of the sanctuary renders harmonious and clear past prophetic fulfillments which are otherwise involved in impenetrable obscurity. It gives a definite idea of the position and work of our great High Priest, and brings out the plan of salvation in its destinctive and beautiful features. It reins us up, as no other subject does, to the realities of the judgment, and shows the preparation we need to be able to stand in the coming day. It shows us that we are in the waiting time, and puts us upon our watch, for we do not know how soon the work will be finished, and our Lord appear. Watch, lest coming suddenly He find you sleeping.

After stating the great events connected with our Lord's mission here upon the earth, the prophet in the last part of Daniel 9: 27 speaks of the soon-following destruction of Jerusalem by the Roman power; and finally of the destruction of that power itself, called in the margin "the desolator."

 R. M. ELDRIDGE, ARTIST

DANIEL ASSISTED BY THE ANGEL

"Are they not all ministering spirits, sent forth to minister for them who shall be heirs of salvation?" Hebrews 1: 14.

CHAPTER X

GOD INTERVENES IN WORLD AFFAIRS

VERSE 1 In the third year of Cyrus king of Persia a thing was revealed unto Daniel, whose name was called Belteshazzar; and the thing was true, but the time appointed was long: and he understood the thing, and had understanding of the vision.

THIS verse introduces the last recorded vision of the prophet Daniel, the instruction imparted to him at this time being continued through Daniel 11 and 12. The death of Daniel is supposed to have occurred soon after this, he being at this time, according to Prideaux, not less than ninety years of age.

VERSE 2 In those days I Daniel was mourning three full weeks. 3 I ate no pleasant bread, neither came flesh nor wine in my mouth, neither did I anoint myself at all, till three whole weeks were fulfilled.

Daniel's Sorrow.—The marginal reading for "three full weeks" is "weeks of days," here used to distinguish the time spoken of from the *weeks of years* brought to view in the preceding chapter.

For what purpose did this aged servant of God thus humble himself and afflict his soul?—Evidently to understand more fully the divine purpose concerning events that were to befall the church of God. The divine messenger sent to instruct him says, "From the first day that thou didst set thine heart to *understand.*" Verse 12. There was still something, then, which Daniel did not understand. What was it? Undoubtedly it was some part of his preceding vision, that of Daniel 9, and through that of the vision of Daniel 8, of which Daniel 9 was but a further explanation. As the result of his supplication, he now receives more minute information respecting the events included in the great outlines of his former visions.

This mourning of the prophet is supposed to have been accompanied with fasting, not an absolute abstinence from food, but a use of only the plainest and most simple articles of diet. He ate no pleasant bread, no delicacies or dainties; he used no flesh or wine; and he did not anoint his head, which was to the Jews an outward sign of fasting. How long he would have continued this fast had he not received the answer to his prayer, we do not know, but his course in continuing it for three full weeks shows that he was not a person to cease his supplications till his petition was granted.

VERSE 4 And in the four and twentieth day of the first month, as I was by the side of the great river, which is Hiddekel; 5 then I lifted up mine eyes, and looked, and behold a certain man clothed in linen, whose loins were girded with fine gold of Uphaz: 6 His body also was like the beryl, and His face as the appearance of lightning, and His eyes as lamps of fire, and His arms and His feet like in color to polished brass, and the voice of His words like the voice of a multitude. 7 And I Daniel alone saw the vision: for the men that were with me saw not the vision; but a great quaking fell upon them, so that they fled to hide themselves. 8 Therefore I was left alone, and saw this great vision, and there remained no strength in me: for my comeliness was turned in me into corruption, and I retained no strength. 9 Yet heard I the voice of His words: and when I heard the voice of His words, then was I in a deep sleep on my face, and my face toward the ground.

The word Hiddekel in the Syriac is applied to the Euphrates River; in the Vulgate, Greek, and Arabic, to the Tigris; therefore some conclude that the prophet had this vision where these rivers unite, near the Persian Gulf.

A most majestic being visited Daniel on this occasion. The description here given of him is almost parallel to the description of Christ in Revelation 1: 14-16. Also, since the effect on Daniel was similar to that experienced by Paul and his companions when the Lord appeared to them on the road to Damascus (Acts 9: 1-7), we conclude that Christ Himself appeared to Daniel. We learn in verse 13 that Michael had come to assist Gabriel in influencing the Persian king. How natural then that He should show Himself to Daniel on this occasion.

VERSE 10 And, behold, an hand touched me, which set me upon my knees and upon the palms of my hands. 11 And he said unto me, O Daniel, a man greatly beloved, understand the words that I speak unto thee, and stand upright: for unto thee am I now sent. And when he had spoken this word unto me, I stood trembling. 12 Then said he unto me, Fear not, Daniel: for from the first day that thou didst set thine heart to understand, and to chasten thyself before thy God, thy words were heard, and I am come for thy words.

Gabriel Encourages Daniel.—After Daniel had fallen at the majestic appearance of Christ, the angel Gabriel, obviously the speaker in verses 11-13, laid his hand upon him to give him assurance and confidence. He told Daniel that he was a man greatly beloved. Wonderful declaration! A member of the human family, one of the same race with us, loved, not merely in the general sense in which God loved the whole world when He gave His Son to die for mankind, but loved as an individual, and that greatly! Well might the prophet receive confidence from such a declaration as that! He tells him, moreover, that he is come for the purpose of an interview with him, and he wishes him to bring his mind into a proper state to understand his words. Being thus assured, the holy and beloved prophet stood trembling, before the angel.

"Fear not, Daniel," continued Gabriel. He had no occasion to fear before one, even though a heavenly being, who had been sent to him because he was greatly beloved, and in answer to his earnest prayer. Nor ought the people of God of any age to entertain a servile fear of any of those agents who are sent forth to minister to their salvation. There is, however, a disposition manifested among far too many to conceive of Jesus and His angels as only stern ministers of justice, rather than as beings who are earnestly working for their salvation. The presence of an angel, should he appear bodily before them, would strike them with terror, and the thought that Christ is soon to appear distresses and alarms them. We recommend to such more of that perfect love which casts out all fear.

VERSE 13 But the prince of the kingdom of Persia withstood me one and twenty days: but, lo, Michael, one of the chief princes, came to help me; and I remained there with the kings of Persia.

Gabriel Delayed by the King of Persia.—How often the prayers of God's people are heard while as yet there is no apparent answer! It was even so in this case with Daniel. The angel told him that from the *first day* he set his heart to understand, his words were heard. Yet Daniel continued to afflict his soul with fasting, and to wrestle with God for three full weeks, unaware that any respect had been paid to his petition. But why was the delay? The king of Persia withstood the angel. The answer to Daniel's prayer involved some action on the part of that king. This action he must be influenced to perform. It doubtless pertained to the work which he was to do, and had already begun to do, in behalf of the temple at Jerusalem and the Jews, his decree for the building of that temple being the first of the series which finally constituted that notable commandment to restore and build Jerusalem, at the going forth of which the great prophetic period of 2300 days was to begin. The angel was dispatched to influence him to go forward in accordance with the divine will.

How little do we realize what is going on in the unseen world in relation to human affairs! Here the curtain is for a moment lifted, and we catch a glimpse of the movements within. Daniel prays. The Creator of the universe hears. The command is issued to Gabriel to go to his relief. But the king of Persia must act before Daniel's prayer is answered, and the angel hastens to the Persian king. Satan no doubt musters his forces to oppose. They meet in the royal palace of Persia. All the motives of selfish interest and worldly policy which Satan can play upon, he doubtless uses to the best advantage to influence the king against compliance with God's will, while Gabriel brings to bear his influence in the other direction. The king struggles between conflicting emotions. He hesitates; he delays. Day after day passes away, yet Daniel prays on. The king still refuses to yield to the influence of the angel. Three weeks expire, and lo, a mightier than Gabriel joins him in the palace of the king, and then they come to Daniel to acquaint him with the progress of events. From the first, said Gabriel, your prayer was heard; but during these three weeks which you have devoted to prayer and fasting, the king of Persia has resisted my influence and prevented my coming.

Such was the effect of prayer. God has erected no barriers between Himself and His people since Daniel's time. It is still their privilege to offer up prayer as fervent and effectual as his, and, like Jacob, to have power with God, and to prevail.

Who was Michael, who here came to Gabriel's assistance? The term signifies, "He who is like God," and the Scriptures clearly show that Christ is the one who bears this name. Jude (verse 9) declares that Michael is the Archangel. This word signifies "head, or chief, angel," and in our text Gabriel calls Him "one [or, as the margin reads, *the first*] of the chief princes." There can be but one archangel, and hence it is manifestly improper to use the word in the plural as some do. The Scriptures never so use it. In 1 Thessalonians 4: 16, Paul states that when the Lord appears the second time to raise the dead, the voice of the archangel is heard. Whose voice is heard when the dead are raised?—The voice of the Son of God. (John 5: 28.) Putting these scriptures together, they prove that the dead are called from their graves by the voice of the Son of God, that the voice which is then heard is the voice of the Archangel, proving that the Archangel is the Son of God, and that the Archangel is called Michael, from which it follows that Michael is the Son of God. In the last verse of Daniel 10, He is called "your Prince," and in the first of Daniel 12, "the great Prince which standeth for the children of thy people," expressions which can appropriately be applied to Christ, but to no other being.

VERSE 14 Now I am come to make thee understand what shall befall thy people in the latter days: for yet the vision is for many days.

The expression, "yet the vision is for many days," reaching far into the future, and embracing what should befall the people of God even in the latter days, shows conclusively that the 2300 days given in that vision cannot mean literal days, but must be days of years. (See comments on Daniel 9: 25-27.)

VERSE 15 And when he had spoken such words unto me, I set my face toward the ground, and I became dumb. 16 And, behold, one like the similitude of the sons of men touched my lips: then I opened my mouth, and spake, and said unto him that stood before me, O my lord, by the vision my sorrows are turned upon me, and I have retained no strength. 17 For how can the servant of this my lord talk with this my lord? For as for me, straightway there remained no strength in me, neither is there breath left in me.

One of the most marked characteristics manifested by Daniel was the tender solicitude he felt for his people. Having come now clearly to comprehend that the vision portended long ages of oppression and suffering for the church, he was so affected by the view that his strength departed from him, his breath ceased, and the power of speech was gone. The vision of verse 16 doubtless refers to the former vision of Daniel 8.

VERSE 18 Then there came again and touched me one like the appearance of a man, and he strengthened me, 19 and said, O man greatly beloved, fear not: peace be unto thee, be strong, yea, be strong. And when he had spoken unto me, I was strengthened, and said, Let my lord speak; for thou hast strengthened me. 20 Then said he, Knowest thou wherefore I come unto thee? And now will I return to fight with the prince of Persia: and when I am gone forth, lo, the prince of Grecia shall come. 21 But I will show thee that which is noted in the Scripture of truth: and there is none that holdeth with me in these things, but Michael your Prince.

The prophet is at length strengthened to hear in full the communication which the angel has to make. Gabriel says, "Knowest thou wherefore I come unto thee?" Do you understand my purpose so that you will no more fear? He then announced his intention to return, as soon as his communication was complete, to fight with the king of Persia. The word עִם, *im*, signifying "with," is, in the Septuagint, μετά, *meta*, and signifies, not "against," but "in common with, alongside of;" that is, the angel of God would stand on the side of the Persian kingdom as long as it was in the providence of God that that kingdom should continue. "And when I am gone forth," continued Gabriel, "lo, the prince of Grecia shall come." That is, when he withdraws his support from that kingdom, and the providence of God operates in behalf of another kingdom, the prince of Grecia shall come, and the Persian monarchy shall be overthrown.

Gabriel then announced that none had an understanding with him in the matters he was about to communicate except Michael the Prince. After he had made them known to Daniel, there were four beings in the universe who possessed a knowledge of these important truths—Daniel, Gabriel, Christ, and God. Four links appear in this chain of witnesses—the first, Daniel, a member of the human family; the last, Jehovah, the God of all!

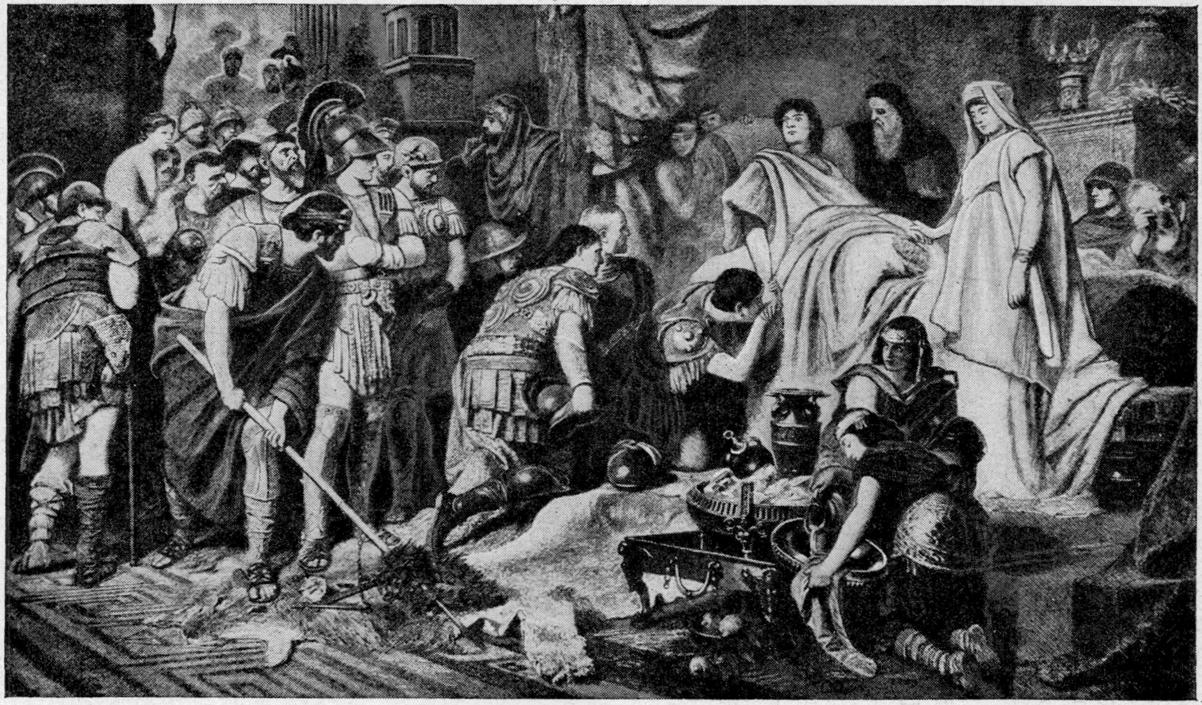

THE DEATH OF ALEXANDER THE GREAT

CHAPTER XI

UNROLLING THE SCROLL OF THE FUTURE

VERSE 1 Also I in the first year of Darius the Mede, even I, stood to confirm and to strengthen him. 2 And now will I show thee the truth. Behold, there shall stand up yet three kings in Persia; and the fourth shall be far richer than they all: and by his strength through his riches he shall stir up all against the realm of Grecia.

WE NOW enter upon a prophecy of future events, clothed not in figures and symbols, as in the visions of Daniel 2, 7, and 8, but given mostly in plain language. Many of the signal events of the world's history from the days of Daniel to the end of the world, are here brought to view. This prophecy, as Thomas Newton says, may not improperly be said to be a comment on and explanation of the vision of Daniel 8, a statement showing how clearly he perceived the connection between that vision and the rest of the book of Daniel.[1]

Daniel's Last Vision Interpreted.—The angel Gabriel, after stating that he had stood in the first year of Darius to confirm and strengthen him, turns his attention to the future. Darius was dead, and Cyrus was now reigning. Three kings would yet stand up, or reign, in Persia, doubtless the immediate successors of Cyrus. These were Cambyses, son of Cyrus; Smerdis, an impostor; and Darius Hystaspes.

Xerxes Invades Greece.—The fourth king after Cyrus was Xerxes, son of Darius Hystaspes. He was famous for his wealth, a direct fulfillment of the prophecy stating that he should be "far richer than they all." He was determined to conquer the Greeks, therefore he set about organizing a mighty army, which Herodotus says numbered 5,283,220 men.

[1] Thomas Newton, *Dissertations on the Prophecies*, Vol. I, p. 335.

Xerxes was not content to stir up the East alone. He also enlisted the support of Carthage in the West. The Persian king fought Greece successfully at the famous battle of Thermopylæ; but the mighty army was able to overrun the country only when the three hundred brave Spartans who held the pass were betrayed by traitors. Xerxes finally suffered disastrous defeat at the battle of Salamis in the year 480 B. C., and the Persian army made its way back again to its own country.

VERSE 3 And a mighty king shall stand up, that shall rule with great dominion, and do according to his will. 4 And when he shall stand up, his kingdom shall be broken, and shall be divided toward the four winds of heaven; and not to his posterity, nor according to his dominion which he ruled: for his kingdom shall be plucked up, even for others beside those.

Xerxes was the last Persian king to invade Greece; and now the prophecy passes over nine minor rulers to introduce the "mighty king," Alexander the Great.

After overthrowing the Persian Empire, Alexander "became absolute lord of that empire in the utmost extent in which it was ever possessed by any of the Persian kings."[2] His dominion comprised "the greater portion of the then-known habitable world." How well he has been described as "a mighty king, . . . that shall rule with great dominion, and do according to his will"! But he exhausted his energies in rioting and drunkenness, and when he died in 323 B. C., his vainglorious and ambitious projects went into sudden and total eclipse. The Grecian Empire did not go to Alexander's sons. Within a few years after his death, all his posterity had fallen victims to the jealousy and ambition of his leading generals, who tore the kingdom into four parts. How short is the transit from the highest pinnacle of earthly glory to the lowest depths of oblivion and death! Alexander's four leading generals—Cassander, Lysimachus, Seleucus, and Ptolemy—took possession of the empire.

---

[2] Humphrey Prideaux, *The Old and New Testament Connected in the History of the Jews*, Vol. I, p. 378.

"After the death of Antigonus [301 B. C.], the four confederated princes divided his dominions between them; and hereby the whole empire of Alexander became parted, and settled into four kingdoms. Ptolemy had Egypt, Libya, Arabia, Cœle-Syria, and Palestine; Cassander, Macedon and Greece; Lysimachus, Thrace, Bithynia, and some other of the provinces beyond the Hellespont and the Bosphorus; and Seleucus all the rest. And these four were the four horns of the he-goat mentioned in the prophecies of the prophet Daniel, which grew up after the breaking off of the first horn. That first horn was Alexander, king of Grecia, who overthrew the kingdom of the Medes and Persians; and the other four horns were these four kings, who sprung up after him, and divided the empire between them. And these also were the four heads of the leopard, spoken of in another place of the same prophecies. And their four kingdoms were the four parts, into which, according to the same prophet, the 'kingdom of the mighty king (*i. e.* of Alexander) should be broken, and divided toward (*i. e.* according to the number of) the four winds of heaven,' among those four kings, 'who should not be of his posterity,' as neither of the four above-mentioned were. And therefore, by this last partition of the empire of Alexander, were all these prophecies exactly fulfilled." [3]

VERSE 5 And the king of the south shall be strong, and one of his princes; and he shall be strong above him, and have dominion; his dominion shall be a great dominion.

King of the South.—The king of the north and the king of the south are many times referred to in the rest of this chapter. Therefore it is essential to an understanding of the prophecy to identify these powers clearly. When Alexander's empire was divided, the portions lay toward the four winds of heaven —north, south, east, and west. These divisions may well be reckoned from Palestine, the central part of the empire. That division of the empire lying west of Palestine would thus con-

[3] *Ibid.*, p. 415.

stitute the kingdom of the west; that lying north, the kingdom of the north; that lying east, the kingdom of the east; and that lying south, the kingdom of the south.

During the wars and revolutions which followed for long ages, geographical boundaries were frequently changed or obliterated; old ones were wiped out, and new ones instituted. But whatever changes might occur, these *first* divisions of the empire must determine the names which these portions of territory should ever afterward bear, or we have no standard by which to test the application of the prophecy. In other words, whatever power at any time should occupy the territory which at first constituted the kingdom of the north, that power would be king of the north as long as it occupied that territory. Whatever power should occupy that which at first constituted the kingdom of the south, that power would so long be the king of the south. We speak of only these two, because they are the only ones afterward spoken of in the prophecy, and because, in fact, almost the whole of Alexander's empire finally resolved itself into these two divisions.

The successors of Cassander were very soon conquered by Lysimachus, and his kingdom, Greece and Macedon, was annexed to Thrace. Lysimachus was in turn conquered by Seleucus, and Macedon and Thrace were annexed to Syria.

These facts prepare the way for an application of the text before us. The king of the south, Egypt, shall be strong. Ptolemy Soter annexed Cyprus, Phœnicia, Caria, Cyrene, and many islands and cities to Egypt. Thus was his kingdom made strong. But another of Alexander's princes is introduced in the expression, "one of his princes." This must refer to Seleucus Nicator, who, as already stated, by annexing Macedon and Thrace to Syria became possessor of three parts out of four of Alexander's dominion, and established a more powerful kingdom than that of Egypt.

VERSE 6 And in the end of years they shall join themselves together; for the king's daughter of the south shall come to the king of the north to make an agreement: but she shall not retain the power of the arm; neither shall he stand, nor his arm; but she shall be given up, and they that brought her, and he that begat her, and he that strengthened her in these times.

King of the North.—There were frequent wars between the kings of Egypt and of Syria. Especially was this the case with Ptolemy Philadelphus, the second king of Egypt, and Antiochus Theos, third king of Syria. They at length agreed to make peace upon condition that Antiochus should put away his former wife, Laodice, and her two sons, and should marry Berenice, the daughter of Ptolemy Philadelphus. Ptolemy accordingly brought his daughter to Antiochus, bestowing with her an immense dowry.

"But she shall not retain the power of the arm;" that is, her interest and power with Antiochus. So it proved; for shortly afterward, Antiochus brought back to the court his former wife Laodice and her children. Then says the prophecy, "Neither shall *he* [Antiochus] stand, nor his arm," or posterity. Laodice, being restored to favor and power, feared lest in the fickleness of his temper Antiochus should again disgrace her by recalling Berenice. Concluding that nothing short of his death would be an effectual safeguard against such a contingency, she caused him to be poisoned shortly afterward. Neither did his children by Berenice succeed him in the kingdom, for Laodice so managed affairs as to obtain the throne for her eldest son Seleucus Callinicus.

"But she [Berenice] shall be given up." Laodice, not content with poisoning her husband Antiochus, caused Berenice and her infant son to be murdered. "They that brought her." All of her Egyptian women and attendants, in endeavoring to defend her, were slain with her. "He that begat her," margin, "whom she brought forth," that is, her son, who was murdered at the same time by order of Laodice. "He that strengthened her in these times," was doubtless her husband, Antiochus, or those who took her part and defended her.

VERSE 7 But out of a branch of her roots shall one stand up in his estate, which shall come with an army, and shall enter into the fortress of the king of the north, and shall deal against them, and shall prevail: 8 and shall also carry captives into Egypt their gods, with their princes, and with their precious vessels of silver and of gold; and he shall continue more years than the king of the north. 9 So the king of the south shall come into his kingdom, and shall return into his own land.

The branch out of the same root with Berenice was her brother, Ptolemy Euergetes. He had no sooner succeeded his father Ptolemy Philadelphus in the kingdom of Egypt, than, burning to avenge the death of his sister Berenice, he raised an immense army and invaded the territory of the king of the north, Seleucus Callinicus, who with his mother Laodice reigned in Syria. He prevailed against them, even to the conquering of Syria, Cilicia, the upper parts beyond the Euphrates, and eastward to Babylon. But hearing that a sedition was raised in Egypt requiring his return home, he plundered the kingdom of Seleucus by taking forty thousand talents of silver and precious vessels and two thousand five hundred images of the gods. Among these were the images which Cambyses had formerly taken from Egypt and carried into Persia. The Egyptians, being wholly given to idolatry, bestowed upon Ptolemy the title Euergetes, or the Benefactor, as a compliment for restoring their captive gods after many years.

"There are authors still extant," says Thomas Newton, "who confirm several of the same particulars. Appian informs us that Laodice having killed Antiochus, and after him both Berenice and her child, Ptolemy the son of Philadelphus to revenge these murders invaded Syria, slew Laodice, and proceeded as far as to Babylon. From Polybius we learn that Ptolemy, surnamed Euergetes, being greatly incensed at the cruel treatment of his sister, Berenice, marched with an army into Syria, and took the city of Seleucia, which was kept for some years afterward by the garrisons of the kings of Egypt. Thus did he 'enter into the fortress of the king of the north.' Polyænus affirms that Ptolemy made himself master of all the country from Mount Taurus as far as to India without war or battle; but he ascribes it by mistake to the father instead of the son. Justin asserts that if Ptolemy had not been recalled by a domestic sedition into Egypt, he would have possessed the whole kingdom of Seleucus. So the king of the south came into the kingdom of the north, and then returned into his own land. He likewise 'continued more years than the king of the north;' for Seleucus Callinicus died in exile of a fall from his horse, and Ptolemy Euergetes survived him about four or five years."[4]

VERSE 10 But his sons shall be stirred up, and shall assemble a multitude of great forces: and one shall certainly come, and overflow, and pass through: then shall he return, and be stirred up, even to his fortress.

The first part of this verse speaks of sons, in the plural; the last part, of one, in the singular. The sons of Seleucus Callinicus were Seleucus Ceraunus and Antiochus Magnus. These both entered with zeal upon the work of vindicating and avenging the cause of their father and their country. The elder of these, Seleucus, first took the throne. He assembled a great multitude to recover his father's dominions; but was poisoned by his generals after a short, inglorious reign. His more capable brother, Antiochus Magnus, was thereupon proclaimed king. He took charge of the army, recovered Seleucia and Syria, and made himself master of some places by treaty and of others by force of arms. Antiochus overcame Nicolas, the Egyptian general, in battle and had thoughts of invading Egypt itself. However, a truce followed, wherein both sides treated for peace, yet prepared for war. Here is the "one" who should certainly "overflow and pass through."

VERSE 11 And the king of the south shall be moved with choler, and shall come forth and fight with him, even with the king of the north: and he shall set forth a great multitude; but the multitude shall be given into his hand.

Kings of the North and the South in Conflict.—Ptolemy Philopator succeeded his father Euergetes in the kingdom of Egypt, being advanced to the crown not long after Antiochus Magnus had succeeded his brother in the government of Syria. He was an ease-loving and vicious prince, but was at length aroused at

[4] Thomas Newton, *Dissertations on the Prophecies*, Vol. I, pp. 345, 346.

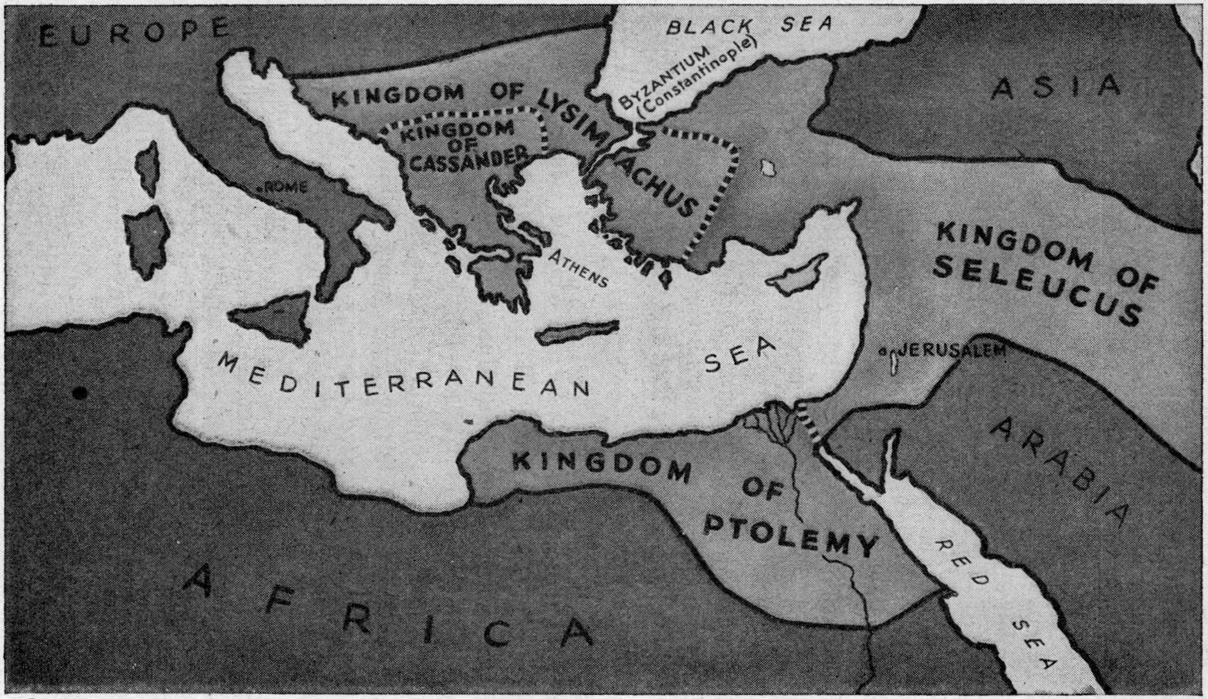

R. M. ELDRIDGE, ARTIST

ALEXANDER'S EMPIRE DIVIDED

After the death of Alexander, his empire was divided among his four generals: Lysimachus, Cassander, Seleucus, and Ptolemy.

the prospect of an invasion of Egypt by Antiochus. He was indeed "moved with choler" because of the losses he had sustained and the danger which threatened him. He marshaled a large army to check the progress of the Syrian king, but the king of the north was also "to set forth a great multitude." The army of Antiochus, according to Polybius, amounted to 62,000 footmen, 6,000 horsemen, and 102 elephants. In this conflict, the Battle of Raphia, Antiochus was defeated, with nearly 14,000 soldiers slain and 4,000 taken prisoner, and his army was given into the hands of the king of the south—a fulfillment of prophecy.

VERSE 12 And when he hath taken away the multitude, his heart shall be lifted up; and he shall cast down many ten thousands; but he shall not be strengthened by it.

Ptolemy lacked the prudence to make good use of his victory. Had he followed up his success, he would probably have become master of the whole kingdom of Antiochus; but after making only a few threats, he made peace that he might be able to give himself up to the uninterrupted and uncontrolled indulgence of his brutish passions. Thus having conquered his enemies, he was overcome by his vices, and forgetful of the great name which he might have established, he spent his time in feasting and sensuality.

His heart was lifted up by his success, but he was far from being strengthened by it, for the inglorious use he made of it caused his own subjects to rebel against him. But the lifting up of his heart was especially made manifest in his transactions with the Jews. Coming to Jerusalem, he offered sacrifices, and was desirous of entering into the most holy place of the temple contrary to the law and religion of the Jews. But being restrained with great difficulty, he left the place, burning with anger against the whole nation of the Jews, and immediately began against them a relentless persecution. In Alexandria, where Jews had resided since the days of Alexander, enjoying the privileges of the most favored citizens, forty thousand according to Eusebius, sixty thousand according to Jerome, were slain. The rebellion of the Egyptians and the massacre of the Jews certainly were not calculated to strengthen Ptolemy in his kingdom, but were sufficient rather to ruin it almost totally.

VERSE 13 For the king of the north shall return, and shall set forth a multitude greater than the former, and shall certainly come after certain years with a great army and much riches.

The events predicted in this verse were to occur "after certain years." The peace concluded between Ptolemy Philopater and Antiochus Magnus lasted fourteen years. Meanwhile Ptolemy died from intemperance and debauchery, and was succeeded by his son Ptolemy Epiphanes, then five years old. Antiochus suppressed rebellion in his kingdom during the same time, and reduced the eastern provinces to obedience. He was then at leisure for any enterprise when young Epiphanes came to the throne of Egypt. Thinking this too good an opportunity for enlarging his dominion to let slip, he raised an immense army, "greater than the former," and set out against Egypt, expecting to have an easy victory over the infant king.

VERSE 14 And in those times there shall many stand up against the king of the south: also the robbers of thy people shall exalt themselves to establish the vision; but they shall fall.

Antiochus Magnus was not the only one who rose up against the infant Ptolemy. Agathocles, his prime minister, having possession of the king's person and conducting the affairs of the kingdom in his stead, was so dissolute and proud in the exercise of his power that the provinces which before were subject to Egypt, rebelled. Egypt itself was disturbed by seditions, and the Alexandrians, rising up against Agathocles, caused him, his sister, his mother, and their associates, to be put to death. At the same time, Philip of Macedon entered into a league with Antiochus to divide the dominions of Ptolemy between them, each proposing to take the parts which lay nearest and most convenient to him. Here was a rising up against the king of the south sufficient to fulfill the prophecy, and it resulted, beyond doubt, in the exact events which the prophecy forecast.

A new power is now introduced—"the robbers of thy people;" literally, says Thomas Newton, "the sons of the breakers . . . of thy people." [5] Far away on the banks of the Tiber, a kingdom had been nourishing ambitious projects and dark designs. Small and weak at first, it grew in strength and vigor with marvelous rapidity, reaching out cautiously here and there to try its prowess and test its warlike arm, until with consciousness of its power it boldly reared its head among the nations of the earth, and seized with invincible hand the helm of affairs. Henceforth the name of Rome stands upon the page of history, destined for long ages to control the world, and to exert a mighty influence among the nations even to the end of time.

Rome spoke—and Syria and Macedonia soon found a change coming over the aspect of their dream. The Romans interfered in behalf of the young king of Egypt, determined that he should be protected from the ruin devised by Antiochus and Philip. This was 200 B. C., and was one of the first important interferences of the Romans in the affairs of Syria and Egypt. Rollin furnishes the following succinct account of this matter:

"Antiochus, king of Syria, and Philip, king of Macedonia, during the reign of Ptolemy Philopator, had discovered the strongest zeal for the interest of that monarch, and were ready to assist him on all occasions. Yet no sooner was he dead, leaving behind him an infant, whom the laws of humanity and justice enjoined them not to disturb in the possession of his father's kingdom, than they immediately join in a criminal alliance, and excite each other to take off the lawful heir, and divide his dominions between them. Philip was to have Caria, Libya, Cyrenaica, and Egypt; and Antiochus, all the rest. With this view, the latter entered Cœle-Syria and Palestine,

[5] Thomas Newton, *Dissertations on the Prophecies*, Vol. I, p. 352.

and in less than two campaigns made an entire conquest of those two provinces, with all their cities and dependencies. Their guilt, says Polybius, would not have been quite so glaring, had they, like tyrants, endeavored to gloss over their crimes with some specious pretense; but so far from doing this, their injustice and cruelty were so barefaced, that to them was applied what is generally said of fishes, that the large ones, though of the same species, prey on the lesser. One would be tempted, continues the same author, at seeing the most sacred laws of society so openly violated, to accuse Providence of being indifferent and insensible to the most horrid crimes; but it fully justified its conduct by punishing those two kings according to their deserts; and made such an example of them as ought in all succeeding ages to deter others from following their example. For, whilst they are meditating to dispossess a weak and helpless infant of his kingdom by piecemeal, Providence raised up the Romans against them, who entirely subverted the kingdoms of Philip and Antiochus, and reduced their successors to almost as great calamities as those with which they intended to crush the infant king."[6]

"To establish the vision." The Romans more than any other people are the subject of Daniel's prophecy. Their first interference in the affairs of these kingdoms is here referred to as being the establishment, or demonstration, of the truth of the vision which predicted the existence of such a power.

"But they shall fall" is referred by some to those mentioned in the first part of the verse, who should stand up against the king of the south; others, to the robbers of Daniel's people, the Romans. It is true in either case. If those who combined against Ptolemy are referred to, all that need be said is that they did speedily fall. If it applies to the Romans, the prophecy simply pointed to the period of their final overthrow.

VERSE 15 So the king of the north shall come, and cast up a mount, and take the most fenced cities: and the arms of the south shall not withstand, neither his chosen people, neither shall there be any strength to withstand.

---

[6] Charles Rollin, *Ancient History*, Vol. V, pp. 305, 306.

The education of the young king of Egypt was entrusted by the Roman Senate to M. Emilius Lepidus, who appointed Aristomenes, an old and experienced minister of that court, to be his guardian. His first act was to provide against the threatened invasion of the two confederated kings, Philip and Antiochus.

To this end he dispatched Scopas, a famous general of Ætolia then in the service of the Egyptians, into his native country to raise reinforcements for the army. After equipping an army, he marched into Palestine and Cœle-Syria (Antiochus being engaged in a war with Attalus in Lesser Asia), and reduced all Judea to the authority of Egypt.

Thus affairs were brought about for the fulfillment of the verse before us. Desisting from his war with Attalus at the dictation of the Romans, Antiochus took speedy steps for the recovery of Palestine and Cœle-Syria from the hands of the Egyptians. Scopas was sent to oppose him. Near the sources of the Jordan, the two armies met. Scopas was defeated, pursued to Sidon, and there closely besieged. Three of the ablest generals of Egypt, with their best forces, were sent to raise the siege, but without success. At length Scopas, meeting a foe in the specter of famine with which he was unable to cope, was forced to surrender on the dishonorable terms of life only. He and his ten thousand men were permitted to depart, stripped and destitute. Here was the taking of the "most fenced cities by the king of the north, for Sidon was in its situation and defenses one of the strongest cities of those times. Here was the failure of the arms of the south to withstand, and the failure also of the people which the king of the south had chosen; namely, Scopas and his Ætolian forces.

VERSE 16 But he that cometh against him shall do according to his own will, and none shall stand before him: and he shall stand in the glorious land, which by his hand shall be consumed.

Rome Conquers Syria and Palestine.—Although Egypt had not been able to stand before Antiochus Magnus, the king of the north, Antiochus Asiaticus could not stand before the Romans, who came against him. No kingdoms could resist this rising power. Syria was conquered, and added to the Roman Empire, when Pompey in 65 B. C. deprived Antiochus Asiaticus of his possessions and reduced Syria to a Roman province.

The same power was also to stand in the Holy Land, and consume it. The Romans became connected with the people of God, the Jews, by alliance in 161 B. C. From this date Rome held a prominent place in the prophetic calendar. It did not, however, acquire jurisdiction over Judea by actual conquest until 63 B. C.

On Pompey's return from his expedition against Mithridates Eupator, king of Pontus, two competitors, sons of the high priest of the Jews in Palestine, Hyrcanus and Aristobulus, were struggling for the crown of Judea. Their cause came before Pompey, who soon perceived the injustice of the claims of Aristobulus, but he wished to defer decision in the matter until after his long-desired expedition into Arabia. He promised then to return, and settle their affairs as should seem just and proper. Aristobulus, fathoming Pompey's real sentiments, hastened back to Judea, armed his subjects, and prepared for a vigorous defense, determined at all hazards to keep the crown which he foresaw would be adjudicated to another. After his Arabian campaign against King Aretas, Pompey learned of these warlike preparations and marched on Judea. As he approached Jerusalem, Aristobulus, beginning to repent of his course, came out to meet Pompey, and endeavored to arrange matters by promising entire submission and large sums of money. Accepting this offer, Pompey sent Gabinius at the head of a detachment of soldiers, to receive the money. But when that lieutenant arrived at Jerusalem, he found the gates shut against him, and was told from the top of the walls that the city would not stand by the agreement.

Not to be deceived in this way with impunity, Pompey put Aristobulus in irons, and immediately marched against Jerusalem with his whole army. The partisans of Aristobulus were for defending the city; those of Hyrcanus, for opening the gates. The latter, however, being in the majority, prevailed, and Pompey was given free entrance into the city. Whereupon the adherents of Aristobulus retired to the temple fortress, as fully determined to defend that place as Pompey was to reduce it. At the end of three months a breach was made in the wall sufficient for an assault, and the place was carried at the point of the sword. In the terrible slaughter that ensued, twelve thousand persons were slain. It was an affecting sight, observes the historian, to see the priests, engaged at the time in divine service, with calm hand and steady purpose pursue their accustomed work, apparently unconscious of the wild tumult, until their own blood was mingled with that of the sacrifices they were offering.

After putting an end to the war, Pompey demolished the walls of Jerusalem, transferred several cities from the jurisdiction of Judea to that of Syria, and imposed tribute on the Jews. For the first time Jerusalem was by conquest placed in the hands of Rome, that power which was to hold the "glorious land" in its iron grasp till it had utterly consumed it.

VERSE 17 He shall also set his face to enter with the strength of his whole kingdom, and upright ones with him; thus shall he do: and he shall give him the daughter of women, corrupting her: but she shall not stand on his side, neither be for him.

Thomas Newton furnishes another reading for this verse, which seems to express more clearly the meaning: "He shall also set his face to enter by force the whole kingdom."[7]

Rome Overruns the Kingdom of the South.—Verse 16 brought us to the conquest of Syria and Judea by the Romans. Rome had previously conquered Macedon and Thrace. Egypt was now all that remained of the "whole kingdom" of Alexander which had not been brought into subjection to the Roman power. Rome now set her face to enter by force into the land of Egypt.

Ptolemy Auletes died in 51 B. C. He left the crown and kingdom of Egypt to his eldest surviving daughter, Cleopatra,

[7] Thomas Newton, *Dissertations on the Prophecies*, Vol. I, p. 356.

and his elder son, Ptolemy XII, a lad of nine or ten years. It was provided in his will that they should marry each other and reign jointly. Because they were young, they were placed under the guardianship of the Romans. The Roman people accepted the charge, and appointed Pompey as guardian of the young heirs of Egypt.

Soon a quarrel broke out between Pompey and Julius Cæsar, which reached its climax in the famous battle of Pharsalus. Pompey, being defeated, fled into Egypt. Cæsar immediately followed him thither; but before his arrival Pompey was basely murdered at the instigation of Ptolemy. Cæsar now assumed the guardianship of Ptolemy and Cleopatra. He found Egypt in commotion from internal disturbances, for Ptolemy and Cleopatra had become hostile to each other, since she had been deprived of her share in the government.

The troubles daily increasing, Cæsar found his small force insufficient to maintain his position, and being unable to leave Egypt on account of the north wind which blew at that season, he sent into Asia for all the troops he had in that region.

Julius Cæsar decreed that Ptolemy and Cleopatra should disband their armies, appear before him for a settlement of their differences, and abide by his decision. Since Egypt was an independent kingdom, this haughty decree was considered an affront to its royal dignity, and the Egyptians, highly incensed, took up arms. Cæsar replied that he acted by the authority of the will of their father, Ptolemy Auletes, who had put his children under the guardianship of the senate and people of Rome.

The matter was finally brought before him, and advocates appointed to plead the cause of the respective parties. Cleopatra, aware of the foible of the great Roman general, decided to appear before him in person. To reach his presence undetected, she had recourse to the following stratagem: She laid herself at full length in a carpet and, Apollodorus, her Sicilian servant, wrapped her up in a cloth, tied the bundle with a thong, and raising it upon his Herculean shoulders, sought the apartments of Cæsar. Claiming to have a present for the Roman general, he was admitted into the presence of Cæsar, and deposited the burden at his feet. When Cæsar unbound this animated bundle, the beautiful Cleopatra stood before him.

Of this incident F. E. Adcock writes: "Cleopatra had a right to be heard if Cæsar was to be judge, and she contrived to reach the city and to find a boatman to take her to him. She came, saw, and conquered. To the military difficulties of withdrawal in the face of the Egyptian army was added the fact that Cæsar no longer wished to go. He was past fifty, but he retained an imperious susceptibility which evoked the admiration of his soldiers. Cleopatra was twenty-two, as ambitious and high-mettled as Cæsar himself, a woman whom he would find it easy to understand and admire as well as to love."[8]

Cæsar at length decreed that the brother and the sister should occupy the throne jointly, according to the intent of the will. Pothinus, the chief minister of state, principally instrumental in expelling Cleopatra from the throne, feared the result of her restoration. He therefore began to excite jealousy and hostility against Cæsar by insinuating among the populace that he designed eventually to give Cleopatra the sole power. Open sedition soon followed. The Egyptians undertook to destroy the Roman fleet. Cæsar retorted by burning theirs. Some of the burning vessels being driven near the quay, several of the buildings of the city took fire, and the famous Alexandrian library, containing nearly 400,000 volumes, was destroyed. Antipater the Idumean joined him with 3,000 Jews. The Jews, who held the frontier gateways into Egypt, permitted the Roman army to pass without interruption. The arrival of this army of Jews under Antipater helped decide the contest.

---

[8] *The Cambridge Ancient History*, Vol. IX, p. 670. By permission of the Macmillan Company, publishers in the United States.

J. L. JEROME, ARTIST

THE DEATH OF JULIUS CÆSAR

After expanding his dominion over vast areas, Cæsar met his death in a conspiracy in the Roman senate.

A decisive battle was fought near the Nile by the fleets of Egypt and Rome, resulting in a complete victory for Cæsar. Ptolemy, attempting to escape, was drowned in the river. Alexandria and all Egypt then submitted to the victor. Rome had now entered into and absorbed the entire original kingdom of Alexander.

By the "upright ones" of the text are doubtless meant the Jews, who gave Cæsar the assistance already mentioned. Without this, he must have failed; with it, he completely subdued Egypt in 47 B. C.

"The daughter of women, corrupting her" was Cleopatra, who had been Cæsar's mistress and was the mother of his son. His infatuation for the queen kept him much longer in Egypt than his affairs required. He spent whole nights in feasting and carousing with the dissolute queen. "But," said the prophet, "she shall not stand on his side, neither be for him." Cleopatra afterward joined herself to Antony, the enemy of Augustus Cæsar, and exerted her whole power against Rome.

VERSE 18 After this shall he turn his face unto the isles, and shall take many: but a prince for his own behalf shall cause the reproach offered by him to cease; without his own reproach he shall cause it to turn upon him.

War in Syria and Asia Minor against Pharnaces, king of the Cimmerian Bosphorus, drew Julius Cæsar away from Egypt. "On his arrival where the enemy was," says Prideaux, "he, without giving any respite either to himself or them, immediately fell on, and gained an absolute victory over them; an account whereof he wrote to a friend of his in these three words: *Veni, vidi, vici!* 'I came, I saw, I overcame.'"[9] The latter part of this verse is involved in some obscurity, and there is difference of opinion in regard to its application. Some apply it further back in Cæsar's life, and think they find a fulfillment in his quarrel with Pompey. But preceding and subsequent events clearly defined in the prophecy, compel us to look for the fulfillment of this part of the prediction between the

[9] Humphrey Prideaux, *The Old and New Testament Connected in the History of the Jews*, Vol. II, p. 312.

victory over Pharnaces, and Cæsar's death at Rome, as brought to view in the following verse.

VERSE 19 Then he shall turn his face toward the fort of his own land: but he shall stumble and fall, and not be found.

After his conquest of Asia Minor, Cæsar defeated the last remaining fragments of Pompey's party, Cato and Scipio in Africa, and Labienus and Varus in Spain. Returning to Rome, the "fort of his own land," he was made dictator for life. Other powers and honors were granted him which made him in fact the absolute sovereign of the empire. But the prophet had said that he should stumble and fall. The language implies that his overthrow would be sudden and unexpected, like a person accidentally stumbling in his walk. So this man, who it is said had fought and won fifty battles, taken one thousand cities, and slain one million one hundred ninety-two thousand men, fell, not in the din of battle and the hour of strife, but when he thought his pathway was smooth and danger far away.

"On the evening before the Ides Cæsar dined with Lepidus, and as the guests sat at their wine someone asked the question, 'What is the best death to die?' Cæsar who was busy signing letters said, 'A sudden one.' By noon the next day, despite dreams and omens, he sat in his chair in the Senate House, surrounded by men he had cared for, had promoted, or had spared, and was struck down, struggling, till he fell dead at the foot of Pompey's statue."[10] Thus he suddenly stumbled and fell, and was not found, in 44 B.C.

VERSE 20 Then shall stand up in his estate a raiser of taxes in the glory of the kingdom: but within few days he shall be destroyed, neither in anger, nor in battle.

Augustus the Raiser of Taxes Appears.—Octavius succeeded his uncle, Julius, by whom he had been adopted. He publicly announced his adoption by his uncle, and took his name. He

[10] *The Cambridge Ancient History*, Vol. IX, p. 738. By permission of the Macmillan Company, publishers in the United States.

joined Mark Antony and Lepidus to avenge the death of Julius Cæsar. The three formed what is called the *triumvirate* form of government. After Octavius was firmly established in the empire, the senate conferred upon him the title "Augustus," and the other members of the triumvirate now being dead, he became supreme ruler.

He was emphatically a raiser of taxes. Luke, speaking of events that took place at the time when Christ was born, says: "It came to pass in those days, that there went out a decree from Cæsar Augustus, that all the world should be taxed." Luke 2: 1. That taxing which embraced all the world was an event worthy of notice, for the person who enforced it has certainly a claim above every other competitor to the title of "a raiser of taxes." During the reign of Augustus "fresh taxation was imposed, one quarter of the annual income from all citizens and a capital levy of one eighth on all freedmen."[11]

He stood up "in the glory of the kingdom." Rome reached the pinnacle of its greatness and power during the "Augustan Age." The empire never saw a brighter hour. Peace was promoted, justice maintained, luxury curbed, discipline established, and learning encouraged. During his reign, the temple of Janus was shut three times, signifying that all the world was at peace. Since the founding of the Roman Empire this temple had been closed but twice previously. At this auspicious hour our Lord was born in Bethlehem of Judea. In a little less than eighteen years after the taxing brought to view, seeming but a "few days" to the distant gaze of the prophet, Augustus died in A. D. 14, in the seventy-sixth year of his age. His life ended not in anger or in battle, but peacefully in his bed, at Nola, whither he had gone to seek repose and health.

VERSE 21 And in his estate shall stand up a vile person, to whom they shall not give the honor of the kingdom: but he shall come in peaceably, and obtain the kingdom by flatteries.

---

[11] *Ibid.*, Vol. X, pp. 96, 97.

MERSON, ARTIST

AUGUSTUS CÆSAR THE TAX COLLECTOR

To be enrolled for taxation, Joseph and Mary went from Nazareth to Bethlehem, where Jesus was born in fulfillment of prophecy.

Tiberius Cuts Off the Prince of the Covenant.—Tiberius Cæsar followed Augustus on the Roman throne. He was raised to the consulate at the age of twenty-nine. It is recorded that as Augustus was about to nominate his successor, his wife, Livia, besought him to nominate Tiberius, her son by a former husband. But the emperor said, "Your son is too *vile* to wear the purple of Rome." Instead, the nomination was given to Agrippa, a virtuous and much-respected Roman citizen. But the prophecy had foreseen that a vile person should succeed Augustus. Agrippa died; and Augustus was again under the necessity of choosing a successor. Livia renewed her intercessions for Tiberius, and Augustus, weakened by age and sickness, was more easily flattered, and finally he consented to nominate that "vile" young man as his colleague and successor. But the citizens never gave him the love, respect, and "honor of the kingdom" due to an upright and faithful sovereign.

How clear a fulfillment is this of the prediction that they should not give him the honor of the kingdom. But he was to come in peaceably, and obtain the kingdom by flatteries. A paragraph from the *Encyclopædia Americana* shows how this was fulfilled:

"During the remainder of the life of Augustus, he [Tiberius] behaved with great prudence and ability, concluding a war with the Germans in such a manner as to merit a triumph. After the defeat of Varus and his legions, he was sent to check the progress of the victorious Germans, and acted in that war with equal spirit and prudence. On the death of Augustus, he succeeded (A. D. 14), without opposition, to the sovereignty of the empire; which, however, with his characteristic dissimulation, he affected to decline, until repeatedly solicited by the servile senate."[12]

Dissimulation on his part, flattery on the part of the "servile senate," and a possession of the kingdom without

---

[12] *Encyclopædia Americana*, 1849 ed., Vol. XII, p. 251, art. "Tiberius."

opposition were the circumstances attending his accession to the throne, thus fulfilling the words of the prophecy.

The person brought to view in the text is called "a vile person." Was such the character sustained by Tiberius? Let another paragraph from the *Encyclopædia Americana* answer:

"Tacitus records the events of this reign, including the suspicious death of Germanicus, the detestable administration of Sejanus, the poisoning of Drusus, with all the extraordinary mixture of tyranny with occasional wisdom and good sense which distinguished the conduct of Tiberius, until his infamous and dissolute retirement (A. D 26), to the isle of Capreæ, in the bay of Naples, never to return to Rome. . . . The remainder of the reign of this tyrant is little more than a disgusting narrative of servility on the one hand, and of despotic ferocity on the other. That he himself endured as much misery as he inflicted, is evident from the following commencement of one of his letters to the senate: 'What I shall write to you, conscript fathers, or what I shall not write, or why I should write at all, may the gods and goddesses plague me more than I feel daily that they are doing, if I can tell.' 'What mental torture,' observes Tacitus, in reference to this passage, 'which could extort such a confession!' "[13]

Tyranny, hypocrisy, debauchery, and uninterrupted intoxication—if these traits and practices show a man to be vile, Tiberius exhibited that character to perfection.

VERSE 22 And with the arms of a flood shall they be overflown from before him, and shall be broken; yea, also the Prince of the covenant.

Thomas Newton presents the following reading of the text as a more accurate translation of the original: "And the arms of the overflower shall be overflown from before him, and shall be broken."[14] This signifies revolution and violence; and in fulfillment we should look for the arms of Tiberius the overflower to be overflown, or, in other words, for him to suffer a

---

[13] *Ibid.*

[14] Thomas Newton, *Dissertations on the Prophecies*, Vol. I, p. 363.

violent death. To show how this was accomplished, we again cite the *Encyclopædia Americana:*

"Acting the hypocrite to the last, he disguised his increasing debility as much as he was able, even affecting to join in the sports and exercises of the soldiers of his guard. At length, leaving his favorite island, the scene of the most disgusting debaucheries, he stopped at a country house near the promontory of Micenum, where, on the sixteenth of March, 37, he sunk into a lethargy, in which he appeared dead; and Caligula was preparing with a numerous escort to take possession of the empire, when his sudden revival threw them into consternation. At this critical instant, Macro, the pretorian prefect, caused him to be *suffocated with pillows.* Thus expired the emperor Tiberius, in the seventy-eighth year of his age, and twenty-third of his reign, universally execrated."[15]

After taking us down to the death of Tiberius, the prophet now mentions an event to take place during his reign which is so important that it should not be passed over. It is the cutting off of the "Prince of the covenant," or the death of our Lord Jesus Christ, "the Messiah the Prince," who was to "confirm the covenant" one week with His people. (Daniel 9: 25-27.)

According to the Scripture, Christ's death took place in the reign of Tiberius. Luke informs us that in the fifteenth year of the reign of Tiberius Cæsar, John the Baptist began his ministry. (Luke 3: 1-3.) According to Prideaux,[16] Dr. Hales,[17] and others, the reign of Tiberius is to be reckoned from his elevation to the throne to reign jointly with Augustus, his stepfather, in August, A. D. 12. His fifteenth year would therefore be from August, A. D. 26, to August, A. D. 27. Christ was six months younger than John, and is supposed to have begun His ministry six months later, both, according to the law of the priesthood, entering upon their work when they were thirty years of age. If John began in the spring, in the

[15] *Encyclopædia Americana*, 1849 ed., Vol. XII, pp. 251, 252, art. "Tiberius."

[16] Humphrey Prideaux, *The Old and New Testament Connected in the History of the Jews*, Vol. II, p. 423.

[17] William Hales, *A New Analysis of Chronology*, Vol. III, p. 1.

latter part of the fifteenth year of Tiberius, it would bring the beginning of Christ's ministry in the autumn of A. D. 27. Right here the best authorities place the baptism of Christ, the exact point where the 483 years from 457 B. C., which were to extend to the Messiah the Prince, terminated. Christ then went forth proclaiming that the time was fulfilled. From this point we go forward three years and a half to find the date of the crucifixion, for Christ attended but four Passovers, and was crucified at the last one. Three and a half years from the autumn of A. D. 27 brings us to the spring of A. D. 31. The death of Tiberius is placed but six years later, in A. D. 37. (See comments on Daniel 9: 25-27.)

VERSE 23 And after the league made with him he shall work deceitfully: for he shall come up, and shall become strong with a small people.

Rome Makes a League With the Jews.—The "him" with whom the league is made, must be the same power which has been the subject of the prophecy from the 14th verse, the Roman Empire. That this is true has been shown in the fulfillment of the prophecy in the three individuals who successively ruled over the empire—Julius, Augustus, and Tiberius Cæsar.

Now that the prophet has taken us through the secular events of the Roman Empire to the end of the seventy weeks of Daniel 9: 24, he takes us back to the time when the Romans became directly connected with the people of God by the Jewish league in 161 B. C. From this point we are then taken through a direct line of events to the final triumph of the church and the setting up of God's everlasting kingdom. Grievously oppressed by the Syrian kings, the Jews sent an embassy to Rome to solicit the aid of the Romans and to join themselves in "a league of amity and confederacy with them." [18] The Romans listened to the request of the Jews, and granted them a decree couched in these words:

---

[18] See 1 Maccabees 8; Humphrey Prideaux, *The Old and New Testament Connected in the History of the Jews*, Vol. II, p. 166.

" 'The decree of the senate concerning a league of assistance and friendship with the nation of the Jews. It shall not be lawful for any that are subject to the Romans to make war with the nation of the Jews, nor to assist those that do so, either by sending them corn, or ships, or money; and if any attack be made upon the Jews, the Romans shall assist them, as far as they are able; and again, if any attack be made upon the Romans, the Jews shall assist them. And if the Jews have a mind to add to, or to take away anything from, this league of assistance, that shall be done with the common consent of the Romans. And whatsoever addition shall thus be made, it shall be of force.' This decree "was written by Eupolemus, the son of John, and by Jason, the son of Eleazer, when Judas was high priest of the nation, and Simon, his brother, was general of the army. And this was the first league that the Romans made with the Jews, and was managed after this manner."[19]

At this time the Romans were a small people, and began to work deceitfully, or with cunning, as the word signifies. But from this time they rose steadily and rapidly to the height of power.

VERSE 24 He shall enter peaceably even upon the fattest places of the province; and he shall do that which his fathers have not done, nor his fathers' fathers; he shall scatter among them the prey, and spoil, and riches: yea, and he shall forecast his devices against the strongholds, even for a time.

Before the days of Rome, nations entered upon valuable provinces and rich territory by war and conquest. Rome was now to do what had not been done by the fathers or the fathers' fathers, namely, receive these acquisitions through peaceful means. The custom was now inaugurated of kings' leaving their kingdoms to the Romans by legacy. Rome came into possession of large provinces in this manner.

Those who thus came under the dominion of Rome derived no small advantage. They were treated with kindness and leniency. It was like having the prey and spoil distributed

---

[19] Flavius Josephus, "Antiquities of the Jews," book 12, chap. 10, sec. 6, *The Works of Flavius Josephus*, p. 374.

among them. They were protected from their enemies, and they rested in peace and safety under the ægis of the Roman power.

To the latter part of this verse, Thomas Newton gives the thought of forecasting devices *from* strongholds, instead of *against* them. This the Romans did from the strong fortress of their seven-hilled city. "Even for a time" doubtless refers to a prophetic time, 360 years. From what point are these years to be dated? Probably from the event brought to view in the following verse.

VERSE 25 And he shall stir up his power and his courage against the king of the south with a great army; and the king of the south shall be stirred up to battle with a very great and mighty army; but he shall not stand: for they shall forecast devices against him.

Rome Contends With the King of the South.—By verses 23 and 24 we are brought down this side of the league made between the Jews and the Romans, in 161 B. C., to the time when Rome had acquired universal dominion. The verse now before us brings to view a vigorous campaign against the king of the south, Egypt, and a notable battle between mighty armies. Did such events as these take place in the history of Rome about this time?—They did. The war was the war between Egypt and Rome, and the battle was the battle of Actium. Let us consider briefly the circumstances leading to this conflict.

Mark Antony, Augustus Cæsar, and Lepidus constituted the triumvirate which had sworn to avenge the death of Julius Cæsar. Antony became the brother-in-law of Augustus by marrying his sister Octavia. Antony was sent into Egypt on government business, but fell a victim to the charms of Cleopatra, Egypt's dissolute queen. So strong was the passion he conceived for her that he finally espoused the Egyptian interests, rejected his wife Octavia to please Cleopatra, and bestowed province after province upon her. He celebrated triumphs at Alexandria instead of at Rome, and otherwise so affronted the Roman people that Augustus had no difficulty in leading them to engage heartily in a war against Egypt. This war was ostensibly against Egypt and Cleopatra, but it was really against Antony, who now stood at the head of Egyptian affairs. The true cause of their controversy, says Prideaux, was that neither of them could be content with only half of the Roman Empire. Lepidus had been deposed from the triumvirate, and the rule of the empire now lay between the other two. Each being determined to possess the whole, they cast the die of war for its possession.

Antony assembled his fleet at Samos. Five hundred ships of war of extraordinary size and structure, having several decks one above another, with towers upon the head and stern, made an imposing and formidable array. These ships carried about one hundred twenty-five thousand soldiers. The kings of Libya, Cilicia, Cappadocia, Paphlagonia, Comagena, and Thrace, were there in person, and those of Pontus, Judea, Lycaonia, Galatia, and Media, had sent their troops. A more splendid military spectacle than this fleet of war ships as they spread their sails and moved out to sea, the world has rarely seen. Surpassing all in magnificence came the galley of Cleopatra, floating like a palace of gold beneath a cloud of purple sails. Its flags and streamers fluttered in the wind, and trumpets and other musical instruments of war made the heavens resound with notes of joy and triumph. Antony followed close behind her in a galley of almost equal magnificence.

Augustus, on the other hand, displayed less pomp but more utility. He had but half as many ships as Antony, and only eighty thousand foot soldiers. But all his troops were chosen men, and on board his fleet were none but experienced seamen; whereas Antony, not finding sufficient mariners, had been obliged to man his vessels with artisans of every class, men inexperienced and better calculated to cause trouble than to do real service in time of battle. The season being far consumed in these preparations, Augustus made his rendezvous at Brundusium, and Antony at Corcyra, till the following year.

The next spring, both armies were put in motion on land and sea. The fleets at length entered the Ambracian Gulf in Epirus, and the land forces were drawn up on either shore in plain view. Antony's most experienced generals advised him not to hazard a battle by sea with his inexperienced mariners, but send Cleopatra back to Egypt, and hasten at once into Thrace or Macedonia, and trust the issue to his land forces, who were composed of veteran troops. But illustrating the old adage, *Quem Deus perdere vult, prius dementat* ("Him whom God wishes to destroy He first makes mad"), and infatuated by Cleopatra, he seemed desirous only of pleasing her; while she, trusting to appearances only, deemed her fleet invincible, and advised immediate action.

The battle was fought September 2, 31 B. C., at the mouth of the gulf of Ambracia, near the city of Actium. The world was the stake for which these stern warriors, Antony and Augustus, now played. The contest, long doubtful, was at length decided by the course which Cleopatra pursued. Frightened at the din of battle, she took to flight when there was no danger, and drew after her the Egyptian squadron numbering sixty ships. Antony, beholding this movement, and lost to everything but his blind passion for her, precipitately followed, and yielded a victory to Augustus, which, had his Egyptian forces proved true to him, and had he proved true to his own manhood, he might have gained.

This battle doubtless marks the beginning of the "time" mentioned in verse 24. As during this "time" devices were to be forecast from the stronghold, or Rome, we should conclude that at the end of that period western supremacy would cease, or such a change take place in the empire that that city would no longer be considered the seat of government. From 31 B. C., a prophetic "time," or 360 years, would bring us to A. D. 330. Hence it becomes a noteworthy fact that the seat of empire was removed from Rome to Constantinople by Constantine the Great in that very year.[20]

---

[20] See *Encyclopædia Britannica*, 11th edition, Vol. VII, p. 3, art., "Constantinople."

VERSE 26 Yea, they that feed of the portion of his meat shall destroy him, and his army shall overflow: and many shall fall down slain.

Antony was deserted by his allies and friends, those that fed "of the portion of his meat." Cleopatra as already described suddenly withdrew from the battle, taking sixty ships of the line with her. The land army, disgusted with the infatuation of Antony, went over to Augustus, who received the soldiers with open arms. When Antony arrived at Libya, he found that the forces which he had left there under Scarpus to guard the frontier, had declared for Augustus, and in Egypt his forces surrendered. In rage and despair, Antony then took his own life.

VERSE 27 And both these kings' hearts shall be to do mischief, and they shall speak lies at one table; but it shall not prosper: for yet the end shall be at the time appointed.

Antony and Augustus were formerly in alliance. Yet under the garb of friendship, they were both aspiring and intriguing for universal dominion. Their protestations of friendship for each other were the utterances of hypocrites. They spoke lies at one table. Octavia, the wife of Antony and sister of Augustus, declared to the people of Rome at the time Antony divorced her, that she had consented to marry him solely with the hope that it would prove a pledge of union between Augustus and Antony. But that counsel did not prosper. The rupture came, and in the conflict that ensued Augustus was entirely victorious.

VERSE 28 Then shall he return into his land with great riches; and his heart shall be against the holy covenant; and he shall do exploits, and return to his own land.

Two returnings from foreign conquest are here brought to view. The first was after the events narrated in verses 26, 27, and the second, after this power had had indignation against the holy covenant, and had performed exploits. The first was fulfilled in the return of Augustus after his expedition against Egypt and Antony. He arrived in Rome with abundant honor and riches, for "at this time such vast riches were brought to Rome from Egypt on the reducing of that country, and the return of Octavianus [Augustus] and his army from thence, that the value of money fell one half, and the prices of provisions and all vendible wares were doubled thereon."[21]

Augustus celebrated his victories in a three-days' triumph —a triumph which Cleopatra herself would have graced as one of the royal captives, had she not artfully caused herself to be bitten fatally by an asp.

Rome Destroys Jerusalem.—The next great enterprise of the Romans after the overthrow of Egypt, was the expedition against Judea and the capture and destruction of Jerusalem. The holy covenant is doubtless the covenant which God has maintained with His people under different forms in different ages of the world. The Jews rejected Christ, and according to the prophecy that all who would not hear that Prophet should be cut off, they were destroyed out of their own land and scattered to every nation under heaven. While Jews and Christians alike suffered under the oppressive hand of the Romans, it was doubtless in the reduction of Judea especially that the exploits which are mentioned in the sacred text were exhibited.

Under Vespasian the Romans invaded Judea, and took the cities of Galilee, Chorazin, Bethsaida, and Capernaum, where Christ had been rejected. They destroyed the inhabitants, and left nothing but ruin and desolation. Titus besieged Jerusalem, and drew a trench around it, according to the prediction of the Saviour. A terrible famine ensued. Moses had predicted that appalling calamities would come upon the Jews if they departed from God. It had been prophesied that even the tender and delicate woman would eat her own children in the straitness of the siege. (Deuteronomy 28: 52-55.) Under the siege of Jerusalem by Titus, a literal fulfillment of this prediction occurred. Hearing of the inhuman deeds, but forget-

[21] Humphrey Prideaux, ***The Old and New Testament Connected in the History of the Jews,*** **Vol. II, p. 380.**

E. J. POYNTER. ARTIST

THE DESTRUCTION OF JERUSALEM IN A. D. 70

Using battering rams, the Romans fulfilled Christ's prediction: "There shall not be left here one stone upon another, that shall not be thrown down." Matthew 24: 2.

ting that he was the one who was driving the people to such direful extremities, he swore the eternal extirpation of the accursed city and people.

Jerusalem fell in A. D. 70. As an honor to himself, the Roman commander had determined to save the temple, but the Lord had said, "There shall not be left here one stone upon another, that shall not be thrown down." Matthew 24: 2. A Roman soldier seized a brand of fire, and climbing upon the shoulders of his comrades, thrust it into one of the windows of the beautiful structure. It was soon ablaze, and the frantic efforts of the Jews to extinguish the flames, seconded by Titus himself, were all in vain. Seeing that the temple would be destroyed, Titus rushed in and bore away the golden candlestick, the table of showbread, and the volume of the law, wrapped in gold tissue. The candlestick was afterward deposited in Vespasian's Temple of Peace and copied on the triumphal arch of Titus, where its mutilated image is yet to be seen.

The siege of Jerusalem lasted five months. In that siege eleven hundred thousand Jews perished, and ninety-seven thousand were taken prisoners. The city was so amazingly strong that Titus exclaimed when viewing the ruins, "We have fought with the assistance of God." It was completely leveled, and the foundations of the temple were plowed up by Tarentius Rufus. The duration of the whole war was seven years, and almost a million and a half persons are said to have fallen victims to its awful horrors.

Thus this power performed great exploits, and again returned to his own land.

VERSE 29 At the time appointed he shall return, and come toward the south; but it shall not be as the former, or as the latter.

The time appointed is probably the prophetic time of verse 24, which has been previously mentioned. It closed, as already shown, in A. D. 330, at which time this power was to return and come again toward the south, but not as on the former occasion, when it went to Egypt, nor as the latter, when it went to Judea. Those were expeditions which resulted in conquest and glory. This one led to demoralization and ruin. The removal of the seat of empire to Constantinople was the signal for the downfall of the empire. Rome then lost its prestige. The western division was exposed to the incursions of foreign enemies. On the death of Constantine, the Roman Empire was divided among his three sons, Constantius, Constantine II, and Constans. Constantine II and Constans quarreled, and the victorious Constans gained the supremacy of the entire West. The barbarians of the North soon began their incursions and extended their conquests until the imperial power of the West expired in A. D. 476.

VERSE 30 For the ships of Chittim shall come against him: therefore he shall be grieved, and return, and have indignation against the holy covenant: so shall he do; he shall even return, and have intelligence with them that forsake the holy covenant.

Rome Pillaged by Barbarians.—The prophetic narrative still has reference to the power which has been the subject of the prophecy from the sixteenth verse; namely, Rome. What were the ships of Chittim that came against this power, and when was this movement made? What country or power is meant by Chittim? Adam Clarke has this note on Isaiah 23: 1, "From the land of Chittim it is revealed to them:" "The news of the destruction of Tyre by Nebuchadnezzar is said to be brought to them from Chittim, the islands and coasts of the Mediterranean; 'for the Tyrians,' says Jerome on verse 6, 'when they saw they had no other means of escaping, fled in their ships, and took refuge in Carthage and in the islands of the Ionian and Ægean sea.' . . . So also Jarchi on the same place."[22] Kitto[23] gives the same locality to Chittim, the coast and islands of the Mediterranean; and the mind is carried by the testimony of Jerome to a definite and celebrated city situated in that region, that is, Carthage.

Was a naval warfare with Carthage as a base of operations ever waged against the Roman Empire? We think of the terrible onslaught of the Vandals upon Rome under the fierce Genseric, and answer readily in the affirmative. Every spring he sallied forth from the port of Carthage at the head of his large and well-disciplined naval forces, spreading consternation through all the maritime provinces of the empire. That this is the work brought to view is further evident when we consider that we are brought down in the prophecy to this very time. In verse 29, the transfer of empire to Constantinople we understood to be mentioned. Following in due course of time as the next remarkable revolution, came the irruptions of the barbarians of the North, prominent among which was

[22] Adam Clarke, *Commentary on the Old Testament*, Vol. IV, pp. 109, 110, note on Isaiah 23: 1.

[23] See John Kitto, *Cyclopædia of Biblical Literature*, art. "Chittim," p. 196.

the Vandal war already mentioned. The years A. D. 428-477 mark the career of Genseric.

"He shall be grieved, and return" may have reference to the desperate efforts which were made to dispossess Genseric of the sovereignty of the seas, the first by Majorian, the second by Pope Leo I, both of which were utter failures. Rome was obliged to submit to the humiliation of seeing its provinces ravaged, and its "eternal city" pillaged by the enemy. (See comments on Revelation 8: 8.)

"Indignation against the holy covenant." This doubtless refers to attempts to destroy God's covenant by attacking the Holy Scriptures, the book of the covenant. A revolution of this nature was accomplished in Rome. The Heruli, Goths, and Vandals, who conquered Rome, embraced the Arian faith, and became enemies of the Catholic Church. It was especially for the purpose of exterminating this heresy that Justinian decreed the pope to be the head of the church and the corrector of heretics. The Bible soon came to be regarded as a dangerous book that should not be read by the common people, but all questions in dispute were to be submitted to the pope. Thus was indignity heaped upon God's word.

Says the historian, in commenting upon the attitude of the Catholic Church toward the Scriptures:

"One would have thought that the Church of Rome had removed her people to a safe distance from the Scriptures. She has placed the gulf of tradition between them and the Word of God. She has removed them still farther from the sphere of danger, by providing an infallible interpreter, whose duty it is to take care that the Bible shall express no sense hostile to Rome. But, as if this were not enough, she has laboured by all means in her power to prevent the Scriptures coming in any shape into the hands of her people. Before the Reformation she kept the Bible locked up in a dead language, and severe laws were enacted against the reading of it. The Reformation unsealed the precious volume. Tyndale and Luther, the one from his retreat at Vildorfe in the Low Countries, and the other from amid the deep shades of the Thuringian forest, sent forth the Bible to the nations in the vernacular tongues of England and Germany. A thirst was thus awakened for the Scriptures, which the Church of Rome deemed it imprudent openly to oppose. The Council of Trent enacted ten rules regarding prohibited books, which, while they appeared to gratify, were insidiously framed to check, the growing desire for the Word of God. In the fourth rule, the Council prohibits any one from reading the Bible without a license from his bishop or inquisitor; that license to be founded on a certificate from his confessor that he is in no danger of receiving injury from so doing. The Council adds these emphatic words:—'That if any one shall dare to read or keep in his possession that book, without such a license, he shall not receive absolution till he has given it up to his ordinary.' These rules are followed by the bull of Pius IV., in which he declares that those who shall violate them shall be held guilty of mortal sin. Thus did the Church of Rome attempt to regulate what she found it impossible wholly to prevent. The fact that no Papist is allowed to read the Bible without a license does not appear in the catechisms and other books in common use among Roman Catholics in this country; but it is incontrovertible that it forms the law of that Church. And, in accordance therewith, we find that the uniform practice of the priests of Rome, from the popes downwards, is to prevent the circulation of the Bible,—to prevent it wholly in those countries, such as Italy and Spain, where they have the power, and in other countries, such as our own, to all the extent to which their power enables them. Their uniform policy is to discourage the reading of the Scriptures in every possible way; and when they dare not employ force to effect this object, they scruple not to press into their service the ghostly power of their Church, by declaring that those who presume to contravene the will of Rome in this matter are guilty of mortal sin."[24]

---

[24] J. A. Wylie, *The Papacy*, pp. 180, 181.

The emperors of Rome, the eastern division of which still continued, had intelligence, or connived, with the church of Rome, which had forsaken the covenant and constituted the great apostasy, for the purpose of putting down "heresy." The man of sin was raised to his presumptuous throne by the defeat of the Arian Goths, who then held possession of Rome, in A. D. 538.

VERSE 31 And arms shall stand on his part, and they shall pollute the sanctuary of strength, and shall take away the daily sacrifice, and they shall place the abomination that maketh desolate.

They shall pollute the sanctuary of strength," or Rome. If this applies to the barbarians, it was literally fulfilled; for Rome was sacked by the Goths and Vandals, and the imperial power of the West ceased through the conquest of Rome by Odoacer. Or if it refers to those rulers of the empire who were working in behalf of the papacy against the pagan and all other opposing religions, it would signify the removal of the seat of empire from Rome to Constantinople, which contributed its measure of influence to the downfall of Rome. The passage would then be parallel to Daniel 8: 11 and Revelation 13: 2.

Papacy Takes Away "the Daily."—It was shown in comments on Daniel 8: 13, that "sacrifice" is a word erroneously supplied. It should be "desolation." The expression denotes a desolating power, of which the abomination of desolation is but the counterpart, and to which it succeeds in point of time. It seems clear therefore that the "daily" desolation was paganism, and the "abomination of desolation" is the papacy. But it may be asked, How can this be the papacy since Christ spoke of it in connection with the destruction of Jerusalem? The answer is, Christ evidently referred to Daniel 9, which predicts the destruction of Jerusalem, and not to this verse in Daniel 11, which does not refer to that event. In the ninth chapter, Daniel speaks of desolations and abominations in the plural. More than one abomination, therefore, treads down the church; that is, as far as the church is concerned, both paganism and the papacy are abominations. But as distinguished from each other, the language is restricted. One is the "daily" desolation, and the other is pre-eminently the transgression or "abomination" of desolation.

How was the "daily," or paganism, taken away? As this is spoken of in connection with the placing or setting up of the abomination of desolation, or the papacy, it must denote, not merely the nominal change of the religion of the empire from paganism to Christianity, as on the so-called conversion of Constantine, but to such an eradication of paganism from all the elements of the empire that the way would be entirely open for the papal abomination to arise and assert its arrogant claims. Such a revolution as this was accomplished, but not for nearly two hundred years after the death of Constantine.

As we approach the year A. D. 508, we behold a mighty crisis ripening between Catholicism and the pagan influences still existing in the empire. Up to the time of the conversion of Clovis, king of France, in A. D. 496, the French and other nations of Western Rome were pagan; but following that event, the efforts to convert idolaters to Romanism were crowned with great success. The conversion of Clovis is said to have been the occasion of bestowing upon the French monarch the titles "Most Christian Majesty" and "Eldest Son of the Church." Between that time and A. D. 508, by alliances, capitulations, and conquests, the Arborici, the Roman garrisons in the West, Brittany, the Burgundians, and the Visigoths, were brought into subjection.

From the time when these successes were fully accomplished, in A. D. 508, the papacy was triumphant so far as paganism was concerned; for though the latter doubtless retarded the progress of the Catholic faith, yet it had not the power, if it had the disposition, to suppress the faith, and hinder the encroachments of the Roman pontiff. When the prominent powers of Europe gave up their attachment to paganism, it was only to perpetuate its abominations in another form; for Christianity as exhibited in the Roman

Catholic Church was, and is, only paganism baptized.

The status of the see of Rome was also peculiar at this time. In 498, Symmachus ascended the pontifical throne as a recent convert from paganism. He found his way to the papal chair by striving with his competitor even unto blood. He received adulation as the successor of St. Peter, and struck the keynote of papal assumption by presuming to excommunicate the Emperor Anastasius.[25] The most servile flatterers of the pope now began to maintain that he was constituted judge in the place of God, and that he was the vicegerent of the Most High.

Such was the direction in which events were tending in the West. In what state were affairs at the same time in the East? A strong papal party now existed in all parts of the empire. The adherents of this cause in Constantinople, encouraged by the success of their brethren in the West, deemed it safe to begin open hostilities in behalf of their master at Rome.

Let it be marked that soon after the year 508, paganism had so far declined, and Catholicism had so far relatively increased in strength, that the Catholic Church for the first time was able to wage a successful war against both the civil authority of the empire and the church of the East, which had for the most part embraced the Monophysite doctrine, which Rome counted heresy. Partisan zeal culminated in a whirlwind of fanaticism and civil war, which swept in fire and blood through Constantinople. The extermination of 65,000 heretics was the result. That such a war took place a few years later will be seen in the following quotation from Gibbon in his account of events under the years 508-518:

"The statues of the emperor were broken, and his person was concealed in a suburb, till, at the end of three days, he dared to implore the mercy of his subjects. Without his diadem, and in the posture of a suppliant, Anastasius appeared on the throne of the circus. The Catholics, before his face,

---

[25] See Louis E. Dupin, *A New History of Ecclesiastical Writers*, Vol. V, pp. 1-3, "Pope Symmachus."

rehearsed their genuine Trisagion; they exulted in the offer, which he proclaimed by the voice of a herald, of abdicating the purple; they listened to the admonition, that, since *all* could not reign, they should previously agree in the choice of a sovereign; and they accepted the blood of two unpopular ministers, whom their master, without hesitation, condemned to the lions. These furious but transient seditions were encouraged by the success of Vitalian, who, with an army of Huns and Bulgarians, for the most part idolaters, declared himself the champion of the Catholic faith. In this pious rebellion he depopulated Thrace, besieged Constantinople, exterminated sixty-five thousand of his fellow Christians, till he obtained the recall of the bishops, the satisfaction of the pope, and the establishment of the Council of Chalcedon, an orthodox treaty, reluctantly signed by the dying Anastasius, and more faithfully performed by the uncle of Justinian. And such was the event of the *first* of the religious wars which have been waged in the name, and by the disciples, of the God of Peace."[26]

We think it clear that the daily was taken away by A. D. 508. This was preparatory to the setting up, or establishment, of the papacy, which was a separate and subsequent event. Of this the prophetic narrative now leads us to speak.

Papacy Sets Up an Abomination.—"They shall place the abomination that maketh desolate." Having shown quite fully what we think constitutes the taking away of the daily, or paganism, we now inquire, When was the abomination that maketh desolate, or the papacy, placed, or set up? The little horn that had eyes like the eyes of man was not slow to see when the way was open for his advancement and elevation. From the year 508 his progress toward universal supremacy was without a parallel.

When Justinian was about to begin the Vandal war in A. D. 533, an enterprise of no small magnitude and difficulty,

---

[26] Edward Gibbon, *The Decline and Fall of the Roman Empire*, Vol. IV, chap. 47, p. 526.

BENJAMIN CONSTANT, ARTIST

JUSTINIAN AND HIS COUNCIL

Justinian recognized the supremacy of the bishop of Rome, and organized a military campaign against the

he wished to secure the influence of the bishop of Rome, who had then attained a position in which his opinion had great weight throughout a large part of Christendom. Justinian therefore took it upon himself to decide the contest which had long existed between the sees of Rome and Constantinople as to which should have the precedence, by giving the preference to Rome in an official letter to the pope, declaring in the fullest and most unequivocal terms that the bishop of that city should be chief of the whole ecclesiastical body of the empire.

Justinian's letter reads: "Justinian, victor, pious, fortunate, famous, triumphant, ever Augustus, to John, the most holy Archbishop and Patriarch of the noble city of Rome. Paying honor to the Apostolic See and to Your Holiness, as always has been and is our desire, and honoring your blessedness as a father, we hasten to bring to the knowledge of Your Holiness all that pertains to the condition of the churches, since it has always been our great aim to safeguard the unity of your Apostolic See and the position of the holy churches of God which now prevails and abides securely without any disturbing trouble. Therefore we have been sedulous to subject and unite all the priests of the Orient throughout its whole extent to the see of Your Holiness. Whatever questions happen to be mooted at present, we have thought necessary to be brought to Your Holiness's knowledge, however clear and unquestionable they may be, and though firmly held and taught by all the clergy in accordance with the doctrine of your Apostolic See; for we do not suffer that anything which is mooted, however clear and unquestionable, pertaining to the state of the churches, should fail to be made known to Your Holiness, as being the head of all the churches. For, as we have said before, we are zealous for the increase of the honor and authority of your see in all respects."[27]

"The emperor's letter must have been sent before the 25th of March, 533. For, in his letter of that date to Epiphanius he

[27] *Codex Justiniani*, lib. 1, tit. 1; translation as given by R. F. Littledale, *The Petrine Claims* p. 293.

speaks of its having been already dispatched, and repeats his decision that all affairs touching the church shall be referred to the pope, 'head of all bishops, and the true and effective *corrector of heretics.*' "[28]

"In the same month of the following year, 534, the pope returned an answer repeating the language of the emperor, applauding his homage to the see, and adopting the titles of the imperial mandate. He observes that, among the virtues of Justinian, 'one shines as a star, his reverence for the Apostolic chair, to which he has subjected and united all the churches, it being truly the Head of all; as was testified by the rules of the Fathers, the laws of the Princes, and the declarations of the Emperor's piety.'

"The authenticity of the title receives unanswerable proof from the edicts in the 'Novellæ' of the Justinian code. The preamble of the 9th states that 'as the elder Rome was the founder of the laws; so was it not to be questioned that in her was the supremacy of the pontificate.' The 131st, On the ecclesiastical titles and privileges, chapter ii, states: 'We therefore decree that the most holy Pope of the elder Rome is the first of all the priesthood, and that the most blessed Archbishop of Constantinople, the new Rome, shall hold the second rank after the holy Apostolic chair of the elder Rome.' "[29]

Toward the close of the sixth century, John of Constantinople denied the Roman supremacy, and assumed for himself the title of universal bishop; whereupon Gregory the Great, indignant at the usurpation, denounced John and declared, without being aware of the truth of his statement, that he who would assume the title of universal bishop was Antichrist. In 606, Phocas suppressed the claim of the bishop of Constantinople, and vindicated that of the bishop of Rome. But Phocas was not the founder of papal supremacy. "That Phocas repressed the claim of the bishop of Constantinople is beyond a doubt. But the highest authorities among the

---

[28] George Croly, *The Apocalypse of St. John,* p. 170.
[29] *Ibid.,* pp. 170, 171.

civilians and annalists of Rome spurn the idea that Phocas was the founder of the supremacy of Rome; they ascend to Justinian as the only legitimate source, and rightly date the title from the memorable year 533."[30]

George Croly makes this further statement: "On reference to Baronius, the established authority among the Roman Catholic annalists, I found Justinian's grant of supremacy to the pope formally fixed to that period. . . . The entire transaction was of the most authentic and regular kind, and suitable to the importance of the transfer."[31]

Such were the circumstances attending the decree of Justinian. But the provisions of this decree could not at once be carried into effect; for Rome and Italy were held by the Ostrogoths, who were Arians in faith, and strongly opposed to the religion of Justinian and the pope. It was therefore evident that the Ostrogoths must be rooted out of Rome before the pope could exercise the power with which he had been clothed. To accomplish this object, the Italian war began in 534. The management of the campaign was entrusted to Belisarius. On his approach toward Rome, several cities forsook Vitiges, their Gothic and heretical sovereign, and joined the armies of the Catholic emperor. The Goths, deciding to delay offensive operations until spring, allowed Belisarius to enter Rome without opposition. The deputies of the pope and the clergy, of the senate and the people, invited the lieutenant of Justinian to accept their voluntary allegiance.

Belisarius entered Rome on December 10, 536. But this was not an end of the struggle, for the Goths rallied their forces and resolved to dispute his possession of the city by a regular siege, which they began in March, 537. Belisarius feared despair and treachery on the part of the people. Several senators, and Pope Silverius, on proof or suspicion of treason, were sent into exile. The emperor commanded the clergy to elect a new bishop. After solemnly invoking the Holy

[30] *Ibid.*, p. 172, 173.
[31] *Ibid.*, pp. 12, 13.

Ghost they elected the deacon Vigilius, who, by a bribe of two hundred pounds of gold, had purchased the honor.[32]

The whole nation of the Ostrogoths had been assembled for the siege of Rome, but success did not attend their efforts. Their hosts melted away in frequent and bloody combats under the city walls, and the year and nine days during which the siege lasted, witnessed almost the entire destruction of the nation. In the month of March, 538, dangers beginning to threaten them from other quarters, they raised the siege, burned their tents, and retired in tumult and confusion from the city, with numbers scarcely sufficient to preserve their existence as a nation or their identity as a people.

Thus the Gothic horn, the last of the three, was plucked up before the little horn of Daniel 7. Nothing now stood in the way of the pope to prevent his exercising the power conferred upon him by Justinian five years before. The saints, times, and laws were now in his hands, not in purpose only, but in fact. This must therefore be taken as the year when this abomination was placed, or set up, and as the point from which to date the beginning of the prophetic period of 1260 years of papal supremacy.

VERSE 32 And such as do wickedly against the covenant shall he corrupt by flatteries: but the people that do know their God shall be strong, and do exploits.

A People Who "Know Their God."—Those who forsake the book of the covenant, the Holy Scriptures, who think more of the decree of popes and the decisions of councils than they do of the word of God—these shall he, the pope, corrupt by flatteries. That is, they shall be led on in their partisan zeal for the pope by the bestowment of wealth, position, and honors.

At the same time a people shall exist who know their God, and these shall be strong, and do exploits. These were Christians who kept pure religion alive in the earth during the Dark

---

[32] See Edward Gibbon, *The Decline and Fall of the Roman Empire*, Vol. IV, chap. 41, pp. 168, 169.

Ages of papal tyranny, and performed marvelous acts of self-sacrifice and religious heroism in behalf of their faith. Prominent among these stand the Waldenses, the Albigenses, and the Huguenots.

VERSE 33 And they that understand among the people shall instruct many; yet they shall fall by the sword, and by flame, by captivity, and by spoil, many days.

The long period of papal persecution against those who were struggling to maintain the truth and instruct their fellow men in ways of righteousness, is here brought to view. The number of the days during which they were thus to fall is given in Daniel 7: 25; 12: 7; Revelation 12: 6, 14; 13: 5. The period is called, "a time, and times, and the dividing of time;" "a time, times, and a half;" "a thousand two hundred and threescore days;" and "forty and two months." All these expressions are various ways of denoting the same 1260 years of papal supremacy.

VERSE 34 Now when they shall fall, they shall be holpen with a little help; but many shall cleave to them with flatteries.

In Revelation 12, where this same papal persecution is brought to view, we read that the earth helped the woman by opening her mouth and swallowing up the flood which the dragon cast out after her. The Protestant Reformation led by Martin Luther and his co-workers furnished the help here foretold. The German states espoused the Protestant cause, protected the reformers, and restrained the work of persecution carried on by the papal church. But when the Protestants were helped, and when their cause began to be popular, many were to cleave unto them with flatteries, or embrace the faith from unworthy motives.

VERSE 35 And some of them of understanding shall fall, to try them, and to purge, and to make them white, even to the time of the end: because it is yet for a time appointed.

Though restrained, the spirit of persecution was not destroyed. It broke out whenever there was opportunity.

Especially was this the case in England. The religious state of that kingdom was fluctuating, it being sometimes under Protestant and sometimes under papal jurisdiction, according to the religion of the ruling monarch. "Bloody Queen Mary" was a mortal enemy to the Protestant cause, and multitudes fell victims to her relentless persecutions. This condition of affairs was to last more or less "to the time of the end." The natural conclusion would be that when the time of the end should come, this power which the Church of Rome had possessed to punish heretics, which had been the cause of so much persecution, and which for a time had been restrained, would now be taken entirely away. The conclusion would be equally evident that this taking away of the papal supremacy would mark the beginning of the period here called the "time of the end." If this application is correct, the time of the end began in 1798; for then, as already noticed, the papacy was overthrown by the French, and has never since been able to wield all the power it before possessed. The oppression of the church by the papacy is evidently referred to here because that is the only one, with the possible exception of Revelation 2: 10, connected with "a time appointed," or a prophetic period.

VERSE 36 And the king shall do according to his will; and he shall exalt himself, and magnify himself above every god, and shall speak marvelous things against the God of gods, and shall prosper till the indignation be accomplished: for that that is determined shall be done.

A King Magnifies Himself Above Every God.—The king here introduced cannot denote the same power that was last noticed, namely, the papal power; for the specifications will not hold good if applied to that power.

Take a declaration in the next verse: "Nor regard any god." This has never been true of the papacy. God and Christ, though often placed in a false position, have never been professedly set aside and rejected from that system of religion.

Three peculiar features must appear in the power which fulfills this prophecy: It must assume the character here delineated near the beginning of the time of the end, to which we were brought down in the preceding verse. It must be a willful power. It must be an atheistical power. Perhaps the two latter specifications might be united by saying that its willfulness would be manifested in the direction of atheism.

France Fulfills the Prophecy.—A revolution exactly answering to this description did take place in France at the time indicated in the prophecy. Atheists sowed the seeds which bore their logical and baleful fruit. Voltaire, in his pompous but impotent self-conceit, had said, "I am weary of hearing people repeat that twelve men established the Christian religion. I will prove that one man may suffice to overthrow it." Associating with himself such men as Rousseau, D'Alembert, Diderot, and others, he undertook to accomplish his threat. They sowed to the wind, and reaped the whirlwind. Then, too, the Roman Catholic Church was notoriously corrupt in France during this period, and the people were anxious to break the yoke of ecclesiastical oppression. Their efforts culminated in the "reign of terror" of 1793, when France discarded the Bible and denied the existence of the Deity.

A modern historian thus describes this great religious change:

"Certain members of the Convention, too, had been the first to attempt to replace Christian worship in the provinces by civic ceremonial, in the autumn of 1793. At Abbeville, Dumont, having informed the populace that the priests were 'harlequins and clowns in black garments, who showed off marionettes,' had set up the Worship of Reason, and, with a not uncommon inconsistency, organized a 'marionette show' of his own of a most imposing description, with dances in the cathedral every *décadi*, and civic festivals on the 'observance' of which he greatly insisted. Fouché was the next to abolish Christian worship; speaking from the pulpit of the cathedral at Nevers he formally erased all spiritualism from the republican programme, promulgated the famous order which declared 'death an eternal slumber,' and thus turned the key

C. PILOTY, ARTIST

VICTIMS OF THE REIGN OF TERROR

While women knitted, the king and nobility of France were publicly slaughtered by the guillotine.

on heaven and hell alike. . . . In his congratulatory address to the ex-bishop, the President declared that as *the Supreme Being 'desired no worship other than the worship of Reason, that should in future be the national religion!'* "[33]

But there are other and still more striking specifications which were fulfilled by France.

VERSE 37 Neither shall he regard the God of his fathers, nor the desire of women, nor regard any god: for he shall magnify himself above all.

The Hebrew word for *woman* is also translated *wife;* and Thomas Newton observes that this passage would be more properly rendered "the desire of wives."[34] This would seem to indicate that this government, at the same time it declared that God did not exist, would trample underfoot the law which God had given to regulate the marriage institution. And we find that the historian has, unconsciously perhaps, and if so all the more significantly, coupled together the atheism and licentiousness of this government in the same order in which they are presented in the prophecy. He says:

"The family had been destroyed. Under the old regime it had been the very foundation of society. . . . The decree of September 20, 1792 which established divorce, and was carried still further by the Convention in 1794, had borne fruit within four years of which the Legislature itself had never dreamt: an immediate divorce could be pronounced on the score of incompatibility of temper, to come into force within a year at farthest, if either of the couple should refuse to separate before that period elapsed.

"There had been a rush for divorce: by the end of 1793—fifteen months after the passing of the decree—5,994 divorces had been granted in Paris. . . . Under the Directory we see women passed from hand to hand by a legal process. What was the fate of the children born of these successive unions? Some people got rid of them: the number of foundlings in the Year V rose to 4,000 in Paris and to 44,000 in the other depart-

[33] Louis Madelin, *The French Revolution*, pp. 387, 388.
[34] Thomas Newton, *Dissertations on the Prophecies*, Vol. I, pp. 388-390.

ments. When the parents kept the children a tragi-comical confusion was the result. A man would marry several sisters, one after the other: one citizen presented a petition to the Five Hundred for leave to marry the mother of the two wives he had already possessed. . . . The family was dissolved."[35]

"Nor regard any god." In addition to the testimony already presented to show the utter atheism of the nation at this time, we present the following:

The "constitutional bishop of Paris was brought forward to play the principal part in the most impudent and scandalous farce ever acted in the face of a national representation. . . . He was brought forward in full procession, to declare to the Convention that the religion which he had taught so many years was, in every respect, a piece of priestcraft, which had no foundation either in history or sacred truth. He disowned, in solemn and explicit terms, the existence of the Deity to whose worship he had been consecrated, and devoted himself in future to the homage of liberty, equality, virtue, and morality. He then laid on the table his episcopal decorations, and received a fraternal embrace from the president of the Convention. Several apostate priests followed the example of this prelate."[36]

"Hébert, Chaumette, and their associates appeared at the bar, and declared that 'God did not exist.' "[37]

The fear of God was said to be so far from the beginning of wisdom that it was the beginning of folly. All worship was prohibited except that of liberty and the country. The gold and silver plate of the churches was seized and desecrated. The churches were closed. The bells were broken and cast into cannon. The Bible was publicly burned. The sacramental vessels were paraded through the streets on an ass, in token of contempt. A week of ten days instead of seven was established, and death was declared, in conspicuous letters posted over

---

[35] Louis Madelin, *The French Revolution*, pp. 552, 553.

[36] Sir Walter Scott, *Life of Napoleon Buonaparte*, Vol. 1, p. 239.

[37] Archibald Alison, *History of Europe*, Vol. III, p. 22.

burial places, to be an eternal sleep. But the crowning blasphemy, if these orgies of hell admit of degrees, remained to be performed by the comedian Monvel, who, as a priest of Illuminism, said:

" 'God! if you exist, . . . avenge your injured name. I bid you defiance. You remain silent; you dare not launch your thunders; who, after this, will believe in your *existence?*' "[38]

Behold what man is when left to himself, and what infidelity is when the restraints of law are thrown off, and it has the power in its own hands! Can it be doubted that these scenes are what the Omniscient One foresaw and noted on the sacred page, when He pointed out a kingdom to arise which should exalt itself above every god, and disregard them all?

VERSE 38 But in his estate shall he honor the God of forces: and a god whom his fathers knew not shall he honor with gold, and silver, and with precious stones, and pleasant things.

We meet a seeming contradiction in this verse. How can a nation disregard every god, and yet honor the god of forces? It could not at one and the same time hold both these positions, but it might for a time disregard all gods, and then subsequently introduce another worship and regard the god of forces. Did such a change occur in France at this time?—It did. The attempt to make France a godless nation produced such anarchy that the rulers feared the power would pass entirely out of their hands, and therefore perceived that as a political necessity, some kind of worship must be introduced. But they did not intend to introduce any movement which would increase devotion, or develop any true spiritual character among the people, but only such as would keep themselves in power, and give them control of the national forces. A few extracts from history will show this. Liberty and country were at first the objects of adoration. "Liberty, equality, virtue, and morality," the very opposites of anything they possessed in fact

[38] *Ibid.*, p. 24.

or exhibited in practice, were words which they set forth as describing the deity of the nation. In 1793 the worship of the Goddess of Reason was introduced, and is thus described by the historian:

"One of the ceremonies of this insane time stands unrivaled for absurdity combined with impiety. The doors of the Convention were thrown open to a band of musicians, preceded by whom, the members of the Municipal Body entered in solemn procession, singing a hymn in praise of liberty, and escorting, as the object of their future worship, a veiled female, whom they termed the Goddess of Reason. Being brought within the bar, she was unveiled with great form, and placed on the right hand of the president; when she was generally recognized as a dancing girl of the opera, with whose charms most of the persons present were acquainted from her appearance on the stage, while the experience of individuals was farther extended. To this person, as the fittest representative of that Reason whom they worshiped, the National Convention of France rendered public homage. This impious and ridiculous mummery had a certain fashion; and the installation of the Goddess of Reason was renewed and imitated throughout the nation, in such places where the inhabitants desired to show themselves equal to all the heights of the Revolution."[39]

The modern French historian, Louis Madelin, writes:

"The Assembly having excused itself from attendance on the score of business, a procession (of a very mixed description) attended the goddess to the Tuileries, and in her presence forced the deputies to decree the transformation of Notre Dame into the *Temple of Reason.* This not being deemed sufficient, another goddess of Reason, the wife of Momoro, a member of the Convention, was installed at Saint-Sulpice on the following *décadi.* Before long these *Liberties* and *Reasons* were swarming all over France: wantons, only too often, with here and there a goddess of good family and decent behaviour.

---

[39] Sir Walter Scott, *The Life of Napoleon Buonaparte*, Vol. I, pp. 239, 240.

If it be true that the brow of one of these Liberties was bound with a fillet bearing the words '*Turn me not into Licence!*' the suggestion, we may say, would hardly have been superfluous in any part of France: for saturnalia of the most repulsive kind were the invariable rule: at Lyons, we are told, an ass was given drink out of a chalice. . . . Payan cried out upon 'these goddesses, more degraded than those of fable.' "[40]

During the time while the fantastic worship of reason was the national craze, the leaders of the revolution are known to history as "the atheists." But it was soon perceived that a religion with more powerful sanctions than the one then in vogue must be instituted to hold the people. A form of worship therefore followed in which the object of adoration was the "Supreme Being." It was equally hollow so far as any reformation of life and vital godliness were concerned, but it took hold upon the supernatural. And while the Goddess of Reason was indeed a "strange god," the statement in regard to honoring the "God of forces," may perhaps more appropriately be referred to this latter phase.

VERSE 39 Thus shall he do in the most strongholds with a strange god, whom he shall acknowledge and increase with glory: and he shall cause them to rule over many, and shall divide the land for gain.

The system of paganism which had been introduced into France, as exemplified in the worship of the idol set up in the person of the Goddess of Reason, and regulated by a heathen ritual which had been enacted by the National Assembly for the use of the French people, continued in force till the appointment of Napoleon to the provisional consulate of France in 1799. The adherents of this strange religion occupied the fortified places, the strongholds of the nation, as expressed in this verse.

But that which serves to identify the application of this prophecy to France perhaps as clearly as any other particular, is the statement made in the last clause of the verse, that they

[40] Louis Madelin, *The French Revolution*, p. 389.

should "divide the land for gain." Previous to the Revolution, the landed property of France was owned by the Catholic Church and by a few landlords in immense estates. These estates were required by the law to remain undivided, so that no heirs or creditors could partition them. But revolution knows no law, and in the anarchy that now reigned, as noted also in Revelation 11, the titles of the nobility were abolished, and their lands disposed of in small parcels for the benefit of the public exchequer. The government was in need of funds, and these large landed estates were confiscated, and sold at auction in parcels to suit purchasers. The historian thus records this unique transaction:

"The confiscation of two thirds of the landed property in the kingdom, which arose from the decrees of the Convention against the emigrants, clergy, and persons convicted at the Revolutionary Tribunals . . . placed funds worth above £700,000,000 sterling at the disposal of the government."[41]

When did ever an event take place and in what country, fulfilling a prophecy more completely than this?

As the nation began to come to itself, a more rational religion was demanded, and the heathen ritual was abolished. The historian thus describes that event:

"A third and a bolder measure was the discarding of the heathen ritual, and reopening the churches for Christian worship; and of this the credit was wholly Napoleon's, who had to oppose the *philosophic* prejudices of almost all his colleagues. He, in his conversations with them, made no attempt to represent himself as a believer in Christianity; but stood only on the necessity of providing the people with the regular means of worship wherever it is meant to have a state of tranquillity. The priests who chose to take the oath of fidelity to government were readmitted to their functions; and this wise measure was followed by the adherence of not less than 20,000 of

[41] Archibald Alison, *History of Europe*, Vol. III, pp. 25, 26.

these ministers of religion, who had hitherto languished in the prisons of France."[42]

Thus terminated the Reign of Terror and the French Revolution. Out of the ruins rose Bonaparte, to guide the tumult to his own elevation, place himself at the head of the French government, and strike terror to the hearts of nations.

VERSE 40 And at the time of the end shall the king of the south push at him: and the king of the north shall come against him like a whirlwind, with chariots, and with horsemen, and with many ships; and he shall enter into the countries, and shall overflow and pass over.

Kings of South and North Again in Conflict.—After a long interval, the king of the south and the king of the north again appear on the stage of action. We have met with nothing to indicate that we are to look to any locations for these powers other than those which shortly after the death of Alexander constituted respectively the southern and the northern divisions of his empire. The king of the south was at that time Egypt, and the king of the north was Syria, including Thrace and Asia Minor. Egypt continued to rule in the territory designated as belonging to the king of the south, and Turkey for more than four hundred years ruled over the territory which first constituted the domain of the king of the north.

This application of the prophecy calls for a conflict to spring up between Egypt and France, and between Turkey and France, in 1798, which year, as we have seen, marked the beginning of the time of the end. If history testifies that such a triangular war did break out in that year, it will be conclusive proof of the correctness of the application.

We inquire, therefore, Is it a fact that at the time of the end, Egypt did "push," or make a comparatively feeble resistance, while Turkey did come like a resistless "whirlwind," against "him," that is, the government of France? We have already produced some evidence that the time of the end began in 1798; and no reader of history need be informed that in

[42] John Gibson Lockhart, *The History of Napoleon Buonaparte*, Vol. I, p. 154.

that year a state of open hostility between France and Egypt was developed.

To what extent this conflict owed its origin to the dreams of glory deliriously cherished in the ambitious brain of Napoleon Bonaparte, the historian will form his own opinion; but the French, or Napoleon at least, contrived to make Egypt the aggressor. "In a skillfully worded proclamation he [Napoleon] assured the peoples of Egypt that he had come to chastise only the governing caste of Mamelukes for their depredations on French merchants; that, far from wishing to destroy the religion of the Muslim, he had more respect for God, Mohammed, and the Koran than the Mamelukes had shown; that the French had destroyed the Pope and the Knights of Malta who levied war on the Muslim; thrice blessed, therefore, would be those who sided with the French, blessed even those who remained neutral, and thrice unhappy those who fought against them."[43]

The beginning of the year 1798 found France indulging in immense projects against the English. The Directory desired Bonaparte to undertake at once the crossing of the Channel and an attack upon England; but he saw that no direct operations of that kind could be judiciously undertaken before the autumn, and he was unwilling to hazard his growing reputation by spending the summer in idleness. "But," says the historian, "he saw a far-off land, where a glory was to be won which would gain a new charm in the eyes of his countrymen by the romance and mystery which hung upon the scene. Egypt, the land of the Pharaohs and Ptolemies, would be a noble field for new triumphs."[44]

But while still broader visions of glory opened before the eyes of Bonaparte in those Eastern historic lands, covering not Egypt only, but Syria, Persia, Hindustan, even to the Ganges itself, he had no difficulty in persuading the Directory that

---

[43] *The Cambridge Modern History*, Vol. VIII, p. 599. By permission of the Macmillan Company, publishers in the United States.

[44] James White, *History of France*, p. 469.

Egypt was the vulnerable point through which to strike at England by intercepting her Eastern trade. Hence on the pretext above mentioned, the Egyptian campaign was undertaken.

The downfall of the papacy, which marked the termination of the 1260 years, and according to verse 35 showed the beginning of the time of the end, occurred in February, 1798, when Rome fell into the hands of Berthier, the general of the French. On the 5th of March following, Bonaparte received the decree of the Directory relative to the expedition against Egypt. He left Paris May 3, and set sail from Toulon the 19th, with a large naval armament consisting of "thirteen ships-of-the-line, fourteen frigates (some of them unarmed), a large number of smaller vessels of war, and about 300 transports. Upwards of 35,000 troops were on board, along with 1230 horses. If we include the crews, the commission of *savants* sent to explore the wonders of Egypt, and the attendants, the total number of persons aboard was about 50,000; it has even been placed as high as 54,000."[45]

July 2, Alexandria was taken, and immediately fortified. On the 21st the decisive Battle of the Pyramids was fought, in which the Mamelukes contested the field with valor and desperation, but were no match for the disciplined legions of the French. Murad Bey lost all his cannon, 400 camels, and 3,000 men. The loss of the French was comparatively slight. On the 25th, Bonaparte entered Cairo, the capital of Egypt, and only waited the subsidence of the floods of the Nile to pursue Murad Bey to Upper Egypt, whither he had retired with his shattered cavalry, and so make a conquest of the whole country. Thus the king of the south was able to make but a feeble resistance.

At this juncture, however, the situation of Napoleon began to grow precarious. The French fleet, which was his only channel of communication with France, was destroyed by the

---

[45] *The Cambridge Modern History*, Vol. VIII, pp. 597, 598. By permission of the Macmillan Company, publishers in the United States.

J. L. JEROME, ARTIST

NAPOLEON IN EGYPT

In an effort to conquer the world, Napoleon "pushed" eastward into Egypt and Syria.

English under Nelson at Aboukir. On September 11, 1798, the sultan of Turkey, under feelings of jealousy against France, artfully fostered by the English ambassadors at Constantinople, and exasperated that Egypt, so long a semi-dependency of the Ottoman Empire, should be transformed into a French province, declared war against France. Thus the king of the north (Turkey) came against him (France) in the same year that the king of the south (Egypt) "pushed," and both "at the time of the end." This is another conclusive proof that the year 1798 is the year which begins that period—all of which is a demonstration that this application of the prophecy is correct. So many events meeting so accurately the specifications of the prophecy could not take place together and not constitute a fulfillment of the prophecy.

Was the coming of the king of the north, or Turkey, like a whirlwind in comparison with the pushing of Egypt? Napoleon had crushed the armies of Egypt, and essayed to do the same thing with the armies of the sultan which were threatening an attack from the side of Asia. He began his march from Cairo to Syria, February 27, 1799, with 18,000 men. He first took the Fort El-Arish in the desert, then Jaffa (the Joppa of the Bible), conquered the inhabitants of Naplous at Zeta, and was again victorious at Jafet. Meanwhile, a strong body of Turks had intrenched themselves at St. Jean d'Acre, while swarms of Mussulmans gathered in the mountains of Samaria, ready to swoop down upon the French when they should besiege Acre. Sir Sidney Smith at the same time appeared before St. Jean d'Acre with two English ships, reinforced the Turkish garrison of that place, and captured the apparatus for the siege which Napoleon had sent across by sea from Alexandria. A Turkish fleet soon appeared in the offing, which with the Russian and English vessels then co-operating with them constituted the "many ships" of the king of the north.

On the 18th of March the siege began. Napoleon was twice called away to save some French divisions from falling into the hands of the Mussulman hordes that filled the country. Twice also a breach was made in the wall of the city, but the assailants were met with such fury by the garrison that they were obliged, despite their best efforts, to give over the struggle. After a continuance of sixty days, Napoleon raised the siege, sounded the note of retreat, for the first time in his career, and on the 21st of May, 1799, began to retrace his steps to Egypt.

"He . . . shall overflow and pass over." We have found events which furnish a very striking fulfillment of the pushing of the king of the south, and the whirlwind onset of the king of the north against the French power. Thus far there is quite a general agreement in the application of the prophecy. We now reach a point where the views of expositors begin to diverge. To whom do the words he "shall overflow and pass over," refer—to France or to the king of the north? The application of the remainder of this chapter depends upon the answer to this question. From this point two lines of interpretation are maintained. Some apply the words to France, and endeavor to find a fulfillment in the career of Napoleon. Others apply them to the king of the north, and accordingly point for a fulfillment to events in the history of Turkey. We speak of these two positions only, as the attempt which some make to bring in the papacy here is so evidently wide of the mark that it need not be considered. If neither of these positions is free from difficulty, as we presume no one will claim that it is absolutely, it only remains that we take that one which has the weight of evidence in its favor. We shall find one in favor of which the evidence does so greatly preponderate to the exclusion of all others, as scarcely to leave any room for doubt in regard to the view here mentioned.

Turkey Becomes King of the North.—Respecting the application of this portion of the prophecy to Napoleon or to France under his leadership, we do not find events which we can urge with any degree of assurance as the fulfillment of the remaining part of this chapter. Hence we do not see how it can be thus applied. It must, then, be fulfilled by Turkey, unless it can be shown that the expression "king of the north" does not apply to Turkey, or that there is some other power besides either France or the king of the north which fulfilled this part of the prediction. But if Turkey, now occupying the territory which constituted the northern division of Alexander's empire, is not the king of the north of this prophecy, then we are left without any principle to guide us in the interpretation. We presume all will agree that there is no room for the introduction of any other power here. France and the king of the north are the only ones to whom the prediction can apply. The fulfillment must lie between them.

Some considerations certainly favor the idea that there is in the latter part of verse 40 a transfer of the burden of the prophecy from the French power to the king of the north. The latter is introduced just before as coming forth like a whirlwind, with chariots, horsemen, and many ships. The collision between this power and the French we have already noticed. The king of the north with the aid of his allies gained the day in this contest; and the French, foiled in their efforts, were driven back into Egypt. Now it would seem to be the more natural application to refer the "overflowing and passing over" to that power which emerged in triumph from that struggle, and that power was Turkey.

VERSE 41 He shall enter also into the glorious land, and many countries shall be overthrown: but these shall escape out of his hand, even Edom, and Moab, and the chief of the children of Ammon.

Abandoning a campaign in which one third of the army had fallen victims to war and the plague, the French retired from St. Jean d'Acre, and after a fatiguing march of twenty-six days re-entered Cairo in Egypt. They thus abandoned all the conquests they had made in Judea, and the "glorious land," Palestine, with all its provinces, here called "countries," fell back again under the oppressive rule of the Turk. Edom, Moab, and Ammon, lying outside the limits of Palestine, south and east of the Dead Sea and the Jordan, were out of the line of march of the Turks from Syria to Egypt, and so escaped the ravages of that campaign. On this passage, Adam Clarke has the following note: "These and other Arabians, they [the Turks] have never been able to subdue. They still occupy the deserts, and receive a yearly pension of *forty thousand* crowns of gold from the Ottoman emperors to permit the caravans with the pilgrims for Mecca to have a free passage."[46]

VERSE 42 He shall stretch forth his hand also upon the countries: and the land of Egypt shall not escape.

On the retreat of the French to Egypt, a Turkish fleet landed 10,000 men at Aboukir. Napoleon immediately attacked the place, completely routing the Turks, and re-establishing his authority in Egypt. But at this point, severe reverses to the French arms in Europe called Napoleon home to look after the interests of his own country. The command of the troops in Egypt was left with General Kleber, who, after a period of untiring activity for the benefit of the army, was murdered by a Turk in Cairo, and the command was left with Abdallah Menou. With an army which could not be recruited, every loss was serious.

Meanwhile, the English government, as the ally of the Turks, had resolved to wrest Egypt from the French. March 13, 1801, an English fleet disembarked a body of troops at Aboukir. The French gave battle the next day, but were forced to retire. On the 18th Aboukir surrendered. On the 28th reinforcements were brought by a Turkish fleet and the grand vizier approached from Syria with a large army. On the 19th, Rosetta surrendered to the combined forces of the English and the Turks. At Ramanieh a French corps of 4,000 men was defeated by 8,000 English and 6,000 Turks. At Elmenayer 5,000 French were obliged to retreat, May 16, by the vizier, who was pressing forward to Cairo with 20,000 men. The whole French army was now shut up in Cairo and Alexandria. Cairo capitulated June 27, and Alexandria,

[46] Adam Clarke, *Commentary on the Old Testament*, Vol. IV, p. 618, note on Daniel 11: 41.

September 2. Four weeks afterward, October 1, 1801, the preliminaries of peace were signed in London.

"Egypt shall not escape" were the words of the prophecy. This language seems to imply that Egypt would be brought into subjection to some power from whose dominion it would desire to be released. As between the French and the Turks, how did this question stand with the Egyptians?—They preferred French rule. In R. R. Madden's *Travels in Turkey, Egypt, Nubia, and Palestine* it is stated that the French were much regarded by the Egyptians, and extolled as benefactors; that for the short period they remained, they left traces of amelioration; and that, if they could have established their power, Egypt would now be comparatively civilized.[47] In view of this testimony, the language of the Scripture would not be appropriate if applied to the French, for the Egyptians did not desire to escape out of their hands. They did desire to escape from the hands of the Turks, but could not.

VERSE 43 But he shall have power over the treasures of gold and of silver, and over all the precious things of Egypt: and the Libyans and the Ethiopians shall be at his steps.

In illustration of this verse we quote the following statement from the historian concerning Mehemet Ali, the Turkish governor of Egypt who rose to power after the defeat of the French:

"The new Pasha set about strengthening himself in his position so as to insure a permanent hold upon the government of Egypt for himself and his family. First, he saw that he must exact a large revenue from his subjects, in order to send such sums of tribute to Constantinople as would propitiate the Sultan, and make it clearly for his interest to sustain the power of the Egyptian governor. Acting upon this principle he used many unjust means to obtain possession of large estates; he denied the legitimacy of many successions; he burned title deeds, and seized properties; in short, he set at defiance all

---

[47] Richard Robert Madden, *Travels in Turkey, Egypt, Nubia, and Palestine*, Vol. I, p.231.

universally acknowledged rights of landholders. Great disturbances followed, but Mohammed Ali was prepared for these, and, by his wonderful firmness he made it appear that the bare assertion of claims was an aggression on the part of the Sheikhs. The taxes were constantly increased, and their collection put into the hands of the military governors; by this means the peasantry were ground to the very lowest point."[48]

VERSE 44 But tidings out of the east and out of the north shall trouble him: therefore he shall go forth with great fury to destroy, and utterly to make away many.

King of the North in Trouble.—On this verse Adam Clarke has a note which is worthy of mention. He says: "This part of the prophecy is allowed to be yet unfulfilled."[49] His note was printed in 1825. In another part of his comment, he says: "If the Turkish power be understood, as in the preceding verses, it may mean that the Persians on the *east*, and the Russians on the *north*, will at some time greatly embarrass the Ottoman government."

Between this conjecture by Adam Clarke, written in 1825, and the Crimean War of 1853-1856, there is certainly a striking coincidence, inasmuch as the very powers he mentions, the Persians on the east and the Russians on the north, were the ones which instigated that conflict. Tidings from these powers troubled him (Turkey). Their attitude and movements incited the sultan to anger and revenge. Russia, being the more aggressive party, was the object of attack. Turkey declared war on her powerful northern neighbor in 1853. The world looked on in amazement to see a government which had long been called "the Sick Man of the East," a government whose army was dispirited and demoralized, whose treasuries were empty, whose rulers were vile and imbecile, and whose subjects were rebellious and threatening secession, rush with such impetuosity into the conflict. The prophecy said that they

[48] Clara Erskine Clement, *Egypt*, pp. 389, 390.

[49] Adam Clarke, *Commentary on the Old Testament*, Vol. IV, p. 618, note on Daniel 11:44.

should go forth with "great fury," and when they thus went forth in the war aforesaid, they were described, in the profane vernacular of an American writer, as "fighting like devils." England and France, it is true, soon came to the help of Turkey; but she went forth in the manner described, and as reported, gained important victories before receiving the assistance of these powers.

VERSE 45 And he shall plant the tabernacles of his palace between the seas in the glorious holy mountain; yet he shall come to his end, and none shall help him.

King of the North to Come to His End.—We have now traced the prophecy of the 11th chapter of Daniel step by step to this last verse. As we see the divine predictions meeting their fulfillment in history, our faith is strengthened in the final accomplishment of God's prophetic word.

The prophecy of verse 45 centers in that power known as the king of the north. It is the power that shall hold the territory possessed originally by the king of the north. (See pages 235, 236.)

It is predicted of the king of the north that "he shall come to his end, and none shall help him." Just how and when and where his end will come, we may watch with solemn interest, knowing that the hand of Providence guides the destiny of nations.

Time will soon determine this matter. When this event takes place, what follows?—events of the most momentous interest to all the inhabitants of this world, as the next chapter immediately shows.

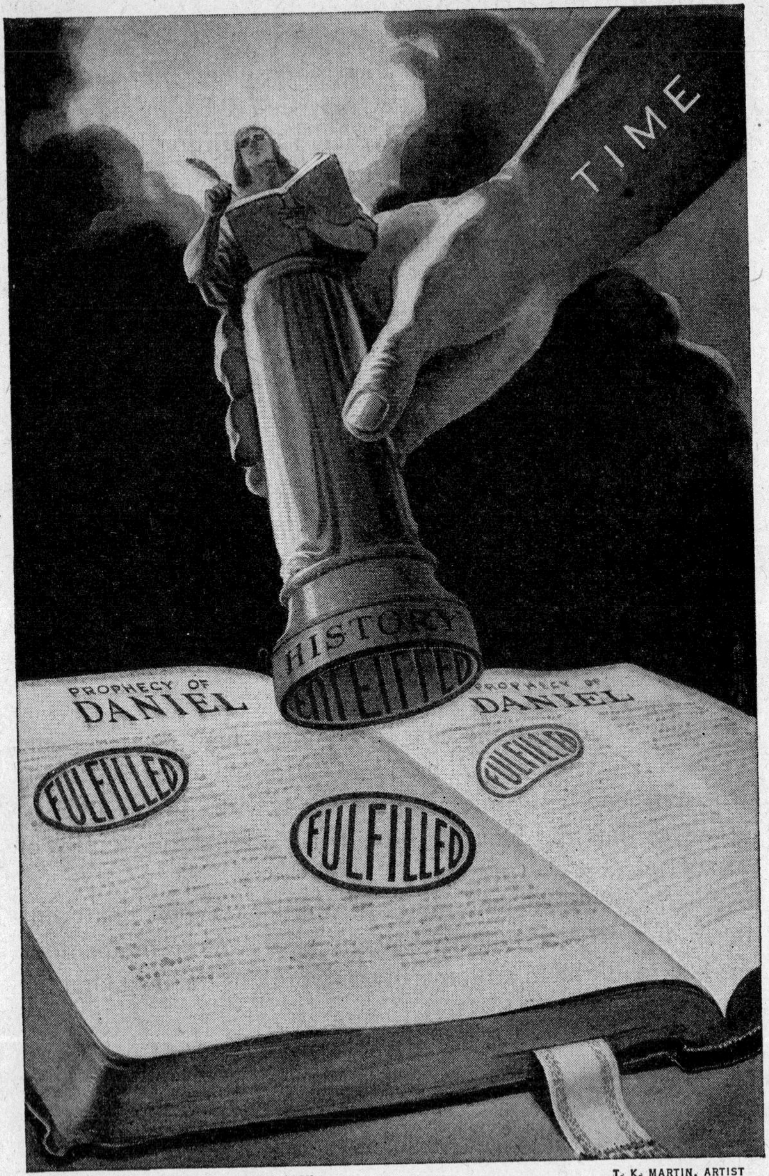

T. K. MARTIN, ARTIST

HISTORY IN THE HAND OF TIME

History has set its seal to the words of the holy prophets, revealing that God has faithfully declared through them the end from the beginning.

CHAPTER XII

HISTORY'S COMING CLIMAX

VERSE 1 And at that time shall Michael stand up, the great prince which standeth for the children of thy people: and there shall be a time of trouble, such as never was since there was a nation even to that same time: and at that time thy people shall be delivered, every one that shall be found written in the book.

A DEFINITE time is specified in this verse, not a particular year or month or day, but a time made definite by the occurrence of a certain event with which it is connected. "At that time." What time?—The time to which we are brought by the closing verse of the preceding chapter—the time when the king of the north shall plant the tabernacles of his palace in the glorious holy mountain. When this event takes place, he is to come to his end; and *then*, according to this verse, we look for the standing up of Michael, the great Prince.

Michael Stands Up.—Who is Michael, and what is his standing up?—Michael is called the "archangel" in Jude 9. This means the chief angel, or the head over the angels. There is but one. Who is he?—He is the one whose voice is heard from heaven when the dead are raised. (1 Thessalonians 4: 16.) Whose voice is heard in connection with that event?—The voice of our Lord Jesus Christ. (John 5: 28.) Tracing back the evidence with this fact as a basis, we reach the following conclusion: The voice of the Son of God is the voice of the Archangel; the Archangel, then, must be the Son of God. But the Archangel is called Michael; hence Michael must be the name given to the Son of God. The expression in verse 1, "the great Prince which standeth for the children of thy people," is sufficient alone to identify the one here spoken of as the Saviour of men. He is "the Prince of life," and "a Prince and a Saviour." Acts 3:15; 5:31. He is the great Prince.

He "standeth for the children of thy people." He condescends to take the servants of God in this poor mortal state, and redeem them for the subjects of His future kingdom. He stands for us who believe. His people are essential to His future purposes, an inseparable part of the purchased inheritance. They are to be the chief agents of that joy which Christ foresaw, and which caused Him to endure all the sacrifice and suffering which have marked His intervention in behalf of the fallen race. Amazing honor! Be everlasting gratitude repaid Him for His condescension and mercy to us! Be His the kingdom, power, and glory, forever and ever!

We now come to the second question, What is the standing up of Michael? The key to the interpretation of this expression is given us: "There shall stand up yet three kings in Persia;" "A mighty king shall stand up, that shall rule with great dominion." Daniel 11: 2, 3. There can be no doubt as to the meaning of these expressions in these instances. They signify to take the kingdom, to reign. This expression in the verse under consideration must mean the same. At that time Michael shall stand up, shall take the kingdom, shall begin to reign.

But is not Christ reigning now?—Yes, associated with His Father on the throne of universal dominion. (Ephesians 1: 20-22; Revelation 3: 21.) But this throne, or kingdom, He gives up at His coming. (1 Corinthians 15: 24.) Then begins His reign, brought to view in the text, when He stands up, or takes His own kingdom, the long-promised throne of His father David, and establishes a dominion of which there shall be no end. (Luke 1: 32, 33.)

The kingdoms of this world shall become the kingdom "of our Lord and of His Christ." His priestly robes are to be laid aside for royal vesture. The work of mercy will be finished and the probation of the human race ended. Then he that is filthy is beyond hope of cleansing; and he that is holy is beyond the danger of falling. All cases are forever decided. From that time on until Christ comes in the clouds of heaven, the nations are broken as with a rod of iron, and dashed in pieces like a potter's vessel, by an unparalleled time of trouble. There will be a series of divine judgments upon men who have rejected God. Then shall the Lord Jesus Christ be revealed from heaven "in flaming fire taking vengeance on them that know not God, and that obey not the gospel." 2 Thessalonians 1: 8. (See also Revelation 11: 15; 22: 11, 12.)

Momentous are the events introduced by the standing up of Michael. He stands up, or takes the kingdom, some length of time before He returns personally to this earth. How important, then, that we have a knowledge of His position, that we may be able to trace the progress of His work, and understand when that thrilling moment draws near which ends His intercession in behalf of mankind, and fixes the destiny of all forever.

But how are we to know this? How are we to determine what is taking place in the sanctuary above? God has been so good as to place in our hands the means of knowing this. He has told us that when certain great events take place on earth, important decisions which synchronize with them are being made in heaven. By these things which are seen, we thus learn of things that are unseen. As we "look through nature up to nature's God," so through terrestrial phenomena and events we trace great movements in the heavenly kingdom. When the king of the north shall plant the tabernacles of his palace between the seas in the glorious holy mountain, then Michael our Lord stands up, or receives from His Father the kingdom, preparatory to His return to this earth. Or it might be expressed in words like these: Then our Lord ceases His work as our great High Priest, and the probation of the world is finished. The great prophecy of the 2300 days gives us the definite beginning of the final division of the work in the sanctuary in heaven. The verse before us gives us data whereby we can discover approximately the time of its close.

Time of Trouble.—In connection with the standing up of Michael, there occurs a time of trouble such as never was. In

© PACIFIC PRESS PUBLISHING ASSN. PAUL REMMEY, ARTIST

"AT THAT TIME SHALL MICHAEL STAND UP"

The patient Saviour has long waited for the harvest of the earth. He will soon come as a mighty reaper.

Matthew 24: 21 we read of a period of tribulation such as never was before it, nor should be after it. This tribulation, fulfilled in the oppression and slaughter of the church by the papal power, is already past; while the time of trouble of Daniel 12: 1 is still future, according to the view we take. How can there be two times of trouble, many years apart, each of them greater than any that had been before it, or should be after it?

To avoid difficulty here, let this distinction be carefully noticed: The tribulation spoken of in Matthew is tribulation upon the church. Christ is there speaking to His disciples, and of His disciples in coming time. They were the ones involved, and for their sake the days of tribulation were to be shortened. (Matthew 24: 22.) The time of trouble mentioned in Daniel is not a time of religious persecution, but of international calamity. There has been nothing like it since there was—not a church, but—a nation. This is the last trouble to come upon the world in its present state. In Matthew there is reference made to time beyond that tribulation; for after it is past, the people of God shall never go through another period of suffering like it. But there is no reference here in Daniel to future time after the trouble here mentioned, for it closes this world's history. It includes the seven last plagues of Revelation 16, and culminates in the revelation of the Lord Jesus, coming in clouds of flaming fire, to visit destruction upon His enemies. But out of this tribulation everyone shall be delivered who shall be found written in the book—the book of life; "for in Mount Zion . . . shall be deliverance, as the Lord hath said, and in the remnant whom the Lord shall call." Joel 2: 32.

VERSE 2 And many of them that sleep in the dust of the earth shall awake, some to everlasting life, and some to shame and everlasting contempt.

This verse reveals the importance of the standing up of Michael, or the beginning of the reign of Christ, for at this time there shall be a resurrection of the dead. Is this the general resurrection which takes place at the second coming of Christ? Or is there to intervene between Christ's reception of the kingdom and His revelation to earth in all His advent glory (Luke 21: 27) a special resurrection answering to the description here given?

Why may it not be the former, or the resurrection which occurs at the last trump?—Because only the righteous, to the exclusion of all the wicked, have part in that resurrection. Those who sleep in Christ then come forth, but the rest of the dead live not again for a thousand years. (Revelation 20: 5.) The *general* resurrection of the whole race, then, is divided into two great events—first, of the righteous exclusively at the coming of Christ; second, of the wicked exclusively a thousand years thereafter. The general resurrection is not a resurrection of both the righteous and the wicked at the same time. Each of these two classes is set off by itself, and the time which elapses between the respective resurrections is plainly stated to be a thousand years.

In the resurrection brought to view in the verse before us, however, many of both righteous and wicked come up together. It cannot therefore be the first resurrection, which includes the righteous only, nor the second resurrection, which is as distinctly confined to the wicked. If the text read, Many of them that sleep in the dust of the earth shall awake to everlasting life, then the "many" might be interpreted as including all the righteous, and the resurrection be that of the just at the second coming of Christ. But the fact that some of the many are wicked, and rise to shame and everlasting contempt, bars the way to such an application.

Is there, then, any place for a special, or limited, resurrection? Is there elsewhere any intimation of such an event, before the Lord appears? The resurrection here predicted takes place when God's people are delivered from the great time of trouble with which the history of this world terminates, and it seems from Revelation 22: 11 that this deliverance is given before the Lord appears. The awful moment arrives when he that is filthy and unjust is pronounced unjust still, and he that is righteous and holy is pronounced holy still. Then the cases of all are forever decided. When this sentence is pronounced upon the righteous, it must be deliverance to them, for then they are placed beyond all reach of danger or fear of evil. But the Lord has not at that time made His appearance, for He immediately adds, "Behold, I come quickly."

The utterance of this solemn fiat seals the righteous to everlasting life and the wicked to eternal death. A voice goes forth from the throne of God, saying, "It is done!" Revelation 16: 17. This is evidently the voice of God, so often alluded to in descriptions of the scenes connected with the last day. Joel speaks of it, and says: "The Lord also shall roar out of Zion, and utter His voice from Jerusalem; and the heavens and the earth shall shake: but the Lord will be the hope of His people, and the strength of the children of Israel." Joel 3: 16. The margin reads instead of "hope," "place of repair, or harbor." Then at this time, when God's voice is heard from heaven just previous to the coming of the Son of man, God is a harbor for His people, or, which is the same thing, provides them deliverance. The last stupendous scene is about to open upon a doomed world. God gives to the astonished nations another evidence and pledge of His power, and raises from the dead a multitude who have long slept in the dust of the earth.

Thus we see that there is a time and place for the resurrection of Daniel 12: 2. A verse in the book of Revelation makes it clear that a resurrection of this kind must take place. "Behold, He cometh with clouds [this is unquestionably the second advent]; and every eye shall see Him [of the nations then living on the earth], and they also which pierced Him [those who took an active part in the terrible work of His crucifixion]; and all kindreds of the earth shall wail because of Him." Revelation 1: 7. Those who crucified the Lord, would, unless there was an exception made in their cases, remain in their graves until the end of the thousand years and come up in the general assembly of the wicked at that time.

But here it is stated that they behold the Lord at His second advent. There must, therefore, be a special resurrection for that purpose.

It is certainly most appropriate that some who were eminent in holiness, who labored and suffered for their hope of a coming Saviour, but died without seeing Him, should be raised a little before, to witness the scenes attending His glorious epiphany; as, in like manner, a goodly company came out of their graves at His resurrection to behold His risen glory (Matthew 27: 52, 53), and to escort Him in triumph to the right hand of the throne of the Majesty on high (Ephesians 4: 8, margin). There will be also some, eminent in wickedness, who have done most to reproach the name of Christ and injure His cause, especially those who caused His cruel death upon the cross, and mocked and derided Him in His dying agonies, who will be raised, as part of their judicial punishment, to behold His return in the clouds of heaven, a celestial victor, in great majesty and splendor unendurable to them.

What is here said is supposed by some to furnish good evidence of the eternal conscious suffering of the wicked, because those of this character who are spoken of come forth to shame and everlasting contempt. How can they forever suffer shame and contempt, unless they are forever conscious? It has already been stated that shame implies their consciousness, but it will be noticed that this is not said to be everlasting. This qualifying word is not inserted until we come to the contempt, which is an emotion felt by others toward the guilty, and does not render necessary the consciousness of those against whom it is directed. Shame for their wickedness and corruption will burn into their very souls as long as they are conscious. When they pass away, consumed for their iniquities, their loathsome characters and their guilty deeds excite only contempt on the part of all the righteous, as long as they hold them in remembrance. The text therefore furnishes no proof of the eternal suffering of the wicked.

VERSE 3 And they that be wise shall shine as the brightness of the firmament; and they that turn many to righteousness as the stars forever and ever.

A Glorious Inheritance.—The margin reads "teachers" in the place of "wise." "They that be *teachers* shall shine as the brightness of the firmament." That is, of course, those who teach the truth, and lead others to a knowledge of it just previous to the time when the events recorded in the foregoing verses are to be fulfilled. As the world estimates loss and profit, it costs something to be teachers of truth in these days. It costs reputation, ease, comfort, and often property. It involves labors, crosses, sacrifices, loss of friendship, ridicule, and not infrequently, persecution.

The question is often asked, How can you afford to keep the true Sabbath, and perhaps lose a situation, reduce your income, or even hazard your means of support? Oh, what shortsightedness, to make obedience to what God requires a matter of pecuniary consideration! How unlike is this to the noble martyrs who loved not their lives unto the death! When God commands, we cannot afford to disobey. If we are asked, How can you afford to keep the Sabbath, and do other duties involved in rendering obedience to the truth? we have only to ask in reply, How can you afford *not* to do them?

In the coming day, when those who have sought to save their lives shall lose them, and those who have been willing to hazard all for the sake of the truth and its divine Lord, shall receive the glorious reward promised in the text, and be raised up to shine as the firmament, and as the imperishable stars forever and ever, it will then be seen who have been wise, and who, on the contrary, have made the choice of blindness and folly. The wicked and worldly now look upon Christians as fools and madmen, and congratulate themselves upon their superior shrewdness in shunning what they call their folly, and avoiding their losses. We need make no response, for those who now render this decision will soon themselves reverse it, and that with terrible though unavailing earnestness.

Meanwhile, it is the Christian's privilege to dwell upon the consolations of this marvelous promise. A conception of its magnitude can be gathered only from the stellar worlds themselves. What are those stars, in the likeness of which the teachers of righteousness are to shine forever and ever? How much of brightness, and majesty, and length of days, is involved in this comparison?

The sun of our own solar system is one of these stars. If we compare it with this globe upon which we live (our handiest standard of measurement), we find it an orb of no small magnitude and magnificence. Our earth is nearly eight thousand miles in diameter, but the sun's diameter is eight hundred sixty-four thousand miles. In size it is one million three hundred thousand times as large as our globe. In the matter of its substance, it would balance three hundred thirty-two thousand worlds like ours. What immensity is this!

Yet this is far from being the largest or the brightest of the orbs in the heavens. The sun's proximity, only some ninety-three million miles from us, gives him with us a controlling presence and influence. But far away in the depths of space, so far that they appear like mere points of light, blaze other orbs of vaster size and greater glory. The nearest fixed star, Proxima Centauri, in the southern hemisphere, is found to be about twenty-five million million miles away. But the polestar system is about a hundred times as remote, or two thousand five hundred trillion miles; and it shines with a luster equal to that of 2500 of our suns. Others are also more luminous, as, for instance, Arcturus, which emits light equivalent to one hundred fifty-eight of our suns; Capella, one hundred eighty-five; and so on, until at last we reach the great star Rigel, in the constellation Orion, which floods the celestial spaces with a brilliance fifteen thousand times that of the ponderous orb which lights and controls our solar system![1] Why, then, does it not appear more luminous to us? Ah, its distance is equivalent to thirty-three million diame-

[1] James H. Jeans, *The Stars in Their Courses*, p. 165.

ters of the earth's orbit; and the latter is one hundred eighty-six million miles! Figures are weak to express such distances. It will be sufficient to say that its glowing light must traverse space as only light travels—one hundred eighty-six thousand miles a second—for a period of more than ten years before it reaches this world of ours. There are many other stars which are hundreds of light-years from our solar system.

Some of these monarchs of the skies rule singly, like our own sun. Some are double; that is, what appears to us like one star is found to consist of two stars—two suns with their retinue of planets, revolving around each other. Others are triple, some are quadruple, and one at least is sextuple.

Besides this, they show colors of the rainbow. Some systems are white, some blue, some red, some yellow, some green. In some, the different suns belonging to the same system are variously colored. Says Dr. Burr: "And, as if to make that Southern Cross the fairest object in all the heavens, we find in it a group of more than a hundred variously colored red, green, blue, and bluish-green suns, so closely thronged together as to appear in a powerful telescope like a superb bouquet, or piece of fancy jewelry." [2]

A few years pass away, and all things earthly gather the mold of age and the odor of decay. But the stars shine on in their glory as in the beginning. Centuries and cycles have gone by, kingdoms have arisen and slowly passed away. We go back beyond the dim and shadowy horizon of history, go back even to the earliest moment when order was evoked out of chaos, and "the morning stars sang together, and all the sons of God shouted for joy" (Job 38: 7)—even then the stars were on their stately marches. How long before this we know not. Astronomers tell us of nebulæ lying on the farthest outposts of telescopic vision, whose light in its never ceasing flight would consume five million years in reaching this planet. Yet their brightness is not dimmed, nor their force abated. The dew of youth still seems fresh upon them. No faltering motion

---

[2] Enoch Fitch Burr, *Ecce Cœlum*, p. 136.

FRANKLIN BOOTH, ARTIST

DANIEL SPEAKS IN THE TIME OF THE END

"Thou, O Daniel, shut up the words, and seal the book, even to the time of the end: many shall run to and fro, and knowledge shall be increased." Daniel 12: 4.

reveals the decrepitude of age. These shine on in undiminished glory through all eternity.

Thus shall they shine who turn many to righteousness. They shall bring joy even to the heart of the Redeemer. Thus shall their years roll on forever and ever.

VERSE 4 But thou, O Daniel, shut up the words, and seal the book, even to the time of the end: many shall run to and fro, and knowledge shall be increased.

Book of Daniel Sealed.—The "words" and "book" here spoken of doubtless refer to the things which had been revealed to Daniel in this prophecy. These things were to be shut up and sealed until the time of the end; that is, they were not to be specially studied, or to any great extent understood, until that time. The time of the end, as has already been shown, began in 1798. As the book was closed up and sealed *to* that time, the plain inference is that at that time, or from that point, the book would be unsealed. People would be better able to understand it, and would have their attention specially called to this part of the inspired word. Of what has been done on the subject of prophecy since that time, it is unnecessary to remind the reader. The prophecies, especially Daniel's prophecy, have been under examination by all students of the word wherever civilization has spread abroad its light upon the earth. So the remainder of the verse, being a prediction of what should take place after the time of the end, begins, "Many shall run to and fro." Whether this running to and fro refers to the passing of people from place to place, and the great improvements in the facilities for transportation and travel made within the past century, or whether it means, as some understand it, a turning to and fro in the prophecies, that is, a diligent and earnest search into prophetic truth, the fulfillment is certainly and surely before our eyes. It must have its application in at least one of these two ways, and in both of these respects the present age is very strongly marked.

Increase of Knowledge.—"And knowledge shall be increased." This must refer either to the increase of knowledge in general, the development of the arts and sciences, or an increase of knowledge in reference to those things revealed to Daniel, which were closed and sealed to the time of the end. Here, again, apply it which way we will, the fulfillment is most marked and complete. Look at the marvelous achievements of the human mind, and the cunning works of men's hands, rivaling the magician's wildest dreams, which have been accomplished within the past hundred years or more. Within this time more advancement has been made in all scientific attainments, more progress has been made in human comforts, in the rapid transaction of business among men, in the transmission of thoughts and words from one to another, and in the means of rapid transit from place to place and even from continent to continent, than all that was done for three thousand years previously.

Harvesting Machinery.—Compare the harvesting methods of our day with the old method of hand reaping which was in use in the days of our grandfathers. Today one machine cuts and gathers, threshes and sacks the grain ready for the market.

Modern Battleships and Mechanized Warcraft.—Modern warfare uses naval armored surface and underseas boats and fighting and bombing airplanes undreamed of at the middle of the past century. Tanks and motor trucks, motorized guns, and other equipment replace the animals and battering-rams of the ancients.

The Steam Railway.—The first American-built locomotive was made at the West Point Foundry, New York, and put into service in 1830. In the present day, improvements have made possible speeds of more than one hundred miles an hour by streamlined trains.

Ocean Steamships.—After little more than a century of steam-powered ships, the largest ocean liners built can cross the Atlantic in four days, and supply every luxury found in the finest hotels.

Television.—Then came wireless, a miracle, in 1896. By 1921, this discovery had developed into radio broadcasting.

Now television—the wireless transmission of sight and sound, the sending forth of motion pictures on air waves—is a household reality.

The Automobile.—Only a few years ago the automobile was unknown. Now the entire population of the United States could ride at one time, and racing cars have made speeds of more than three hundred miles an hour. Huge passenger buses span the continents, and in the large cities double-decked busses have largely replaced electric street cars.

The Typewriter.—The first model of the modern typewriter was put on the market in 1874. Now speedy and noiseless machines, in both office and portable style, are adapted to every type of writing and tabulation, and have become an indispensable part of general business and office equipment everywhere.

The Modern Printing Press.—Contrast the hand printing press of Benjamin Franklin with the high-speed rotary printing press, capable of printing news at more than twice the speed of machine-gun fire.

The Photographic Camera.—The first sunlight picture of a human face was made by Professor John William Draper of New York, in 1840, by an improvement of the process of Daguerre, the French pioneer in photography. Since 1924, by means of improved lenses, photographs have been taken from great distances, over wide areas, and from airplanes high in the sky. Photographs can be taken of objects invisible to the eye by means of X rays and infrared rays. Color photography has made vast advances. Beginning in 1895, the motion picture has become a mighty influence in the lives of millions. Movie and color cameras have been perfected and made cheap enough for use by multitudes.

Air Navigation.—Man's conquest of the air was achieved by the airplane in 1903. It is one of the most noteworthy triumphs of any age. Regular transoceanic passenger and mail service between North and South America and Europe and the Orient has been established.

The Telephone.—The first patent on the telephone was granted Alexander Graham Bell in 1876. Since then intricate networks of telephones have been spread over the continents to link all people together.

Typesetting Machines.—These have worked a revolution in the art of printing. The first machine to set type mechanically was patented in England in 1822 by Dr. William Church. Out of many kinds since introduced, those chiefly used at the present are the type-casting machines, such as the Linotype, invented by Mergenthaler in 1878, and the Monotype, invented by Lanston in 1885.

The Teletypesetter.—By a combination of the telegraph and line-casting machines, it is now possible for one operator at a central station simultaneously to operate type-casting machines by telegraph at any distance or in as many places as are in connection. This puts news into type at an increase in speed of from 50 to 100 per cent.

The Suspension Bridge.—The first suspension bridge of note in this country was built across the Niagara River in 1855. The Golden Gate Bridge across the entrance to San Francisco Bay, finished in 1937 at a cost of $35,000,000, has the longest single span in the world, 4,200 feet. Similar accomplishments in bridge construction have been attained in all progressive countries of the world.

The following is a partial list of advances in knowledge since the time of the end began in 1798:

Gas lighting, 1798; steel pens, 1803; friction matches, 1820; electrotyping, 1837; sewing machine, 1841; anesthesia by ether and by chloroform, 1846, 1848; ocean cable, 1858; Gatling gun, 1861; Monitor warship, 1862; automatic air brakes on trains, 1872; seismograph, 1880; steam turbine, 1883; X ray, 1895; radium, 1898; transcontinental telephone, 1915.

What a galaxy of wonders to originate in a single age! How marvelous the scientific attainments of the present day, upon which all these discoveries and achievements concentrate their light! Viewed from this standpoint, we have truly reached the age of the increase of knowledge.

To the honor of Christianity let it be noted in what lands and by whom, these discoveries have been made which have done so much to add to the facilities and comforts of life. It is in Christian lands, among Christian men. Not in the Dark Ages, which furnished only a travesty on Christianity; not to pagans, who in their ignorance know not God, nor to those who in Christian lands deny Him, is the credit of this progress due. Indeed, it is the very spirit of equality and individual liberty inculcated in the gospel of Christ when preached in its purity, which unshackles human limbs, unfetters human minds, invites them to the highest use of their powers, and makes possible such an age of free thought and action in which these wonders can be achieved.

Increase of Bible Knowledge.—But if we take the other standpoint, and refer the increase of knowledge to an increase of Bible knowledge, we have only to look at the wonderful light which within the past one hundred and fifty years has shone upon the Scriptures. The fulfillment of prophecy has been revealed in the light of history. The use of a better principle of interpretation has led to conclusions showing beyond dispute that the end of all things is near. Truly the seal has been taken from the book, and knowledge respecting what God has revealed in His word, is wonderfully increased. We think it is in this respect that the prophecy is more especially fulfilled, but only in an age of unparalleled facilities like the present could the prophecy be accomplished.

That we are in the time of the end is shown by Revelation 10: 1, 2, where a mighty angel is seen to come down from heaven with a little book open in his hand. Then the book of this prophecy should be no longer sealed. It was to be opened and understood. For proof that the little book to be opened is the book here closed and sealed when Daniel wrote, and that that angel delivers his message in this generation, see comments on Revelation 10: 2.

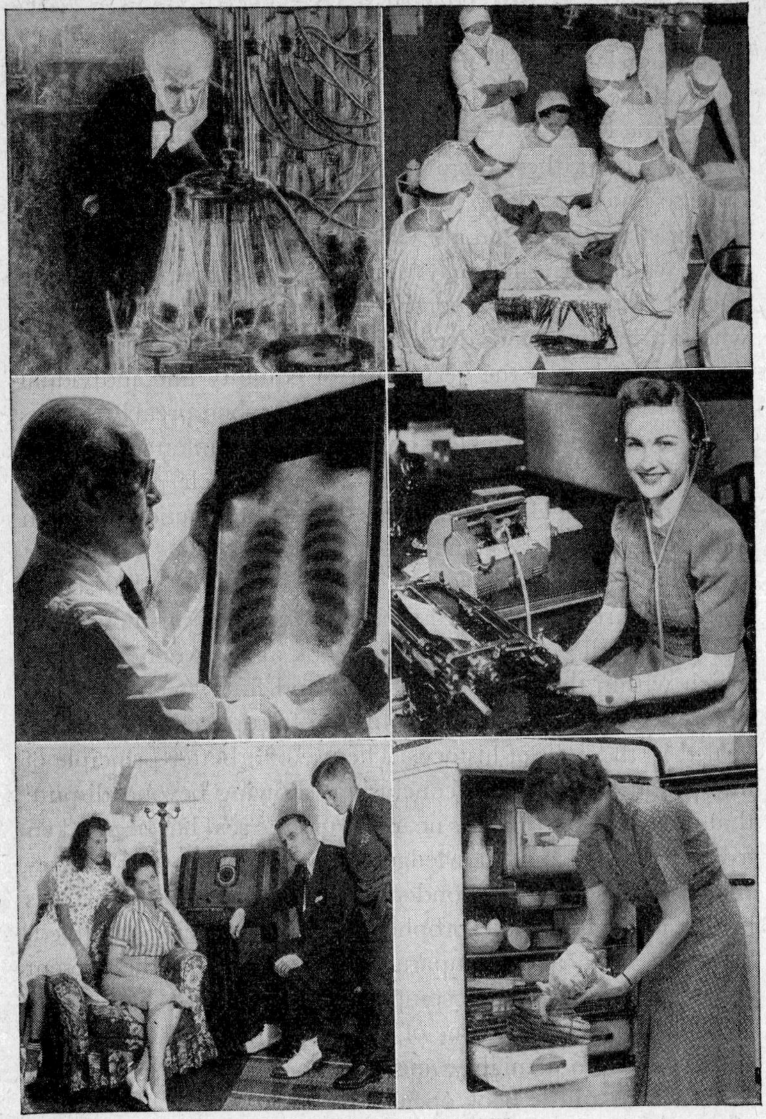

PHOTOGRAPHS BY FISHER SCIENTIFIC CO., ROBERTS, KEYSTONE, LAMBERT

"KNOWLEDGE SHALL BE INCREASED"

The scientific laboratory is a symbol of modern intellectual advancement. Its contributions to medicine, business, and home comforts are common to all.

PHOTOGRAPHS BY B. & O. RY., SHRIBER, LATOUR, PAN-AMER. AIR., ROBERTS, GALLOWAY

"MANY SHALL RUN TO AND FRO"

The speed of modern transportation and communication, and the marvels of engineering, are reminders that we are living in an age of mechanical miracles.

VERSE 5 Then I Daniel looked, and, behold, there stood other two, the one on this side of the bank of the river, and the other on that side of the bank of the river. 6 And one said to the man clothed in linen, which was upon the waters of the river, How long shall it be to the end of these wonders? 7 And I heard the man clothed in linen, which was upon the waters of the river, when he held up his right hand and his left hand unto heaven, and sware by Him that liveth forever that it shall be for a time, times, and a half; and when he shall have accomplished to scatter the power of the holy people, all these things shall be finished.

How Long to the End?—The question, "How long shall it be to the end of these wonders?" undoubtedly has reference to all that has previously been mentioned, including the standing up of Michael, the time of trouble, the deliverance of God's people, and the special resurrection of verse 2. The answer seems to be given in two divisions: First, a specific prophetic period is marked off, and then an indefinite period follows before the conclusion of all these things is reached, just as we have it in Daniel 8: 13, 14. When the question was asked, "How long . . . the vision . . . to give both the sanctuary and the host to be trodden underfoot?" the answer mentioned a definite period of 2300 days, followed by an indefinite period in the cleansing of the sanctuary. So in the text before us, there is given the period of a time, times, and a half, or 1260 years, and then an indefinite period for the continuance of the scattering of the power of the holy people, before the consummation.

The 1260 years mark the period of papal supremacy. Why is this period here introduced?—Probably because this power is the one which does more than any other in the world's history toward scattering the power of the holy people, or oppressing the church of God. But what shall we understand by the expression, "When he shall have accomplished to scatter the power of the holy people"? To whom does the pronoun "he" refer? According to the wording of this scripture, the antecedent would at first seem to be "Him that liveth forever," or Jehovah; but, as an eminent expositor of the prophecies judiciously remarks, in considering the pronouns of the Bible we are to interpret them according to the facts of the case, and hence must frequently refer them to an antecedent understood, rather than to some noun which is expressed. So, here, the little horn, or man of sin, after being introduced by the particular mention of the time of his supremacy, 1260 years, may be the power referred to by the pronoun "he." For 1260 years he had grievously oppressed the church, or scattered its power. After his supremacy is taken away, his disposition toward the truth and its advocates still remains, his power is still felt to a certain extent, and he continues his work of oppression as far as he is able, until when?—Until the last of the events brought to view in verse 1, the deliverance of God's people. When they are thus delivered, persecuting powers are no longer able to oppress them, their power is no longer scattered, the end of the wonders described in this great prophecy is reached, and all its predictions are accomplished.

Or without particularly altering the sense, we may refer the pronoun "he" to the one mentioned in the oath of verse 7, as "Him that liveth forever;" that is, God, since He employs the agency of earthly powers in chastising and disciplining His people, and in that sense may be said Himself to scatter their power. By His prophet He said concerning the kingdom of Israel, "I will overturn, overturn, overturn it, . . . until He come whose right it is." Ezekiel 21: 27. Again, "Jerusalem shall be trodden down of the Gentiles, until the times of the Gentiles be fulfilled." Luke 21: 24. Of like import is the prophecy of Daniel 8: 13: "How long . . . the vision . . . *to give* both the sanctuary and the host to be trodden under foot?" Who gives them to this condition?—God. Why?—To discipline, to "purify and make white" His people. How long? —Until the sanctuary is cleansed.

VERSE 8 And I heard, but I understood not: then said I, O my lord, what shall be the end of these things? 9 And he said, Go thy way, Daniel: for the words are closed up and sealed till the time of the end. 10 Many shall be purified, and made white, and tried; but the wicked shall do wickedly: and none of the wicked shall understand; but the wise shall understand.

The Book Sealed Until the Time of the End.—By Daniel's solicitude to understand fully all that had been shown him, we are forcibly reminded of Peter's words where he speaks of the prophets' inquiring and searching diligently to understand the predictions concerning the sufferings of Christ and the glory that should follow; as also of the fact "that not unto themselves, but unto us they did minister." 1 Peter 1: 12. How little of what they wrote were some of the prophets permitted to understand! But they did not therefore refuse to write. If God required it, they knew that in due time He would see that His people derived from their writings all the benefit that He intended.

So the language here used to Daniel was the same as telling him that when the right time should come, the wise would understand the meaning of what he had written, and profit thereby. The time of the end was the time in which the Spirit of God was to break the seal of this book. Consequently this was the time during which the wise should understand, while the wicked, lost to all sense of the value of eternal truth, with hearts callous and hardened in sin, would grow continually more wicked and more blind. None of the wicked understand. The efforts which the wise put forth to understand, the wicked call folly and presumption, and ask in sneering phrase, "Where is the promise of His coming?" Should the question be raised, Of what time and what generation does the prophet speak? the solemn answer would be, Of the present time, and of the generation now before us. This language of the prophet is now receiving a most striking fulfillment.

The phraseology of verse 10 seems at first sight to be rather peculiar: "Many shall be purified, and made white, and tried." How, it may be asked, can they be made white and then tried (as the language would seem to imply), when it is by being tried that they are purified and made white? The language doubtless describes a process which is many times repeated in the experience of those, who, during this time, are being made ready for the coming and kingdom of the Lord.

They are purified and made white, as compared with their former condition. Then they are again tried. Greater tests are brought to bear upon them. If they endure these, the work of purification is thus carried on to a still greater extent until they attain to a purer character. After reaching this state, they are tried again, and further purified and made white. Thus the process goes on until characters are developed which will stand the test of the day of judgment and a spiritual condition is reached which needs no further trial.

VERSE 11 And from the time that the daily sacrifice shall be taken away, and the abomination that maketh desolate set up, there shall be a thousand two hundred and ninety days.

The 1290 Prophetic Days.—We have here a new prophetic period introduced, 1290 prophetic days, which according to Bible authority would denote the same number of literal years. From the reading of the text, some have inferred that this period begins with the setting up of the abomination of desolation, or the papal power, in A. D. 538, and consequently extends to 1828. We find nothing in the latter year to mark its termination, but we do find evidence in the margin that it begins *before* the setting up of the papal abomination. The margin reads, "*To* set up the abomination." With this reading the text would stand thus: "From the time that the daily sacrifice shall be taken away to set up [or in order to set up] the abomination that maketh desolate, there shall be a thousand two hundred and ninety days."

The Year A. D. 508.—We are not told directly to what event these 1290 days reach; but inasmuch as their beginning is marked by a work which takes place to prepare the way for the setting up of the papacy, it would be natural to conclude that their end would be marked by the cessation of papal supremacy. Counting back, then, 1290 years from 1798, we have the year 508. This period is doubtless given to show the date of the taking away of the daily, and it is the only one which does this. The two periods, therefore, the 1290 and the 1260 days, terminate together in 1798, the latter beginning in 538, and the former in 508, thirty years previous. In support of the date A. D. 508 the following historical quotations are given:

Baptism of Clovis.—"As to the writings of Anastasius, . . . there is one from him to Clovis, king of the Franks, congratulating that prince on his conversion to the Christian religion. For Clovis, the first Christian king of the Franks, was baptized on Christmas Day 496, the very day, according to some, on which the pope was ordained."[3]

Thomas Hodgkin says:

"The result of this ceremony was to change the political relations of every state in Gaul. Though the Franks were among the roughest and most uncivilized of the tribes that had poured westwards across the Rhine, as Catholics they were now sure of a welcome from the Catholic clergy of every city, and where the clergy led, the 'Roman' provincials, or in other words the Latin-speaking laity, generally followed. Immediately after his baptism Clovis received a letter of enthusiastic welcome into the true fold, written by Avitus, Bishop of Vienne, the most eminent ecclesiastic of the Burgundian kingdom."[4]

Clovis the First Catholic Prince.—"It is observable, that Clovis was, at this time [496], the only Catholic prince in the known world, as the word Catholic was then understood. Anastasius, Emperor of the East, was a professed Eutychian. Theodoric, King of the Ostrogoths in Italy; Alaric, King of the Visigoths, master of all Spain, and of the third part of Gaul; the kings of the Burgundians, Suevians, and Vandals, in Gaul, Spain, and Africa; were all zealous followers of Arius. As for the other kings of the Franks settled in Gaul, they were still pagans. Clovis was not only the sole Catholic prince at this time in the world; but the first king that ever embraced the Catholic religion; which has procured to the French king the title of the 'most Christian,' and that of 'the eldest son of the Church.' But were we to compare the conduct and actions of Clovis, the Catholic, with those of the Arian King

[3] Archibald Bower, *The History of the Popes*, Vol. I, p. 295.

[4] Thomas Hodgkin, *Theodoric the Goth*, pp. 190, 191.

Theodoric, such a comparison would no ways redound to the honor of the Catholic faith."[5]

Popes Endangered by Arian Princes.—Ephraim Emerton, former professor of history at Harvard University, says:

"By the time the Franks had fought the battle of Strassburg the bishops of the city of Rome had come to be looked up to as the leaders of the Church in what had been the Western Empire. They had come to be called popes, and were trying hard to govern the Church of the West just as a king might govern his people. We have seen how much respect a venerable pope like Leo could command even from such rude destroyers as Attila and Gaiseric. Now the popes had always been devoted Catholics, opposed to Arianism wherever it appeared. At the moment of the Frankish conversion they were in constant danger from the Arian Ostrogoths who had just got a firm hold upon Italy. Theodoric had not disturbed the religion of Rome, but a new king might arise who should try to force Arianism upon the whole of Italy. The pope was therefore overjoyed to hear that the newly converted Franks had taken his form of the Christian belief. He was ready to bless every undertaking of theirs as the work of God, if only it might be against the worse than heathen Arians. Thus began as early as the year 500 an understanding between the Roman Papacy and the Frankish kingdom which was to ripen into an intimate alliance and to do very much towards shaping all the future history of Europe."[6]

Clovis's Conversion a Check on the Arians.—"The event which intensified the fears of all these Arian kings, and which left to each one little more than the hope that he might be the last to be devoured, was the conversion to Catholicism of Clovis, the heathen king of the Franks."[7]

Barbarian League Against Clovis.—"The kings of the barbarians were . . . invited to join in a 'League of Peace,' in

---

[5] Archibald Bower, *The History of the Popes*, Vol. I, p. 296, footnote. See also Henry Hart Milman, *History of Latin Christianity*, Vol. I, pp. 381-388.

[6] Ephraim Emerton, *Introduction to the Study of the Middle Ages*, pp. 65, 66.

[7] Thomas Hodgkin, *Theodoric the Goth*, p. 186.

order to check the lawless aggressions of Clovis which threatened danger to all."[8]

"To form such a confederacy and to league together all the older Arian monarchies against this one aspiring Catholic state which threatened to absorb them all, was now the main purpose of Theodoric."[9]

Clovis Launches a Religious War.—"The diplomatic action of Theodoric was powerless to avert the war; possibly even it may have stimulated Clovis to strike rapidly before a hostile coalition could be formed against him. At an assembly of his nation (perhaps the 'Camp of March') in the early part of 507, he impetuously declared: 'I take it grievously amiss that these Arians should hold so large a part of Gaul. Let us go and overcome them with God's help, and bring the land into subjection to us.' The saying pleased the whole multitude, and the collected army marched southward to the Loire."[10]

Clovis Defeats the Visigoths.—"The next campaign of the Frankish king was one of far greater importance and success. He was set on trying his fortune against the young king of the Visigoths, whose personal weakness and unpopularity with his Roman subjects tempted him to an invasion of Aquitaine. It would seem that Chlodovech [Clovis] carefully chose as a *casus belli* the Arian persecutions of Alaric, who, like his father Euric, was a bad master to his Catholic subjects. . . . *In 507 Chlodovech declared war on the Visigoths.*"[11]

"Why the explosion was delayed until the year 507 is unknown. That the king of the Franks was the aggressor is certain. He easily found a pretext for beginning the war as a champion and protector of Catholic Christianity against the absolutely just measures which Alaric took against his treacherous orthodox clergy. . . . In the spring of 507 he [Clovis] suddenly crossed the Loire and marched toward Poitiers. . . .

---

[8] *Ibid.*, pp. 198, 199.
[9] *Ibid.*, p. 194.
[10] *Ibid.*, p. 199.
[11] Charles Oman, *The Dark Ages*, p. 62.

Ten miles from Poitiers, the Visigoths had taken up their position. Alaric put off beginning battle because he was waiting for the Ostrogoth troops, but as they were hindered by the appearance of a Byzantine fleet in Italian waters he determined to fight instead of beating a retreat, as it would have been wise to do. After a short engagement the Goths turned and fled. In the pursuit the king of the Goths was killed, it was said by Clovis's own hand (507). With this overthrow the rule of the Visigoths in Gaul was ended forever."[12]

"It is evident, from the language of Gregory of Tours, that this conflict between the Franks and Visigoths was regarded by the Orthodox party of his own and preceding ages as a religious war, on which, humanly speaking, *the prevalence of the Catholic or the Arian creed in Western Europe depended.*"[13]

"A. D. 508. A short time after these events, Clovis received the titles and dignity of Roman patricius and consul from the Greek emperor Anastasius; who appears to have been prompted to this act more by motives of jealousy and hatred towards Theodoric the Ostrogoth, than by any love he bore for the restless and encroaching Frank. The meaning of these obsolete titles, as applied to those who stood in no direct relation to either division of the Roman Empire, has never been sufficiently explained. . . . The sun of Rome was set, but the twilight of her greatness still rested on the world. The German kings and warriors received with pleasure, and wore with pride, a title which brought them into connection with that imperial city, of whose universal dominion, of whose skill in armies and arts, the traces lay everywhere around them."[14]

"In 508 Clovis received at Tours the insignia of the consulship from the eastern emperor, Anastasius, but the title was purely honorific. The last years of his life Clovis spent in

---

[12] *The Cambridge Medieval History,* Vol. I, p. 286. By permission of the Macmillan Company, publishers in the United States.

[13] Walter C. Perry, *The Franks, From Their First Appearance in History to the Death of King Pepin,* p. 85.

[14] *Ibid.,* pp. 88, 89.

Paris, which he made the capital of his kingdom."[15]

End of Arian Resistance.—This disposed of the Visigothic kingdom, but there yet remained the league of Arian powers under Theodoric. Alaric had counted on the assistance of Theodoric, but the latter failed him. The next year, A. D. 508, however, Theodoric came against Clovis and gained a victory, after which he unaccountably made peace with him, and the resistance of the Arian powers was at an end.[16]

Significance of Clovis's Victories.—The eminence which Clovis had attained in the year 508, and the significance of his victories to the future of Europe and the church, were so great that historians cannot forbear commenting on them.

"Nor was his a temporary conquest. The kingdom of the West Goths and the Burgundians had become the kingdom of the Franks. The invaders had at length arrived, who were to remain. It was decided that the Franks, and not the Goths, were to direct the future destinies of Gaul and Germany, and that the Catholic faith, and not Arianism, was to be the religion of these great realms."[17]

"Clovis was the first to unite all the elements from which the new social order was to be formed,—namely, the barbarians, whom he established in power; the Roman civilization, to which he rendered homage by receiving the insignia of patrician and of consul from the Emperor Anastasius; and finally, the Catholic Church, with which he formed that fruitful alliance which was continued by his successors."[18]

Paved the Way for Alliance of Church and State.—"In him [Clovis] met two religions, and two ages of the world. At his birth the Roman world was still a power; his death marks the dawn of the Middle Ages. He stepped into the vacant place of the Eastern emperor, and paved the way for what Charle-

---

15 *Encyclopædia Britannica,* 11th ed., art. "Clovis," Vol. VI, p. 563.

16 See Thomas Hodgkin, *Theodoric the Goth,* pp. 202, 203; Nugent Robinson, *A History of the World,* Vol. I, pp. 75-79, 81, 82.

17 Richard W. Church, *The Beginning of the Middle Ages,* pp. 38, 39.

18 Victor Duruy, *The History of the Middle Ages,* p. 32.

magne perfected—the fusion of Roman and German civilization, the alliance of church and state."[19]

Clovis Saved the Church From Paganism and Arianism.—"He [Clovis] had on all occasions shown himself the heartless ruffian, the greedy conqueror, the bloodthirsty tyrant; but by his conversion he had led the way to the triumph of Catholicism; he had saved the Roman Church from the Scylla and Charybdis of heresy and paganism, planted it on a rock in the very center of Europe, and fixed its doctrines and traditions in the hearts of the conquerors of the West."[20]

Foundations of the Medieval Church.—"The results of their [the Franks'] occupation of Gaul were so important, the empire which they founded, their alliance with the church, their legal notions and political institutions were all of such decisive influence upon the future that their history deserves separate treatment. . . . It is to them that the political inheritance of the Roman Empire passed; to them came the honor of taking up and carrying on, roughly, to be sure, and far less extensively and effectively, but nevertheless of actually carrying on the political work which Rome had been doing. They alone represent that unity which Rome had established, and so far as that unity was maintained at all as a definite fact, it is the Franks who maintained it. . . . It is only at the end of the fifth century that their career really begins, and then, as so often in similar cases, it is the genius of one man, a great leader, which creates the nation. . . . Clovis . . . appears as one of the great creative spirits who give a new direction to the currents of history. . . . A third step of great importance in this process of union was also taken by Clovis. One institution, produced in the ancient world before the Germans entered it, had continued with vigorous life and wide influence, indeed, with slowly increasing power, through all the changes of this chaotic period. It was to be in the future a still greater

---

[19] Julius von Pflugk-Harttung, in *A History of All Nations*, Vol. VII, p. 72.

[20] Walter C. Perry, *The Franks, From Their First Appearance in History to the Death of King Pepin*, p. 97.

power and to exert an influence even wider and more permanent than that of the Franks. . . . This was the Roman Church. *It was to be the great ecclesiastical power of the future.* It was therefore a most essential question whether the Franks, *who were to grow on their side into the great political power of the future*, should do so in alliance with this other power or in opposition to it. . . .

"This question Clovis settled, not long after the beginning of his career, by his conversion to Catholic Christianity. . . . In these three ways, therefore, the work of Clovis was of creative influence upon the future. He brought together the Roman and the German upon equal terms, each preserving the sources of his strength, to form a new civilization. He founded a political power which was to unite nearly all the continent in itself, and to bring the period of the invasions to an end. He established a close alliance between the two great controlling forces of the future, the two empires which continued the unity which Rome had created, the political empire and the ecclesiastical."[21]

Thus in A. D. 508 terminated united resistance to the development of the papacy. The question of supremacy between Frank and Goth, between the Catholic and the Arian religions, had then been settled in favor of the Catholics.

VERSE 12 Blessed is he that waiteth, and cometh to the thousand three hundred and five and thirty days. 13 But go thou thy way till the end be: for thou shalt rest, and stand in thy lot at the end of the days.

The 1335 Prophetic Days.—Still another prophetic period is here introduced, denoting 1335 years. Can we tell when this period begins and ends? The only clue we have to the solution of this question, is the fact that it is spoken of in immediate connection with the 1290 years, which began in 508 as shown above. From that point there shall be, says the prophet, 1290 days. The very next sentence reads, "Blessed is he that waiteth, and cometh to the 1335 days." From what point?—

---

[21] George Burton Adams, *Civilization During the Middle Ages*, pp. 137-144.

From the same point, undoubtedly, as that from which the 1290 date, namely, A. D. 508. Unless they are to be reckoned from this point, it is impossible to locate them, and they must be excepted from the prophecy of Daniel when we apply to it the words of Christ, "Whoso readeth, let him understand." Matthew 24: 15. From this point they would extend to 1843, for 1335 added to 508 make 1843. Beginning in the spring of the former year, they ended in the spring of the latter.

But how can it be that they have ended, it may be asked, since at the end of these days Daniel stands in his lot, which is by some supposed to refer to his resurrection from the dead? This question is founded on a misapprehension in two respects: First, that the days at the end of which Daniel stands in his lot are the 1335 days; and second, that the standing of Daniel in his lot is his resurrection, which also cannot be sustained. The only thing promised at the end of the 1335 days is a blessing to those who wait and come to that time; that is, those who are then living. What is this blessing? Looking at the year 1843, when these years expired, what do we behold? We see a remarkable fulfillment of prophecy in the great proclamation of the second coming of Christ. Forty-five years before this, the time of the end began, the book was unsealed, and light began to increase. About the year 1843, there was a grand culmination of all the light that had been shed on prophetic subjects up to that time. The proclamation went forth in power. The new and stirring doctrine of the setting up of the kingdom of God shook the world. New life was imparted to the true disciples of Christ. The unbelieving were condemned, the churches were tested, and a spirit of revival was awakened which has had no parallel since.

Was this the blessing? Listen to the Saviour's words: "Blessed are your eyes," said He to His disciples, "for they see; and your ears, for they hear." Matthew 13: 16. Again He told His followers that prophets and kings had desired to see the things which they saw, and had not seen them. But "blessed," said He to them, "are the eyes which see the things that ye see." Luke 10: 23, 24. If a new and glorious truth was a blessing in the days of Christ to those who received it, why was it not equally so in A. D. 1843?

It may be objected that those who engaged in this movement were disappointed in their expectations; so were the disciples of Christ at His first advent, in an equal degree. They shouted before Him as He rode into Jerusalem, expecting that He would then take the kingdom. But the only throne to which He then went was the cross, and instead of being hailed as king in a royal palace, He was laid a lifeless form in Joseph's new sepulcher. Nevertheless, they were "blessed" in receiving the truths they had heard.

It may be objected further that this was not a sufficient blessing to be marked by a prophetic period. Why not, since the period in which it was to occur, the time of the end, is introduced by a prophetic period; since our Lord, in verse 14 of His great prophecy of Matthew 24, makes a special announcement of this movement; and since it is still further set forth in Revelation 14: 6, 7, under the symbol of an angel flying through midheaven with a special anouncement of the everlasting gospel to the inhabitants of the earth? Surely the Bible gives great prominence to this movement.

Two more questions remain to be noticed briefly: What days are referred to in verse 13? What is meant by Daniel's standing in his lot? Those who claim that the days are the 1335, are led to that application by looking back no further than to the preceding verse, where the 1335 days are mentioned; whereas, in making an application of these days so indefinitely introduced, the whole scope of the prophecy should certainly be taken in from Daniel 8. Chapters 9, 10, 11, and 12 are clearly a continuation and explanation of the vision of Daniel 8; hence we may say that in the vision of chapter 8, as carried out and explained, there are four prophetic periods: the 2300, 1260, 1290, and 1335 days. The first is the principal and longest period; the others are but intermediate parts and subdivisions of this. Now, when the angel tells Daniel at the conclusion of his instructions that he shall stand in his lot at the end of the days, without specifying which period was meant, would not Daniel's mind naturally turn to the principal and longest period, the 2300 days, rather than to any of its subdivisions? If this is so, the 2300 are the days intended. The reading of the Septuagint seems to look plainly in this direction: "But go thy way and rest; for there are yet days and seasons to the full accomplishment [of these things]; and thou shalt stand in thy lot at the end of the days." This certainly carries the mind back to the long period contained in the first vision, in relation to which the subsequent instructions were given.

The 2300 days, as has been already shown, terminated in 1844, and brought us to the cleansing of the sanctuary. How did Daniel at that time stand in his lot? In the person of his Advocate, our great High Priest, as He presents the cases of the righteous for acceptance to His Father. The word here translated "lot" does not mean a piece of real estate, a "lot" of land, but the "decisions of chance" or the "determinations of Providence." At the end of the days, the lot, so to speak, was to be cast. In other words, a determination was to be made in reference to those who should be accounted worthy of a possession in the heavenly inheritance. When Daniel's case comes up for examination, he is found righteous, stands in his lot, is assigned a place in the heavenly Canaan.

When Israel was about to enter into the Promised Land, the lot was cast, and the possession of each tribe was assigned. The tribes thus stood in their respective "lots" long before they entered upon the actual possession of the land. The time of the cleansing of the sanctuary corresponds to this period of Israel's history. We now stand upon the borders of the heavenly Canaan, and decisions are being made, assigning to some a place in the eternal kingdom, and barring others forever. In the decision of his case, Daniel's portion in the celestial inheritance will be made sure to him. With him all the faithful will also stand. When this devoted servant of God, who filled up a long life with the noblest deeds of service to his Maker, though cumbered with the weightiest cares of this life, shall enter upon his reward for well-doing, we too may enter with him into rest.

We draw the study of this prophecy to a close, with the remark that it has been with no small degree of satisfaction that we have spent what time and study we have on this wonderful prophecy, and in contemplating the character of this most beloved of men and most illustrious of prophets. God is no respecter of persons, and a reproduction of Daniel's character will secure the divine favor as signally even now. Let us emulate his virtues, that we, like him, may have the approbation of God while here, and dwell amid the creations of His infinite glory in the long hereafter.

THE RESPONSE OF HISTORY TO THE REVELATION

"We have also a more sure word of prophecy; whereunto ye do well that ye take heed, as unto a light that shineth in a dark place, until the day dawn, and the day star arise in your hearts." 2 Peter 1: 19.

INTRODUCTION

THE REVELATION, usually termed "The Apocalypse," from its Greek name, 'Αποκάλυψις, *Apokalypsis*, meaning "a disclosure, a revelation," has been described to be "a panorama of the glory of Christ." In the Evangelists we have the record of His humiliation, His condescension, His toil and sufferings, His patience, His mockings by those who should have done Him reverence, and finally His death upon the shameful cross—a death esteemed in that age to be the most ignominious that men could inflict. In the Revelation we have the gospel of His enthronement in glory, His association with the Father upon the throne of universal dominion, His overruling providence among the nations of the earth, and His coming again, not a homeless stranger, but in power and great glory, to punish His enemies and reward His followers.

Scenes of glory surpassing fable are unveiled before us in this book. Appeals of unwonted power bear down upon the impenitent from its sacred pages in threatenings of judgment that have no parallel in any other portion of the book of God. Consolation which no language can describe is here given to the humble followers of Christ in this world. No other book takes us at once, and so irresistibly, into another sphere. Long vistas are here opened before us, which are bounded by no terrestrial objects, but carry us forward into other worlds. And if ever themes of thrilling and impressive interest, and grand and lofty imagery, and sublime and magnificent description, can invite the attention of mankind, then the Revelation invites us to a careful study of its pages, which urge upon our notice the realities of a momentous future and an unseen world.

 FRANKLIN BOOTH, ARTIST

HOW PROPHECY IS GIVEN

"Blessed is he that readeth, and they that hear the words of this prophecy, and keep those things which are written therein." Revelation 1: 3.

CHAPTER I

THE DIVINE METHOD OF PROPHETIC REVELATION

THE BOOK of the Revelation opens with the announcement of its title, and with a benediction on those who give diligent heed to its solemn prophetic utterances:

VERSE 1 The Revelation of Jesus Christ, which God gave unto Him, to show unto His servants things which must shortly come to pass; and He sent and signified it by His angel unto His servant John: 2 who bare record of the word of God, and of the testimony of Jesus Christ, and of all things that he saw. 3 Blessed is he that readeth, and they that hear the words of this prophecy, and keep those things which are written therein: for the time is at hand.

The Title.—The translators of the King James Version of the Bible have given this book the title, "The Revelation of St. John the Divine." In this they contradict the very first words of the book itself, which declare it to be "The Revelation of Jesus Christ." Jesus Christ is the Revelator, not John. John is but the penman employed by Christ to write out this Revelation for the benefit of His church. John is the disciple of Jesus who was beloved and highly favored among the twelve. He was evangelist and apostle, and the writer of the Gospel and the epistles which bear his name. To his previous titles must now be added that of prophet; for the Revelation is a prophecy, and John so denominates it. But the content of this book has its origin in a still higher source. It is not only the Revelation of Jesus Christ, but it is the Revelation which God gave unto Him. It comes first from the great Fountain of all wisdom and truth, God the Father; by Him it was communicated to Jesus Christ, the Son; and Christ sent and signified it by His angel to His servant John.

The Character of the Book.—This is expressed in one word, "Revelation." A revelation is something revealed or made known, not something hidden and concealed. Moses tells us that "the secret things belong unto the Lord our God: but those things which *are revealed* belong unto us and to our children forever." Deuteronomy 29: 29. The very title of the book, then, is a sufficient refutation of the opinion sometimes expressed that this book is among the mysteries of God, and cannot be understood. Were this the case, it should bear some such title as "The Mystery" or "The Hidden Book," certainly not "The Revelation."

Its Object.—"To show unto His servants things which must shortly come to pass." His servants—who are they? For whose benefit was the Revelation given? Was it to be for any specified persons, for any particular churches, for any special period of time? No, it is for all the church in all time, as long as any of the events predicted within the book remain to be accomplished. It is for all those who can claim the appellation, "His servants," wherever or whenever they may live.

God says that this prophecy was given to reveal coming events to His servants, yet many of the expositors of His word tell us that no man can understand it! This is as if God would undertake to make known to mankind important truths, yet fall into the worse than earthly folly of clothing them in language or in figures which human minds could not comprehend! It is as if He would command a person to behold some distant object, and then erect an impenetrable barrier between him and the object! Or as if He would give His servants a light to guide them through the gloom of night, yet throw over that light a pall so thick and heavy that not a ray of its brightness could penetrate the obscuring folds! How men dishonor God who thus trifle with His word! No; the Revelation will accomplish the object for which it was given, and "His servants" will learn from it the "things which must shortly come to pass," and which concern their eternal salvation.

His Angel.—Christ sent and made known the Revelation to John by "His angel." A particular angel seems to be brought to view here. What angel could appropriately be called

Christ's angel? We found an answer to this question in our study, as will be seen in the comments on Daniel 10: 21. From that study we concluded that the truths to be revealed to Daniel were committed exclusively to Christ, and to an angel whose name was Gabriel. Similar to the work of communicating important truth to the "beloved prophet" is the work of Christ in the book of the Revelation—transmitting important truth to the "beloved disciple." Who in this work can be *His* angel but the one who was engaged with Daniel in the former work of prophecy, that is, the angel Gabriel? It would also seem most appropriate that the same angel who was employed to carry messages to the "beloved" prophet of ancient times, should perform the same office for the prophet John in the gospel age. (See comments on Revelation 19: 10.)

Blessing on the Reader.—"Blessed is he that readeth, and they that hear the words of this prophecy." Is there so direct and formal a blessing pronounced upon the reading and observance of any other part of the word of God? What encouragement we have for its study! Shall we say that it cannot be understood? Is a blessing offered for the study of a book which it can do us no good to study?

God has pronounced His blessing upon the reader of this prophecy, and has set the seal of His approbation to an earnest study of its marvelous pages. With such encouragement from a divine source, the child of God will be unmoved by a thousand feeble counterblasts from men.

Every fulfillment of prophecy brings its duties. There are things in the Revelation to be observed, or performed. Practical duties are to be fulfilled as the result of an understanding and accomplishment of the prophecy. A notable instance of this kind may be seen in Revelation 14: 12, where it is said, "Here are they that keep the commandments of God, and the faith of Jesus."

"The time is at hand," writes John, and in so doing he gives another motive for the study of this book. It becomes more and more important, as we draw near the great consummation. On this point we offer the impressive thoughts of another: "The importance of studying the Apocalypse increases with the lapse of time. Here are 'things which must shortly come to pass.' . . . Even when John bare record of the word of God, and of the testimony of Jesus Christ, and of all things that he saw, the long period within which those successive scenes were to be realized was at hand. The first in the connected series was on the eve of accomplishment. If proximity then constituted a motive for heeding these contents, how much more does it now! Every revolving century, every closing year, adds to the urgency with which attention is challenged to the concluding portion of Holy Writ. And does not that intensity of devotion to the present, which characterizes our times and our country, enhance the reasonableness of this claim? Never, surely, was there a period when some mighty counteracting power was more needed. The Revelation of Jesus Christ duly studied supplies an appropriate corrective influence. Would that all Christians might in fullest measure receive the blessing of 'them that hear the words of this prophecy, and that keep the things which are written therein; for the time is at hand.' "[1]

The Dedication.—Following the blessing, we have the dedication in these words:

VERSE 4 John to the seven churches which are in Asia: Grace be unto you, and peace, from Him which is, and which was, and which is to come; and from the seven Spirits which are before His throne; 5 and from Jesus Christ, who is the faithful witness, and the first begotten of the dead, and the prince of the kings of the earth. Unto Him that loved us, and washed us from our sins in His own blood, 6 and hath made us kings and priests unto God and His Father; to Him be glory and dominion forever and ever. Amen.

The Churches in Asia.—There were more churches in Asia than seven. We may confine ourselves to that western fraction of Asia known as Asia Minor, or we may include still less territory than that. Even in that small part of Asia Minor where the seven churches were located, and right in their very

---

[1] Augustus C. Thompson, *Morning Hours in Patmos*, pp. 28, 29.

midst, there were other important churches. Colosse, to the Christians of which place Paul addressed his epistle to the Colossians, was but a short distance from Laodicea. Miletus was nearer than any of the seven to Patmos, where John had his vision. Furthermore, it was an important center of Christianity, as we may judge from the fact that during one of his stays there Paul sent for the elders of the church of Ephesus to meet him at that place. (Acts 20: 17-38.) At the same place he also left in good Christian hands, his disciple Trophimus, sick. (2 Timothy 4: 20.) Troas, where Paul spent a season with the disciples, and whence after waiting until the Sabbath was past he started upon his journey, was not far removed from Pergamos, named among the seven.

It becomes therefore an interesting question to determine why seven of the churches of Asia Minor were selected as the ones to which the Revelation should be dedicated. Does the salutation to the seven churches in Revelation 1, and the admonitions to them in Revelation 2 and 3, have reference solely to the seven literal churches named? Are things described only as they then existed, and portrayed as they were to come to them alone? We cannot so conclude, for good and substantial reasons:

The entire book of Revelation was dedicated to the seven churches. (See Revelation 1: 3, 11, 19; 22: 18, 19.) The book was no more applicable to them than to other Christians in Asia Minor—those, for instance, who dwelt in Pontus, Galatia, Cappadocia, and Bithynia, who were addressed in Peter's epistle (1 Peter 1: 1); or the Christians of Colosse, Troas, and Miletus, in the very midst of the churches named.

Only a small part of the book could have individually concerned the seven churches, or any of the Christians of John's day, for most of the events it brings to view were so far in the future as to lie far beyond the lifetime of the generation then living, or even the time during which those churches would continue. Consequently those churches could have no direct connection with them.

The seven stars which the Son of man held in His right hand are declared to be the angels of the seven churches. (Verse 20.) The *angels* of the churches, doubtless all will agree, are the *ministers* of the churches. Their being held in the right hand of the Son of man denotes the sustaining power, guidance, and protection vouchsafed to them. But there were only seven of them in His right hand. Are there only seven thus cared for by the great Master of assemblies? May not *all* the true ministers of the entire gospel age derive from this representation the consolation of knowing that they are upheld and guided by the right hand of the great Head of the church? Such would seem to be the only consistent conclusion to be reached.

Again, John, looking into the Christian Era, saw only seven candlesticks, representing seven churches, in the midst of which stood the Son of man. The position of the Son of man among them must denote His presence with them, His watch-care over them, and His searching scrutiny of all their works. But does He thus take cognizance of only seven individual churches? May we not rather conclude that this scene represents His position in reference to all His churches during the gospel age? Then why were only seven mentioned? Seven, as used in the Scriptures, is a number denoting fullness and completeness. Therefore the seven candlesticks denote the entire gospel church in seven periods, and the seven churches may be applied in the same manner.

Why, then, were the seven particular churches chosen that are mentioned? For the reason, doubtless, that in the names of these churches, according to the definitions of the words, are brought out the religious features of those periods of the gospel age which they respectively were to represent.

"The seven churches," therefore, are easily understood to mean not merely the seven literal churches of Asia which went by the names mentioned, but seven periods of the Christian church, from the days of the apostles to the close of probation. (See comments on Revelation 2: 1.)

The Source of Blessing.—"From Him which is, and which was, and which is to come," or is to be—an expression which in this connection refers to God the Father, since the Holy Spirit and Christ are mentioned separately in the immediate context.

The Seven Spirits.—This expression probably has no reference to angels, but to the Spirit of God. It is one of the sources from which grace and peace are invoked for the church. On the interesting subject of the seven spirits, Thompson remarks: "That is, from the Holy Spirit, denominated 'the seven spirits,' because seven is a sacred and perfect number; not thus named . . . as denoting interior plurality, but the fullness and perfection of His gifts and operations."[2] Albert Barnes says, "The number seven, therefore, may have been given to the Holy Spirit with reference to the *diversity* or the *fullness* of His operations on the souls of men, and to His manifold agency on the affairs of the world, as further developed in this book."[3]

His Throne.—This refers to the throne of God the Father, for Christ has not yet taken His own throne. The seven spirits being *before* the throne "may be intended to designate the fact that the Divine Spirit was, as it were, prepared to go forth, or to be *sent* forth, in accordance with a common representation in the Scriptures, to accomplish important purposes in human affairs."[4]

"And From Jesus Christ."—Some of the chief characteristics which pertain to Christ are here mentioned. He is "the faithful Witness." Whatever He bears witness to is true. Whatever He promises, He will surely fulfill.

"The first begotten of the dead" is an expression parallel to 1 Corinthians 15: 20, 23; Hebrews 1: 6; Romans 8: 29; and Colossians 1: 15, 18, where we find such expressions applied to Christ as "the first fruits of them that slept," "the

[2] *Ibid.*, pp. 34, 35.

[3] Albert Barnes, *Notes on Revelation*, p. 62, comment on Revelation 1: 4. See also S. T. Bloomfield, D. D., *The Greek Testament With English Notes*, Vol. II, p. 565, comment on Revelation 1: 4.

[4] Albert Barnes, *Notes on Revelation*, p. 62, comment on Revelation 1: 4.

firstborn among many brethren," "the firstborn of every creature," and "the firstborn from the dead." But these expressions do not denote that He was the first in point of time to be raised from the dead; for others were raised before Him. Moreover, that is a very unimportant point. But He was the chief and central figure of all who have come up from the grave, for it was by virtue of Christ's coming, work, and resurrection, that any were raised before His time. In the purpose of God He was the first in point of time as well as in importance, for it was not until after the purpose of Christ's triumph over the grave was formed in the mind of God, who "calleth those things which be not as though they were" (Romans 4: 17), that any were released from the power of death by virtue of that great purpose which was in due time to be accomplished.

Christ is "the Prince of the kings of the earth." In a certain sense He is that now. Paul informs us, in Ephesians 1: 20, 21, that He has been set at the right hand of God in the heavenly places, "far above all principality, and power, and might, and dominion, and every name that is named, not only in this world, but also in that which is to come." The highest names in this world are those of princes, kings, emperors, and potentates of earth. But Christ is placed far above them. He is seated with His Father upon the throne of universal dominion, and ranks equally with Him in the overruling and the controlling of the affairs of all nations of earth. (Revelation 3: 21.)

In a more particular sense, Christ is to be Prince of the kings of the earth when He takes His own throne, and the kingdoms of this world *become* the "kingdoms of our Lord and of His Christ," when they are given by the Father into His hands, and He comes forth bearing upon His vesture the title of "King of kings and Lord of lords," to dash them in pieces like a potter's vessel. (Revelation 19: 16; 2: 27; Psalm 2: 8, 9.)

Christ is spoken of further as "Him that loved us, and washed us from our sins in His own blood." We have thought that earthly friends loved us—a father, a mother, brothers and sisters, or bosom friends—but we see that no love is worthy of the name compared with the love of Christ for us. The following sentence adds intensity of meaning to the previous words: "And washed us from our sins in His own blood." What love is this! "Greater love," says the apostle, "hath no man than this, that a man lay down his life for his friends." John 15: 13. But Christ has commended His love for us in that He died for us "while we were yet sinners." But more than this, He "hath made us kings and priests unto God and His Father." From being leprous with sin, we are made clean in His sight; from being enemies, we are not only made friends, but raised to positions of honor and dignity. What matchless love! What matchless provision God has made that we might be cleansed from sin! Consider for a moment the sanctuary service and its beautiful significance. When a sinner confesses his sins, and receives forgiveness, he lays them on Christ, the Lamb of God, which taketh away the sin of the world. In the books of heaven where they are recorded, the blood of Christ covers them, and if the follower of God is faithful to his profession, those sins will never be revealed, but will be destroyed by the fires that purify the earth when sin and sinners are consumed. Says the prophet Isaiah, "Thou hast cast all my sins behind Thy back." Isaiah 38: 17. Then will apply the statement of the Lord through Jeremiah, "I will remember their sin no more." Jeremiah 31: 34.

No wonder the loving and beloved disciple John ascribed to this Being who has done so much for us, glory and dominion, forever and ever!

VERSE 7 Behold, He cometh with clouds; and every eye shall see Him, and they also which pierced Him: and all kindreds of the earth shall wail because of Him. Even so, Amen.

Here John carries us forward to the second advent of Christ in glory, the climax and crowning event of His intervention in behalf of this fallen world. Once He came in weakness, now He comes in power; once in humility, now in glory.

 FRANKLIN BOOTH, ARTIST

"EVERY EYE SHALL SEE HIM"

The second coming of Christ will not be a secret rapture. It will be a visible advent of indescribable glory.

He comes with clouds, in like manner as He ascended. (Acts 1: 9, 11.)

His Coming Visible.—"Every eye shall see Him." All who are alive at the time of His coming shall see Jesus. We know of no personal coming of Christ that will be as the stillness of midnight, or take place only in the desert or the secret chamber. He comes not as a thief in the sense of stealing in secretly and quietly upon the world. But He comes to take to Himself His dearest treasure, His sleeping and living saints, whom He has purchased with His own precious blood; whom He has wrested from the power of death in fair and open conflict; and for whom His coming will be no less open and triumphant. It will be with the brilliancy and splendor of the lightning as it shines from the east to the west. (Matthew 24: 27.) It will be with the sound of a trumpet that will pierce to earth's lowest depths, and with a mighty voice that shall wake the sainted sleepers from their dusty beds. (Matthew 24: 31, margin; 1 Thessalonians 4: 16.) He will come upon the wicked as a thief, only because they persistently shut their eyes to the tokens of His approach, and will not believe the declarations of His word that He is at the door. To represent two comings, a private and a public one, in connection with the second advent, as some do, is wholly unwarranted from the Scriptures.

"*They Also Which Pierced Him.*"—They also (in addition to the "every eye" before mentioned) who were chiefly concerned in the tragedy of His death shall behold Him returning to earth in triumph and glory. But how is this? They are not now living, and how then shall they behold Him when He comes? There will be a resurrection from the dead. This is the only possible avenue to life to those who have once been laid in the grave. But how is it that these wicked persons come up at this time, since the general resurrection of the wicked does not take place until a thousand years after the second advent? (Revelation 20: 1-6.) On this point Daniel says further:

"At that time shall Michael stand up, the great Prince which standeth for the children of thy people: and there shall be a time of trouble, such as never was since there was a nation even to that same time: and at that time thy people shall be delivered, everyone that shall be found written in the book. And many of them that sleep in the dust of the earth shall awake, some to everlasting life, and some to shame and everlasting contempt." Daniel 12: 1, 2.

Here a partial resurrection is brought to view, a resurrection of a certain group of both righteous and wicked. This takes place before the general resurrection of either group. *Many*, not all, that sleep shall awake—*some* of the righteous, not all of them, to everlasting life, and *some* of the wicked, not all of them, to shame and everlasting contempt. This resurrection takes place in connection with the great time of trouble such as never was, which precedes the coming of the Lord. May not "they also which pierced Him" be among those who then come up to shame and everlasting contempt? What could be more appropriate than that those who took part in our Lord's greatest humiliation, and other special leaders in crime against Him, should be raised to behold His terrible majesty as He comes triumphantly in flaming fire to take vengeance on them that know not God, and obey not His gospel?

The response of the church is, "Even so, Amen." Though this coming of Christ is to the wicked a scene of terror and destruction, it is to the righteous a scene of joy and triumph. This coming, which is with flaming fire, and for the purpose of taking vengeance on the wicked, is to recompense all those who believe. (2 Thessalonians 1: 6-10.) Every friend and lover of Christ will hail every declaration and every token of His return as glad tidings of great joy.

VERSE 8 I am Alpha and Omega, the beginning and the ending, saith the Lord, which is, and which was, and which is to come, the Almighty.

Here another speaker than John is introduced. In declaring who He is, He uses two of the same characterizations,

"Alpha and Omega, the beginning and the ending," as are found in Revelation 22: 13, where according to verses 12 and 16 of that chapter, it is plainly Christ who is speaking. We conclude, then, that it is Christ who is speaking in verse 8.

VERSE 9 I John, who also am your brother, and companion in tribulation, and in the kingdom and patience of Jesus Christ, was in the isle that is called Patmos, for the word of God, and for the testimony of Jesus Christ.

The subject here changes, for John introduces the place and the circumstances under which the Revelation was given. He first sets himself forth as a brother of the universal church, their companion in the tribulations of the Christian.

In this passage John evidently has reference to the future kingdom of glory. He introduces the thought of tribulation as part of the necessary preparation for entry into the kingdom of God. This idea is emphasized in such scriptures as: "We must through much tribulation enter into the kingdom of God." Acts 14: 22. "If we suffer, we shall also reign with Him." 2 Timothy 2: 12. It is true that while here in the flesh, believers in Christ have access to the throne of grace. This is the throne of the kingdom of grace into which we are inducted at conversion, for He "hath translated us into the kingdom of His dear Son." Colossians 1: 13. But at the second advent of the Saviour, when the kingdom of glory will be inaugurated, then the saints, members of the kingdom of grace here, redeemed from this present evil world, will have access to the throne of His glory. Then tribulation will be over, and the children of God will bask in the sunlight of the presence of the King of kings throughout eternity.

The Place of the Writing.—Patmos is a small, barren island off the west coast of Asia Minor, between the island of Icaria and the promontory of Miletus, where in John's day was located the nearest Christian church. It is about ten miles long, six miles wide at its greatest breadth. Its present name is Patmo. The coast is high, and consists of a succession of capes, which form many ports. The only one now in use is a deep bay sheltered by high mountains on every side but one, where it is protected by a projecting cape. The town attached to this port is situated upon a high, rocky mountain rising immediately from the sea. About halfway up the mountain on which this town is built there is shown a natural grotto in the rock where tradition says that John had his vision and wrote the Revelation. On account of the stern and desolate character of this island, it was used under the Roman Empire as a place of banishment. This accounts for the exile of John there. The banishment of the apostle took place under the emperor Domitian about the year A. D. 94; and from this supposition the date assigned to the writing of the Revelation is A. D. 95 or 96.

The Cause of Banishment.—"For the word of God, and for the testimony of Jesus Christ." This was John's high crime and misdemeanor. The tyrant Domitian, who was then invested with the imperial purple of Rome, more eminent for his vices than even for his civil position, quailed before this aged but dauntless apostle. He dared not permit the promulgation of the gospel within the bounds of his kingdom. He exiled John to lonely Patmos, where, if anywhere this side of death, he might be said to be out of the world. After confining him to that barren spot, and to the cruel labor of the mines, the emperor doubtless thought that this preacher of righteousness was finally disposed of, and that the world would hear of him no more.

Probably the persecutors of John Bunyan thought the same when they had shut him up in Bedford jail. But when man thinks he has buried the truth in eternal oblivion, the Lord gives it a resurrection in tenfold glory and power. From Bunyan's dark and narrow cell there blazed forth a spiritual light, through the *Pilgrim's Progress*, which for almost three hundred years has built up the interests of the gospel. From the barren Isle of Patmos, where Domitian thought he had forever extinguished at least one torch of truth, there arose the most magnificent revelation of all the sacred canon, to shed its divine luster over the whole Christian world until the end of time. How many will revere the name of the beloved disciple, and thrill with delight at his enraptured visions of heavenly glory, who will never learn the name of the monster who caused his banishment! Verily those words of the Scriptures are sometimes applicable to the present life, which declare that "the righteous shall be in everlasting remembrance," but "the name of the wicked shall rot." (Psalm 112: 6; Proverbs 10: 7.)

VERSE 10 I was in the Spirit on the Lord's day, and heard behind me a great voice, as of a trumpet.

Though John was exiled from all of like faith, and almost from the world, he was not exiled from God, nor from Christ, nor from the Holy Spirit, nor from angels. He still had communion with his divine Lord. The expression "in the Spirit" seems to denote the highest state of spiritual elevation into which a person can be brought by the Spirit of God. It marked the beginning of his vision.

"*On the Lord's Day.*"—What day is intended by this designation? On this question four different positions are taken by various classes. One class holds that the expression "the Lord's day" covers the whole gospel age, and does not mean any particular twenty-four-hour day. Another class holds that the Lord's day is the day of judgment, the future "day of the Lord," so often brought to view in the Scriptures. A third view is that the expression refers to the first day of the week. Still another class holds that it means the seventh day, the Sabbath of the Lord.

To the first of these positions it is sufficient to reply that the book of Revelation is dated by John on the Isle of Patmos, and upon the Lord's day. The writer, the place where it was written, and the day upon which it was dated, have each a real existence, not merely a symbolical or mystical one. But if we say that the day means the gospel age, we give it a symbolical or mystical meaning, which is not admissible. Why would it be necessary for John to explain that he was writing in the "Lord's day" if it meant the gospel age? It is well known that the book of Revelation was written some sixty-five years after the death of Christ.

The second position, that it is the day of judgment, cannot be correct. Though John might have had a vision *concerning* the day of judgment, he could not have had one *on* that day when it is yet future. The word translated "on" is ἐν, *en*, and is defined by Thayer when relating to time: "Periods and portions of time in which anything occurs, *in, on, at, during*." It never means "about" or "concerning." Hence those who refer it to the judgment day either contradict the language used, making it mean "concerning" instead of "on," or they make John state a strange falsehood by saying that he had a vision upon the Isle of Patmos, nearly eighteen hundred years ago, *on* the day of judgment which is yet future!

The third view, that by "Lord's day" is meant the first day of the week, is the one most generally entertained. On this we inquire for the proof. What evidence have we for this assertion? The text itself does not define the term "the Lord's day;" hence if it means the first day of the week, we must look elsewhere in the Bible for the proof that that day of the week is ever so designated. The only other inspired writers who speak of the first day at all, are Matthew, Mark, Luke, and Paul; and they speak of it simply as "the first day of the week." They never speak of it in a manner to distinguish it above any other of the six working days. This is the more remarkable, viewed from the popular standpoint, as three of them speak of it at the very time when it is said to have become the Lord's day by the resurrection of the Lord upon the first day of the week, and two of them mention it some thirty years after that event.

If it is said that "the Lord's day" was the usual term for the first day of the week in John's day, we ask, Where is the proof of this? It cannot be found. In truth, we have proof of the contrary. If this were the universal designation of the first day of the week at the time the Revelation was written, the same writer would most assuredly call it so in all his subsequent writings. But John wrote his Gospel *after* he wrote the Revelation, and yet in that Gospel he calls the first day of the week, not "the Lord's day," but simply "the first day of the week." For proof that John's Gospel was written at a period subsequent to the Revelation, the reader is referred to standard authorities.

The claim here set up in behalf of the first day, is still further disproved by the fact that neither the Father nor the Son has ever claimed the first day as His own in any higher sense than He has each or any of the other laboring days. Neither of them has ever placed any blessing upon it, or attached any sanctity to it. If it were to be called the Lord's day from the fact of Christ's resurrection upon it, Inspiration would doubtless have somewhere so informed us. But there are other events equally essential to the plan of salvation, such as the crucifixion and the ascension; and in the absence of all instruction upon the point, why not call the day upon which either of these occurred, the Lord's day, as well as the day upon which He rose from the dead?

Since the three positions already examined have been disproved, the fourth—that by Lord's day is meant the Sabbath of the Lord—now demands attention. This of itself is susceptible of the clearest proof. When God gave to man in the beginning six days of the week for labor, He expressly reserved the seventh day to Himself, placed His blessing upon it, and claimed it as His holy day. (Genesis 2: 1-3.) Moses told Israel in the wilderness of Sin on the sixth day of the week, "Tomorrow is the rest of the holy Sabbath unto the Lord." Exodus 16: 23.

We come to Sinai, where the great Lawgiver proclaimed His moral precepts in awful grandeur; and in that supreme code He thus lays claim to His hallowed day: "The seventh day is the Sabbath *of the Lord thy God:* . . . for in six days the Lord made heaven and earth, the sea, and all that in them is, and rested the seventh day: wherefore the Lord blessed the Sabbath day, and hallowed it." By the prophet Isaiah, about

CHRIST AMONG THE CANDLESTICKS

[illegible] adoration, John fell at the feet of the blessed Saviour.

eight hundred years later, God spoke as follows: "If thou turn away thy foot from *the* Sabbath, from doing thy pleasure on *My holy day*, . . . then shalt thou delight thyself in the Lord." Isaiah 58: 13.

We come to New Testament times, and He who is one with the Father declares expressly, "The Son of man is *Lord* also of the Sabbath." Mark 2: 27. Can any man deny that that day is the *Lord's day*, of which He has emphatically declared that He is the *Lord?* Thus we see that whether it be the Father or the Son whose title is involved, no other day can be called the Lord's day but the Sabbath of the great Creator.

There is in the Christian Era one day distinguished above the other days of the week as "the Lord's day." How completely this great fact disproves the claim put forth by some that there is no Sabbath in the gospel age but that all days are alike! By calling it the Lord's day, the apostle has given us, near the close of the first century, apostolic sanction for the observance of the only day which can be called the Lord's day, which is the seventh day of the week.

When Christ was on earth, He clearly designated which day was His day by saying, "The Son of man is Lord even of the Sabbath day." Matthew 12: 8. If He had said instead, "The Son of man is Lord of the first day of the week," would not that now be set forth as conclusive proof that Sunday is the Lord's day?—Certainly, and with good reason. Then it ought to be allowed to have the same weight for the seventh day, in reference to which it *was* spoken.

VERSE 11 Saying, I am Alpha and Omega, the first and the last: and, What thou seest, write in a book, and send it unto the seven churches which are in Asia; unto Ephesus, and unto Symrna, and unto Pergamos, and unto Thyatira, and unto Sardis, and unto Philadelphia, and unto Laodicea. 12 And I turned to see the voice that spake with me. And being turned, I saw seven golden candlesticks; 13 and in the midst of the seven candlesticks one like unto the Son of man, clothed with a garment down to the foot, and girt about the paps with a golden girdle. 14 His head and His hairs were white like wool, as white as snow; and His eyes were as a flame of fire; 15 and His feet like unto fine brass, as if they burned in a furnace; and His voice as the sound of many waters. 16 And He had in His right hand seven stars: and out of His mouth went a sharp twoedged sword: and His countenance was as the sun shineth in His strength. 17 And when I saw Him, I fell at His feet as dead. And He laid His right hand upon me, saying unto me, Fear not; I am the first and the last: 18 I am He that liveth, and was dead; and, behold, I am alive forevermore, Amen; and have the keys of hell and of death.

The expression, "I turned to see the voice," refers to the person from whom the voice came.

Seven Golden Candlesticks.—These cannot be the antitype of the golden candlestick of the ancient typical temple service, for that was but *one* candlestick with seven branches. That is ever spoken of in the singular number. But here are *seven*, and these are more properly "lamp stands" than simply candlesticks, stands upon which lamps are set to give light in the room. They bear no resemblance to the candlestick of the ancient tabernacle. On the contrary the stands are so distinct, and so far separated one from another, that the Son of man is seen walking about in the midst of them.

The Son of Man.—The central and all-attractive figure of the scene now opened before John's vision is the majestic form of the Son of man, Jesus Christ. The description here given of Him, with His flowing robe, His hair white, not with age, but with the brightness of heavenly glory, His flaming eyes, His feet glowing like molten brass, and His voice as the sound of many waters, cannot be excelled for grandeur and sublimity. Overcome by the presence of this august Being, and perhaps under a keen sense of all human unworthiness, John fell at His feet as dead, but a comforting hand is laid upon him, and a voice of sweet assurance tells him not to fear. It is equally the privilege of Christians today to feel the same hand laid upon them to strengthen and comfort them in hours of trial and affliction, and to hear the same voice saying to them, "Fear not."

But the most cheering assurance in all these words of consolation is the declaration of this exalted one who is alive forevermore, that He is the arbiter of death and the grave. I have, He says, "the keys of hell [ᾅδης, *hades*, the grave] and of death." Death is a conquered tyrant. He may gather to the grave the precious of earth, and gloat for a season over his apparent triumph. But he is performing a fruitless task, for the key to his dark prison house has been wrenched from his grasp, and is now held in the hands of a mightier than he. He is compelled to deposit his trophies in a region over which another has absolute control; and this one is the unchanging Friend and the pledged Redeemer of His people. Then grieve not for the righteous dead; they are in safekeeping. An enemy takes them away for a while, but a friend holds the key to the place of their temporary confinement.

VERSE 19 Write the things which thou hast seen, and the things which are, and the things which shall be hereafter.

A more definite command is given in this verse to John to write the entire Revelation, which would relate chiefly to things which were then in the future. In some few instances, events then in the past or then taking place were referred to; but these references were simply for the purpose of introducing events to be fulfilled after that time, so that no link in the chain might be lacking.

VERSE 20 The mystery of the seven stars which thou sawest in My right hand, and the seven golden candlesticks. The seven stars are the angels of the seven churches: and the seven candlesticks which thou sawest are the seven churches.

To represent the Son of man as holding in His hand only the ministers of seven literal churches in Asia Minor, and walking in the midst of only those seven churches, would be to reduce the sublime representations and declarations of this and following chapters to comparative insignificance. The providential care and presence of the Lord are not with a specified number of churches only, but with all His people; not in the days of John merely, but through all time. "Lo, I am with you alway," said He to His disciples, "even unto the end of the world." (See remarks on verse 4.)

JAMES ARCHER, ARTIST

"YOU A CHRISTIAN!"

It required faith to be a follower of Christ in the early centuries, when the church was brought into conflict with Roman paganism,

CHAPTER II

THE LETTERS OF JESUS TO THE CHURCHES

IN THE first chapter, the prophet outlined the subject of the seven churches, represented by the seven candlesticks, and the ministry of the churches, represented by the seven stars. He now takes up each church particularly, and writes the message designed for it, addressing the epistle in every case to the angel, or the ministry, of the church.

VERSE 1 Unto the angel of the church of Ephesus write: These things saith He that holdeth the seven stars in His right hand, who walketh in the midst of the seven golden candlesticks; 2 I know thy works, and thy labor, and thy patience, and how thou canst not bear them which are evil: and thou hast tried them which say they are apostles, and are not, and hast found them liars: 3 and hast borne, and hast patience, and for My name's sake hast labored, and hast not fainted. 4 Nevertheless I have somewhat against thee, because thou hast left thy first love. 5 Remember therefore from whence thou art fallen, and repent, and do the first works; or else I will come unto thee quickly, and will remove thy candlestick out of his place, except thou repent. 6 But this thou hast, that thou hatest the deeds of the Nicolaitanes, which I also hate. 7 He that hath an ear, let him hear what the Spirit saith unto the churches: To him that overcometh will I give to eat of the tree of life, which is in the midst of the Paradise of God.

The Church of Ephesus.—Some reasons why the messages to the seven churches should be regarded as prophetic, having their application to seven distinct periods covering the Christian age, have been given in the remarks on Revelation 1:4. It may be added here that this view is not new. Thomas Newton says, "Many contend, and among them such learned men as More and Vitringa, that the seven epistles are prophetical of so many successive periods and states of the church from the beginning to the conclusion of all."[1]

Thomas Scott says: "Many expositors have imagined that these epistles to the seven churches were mystical prophecies

[1] Thomas Newton, *Dissertations on the Prophecies*, Vol. II, p. 167.

of seven distinct periods, into which the whole term, from the apostles' days to the end of the world, would be divided."[2]

Although Newton and Scott do not themselves hold this view, their testimony is good as showing that such has been the view of *many expositors*. Two of them say:

"The earliest commentator on the Apocalypse, whose work has come down to us, was Victorinus, Bishop of Pettau, or Petavium, who died a martyr in the year 303. He was the contemporary of Irenæus, and a man of piety, diligence in setting forth the teachings of the Scriptures, and vigorous in his perceptions of the meaning of the sacred writers. Most of his writings have been lost, except some fragments. His comments on the Apocalypse survive, in a text less pure than we could wish, but sufficiently giving the substance of his views. In his *Scholia in Apocalypsin*, he says that what John addresses to one Church he addresses to all; that Paul was the first to teach that *there are seven Churches in the whole world*, and that *the seven Churches named mean the Church Catholic;* and that John, to observe the same method, has not exceeded the number seven.

"What Victorinus means, is that Paul, in writing to *seven* Churches, and to seven only, intended to have it understood that all the Churches of all time are comprehended in seven; and that, in the same way, the seven Churches in the Apocalypse are meant to comprise all the Churches in the world: that is, the Church Catholic of all ages. This was also the view of Tichænius, of the fourth century; Arethas of Cappadocia, and Primasius of Adrumetum, in the sixth; and Vitringa, Mede, More, Girdlestone, and a large body of divines, of later periods."[3]

"Mede expounded the Seven Epistles as prophetic of the *Seven Ages* of the Church, so that all good should there be prophesied of themselves and all evil of Rome (see Trench, *l.c.*, p. 228). Later still Vitringa expounded the Epistles on

---

[2] Thomas Scott, *Commentary*, Vol. II, p. 754, note on Revelation 2: 1.

[3] Joseph A. Seiss, *The Apocalypse*, Vol. I, pp. 128, 129.

the same principle; and he writes (pp. 32-36): 'Existimo Spiritum S. sub typo et emblemate Septem Ecclesiarum Asiæ nobis . . . voluisse depingere septem variantes status Ecclesiæ Christianæ . . . usque ad Adventum Domini'; adding—'demonstratur illas *Prophetice* non *Dogmatice* esse exponendas.'

"Mede ('Works,' *Advert.*, ch. x, p. 905) states his opinion more fully as follows: 'If we consider their number being Seven, which is a number of revolution of times, or if we consider the choice of the Holy Ghost in that he taketh neither all, no nor the most famous Churches in the world, as Antioch, Alexandria, Rome, . . . If these things be well considered, may it not seem that these Seven Churches, besides their literal respect, were intended to be as patterns and types of the several *Ages* of the Catholic Church *a principio ad finem?* that so these Seven Churches should prophetically sample unto us a Sevenfold successive temper and condition of the whole visible Church according to the several *Ages* thereof. . . . And if this were granted . . . then surely the First Church (viz., the Ephesian state) must be the first, and the Last be the last. . . . The mention of false Jews and the synagogue of Satan, &c. (Apoc.ii) in the Five middle ones, will argue that they belong to the times of the Beast and Babylon. And for the *Sixth* in special we have a good character where to place it, viz., partly about the time the Beast is falling, and partly after his destruction, when the New Jerusalem cometh.' "[4]

It appears from the authors above cited, that what has led commentators of more modern times to discard the view of the prophetical nature of the messages to the seven churches, is the comparatively recent and unscriptural doctrine of the temporal millennium. The last stage of the church, as described in Revelation 3: 15-17, was deemed to be incompatible with the glorious state of things which would exist here on this earth for a thousand years, with all the world converted to God.

[4] F. C. Cook, editor, *The Bible Commentary*, New Testament, Vol. IV, pp. 530, 531.

Hence in this case, as in many others, the Scriptural view is made to yield to the more pleasing. The hearts of men, as in ancient times, still love smooth things, and their ears are ever favorably open to those who will prophesy peace.

The first church named is Ephesus. According to the application here made, this would cover the first, or apostolic age of the church. The definition of the word "Ephesus" is "desirable," which may well be taken as a good descriptive term of the character and condition of the church in its first state. Those early Christians had received the doctrine of Christ in its purity. They enjoyed the benefits and blessings of the gifts of the Holy Spirit. They were noted for their works, labor, and patience. In faithfulness to the pure principles taught by Christ, they could not bear those that were evil, and they tested false apostles, searched out their true characters, and found them liars. That this work was done by the literal and particular church at Ephesus more than by other churches of that time, we have no evidence. There is nothing said about it by Paul in his epistle to that church. But this work *was* carried on by the Christian church as a whole, in that age, and was a most appropriate work at that time. (See Acts 15; 2 Corinthians 11: 13.)

The Angel of the Church.—The angel of a church must denote a messenger, or minister, of that church. As each church covers a period of time, the angel of each church must denote the *ministry*, or all the true ministers of Christ during the period covered by that church. The different messages, though addressed to the ministers, cannot be understood to be applicable to them alone, but are appropriately addressed to the church through them.

The Cause of Complaint.—"I have somewhat against thee," says Christ, "because thou hast left thy first love." "Not less worthy of warning than departure from fundamental doctrine or from Scriptural morality, is the leaving of first love. The charge here is not that of falling from grace, nor that love is extinguished, but diminished. No zeal, no suffering, can atone for the want of first love."[5] The time never should come in a Christian's experience, when, if he were asked to mention the period of his greatest love to Christ, he would not say, The present moment. But if such a time does come, then he should remember whence he is fallen, meditate upon it, carefully call up the state of his former acceptance with God, and hasten to repent and retrace his steps to that desirable position. Love, like faith, is manifested by works; and first love, when it is attained, will always bring forth corresponding works.

The Admonition.—"I will come unto thee quickly, and will remove thy candlestick out of his place, except thou repent." The coming here mentioned must be a figurative coming, signifying a visitation of judgment, inasmuch as it is conditional. The removal of the candlestick would denote the taking away from the church of the light and privileges of the gospel, and the committing of these advantages to other hands, unless the church should better fulfill the responsibilities of the trust committed to it. It would be the rejection of them by Christ as His representatives, to bear the light of His truth and gospel before the world. This threatening would be just as applicable to individuals as to the church as a body. How many who professed Christianity during that period came short and were rejected, we do not know, but doubtless many. Thus things would go on, some remaining steadfast, some backsliding and becoming no longer light-bearers in the world, new converts meanwhile filling up the vacancies made by death and apostasy, until the church reached a new era in her experience, marked off as another period in her history, and covered by another message.

The Nicolaitanes.—How ready is Christ to commend His people for whatever good qualities they may possess! If there is anything of which He approves, He mentions that first. In this message to the church of Ephesus, after first mentioning their commendable traits and then their failures, as if unwilling

[5] Augustus C. Thompson, *Morning Hours in Patmos*, pp. 122, 123.

to pass by any of their good qualities, He says that they hated the deeds of the Nicolaitanes, which He also hated. In verse 15 the doctrines of the same characters are condemned. It appears that they were a class of persons whose deeds and doctrines were both abominable in the sight of Heaven. Their origin is involved in some doubt. Some say that they sprang from Nicholas of Antioch, one of the seven deacons (Acts 6: 5); some, that they only attribute their origin to him to gain the prestige of his name; and others, that the sect took its name from one Nicholas of later date. The latter theory is probably more nearly correct. Concerning their doctrines and practices, there seems to be a general agreement that they held to a community of wives, regarded adultery and fornication as matters of indifference, and permitted the eating of things offered to idols. (See Clarke, Kitto, and other commentators.)

The Summons to Attention.—"He that hath an ear, let him hear what the Spirit saith unto the churches." This is a solemn manner of calling universal attention to that which is of general and most momentous importance. The same language is used to each of the seven churches. Christ, when upon earth, made use of the same form of speech in calling the attention of the people to the most important of His teachings. He used it in reference to the mission of John (Matthew 11: 15), the parable of the sower (Matthew 13: 9), and the parable of the tares, setting forth the end of the world (Matthew 13: 43). It is also used in relation to an important prophetic fulfillment in Revelation 13: 9.

The Promise to the Overcomer.—To the victor it is promised that he shall eat of the tree of life that grows in the midst of Paradise, or the garden, of God. Where is this Paradise? It is in the third heaven. Paul writes, in 2 Corinthians 12: 2, that he knew a man (referring to himself) caught up to the third heaven. In verse 4 he says that he was caught up *into* "Paradise," leaving only one conclusion to be drawn, which is that Paradise is in the third heaven. In this Paradise, it seems, is the tree of life. There is but one tree of life brought to view in the Bible. It is mentioned six times, three times in Genesis, and three times in the Revelation; but it is used every time with the definite article "the." It is *the* tree of life in the first book of the Bible, *the* tree of life in the last; *the* tree of life in the "Paradise" (the term used for "garden" in the Greek translation of Genesis) in Eden at the beginning, and *the* tree of life in the Paradise of which John now speaks, in heaven above. If there is but one tree, and that was at first upon earth, it may be asked how it has now come to be in heaven. The answer would be that it must have been taken up to the Paradise above. There is no possible way that the identical body which is situated in one place can be located in another, but by being transported there bodily. That the tree of life and Paradise have been removed from earth to heaven there is a very good reason to believe. One commentator remarks on this point:

"The act of God in appointing the cherubim 'to keep the way of the tree of life' (Genesis 3: 24) in the garden of Eden, likewise appears not only in an aspect indicating judicial severity, but also in one which conveys a promise full of consolation. The blessed abode from which man is expelled, is neither annihilated nor even abandoned to desolation and ruin, but withdrawn from the earth and from man, and consigned to the care of the most perfect creatures of God, in order that it may be ultimately restored to man when he is redeemed. (Revelation 22: 2.) The garden, as it existed before God 'planted,' or adorned it, came under the curse, like the remainder of the earth, but the celestial and paradisaical addition was exempted, and entrusted to the cherubim. The true (ideal) Paradise is now translated to the invisible world. At least a symbolical copy of it, established in the holy of holies in the tabernacle is already granted to the people of Israel, after the pattern which Moses saw in the mount (Exodus 25: 9, 40); and the original itself, as the renewed habitation of redeemed man, will hereafter descend to the earth. (Revelation 21:10.)"[6]

---

[6] John H. Kurtz, *Manual of Sacred History*, p. 50.

To the overcomer, then, is promised a restoration that will include more than Adam lost. Not to the overcomers of that state of the church merely, but to all overcomers of every age is the promise made, for in the great rewards of heaven there are no restrictions. Reader, strive to be an overcomer, for he who gains access to the tree of life in the midst of the Paradise of God, shall die no more.

The Time of the Church.—The time covered by this first church may be considered the period from the resurrection of Christ to the close of the first century, or to the death of the last of the apostles.

VERSE 8 And unto the angel of the church in Smyrna write: These things saith the First and the Last, which was dead, and is alive: 9 I know thy works, and tribulation, and poverty, (but thou art rich) and I know the blasphemy of them which say they are Jews, and are not, but are the synagogue of Satan. 10 Fear none of those things which thou shalt suffer: behold, the devil shall cast some of you into prison, that ye may be tried; and ye shall have tribulation ten days: be thou faithful unto death, and I will give thee a crown of life. 11 He that hath an ear, let him hear what the Spirit saith unto the churches: He that overcometh shall not be hurt of the second death.

The Church of Smyrna.—It will be noticed that the Lord introduces Himself to each church by mentioning some of His characteristics which show Him to be peculiarly fitted to bear to them the testimony which He utters. To the Smyrna church, about to pass through the fiery ordeal of persecution, He reveals Himself as one who was dead, but is now alive. If they should be called to seal their testimony with their blood, they were to remember that the eyes of One were upon them who had shared the same fate, but had triumphed over death, and was able to bring them up from a martyr's grave.

Poverty and Riches.—"I know thy . . . poverty," says Christ to them, "but thou art rich." Strange paradox this may seem at first. But who are the truly rich in this world?—Those who are "rich in faith" and "heirs of the kingdom." The wealth of this world, for which men so eagerly strive, and so often barter away present happiness and future endless life, is "coin not current in heaven." One writer has well said, "There is many a rich poor man, and many a poor rich man."

"*Say They Are Jews, and Are Not.*"—That the term Jew is not here used in a literal sense, is very evident. It denotes some character which was approved by the gospel standard. Paul's language will make this point plain. He says: "He is not a Jew, which is one outwardly; neither is that circumcision, which is outward in the flesh: but he is a Jew [in the true Christian sense], which is one inwardly; and circumcision is that of the heart, in the spirit, and not in the letter, whose praise is not of men, but of God." Romans 2: 28, 29. Again he says: "For they are not all Israel, which are of Israel; neither, because they are the seed of Abraham, are they all children." Romans 9: 6, 7. In Galatians 3: 28, 29, Paul further tells us that in Christ there are no such outward distinctions as Jew or Greek; but if we are Christ's, then are we "Abraham's seed" (in the true sense), and heirs according to the promise. To say, as some do, that the term Jew is never applied to Christians, is to contradict all these inspired declarations of Paul, and the testimony of the faithful and true Witness to the Smyrna church. Some were hypocritically pretending to be Jews in this Christian sense, when they possessed none of the necessary characteristics. Such were of the synagogue of Satan.

Tribulation Ten Days.—As this message is prophetic, the time mentioned in it must also be regarded as prophetic. Since a prophetic day stands for a literal year, the ten days would denote ten years. It is a noticeable fact that the last and most bloody of the ten great persecutions of the Christian church continued just ten years from A. D. 303 to 313, beginning under Diocletian.

It would be difficult to make an application of this language on the ground that these messages are not prophetic; for in that case only ten literal days could be meant. It would not seem probable that a persecution of only ten days, or only a single church, would be made a matter of prophecy; and no mention of any such case of limited persecution can be found.

EDWIN LONG, ARTIST

CHRIST OR DIANA?

The early church was in great tribulation. Many remained faithful when by merely casting a bit of incense upon a pagan altar they could have denied Christ.

Again, apply this persecution to any of the notable ones of that period, and how could it be spoken of as the fate of one church alone? All the churches suffered in them. Where, then, would be the propriety of singling out one particular group, to the exclusion of the others, as being the only one involved in such a calamity?

The Admonition.—"Be thou faithful unto death." Some have endeavored to base a criticism on the use of the word "unto," instead of "until," as though the idea of time was not involved. But the original word, ἄχρι, *achri*, here rendered "unto," signifies primarily "until." No argument, however, can be drawn from this for consciousness in death. The vital point for that argument is still lacking, for it is not affirmed that the crown of life is bestowed immediately at death. We must consequently look to other scriptures to learn when the crown of life is given; and other scriptures inform us fully. Paul declares that this crown is to be given at the day of Christ's appearing (2 Timothy 4: 8); at the last trump (1 Corinthians 15: 51-54); when the Lord shall Himself descend from heaven (1 Thessalonians 4: 16, 17); when the Chief Shepherd shall appear, says Peter (1 Peter 5: 4); at the resurrection of the just, says Christ (Luke 14: 14); and when He shall return to take His people to the mansions prepared for them, that they may ever be with Him (John 14: 3). "Be thou faithful until death," and having been thus faithful, when the time comes that the saints of God are rewarded, you shall receive a crown of life.

The Promise to the Overcomer.—"He shall not be hurt of the second death." Is not the language Christ here uses a good comment upon what He taught His disciples when He said, "Fear not them which kill the body, but are not able to kill the soul: but rather fear Him which is able to destroy both soul and body in hell"? Matthew 10: 28. The Smyrna church members might be put to death here, but the future life which was to be given them, man *could* not take away, and God *would* not. Hence they were to fear not those who could kill the body, fear none of the things which they should suffer, for their eternal existence was assured.

The Meaning and the Time of the Church.—Smyrna signifies "myrrh," fit appellation for the church of God while passing through the fiery furnace of persecution, and proving herself a "sweet-smelling savor" unto Him. But we soon reach the days of Constantine, when the church presents a new phase, rendering a far different name and another message applicable to her history.

According to the foregoing application, the date of the Smyrna church would be A. D. 100-323.

VERSE 12 And to the angel of the church in Pergamos write: These things saith He which hath the sharp sword with two edges: 13 I know thy works, and where thou dwellest, even where Satan's seat is: and thou holdest fast My name, and hast not denied My faith, even in those days wherein Antipas was My faithful martyr, who was slain among you, where Satan dwelleth. 14 But I have a few things against thee, because thou hast there them that hold the doctrine of Balaam, who taught Balak to cast a stumbling-block before the children of Israel, to eat things sacrificed unto idols, and to commit fornication. 15 So hast thou also them that hold the doctrine of the Nicolaitanes, which thing I hate. 16 Repent; or else I will come unto thee quickly, and will fight against them with the sword of My mouth. 17 He that hath an ear, let him hear what the Spirit saith unto the churches: To him that overcometh will I give to eat of the hidden manna, and will give him a white stone, and in the stone a new name written, which no man knoweth saving he that receiveth it.

The Church of Pergamos.—Against the preceding church there was no word of condemnation uttered. Persecution is ever calculated to keep the church pure, and incite its members to piety and godliness. But we now reach the period of the Pergamos church, when influences began to work which brought errors and evils into the church.

The word "Pergamos" signifies "height, elevation." It was a period in which the true servants of God had to struggle against a spirit of worldly policy, pride, and popularity among the professed followers of Christ, and against the virulent workings of the mystery of iniquity, which finally resulted in the full development of the papal "man of sin." 2 Thessalonians 2: 3.

The Commendation.—"Where Satan's seat is." Christ takes cognizance of the unfavorable situation of His people during this period. The language is probably not designed to denote location. As to place, Satan works wherever Christians dwell. But surely there are times and seasons when he works with special power, and the period covered by the church of Pergamos was one of these. During this period, the doctrine of Christ was being corrupted, the mystery of iniquity was working, and Satan was laying the foundation of a stupendous system of apostasy, the papacy. Here was the falling away foretold by Paul in 2 Thessalonians 2: 3, cited already.

It is interesting to note that the city of Pergamos became the seat of ancient Babylonian sun worship. "The Chaldean Magi enjoyed a long period of prosperity at Babylon. A pontiff appointed by the sovereign ruled over a college of seventy-two hierophants. . . . [After the Medo-Persian occupation], the defeated Chaldeans fled to Asia Minor, and fixed their central college at Pergamos, and took the Palladium of Babylon, the cubic stone, with them. Here, independent of state control, they carried on the rites of their religion, and plotted against the peace of the Persian Empire, caballing with the Greeks for that purpose."[7]

Antipas.—That a class of persons is referred to by this name, and not an individual, there is good reason to believe; for no authentic information respecting such an individual is now to be found. On this point William Miller says:

"It is supposed that Antipas was not an individual, but a class of men who opposed the power of the bishops, or popes, in that day, being a combination of two words, 'Anti,' *opposed*, and 'Papas,' *father*, or *pope;* and many of them suffered martyrdom at that time in Constantinople and Rome, where the bishops and popes began to exercise the power which soon after brought into subjection the kings of the earth, and trampled on the rights of the church of Christ. And for

[7] William B. Barker, *Lares and Penates,* pp. 232, 233.

myself, I see no reason to reject this explanation of the word 'Antipas' in this text, as the history of those times are [is] perfectly silent respecting such an individual as is here named."[8]

Watson's *Biblical Dictionary* says, "Ancient ecclesiastical history furnishes no account of this Antipas."[9] Adam Clarke mentions a work as extant called the "Acts of Antipas," but gives us to understand that it is entitled to no credit.[10]

The Cause of Complaint.—Disadvantages in situation are no excuse for wrongs in the church. Although this church existed at a time when Satan was making strong delusions, it was the duty of its members to keep themselves free from his evil doctrines. Hence they were censured for harboring among them those who held the doctrines of Balaam and the Nicolaitanes. (See comments on the Nicolaitanes, verse 6.) The doctrine of Balaam is here partly revealed. He taught Balak to cast a stumbling block before the children of Israel. (See a full account of his work and its results in Numbers 22-25; 31: 13-16.) It appears that Balaam desired to curse Israel for the sake of the rich reward which Balak offered him. But not being permitted by the Lord to curse them, he resolved to accomplish essentially the same thing in another way. He therefore counseled Balak to seduce them, by means of the women of Moab, to participate in the celebration of the rites of idolatry and all its licentious accompaniments. The plan succeeded. The abominations of idolatry spread through the camp of Israel, the curse of God was called down upon them by their sins, and twenty-four thousand persons died.

The doctrines complained of in the church of Pergamos were of course similar in their tendency, leading to spiritual idolatry and an unlawful connection between the church and the world. Out of this spirit was finally produced the union

---

[8] William Miller, *Evidence From Scripture and History of the Second Coming of Christ*, pp 135, 136.

[9] Richard Watson, *A Biblical and Theological Dictionary*, p. 69, art. "Antipas."

[10] Adam Clarke, *Commentary on the New Testament*, Vol. II, p. 978, note on Revelation 2: 13.

of civil and ecclesiastical powers which culminated in the formation of the papacy.

The Admonition.—Christ declared that if they did not repent, He would take the matter into His own hands, and come unto them (in judgment), and fight against them (those who held these evil doctrines); and the whole church would be held responsible for the wrongs of those heretical ones whom they harbored in their midst.

Promise to the Overcomer.—The overcomer is promised that he shall eat of the hidden manna, and receive from his approving Lord a white stone, with a new and precious name engraved on it. Most commentators apply the manna, white stone, and new name, to spiritual blessings to be enjoyed in this life; but like all the other promises to the overcomer, this doubtless refers to the future, and is to be given when the time comes for the saints to be rewarded. Perhaps the following comment is as satisfactory as anything that has ever been written upon these several particulars:

"It is generally supposed by commentators that this refers to an ancient judicial custom of dropping a black stone into an urn when it is intended to condemn, and a white stone when the prisoner was acquitted. But this is an act so distinct from that described in the scripture before us, 'I will give him a white stone,' that we are disposed to agree with those who think it refers rather to a custom of a very different kind, and not unknown to the classical reader, according with beautiful propriety to the case before us. In primitive times, when traveling was rendered difficult from want of places of public entertainment, hospitality was exercised by private individuals to a very great extent, of which indeed we find frequent traces in all history, and in none more than the Old Testament. Persons who partook of this hospitality, and those who practiced it, frequently contracted habits of friendship and regard for each other; and it became a well-established custom both among the Greeks and Romans, to provide their guests with some particular mark, which was handed down from father to son, and ensured hospitality and kind treatment whenever it was presented. This mark was usually a small stone or pebble, cut in half, upon the halves of which the host and guest mutually inscribed their names, and then interchanged with each other. The production of this tessera was quite sufficient to insure friendship for themselves or their descendants whenever they traveled again in the same direction; while it is evident that these stones required to be privately kept, and the names written upon them carefully concealed, lest others should obtain the privileges instead of the persons for whom they were intended.

"How natural, then, is the allusion to this custom in the words of the text, 'I will give him to eat of the hidden manna;' and having done so, having made him partaker of my hospitality, having recognized him as my guest, my friend, I will present him with the 'white stone, and in the stone a new name written, which no man knoweth, save he who receiveth it.' I will give him a pledge of my friendship, sacred and inviolable, known only to himself."[11]

On the new name, John Wesley very appropriately says:

"Jacob, after his victory, gained the new name of Israel. Wouldst thou know what thy new name will be? The way to this is plain—overcome. Till then all thy inquiries are vain. Thou wilt then read it on the white stone."[12]

The Time of the Church.—The period covered by this church extends from the days of Constantine, or perhaps, rather, from his professed conversion to Christianity in A. D. 323, to the establishment of the papacy in A. D. 538.

VERSE 18 And unto the angel of the church in Thyatira write: These things saith the Son of God, who hath His eyes like unto a flame of fire, and His feet are like fine brass: 19 I know thy works, and charity, and service, and faith, and thy patience, and thy works; and the last to be more than the first. 20 Notwithstanding I have a few things against thee, because thou sufferest that woman Jezebel, which calleth herself a prophetess, to teach

[11] Henry Blunt, *A Practical Exposition of the Epistles to the Seven Churches of Asia*, pp. 116-119.

[12] John Wesley, *Explanatory Notes Upon the New Testament*, p. 689, comment on Revelation 2: 17.

and to seduce My servants to commit fornication, and to eat things sacrificed unto idols. 21 And I gave her space to repent of her fornication; and she repented not. 22 Behold, I will cast her into a bed, and them that commit adultery with her into great tribulation, except they repent of their deeds. 23 And I will kill her children with death; and all the churches shall know that I am He which searcheth the reins and hearts: and I will give unto every one of you according to your works. 24 But unto you I say, and unto the rest in Thyatira, as many as have not this doctrine, and which have not known the depths of Satan, as they speak; I will put upon you none other burden. 25 But that which ye have already hold fast till I come. 26 And he that overcometh, and keepeth My works unto the end, to him will I give power over the nations: 27 and he shall rule them with a rod of iron; as the vessels of a potter shall they be broken to shivers: even as I received of My Father. 28 And I will give him the morning star. 29 He that hath an ear, let him hear what the Spirit saith unto the churches.

If the period covered by the Pergamos church has been correctly located, it terminated with the setting up of the papacy in A. D. 538. The most natural division to be assigned to the church of Thyatira would be the time of the continuance of this power through the 1260 years of its supremacy, or from A. D. 538 to A. D. 1798.

The Church of Thyatira.—Thyatira signifies "sweet savor of labor," or "sacrifice of contrition." This well describes the state of the church of Jesus Christ during the long period of papal triumph and persecution. This age of dreadful tribulation for the church such as never was (Matthew 24: 21), improved the religious condition of believers. Hence for their works—charity, service, faith, and patience—they receive the commendation of Him whose eyes are as a flame of fire. Works are again mentioned, as if worthy of double commendation, and the last were more than the first. There had been an improvement in their condition, a growth of grace, an increase in all these elements of Christianity. This progress, under such conditions, was commended by the Lord.

This church is the only one that is commended for an improvement in spiritual things. But as in the church of Pergamos unfavorable circumstances were no apology for false doctrines in the church, so in this church, no amount of labor, charity, service, faith, or patience could compensate for a like sin. A rebuke is therefore given them for suffering an agent of Satan to remain in their midst.

The Cause of Complaint.—"That woman Jezebel." As in the preceding church Antipas denoted, not an individual, but a class of persons, so, doubtless, Jezebel is here to be understood in the same sense. Watson's *Biblical Dictionary* says, "The name of Jezebel is used proverbially. Revelation 2: 20."[13] William Miller speaks as follows:

"Jezebel is a figurative name, alluding to Ahab's wife, who slew the prophets of the Lord, led her husband into idolatry, and fed the prophets of Baal at her own table. A more striking figure could not have been used to describe the papal abominations. (See 1 Kings 18, 19, and 21. . . .) It is very evident from history, as well as from this verse in Revelation, that the church of Christ did suffer some of the papal monks to preach and teach among them."[14]

The *Comprehensive Commentary* has the following remark upon verse 23: "Children are spoken of, which confirms the idea that a sect and its proselytes are meant."[15]

The judgments here threatened against this woman are in harmony with the threatenings in other parts of this book against the Roman Catholic Church under the symbol of a corrupt woman, the mother of harlots and abominations of the earth. (See Revelation 17-19.) The death which is threatened is doubtless the second death, at the end of the one thousand years of Revelation 20, when the righteous retribution from the Searcher of "the reins and hearts" of all men will be given. Further, the declaration, "I will give unto every one of you according to your works," is proof that the address to this church looks forward prophetically to the final reward or punishment of all accountable beings.

"All the Churches Shall Know."—It has been argued from this expression that these churches could not denote seven *suc-*

---

[13] Richard Watson, *A Biblical and Theological Dictionary*, p. 535, art. "Jezebel."

[14] William Miller, *Evidence From Scripture and History of the Second Coming of Christ*, p. 139

[15] William Jenks, *Comprehensive Commentary*, Vol. V, p. 674, note on Revelation 2: 23.

cessive periods of the gospel age, but must exist contemporaneously, as otherwise *all* the churches could not know that Christ was the searcher of "the reins and hearts" from seeing His judgments upon Jezebel and her children. But when is it that all the churches are to know this?—It is when these children are punished with death. If this is at the time when the second death is inflicted upon all the wicked, then indeed will "all the churches," as they behold the infliction of the judgment, know that no secret thing, no evil thought or purpose of the heart has escaped the knowledge of Him who, with eyes like flames of fire, searches the hearts of men.

"I will put upon you none other burden." We believe this refers to a respite promised the church from the burden so long her portion, the weight of papal oppression. It cannot be applied to the reception of new truths, for truth is not a burden to any accountable being. But the days of tribulation that came upon that church were to be shortened for the elect's sake. (Matthew 24: 22.) "They shall be holpen," says the prophet, "with a little help." Daniel 11: 34. "The earth helped the woman," says John. Revelation 12: 16.

The Admonition.—"Hold fast till I come." These are the words of the "Son of God," and bring to our view an unconditional coming. To the churches of Ephesus and Pergamos, certain comings were threatened on conditions: "Repent, or *else* I will come unto thee," implying visitations of judgment. But here a coming of a different nature is brought to view. It is not a threatening of punishment. It is suspended upon no conditions. It is set before the believer as a matter of hope, and can refer to no event other than the future second advent of the Lord in glory, when the Christian's trials will cease, and his efforts in the race for life, and his warfare for a crown of righteousness, will be rewarded with everlasting success.

This church brings us down to the time when the more immediate signs of the soon-coming advent began to be fulfilled. In 1780, eighteen years before the close of this period, the predicted signs in the sun and moon were fulfilled. (See comments on Revelation 6: 12.) In reference to these signs the Saviour said: "When these things begin to come to pass, then look up, and lift up your heads; for your redemption draweth nigh." Luke 21: 28. In the history of this church we reach a point when the end is drawing so near that the attention of the people could properly be called more particularly to that event. Christ has ever said to His followers, "Occupy till I come." Luke 19: 13. Now He says, "Hold fast till I come."

The Promise to the Overcomer.—"Unto the end." This must denote the end of the Christian age. "He that shall endure unto the end," says Christ, "the same shall be saved." Matthew 24: 13. Is there not here a like promise to those who keep the works of Christ, do the things He has enjoined, and keep the faith of Jesus? (Revelation 14: 12.)

"*Power Over the Nations.*"—In this world the wicked bear rule, and the servants of Christ are of no esteem. But the time is coming when righteousness will be in the ascendency; when all ungodliness will be seen in its true light, and be at a heavy discount; and when the scepter of power will be in the hands of the people of God. This promise will be explained by the following facts and scriptures: The nations are to be given by the Father into the hands of Christ, to be ruled with a rod of iron, and dashed in pieces like a potter's vessel. (Psalm 2: 8, 9.) Associated with Christ when He thus enters upon His own work of power and judgment, are to be His saints. (Revelation 3: 21.) They are to reign with Him in this capacity for one thousand years. (Revelation 20: 4.) During this period, the degree of judgment upon wicked men and evil angels is determined. (1 Corinthians 6: 2, 3.) At the end of the one thousand years, they have the honor of sharing with Christ in the execution of the sentence written. (Psalm 149: 9.)

The Morning Star.—Christ says in Revelation 22: 16 that He is Himself the morning star, the immediate forerunner of the day. What is here called the "morning star," is called the "daystar" in 2 Peter 1: 19, where it is associated with the dawn of the day: "Until the day dawn, and the daystar arise."

During the saints' weary night of watching, they have the word of God to shed its needful light upon their path. But when the daystar shall arise in their hearts, or the morning star be given to the overcomers, they will be taken into so close a relationship to Christ that their hearts will be fully illuminated with His Spirit, and they will walk in His light. Then they will no longer need the sure word of prophecy, which now shines as a light in a dark place. Hasten on, O glorious hour, when the light of heaven's bright day shall rise upon the pathway of the faithful, and beams of glory from the eternal world shall gild their banners!

FRANKLIN BOOTH, ARTIST

"I STAND AT THE DOOR, AND KNOCK"

Today Christ is knocking at the door of every heart. Hark! He knocks at your heart. Let Him in.

CHAPTER III

"BEHOLD, I STAND AT THE DOOR AND KNOCK"

VERSE 1 And unto the angel of the church in Sardis write: These things saith He that hath the seven Spirits of God, and the seven stars: I know thy works, that thou hast a name that thou livest, and art dead. 2 Be watchful, and strengthen the things which remain, that are ready to die: for I have not found thy works perfect before God. 3 Remember therefore how thou hast received and heard, and hold fast, and repent. If therefore thou shalt not watch, I will come on thee as a thief, and thou shalt not know what hour I will come upon thee. 4 Thou hast a few names even in Sardis which have not defiled their garments; and they shall walk with Me in white: for they are worthy. 5 He that overcometh, the same shall be clothed in white raiment; and I will not blot out his name out of the book of life, but I will confess his name before My Father, and before His angels. 6 He that hath an ear, let him hear what the Spirit saith unto the churches.

Church in Sardis.—If the dates of the preceding churches have been correctly fixed, the period covered by the church of Sardis must begin about 1798. "Sardis" signifies "prince or song of joy," or "that which remains." We then have the reformed churches before us as constituting this church, from the date above named to the great movement which marked another era in the history of the people of God.

The Cause of Complaint.—The great fault found with Sardis is that it has a name to live, but is dead. What a high position, in a worldly point of view, has the nominal church occupied during this period! Look at her high-sounding titles, and her favor with the world. But how pride and popularity have grown apace, until spirituality is destroyed, the line of distinction between the church and the world is obliterated, and the different popular bodies are churches of Christ only in name!

This church was to hear the proclamation of the doctrine of the second advent. "If therefore thou shalt not watch, I will come on thee as a thief." Verse 3. This implies that the doctrine of the advent would be proclaimed, and the duty of watching would be enjoined upon the church. The coming spoken of is unconditional; the manner only in which it would come upon them is conditional. Their not watching would not prevent the coming of the Lord; but by watching they could avoid being overtaken as by a thief. It is only to those who are in this condition that the day of the Lord comes unawares. "Ye, brethren," says Paul, "are not in darkness, that that day should overtake you as a thief." 1 Thessalonians 5: 4.

"A few names even in Sardis," would seem to imply a period of unparalleled worldliness in the church. But even in this state of things, there are some whose garments are not defiled, some who have kept themselves free from the contaminating influence of sin. James says, "*Pure* religion and undefiled before God and the Father is this, To visit the fatherless and widows in their affliction, and to keep himself *unspotted from the world.*" James 1: 27.

The Promise to the Overcomer.—"Shall walk with Me in white." The Lord does not overlook His people in any place, however few their numbers. Lonely Christian, with none of like precious faith with whom to commune, do you ever feel as if the hosts of unbelievers would swallow you up? You are not unnoticed or forgotten by your Lord. The multitude of the wicked around you cannot be so great as to hide you from His view. If you keep yourself unspotted from surrounding evil, the promise is sure. You shall be clothed in white, the white raiment of the overcomer. You shall walk with your Lord in glory. "The Lamb which is in the midst of the throne shall feed them, and shall lead them unto living fountains of waters; and God shall wipe away all tears from their eyes." Revelation 7: 17.

Being clothed with white raiment is explained in other scriptures to be a symbol of exchanging iniquity for righteousness. (See Zechariah 3: 4, 5.) "Take away the filthy garments from him," is explained by the language that follows, "Behold, I have caused thine iniquity to pass from thee."

"The fine linen," or the white raiment, "is the righteousness of saints." Revelation 19: 8.

The Book of Life.—Here is introduced an object of thrilling interest. Ponderous volume, in which are enrolled the names of all the candidates for everlasting life! Is there danger, after our names have once been entered in that heavenly journal, that they may be blotted out? Yes; or this warning would never have been penned. Even Paul feared that he himself might become a castaway. (1 Corinthians 9: 27.) It is only by being overcomers to the end that our names can be retained in that book. But all will not gain the victory. Their names, of course, will be blotted out. Reference is here made to some definite point of time in the future for this work. "I *will not*," says Christ, blot out the names of the overcomers, which is also saying, by implication, that at the same time He *will* blot out the names of those who do not overcome. Is not this the same time mentioned by Peter? "Repent ye therefore, and be converted, that your *sins* may be *blotted out* when the times of refreshing shall come from the presence of the Lord." Acts 3: 19.

To say to the overcomer that his name shall not be blotted out of the book of life, is to say also that his sins shall be blotted out of the book wherein they are recorded, to be remembered against him no more forever. (Hebrews 8: 12.) It means that either his name or his sins will be blotted out from the heavenly records. What a precious thought it is that *now* we are forgiven if we confess our transgressions! Then if we remain faithful to God these sins will be blotted out at the coming of Jesus.

When that hour of decision shall come, which cannot now be a great way in the future, how, reader, will it be with you? Will your sins be blotted out, and your name be retained in the book of life? Or will your name be blotted out of the book of life, and your sins be left to bear their fearful record against you?

The Presentation in Glory.—"I will confess his name before My Father, and before His angels." Christ taught that as men confessed or denied, despised or honored Him here, they would be confessed or denied by Him before His Father in heaven and before the holy angels. (Matthew 10: 32, 33; Mark 8: 38; Luke 12: 8, 9.) Who can fathom the honor of being approved before the heavenly hosts! Who can conceive of the bliss of that moment when we shall be owned by the Lord of life before His Father as those who have done His will, fought the good fight, run the race, honored Him before men, overcome, and whose names are worthy through His merits to stand upon the imperishable record of the book of life forever and ever!

VERSE 7 And to the angel of the church in Philadelphia write: These things saith He that is holy, He that is true, He that hath the key of David, He that openeth, and no man shutteth; and shutteth, and no man openeth:
8 I know thy works: behold, I have set before thee an open door, and no man can shut it: for thou hast a little strength, and hast kept My word, and hast not denied My name. 9 Behold, I will make them of the synagogue of Satan, which say they are Jews, and are not, but do lie; behold, I will make them to come and worship before thy feet, and to know that I have loved thee. 10 Because thou hast kept the word of My patience, I also will keep thee from the hour of temptation, which shall come upon all the world, to try them that dwell upon the earth. 11 Behold, I come quickly: hold that fast which thou hast, that no man take thy crown. 12 Him that overcometh will I make a pillar in the temple of My God, and he shall go no more out: and I will write upon him the name of My God, and the name of the city of My God, which is New Jerusalem, which cometh down out of heaven from My God: and I will write upon him My new name. 13 He that hath an ear, let him hear what the Spirit saith unto the churches.

The Church of Philadelphia.—The word "Philadelphia" signifies "brotherly love," and expresses the position and spirit of those who received the Advent message up to the autumn of 1844. The great religious awakening in the early part of the nineteenth century which resulted from a study of the prophecies, culminated in this advent movement. Men from all denominations were convinced that the coming of Christ was near. As they came out of the various churches, they left sectarian names and feelings behind, and every heart beat in unison as all joined to give the alarm to the churches and to the world, and pointed to the coming of the Son of man as the believer's true hope. Selfishness and covetousness were laid aside, and a spirit of consecration and sacrifice was cherished. The Spirit of God was with every true believer, and His praise upon every tongue. Those who were not in that movement cannot fully realize how great was the searching of heart, the consecration to God, the peace and joy in the Holy Spirit, and the pure, fervent love for one another which true believers enjoyed.

"*The Key of David.*"—A key is a symbol of power. The Son of God is the rightful heir to David's throne; and He is about to take to Himself His great power and to reign; hence He is represented as having the key of David. The throne of David, or of Christ, on which He is to reign, is included in the capital of His kingdom, the New Jerusalem, now above, but which is to be located on this earth, where He is to reign forever and ever. (Revelation 21: 1-5; Luke 1: 32, 33.)

"*He That Openeth, and No Man Shutteth.*"—To understand this language, it is necessary to look at Christ's position and work as connected with His ministry in the sanctuary, or true tabernacle above. (Hebrews 8: 2.) A figure, or pattern, of this heavenly sanctuary once existed here upon earth in the sanctuary built by Moses. (Exodus 25: 8, 9; Acts 7: 44; Hebrews 9: 1, 21, 23, 24.) The earthly building had two apartments,—the holy place and the most holy place. (Exodus 26: 33, 34.) In the first apartment were the candlestick, the table of showbread, and the altar of incense. In the second were the ark, which contained the tables of the covenant, or the ten commandments, and the cherubim. (Hebrews 9: 1-5.) In like manner the sanctuary in which Christ ministers in heaven has two apartments, for it is clearly stated in Hebrews 9: 21-24 that "both the tabernacle and all the vessels of the ministry" were "patterns of things in the heavens." As all things were made after their pattern, the heavenly sanctuary has also furniture similar to that of the earthly. For the antitype of the golden candlestick and altar of incense, in the first apartment, see Revelation 4: 5; 8: 3; and for the antitype of the ark of the covenant, with its ten commandments, see Revelation 11: 19.

In the earthly sanctuary the priests ministered. (Exodus 28: 41, 43; Hebrews 9: 6, 7; 13: 11.) The ministry of these priests was a shadow of the ministry of Christ in the sanctuary in heaven. (Hebrews 8: 4, 5.)

A complete round of service was performed in the earthly tabernacle once every year. (Hebrews 9: 7.) But in the tabernacle above the service is performed once for all. (Hebrews 7: 27; 9: 12.) At the close of the yearly typical service, the high priest entered the second apartment, the most holy place of the sanctuary, to make an atonement; and this work is appropriately called the cleansing of the sanctuary. (Leviticus 16: 20, 30, 33; Ezekiel 45: 18.) When the ministry in the most holy place began, that in the holy place ceased; and no service was performed there so long as the priest was engaged in the most holy place. (Leviticus 16: 17.)

A similar opening and shutting, or change of ministration, must be accomplished by Christ when the time comes for the cleansing of the heavenly sanctuary. The time did come for this service to begin at the close of the 2300 days, in 1844. To this event the opening and shutting mentioned in the text under consideration can appropriately apply, the opening being that of Christ's ministration in the most holy place, and the shutting, its cessation in the first apartment, or holy place. (See exposition of the subject of the sanctuary and its cleansing, under Daniel 8: 14.)

Verse 9 probably applies to those who do not keep pace with the advancing light of truth, and who oppose Christians who do. Such shall yet be made to feel and confess that God loves those who obey His word, and follow in the knowledge of His truth.

"*The Word of My Patience.*"—John says in Revelation 14: 12: "Here is the patience of the saints; here are they that keep the commandments of God, and the faith of Jesus." Those who now live in patient, faithful obedience to the commandments of God and the faith of Jesus, will be kept in the hour of temptation and peril. (See the comments on Revelation 13: 13-17.)

"*Behold, I Come Quickly.*"—The second coming of Christ is here again brought to view, and with more startling emphasis than in any of the preceding messages. The nearness of that event is here urged upon the attention of believers. The message applies to a period when this great event is impending. In this we have indubitable evidence of the prophetic nature of these messages. What is said of the first three churches contains no allusion to the second coming of Christ, from the fact that they do not cover a period in which that event could be Scripturally expected. But with the Thyatira church, the time had come when this great hope was just beginning to dawn upon the church. The mind is carried forward to this hope by a single allusion: "Hold fast till I come."

The next state of the church, the Sardis period, finds the church occupying a position still nearer that event, and the great proclamation is brought to view which was to herald Christ's coming, and the duty of watching is enjoined upon the church: "If thou shalt not watch, I will come on thee as a thief." We reach the Philadelphia church still later, and the nearness of the same great event then leads Him who "is holy and true" to utter the stirring declaration, "Behold, I come quickly."

It is evident from this that these churches occupy positions successively nearer the great day of the Lord, as in each succeeding one, and in a continually increasing ratio, this great event is made more and more prominent, and is more definitely and impressively urged upon the attention of the church. Here indeed they see the day approaching. (Hebrews 10: 25.)

The Admonition.—"Hold that fast which thou hast, that no man take thy crown." By our faithfulness we are not depriving anyone else of a crown. The verb rendered "to take" has a number of definitions, one of which is "to take away, snatch from, *deprive of.*" Let no one, and no thing, induce you to yield the truth, or pervert you from the right ways of the Lord, for by so doing it will cause you to lose the reward.

The Promise to the Overcomer.—The overcomer is to be a pillar in the temple of God, and go out no more. The temple here must denote the church, and the promise of being made a pillar in it is the promise of a place of honor, permanence, and safety in the church, under the figure of a heavenly building. When the time comes for this part of the promise to be fulfilled, probation is past, and the overcomer is fully established in the truth, and sealed. "He shall go no more out," that is, there is no more danger of his falling away, he is the Lord's forever, and his salvation is sure.

From the moment the Christians overcome and are sealed for heaven, they are labeled, if we may so express it, as belonging to God and Christ, and addressed to their destination, the New Jerusalem. They are to have written upon them the name of God, whose property they are, the name of the New Jerusalem, to which place they are going, not old Jerusalem where some are vainly looking. They also have upon them the new name of Christ, by whose authority they are to receive everlasting life, and enter into the kingdom. Thus sealed and labeled, the saints of God are safe. No enemy will be able to prevent their reaching their destination, the glorious haven of rest, the New Jerusalem above.

VERSE 14 And unto the angel of the church of the Laodiceans write: These things saith the Amen, the faithful and true Witness, the beginning of the creation of God: 15 I know thy works, that thou art neither cold nor hot: I would thou wert cold or hot. 16 So then because thou art lukewarm, and neither cold nor hot, I will spue thee out of My mouth. 17 Because thou sayest, I am rich, and increased with goods, and have need of nothing; and knowest not that thou art wretched, and miserable, and poor, and blind, and naked: 18 I counsel thee to buy of Me gold tried in the fire, that thou mayest be rich; and white raiment, that thou mayest be clothed, and that the shame of thy nakedness do not appear; and anoint thine eyes with eyesalve, that thou mayest see. 19 As many as I love, I rebuke and chasten: be zealous therefore, and repent. 20 Behold, I stand at the door, and knock: if any man hear My voice, and open the door, I will come in to him, and will sup with him, and he with Me. 21 To him that overcometh will I grant to sit with Me in My throne, even as I also overcame, and am set down with My Father in His throne. 22 He that hath an ear, let him hear what the Spirit saith unto the churches.

The Church of Laodicea.—"Laodicea" signifies "the judging of the people," or, according to Cruden, "a just people." The message to this church brings to view the closing scenes of probation. It reveals a period of judgment. It is the last stage of the church. Consequently it applies to believers under the third angel's message, the last message of mercy before the coming of Christ. (Revelation 14: 9-14.) While the work of the great Day of Atonement is in progress, and the investigative judgment is going forward upon the house of God, there is a period during which the just and holy law of God is taken by the waiting church as their rule of life.

"*These Things Saith the Amen.*"—This is, then, the final message to the churches before the close of probation. The description given of the indifferent Laodiceans is fearful and startling. Nevertheless, it cannot be denied, for the Witness is "faithful and true." Moreover, He is "the beginning of the creation of God." Some attempt by this language to uphold the error that Christ is a created being, dating His existence anterior to that of any other created being or thing, next to the self-existent and eternal God. But the language does not imply that He was created; for the words, "the beginning of the creation," may simply signify that the work of creation, strictly speaking, was begun by Him. "Without Him was not anything made." Others, however, and more properly we think, take the word ἀρχή, *arche*, to mean the "agent" or "efficient cause," which is one of the definitions of the word, understanding that Christ is the agent through whom God has created all things.

The Cause of Complaint.—The charge He brings against the Laodiceans is that they are lukewarm, neither hot nor cold. They lack that religious fervor and devotion which is demanded by their position in the world's closing history with the light of prophecy beaming upon their pathway. This lukewarmness is shown by a lack of good works, for it is from a knowledge of their works that the faithful and true Witness brings this fearful charge against them.

"I KNOW THY WORKS"

"Thou hast a name that thou livest, and art dead. Be watchful, . . ; and repent." Revelation 3: 1-3.

"*I Would Thou Wert Cold or Hot.*"—Three spiritual conditions are brought to view in this message—the cold, the lukewarm, and the hot. It is important to determine what condition they each denote, in order to guard against wrong conclusions. Three spiritual conditions which pertain to the church, not to the world, are to be considered. What the term "hot" means it is not difficult to conceive. The mind at once calls up a state of intense zeal, when all the affections, raised to the highest pitch, are drawn out for God and His cause, and manifest themselves in corresponding works. To be lukewarm is to lack this zeal, to be in a state in which heart and earnestness are wanting, in which there is no self-denial that costs anything, no cross-bearing that is felt, no determined witnessing for Christ, and no valiant aggression that keeps the armor bright. Worst of all, it implies entire *satisfaction* with that condition. But to be cold—what is that? Does it denote a state of corruption, wickedness, and sin, such as characterizes the world of unbelievers? We cannot so regard it, for several reasons:

It would seem harsh and repulsive to represent Christ as wishing under any circumstances that persons should be in such a condition, but He says, "I *would* thou wert *cold* or hot."

No state can be more offensive to Christ than that of the sinner in open rebellion, with a heart filled with every evil. It would therefore be incorrect to represent Christ as preferring that state to any position which His people can occupy while they are still retained as His.

The threat of rejection in verse 16 is *because* they are *neither* cold nor hot. It is as much as to say that if they were *either* cold or hot, they would not be rejected. But if by *cold* is meant a state of open worldly wickedness, they would be rejected very speedily. Hence such cannot be its meaning.

We are brought to the conclusion that by this language our Lord has no reference whatever to those outside His church, but that He refers to three degrees of spiritual affections, two of which are more acceptable to Him than the third. Heat and cold are preferable to lukewarmness. But what kind of spiritual state is denoted by the term "cold"? We may remark first that it is a state of *feeling*. In this respect it is superior to lukewarmness, which is a state of comparative insensibility, indifference, and supreme self-satisfaction. To be hot is also to be in a state of feeling. As "hot" denotes joyous fervor, and a lively exercise of all the affections, with a heart buoyant with the sensible presence and love of God, so "cold" would seem to denote a spiritual condition characterized by a destitution of these traits, yet one in which the individual *feels* such destitution. This state is well expressed by the language of Job, "Oh that I knew where I might find Him!" Job 23: 3.

In this state there is not indifference, nor is there content; but there is a sense of coldness, unfitness, and discomfort, and a groping and seeking after something better. There is hope for a person in this condition. What a man feels that he lacks and wants, he will earnestly strive to obtain. The most discouraging feature of the lukewarm is that they are conscious of no lack, and feel that they have need of nothing. Hence it is easy to see why our Lord should prefer to behold His church in a state of comfortless coldness, rather than in a state of comfortable, easy, indifferent lukewarmness. A person will not long remain cold. His efforts will soon lead him to the fervid state. But if lukewarm, there is danger of his remaining till the faithful and true Witness is obliged to reject him as a nauseous and loathsome thing.

"*I Will Spue Thee Out of My Mouth.*"—Here the figure is still further carried out, and the rejection of the lukewarm expressed by the nauseating effects of tepid water. This denotes a final rejection, an utter separation from His church.

"*Rich, and Increased With Goods.*"—Such the Laodiceans think is their condition. They are not hypocrites, because they *know not* that they are poor, miserable, blind, and naked.

The Admonition.—"Buy of Me," says the true Witness, "gold tried in the fire, that thou mayest be rich; and white raiment, that thou mayest be clothed; . . . and anoint thine eyes with eyesalve, that thou mayest see." This shows at once to the deceived Laodiceans the things they lack, and the extent of their destitution. It shows, too, where they can obtain those things in which they are so fearfully poor, and brings before them the necessity of speedily obtaining them. The case is so urgent that our great Advocate in the court above sends us special counsel on this point. The fact that He who has condescended to point out our lack and counsel us to buy, is the one who has these things to bestow and invites us to come to Him for them, is the best possible guarantee that our application will be respected and our requests granted.

But by what means can we buy these things?—Just as we buy all other gospel graces. "Ho, every one that thirsteth, come ye to the waters, and he that hath no money; come ye, buy, and eat; yea, come, buy wine and milk without money and without price." Isaiah 55: 1. We thus buy by the asking, buy by throwing away the worthless baubles of earth and receiving priceless treasures in their stead, buy by simply coming and receiving, buy, giving nothing in return. What do we buy on these gracious terms?—Bread that perishes not, spotless raiment that soils not, riches that corrupt not, and an inheritance that fades not away. Strange transaction, this! Yet the Lord condescends to deal thus with His people. He might compel us to come in the manner and with the mien of beggars, but instead of this He gives us the treasures of His grace, and in return receives our worthlessness, that we may take the blessings He has to bestow, not as pittances dealt out to mendicants, but as the legitimate possessions of honorable purchase. The things to be obtained demand special notice.

"*Gold Tried in the Fire.*"—Gold literally considered is the comprehensive name for all worldly wealth and riches. Figuratively, it must denote that which constitutes spiritual riches. What grace, then, is represented by the gold, or rather, what graces? Doubtless no one single grace can be said to answer to the full import of that term. The Lord said to the church of Smyrna that He knew their poverty, but they were rich. That testimony shows that their riches consisted of that which was finally to put them in possession of a crown of life. Says James, "Hearken, my beloved brethren, Hath not God chosen the poor of this world, *rich in faith*, and heirs of the kingdom which He hath promised to them that love Him?" James 2: 5. "Faith," says Paul, "is the substance of things hoped for, the evidence of things not seen." Hebrews 11: 1. To be "rich toward God," rich in the spiritual sense, is to have a clear title to the promises, to be an heir of that "inheritance incorruptible, and undefiled, and that fadeth not away, reserved in heaven for you." 1 Peter 1: 4. "If ye be Christ's, then are ye Abraham's seed, and heirs according to the promise." Galatians 3: 29. How do we obtain this heirship?—In the same way that Abraham obtained the promise, that is, through faith. (Romans 4: 13, 14.)

No wonder, then, that the entire eleventh chapter of Hebrews should be devoted to this important subject, setting forth the mighty achievements that have been accomplished, and the precious promises that have been obtained, through faith. In Hebrews 12: 1, the grand conclusion of the argument is given when Christians are exhorted to lay aside every weight, and the sin (of unbelief) that so easily besets them.

Nothing will sooner dry up the springs of spirituality, and sink us into utter poverty in reference to the things of the kingdom of God, than to let faith go out and unbelief come in. Faith must enter into every action that is pleasing in His sight. In coming to Him, the first thing is to believe that He is. It is through faith, as the chief agent under the grace which is the gift of God, that we are to be saved. (Hebrews 11: 6; Ephesians 2: 8.)

From this it would seem that faith is a principal element of spiritual wealth. But if, as already remarked, no one grace can answer to the full import of the term "gold," so doubtless other things are included with faith. "Faith is the substance of things hoped for." Hence hope is an inseparable accompaniment of faith. (Hebrews 11: 1; Romans 8: 24, 25.) Again

Paul tells us that faith works by love, and speaks in another place of being "rich in good works." (Galatians 5: 6; 1 Timothy 6: 18.) Hence love cannot be separated from faith. We then have before us the three things associated together by Paul in 1 Corinthians 13—faith, hope, and charity, or love; and the greatest of these is charity, which is "rich in good works." Such is the gold tried by fire which we are counseled to buy.

"*White Raiment.*"—On this point there would not seem to be much room for controversy. A few texts will furnish a key to the understanding of this expression. Says the prophet, "All our righteousnesses are as filthy rags." Isaiah 64: 6. We are counseled to buy the opposite of filthy rags, which would be complete and spotless raiment. The same figure is used in Zechariah 3: 3, 4. John, in Revelation 19: 8, says plainly that "the fine linen is the righteousness of saints."

The Eyesalve.—On the eyesalve there is as little room for a diversity of opinion as upon the white raiment. The anointing of the eyes is certainly not to be taken in a literal sense, for reference is being made to spiritual things. The eyesalve must denote that by which our spiritual discernment is quickened. There is but one agent revealed to us in the word of God by which this is accomplished, and that is the Holy Spirit. In Acts 10: 38 we read that "God anointed Jesus of Nazareth with the Holy Ghost." The same writer through whom came this Revelation from Jesus Christ which we are studying, wrote to the church in his first epistle as follows: "But ye have an unction from the Holy One, and ye know all things. . . . But the anointing which ye have received of Him abideth in you, and ye need not that any man teach you: but as the same anointing teacheth you of all things, and is truth, and is no lie, and even as it hath taught you, ye shall abide in Him." 1 John 2: 20, 27. By referring to his Gospel, it is found that the work which John here sets forth as accomplished by the anointing is exactly the same that he there attributes to the Holy Spirit. "The Comforter, which is the Holy Ghost, whom the Father will send in My name, He shall teach you all things, and bring all things to your remembrance, whatsoever I have said unto you." John 14: 26. (See also John 16: 13.)

Thus in a formal and solemn manner are we counseled by the faithful and true Witness, under the figures of gold, white raiment, and eyesalve, to seek from Him an increase of the heavenly graces of faith, hope, charity, that righteousness which He alone can furnish, and an unction from the Holy Spirit. But how is it possible that a people lacking these things should think themselves rich and increased with goods? A plausible inference may here be drawn, which is perhaps also a necessary one, as there is room for no other. It will be observed that no fault is found with the Laodiceans on account of the doctrines they hold. They are not accused of harboring a Jezebel in their midst, or of countenancing the doctrines of Balaam or the Nicolaitanes. So far as we can learn, their belief is correct, and their doctrine sound.

The inference therefore is that having a correct doctrine, they are content. They are satisfied with a correct form of religion without its power. Having received light concerning the closing events of the gospel era, and having a correct theoretical knowledge of the truths that pertain to the last generation of men, they are inclined to rest in this to the neglect of spiritual power which changes the life and builds strong character. It is by their actions, doubtless, not by their words, that they say they are rich and increased with goods. Having so much light and so much truth, what can they want besides? If they defend the theory, and as far as their outward life is concerned, conform to the increasing light upon the commandments of God and the faith of Jesus, is not their righteousness complete? Are they not rich, and increased with goods, and in need of nothing? Here is their failure. Their whole being should cry out for the spirit, the zeal, the fervency, the life, the power, of a living Christianity.

The Token of Love.—As strange as it may seem, the token of love is chastisement. "As many as I love, I rebuke and chasten." If we are without chastisement, we are not sons. (Hebrews 12: 8.) "A general law of His gracious economy," says Augustus C. Thompson, "is here set forth. . . . As all need chastisement in some measure, they in some measure receive it, and thus have proof of the Saviour's attachment. This is a hard lesson to learn, and believers are dull scholars; yet here and throughout God's word and providence it stands, that trials are His benedictions, and that no child escapes the rod. The incorrigibly misshapen and coarse-grained blocks are rejected, whilst those chosen for the glorious structure are subjected to the chisel and the hammer. There is no cluster on the true vine but must pass through the winepress. 'For myself,' said an old divine under affliction—'for myself, I bless God I have observed and felt so much mercy in this angry dispensation of God that I am almost transported. I am sure highly pleased with thinking how infinitely sweet His mercies are, when His judgments are so gracious.' In view, then, of the origin and design of the chastisements you receive, 'Be zealous and repent.' Lose no time; lose not a blow of the rod, but repent at once. Be fervent in spirit. Such is the first appliance of encouragement."[1]

Be Zealous and Repent.—Although, as we have seen, the condition represented by coldness is preferable to one of lukewarmness, yet that is not a state in which our Lord ever desires to find us. We are never exhorted to seek that state. There is a far better one which we are counseled to attain; and that is to be zealous, to be fervent, and to have our hearts all aglow in the service of our Master.

Christ Knocking at the Door.—"Here is the heart of hearts," says Augustus C. Thompson. "Notwithstanding their offensive attitude, their unlovely character, such is His love to their souls that He humbles Himself to solicit the privilege of making them blessed. 'Behold, I stand at the door, and knock.' Why does He? Not because He is without home elsewhere.

[1] Augustus C. Thompson, *Morning Hours in Patmos*, pp. 260, 261.

© PACIFIC PRESS PUBLISHING ASSN. FRANKLIN BOOTH. ARTIST

A HEAVENLY GUEST

"If any man . . . open the door, I will come in to him, and will sup with him." Revelation 3: 20. Come, yes, come into our homes, Lord Jesus.

. . . Among the mansions in His Father's house there is not one entrance closed to Him. He is the life of every heart, the light in every eye, the song on every tongue, in glory. But He goes round from door to door in Laodicea. He stands at each, and knocks, because He came to seek and to save that which is lost, because He cannot give up the purpose of communicating eternal life to as many as the Father hath given Him, and because He cannot become known to the inmate unless the door be opened and a welcome given Him. Have you bought a piece of ground, have you bought five yoke of oxen, is your hat in your hand, and do you pray to be excused? He knocks and knocks. But you cannot receive company at present; you are worn out with labor; you have wheeled round the sofa; you are making yourself comfortable, and you send word you are engaged. He knocks and knocks. . . . It is the hour for church prayer meeting or for monthly concert; there is opportunity to pay a Christian visit to an individual or a family; but you move not. . . . Oh, nauseous lukewarmness! Oh, fatal worldliness! The Lord of glory comes all the way from His celestial palace—comes in poverty, in sweat, in blood—comes to the door of a professed friend, who owes all to Him, and cannot get in!—comes to rescue a man whose house is on fire, and he will not admit Him! Oh, the height, the depth, of Jesus Christ's forbearance! Even the heathen Publius received Paul, and lodged him three days courteously. Shall nominal Christians tell the Lord of apostles they have no room for Him?"[2]

"*If Any Man Hear My Voice.*"—The Lord entreats, then, as well as knocks. The word "if" implies that some will not hear. Though He stands and knocks, yet some will close their ears to His tender entreaties. But it is not enough simply to hear. We must open the door. Many who at first hear the voice, and for a time feel inclined to heed, will, alas! fail in the end to do that which is necessary to secure to themselves the communion of the heavenly Guest.

---

[2] *Ibid.*, pp. 261-264.

Reader, are your ears open to the entreaties which the Saviour directs to you? Is His voice a welcome sound to you? Will you heed it? Will you open the door and let Him in? Or is the door of your heart held fast by heaps of this world's rubbish, which you are unwilling to remove? Remember that the Lord of life never forces an entrance. He condescends to come and knock, and seek admittance; but He takes up His abode in those hearts only where He is then a welcome and invited guest.

Then the promise! "I will come in to him, and will sup with him, and he with Me." How forcible and touching is the figure! Friend with friend, partaking of the cheerful and social meal! Mind with mind, holding free and intimate converse! What a festal scene must that be where the King of glory is a guest! No common degree of union, no ordinary blessing, no usual privilege, is denoted by this language. Who can remain indifferent under such tender entreaty and so gracious a promise? Nor are we required to furnish the table for this exalted Guest. This He does Himself, not with the gross nutriment of earth, but with viands from His own heavenly storehouse. Here He sets before us foretastes of the glory soon to be revealed. Here He gives us an earnest of our future inheritance, which is "incorruptible, and undefiled, and that fadeth not away." Verily, when we comply with the conditions and receive this promise, we shall experience the rising of the day star in our hearts, and behold the dawn of a glorious morning for the church of God.

The Promise to the Overcomer.—The promise of supping with His disciples is made by the Lord before the final promise to the overcomer is given. This shows that the blessings included in that promise are to be enjoyed in this probationary state. Now, added to all these, is the promise to the overcomer: "To him that overcometh will I grant to sit with Me in My throne, even as I also overcame, and am set down with My Father in His throne." Here the promises of the Lord culminate. From being at first rebellious, and then fallen, degraded, and polluted, man is brought back into reconciliation with God through the work of the Redeemer. He is cleansed from his pollutions, redeemed from the fall, made immortal, and finally raised to a seat upon the throne of his Saviour. Honor and exaltation can go no farther. Human minds cannot conceive that state, human language cannot describe it. We can only labor on until, if overcomers, we shall know what it is.

In this verse there is not only a glorious promise, but there is also an important doctrine. We learn by this that Christ reigns consecutively upon two thrones. One is the throne of His Father, the other is His own throne. He declares in this verse that He has overcome, and is now set down with His Father in His throne. He is now associated with the Father in the throne of universal dominion, placed at His right hand, far above all principality, power, might, and dominion. (Ephesians 1: 20-22.) While in this position, He is a priest-king. He is a priest, "a minister of the sanctuary;" but at the same time He is "on the right hand of the *throne* of the Majesty in the heavens." Hebrews 8: 1, 2. This position and work of our Lord was thus predicted by the prophet Zechariah: "Speak unto him, saying, Thus speaketh the Lord of hosts [God], saying, Behold the man whose name is The Branch [Christ]; and He shall grow up out of His place, and He shall build the temple of the Lord: . . . and He [Christ] shall bear the glory, and shall sit and rule upon His [God's] throne; and He [Christ] shall be a priest upon His [God's] throne: and the counsel of peace [in the sacrifice and priestly work of Christ in behalf of repenting man] shall be between them both." Zechariah 6: 12, 13.

But the time is coming when He is to change His position, and leaving the throne of His Father, take His own throne. This must be when the time comes for the reward of the overcomers, for when they enter upon their reward, they are to sit with Christ on His throne, as He has overcome, and is now seated with the Father upon His throne. This change in the position of Christ is set forth by Paul:

"Then cometh the end, when He shall have delivered up the kingdom to God, even the Father; when He shall have put down all rule and all authority and power. For He must reign, till He hath put all enemies under His feet. The last enemy that shall be destroyed is death. For He hath put all things under His feet. But when He saith all things are put under Him, it is manifest that He is excepted, which did put all things under Him. And when all things shall be subdued unto Him, then shall the Son also Himself be subject unto Him that put all things under Him, that God may be all in all." 1 Corinthians 15: 24-28.

The truths taught in this scripture may perhaps be most briefly expressed by a paraphrase, and by giving, in every instance, instead of the pronouns, the nouns to which they respectively refer. Thus:

"Then cometh the end (of the present age), when Christ shall have delivered up the kingdom (which He now holds conjointly with the Father) to God, even the Father; when God shall have put down all rule and all authority and power (that is opposed to the work of the Son). For Christ must reign (on the throne of His Father) till the Father hath put all enemies under Christ's feet. [See Psalm 110: 1.] The last enemy that shall be destroyed is death. For God (then) hath put all things under Christ's feet. But when God saith, All things are put under Christ (and He begins His reign upon His own throne), it is manifest that God is excepted, who did put all things under Christ. And when all things shall be subdued unto Christ, then shall Christ also Himself be subject unto God that put all things under Him, that God may be all in all."

From this it will be seen that the kingdom which Christ delivers up to the Father is that which He holds at the present time upon His Father's throne, where He tells us He is now seated. He delivers up this kingdom at the end of His priestly mediation, when the time comes for Him to take His own throne. After this He reigns on the throne of His father David, and is subject only to God, who still retains His position upon the throne of universal dominion. In this reign of Christ the saints participate. "To him that overcometh will I grant to sit with Me in My throne." "They lived," says John, dating from the first resurrection, "and reigned with Christ a thousand years." Revelation 20: 4. This we understand to be a special reign, or for a special purpose, as will be noticed in that chapter, for the actual reign of the saints is to be "forever and ever." Daniel 7: 18, 27. How can any earthly attraction divert our gaze from this enduring and heavenly prospect?

Thus close the messages to the seven churches. How pointed and searching is their testimony! What lessons they contain for all Christians in all ages! It is as true with the last church as with the first, that all their works are known to Him who walks in the midst of the seven golden candlesticks. From His scrutinizing gaze nothing can be hidden. While His threatenings to the hypocrites and evil workers are awful, as in justice they may be, how ample, how comforting, how gracious, how glorious are His promises to those who love and follow Him with singleness of heart!

ADAPTED FROM G. DORE, ARTIST

"HOLY, HOLY, HOLY, LORD GOD ALMIGHTY!"

"Thou art worthy, O Lord, to receive glory and honor and power: for Thou hast created all things." Revelation 4: 11.

CHAPTER IV

BEFORE THE THRONE OF GOD

VERSE 1 After this I looked, and, behold, a door was opened in heaven: and the first voice which I heard was as it were of a trumpet talking with me; which said, Come up hither, and I will show thee things which must be hereafter.

IN THE first three chapters, John presented the vision he had of the Son of man. He described His majestic person, and recorded the words which He uttered with a voice as the sound of many waters. A new scene and a new vision now open before us. The expression "after this" does not denote that what is recorded in Revelation 4 and onward was to take place after the *fulfillment* of everything recorded in the three preceding chapters. It means only that after the prophet had seen and heard what is there recorded, he had the new view which he now introduces.

"*A Door Was Opened in Heaven.*"—Let it be noticed that John says, "A door was opened *in* heaven," not *into* heaven. This expression reads literally in the Greek, "Behold, a door open in heaven." It was not an opening of heaven itself before the mind of John, as in the case of Stephen (Acts 7: 56), but some place in heaven was open before him, and he was permitted to behold what was taking place within. That what John saw open was the heavenly sanctuary, will plainly appear from other parts of the book.

"*Things Which Must Be Hereafter.*"—Compare this with Revelation 1: 1. The great object of the Revelation seems to be the presentation of future events which will inform, edify, and comfort the church.

VERSE 2 And immediately I was in the Spirit: and, behold, a throne was set in heaven, and One sat on the throne. 3 And He that sat was to look upon like a jasper and a sardine stone: and there was a rainbow round about the throne, in sight like unto an emerald. 4 And round about the throne were four and twenty seats: and upon the seats I saw four and twenty elders sitting, clothed in white raiment; and they had on their heads crowns of gold. 5 And out of the throne proceeded lightnings and thunderings and voices: and there were seven lamps of fire burning before the throne, which are the seven Spirits of God.

In the Spirit.—Once before in this book we have had the expression, "I was in the Spirit on the Lord's day" (Revelation 1: 10), where it was taken to express the fact that John had a vision upon the Sabbath, or true Lord's day. If it there expressed the state of being in vision, it would denote the same thing here. Consequently the first vision ended with Revelation 3, and a new one is here introduced. Nor is it any objection to this view that previous to this, as is learned from the first verse of this chapter, John was in such a spiritual state as to be able to look up and see a door open in heaven, and to hear a voice like the mighty sound of a trumpet calling him up to a nearer prospect of heavenly things. Stephen, also, full of the Holy Ghost, looked up and saw the heavens open, and the Son of man on the right hand of God. To be in the Spirit denotes a high state of spiritual elevation. On what day this vision was given, we are not informed.

Being again in heavenly vision, John first beheld a throne set in heaven, and the Divine Being seated upon it. The description of the appearance of this personage, clothed in garments of mingled colors, is such as at once to suggest to the mind a monarch vested with his royal robes. About the throne there was a rainbow, which added grandeur to the scene, and reminds us that though He who sits upon the throne is an almighty and absolute ruler, He is nevertheless the covenant-keeping God.

The Four and Twenty Elders.—Who are these beings who surround the throne of glory? It will be observed that they are clothed in white raiment and have on their heads crowns of gold, which are tokens of both a conflict completed and a victory gained. From this we conclude that they were once participants in the Christian warfare, they once trod the earthly way with all saints; but they have been overcomers, and in advance of the great multitude of the redeemed, are wearing their victor crowns in the heavenly world. Indeed, they plainly tell us this in the song of praise which they ascribe to the Lamb: "They sung a new song, saying, Thou art worthy to take the book, and to open the seals thereof: for Thou wast slain, and hast redeemed us to God by Thy blood out of every kindred, and tongue, and people, and nation." Revelation 5: 9. This song is sung before any of the events in the prophecy of the seven seals take place; for it is sung to set forth the worthiness of the Lamb to take the book and to open the seals, on the ground of what He had already accomplished—their redemption. It is not therefore thrown in here by anticipation, having its application in the future, but it expresses an absolute and finished fact in the history of those who sang it. These, then, were a class of redeemed persons—redeemed from this earth, redeemed as all others must be redeemed, by the precious blood of Christ.

Do we in any other place read of such a class of redeemed ones? We think Paul refers to the same company when he writes to the Ephesians thus: "Wherefore He saith, When He [Christ] ascended up on high, He led captivity captive, and gave gifts unto men." The marginal reading is, He led a "multitude of captives." Ephesians 4: 8. Going back to the events that occurred in connection with the crucifixion and the resurrection of Christ, we read: "The graves were opened; and many bodies of the saints which slept arose, and came out of the graves after His resurrection, and went into the holy city, and appeared unto many." Matthew 27: 52, 53. Thus the answer to our question comes unmistakably from the sacred page. These are some of those who came out of their graves at the resurrection of Christ, and who were numbered with the illustrious multitude which Jesus led up from the captivity of Death's dark domain when He ascended in triumph on high. Matthew records their resurrection, Paul their ascension, and John beholds them in heaven, performing the sacred duties which they were raised up to accomplish.

In this view we are not alone. John Wesley spoke as follows concerning the four and twenty elders: " 'Clothed in white raiment'—This and their golden crowns show that they had already finished their course, and taken their places among the citizens of heaven. They are never termed souls, and hence it is probable that they had glorified bodies already. Compare Matthew 27: 52."[1]

Particular attention must be given to the fact that the four and twenty elders are said to be seated on thrones. Our translation reads "seats;" but the Greek is θρόνοι, *thronoi*, thrones, the same word as is used three times in verses 2 and 3 and once in verse 4 immediately preceding. Thus the Revised Version reads: "Round about the throne were four and twenty thrones, and upon the thrones I saw four and twenty elders sitting." Consequently this passage throws light on the expression found in Daniel 7: 9, "I beheld till the thrones were cast down." These are the same thrones, and as has been shown in comments upon that passage, the meaning is not that the thrones were overturned, or cast down, in the ordinary sense of that expression, but placed, or set. The figure is taken from the Eastern custom of placing mats or divans for distinguished guests to sit upon. These four and twenty elders (see comments on Revelation 5) are evidently assistants of Christ in His mediatorial work in the sanctuary on high. When the judgment scene described in Daniel 7: 9 began in the most holy place, their thrones were placed there, according to the testimony of that passage.

The Seven Lamps of Fire.—In these lamps of fire we have the antitype of the golden candlestick of the typical sanctuary, with its seven ever-burning lamps. This candlestick was placed by divine direction in the first apartment of the earthly sanctuary. (Exodus 25: 31, 32, 37; 26: 35; 27: 20.) Now when John tells us that a door was open in heaven, and in the apartment thus disclosed to view he sees the antitype of the candlestick of

[1] John Wesley, *Explanatory Notes Upon the New Testament*, p. 695, comment on Revelation 4: 4.

the earthly sanctuary, it is good proof that he is looking into the first apartment of the sanctuary above.

VERSE 6 And before the throne there was a sea of glass like unto crystal: and in the midst of the throne, and round about the throne, were four beasts full of eyes before and behind. 7 And the first beast was like a lion, and the second beast like a calf, and the third beast had a face as a man, and the fourth beast was like a flying eagle. 8 And the four beasts had each of them six wings about him; and they were full of eyes within: and they rest not day and night, saying, Holy, holy, holy, Lord God Almighty, which was, and is, and is to come. 9 And when those beasts give glory and honor and thanks to Him that sat on the throne, who liveth forever and ever, 10 the four and twenty elders fall down before Him that sat on the throne, and worship Him that liveth forever and ever, and cast their crowns before the throne, saying, 11 Thou art worthy, O Lord, to receive glory and honor and power: for Thou hast created all things, and for Thy pleasure they are and were created.

The Sea of Glass.—Not composed of glass, but a broad expanse resembling glass—"glassy, i.e., transparent," as James Strong says in his *Greek Dictionary.* This idea is further carried out by the likening of the sea to crystal, which is defined to mean "anything concrete and pellucid, like ice or glass." The position of this sea is such as to show that it bears no analogy to the laver of the ancient typical service. It may extend under, and be the foundation of, the throne and even of the city itself. It is again brought to view in Revelation 15: 2, as the place where the overcomers, in the ecstatic joy of final victory, will soon stand. There we shall praise Him who has given us the victory.

The Four Living Creatures.—It is an unhappy translation which has given us the word "beasts" in this verse. The Greek word ζῶον, *zoon,* denotes properly "a living creature." Bloomfield says in his comment, " 'Four living creatures' (not *beasts*). So Heinr. renders it. . . . The propriety of this correction, is now, I believe, generally agreed upon by commentators. The word is very different from θηρίον, [*therion,* wild beast], used to designate the prophetic beasts in the 13th and following chapters. (Scholefield.) It may be added, that Bulkeley adduces several examples of ζῶον, to denote, not only creature, but even a human being, especially one from Origen, who uses it of our Lord Jesus."[2]

Similar imagery is used in the first chapter of Ezekiel. The qualities which would seem to be signified by the emblems are strength, perseverance, reason, and swiftness—strength of affection, perseverance in carrying out the requirements of duty, reason in comprehending the divine will, and swiftness in obeying. These living beings are even more intimately connected with the throne than are the four and twenty elders, being represented as in the midst of it, and round about it. Like the elders, these in their song to the Lamb ascribe to Him praise for having redeemed them from the earth. They therefore belong to the same company, and represent a part of the great multitude, who, as already described (see remarks on verse 4), have been led up on high from the captivity of death. Concerning the object of their redemption, see remarks on Revelation 5: 8.

They Rest Not.—"O happy unrest!" beautifully exclaims John Wesley. The theme of their constant worship is, "Holy, holy, holy, Lord God Almighty, which was, and is, and is to come." No sublimer strain ever issued from created lips. They repeat it "day and night," or continually, these terms only denoting the manner in which time is reckoned here, for there can be no night where the throne of God is. (Revelation 21: 23, 25.)

We mortals are likely to tire of the repetition of the simple testimony we bear here to the goodness and mercy of God. We are sometimes tempted to say nothing, because we cannot continually say something new. But may we not learn a profitable lesson from the course of these holy beings above, who never grow weary of the ceaseless repetition of these words, "Holy, holy, holy, Lord God Almighty;" and to whom these words never grow old, because their hearts ever glow with a sense of His holiness, goodness, and love? Praise does not be-

---

[2] S. T. Bloomfield, *The Greek Testament With English Notes*, Vol. II, p. 574, comment on Revelation 4: 6.

come to them monotonous, for with every utterance they gain a new view of the attributes of the Almighty. They reach a greater height of comprehension in their vision of His perfections; the horizon expands before them; their hearts enlarge; and the new emotions of adoration draw from them a fresh utterance of their holy salutation, new even to themselves, "Holy, holy, holy, Lord God Almighty!"

So, even with us here, though words are often repeated concerning the goodness, the mercy, and the love of God, the value of His truth, and the attractions of the world to come, these should not grow stale upon the ear. We should all our lives be rising to new conceptions of the blessings embraced in these glorious themes.

"Thou art worthy, O Lord, to receive glory and honor and power." How worthy, we never shall be able to realize until, like the holy beings who utter this language, changed to immortality, we are presented "faultless before the presence of His glory." Jude 24.

"*Thou Hast Created All Things.*"—The works of creation furnish the foundation for the honor, glory, and power ascribed to God. "For Thy pleasure [or through Thy will, *διὰ τὸ θέλημά σου, dia to thelema sou*], they are, and were created." God willed, and all things came into existence; and by the same power they are preserved and sustained.

 PAUL REMMEY, ARTIST

A CHALLENGE FROM HEAVEN

"Who is worthy to open the book? . . . No man in heaven, nor in earth, . . . was able to open the book." Revelation 5: 2, 3.

CHAPTER V

THE CHALLENGE OF THE SEALED BOOK

VERSE 1 And I saw in the right hand of Him that sat on the throne a book written within and on the backside, sealed with seven seals.

AS A NEW chapter opens, the same view is still before the mind of the apostle. By the words, "Him that sat on the throne," is evidently meant the Father, as the Son is later introduced as "a Lamb as it had been slain." The book which John here saw, contained a revelation of scenes that were to be enacted in the history of the church to the end of time. That the volume is held in the right hand of Him that sat on the throne may signify that a knowledge of the future rests with God alone, except so far as He sees fit to reveal it to others.

The Sealed Book.—The books in use at the time the Revelation was given were not in the form of books as now made. They did not consist of a series of leaves bound together, but were composed of strips of parchment or other material, rolled up. On this point, John Wesley remarks:

"The usual books of the ancients were not like ours, but were volumes, or long pieces of parchment, rolled upon a long stick, as we frequently roll silks. Such was this represented, which was sealed with seven seals. Not as if the apostle saw all the seals at once: for there were seven volumes wrapped up one within another, each of which was sealed: so that upon opening and unrolling the first, the second appeared to be sealed up till that was opened, and so on to the seventh." [1]

This book was not written within and on the backside, as the punctuation of our common version makes it read.

[1] John Wesley, *Explanatory Notes Upon the New Testament*, p. 697, comment on Revelation 5: 1.

"Grotius, Lowman, Fuller, etc.," says the *Cottage Bible*, "remove the comma thus: 'Written within, and on the back (or outside) sealed.'"[2] How these seals were placed, is sufficiently explained.

VERSE 2 And I saw a strong angel proclaiming with a loud voice, Who is worthy to open the book, and to loose the seals thereof? 3 And no man in heaven, nor in earth, neither under the earth, was able to open the book, neither to look thereon. 4 And I wept much, because no man was found worthy to open and to read the book, neither to look thereon.

The Challenge.—In the vision God, as it were, held forth this book to the view of the universe, and a strong angel, one doubtless of great eminence and power, came forth as a crier, and with a mighty voice challenged all creatures in the universe to try the strength of their wisdom in opening the counsels of God. Who could be found worthy to open the book, and to loose the seals thereof? A pause ensued. In silence the universe owned its inability and unworthiness to enter into the counsels of the Creator. "No man in heaven," οὐδείς, *oudeis*, no one, signifies not merely no man, but no one, no being, in heaven. Is not this proof that the faculties of angels are limited, like those of man, in respect to penetrating the future and disclosing what is to come? When the apostle saw that no one came forward to open the book, he greatly feared that the counsels of God which it contained in reference to his people would never be disclosed. In the natural tenderness of his feelings, and his concern for the church, he wept much. "How far are they," says John Wesley, "from the temper of St. John, who inquire after anything rather than the contents of this book!"[3]

Upon the words, "I wept much," Joseph Benson offers the following beautiful remarks: "Being greatly affected with the thought that no being whatever was to be found able to understand, reveal, and accomplish the divine counsels, fearing they would still remain concealed from the church. This weeping

[2] *The Cottage Bible*, Vol. II, p. 1391, note on Revelation 5: 1.

[3] John Wesley, *Explanatory Notes Upon the New Testament*, p. 698, comment on Revelation 5: 4.

of the apostle sprang from greatness of mind. The tenderness of heart which he always had, appeared more clearly now he was out of his own power. The Revelation was not written without tears: neither without tears will it be understood."[4]

VERSE 5 And one of the elders saith unto me, Weep not: behold, the Lion of the tribe of Judah, the Root of David, hath prevailed to open the book, and to loose the seven seals thereof. 6 And I beheld, and, lo, in the midst of the throne and of the four beasts, and in the midst of the elders, stood a Lamb as it had been slain, having seven horns and seven eyes, which are the seven Spirits of God sent forth into all the earth. 7 And He came and took the book out of the right hand of Him that sat upon the throne.

John is not permitted to weep for long. God is not willing that any knowledge which can benefit His people shall be withheld from them. Provision is made for the opening of the book. Hence one of the elders counsels John, "Weep not: behold, the Lion of the tribe of Judah, the Root of David, hath prevailed to open the book, and to loose the seven seals thereof." Why one of the elders in preference to some other being, should impart this information to John, does not appear, unless it is that having been redeemed, they had an acquaintance with Christ, and would be especially interested in all that pertained to the welfare of the church on earth.

Christ is here called the "Lion of the tribe of Judah." Why called a lion? And why of the tribe of Judah?—As to the first question, it is probably to denote His strength. As the lion is the king of beasts, the monarch of the forest, he thus becomes a fit emblem of kingly authority and power. As to being "of the tribe of Judah," He doubtless receives this appellation from the prophecy in Genesis 49: 9, 10.

"*The Root of David.*"—Christ was the source and sustainer of David in his position and power. That David's position was specially ordained of Christ, and that he was specially sustained by Him, there can be no doubt. David was the type, Christ the antitype. David's throne and reign over Israel was a type of Christ's reign over His people. He shall reign

[4] Joseph Benson, *Commentary on the New Testament*, Vol. II, p. 721, note on Revelation 5: 4.

upon "the throne of His father David." Luke 1: 32, 33. As Christ appeared in the line of David's descendants when He took upon Himself our nature, He is also called "the offspring of David," and "a rod out of the stem of Jesse." Isaiah 11: 1, 10; Revelation 22: 16. His connection with the throne of David being thus set forth, and His right thus shown to rule over the people of God, there was a propriety in entrusting to Him the opening of the seals.

"*Hath Prevailed.*"—These words indicate that the right to open the book was acquired by a victory gained in some previous conflict. We find the account of this triumph set forth later in this chapter. The next scene introduces us to the great work of Christ as the Redeemer of the world, and the shedding of His blood for the remission of sin and the salvation of man. In this work He was subjected to the fiercest assaults of Satan. But He endured temptation, bore the agonies of the cross, rose a victor over death and the grave, made the way of redemption sure—triumphed! Hence the four living beings and the four and twenty elders sing, "Thou art worthy to take the book, and to open the seals thereof: for Thou wast slain, and hast redeemed us to God by Thy blood."

John looks for the Lion of the tribe of Judah and beholds a Lamb in the midst of the throne and of the four living beings and the elders, as it had been slain.

"*In the Midst of the Throne.*"—Philip Doddridge translates thus: "I beheld . . . in the middle space between the throne and the four living creatures, and in the midst of the elders, . . . there stood . . . . a Lamb." [5] In the center of the scene was the throne of the Father, and standing in the open space which surrounded it was the Son, set forth under the symbol of a slain lamb. Around these there stood those saints who had been redeemed: first, those represented by the four living creatures, then the elders forming the second circle, and the angels (verse 11) forming a third circle. The worthiness of Christ as

[5] Philip Doddridge, *The Family Expositor*, Vol. VI, p. 405, paraphrase of Revelation 5:5.

He thus stands forth under the figure of a slain lamb, is the admiration of all the holy throng.

"*As It Had Been Slain.*"—John C. Woodhouse, as quoted in the *Comprehensive Commentary*, says: "The Greek implies that the Lamb appeared with a wounded neck and throat, as if smitten at the altar as a victim."[6] On this phrase, Adam Clarke says: "As if now in the act of being offered. This is very remarkable; so important is the sacrificial offering of Christ in the sight of God, that He is still represented as being in the very act of pouring out His blood for the offenses of man."[7]

"*Seven Horns and Seven Eyes.*"—Horns are symbols of power and eyes typify wisdom. Seven is a number denoting completeness, or perfection. We are thus taught that perfect power and perfect wisdom inhere in the Lamb.

"*He Came and Took the Book.*"—Commentators have found an incongruity in the idea that the book was taken by the Lamb, and have had recourse to several expedients to avoid the difficulty. But is it not a well-established principle that any action which could be performed by the person or being represented by a symbol, may be attributed to the symbol? Is not this all the explanation that the passage needs? The Lamb, we know, is a symbol of Christ. We know there is nothing incongruous in Christ's taking a book, and when we read that the book was taken, we think of the action, not as performed by a lamb, but by the one of whom the lamb is a symbol.

VERSE 8 And when He had taken the book, the four beasts and four and twenty elders fell down before the Lamb, having every one of them harps, and golden vials full of odors, which are the prayers of saints. 9 And they sung a new song, saying, Thou art worthy to take the book, and to open the seals thereof: for Thou wast slain, and hast redeemed us to God by Thy blood out of every kindred, and tongue, and people, and nation; 10 and hast made us unto our God kings and priests: and we shall reign on the earth.

"*Vials Full of Odors.*"—From this expression we form an idea of the employment of those redeemed ones represented by

---

[6] William Jenks, *Comprehensive Commentary*, Vol. V. p. 684, note on Revelation 5: 6.

[7] Adam Clarke, *Commentary on the New Testament*, Vol. II, p. 991, note on Revelation 5: 6.

the four living creatures and the four and twenty elders. They have golden vials, or vessels, full of odors—or, as the margin reads, incense—which are the prayers of saints. This is a work of ministry such as pertains to priests.

The reader will remember that in the ancient typical service the high priest had many assistants. When we consider that we are now looking into the sanctuary in heaven, the conclusion at once follows that these redeemed ones are the assistants of our great High Priest above. For this purpose they were doubtless redeemed. What could be more appropriate than that our Lord should be assisted in His priestly work for the human race by noble members of that race whose holiness of life, and purity of character, had fitted them to be raised up for that purpose? (See remarks on Revelation 4: 4.)

We are aware that many entertain a great aversion to the idea of there being anything real and tangible in heaven. But though the Revelation deals largely in *figures*, it does not deal in *fictions*. There is reality in all the things described, and we gain an understanding of the reality when we get a correct interpretation of the figures. Thus, in this vision we know that the One upon the throne is God. He is really there. We know the Lamb symbolizes Christ. He too is really there. He ascended with a literal, tangible body, and who can say that He does not still retain it?

If, then, our great High Priest is a literal being, He must have a literal place in which to minister. If the four living creatures and the four and twenty elders represent those whom Christ led up from the captivity of death at the time of His resurrection and ascension, why are they not just as literal beings while there in heaven as they were when they ascended?

The Song.—It is called "a new song," new, probably, in respect to the occasion and the composition. They were the first that could sing it, being the first that were redeemed. They call themselves "kings and priests." In what sense they are priests has already been noticed. They assist Christ in His priestly work. In the same sense doubtlesss they are also kings, for Christ is set down with His Father on His throne, and doubtless these as ministers of His have some part to act in connection with the government of heaven in its relation to this world.

The Anticipation.—"We shall reign on the earth." Thus, notwithstanding they are redeemed and surround the throne of God and of the Lamb, where all is glory ineffable, their song contemplates a still higher state when the great work of redemption shall be completed, and they, with the whole redeemed family of God, shall reign on the earth, the promised inheritance and the eternal residence of the saints. (Romans 4: 13; Galatians 3: 29; Psalm 37: 11; Matthew 5: 5; 2 Peter 3: 13; Isaiah 65: 17-25; Revelation 21: 1-5.)

VERSE 11 And I beheld, and I heard the voice of many angels round about the throne and the beasts and the elders: and the number of them was ten thousand times ten thousand, and thousands of thousands; 12 saying with a loud voice, Worthy is the Lamb that was slain to receive power, and riches, and wisdom, and strength, and honor, and glory, and blessing.

The Heavenly Sanctuary.—How little conception we have of the magnitude and glory of the heavenly temple! Into that temple John was introduced at the opening of Revelation 4, by the door which was open in heaven. Into the same temple, he is still looking in Revelation 5: 11, 12. Now he beholds the heavenly hosts. About the throne are those represented by the four living creatures. Next come the four and twenty elders. Then John views a multitude of the heavenly angels surrounding the whole. How many? How many would we suppose could convene within the heavenly temple? "Ten thousand times ten thousand!" exclaims the seer. In this expression alone we have one hundred million! Then, as if no numerical expression is adequate to embrace the countless throng, he further adds, "And thousands of thousands!" Well might the writer of Hebrews call this "an innumerable company of angels." Hebrews 12: 22. These were in the sanctuary above.

Such was the company that John saw assembled at the place where the worship of a universe centers, and where the wondrous plan of human redemption is going forward to completion. The central figure in this innumerable and holy throng was the Lamb of God, and the central act of His life which claimed their admiration was the shedding of His blood for the salvation of fallen man. Every voice in all that heavenly host joined in the ascription which was raised, "Worthy is the Lamb that was *slain* to receive power, and riches, and wisdom, and strength, and honor, and glory, and blessing." Fitting assemblage for such a place! Fitting song of adoration to be raised to Him who by the shedding of His blood became a ransom for many, and who as our great High Priest in the sanctuary above still pleads the merits of His sacrifice in our behalf. Here, before such an august assemblage, must our life record soon come up in final review. What shall fit us for the searching ordeal? What shall enable us to rise and stand at last with the sinless throng above? O infinite merit of the blood of Christ, which can cleanse us from all our pollutions, and make us meet to tread the holy hill of Zion! O infinite grace of God, which can prepare us to endure the glory, and give us boldness to enter into His presence, even with exceeding joy!

VERSE 13 And every creature which is in heaven, and on the earth, and under the earth, and such as are in the sea, and all that are in them, heard I saying, Blessing, and honor, and glory, and power, be unto Him that sitteth upon the throne, and unto the Lamb forever and ever. 14 And the four beasts said, Amen. And the four and twenty elders fell down and worshiped Him that liveth forever and ever.

A Clean Universe.—In verse 13 we have a declaration thrown in out of its chronological order for the purpose of following out to its completion the previous statement or allusion. This occurs frequently in the Bible. In this instance the time is anticipated when the work of redemption is finished. In verse 10 the four living creatures and four and twenty elders had declared, "We shall reign on the earth." Now the prophet's mind is carried forward to that event. He looks forward to the time when the number of the redeemed shall be made up, the universe be freed from sin and sinners, and a universal song of adoration go up to God and the Lamb.

It is futile to attempt to apply this to the church in its present state, or to any time in the past since sin entered the world, or even since Satan fell from his high position as an angel of light and love in heaven. For at the time of which John speaks, *every creature* in heaven and on earth without any exception was sending up its anthem of blessings to God. But to speak only of this world since the fall, cursings instead of blessings have been breathed out against God and His throne from the great majority of our apostate race. So it will ever be while sin reigns.

We find, then, no place for this scene which John describes, unless we go forward to the time when the plan of redemption is completed, and the saints enter upon their promised reign on the earth.

To the Lamb, equally with the Father who sits upon the throne, praise is ascribed in this song of adoration. "Blessing, and honor, and glory, and power, be unto Him that sitteth upon the throne, and unto the Lamb forever and ever." Revelation 5: 13.

Coming back from the glorious scene anticipated in verse 13 to events taking place in the heavenly sanctuary before him, the prophet hears the four living creatures exclaim, Amen.

 T. K. MARTIN, ARTIST

THE RIDER ON THE WHITE HORSE

Armed with the word of God and guided by the Holy Spirit, the early church went forth "conquering, and to conquer."

CHAPTER VI

BREAKING THE SEALS ON THE BOOK OF PROPHECY

VERSE 1 And I saw when the Lamb opened one of the seals, and I heard, as it were the noise of thunder, one of the four beasts saying, Come and see. 2 And I saw, and behold a white horse: and he that sat on him had a bow; and a crown was given unto him: and he went forth conquering, and to conquer.

THE LAMB takes the book, and proceeds at once to open the seals. The attention of the apostle is called to the scenes that occur under each seal. The number seven has already been noticed as denoting completeness and perfection in the Scriptures. The seven seals represent events of a religious character, and contain the history of the church from the opening of the Christian Era to the second coming of Christ. When the seals were broken, and the record was brought to light, the scenes were presented before John, not by the reading of the description, but by a representation of what was described in the book being made to pass before his view in living characters, and in the place where the reality was to occur, namely, on the earth.

The First Seal.—The first symbol is a white horse, bearing a rider who carries a bow. A crown is given to him, and he goes forth conquering and to conquer, a fit emblem of the triumphs of the gospel in the first century of the Christian Era. The whiteness of the horse denotes the purity of faith in that age. The crown which was given to the rider, and his going forth as a conqueror to make still further conquests, signify the zeal and success with which the truth was promulgated by its earliest ministers. By what symbols could the work of Christianity better be represented when it went forth as an aggressive principle against the huge systems of error with which it had at first to contend? The rider upon this horse went forth—

where? His commission was unlimited. The gospel was to all the world.

VERSE 3 And when He had opened the second seal, I heard the second beast say, Come and see. 4 And there went out another horse that was red: and power was given to him that sat thereon to take peace from the earth, and that they should kill one another: and there was given unto him a great sword.

The Second Seal.—Perhaps the first feature noticed in these symbols is the contrast in the color of the horses. This doubtless has special significance. If the whiteness of the first horse denoted the purity of the gospel in the period which that symbol covers, the redness of the second horse would signify that in this period that original purity began to be corrupted. The mystery of iniquity already worked in Paul's day, and the professed church of Christ was so far corrupted by this time as to require this change in the color of the symbol. Errors began to arise. Worldliness came in. The ecclesiastical power sought the alliance of the secular. Troubles and commotions were the result.

Speaking of the period of the Christian church from A. D. 100 to 311, the historian remarks:

"We now descend from the primitive apostolic church to the Græco-Roman; from the scene of creation to the work of preservation; from the fountain of divine revelation to the stream of human development; from the inspirations of the apostles and prophets to the productions of enlightened but fallible teachers. The hand of God has drawn a bold line of demarcation between the century of miracles and the succeeding ages, to show, by the abrupt transition and the striking contrast, the difference between the work of God and the work of man."[1] "The second period, from the death of the apostle John to the end of the persecutions, or to the accession of Constantine, the first Christian emperor, is the classic age . . . of heathen persecution, and of Christian martyrdom and heroism. . . . It furnishes a continuous commentary on the

[1] Philip Schaff, *History of the Christian Church,* Vol. II, p. 7.

Saviour's words, 'Behold, I send you forth as sheep in the midst of wolves.' "[2] "The ante-Nicene age . . . is . . . the common root out of which both [Catholicism and Protestantism] have sprung, Catholicism (Greek and Roman) first, and Protestantism afterwards. It is the natural transition from the apostolic age to the Nicene age, yet leaving behind many important truths of the former (especially the Pauline doctrines) which were to be derived and explored in future ages. We can trace in it the elementary forms of the Catholic creed, organization, and worship, and also the germs of nearly all the corruptions of Greek and Roman Christianity."[3]

The spirit of this period perhaps reached its climax as we come to the days of Constantine, the first so-called Christian emperor, whose conversion to Christianity in A. D. 323 brought about a compromise between the church and the Roman Empire. The Edict of Milan in A. D. 313, is said to have granted toleration to Christians and allowed conversions to Christianity. Kenneth S. Latourette declares that the acts immediately preceding and culminating in the Edict of Milan in 313 "still remain the most significant of the many milestones in the road by which the church and the state moved toward co-operation."[4]

This modern scholar of church history further declares:

"Christianity, by bringing the church into existence, developed an institution which in part was a rival of the state. It created a society within the empire which, so many believed, threatened the very existence of the latter. The conflict was very marked in the century or more before Constantine. . . . When Constantine made his peace with the faith, however, it long looked as though the conflict had been resolved by the control of the church by the state. Yet, even in the days of the seeming subordination of the church to the government,

[2] *Ibid.*, p. 8.

[3] *Ibid.*, p. 11.

[4] Kenneth Scott Latourette, *A History of the Expansion of Christianity*, Vol. I, The First Five Centuries, p. 159.

ecclesiastics sought to influence the policies of the latter."[5]

This state of things answers well to the declaration of the prophet that power was given to him that sat on the horse "to take peace from the earth, and that they should kill one another: and there was given unto him a great sword."

VERSE 5 And when He had opened the third seal, I heard the third beast say, Come and see. And I beheld, and lo a black horse; and he that sat on him had a pair of balances in his hand. 6 And I heard a voice in the midst of the four beasts say, A measure of wheat for a penny, and three measures of barley for a penny; and see thou hurt not the oil and the wine.

The Third Seal.—How rapidly the work of corruption progresses! What a contrast in color between this symbol and the first one: A black horse—the very opposite of white! A period of great darkness and moral corruption in the church must be denoted by this symbol. By the events of the second seal the way was fully opened for that state of things to be brought about which is here presented. The time that intervened between the reign of Constantine and the establishment of the papacy in A. D. 538 may be justly noted as the time when the darkest errors and grossest superstitions sprang up in the church. Of a period immediately succeeding the days of Constantine, Mosheim says:

"Those vain fictions, which an attachment to the Platonic philosophy and to popular opinions had engaged the greatest part of the Christian doctors to adopt before the time of Constantine, were now confirmed, enlarged, and embellished in various ways. From hence arose that extravagant veneration for departed saints, and those absurd notions of a certain fire destined to purify separate souls, that now prevailed, and of which the public marks were everywhere to be seen. Hence also the celibacy of priests, the worship of images and relics, which in process of time almost utterly destroyed the Christian religion, or at least eclipsed its luster, and corrupted its very essence in the most deplorable manner. An enormous train of different superstitions were gradually substituted in the place

[5] *Ibid.*, p. 273.

of true religion and genuine piety. This odious revolution was owing to a variety of causes. A ridiculous precipitation in receiving new opinions, a preposterous desire of imitating the pagan rites, and of blending them with the Christian worship, and that idle propensity which the generality of mankind have toward a gaudy and ostentatious religion, all contributed to establish the reign of superstition upon the ruins of Christianity."[6]

Again he says: "A whole volume would be requisite to contain an enumeration of the various frauds which artful knaves practiced, with success, to delude the ignorant, when true religion was almost entirely superseded by horrid superstition."[7]

These quotations from Mosheim contain a description of the period covered by the black horse of the third seal that answers accurately to the prophecy. It is seen by this how paganism was incorporated into Christianity, and how during this period the false system which resulted in the establishment of the papacy, rapidly rounded out its full outlines, and ripened into all its deplorable perfection of strength and stature.

The Balances.—"The balances denoted that religion and civil power would be united in the person who would administer the executive power in the government, and that he would claim the judicial authority both in church and state. This was true among the Roman emperors from the days of Constantine until the reign of Justinian, when he gave the same judicial power to the bishop of Rome."[8]

The Wheat and the Barley.—"The measures of wheat and barley for a penny denote that the members of the church would be eagerly engaged after worldly goods, and the love of money would be the prevailing spirit of the times, for they would dispose of anything for money."[9]

The Oil and the Wine.—These "denote the graces of the Spirit, faith and love, and there was great danger of hurting

---

[6] John L. Mosheim, *An Ecclesiastical History*, Vol. I, pp. 364, 365.
[7] *Ibid.*, p. 368.
[8] William Miller, *Evidence From Scripture and History of the Second Coming of Christ*, p. 176.
[9] *Ibid.*

EDOUARD DEBAT-PONSAN, ARTIST

ALL IN THE NAME OF CHRIST

The gruesome record is that through the centuries the established church has persecuted religious minorities in the name of Christ.

these, under the influence of so much of a worldly spirit. And it is well attested by all historians that the prosperity of the church in this age produced the corruptions which finally terminated in the falling away, and setting up the antichristian abominations."[10]

It will be observed that the voice limiting the amount of wheat for a penny, and saying, "Hurt not the oil and the wine," is not spoken by anyone on earth, but comes from the midst of the four living creatures, signifying that although the undershepherds, the professed ministers of Christ, had no care for the flock, yet the Lord was not unmindful of them in this period of darkness. A voice comes from heaven. He takes care that the spirit of worldliness does not prevail to such a degree that Christianity should be entirely lost, or that the oil and the wine—graces of genuine piety—should perish from the earth.

VERSE 7 And when He had opened the fourth seal, I heard the voice of the fourth beast say, Come and see. 8 And I looked, and behold a pale horse: and his name that sat on him was Death, and Hell followed with him. And power was given unto them over the fourth part of the earth, to kill with sword, and with hunger, and with death, and with the beasts of the earth.

The Fourth Seal.—The color of this horse is remarkable. The original word denotes the "pale or yellowish color" that is seen in blighted or sickly plants. A strange state of things in the professed church must be denoted by this symbol. The rider on this horse is named Death, and Hell (ᾅδης, *hades*, "the grave") followed with him. The mortality is so great during this period that it would seem as if "the pale nations of the dead" had come upon earth, and were following in the wake of this desolating power. The period during which this seal applies can hardly be mistaken. It must refer to the time in which the papacy bore its unrebuked, unrestrained, and persecuting rule, beginning about A. D. 538, and extending to the time when the Reformers began their work of exposing the corruptions of the papal system.

[10] *Ibid.*

"Power was given unto them"—"him," says the margin, that is, the power personified by Death on the pale horse, namely, the papacy. By the fourth part of the earth is doubtless meant the territory over which this power had jurisdiction; and the words "sword," "hunger," "death" (that is, some infliction which causes death, as exposure or torture), and beasts of the earth, are figures denoting the means by which it has put to death millions of martyrs.

VERSE 9 And when He had opened the fifth seal, I saw under the altar the souls of them that were slain for the word of God and for the testimony which they held: 10 and they cried with a loud voice, saying, How long, O Lord, holy and true, dost Thou not judge and avenge our blood on them that dwell on the earth? 11 And white robes were given unto every one of them; and it was said unto them, that they should rest yet for a little season, until their fellow servants also and their brethren, that should be killed as they were, should be fulfilled.

The Fifth Seal.—Under the fifth seal the martyrs cry for vengeance, and white robes are given to them. The questions that at once suggest themselves for solution are, Does this seal cover a period of time, and if so what period? Where is the altar under which these souls were seen? What are these souls, and what is their condition? What is meant by their cry for vengeance? What is meant by white robes being given to them? When do they rest for a little season, and what is signified by their brethren being killed as they were? To all these questions we believe satisfactory answers can be returned.

It seems consistent that this seal, like all the others, should cover a period of time, and that the date of its application cannot be mistaken if the preceding seals have been rightly located. Following the period of the papal persecution, the time covered by this seal would begin when the Reformation began to undermine the papal fabrication, and restrain the persecuting power of the Roman Catholic Church.

The Altar.—This cannot denote any altar in heaven, as it is evidently the place where these victims had been slain—the altar of sacrifice. On this point, Adam Clarke says: "A symbolical vision was exhibited, in which he saw an altar; and under it the souls of these who had been slain for the word of God—martyred for their attachment to Christianity—are represented as being newly slain as victims to idolatry and superstition. *The altar is upon earth, not in heaven.*"[11] A confirmation of this view is found in the fact that John is beholding scenes upon the earth. The souls are represented under the altar, just as victims slain upon it would pour out their blood beneath it, and fall by its side.

The Souls Under the Altar.—This representation is popularly regarded as a strong proof of the doctrine of disembodied spirits and the conscious state of the dead. Here, it is claimed, are souls seen by John in a disembodied state, and yet they were conscious and had knowledge of passing events, for they cried for vengeance on their persecutors. This view of the passages is inadmissible, for several reasons.

The popular view places these souls in heaven, but the altar of sacrifice on which they were slain, and beneath which they were seen, cannot be there. The only altar we read of in heaven is the altar of incense, but it would not be correct to represent victims just slain as under the altar of incense, as that altar was never devoted to such a use.

It would be repugnant to all our ideas of the heavenly state to represent souls in heaven *shut up* under an altar.

Can we suppose that the idea of *vengeance* would so dominate the minds of souls in heaven as to make them, despite the joy and glory of that ineffable state, dissatisfied and uneasy until vengeance was inflicted upon their enemies? Would they not rather rejoice that persecution raised its hand against them, and thus hastened them into the presence of their Redeemer, at whose right hand there is fullness of joy and pleasures forevermore?

But, further, the popular view which puts these souls in heaven, puts the wicked at the same time in the lake of fire, writhing in unutterable torment, and in *full view of* the hea-

---

[11] Adam Clarke, *Commentary on the New Testament*, Vol. I, p. 994, note on Revelation 6: 9.

venly host. Now the souls brought to view under the fifth seal were those who had been slain under the preceding seal, scores of years, and most of them centuries, before. Beyond any question, their persecutors had all passed off the stage of action, and according to the view under consideration were suffering all the torments of hell right before their eyes.

Yet, as if not satisfied with this, they cry to God as though He were delaying vengeance on their murderers. What greater vengeance could they want? Or, if their persecutors were still on the earth, they must know that they would, in a few years at most, join the vast multitude daily pouring through the gate of death into the world of woe. Their amiability is put in no better light even by this supposition. One thing at least is evident: The popular theory concerning the condition of the dead, righteous and wicked, cannot be correct, or the interpretation usually given to this passage is not correct, for they are mutually exclusive.

But it is urged that these souls must be conscious, for they cry to God. This argument would be of weight were there no such figure of speech as personification. But while there is, it will be proper on certain conditions to attribute life, action, and intelligence to inanimate objects. Thus the blood of Abel is said to have cried to God from the ground. (Genesis 4: 9, 10.) The stone cried out of the wall, and the beam out of the timber answered it. (Habakkuk 2: 11.) The hire of the laborers kept back by fraud cried, and the cry entered into the ears of the Lord of sabaoth. (James 5: 4.) So the souls mentioned in our text could cry, and not thereby be proved to be conscious.

The incongruity of the popular view on this verse is apparent, for Albert Barnes makes the following concession: "We are not to suppose that this *literally* occurred, and that John actually saw the souls of the martyrs beneath the altar—for the whole representation is symbolical; nor are we to suppose that the injured and the wronged in heaven actually pray for vengeance on those who wronged them, or that the redeemed in heaven will continue to pray with reference to things on earth; but it may be fairly inferred from this that there will be *as real* a remembrance of the wrongs of the persecuted, the injured, and the oppressed, *as if* such prayer were offered there; and that the oppressor has as much to dread from the divine vengeance *as if* those whom he has injured should cry in heaven to the God who hears prayer, and who takes vengeance."[12]

On such passages as this, the reader is misled by the popular definition of the word "soul." From that definition, he is led to suppose that this text speaks of an immaterial, invisible, immortal essence in man, which soars into its coveted freedom on the death of the mortal body. No instance of the occurrence of the word in the original Hebrew or Greek will sustain such a definition. It most often means "life," and is not infrequently rendered "person." It applies to the dead as well as to the living, as may be seen by reference to Genesis 2: 7, where the word "living" need not have been expressed were life an inseparable attribute of the soul; and to Numbers 19: 13, where the Hebrew concordance reads "dead soul." Moreover, these souls pray that their *blood* may be avenged—an article which the immaterial soul, as popularly understood, is not supposed to possess. The word "souls" may be regarded as here meaning simply the martyrs, those who had been slain, the words "souls of them" being a periphrasis for the whole person. They were represented to John as having been slain upon the altar of papal sacrifice, on this earth, and lying dead beneath it. They certainly were not alive when John saw them under the fifth seal, for he again brings to view the same company, in almost the same language, and assures us that the first time they live after their martyrdom is at the resurrection of the just. (Revelation 20: 4-6.) Lying there victims of papal bloodthirstiness and oppression, they cried to God for vengeance in the same manner that Abel's blood cried to Him from the ground.

[12] Albert Barnes, *Notes on Revelation*, pp. 190, 191, comment on Revelation 6: 9-11.

The White Robes.—These were given as a partial answer to their cry, "How long, O Lord, . . . dost Thou not judge and avenge our blood?" They had gone down to the grave in the most ignominious manner. Their lives had been misrepresented, their reputations tarnished, their names defamed, their motives maligned, and their graves covered with shame and reproach, as containing the dishonored dust of the most vile and despicable of characters. Thus the Church of Rome, which then molded the sentiment of the principal nations of the earth, spared no pains to make her victims an abhorrence to all people.

But the Protestant Reformation began its work. It began to be seen that the church was corrupt and disreputable, and those against whom it vented its rage were the good, the pure, and the true. The work went on among the most enlightened nations, the reputation of the church going down, and that of the martyrs coming up, until the corruptions of the papal abominations were fully exposed. Then that huge system of iniquity stood forth before the world in all its naked deformity, while the martyrs were vindicated from all the aspersions under which that persecuting church had sought to bury them. Then it was seen that they had suffered, not for being vile and criminal, but "for the word of God, and for the testimony which they held." Then their praises were sung, their virtues admired, their fortitude applauded, their names honored, and their memories cherished. White robes were thus given to every one of them.

The Little Season.—The cruel work of Roman Catholicism did not altogether cease, even after the work of the Protestant Reformation had become widespread and well established. Not a few terrible outbursts of hate and persecution were yet to be felt by the true church. Multitudes more were to be punished as heretics, and to join the great army of martyrs. The full vindication of their cause was to be delayed a little season. During this time Rome added hundreds of thousands to the vast throng of whose blood she had already become guilty.

But the spirit of persecution was finally restrained, the cause of the martyrs was vindicated, and the "little season" of the fifth seal came to a close.

VERSE 12 And I beheld when He had opened the sixth seal, and, lo, there was a great earthquake; and the sun became black as sackcloth of hair, and the moon became as blood; 13 and the stars of heaven fell unto the earth, even as a fig tree casteth her untimely figs, when she is shaken of a mighty wind. 14 And the heaven departed as a scroll when it is rolled together; and every mountain and island were moved out of their places. 15 And the kings of the earth, and the great men, and the rich men, and the chief captains, and the mighty men, and every bondman, and every free man, hid themselves in the dens and in the rocks of the mountains; 16 and said to the mountains and rocks, Fall on us, and hide us from the face of Him that sitteth on the throne, and from the wrath of the Lamb: 17 for the great day of His wrath is come; and who shall be able to stand?

The Sixth Seal.—Such are the solemn and sublime scenes which occur under the sixth seal. A thought well calculated to awaken in every heart an intense interest in divine things is the consideration that we are now living amid the momentous events of this seal, as will presently be proved.

Between the fifth and sixth seals there seems to be a sudden and complete change from highly figurative to strictly literal language. Whatever may be the cause, the change cannot well be denied. By no principle of interpretation can the language of the preceding seals be made to be literal, nor can the language of this any more easily be made figurative. We must therefore accept the change, even though we may be unable to explain it. There is a significant fact, however, to which we would here call attention. It was in the period covered by this seal that the prophetic parts of God's word were to be unsealed, and many run to and fro, or give their attention to the understanding of these things, and thereby knowledge on this part of God's word was to be greatly increased. We suggest that it may be for this reason that the change in the language here occurs, and that the events of this seal, taking place at a time when these things were to be fully understood, are not couched in figures, but are laid before us in plain and unmistakable language.

 R. M. ELDRIDGE, ARTIST

THE GREAT LISBON EARTHQUAKE

A terrible earthquake and tidal wave struck Southwestern Europe and North Africa in November, 1755.

The Great Earthquake.—The first event under this seal, and perhaps the one which marks its opening, is a great earthquake. As the most striking fulfillment of this prediction, we refer to the great earthquake of November 1, 1755, known as the earthquake of Lisbon. Of this earthquake, Robert Sears says:

"The great earthquake of 1755 extended over a tract of at least four millions of square miles. Its effects were even extended to the waters, in many places where the shocks were not perceptible. It pervaded the greater portions of the continents of Europe, Africa, and America; but its extreme violence was exercised on the southwestern part of the former."[13] "In Africa, this earthquake was felt almost as severely as it had been in Europe. A great part of the city of Algiers was destroyed. Many houses were thrown down at Fez and Mequinez, and multitudes were buried beneath their ruins. Similar effects were realized in Morocco. Its effects were likewise felt at Tangier, at Tetuan, at Funchal in the Island of Madeira; . . . it is probable . . . that all Africa was shaken by this tremendous convulsion. At the North, it extended to Norway and Sweden; Germany, Holland, France, Great Britain, and Ireland were all more or less agitated by the same great and terrible commotion of the elements."[14] "The city of Lisbon . . . previous to that calamity . . . contained about . . . 150,000 inhabitants. . . . Mr. Barretti says, 'that 90,000 persons are supposed to have been lost on that fatal day.' "[15]

Sir Charles Lyell gives the following graphic description of this remarkable phenomenon:

"In no part of the volcanic region of Southern Europe has so tremendous an earthquake occurred in modern times as that which began on the 1st of November, 1755, at Lisbon. A sound of thunder was heard underground, and immediately afterwards a violent shock threw down the greater part of that

[13] Robert Sears, *Wonders of the World*, p. 50.
[14] *Ibid.*, p. 58.
[15] *Ibid.*, p. 381.

city. In the course of about six minutes, sixty thousand persons perished. The sea first retired, and laid the bar dry; it then rolled in, rising fifty feet above its ordinary level. The mountains of Arrabida, Estrella, Julio, Marvan, and Cintra, being some of the largest in Portugal, were impetuously shaken, as it were, from their very foundations; and some of them opened at their summits, which were split and rent in a wonderful manner, huge masses of them being thrown down into the subjacent valleys. Flames are related to have issued from these mountains, which are supposed to have been electric; they are also said to have smoked; but vast clouds of dust may have given rise to this appearance. . . .

"The great area over which this Lisbon earthquake extended is very remarkable. The movement was most violent in Spain, Portugal, and the north of Africa; but nearly the whole of Europe, and even the West Indies, felt the shock on the same day. A seaport called St. Ubes, about twenty miles south of Lisbon, was engulfed. At Algiers and Fez, in Africa, the agitation of the earth was equally violent, and at the distance of eight leagues from Morocco, a village, with the inhabitants to the number of about eight or ten thousand persons, together with all their cattle, were [was] swallowed up. Soon after, the earth closed again over them.

"The shock was felt at sea, on the deck of a ship to the west of Lisbon, and produced very much the same sensation as on dry land. Off St. Lucar [s], the captain of the ship 'Nancy' felt his vessel shaken so violently that he thought she had struck the ground, but, on heaving the lead, found a great depth of water. Captain Clark, from Denia, in latitude 36° 24′ N., between nine and ten in the morning, had his ship shaken and strained as if she had struck upon a rock. Another ship, forty leagues west of St. Vincent, experienced so violent a concussion that the men were thrown a foot and a half perpendicularly up from the deck. In Antigua and Barbadoes, as also in Norway, Sweden, Germany, Holland, Corsica, Switzerland, and Italy, tremors and slight oscillations of the ground were felt.

"The agitation of lakes, rivers, and springs in Great Britain was remarkable. At Loch Lomond, in Scotland, for example, the water, without the least apparent cause, rose against its banks, and then subsided below its usual level. The greatest perpendicular height of this swell was two feet four inches. It is said that the movement of this earthquake was undulatory, and that it traveled at the rate of twenty miles a minute. A great wave swept over the coast of Spain, and is said to have been sixty feet high at Cadiz. At Tangier, in Africa, it rose and fell eighteen times on the coast; at Funchal, in Madeira, it rose full fifteen feet perpendicular above high-water mark, although the tide, which ebbs and flows there seven feet, was then at half ebb. Besides entering the city and committing great havoc, it overflowed other seaports in the island. At Kinsale, in Ireland, a body of water rushed into the harbor, whirled round several vessels, and poured into the market-place."[16]

If the reader will look in his atlas at the countries mentioned, he will see how large a part of the earth's surface was agitated by this awful convulsion. Other earthquakes may have been as severe in particular localities, but no other supplies all the conditions necessary to constitute it a fitting event to mark the opening of the seal.

The Darkening of the Sun.—Following the earthquake, as announced by the prophecy, "the sun became black as sackcloth of hair." This part of the prediction has also been fulfilled. We need not here enter into a detailed account of the wonderful darkening of the sun, May 19, 1780. Most persons of general reading, it is presumed, have seen some account of it. The following detached declarations from different authorities will give an idea of its nature:

"Dark Day, The. May 19, 1780—so called on account of a remarkable darkness on that day extending over all New England. . . . The obscuration began about ten o'clock in

---

[16] A. R. Spofford and Charles Gibbon, *The Library of Choice Literature*, Vol. VII, pp. 162, 163.

DARKNESS AT NOONDAY

A dense darkness came in the morning of May 19, 1780, and continued until the following night.

the morning, and continued till the middle of the next night, but with differences of degree and duration in different places. . . . The true cause of this remarkable phenomenon is not known."[17]

"In the month of May, 1780, there was a very terrific dark day in New England, when 'all faces seemed to gather blackness,' and the people were filled with fear. There was great distress in the village where Edward Lee lived, 'men's hearts failing them for fear' that the Judgment-day was at hand; and the neighbors all flocked around the holy man, [who] spent the gloomy hours in earnest prayer for the distressed multitude."[18]

"The *time* of this extraordinary darkness was May 19, 1780," says Professor Williams. "It came on between the hours of ten and eleven A. M., and continued until the middle of the next night, but with different appearances at different places. . . .

"The *degree* to which the darkness arose was different in different places. In most parts of the country it was so great that people were unable to read common print, determine the time of day by their clocks or watches, dine, or manage their domestic business, without the light of candles. In some places the darkness was so great that persons could not see to read common print in the open air, for several hours together; but I believe this was not generally the case.

"The *extent* of this darkness was very remarkable. Our intelligence in this respect is not so particular as I could wish; but from the accounts that have been received, it seems to have extended all over the New England States. It was observed as far east as Falmouth [Portland, Maine]. To the westward we hear of its reaching to the furthest parts of Connecticut, and Albany. To the southward it was observed all along the seacoasts, and to the north as far as our settlements extend. It is probable it extended much beyond these limits in some direc-

[17] Noah Webster, "Vocabulary of the Names of Noted . . . Persons and Places," *An American Dictionary of the English Language*, 1882 ed.

[18] "Some Memorials of Edward Lee," *The Publications of the American Tract Society*, Vol. XI, p. 376.

tions, but the exact boundaries cannot be ascertained by any observations that I have been able to collect.

"With regard to its *duration*, it continued in this place at least fourteen hours; but it is probable this was not exactly the same in different parts of the country.

"The *appearance* and *effects* were such as tended to make the prospect extremely dull and gloomy. Candles were lighted up in the houses; the birds, having sung their evening songs, disappeared, and became silent; the fowls retired to roost; the cocks were crowing all around, as at break of day; objects could not be distinguished but at a very little distance; and everything bore the appearance and gloom of night."[19]

"The 19th of May, 1780, was a remarkable dark day. Candles were lighted in many houses; the birds were silent and disappeared, and the fowls retired to roost. . . . A very general opinion prevailed that the day of judgment was at hand."[20]

Whittier, in a well-known poem pictures it thus:

> " 'Twas on a May-day of the far old year
> Seventeen hundred eighty, that there fell
> Over the bloom and sweet life of the Spring,
> Over the fresh earth and the heaven of noon,
> A horror of great darkness, like the night
> In day of which the Norland sagas tell,—
> The Twilight of the Gods. The low-hung sky
> Was black with ominous clouds, save where its rim
> Was fringed with a dull glow, like that which climbs
> The crater's sides from the red hell below.
> Birds ceased to sing, and all the barnyard fowls
> Roosted; the cattle at the pasture bars
> Lowed, and looked homeward; bats on leathern wings
> Flitted abroad; the sounds of labor died;
> Men prayed, and women wept; all ears grew sharp
> To hear the doom-blast of the trumpet shatter
> The black sky, that the dreadful face of Christ
> Might look from the rent clouds, not as he looked
> A loving guest at Bethany, but stern
> As Justice and inexorable Law."[21]

---

[19] Samuel Williams, in *Memoirs of the American Academy of Arts and Sciences*, Vol. I, pp. 234, 235.

[20] Timothy Dwight, quoted by John W. Barber, *Connecticut Historical Collections*, p. 403.

[21] John G. Whittier, "Abraham Davenport," *Complete Poetical Works*, p. 260.

"*The Moon Became as Blood.*"—The darkness of the following night, May 19, 1780, was as unnatural as that of the day had been.

"The darkness of the following evening was probably as gross as ever has been observed since the Almighty fiat gave birth to light. . . . I could not help conceiving at the time, that if every luminous body in the universe had been shrouded in impenetrable shades, or struck out of existence, the darkness could not have been more complete. A sheet of white paper held within a few inches of the eyes, was equally invisible with the blackest velvet."[22]

"In the evening . . . perhaps it never was darker since the children of Israel left the house of bondage. This gross darkness held till about one o'clock, although the moon had fulled but the day before."[23]

This statement respecting the phase of the moon proves the impossibility of an eclipse of the sun at that time. Whenever on this memorable night the moon did appear, as at certain times it did, it had, according to this prophecv, the appearance of blood.

"*The Stars of Heaven Fell.*"—The voice of history still cries, *Fulfilled!* We refer to the great meteoric shower of November 13, 1833. On this point a few testimonies will suffice.

"At the cry, 'Look out of the window,' I sprang from a deep sleep, and with wonder saw the east lighted up with the dawn and meteors. . . . I called to my wife to behold; and while robing, she exclaimed, 'See how the stars fall!' I replied, 'That is the wonder:' and we felt in our hearts that it was a sign of the last days. For truly 'the stars of heaven fell unto the earth, even as a fig tree casteth her untimely figs, when she is shaken of a mighty wind.' Revelation 6: 13. . . .

"And how did they fall? Neither myself nor one of the family heard any report; and were I to hunt through nature

---

[22] Samuel Tenny, in *Collections of Massachusetts Historical Society for the Year 1792*, Vol. I, pp. 97, 98.

[23] Boston *Gazette*, May 29, 1780.

 R. M. ELDRIDGE, ARTIST

THE FALLING STARS

On the night of November 12-13, 1833, occurred the grandest meteoric display ever recorded. The heavens were ablaze with fiery meteors moving swiftly in all directions.

for a simile, I could not find one so apt to illustrate the appearance of the heavens, as that which St. John uses in the prophecy before quoted. 'It rained fire!' says one. Another, 'It was like a shower of fire.' Another, 'It was like the large flakes of falling snow, before a coming storm, or large drops of rain before a shower.' I admit the fitness of these for common accuracy; but they come far short of the accuracy of the figure used by the prophet. 'The stars of heaven fell unto the earth;' they were not sheets, or flakes, or drops of fire; but they were what the world understands by the name of 'falling stars;' and one speaking to his fellow in the midst of the scene, would say, 'See how the stars fall!' and he who heard, would not pause to correct the astronomy of the speaker, any more than he would reply, 'The sun does not move,' to one who should tell him, 'The sun is rising.' The stars fell 'even as a fig tree casteth her untimely figs, when she is shaken of a mighty wind.' Here is the exactness of the prophet. The falling stars did not come, as if from several trees shaken, but from *one:* those which appeared in the east fell toward the east; those which appeared in the north fell toward the north; those which appeared in the west fell toward the west; and those which appeared in the south (for I went out of my residence into the park), fell toward the south; and they fell, not as *ripe* fruit falls. Far from it. But they flew, they were *cast*, like the unripe fruit, which at first refuses to leave the branch; and, when it does break its hold, flies swiftly, *straight off*, descending; and in the multitude falling, some cross the track of others, as they are thrown with more or less force."[24]

"The most sublime phenomenon of shooting stars, of which the world has furnished any record, was witnessed throughout the United States on the morning of the 13th of November, 1833. The entire extent of this astonishing exhibition has not been precisely ascertained, but it covered no inconsiderable portion of the earth's surface. . . . The first appearance was

[24] New York *Journal of Commerce*, Nov. 14, 1833, Vol. VIII, No. 534, p. 2.

that of fireworks of the most imposing grandeur, covering the entire vault of heaven with myriads of fireballs, resembling skyrockets. Their coruscations were bright, gleaming, and incessant, and they fell thick as the flakes in the early snows of December. To the splendors of this celestial exhibition the most brilliant skyrockets and fireworks of art bear less relation than the twinkling of the most tiny star to the broad glare of the sun. The whole heavens seemed in motion, and suggested to some the awful grandeur of the image employed in the Apocalypse, upon the opening of the sixth seal, when 'the stars of heaven fell unto the earth, even as a fig-tree casteth her untimely figs, when she is shaken of a mighty wind.' "[25]

"After collecting and collating the accounts given in all the periodicals of the country, and also in numerous letters addressed either to my scientific friends or to myself, the following appeared to be the *leading facts* attending the phenomenon. The shower pervaded nearly the whole of North America, having appeared in nearly equal splendor from the British possessions on the north, to the West India Islands and Mexico on the south, and from sixty-one degrees of longitude east of the American coast, quite to the Pacific Ocean on the west. Throughout this immense region, the duration was nearly the same. The meteors began to attract attention by their unusual frequency and brilliancy, from *nine to twelve o'clock* in the evening; were most striking in their appearance from *two to five;* arrived at their maximum, in many places, about *four* o'clock; and continued until rendered invisible by the light of day."[26]

"The spectacle must have been of the sublimest order. The apostle John might have had it before him when he indited the passage referring to the opening of the sixth seal: 'And the stars of heaven fell unto the earth, even as a fig tree casteth her untimely figs, when she is shaken of a mighty wind.' "[27]

---

[25] Elijah H. Burritt, *The Geography of the Heavens*, p. 163.
[26] Denison Olmsted, *The Mechanism of the Heavens*, p. 328.
[27] Edwin Dunkin, *The Heavens and the Earth*, p. 186.

"*The Heaven Departed as a Scroll.*"—In this event our minds are turned to the future. From looking at the past, and beholding the word of God fulfilled, we are now called to look at events in the future, which are no less sure to come. Our position is unmistakably defined. We stand between the 13th and 14th verses of this chapter. We wait for the heavens to depart as a scroll when it is rolled together. These are times of unparalleled solemnity and importance, for we do not know how near we may be to the fulfillment of these things.

The departing of the heavens is included in what the writers of the Gospels call, in the same series of events, the shaking of the powers of the heavens. Other scriptures give us further particulars concerning this prediction. From Hebrews 12: 25-27; Joel 3: 16; Jeremiah 25: 30-33; Revelation 16: 17, we learn that it is the voice of God, as He speaks in terrible majesty from His throne in heaven, that causes this fearful commotion in earth and sky. Once the Lord spoke with an audible voice, when He gave His eternal law from Sinai. At that time the earth shook. He is to speak again, and not only the earth will shake, but the heavens also. Then will the earth "reel to and fro like a drunkard." It will be "dissolved" and "utterly broken down." Isaiah 24. Mountains will move from their firm bases. Islands will suddenly change their location in the midst of the sea. From the level plain will arise the precipitous mountain. Rocks will thrust up their ragged forms from earth's broken surface. While the voice of God is reverberating through the earth, the direst confusion will reign over the face of nature.

To show that this is no mere conception of the imagination, the reader is requested to mark the exact phraseology which some of the prophets have used in reference to this time. Isaiah says: "The earth is utterly broken down, the earth is clean dissolved, the earth is moved exceedingly. The earth shall reel to and fro like a drunkard, and shall be removed like a cottage; and the transgression thereof shall be heavy upon it; and it shall fall, and not rise again." Isaiah 24: 19, 20.

Jeremiah in thrilling language describes the scene as follows: "I beheld the earth, and, lo, it was without form, and void; and the heavens, and they had no light. I beheld the mountains, and, lo, they trembled, and all the hills moved lightly. I beheld, and, lo, there was no man, and all the birds of the heavens were fled. . . . For thus hath the Lord said, The whole land shall be desolate." Jeremiah 4: 23-27.

Then will the world's dream of carnal security be effectually broken. Kings who, intoxicated with their own earthly authority, have never dreamed of a higher power than they themselves, now realize that there is One who reigns as King of kings. The great men behold the vanity of all earthly pomp, for there is a greatness above that of earth. The rich men throw their silver and gold to the moles and bats, for it cannot save them in that day. The chief captains forget their brief authority, and the mighty men forget their strength. Every bondman who is in the still worse bondage of sin, and every freeman—all classes of the wicked, from the highest down to the lowest—join in the general wail of consternation and despair.

They who never prayed to Him whose arm could bring salvation, now raise an agonizing prayer to rocks and mountains to bury them forever from the sight of Him whose presence brings to them destruction. Fain would they now avoid reaping what they have sown by a life of lust and sin. Fain would they now shun the fearful treasure of wrath which they have been heaping up for themselves against this day. Fain would they bury themselves and their catalogue of crimes in everlasting darkness. So they flee to the rocks, caves, caverns, and fissures which the broken surface of the earth now presents before them. But it is too late. They cannot conceal their guilt or escape the long-delayed vengeance.

"It will be in vain to call,
'Ye mountains on us fall,'
For His hand will find out all,
In that day."

The day which they thought never would come, has at last taken them as in a snare, and the involuntary language of their anguished hearts is, "The great day of His wrath is come, and who shall be able to stand?" Before that day comes with its fearful scenes, we pray you, reader, give your most serious and candid attention to your salvation.

Many now affect to despise the institution of prayer, but at one time or another all men will pray. Those who will not now pray to God in penitence, will then pray to the rocks and mountains in despair; and this will be the largest prayer meeting ever held.

> Ah! better far
> To cease the unequal war,
> While pardon, hope, and peace may yet be found;
> Nor longer rush upon the embossed shield
> Of the Almighty, but repentant yield,
> And all your weapons of rebellion ground.
> Better pray now in love, than pray erelong in fear.
> Call ye upon Him while He waits to hear;
> So in the coming end,
> When down the parted sky
> The angelic hosts attend
> The Lord of heaven, most high,
> Before whose face the solid earth is rent,
> You may behold a friend omnipotent,
> And safely rest beneath His sheltering wings,
> Amid the ruin of all earthly things.

 FRANKLIN BOOTH, ARTIST

HOLDING BACK THE WINDS OF STRIFE

In His mercy God's restraining angels hold back the winds of destruction from striking in full force upon the world.

CHAPTER VII

THE SEAL OF THE LIVING GOD

VERSE 1 And after these things I saw four angels standing on the four corners of the earth, holding the four winds of the earth, that the wind should not blow on the earth, nor on the sea, nor on any tree. 2 And I saw another angel ascending from the east, having the seal of the living God: and he cried with a loud voice to the four angels, to whom it was given to hurt the earth and the sea, 3 saying, Hurt not the earth, neither the sea, nor the trees, till we have sealed the servants of our God in their foreheads.

THE TIME of the work here introduced is established beyond mistake. The sixth chapter closed with the events of the sixth seal, and the seventh seal is not mentioned until we reach the beginning of Revelation 8. The whole of Revelation 7 is therefore thrown in here parenthetically. Why is it thus introduced at this point? Evidently it is given for the purpose of stating additional particulars concerning the sixth seal. The expression, "after these things," does not mean after the fulfillment of all the events previously described, but after the prophet had been carried in vision to the close of the sixth seal, that the consecutive order of events as given in Revelation 6 might not be broken, his mind is called to what is mentioned in Revelation 7 as further particulars in regard to that seal. We inquire, Between what events in that seal is this work done? It must be accomplished before the departing of the heavens as a scroll, for after that event there is no place for such a work as this. It must take place after the signs in the sun, moon, and stars, for these signs have already been fulfilled, and such a sealing work has not yet been accomplished. It comes in therefore between the 13th and 14th verses of Revelation 6. There, as already shown, is just where we now stand. Hence the first part of Revelation 7 relates to a work the accomplishment of which may be looked for now.

Four Angels.—Angels are ever-present agents in the affairs of the earth. Why may not these be four of those heavenly beings into whose hands God has committed the work of holding the winds while it is God's purpose that they should not blow, and loosing them when the time comes for the hurting of the earth?

Four Corners of the Earth.—This expression denotes the four quarters, or the four points of the compass, and signifies that these angels in their particular sphere have charge of the whole earth.

Four Winds.—Winds in the Bible symbolize political commotion, strife, and war. (Daniel 7: 2; Jeremiah 25: 32.) The *four* winds, held by four angels standing in the four quarters of the earth, must denote all the elements of strife and commotion that exist in the world. When they are all loosed and all blow together, it will constitute the great whirlwind just referred to in the prophecy of Jeremiah.

Angel Ascending From the East.—Another literal angel, having charge of another specific work, is here introduced. Instead of the words "ascending from the east," some translations read, "ascending from the sunrising," which is a more literal translation. The expression evidently refers to manner rather than locality, for as the sun rises with rays at first oblique and comparatively powerless, then increases in strength until it shines in all its meridian power and splendor, so the work of this angel begins in moderation, moves onward with ever-accumulating influence, and closes in strength and power.

Seal of the Living God.—It is the distinguishing characteristic of the ascending angel that he bears with him the seal of the living God. From this fact and the chronology of his work we are to determine if possible what movement is symbolized by his mission. The nature of his work is evidently suggested by his having the seal of the living God. To ascertain what his work is, we must determine what the seal of the living God is.

A seal is *defined* to be an instrument of sealing, that which "is used by individuals, corporate bodies, and states, for making impressions on wax, upon instruments of writing, as an evidence of their authenticity." The original word in this text is defined, "A seal, i. e., a signet ring; a mark, stamp, badge; a token, a pledge." The verb signifies: "To secure to any one, to make sure; to set a seal or mark upon anything in token of its being genuine or approved; to attest, to confirm, to establish, to distinguish by a mark." With these definitions as a basis, we compare Genesis 17: 11 with Romans 4: 11, and Revelation 7: 3 with Ezekiel 9: 4, and find that the words "token," "sign," "seal," and "mark" are used in the Bible as synonymous terms. The seal of God brought to view in our text is to be applied to the servants of God. In this case it is not some literal mark to be made in the flesh, but some institution or observance having special reference to God, which will serve as a "mark of distinction" between the worshipers of God and those who are not His servants, though they may profess to follow Him.

A seal is *used* to render valid or authentic any enactments or laws that a person or power may promulgate. Frequent instances of its use occur in the Scriptures. In 1 Kings 21: 8, we read that Jezebel "wrote letters in Ahab's name, and sealed them with his seal." These letters then had all the authority of King Ahab. Again, in Esther 3: 12: "In the name of King Ahasuerus was it written, and sealed with the king's ring." So also in Esther 8: 8: "The writing which is written in the king's name, and sealed with the king's ring, may no man reverse."

A seal is used in connection with some law or enactment that demands obedience, or upon documents that are to be made legal, or subject to the provisions of law. The idea of law is inseparable from a seal.

We are not to suppose that to the enactments and laws of God binding upon men, there must be attached a literal seal, made with literal instruments. From the definition of the term, and the purpose for which a seal is used, as shown before, we must understand a seal to be strictly that which gives validity and authenticity to enactments and laws. This is found in the name or signature of the lawmaking power, expressed in such terms as to show what the power is, and its right to make laws and demand obedience. Even with a literal seal, the name must always be used as indicated in the references given above. An instance of the use of the name alone seems to occur in Daniel 6: 8: "Now, O king, establish the decree, and *sign* the writing, that it be not changed, according to the law of the Medes and Persians, which altereth not." In other words, affix the signature of royalty, which shows who it is that demands obedience, and what his right is to demand it.

In the prophecy of Isaiah 8, we read: "Bind up the testimony, seal the law among My disciples." This must refer to a work of reviving in the minds of the disciples some of the claims of the law which had been overlooked, or perverted from their true meaning. In the prophecy this is called sealing the law, or restoring to it its seal, which had been taken from it.

The 144,000, who in the chapter before us are said to be sealed with the *seal* of God in their foreheads, are again brought to view in Revelation 14: 1, where they are said to have the Father's *name* written in their foreheads.

What Is the Seal of God?—From the foregoing reasoning, facts, and declarations of Scripture, two conclusions inevitably follow:

1. The seal of God is found in the law of God.
2. The seal of God is that part of His law which contains His name, or descriptive title, showing who He is, the extent of His dominion, and His right to rule.

The law of God is admitted by all the leading evangelical denominations to be summarily contained in the decalogue, or ten commandments. We have, then, but to examine these commandments to see which one it is that constitutes the seal of the law, or in other words, makes known the true God, the lawmaking power.

The first three commandments mention the word "God," but we cannot tell from these who is meant, for there are multitudes of objects to which this name is applied. There are "gods many and lords many," as the apostle says. (1 Corinthians 8: 5.) We pass over the fourth commandment for the time being. The fifth contains the words "Lord" and "God," but does not define them, and the remaining five precepts do not contain the name of God at all. With that part of the law which we have examined, it would be impossible to convict the grossest idolater of sin. The worshiper of images could say, This idol before me is my god, his name is god, and these are his precepts. The worshiper of the heavenly bodies could also say, The sun is my god, and I worship him according to this law. Thus without the fourth commandment the decalogue is null and void, as far as it pertains to the definition of the worship of the true God.

But let us now add the fourth commandment, restore to the law this precept, which many are ready to contend has been expunged, and see how the case will then stand. As we examine this commandment, which contains the declaration, "For in six days the Lord made heaven and earth, the sea, and all that in them is," we see at once that we are reading the requirements of Him who created all things. The sun then is not the God of the decalogue. The true God is He who made the sun. No object in heaven or earth is the being who here demands obedience, for the God of this law is the one who made all created things. Now we have a weapon against idolatry. Now this law can no longer be applied to false gods, who "have not made the heavens and the earth." Jeremiah 10: 11. The Author of this law has declared who He is, the extent of His dominion, and His right to rule; for every created intelligence must at once assent that He who is the Creator of all has a right to demand obedience from all His creatures. Thus with the fourth commandment in its place, this wonderful document, the decalogue, the only document among men which God ever wrote with His own finger, has a signature, it has that which renders it intelligible and authentic, it has a seal. But without the fourth commandment, the law is incomplete and unauthoritative.

VERNON NYE, ARTIST

CHRIST AND THE LAW

The seal of God's authority is in His law, the Ten Commandments. The Saviour Himself confirmed this law.

From the foregoing logic it is evident that the fourth commandment constitutes the seal of the law of God, or the seal of God. The Scriptures give direct testimony on this conclusion.

We have seen already that in Scripture usage, "sign," "seal," "token," and "mark" are synonymous terms. The Lord expressly says that the Sabbath is a *sign* between Him and His people. "Verily My Sabbaths ye shall keep; for it is a *sign* between Me and you throughout your generations; *that ye may know that I am the Lord* that doth sanctify you." Exodus 31: 13. The same fact is again stated in Ezekiel 20: 12, 20. Here the Lord told His people that the very object of their keeping the Sabbath was that they might *know* that He is the true God. This is the same as if the Lord had said, "The Sabbath is a seal. On My part it is the seal of My authority, the sign that I have the right to command obedience; on your part it is a token that you accept Me to be your God."

Should it be said that this principle can have no application to Christians at the present time, as the Sabbath was a sign between God and the Jews only, it would be sufficient to reply that the terms "Jews" and "Israel" in a true Scriptural sense are not confined to the literal seed of Abraham. This patriarch was chosen at first because he was the friend of God while his fathers were idolaters. His posterity were chosen to be God's people, the guardians of His law and the depositaries of His truth, because all others had apostatized from Him. These words respecting the Sabbath were spoken to them while they enjoyed the honor of being thus set apart from all others. But when the middle wall of partition was broken down, and the Gentiles were called in to be partakers of the blessings of Abraham, all God's people, both Jews and Gentiles, were brought into a new and more intimate relation to God through His Son, and are now described by such expressions as "a Jew which is one inwardly," and "an Israelite indeed." Romans 2: 29; John 1: 47. These declarations apply to all such, for they have as much occasion to *know* the Lord as had His people of old.

Thus the Sabbath of the fourth commandment is taken by the Lord as a *sign* between Him and His people, or the *seal* of His law for all time. By keeping that commandment people signify that they are the worshipers of the true God. In the same commandment God makes Himself known as their rightful ruler, inasmuch as He is their Creator.

In harmony with this idea, the significant fact is to be noticed that whenever the sacred writers wish to point out the true God in distinction from false gods of every description, an appeal is made to the great facts of creation, upon which the fourth commandment is based. (See 2 Kings 19: 15; 2 Chronicles 2: 12; Nehemiah 9: 6; Psalm 96: 5; 115: 4-7, 15; 121: 2; 124: 8; 134: 3; 146: 6; Isaiah 37: 16; 42: 5; 44: 24; 45: 12; 51: 13; Job 9: 8; Jeremiah 10: 10-12; 32: 17; 51: 15; Acts 4: 24; 14: 15; 17: 23, 24.)

Notice again that the same company who in Revelation 7 have the seal of the living God in their foreheads, are brought to view again in Revelation 14: 1, having the Father's *name* in their foreheads. This is good proof that the "seal of the living God" and the "Father's name" are used synonymously. The chain of evidence on this point is made complete when it is ascertained that the fourth commandment, which has been shown to be the seal of the law, is spoken of by the Lord as that which contains His name. The proof of this will be seen in Deuteronomy 16: 6: "But at the place which the Lord thy God shall choose to place His *name* in, there shalt thou sacrifice the Passover." What was in the place where they sacrificed the Passover? There was the sanctuary, having in its holiest apartment the ark with the ten commandments, the fourth of which identified the true God, and contained His name. Wherever this fourth commandment was, there God's name was placed, and this was the only thing to which the language could be applied. (See Deuteronomy 12: 5, 11, 21; 14: 23, 24.)

The Sealing Work.—Since we have now ascertained that the seal of God is His holy Sabbath, with which His name is identified, we are prepared to proceed with the application. By the scenes introduced in the verses before us—the four winds apparently about to blow, bringing war and trouble upon the land, and this work restrained until the servants of God should be sealed—we are reminded of the houses of the Israelites marked with the blood of the paschal lamb, and spared as the destroying angel passed over to slay the firstborn of the Egyptians. (Exodus 12.) We are also reminded of the mark made by the man with a writer's inkhorn on all those who were to be spared by the men with the slaughtering weapons who followed after. (Ezekiel 9.) We conclude that the seal of God placed upon His servants is some distinguishing mark, or religious characteristic, through which they will be exempted from the judgments of God that fall on the wicked around them.

As we have found the seal of God in the fourth commandment, the inquiry follows, Does the observance of that commandment involve any peculiarity in religious practice?—Yes, a very marked and striking one. It is one of the most singular facts to be met with in religious history that, in an age of such boasted gospel light as the present, when the influence of Christianity is so powerful and widespread, one of the most striking peculiarities in practice which a person can adopt, and one of the greatest crosses he can take up, is the simple observance of the fourth commandment of God's law. This precept requires the observance of the seventh day of each week as the Sabbath of the Lord; while almost all Christendom, through the combined influences of paganism and the papacy, has been beguiled into the keeping of the first day. A person has only to begin the observance of the day enjoined in the commandment, when a mark of peculiarity is upon him at once. He is distinct from both the professedly religious and the secular world.

We conclude that the angel ascending from the east, having the seal of the living God, is a divine messenger in charge of a work of reform to be carried on among men involving the Sabbath of the fourth commandment. The agents of this work on the earth are of course ministers of Christ, for to men is given the commission of instructing their fellow men in Bible truth. But as there is order in the execution of all the divine counsels, it seems not improbable that a literal angel may have the charge and oversight of this reform.

We have already noticed that the chronology of this work locates it in our own time. This is further evident from the fact that in the next scene after the sealing of these servants of God, they appear before the throne with palms of victory in their hands. The sealing is therefore the last work to be accomplished for them prior to their deliverance from the destruction brought upon the world in connection with the second advent.

Identity of the Sealing Angel.—In Revelation 14 we find the same work again brought to view under the symbol of an angel flying in the midst of heaven with the most terrible warning that ever fell upon the ears of men. While we shall speak of this more fully when we reach that chapter, we refer to it now because it is the last work to be accomplished for the world before the coming of Christ, which is the next event in order in that prophecy, and hence must synchronize with the work here brought to view in Revelation 7: 1-3. The angel with the seal of the living God is therefore the same as the third angel of Revelation 14.

This view strengthens the foregoing exposition of the seal. As the result of the sealing work in Revelation 7, a certain company are sealed with the seal of the living God, while as the result of the third angel's message of Revelation 14 a company of people obey all the "*commandments of God.*" Revelation 14: 12. It is the fourth commandment of the decalogue and that alone which the Christian world is openly violating and teaching men to violate. That this is the vital question in this message is evident from the fact that the keeping of the commandments, including the Lord's Sabbath, is what distinguishes the servants of God from those who worship the beast and receive his mark. As will be hereafter shown, this mark is the observance of a counterfeit sabbath.

After thus briefly noticing the main points of the subject, we now come to the most striking feature of all. In accordance with the foregoing chronological argument, we find this work already in process of fulfillment before our eyes. The third angel's message is going forth. The angel ascending from the east is on his mission. The reform on the Sabbath question has begun; and it is surely, though yet in comparative silence, working its way through the land. It is destined to agitate every country that receives the light of the gospel, and it will result in bringing out a people prepared for the soon coming of the Saviour, and sealed for His everlasting kingdom. The sealing of the servants of God by the angel mentioned in verse 3, is therefore in recognition of their faithfulness in keeping the law of God, who is identified in the fourth commandment as the Creator of heaven and earth, and who established the seventh-day Sabbath in commemoration of that great work.

Holding the Winds.—With one more question we leave these verses, upon which we have dwelt so long. Have we seen among the nations any movements which would indicate that the cry of the ascending angel, "Hurt not" by the blowing of the winds, "till we have sealed the servants of our God," has in any manner been answered? The time during which the winds are held could not from the nature of the case be a time of profound peace. This would not answer to the prophecy, for in order to make it manifest that the winds are being held, there must be disturbance, agitation, anger, and jealousy among the nations, with occasional outbursts of strife, like fitful gusts breaking away from the imprisoned and struggling tempest. These outbursts must be unexpectedly checked. Then, but not otherwise, would it be evident to him who looked at events in the light of prophecy, that for some good purpose the restraining hand of Omnipotence was laid upon the surging elements of strife and war. Such has been the aspect of our times. New and unlooked-for complications have suddenly arisen, throwing the world into apparently inextricable confusion, and threatening immediate and direful war, when suddenly and unaccountably all subsided into quiet again. In the last half of the nineteenth century outstanding examples of such coincidences are found in the sudden conclusion of the Franco-German War in 1871, the Russo-Turkish War in 1878, and the Spanish-American War in 1898.

Then there came in the early part of the present century the devastating World War I when the four winds were permitted to blow over much of the world. It was declared by many writers to be the Armageddon of the Apocalypse. As the years went by, it seemed that this great conflagration would consume the entire world, leaving neither root nor branch. But suddenly the angel cried "Hold," for the sealing work was not yet fully accomplished. On November 11, 1918, the four angels stopped the winds of strife, and a war-sick world, distraught by the terror of four years of blood and carnage, rejoiced once more in apparent peace and safety.

The Armistice was acclaimed as marking the beginning of a golden age of peace and prosperity and good will among men, for had not this been "a war to end war"? Millions believed that another war would never come, that the human race had learned its lesson. But may it not be that the hand of God was moving in the affairs of nations to make possible the completion of the great work depicted in verse 3 of this chapter in the words of the angel, "Until we have sealed the servants of God in their foreheads"?

The period extending from the Armistice in 1918 until the breaking out of the second world war was far from peaceful, for the World Almanac listed no less than seventeen conflicts during this time, which touched four continents. Many of these outbreaks possessed potentialities of expanding into serious proportions. But every time the troubled world began to fear the spread of these conflicts, the troubles unexpectedly subsided. Did this angel interpose in behalf of peace?

Then suddenly the four angels again loosed their hold, and the four winds took on whirlwind velocity in a devastating global conflict we call World War II, and almost the entire world was soon engulfed. In its magnitude and fearful depredations on all that mankind holds dear and precious, this struggle entirely overshadowed World War I.

We are unable to understand or explain the ebb and flow of these currents of war and peace on any other basis than the revelation of Jesus Christ given through the prophet John and recorded in the verses before us. When it suits the plans and purposes of God to permit the winds of strife to blow, then human nature untouched by the grace of God is seen in unbridled display. But when He says, "It is enough," the angel cries, "Hold, Hold, Hold, Hold," and the strife ceases that the work of God may proceed. Thus it will be until the great consummation of the plan of salvation.

Are you troubled, dear reader, over the turmoil and confusion among the nations? Do you desire to know what it all means? You will find the answer in the picture presented in these verses. "The Most High ruleth in the kingdom of men, and giveth it to whomsoever He will." Daniel 4: 32. In His own chosen time He will make "wars to cease unto the end of the earth." Psalm 46: 9.

VERSE 4 And I heard the number of them which were sealed: and there were sealed an hundred and forty and four thousand of all the tribes of the children of Israel. 5 Of the tribe of Juda were sealed twelve thousand. Of the tribe of Reuben were sealed twelve thousand. Of the tribe of Gad were sealed twelve thousand. 6 Of the tribe of Aser were sealed twelve thousand. Of the tribe of Nepthalim were sealed twelve thousand. Of the tribe of Manasses were sealed twelve thousand. 7 Of the tribe of Simeon were sealed twelve thousand. Of the tribe of Levi were sealed twelve thousand. Of the tribe of Issachar were sealed twelve thousand. 8 Of the tribe of Zabulon were sealed twelve thousand. Of the tribe of Joseph were sealed twelve thousand. Of the tribe of Benjamin were sealed twelve thousand.

The Number to Be Sealed.—The number sealed is here stated to be one hundred forty-four thousand. From the fact that twelve thousand are sealed from each of the twelve tribes, many suppose that this work must have been accomplished as far back at least as the beginning of the Christian Era, when these tribes were literally in existence. They do not see how it

© SOUTHERN PUBLISHING ASSN. FRANKLIN BOOTH, ARTIST

THE REDEEMED BEFORE THE THRONE

"Blessing, and glory, and wisdom, and thanksgiving, and honor, and power, and might, be unto our God forever and ever." Revelation 7: 12.

can apply to our own time, when every trace of distinction between these tribes has been so long and so completely obliterated. We refer such persons to the opening language of the Epistle of James: "James, a servant of God and of the Lord Jesus Christ, to the *twelve tribes* which are scattered abroad, greeting. *My brethren*, count it all joy when ye fall into divers temptations." Those whom James here addresses are Christians, for they are his brethren. Some were converts from paganism and others were Jews, yet they are all included in the twelve tribes. How can this be? Paul explains in Romans 11: 17-24. In the striking figure of grafting which the apostle there introduces, the tame olive tree represents Israel.

Some of the branches, the natural descendants of Abraham, were broken off because of unbelief in Christ. Through faith in Christ the wild olive scions, the Gentiles, are grafted into the tame olive stock, and thus the twelve tribes are perpetuated. Here we find an explanation of the language of the same apostle: "They are not all Israel which are of Israel," and "he is not a Jew, which is one outwardly, . . . but he is a Jew, which is one inwardly." Romans 9: 6-8; 2: 28, 29. So we find on the gates of the New Jerusalem—which is a New Testament, or Christian, city—the names of the twelve tribes of the children of Israel. On the foundations of this city are inscribed the names of the twelve apostles of the Lamb. (Revelation 21: 12-14.)

If the twelve tribes belonged exclusively to the Jewish era, the more natural order would have been to have their names on the foundations, and those of the twelve apostles on the gates; but no, the names of the twelve tribes are on the gates. As through these gates, so inscribed, all the redeemed hosts will go in and out, so all the redeemed will be reckoned as belonging to these twelve tribes, whether on earth they were Jews or Gentiles.

It will be observed that the enumeration of the tribes here differs from that given in other places. In the text before us, Ephraim and Dan are omitted, and Levi and Joseph put in their places. The omission of Dan is accounted for by commentators on the ground that that tribe was the one chiefly addicted to idolatry. (See Judges 18.) The tribe of Levi here takes its place with the rest, as in the heavenly Canaan the reasons for their not having an inheritance will not exist as in the earthly. Joseph is probably substituted for Ephraim, it being a name which appears to have been applied to the tribe of either Ephraim or Manasseh. (Numbers 13: 11.)

Twelve thousand were sealed "out of" each of the twelve tribes, showing that not all who in the records of heaven had a place among these tribes when this sealing work began, stood the test and were overcomers at last, for the names of those already in the book of life will be blotted out unless they overcome. (Revelation 3: 5.)

VERSE 9 After this I beheld, and, lo, a great multitude, which no man could number, of all nations, and kindreds, and people, and tongues, stood before the throne, and before the Lamb, clothed with white robes, and palms in their hands; 10 and cried with a loud voice, saying, Salvation to our God which sitteth upon the throne, and unto the Lamb. 11 And all the angels stood round about the throne, and about the elders and the four beasts, and fell before the throne on their faces, and worshiped God, 12 saying, Amen: Blessing, and glory, and wisdom, and thanksgiving, and honor, and power, and might, be unto our God forever and ever. Amen.

After the sealing was accomplished, John beholds a countless multitude worshiping God in rapture before His throne. This vast throng is undoubtedly the saved out of every nation, kindred, tribe, and tongue raised from the dead at the second coming of Christ, showing that the sealing is the last work accomplished for the people of God prior to translation.

VERSE 13 And one of the elders answered, saying unto me, What are these which are arrayed in white robes? And whence came they? 14 And I said unto him, Sir, thou knowest. And he said to me, These are they which came out of great tribulation, and have washed their robes, and made them white in the blood of the Lamb. 15 Therefore are they before the throne of God, and serve Him day and night in His temple: and He that sitteth on the throne shall dwell among them. 16 They shall hunger no more, neither thirst any more; neither shall the sun light on them, nor any heat. 17 For the Lamb which is in the midst of the throne shall feed them, and shall lead them unto living fountains of waters: and God shall wipe away all tears from their eyes.

A Special Company.—The questions put by one of the elders to John, "What are these which are arrayed in white robes? And whence came they?" taken in connection with John's answer, "Sir, thou knowest," implying that John did not know, would seem to be devoid of point if they had reference to all the great multitude now before him. For John did know who they were and whence they came, inasmuch as he had just said that they were people—redeemed of course—out of all nations, kindreds, people, and tongues. John could have answered, These are the redeemed ones from all the nations of the earth. No company is brought to view to which special allusion would more naturally be made than to the company spoken of in the first part of the chapter, the 144,000. John had indeed seen this company in their mortal state as they were receiving the seal of the living God amid the troublous scenes of the last days; but as they here stand among the redeemed throng, the transition is so great, and the condition in which they now appear so different, that he does not recognize them as the special company which he saw sealed upon the earth. To this company, the following specifications seem to be specially applicable.

Came Out of Great Tribulation.—While it is true in some degree of all Christians that they "must through much tribulation enter into the kingdom of God" (Acts 14: 22), it is true of the 144,000 in a very special sense. They pass through the great time of trouble such as never was since there was a nation. (Daniel 12: 1.) They experience the mental anguish of the time of Jacob's trouble. (Jeremiah 30: 4-7.) They are to stand without a mediator through the terrible scenes of the seven last plagues, those exhibitions of God's unmingled wrath in the earth as we shall see in Revelation 15, 16. They pass through the most severe time of trouble the world has ever known, although they shall finally triumph and be delivered.

Wear White Robes.—They have washed their robes and made them white in the blood of the Lamb. To the last generation the counsel is very emphatic on the subject of obtaining the white raiment. (Revelation 3: 5, 18.) The 144,000 refuse to violate the commandments of God. (Revelation 14: 1, 12.) It will be seen that they have rested their hope of life on the merits of the shed blood of their divine Redeemer, making Him their source of righteousness. There is peculiar force in saying of these that they have washed their robes, and made them white in the blood of the Lamb.

Called First Fruits.—Verse 15 describes the post of honor they occupy in the kingdom, and their nearness to God. In another place they are called "the first fruits unto God and the Lamb." Revelation 14: 4.

Shall Hunger No More.—In verse 16 it is said, "They shall hunger no more, neither thirst any more." This shows that they have once suffered hunger and thirst. To what can this refer? As it doubtless has reference to some special experience, may it not refer to their trials in the time of trouble, more especially during the seven last plagues? In this time the righteous will be reduced to bread and water, and that "will be sure" (Isaiah 33: 16), enough for sustenance. Yet may it not be that when the pastures, with all fruits and vegetation, are dried up (Joel 1: 18-20), and the rivers and fountains are turned to blood (Revelation 16: 4-7), to reduce their connection with earth and earthly things to the lowest limit, the saints who pass through that time will be brought occasionally to extreme degrees of hunger and thirst? But the kingdom once gained, "they shall hunger no more, neither thirst any more."

The prophet continues: "Neither shall the sun light on them, nor any heat." The 144,000 live through the time when power is given unto the sun "to scorch men with fire." Revelation 16: 8, 9. Though they are shielded from the deadly effect which it has upon the wicked around them, we cannot suppose that their sensibilities will be so deadened that they will feel no unpleasant sensations from the terrific heat. No, as they enter the fields of the heavenly Canaan, they will be prepared to appreciate the divine assurance that the sun shall not injure them.

The Lamb Shall Lead Them.—Another testimony concerning the same company, and applying at the same time, says, "These are they which follow the Lamb whithersoever He goeth." Revelation 14: 4. Both expressions denote the state of intimate and divine companionship to which the blessed Redeemer admits them.

In the following beautiful passage the psalmist seems to allude to the same promise: "They shall be abundantly satisfied with the fatness of Thy house; and Thou shalt make them drink of the river of Thy pleasures." Psalm 36: 8. The phraseology of this promise to the 144,000 is also partly found in a glowing prophecy from the pen of Isaiah: "He will swallow up death in victory; and the Lord God will wipe away tears from off all faces; and the rebuke of His people shall He take away from off all the earth: for the Lord hath spoken it." Isaiah 25: 8.

© H. A. ROBERTS

THE SUNSET OF THE ROMAN EMPIRE

Like forbidding clouds, fierce northern tribes invaded Rome, eclipsed its glory, and decimated its empire.

CHAPTER VIII

THE COLLAPSE OF THE ROMAN EMPIRE

VERSE 1 And when He had opened the seventh seal, there was silence in heaven about the space of half an hour.

THE FIRST verse of this chapter relates to the events of the preceding chapters, and therefore should not have been separated from them by the division of the chapter. The series of seven seals is here resumed and concluded. The sixth chapter of Revelation closed with the events of the sixth seal, and the eighth chapter begins with the opening of the seventh seal. Hence the seventh chapter stands parenthetically between the sixth and seventh seals, and it appears that the sealing work of Revelation 7 belongs to the sixth seal.

Silence in Heaven.—The sixth seal does not bring us to the second advent of Christ, although it embraces events closely connected with that coming. It introduces the fearful commotions of the elements, described as the heavens rolling together as a scroll, the breaking up of the surface of the earth, and the confession by the wicked that the great day of God's wrath is come. They are doubtless in momentary expectation of seeing the King appear in glory. But the seal stops just short of that event. The personal appearing of Christ must therefore be allotted to the next seal.

When the Lord appears, He comes with all the holy angels with Him. (Matthew 25: 31.) When *all* the heavenly harpers leave the courts above to come to this earth with their divine Lord as He descends to gather the fruit of His redeeming work, will there not be silence in heaven? The length of this period of silence, if we consider it prophetic time, would be about seven days.

VERSE 2 And I saw the seven angels which stood before God; and to them were given seven trumpets.

This verse introduces a new and distinct series of events. In the seals we have had the history of the church during what is called the Christian Era. In the seven trumpets now introduced we have the principal political and warlike events that occur during the same time.

VERSE 3 And another angel came and stood at the altar, having a golden censer; and there was given unto him much incense, that he should offer it with the prayers of all saints upon the golden altar which was before the throne. 4 And the smoke of the incense, which came with the prayers of the saints, ascended up before God out of the angel's hand. 5 And the angel took the censer, and filled it with fire of the altar, and cast it into the earth: and there were voices, and thunderings, and lightnings, and an earthquake.

After introducing the seven angels upon the stage of action in verse 2, John for a moment directs attention to an entirely different scene. The angel who approaches the altar is not one of the seven trumpet angels. The altar is the altar of incense, which in the earthly sanctuary was placed in the first apartment. Here then is another proof that there exists in heaven a sanctuary with its corresponding vessels of service, of which the earthly was a figure, and that we are taken into that sanctuary by the visions of John. A work of ministration for all the saints in the sanctuary above is thus brought to view. Doubtless the entire work of mediation for the people of God during the gospel era is here presented. This is apparent from the fact that the angel offers his incense with the prayers of *all* saints. That we are here carried forward to the end of time, is evident from the act of the angel in filling the censer with fire and casting it unto the earth; by this act he shows that his work is done. No more prayers are to be offered up mingled with incense. This symbolic act can have its application only at the time when the ministration of Christ in the sanctuary in behalf of mankind has forever ceased. Following the angel's act there are voices, thunderings, lightnings, and an earthquake—exactly such occurrences as we are elsewhere informed take place at the close of human probation. (See Revelation 11: 19; 16: 17, 18.)

But why are these verses inserted here? They are a message of hope and comfort for the church. The seven angels with their warlike trumpets had been introduced; terrible scenes were to take place when they should sound; but before they begin to blow, the people of God are directed to behold the work of mediation in their behalf in heaven, and to look to their source of help and strength during this time. Though they should be tossed upon the tumultuous waves of strife and war, they were to know that their great High Priest still ministered for them in the sanctuary in heaven. To that sacred place they could direct their prayers with the assurance that they would be offered with incense to their Father in heaven. Thus could they gain strength and support in all their tribulation.

VERSE 6 And the seven angels which had the seven trumpets prepared themselves to sound.

The Seven Trumpets.—The subject of the seven trumpets is resumed. These trumpets occupy the rest of this chapter and all of Revelation 9. The blowing of the trumpets by the seven angels comes as a complement to the prophecy of Daniel 2 and 7, beginning with the breaking up of the old Roman Empire into its ten divisions. In the first four trumpets, we have a description of the special events which marked Rome's fall.

VERSE 7 The first angel sounded, and there followed hail and fire mingled with blood, and they were cast upon the earth: and the third part of trees was burnt up, and all green grass was burnt up.

Alexander Keith has justly remarked on the subject of this prophecy:

"None could elucidate the texts more clearly, or expound them more fully, than the task has been accomplished by Gibbon. The chapters of the skeptical philosopher that treat directly of the matter, need but a text to be prefixed and a few unholy words to be blotted out, to form a series of expository lectures on the eighth and ninth chapters of the Revelation of Jesus Christ."[1] "Little or nothing is left for the professed interpreter to do but to point to the pages of Gibbon."[2]

The first sore and heavy judgment which fell on Western Rome in its downward course, was the war with the Goths under Alaric, who opened the way for later inroads. The death of Theodosius the Roman emperor, occurred in January, A. D. 395, and before the end of the winter the Goths under Alaric were in arms against the empire.

The first invasion under Alaric ravaged the Eastern Empire. He captured the famous cities and enslaved many of the inhabitants. Thrace, Macedonia, Attica, and the Peloponnesus were conquered, but he did not reach the city of Rome. Later, the Gothic chieftain crossed the Alps and the Apennines and appeared before the walls of the Eternal City, which fell a prey to the fury of the barbarians in A. D. 410.

"Hail and fire mingled with blood" were cast upon the earth. The terrible effects of this Gothic invasion are represented as "hail," from the northern origin of the invaders; "fire," from the destruction by flame of both city and country; and "blood," from the terrible slaughter of the citizens of the empire by the bold and intrepid warriors.

The First Trumpet.—The blast of the first trumpet has its location about the close of the fourth century and onward, and refers to these desolating invasions of the Roman Empire under the Goths.

After quoting at some length from Edward Gibbon's *History of the Decline and Fall of the Roman Empire*, Chapters XXX-XXXIII, concerning the conquests of the Goths, Alexander Keith has presented an admirable summary of the historian's words emphasizing the fulfillment of prophecy:

"Large extracts clearly show how amply and well Gibbon has expounded his text in the history of the first trumpet, the first storm that pervaded the Roman earth, and the first fall of

[1] Alexander Keith, *Signs of the Times*, Vol. I, p. 241.

[2] *Ibid.*

Rome. To use his words in more direct comment, we read thus the sum of the matter: The Gothic nation was in arms at the first sound of the trumpet, and in the uncommon severity of the winter, they rolled their ponderous wagons over the broad and icy back of the river. The fertile fields of Phocis and Bœotia were crowned [sic] with a deluge of barbarians: the males were massacred; the females and cattle of the flaming villages were driven away. The deep and bloody traces of the march of the Goths could easily be discovered after several years. The whole territory of Attica was blasted by the baneful presence of Alaric. The most fortunate of the inhabitants of Corinth, Argos, and Sparta were saved by death from beholding the conflagration of their cities. In a season of such extreme heat that the beds of the rivers were dry, Alaric invaded the dominion of the West. A secluded 'old man of Verona' [the poet Claudian], pathetically lamented the fate of his contemporary *trees*, which must *blaze* in the *conflagration* of the *whole country* [note the words of the prophecy,—'The third part of the *trees* was *burned up*']; and the emperor of the Romans fled before the king of the Goths.

"A furious tempest was excited among the nations of Germany; from the northern extremity of which the barbarians marched almost to the gates of Rome. They achieved the destruction of the West. The dark cloud which was collected along the coasts of the Baltic, burst in thunder upon the banks of the upper Danube. The pastures of Gaul, in which flocks and herds grazed, and the banks of the Rhine, which were covered with elegant houses and well-cultivated farms, formed a scene of peace and plenty, which was suddenly changed into a desert, distinguished from the solitude of nature only by smoking ruins. Many cities were cruelly oppressed, or destroyed. Many thousands were inhumanly massacred. The consuming flames of war spread over the greatest part of the seventeen provinces of Gaul.

"Alaric again stretched his ravages over Italy. During four years the Goths ravaged and reigned over it without control. And in the pillage and fire of Rome, the streets of the city were filled with dead bodies; the flames consumed many public and private buildings; and the ruins of a palace remained, after a century and a half, a stately monument of the Gothic conflagration."[3]

After making this summary, Keith completes the picture by saying:

"The concluding sentence of the thirty-third chapter of Gibbon's History is of itself a clear and comprehensive commentary; for in winding up his own description of this brief but most eventful period, he concentrates, as in a parallel reading, the sum of the history and the substance of the prediction. But the words which precede it are not without their meaning: 'The public devotion of the age was impatient to exalt the saints and martyrs of the Catholic Church on the altars of Diana and Hercules. The *union* of the Roman empire was *dissolved;* its genius was humbled in the dust; and armies of unknown barbarians, issuing from the frozen regions of the North, had established their victorious reign over the fairest provinces of Europe and Africa.'

"The last word—Africa—is the signal for the sounding of the second trumpet. The scene changes from the shores of the Baltic to the southern coast of the Mediterranean, or from the frozen regions of the North to the borders of burning Africa. And instead of a storm of hail being cast upon the earth, a burning mountain was cast into the sea."[4]

VERSE 8 And the second angel sounded, and as it were a great mountain burning with fire was cast into the sea: and the third part of the sea became blood; 9 and the third part of the creatures which were in the sea, and had life, died; and the third part of the ships were destroyed.

The Second Trumpet.—The Roman Empire, after Constantine the Great, was divided into three parts. Hence the frequent remark, "a third part of men," is an allusion to the third part of the empire which was under the scourge. This division

[3] *Ibid.*, p. 251-253.
[4] *Ibid.*, p. 253.

of the Roman kingdom was made at the death of Constantine, among his three sons, Constantius, Constantine II, and Constans. Constantius possessed the East, and fixed his residence at Constantinople, the metropolis of the empire. Constantine II held Britain, Gaul, and Spain. Constans held Illyricum, Africa, and Italy.

The sounding of the second trumpet evidently relates to the invasion and conquest of Africa, and afterward of Italy, by Gaiseric (Genseric), king of the Vandals. His conquests were for the most part *naval*, and his triumphs were "as it were a great mountain burning with fire, cast into the sea." What figure would better, or even so well, illustrate the collision of navies, and the general havoc of war on the maritime coasts? In explaining this trumpet, we are to look for some events which will have a particular bearing on the commercial world. The symbol used naturally leads us to look for agitation and commotion. Nothing but a fierce maritime warfare would fulfill the prediction. If the sounding of the first four trumpets relates to four remarkable events which contributed to the downfall of the Roman Empire, and the first trumpet refers to the ravages of the Goths under Alaric, in this we naturally look for the *next* succeeding act of invasion which shook the Roman power and conduced to its fall. The next great invasion *was* that of Genseric, at the head of the Vandals. His career reached its height between the years A. D. 428-468. This great Vandal chief had his headquarters in Africa. But as Gibbon states, "The discovery and conquest of the black nations [in Africa], that might dwell beneath the torrid zone, could not tempt the rational ambition of Genseric; but he cast his eyes towards the sea; he resolved to create a naval power, and his bold resolution was executed with steady and active perseverance."[5] From the port of Carthage he repeatedly made piratical sallies, preyed on the Roman commerce, and waged war with that empire. To cope with this sea monarch, the

[5] Edward Gibbon, *The Decline and Fall of the Roman Empire*, Vol. III, chap. 36, p. 459.

Roman emperor, Majorian, made extensive naval preparations.

"The woods of the Apennines were felled; the arsenals and manufactures of Ravenna and Misenum were restored; Italy and Gaul vied with each other in liberal contributions to the public service; and the imperial navy of three hundred large galleys, with an adequate proportion of transports and smaller vessels, was collected in the secure and capacious harbor of Carthagena in Spain. . . . But Genseric was saved from impending and inevitable ruin by the treachery of some powerful subjects, envious, or apprehensive, of their master's success. Guided by their secret intelligence, he surprised the unguarded fleet in the Bay of Carthagena: many of the ships were sunk, or taken, or burnt; and the preparations of three years were destroyed in a single day. . . .

"The kingdom of Italy, a name to which the Western Empire was gradually reduced, was afflicted, under the reign of Ricimer, by the incessant depredations of the Vandal pirates. In the spring of each year, they equipped a formidable navy in the port of Carthage; and Genseric himself, though in a very advanced age, still commanded in person the most important expeditions. . . .

"The Vandals repeatedly visited the coasts of Spain, Liguria, Tuscany, Campania, Lucania, Bruttium, Apulia, Calabria, Venetia, Dalmatia, Epirus, Greece, and Sicily. . . .

"The celerity of their motions enabled them, almost at the same time, to threaten and to attack the most distant objects, which attracted their desires; and as they always embarked a sufficient number of horses, they had no sooner landed, than they swept the dismayed country with a body of light cavalry." [6]

A last and desperate attempt to dispossess Genseric of the sovereignty of the seas, was made in the year 468 by Leo I, the emperor of the East. Gibbon bears witness to this as follows:

---

[6] *Ibid.*, pp. 481-486.

"The whole expense of the African campaign, by whatsoever means it was defrayed, amounted to the sum of one hundred and thirty thousand pounds of gold, about five million two hundred thousand pounds sterling. . . . The fleet that sailed from Constantinople to Carthage consisted of eleven hundred and thirteen ships, and the number of soldiers and mariners exceeded one hundred thousand men. . . . The army of Heraclius and the fleet of Marcellinus either joined or seconded the imperial lieutenant. . . . The wind became favorable to the designs of Genseric. He manned his largest ships of war with the bravest of the Moors and Vandals, and they towed after them many large barks filled with combustible materials. In the obscurity of the night, these destructive vessels were impelled against the unguarded and unsuspecting fleet of the Romans, who were awakened by the sense of their instant danger. Their close and crowded order assisted the progress of the fire, which was communicated with rapid and irresistible violence; and the noise of the wind, the crackling of the flames, the dissonant cries of the soldiers and mariners, who could neither command nor obey, increased the horror of the nocturnal tumult. Whilst they labored to extricate themselves from the fire ships, and to save at least a part of the navy, the galleys of Genseric assaulted them with temperate and disciplined valor; and many of the Romans who escaped the fury of the flames, were destroyed or taken by the victorious Vandals. . . . After the failure of this great expedition, Genseric again became the tyrant of the sea; the coasts of Italy, Greece, and Asia were again exposed to his revenge and avarice; Tripoli and Sardinia returned to his obedience; he added Sicily to the number of his provinces; and before he died, in the fullness of years and of glory, he beheld the final extinction of the empire of the West." [7]

Concerning the important part which this bold corsair acted in the downfall of Rome, Gibbon uses this significant

[7] *Ibid.*, pp. 495-498.

ATTILA AND HIS HUNS

By the invaders from the North and the East the mighty empire of Rome was plundered and divided.

language: "Genseric, a name which, in the destruction of the Roman Empire, has deserved an equal rank with the names of Alaric and Attila."[8]

VERSE 10 And the third angel sounded, and there fell a great star from heaven, burning as it were a lamp, and it fell upon the third part of the rivers, and upon the fountains of waters; 11 and the name of the star is called Wormwood: and the third part of the waters became wormwood; and many men died of the waters, because they were made bitter.

The Third Trumpet.—In the interpretation and application of this passage, we are brought to the third important event which resulted in the subversion of the Roman Empire. In revealing the historical fulfillment of this third trumpet, we shall be indebted to the notes of Albert Barnes for a few extracts. In explaining this scripture, it is necessary, as this commentator says, "that there would be some chieftain or warrior who might be compared with a blazing meteor; whose course would be singularly brilliant; who would appear suddenly like a blazing star, and then disappear like a star whose light was quenched in the waters. That the desolating course of that meteor would be mainly on those portions of the world that abounded with springs of water and running streams. That an effect would be produced *as if* those streams and fountains were made bitter; that is, that many persons would perish, and that wide desolations would be caused in the vicinity of those rivers and streams, *as if* a bitter and baleful star should fall into the waters, and death should spread over the lands adjacent to them, and watered by them."[9]

It is here premised that this trumpet has allusion to the desolating wars and furious invasions of Attila, king of the Huns, against the Roman power. Speaking of this warrior, particularly of his personal appearance, Barnes says:

"In the manner of his appearance, he strongly resembled a brilliant meteor flashing in the sky. He came from the East gathering his Huns, and poured them down, as we shall see,

---

[8] *Ibid.*, chap. 33, p. 370.

[9] Albert Barnes, *Notes on Revelation*, p. 239, comment on Revelation 8: 11.

with the rapidity of a flashing meteor, suddenly on the empire. He regarded himself also as devoted to Mars, the god of war, and was accustomed to array himself in a peculiarly brilliant manner, so that his appearance, in the language of his flatterers, was such as to dazzle the eyes of beholders."[10]

In speaking of the *locality* of the events predicted by this trumpet, Barnes has this note:

"It is said particularly that the effect would be on 'the rivers' and on 'the fountains of waters.' If this has a literal application, or if, as was supposed in the case of the second trumpet, the language used was such as had reference to the portion of the empire that would be particularly affected by the hostile invasion, then we may suppose that this refers to those portions of the empire that abounded in rivers and streams, and more particularly those in which the rivers and streams had their origin—for the effect was permanently in the '*fountains* of waters.' As a matter of fact, the principal operations of Attila were in the regions of the Alps, and on the portions of the empire whence the rivers flow down into Italy. The invasion of Attila is described by Gibbon in this general language: 'The whole breadth of Europe, as it extends above five hundred miles from the Euxine to the Adriatic, was at once invaded, and occupied, and desolated by the myriads of barbarians whom Attila led into the field.' "[11]

The Name of the Star Is Called Wormwood.—The word "wormwood" denotes bitter consequences. "These words—which are more intimately connected with the preceding verse, as even the punctuation in our version denotes—recall us for a moment to the character of Attila, to the misery of which he was the author or the instrument, and to the terror that was inspired by his name.

" 'Total extirpation and erasure,' are terms which best denote the calamities he inflicted. . . .

---

[10] *Ibid.*

[11] *Ibid.*, p. 240.

"It was the boast of Attila that the grass never grew on the spot which his horse had trod. 'The scourge of God' was a name that he appropriated to himself, and inserted among his royal titles. He was 'the scourge of his enemies, and the terror of the world.' The Western emperor with the senate and people of Rome, humbly and fearfully deprecated the wrath of Attila. And the concluding paragraph of the chapters which record his history, is entitled, 'Symptoms of the Decay and Ruin of the Roman Government.' The name of the star is called wormwood." [12]

VERSE 12 And the fourth angel sounded, and the third part of the sun was smitten, and the third part of the moon, and the third part of the stars; so as the third part of them was darkened, and the day shone not for a third part of it, and the night likewise.

The Fourth Trumpet.—We understand that this trumpet symbolizes the career of Odoacer, the first barbarian ruler of Italy, who was so intimately connected with the downfall of *Western* Rome. The symbols sun, moon, and stars—for they are undoubtedly here used as symbols—evidently denote the great luminaries of the Roman government, its emperors, senators, and consuls. The last emperor of Western Rome was Romulus, who in derision was called *Augustulus*, or the "diminutive Augustus." Western Rome fell in A. D. 476. Still, however, though the Roman sun was extinguished, its subordinate luminaries shone faintly while the senate and consuls continued. But after many civil reverses and changes of political fortune, at length the whole form of the ancient government was subverted, and Rome itself was reduced from being the empress of the world to a poor dukedom tributary to the Exarch of Ravenna.

The extinction of the Western Empire is recorded by Gibbon as follows:

"The unfortunate Augustulus was made the instrument of his own disgrace: he signified his resignation to the senate; and

[12] Alexander Keith, *Signs of the Times*, Vol. I, pp. 267-269.

that assembly, in their last act of obedience to a Roman prince, still affected the spirit of freedom, and the forms of the constitution. An epistle was addressed, by their unanimous decree, to the emperor Zeno, the son-in-law and successor of Leo, who had lately been restored, after a short rebellion, to the Byzantine throne. They solemnly 'disclaim the necessity, or even the wish of continuing any longer the imperial succession in Italy; since in their opinion the majesty of a sole monarch is sufficient to pervade and to protect, at the same time, both the East and the West. In their own name, and in the name of the people, they consent that the seat of universal empire shall be transferred from Rome to Constantinople; and they basely renounce the right of choosing their master, the only vestige that yet remained of the authority which had given laws to the world.' "[13]

Keith comments on the downfall of Rome:

"The power and the glory of Rome as bearing rule over any nation, became extinct. The name alone remained to the queen of nations. Every token of royalty disappeared from the imperial city. She who had ruled over the nations sat in the dust, like a second Babylon, and there was no throne where the Cæsars had reigned. The last act of obedience to a Roman prince which that once august assembly performed, was the acceptance of the resignation of the last emperor of the West, and the abolition of the imperial succession in Italy. The sun of Rome was smitten. . . .

"A new conqueror of Italy, Theodoric, the Ostrogoth, speedily arose, who unscrupulously assumed the purple, and reigned by the right of conquest. 'The royalty of Theodoric was proclaimed by the Goths (March 5, A. D. 493), with the tardy, reluctant, ambiguous consent of the emperor of the East.' The imperial Roman power, of which either Rome or Constantinople had been jointly or singly the seat, whether in the West or the East, was no longer recognized in Italy, and the 'third

[13] Edward Gibbon, *The Decline and Fall of the Roman Empire*, Vol. III, chap. 36, p. 512.

part of the sun' was smitten till it emitted no longer the faintest rays. The power of the Cæsars was unknown in Italy; and a Gothic king reigned over Rome.

"But though the third part of the sun was smitten, and the Roman imperial power was at an end in the city of the Cæsars, yet the moon and the stars still shone, or glimmered, for a little longer in the Western hemisphere [empire], even in the midst of Gothic darkness. The consulship and the senate ['the moon and the stars'] were not abolished by Theodoric. 'A Gothic historian applauds the consulship of Theodoric as the height of all temporal power and greatness;'—as the moon reigns by night, after the setting of the sun. And instead of abolishing that office, Theodoric himself 'congratulates those annual favorites of fortune, who, without the cares, enjoyed the splendor of the throne.'

"But, in their prophetic order, the consulship and the senate of Rome met their fate, though they fell not by the hands of Vandals or of Goths. The next revolution in Italy was its subjection to Belisarius, the general of Justinian, emperor of the East. He did not spare what barbarians had hallowed. 'The Roman Consulship Extinguished by Justinian, A. D. 541,' is the title of the last paragraph of the fortieth chapter of Gibbon's *History of the Decline and Fall of Rome*. 'The succession of the consuls finally ceased in the thirteenth year of Justinian, whose despotic temper might be gratified by the silent extinction of a title which admonished the Romans of their ancient freedom.' 'The third part of the sun was smitten, and the third part of the moon, and the third part of the stars.' In the political firmament of the ancient world, while under the reign of imperial Rome, the emperorship, the consulate, and the senate shone like the sun, the moon, and the stars. The history of their decline and fall is brought down till the two former were 'extinguished,' in reference to Rome and Italy, which so long had ranked as the first of cities and of countries; and finally, as the fourth trumpet closes, we see the 'extinction of that illustrious assembly,' the Roman senate. The city that

PAUL THUMANN, ARTIST

TRIUMPHING OVER THE ROMANS

Powerful Teutonic tribes began the breakup of the Roman Empire. They first threw off the Roman yoke in Central Europe, and

had ruled the world, as if in mockery of human greatness, was conquered by the eunuch Narses, the successor of Belisarius. He defeated the Goths (A. D. 552*), achieved 'the conquest of Rome,' and the fate of the senate was sealed."[14]

E. B. Elliott speaks of the fulfillment of this part of the prophecy in the extinction of the Western Empire, as follows:

"Thus was the final catastrophe preparing, by which the Western emperors and empire were to become extinct. The glory of Rome had long departed; its provinces one after another been rent from it; the territory still attached to it become like a desert; and its maritime possessions and its fleets and commerce been annihilated. Little remained to it but the vain titles and insignia of sovereignty. And now the time was come when these too should be withdrawn. Some twenty years or more from the death of Attila, and much less from that of Genseric (who, ere his death, had indeed visited and ravaged the eternal city in one of his maritime marauding expeditions, and thus yet more prepared the coming consummation), about this time, I say, Odoacer, chief of the Heruli—a barbarian remnant of the host of Attila, left on the Alpine frontiers of Italy—interposed with his command that the *name* and the *office of Roman Emperor of the West*, should be abolished. The authorities bowed in submission to him. The last phantom of an emperor—one whose name, *Romulus Augustus*, was singularly calculated to bring in contrast before the reflective mind the past glories of Rome and its present degradation—abdicated; and the senate sent away the imperial insignia to Constantinople, professing to the emperor of the East that one emperor was sufficient for the whole of the empire. Thus of the Roman imperial sun, that third which appertained to the Western Empire was eclipsed, and shone no more. I say that *third* of its orb which appertained to the Western empire; for

* Edward Gibbon in *History of the Decline and Fall of the Roman Empire*, Volume IV, chapter 43, pages 273, 274, places the defeat and death of Teias, the last king of the Goths, in A. D. 553. This is the date usually accepted by historians, and is the one used by the author of this book. (See pages 127, 128.)—*Editors.*

[14] Alexander Keith, *Signs of the Times*, Vol. I, pp. 280-283.

the Apocalyptic fraction is literally accurate. In the last arrangement between the two courts, the whole of the Illyrian third had been made over to the *Eastern* division. Thus in the West 'the extinction of the empire' had taken place; the night had fallen.

"Notwithstanding this, however, it must be borne in mind that the authority of the Roman name had not yet entirely ceased. The senate of Rome continued to assemble as usual. The consuls were appointed yearly, one by the Eastern emperor, one by Italy and Rome. Odoacer himself governed Italy under a title (that of *patrician*) conferred on him by the Eastern emperor. And as regarded the more distant Western provinces, or at least considerable districts in them, the tie which had united them to the Roman Empire was not altogether severed. There was still a certain, though often faint, recognition of the supreme imperial authority. The moon and the stars might seem still to shine on the West with a dim reflected light. In the course of the events, however, which rapidly followed one on the other in the next half century, these, too, were extinguished. Theodoric the Ostrogoth, on destroying the Heruli and their kingdom at Rome and Ravenna, ruled in Italy from A. D. 493 to 526 as an independent sovereign; and on Belisarius's and Narses's conquest of Italy from the Ostrogoths (a conquest preceded by wars and desolations in which Italy, and above all its seven-hilled city, were for a time almost made desert), the Roman senate was dissolved, the consulship abrogated. Moreover, as regards the barbaric princes of the Western provinces, their independence of the Roman imperial power became now more distinctly averred and understood. After above a century and [a] half of calamities unexampled almost, as Dr. Robertson most truly represents it, in the history of nations, the statement of Jerome,—a statement couched under the very Apocalyptic figure of the text, but prematurely pronounced on the first taking of Rome by Alaric,—might be considered as at length accomplished: 'Clarissimum terrarum *lumen* extinctum est,' 'The world's glorious *sun* has been extinguished;' or as the modern poet has expressed it, still under the same Apocalyptic imagery—

'She saw her glories star by star expire,'

till not even one star remained, to glimmer on the vacant and dark night."[15]

The fearful ravages of these barbarian hordes who under their bold but cruel and desperate leaders devastated Rome, are vividly portrayed in the following spirited lines:

"And then a deluge of wrath it came,
And the nations shook with dread;
And it swept the earth, till its fields were flame,
And piled with the mingled dead.
Kings were rolled in the wasteful flood,
With the low and crouching slave,
And together lay, in a shroud of blood,
The coward and the brave."

Fearful as were the calamities brought upon the empire by the first incursions of these barbarians, they were light as compared with the calamities which were to follow. They were but as the preliminary drops of a shower before the torrent which was soon to fall upon the Roman world. The three remaining trumpets are overshadowed with a cloud of woe, as set forth in the following verses.

VERSE 13 And I beheld, and heard an angel flying through the midst of heaven, saying with a loud voice, Woe, woe, woe, to the inhabiters of the earth by reason of the other voices of the trumpet of the three angels, which are yet to sound.

This angel is not one of the series of the seven trumpet angels, but simply another heavenly messenger, who announces that the three remaining trumpets are woe trumpets, because of the more terrible events to take place under their sounding. Thus the next, or fifth trumpet, is the first woe; the sixth trumpet, the second woe; and the seventh, the last one in this series of seven trumpets, is the third woe.

---

[15] Edward B. Elliott, *Horæ Apocalypticæ*, Vol. I, pp. 354-356.

JAMES ARCHER, ARTIST

THE MOSLEMS INVADE EUROPE

The fierce Moslem invaders, who had struck terror to Europe, were repulsed at Tours by Charles Martel, and eventually driven from Spain.

CHAPTER IX

THE MOSLEM WORLD IN PROPHECY

VERSE 1 And the fifth angel sounded, and I saw a star fall from heaven unto the earth: and to him was given the key of the bottomless pit.

THE FIFTH *Trumpet.*—For an exposition of this trumpet, we shall again draw from the writings of Alexander Keith. This writer says:

"There is scarcely so uniform an agreement among interpreters concerning any other part of the Apocalypse as respecting the application of the fifth and sixth trumpets, or the first and second woes, to the Saracens and the Turks. It is so obvious that it can scarcely be misunderstood. Instead of a verse or two designating each, the whole of the ninth chapter of the Revelation, in equal portions, is occupied with a description of both.

"The Roman Empire declined, as it arose, by conquest; but the Saracens and the Turks were the instruments by which a false religion became the scourge of an apostate church; and hence, instead of the fifth and sixth trumpets, like the former, being marked by that name alone, they are called woes. . . .

"Constantinople was beseiged for the first time after the extinction of the Western Empire by Chosroes [II], the king of Persia."[1]

The prophet said, "I saw a star fall from heaven unto the earth; and to him was given the key of the bottomless pit."

The historian writes of this time:

"While the Persian monarch [Chosroes II] contemplated the wonders of his art and power, he received an epistle from an obscure citizen of Mecca, inviting him to acknowledge Mahomet as the apostle of God. He rejected the invitation, and tore the epistle. 'It is thus," exclaimed the Arabian

[1] Alexander Keith, *Signs of the Times*, Vol. I, pp. 289, 291.

prophet, 'that God will tear the kingdom, and reject the supplications of Chosroes.' Placed on the verge of the two great empires of the East, Mahomet observed with secret joy the progress of their mutual destruction; and in the midst of the Persian triumphs, he ventured to foretell, that before many years should elapse, victory should again return to the banners of the Romans. At the time when this prediction is said to have been delivered, no prophecy could be more distant from its accomplishment, since the first twelve years of Heraclius announced the approaching dissolution of the empire." [2]

It was not on a single spot that *this* star fell, as did the one that designated Attila, but *upon the earth*.

The provinces of the empire in Asia and Africa were subdued by Chosroes II, and "the Roman Empire was reduced to the walls of Constantinople, with the remnant of Greece, Italy, and Africa, and some maritime cities, from Tyre to Trebizond, of the Asiatic coast. . . . The experience of six years at length persuaded the Persian monarch to renounce the conquest of Constantinople, and to specify the annual tribute or ransom of the Roman Empire; a thousand talents of gold, a thousand talents of silver, a thousand silk robes, a thousand horses, and a thousand virgins. Heraclius subscribed these ignominious terms; but the time and space which he obtained to collect such treasures from the poverty of the East, was industriously employed in the preparation of a bold and desperate attack." [3]

"The king of Persia despised the obscure Saracen, and derided the message of the pretended prophet of Mecca. Even the overthrow of the Roman Empire would not have opened a door for Mahometanism, or for the progress of the Saracenic armed propagators of an imposture, though the monarch of the Persians and *chagan* of the Avars (the successor of Attila) had divided between them the remains of the kingdoms of the Cæsars. Chosroes himself fell. The Persian and Roman mon-

---

[2] Edward Gibbon, *The Decline and Fall of the Roman Empire*, Vol. IV, chap. 46, pp. 463, 464.

[3] *Ibid.*, p. 466.

archies exhausted each other's strength. And before a sword was put into the hands of the false prophet, it was smitten from the hands of those who would have checked his career and crushed his power."[4]

"Since the days of Scipio and Hannibal, no bolder enterprise has been attempted than that which Heraclius achieved for the deliverance of the empire. He . . . explored his perilous way through the Black Sea and the mountains of Armenia, penetrated into the heart of Persia, and recalled the armies of the great king to the defense of their bleeding country. . . .

"In the battle of Nineveh, which was fiercely fought from daybreak to the eleventh hour, twenty-eight standards, besides those which might be broken or torn, were taken from the Persians; the greatest part of their army was cut in pieces, and the victors, concealing their own loss, passed the night on the field. . . . The cities and palaces of Assyria were opened for the first time to the Romans."[5]

"The Roman emperor was not strengthened by the conquests which he achieved; and a way was prepared at the same time, and by the same means, for the multitudes of Saracens from Arabia, like locusts from the same region, who, propagating in their course the dark and delusive Mahometan creed, speedily overspread both the Persian and the Roman empires. More complete illustration of this fact could not be desired than is supplied in the concluding words of the chapter [from Gibbon], from which the preceding extracts are taken."[6]

"Although a victorious army had been formed under the standard of Heraclius, the unnatural effort appears to have exhausted rather than exercised their strength. While the emperor triumphed at Constantinople or Jerusalem, an obscure town on the confines of Syria was pillaged by the Saracens, and they cut in pieces some troops who advanced to its relief, an ordinary and trifling occurrence, had it not been the prelude

[4] Alexander Keith, *Signs of the Times*, Vol. I, p. 293.
[5] Edward Gibbon, *The Decline and Fall of the Roman Empire*, Vol. IV, chap. 46, pp. 470-480.
[6] Alexander Keith, *Signs of the Times*, Vol. I, p. 295.

of a mighty revolution. These robbers were the apostles of Mahomet; their fanatic valor had emerged from the desert; and in the last eight years of his reign, Heraclius lost to the Arabs the same provinces which he had rescued from the Persians."[7]

" 'The spirit of fraud and enthusiasm, whose abode is not in the heavens,' was let loose on earth. The bottomless pit needed but a key to open it, *and that key was the fall of Chosroes.* He had contemptuously torn the letter of an obscure citizen of Mecca. But when from his 'blaze of glory' he sunk into the 'tower of darkness' which no eye could penetrate, the name of Chosroes was suddenly to pass into oblivion before that of Mahomet; and the crescent seemed but to wait its rising till the falling of the star. Chosroes, after his entire discomfiture and loss of empire, was murdered in the year 628; and the year 629 is marked by 'the conquest of Arabia,' and 'the first war of the Mahometans against the Roman Empire.' 'And the fifth angel sounded, and I saw a star fall from heaven unto the earth: and to him was given the key of the bottomless pit. And he opened the bottomless pit.' *He fell unto the earth.* When the strength of the Roman Empire was exhausted, and the great king of the East lay dead in his tower of darkness, the pillage of an obscure town on the borders of Syria was 'the prelude of a mighty revolution.' 'The robbers were the apostles of Mahomet, and their fanatic valor emerged from the desert.' "[8]

The Bottomless Pit.—The meaning of this term may be learned from the Greek *ἄβυσσος*, *abyssos*, which is defined "deep, bottomless, profound," and may refer to any waste, desolate, and uncultivated place. It is applied to the earth in its original state of chaos. (Genesis 1: 2.) In this instance it may appropriately refer to the unknown wastes of the Arabian desert, from the borders of which issued the hordes of Saracens, like swarms of locusts. The fall of Chosroes II the Persian

[7] Edward Gibbon, *The Decline and Fall of the Roman Empire*, Vol. IV, chap. 46, p. 486.
[8] Alexander Keith, *Signs of the Times*, Vol. I, p. 298.

king may well be represented as the opening of the bottomless pit, inasmuch as it prepared the way for the followers of Mohammed to issue from their obscure country and propagate their delusive doctrines with fire and sword until they had spread their darkness over all the Eastern Empire.

VERSE 2 And he opened the bottomless pit; and there arose a smoke out of the pit, as the smoke of a great furnace; and the sun and the air were darkened by reason of the smoke of the pit.

"Like the noxious and even deadly vapors which the winds, particularly from the southwest, diffuse in Arabia, Mahometanism spread from hence its pestilential influence—arose as suddenly and spread as widely as smoke arising out of the pit, the smoke of a great furnace. Such is a suitable symbol of the religion of Mahomet, of itself, or as compared with the pure light of the gospel of Jesus. It was not, like the latter, a light from heaven, but a smoke out of the bottomless pit."[9]

VERSE 3 And there came out of the smoke locusts upon the earth: and unto them was given power, as the scorpions of the earth have power.

"A false religion was set up, which, although the scourge of transgressions and idolatry, filled the world with darkness and delusion; and swarms of Saracens, like locusts, overspread the earth, and speedily extended their ravages over the Roman Empire from east to west. The hail descended from the frozen shores of the Baltic; the burning mountain fell upon the sea from Africa; and the locusts (the fit symbol of the Arabs) issued from Arabia, their native region. They came as destroyers, propagating a new doctrine, and stirred up to rapine and violence by motives of interest and religion."[10]

"A still more specific illustration may be given of the power like unto that of scorpions, which was given them. Not only was their attack speedy and vigorous, but 'the nice sensibility of honor, which weighs the insult rather than the injury, sheds its deadly venom on the quarrels of the Arabs; an indecent

---

[9] *Ibid.*, p. 299.
[10] *Ibid.*, p. 301.

action, a contemptuous word, can be expiated only by the blood of the offender; and such is their patient inveteracy, that they expect whole months and years the opportunity of revenge.' "[11]

VERSE 4 And it was commanded them that they should not hurt the grass of the earth, neither any green thing, neither any tree; but only those men which have not the seal of God in their foreheads.

After the death of Mohammed, he was succeeded in the command by Abu-bekr in A. D. 632, who as soon as he had fairly established his authority and government gathered the Arabian tribes for conquest. When the army was assembled, he instructed his chiefs on methods of conquest:

"When you fight the battles of the Lord, acquit yourselves like men, without turning your backs; but let not your victory be stained with the blood of women or children. Destroy no palm-trees, nor burn any fields of corn. Cut down no fruit-trees, nor do any mischief to cattle, only such as you kill to eat. When you make any covenant, or article, stand to it, and be as good as your word. As you go on, you will find some religious persons who live retired in monasteries, and propose to themselves to serve God that way; let them alone, and neither kill them nor destroy their monasteries: and you will find another sort of people that belong to the synagogue of Satan, who have shaven crowns; be sure you cleave their skulls, and give them no quarter till they either turn Mahometans or pay 'tribute.' "[12]

"It is not said in prophecy or in history that the more humane injunctions were as scrupulously obeyed as the ferocious mandate; but it was so commanded them. And the preceding are the only instructions recorded by Gibbon, and given by Abubeker to the chiefs whose duty it was to issue the commands to all the Saracen hosts. The commands are alike discriminating with the prediction, as if the caliph himself had been acting in known as well as direct obedience to a higher

[11] *Ibid.*, p. 305.

[12] Edward Gibbon, *The Decline and Fall of the Roman Empire*, Vol. V, chap. 51, pp. 189, 190.

mandate than that of mortal man; and in the very act of going forth to fight against the religion of Jesus, and to propagate Mahometanism in its stead, he repeated the words which it was foretold in the Revelation of Jesus Christ that he would say."[13]

Seal of God in Their Foreheads.—In remarks upon Revelation 7: 1-3, we have shown that the seal of God is the Sabbath of the fourth commandment. History is not silent upon the fact that there have been observers of the true seventh-day Sabbath all through the gospel age. But the question has here arisen with many, Who were those men who at this time had the seal of God in their foreheads, and who thereby became exempt from Mohammedan oppression? Let the reader bear in mind the fact already alluded to, that there have been those all through the Christian Era who have had the seal of God in their foreheads, that is, have been intelligent observers of the true Sabbath. Let him consider further that what the prophecy asserts is that the attacks of this desolating Turkish power are not directed against them, but against another class. The subject is thus freed from all difficulty, for this is all that the prophecy really asserts. One class of persons is directly brought to view in the text, namely, those who have not the seal of God in their foreheads. The preservation of those who have the seal of God is brought in only by implication. Accordingly, we do not learn from history that any of these were involved in any of the calamities inflicted by the Saracens upon the objects of their hate. They were commissioned against another class of men. The destruction to come upon this class is not put in contrast with the preservation of other men, but only with that of the fruits and verdure of the earth; thus, Hurt not the grass, trees, nor any green thing, but only a certain class of men. In fulfillment, we have the strange spectacle of an army of invaders sparing those things which such armies usually destroy, the face and productions of nature. In pur-

---

[13] Alexander Keith, *Signs of the Times*, Vol. I, p. 307.

suance of their permission to hurt those men who had not the seal of God in their foreheads, they cleaved the skulls of a class of religionists with shaven crowns, who belonged to the synagogue of Satan. It would seem that these were monks, or some other order of the Roman Catholic Church.

VERSE 5 And to them it was given that they should not kill them, but that they should be tormented five months: and their torment was as the torment of a scorpion, when he striketh a man.

"Their constant incursions into the Roman territory, and frequent assaults on Constantinople itself, were an unceasing torment throughout the empire, which yet they were not able effectually to subdue, notwithstanding the long period, afterward more directly alluded to, during which they continued, by unremitting attacks, grievously to afflict an idolatrous church, of which the pope was the head. . . . Their charge was to torment, and then to hurt, but not to kill, or utterly destroy. The marvel was that they did not."[14] (In reference to the five months, see comments on verse 10.)

VERSE 6 And in those days shall men seek death, and shall not find it; and shall desire to die, and death shall flee from them.

"Men were weary of life, when life was spared only for a renewal of woe, and when all that they accounted sacred was violated, and all that they held dear constantly endangered; and when the savage Saracens domineered over them, or left them only to a momentary repose, ever liable to be suddenly or violently interrupted, as if by the sting of a scorpion."[15]

VERSE 7 And the shapes of the locusts were like unto horses prepared unto battle; and on their heads were as it were crowns like gold, and their faces were as the faces of men.

"The Arabian horse takes the lead throughout the world; and skill in horsemanship is the art and science of Arabia. And the barbed Arabs, swift as locusts and armed like scor-

---

[14] *Ibid.*, pp. 308, 309.
[15] *Ibid.*, p. 309.

pions, ready to dart away in a moment, were ever prepared unto battle.

" 'And on their heads were as it were crowns like gold.' When Mahomet entered Medina (A. D. 622), and was first received as its prince, 'a turban was unfurled before him to supply the deficiency of a standard.' The turbans of the Saracens, like unto a coronet, were their ornament and their boast. The rich booty abundantly supplied and frequently renewed them. To assume the turban is proverbially to turn Mussulman. And the Arabs were anciently distinguished by the miters which they wore."[16]

"And their faces were as the faces of men." "The gravity and firmness of the mind [of the Arab] is conspicuous in his outward demeanor; . . . his only gesture is that of stroking his beard, the venerable symbol of manhood. . . . The honor . . . of their beards is most easily wounded."[17]

VERSE 8 And they had hair as the hair of women, and their teeth were as the teeth of lions.

"Long hair is esteemed an ornament by women. The Arabs, unlike to other men, had their hair as the hair of women, or uncut, as their practice is recorded by Pliny and others. But there was nothing effeminate in their character; for, as denoting their ferocity and strength to devour, their teeth were as the teeth of lions."[18]

VERSE 9 And they had breastplates, as it were breastplates of iron; and the sound of their wings was as the sound of chariots of many horses running to battle.

"The cuirass (or breastplate) was in use among the Arabs in the days of Mahomet. In the battle of Ohud (the second which Mahomet fought) with the Koreish of Mecca (A. D. 624), 'seven hundred of them were armed with cuirasses.' "[19]

---

[16] *Ibid.*, pp. 311, 312.

[17] Edward Gibbon, *The Decline and Fall of the Roman Empire*, Vol. V, chap. 50, pp. 86-88.

[18] Alexander Keith, *Signs of the Times*, Vol. I, p. 312.

[19] *Ibid.*

" 'The charge of the Arabs was not, like that of the Greeks and Romans, the efforts of a firm and compact infantry; their military force was chiefly formed of cavalry and archers.' . . . With a touch of the hand, the Arab horses dart away with the swiftness of the wind. 'The sound of their wings was as the sound of chariots of many horses running to battle.' Their conquests were marvelous both in rapidity and extent, and their attack was instantaneous. Nor was it less successful against the Romans than the Persians."[20]

VERSE 10 And they had tails like unto scorpions, and there were stings in their tails: and their power was to hurt men five months. 11 And they had a king over them, which is the angel of the bottomless pit, whose name in the Hebrew tongue is Abaddon, but in the Greek tongue hath his name Apollyon.

"*To Hurt Men Five Months.*"—The question arises, What men were they to hurt five months?—Undoubtedly the same they were afterward to slay (see verse 15), "the third part of men," or third of the Roman Empire—the Greek division of it.

When were they to begin their work of torment? The eleventh verse answers the question.

"They had a king over them." From the death of Mohammed until near the close of the thirteenth century, the Mohammedans were divided into various factions under several leaders, with no *general* civil government extending over them all. Near the close of the thirteenth century, Othman founded a government which has since been known as the Ottoman government, or empire, which grew until it extended over all the principal Mohammedan tribes, consolidating them into one grand monarchy.

Their king is called "the angel of the bottomless pit." An angel signifies a messenger, a minister, either good or bad, and not always a spiritual being. "The angel of the bottomless pit" would be the chief minister of the religion which came from thence when it was opened. That religion is Mohammedanism, and the sultan was its chief minister.

---

[20] *Ibid.*, p. 313.

His name in the Hebrew tongue is "Abaddon," the destroyer; in Greek, "Apollyon," one that exterminates, or destroys. Having two different names in two languages, it is evident that the character rather than the name of the power is intended to be represented. If so, as expressed in both languages, he is a destroyer. Such has always been the character of the Ottoman government.

But *when* did Othman make his first assault on the Greek empire?—According to Gibbon "it was on the twenty-seventh of July, in the year twelve hundred and ninety-nine of the Christian Era, that Othman first invaded the territory of Nicomædia; and the singular accuracy of the date seems to disclose some foresight of the rapid and destructive growth of the monster."[21]

Von Hammer, the German historian of Turkey, and other authorities have placed this event in 1301. But to what date do the historic sources of this period testify? Pachymeres was a church and state historian, born at Nicæa, which was in the vicinity of the Ottoman invasion; and he wrote his history during this very period. He concluded his work about 1307, so he was a contemporary of Othman.

Possinus, in 1669, worked out a complete chronology of Pachymeres' history, giving the dates for the eclipses of the moon and the sun, as well as other events, recorded by Pachymeres in his work. Concerning the date 1299 Possinus says:

"Now it is our task to give the exact and fundamental epoch of the Ottoman Empire. This we shall try to effect by a thoroughgoing comparison of the dates given by Arab chronologists and the testimony of our Pachymeres. This last-mentioned author reports in the fourth book of this second part, chapter 25, that Atman [Greek name for Othman] grew strong by taking the command over a very strong band of bold and energetic warriors from Paphlagonia. When Muzalo, the Roman army commander, attempted to block his progress, he

[21] Edward Gibbon, *The Decline and Fall of the Roman Empire*, Vol. VI, chap. 64, p. 226.

defeated him in a battle near Nicomedia, the capital of Bithynia. This city the lord of the battlefield henceforth kept as if it were besieged. Now, Pachymeres is very explicit in stating that these events took place in the immediate vicinity of Bapheum, not far from Nicomedia, on the 27th day of July. The year, we asseverate [affirm] in our synopsis, comparing carefully the events, to have been the year of our Lord 1299."[22]

The synopsis to which Possinus refers gives the date of the uniting of these Paphlagonians with Othman's forces, which took place on July 27, as 1299 of the Christian Era, fifth year of Pope Boniface VIII, and the sixth year of Michael Palæologus. The statement is as follows:

"Atman [Othman], the satrap of the Persians, called also Ottomanes, the founder of the still reigning dynasty of the Turcs, grew strong by joining to himself a great number of fierce bandits from Paphlagonia."[23]

The Paphlagonians under the sons of Amurius joined Othman in this attack of July 27, so that Possinus gives the date for this event twice as 1299.

Gregoras, also a contemporary of Othman, supports Gibbon and Pachymeres in establishing the date 1299 in his account of the division of Anatolia. This division among ten Turkish emirs took place in 1300, as supported by reliable historians. Gregoras states that in the division Atman (Othman) got Olympus and certain parts of Bithynia, indicating that Othman had already fought the battle of Bapheum, and had conquered certain parts of this eastern Roman-Greek territory.

"The calculations of some writers have gone upon the supposition that the period should begin with the foundation of the Ottoman Empire; but this is evidently an error; for they not only were to have a king over them, but were to torment men five months. But the period of torment could not begin

---

[22] Possinus, *Observationum Pachymerianarum*, Book III (Chronology), chap. 8, sec. 5, translation made at the Library of Congress.

[23] *Ibid.*, bk. 4, chap. 25.

before the first attack of the tormentors, which was, as above [stated], July 27, 1299."[24]

The calculation which follows, founded on this starting point, was made and first published in a work entitled, *Christ's Second Coming*, by Josiah Litch, in 1838.

" 'And their power was to hurt men five months.' Thus far their commission extended, to torment by constant depredations, but not politically to kill them. 'Five months' [thirty days to a month, one hundred and fifty days], that is, one hundred and fifty years. Commencing July 27, 1299, the one hundred and fifty years reach to 1449. During that whole period the Turks were engaged in an almost perpetual war with the Greek Empire, but yet *without conquering it*. They seized upon and held several of the Greek provinces, but still Greek independence was maintained in Constantinople. But in 1449, the termination of the one hundred and fifty years, a change came,"[25] the history of which will be found under the succeeding trumpet.

VERSE 12 One woe is past; and, behold, there come two woes more hereafter. 13 And the sixth angel sounded, and I heard a voice from the four horns of the golden altar which is before God, 14 saying to the sixth angel which had the trumpet, Loose the four angels which are bound in the great river Euphrates. 15 And the four angels were loosed, which were prepared for an hour, and a day, and a month, and a year, for to slay the third part of men.

The Sixth Trumpet.—"The first woe was to continue from the rise of Mahometanism until the end of the five months. Then the first woe was to end, and the second begin. And when the sixth angel sounded, it was commanded to take off the restraints which had been imposed on the nation, by which they were restricted to the work of *tormenting* men, and their commission extended to slay the third part of men. This command came from the four horns of the golden altar."[26]

---

[24] Josiah Litch, *Prophetic Expositions*, Vol. II, p. 180.
[25] *Ibid.*, p. 181.
[26] *Ibid.*, p. 182.

The Four Angels.—These are the four principal sultanies of which the Ottoman Empire was composed, located in the country watered by the Euphrates. These sultanies were situated at Aleppo, Iconium, Damascus, and Bagdad. Previously they had been restrained; but God commanded, and they were loosed.

Late in the year 1448, as the close of the 150-year period approached, John Palæologus died without leaving a son to follow him on the throne of the Eastern Empire. His brother Constantine, the lawful successor, would not venture to ascend the throne without the consent of the Turkish sultan. Ambassadors therefore went to Adrianople, received the approbation of the sultan, and returned with gifts for the new sovereign. Early in the year 1449, under these ominous circumstances, Constantine, the last of the Greek emperors, was crowned.

The historian Gibbon tells the story:

"On the decease of John Palæologus, . . . the royal family, by the death of Andronicus and the monastic profession of Isidore, was reduced to three princes, Constantine, Demetrius, and Thomas, the surviving sons of the emperor Manuel. Of these the first and the last were far distant in the Morea. . . . The empress-mother, the senate and soldiers, the clergy and people, were unanimous in the cause of the lawful successor: and the despot Thomas, who, ignorant of the change, accidentally returned to the capital, asserted with becoming zeal the interest of his absent brother. An ambassador, the historian Phranza, was immediately dispatched to the court of Adrianople. Amurath received him with honor and dismissed him with gifts; but the gracious approbation of the Turkish sultan announced his supremacy, and the approaching downfall of the Eastern empire. By the hands of two illustrious deputies, the Imperial crown was placed at Sparta on the head of Constantine."[27]

---

[27] Edward Gibbon, *The Decline and Fall of the Roman Empire*, Vol. VI, chap. 67, p. 365.

"Let this historical fact be carefully examined in connection with the prediction [given] above. This was not a violent assault made on the Greeks, by which their empire was overthrown and their independence taken away, but simply a voluntary surrender of that independence into the hands of the Turks, by saying, 'I cannot reign unless you permit.' "[28]

The four angels were loosed for an hour, a day, a month, and a year, to slay the third part of men. This period, during which Ottoman supremacy was to exist, amounts to three hundred ninety-one years and fifteen days. Thus: A prophetic year is three hundred and sixty prophetic days, or three hundred and sixty literal years; a prophetic month, thirty prophetic days, is thirty literal years; one prophetic day is one literal year; and an hour, or the twenty-fourth part of a prophetic day, would be a twenty-fourth part of a literal year, or fifteen days; the whole amounting to three hundred and ninety-one years and fifteen days.

"But although the four angels were thus loosed by the voluntary submission of the Greeks, yet another doom awaited the seat of empire. Amurath, the sultan to whom the submission of Deacozes was made, and by whose permission he reigned in Constantinople, soon after died, and was succeeded in the empire, in 1451, by Mahomet II, who set his heart on Constantinople, and determined to make it a prey.

"He accordingly made preparations for besieging and taking the city. The siege commenced on the 6th of April, 1453, and ended in the taking of the city, and death of the last of the Constantines, on the 16th day of May following. And the eastern city of the Cæsars became the seat of the Ottoman Empire."[29]

The arms and mode of warfare which were used in the siege in which Constantinople was to be overthrown and held in subjection were, as we shall see, distinctly noticed by the prophet.

---

[28] Josiah Litch, *Prophetic Expositions*, Vol. II, pp. 182, 183.
[29] *Ibid.*, p. 183.

 R. M. ELDRIDGE, ARTIST

THE FALL OF CONSTANTINOPLE IN 1453

With the capture of Constantinople by the Turks, the city of Constantine became the seat of the Ottoman Empire.

VERSE 16 And the number of the army of the horsemen were two hundred thousand thousand: and I heard the number of them.

"Innumerable hordes of horses, and them that sat on them! Gibbon describes the first invasion of the Roman territories by the Turks thus: 'The myriads of Turkish horse overspread a frontier of six hundred miles, from Tauris to Azeroum, and the blood of 130,000 Christians was a grateful sacrifice to the Arabian prophet.' Whether the number is designed to convey the idea of any definite number, the reader must judge. Some suppose 200,000 twice told is meant, and then, following some historians, find that number of Turkish warriors in the siege of Constantinople. Some think 200,000,000 to mean all the Turkish warriors during the 391 years fifteen days of their triumph over the Greeks."[30] Nothing can be affirmed on the point. And it is not at all essential.

VERSE 17 And thus I saw the horses in the vision, and them that sat on them, having breastplates of fire, and of jacinth, and brimstone: and the heads of the horses were as the heads of lions; and out of their mouths issued fire and smoke and brimstone.

The first part of this description may have reference to the appearance of these horsemen. Fire, representing a color, stands for red, "as red as fire" being a frequent term of expression; jacinth, or hyacinth, for blue; and brimstone, for yellow. These colors greatly predominated in the dress of these warriors; so that the description, according to this view, would be accurately met in the Turkish uniform, which was composed largely of red, or scarlet, blue, and yellow. The heads of the horses were in appearance as the heads of lions, to denote their strength, courage, and fierceness; while the last part of the verse undoubtedly has reference to the use of gunpowder and firearms for purposes of war, which were then but recently introduced. As the Turks discharged their firearms on horseback, it would appear to the distant beholder that the fire, smoke, and brimstone issued out of the horses' mouths.

---

[30] *Ibid.*, pp. 183, 184.

Quite an agreement exists among commentators in applying the prophecy concerning the fire, smoke, and brimstone to the use of gunpowder by the Turks in their warfare against the Eastern Empire.[31] But they generally allude simply to the heavy ordnance, the large cannon, employed by that power; whereas the prophecy mentions especially the "horses," and the fire "issuing from their mouths," as though smaller arms were used, and used on horseback. Barnes thinks this was the case; and a statement from Gibbon confirms this view. He says: "The incessant volleys of lances and arrows were accompanied with the smoke, the sound, and the fire of their musketry and cannon."[32] Here is good historical evidence that muskets were used by the Turks; and, secondly, it is undisputed that in their general warfare they fought principally on horseback. The inference is therefore well supported that they used firearms on horseback, accurately fulfilling the prophecy, according to the illustration above referred to.

Respecting the use of firearms by the Turks in their campaign against Constantinople, Elliott thus speaks:

"It was to 'the fire and the smoke and the sulphur,' to the artillery and firearms of Mahomet, that the killing of the third part of men, *i. e.*, the capture of Constantinople, and by consequence the destruction of the Greek Empire, was owing. Eleven hundred years and more had now elapsed since her foundation by Constantine. In the course of them, Goths, Huns, Avars, Persians, Bulgarians, Saracens, Russians, and indeed the Ottoman Turks themselves, had made their hostile assaults, or laid siege against it. But the fortifications were impregnable by them. Constantinople survived, *and with it the Greek Empire.* Hence the anxiety of the sultan Mahomet to find that which would remove the obstacle. 'Canst thou cast a cannon,' was his question to the founder of cannon that deserted to him, 'of size sufficient to batter down the wall of

[31] See notes on Revelation 9: 17 in Adam Clarke, *Commentary on the New Testament*, Vol. II, p. 1003; Albert Barnes, *Notes on Revelation*, p. 264; *The Cottage Bible*, Vol. II, p. 1399.

[32] Edward Gibbon, *The Decline and Fall of the Roman Empire*, Vol. VI, chap. 68, p. 388.

Constantinople?' Then the foundry was established at Adrianople, the cannon cast, the artillery prepared, and the siege began.

"It well deserves remark, how Gibbon, always the unconscious commentator on the Apocalyptic prophecy, puts this new instrumentality of war into the foreground of his picture, in his eloquent and striking narrative of the final catastrophe of the Greek Empire. In preparation for it, he gives the history of the recent invention of gunpowder, 'that mixture of saltpeter, sulphur, and charcoal;' tells, as before said, of the foundry of the cannon at Adrianople; then, in the progress of the siege itself, describes how 'the volleys of lances and arrows were accompanied with the smoke, the sound, and the fire of the musketry and cannon;' how 'the long order of Turkish artillery was pointed against the walls, fourteen batteries thundering at once on the most accessible places;' how 'the fortifications which had stood for ages against hostile violence were dismantled on all sides by the Ottoman cannon, many breaches opened, and near the gate of St. Romanus, four towers leveled with the ground:' how, 'as from the lines, the galleys, and the bridge, the Ottoman artillery thundered on all sides, the camp and city, the Greeks and the Turks, were involved in a cloud of smoke, which could only be dispelled by the final deliverance or destruction of the Roman Empire:' and how the besiegers at length 'rushing through the breaches,' 'Constantinople was irretrievably subdued, her empire subverted, and her religion trampled in the dust by the Moslem conquerors.' I say it well deserves observation how markedly and strikingly Gibbon attributes the capture of the city, and so the destruction of the empire, to the Ottoman artillery. For what is it but a comment on the words of the prophecy? 'By these three was the third part of men killed, by the fire, and by the smoke, and by the sulphur, which issued out of their mouths.' "[33]

---

[33] Edward B. Elliott, *Horæ Apocalypticæ*, Vol. I, pp. 478, 479.

VERSE 18 By these three was the third part of men killed, by the fire, and by the smoke, and by the brimstone, which issued out of their mouths. 19 For their power is in their mouth, and in their tails: for their tails were like unto serpents, and had heads, and with them they do hurt.

These verses express the deadly effect of the new mode of warfare introduced. It was by means of these agents—gunpowder, firearms, and cannon—that Constantinople was finally overcome, and given into the hands of the Turks.

In addition to the fire, smoke, and brimstone, which apparently issued out of their mouths, it is said that their power was also in their tails. The meaning of the expression appears to be that horses' tails were the symbol, or emblem, of their authority. It is a remarkable fact that the horse's tail is a well-known Turkish standard, a symbol of office and authority. The image before the mind of John would seem to have been that he saw the horses belching out fire and smoke, and, what was equally strange, he saw that their power of spreading desolation was connected with the tails of the horses. Anyone looking on a body of cavalry with such banners, or ensigns, would be struck with this unusual or remarkable appearance, and would speak of their banners as concentrating and directing their power.

This supremacy of the Mohammedans over the Greeks was to continue, as already noticed, three hundred and ninety-one years and fifteen days. "Commencing when the one hundred and fifty years ended in 1449, the period would end August 11, 1840. Judging from the manner of the commencement of the Ottoman supremacy, that it was by a voluntary acknowledgment on the part of the Greek emperor that he only reigned by permission of the Turkish sultan, we should naturally conclude that the fall or departure of the Ottoman independence would be brought about in the same way; that at the end of the specified period [that is, on the 11th of August, 1840] the sultan would voluntarily surrender his independence into the hands of the Christian powers,"[34] just as he had, three hun-

[34] Josiah Litch, *Prophetic Expositions*, Vol. II, p. 189.

dred ninety-one years and fifteen days before, received it from the hands of the Christian emperor, Constantine XIII

This conclusion was reached, and this application of the prophecy was made by Josiah Litch in 1838, two years before the expected event was to occur. In that year he predicted that the Turkish power would be overthrown "in A. D. 1840, sometime in the month of August;"[35] but a few days before the fulfillment of the prophecy he concluded more definitely from his study that the period allotted to the Turks would come to an end on August 11, 1840. It was then purely a matter of calculation on the prophetic periods of Scripture. It is proper to inquire whether such events did take place according to the calculation. The matter sums itself up in the following inquiry:

When Did Mohammedan Independence in Constantinople End?—For several years previous to 1840, the sultan had been embroiled in war with Mehemet Ali, pasha of Egypt. "In 1838 there was a threatening of war between the sultan and his Egyptian vassal had he not been restrained by the influence of the foreign ambassadors. . . . In 1839 hostilities were again commenced, and were prosecuted until, in a general battle between the armies of the sultan and Mehemet, the sultan's army was entirely cut up and destroyed, and his fleet taken by Mehemet and carried into Egypt. So completely had the sultan's fleet been reduced, that, when hostilities commenced in August, he had only two first-rates and three frigates as the sad remains of the once powerful Turkish fleet. This fleet Mehemet positively refused to give up and return to the sultan, and declared if the powers attempted to take it from him, he would burn it. In this posture affairs stood, when, in 1840, England, Russia, Austria, and Prussia interposed, and determined on a settlement of the difficulty; for it was evident, if let alone, Mehemet would soon become master of the sultan's throne."[36]

---

[35] Josiah Litch, *The Probability of the Second Coming of Christ About A.D. 1843*, p. 157.
[36] *Ibid.*, pp. 192, 193.

The sultan accepted this intervention of the great powers, and thus made a voluntary surrender of the question into their hands. A conference of these powers was held in London, the Sheik Effendi Bey Likgis being present as Ottoman plenipotentiary. An agreement was drawn up to be presented to the pasha of Egypt, whereby the sultan was to offer him the hereditary government of Egypt, and all that part of Syria extending from the Gulf of Suez to the Lake of Tiberias, together with the province of Acre, for life; he on his part to evacuate all other parts of the sultan's dominions then occupied by him, and to return the Ottoman fleet. In case he refused this offer from the sultan, the four powers were to take the matter into their own hands, and use such other means to bring him to terms as they should see fit.

It is obvious that as soon as this ultimatum should be placed under the jurisdiction of Mehemet Ali, pasha of Egypt, the matter would be forever beyond the control of the sultan, and the disposal of his affairs would, from that moment, be in the hands of foreign powers. The sultan dispatched Rifat Bey on a government steamer to Alexandria, to communicate the ultimatum to Mehemet Ali. The ultimatum was placed at his disposal *on the eleventh day of August*, 1840! On the same day, in Constantinople, a note was addressed by the sultan to the ambassadors of the four powers, inquiring what plan was to be adopted in case the pasha should refuse to comply with the terms of the ultimatum, to which they made answer that provision had been made, and *there was no necessity of his alarming himself about any contingency that might arise*.

The facts are substantiated by the following quotations:

"By the French steamer of the 24th, we have advices from Egypt to the 16th. They show no alteration in the resolution of the Pacha. Confiding in the valor of his Arab army, and in the strength of the fortifications which defend his capital, he seems determined to abide by the last alternative; and as recourse to this, therefore, is now inevitable, all hope may be considered as at an end of a termination of the affair without bloodshed. Immediately on the arrival of the Cyclops steamer with the news of the convention of the *four powers*, Mehemet Ali, it is stated, had quitted Alexandria, to make a short tour through Lower Egypt. The object of his absenting himself at such a moment being partly to avoid conferences with the European consuls, but principally to endeavor, by his own presence, to arouse the fanaticism of the Bedouin tribes, and facilitate the raising of his new levies. During the interval of this absence, the *Turkish government steamer, which had reached Alexandria on the 11th, with the envoy Rifat Bey on board*, had been by his orders placed in quarantine, and she was not released from it till the 16th. Previous, however, to the poet's* [boat's] leaving, and on the very day on which he [she] had been admitted to pratique, the above-named functionary had an audience of the Pacha, and had communicated to him the command of the Sultan, with respect to the evacuation of the Syrian provinces, appointing another audience for the next day, when, in the presence of the consuls of the European powers, he would receive from him his definite answer, and inform him of the alternative of his refusing to obey; giving him the ten days which have been allotted him by the convention to decide on the course he should think fit to adopt."[37]

The correspondent of the London *Morning Chronicle*, in a communication dated "Constantinople, August 12, 1840," says:

"I can add but little to my last letter on the subject of the plans of the Four Powers; and I believe that the details I then gave you compose everything that is yet decided on. The portion of the Pacha, as I then stated, is not to extend beyond the line of Acre, and does not include either Arabia or Candia. Egypt alone is to be hereditary in his family, and the province of Acre to be considered as a pachalik, to be governed by his

[37] London *Morning Chronicle*, September 18, 1840, extract from a correspondent's letter dated "Constantinople, August 27, 1840."

*The word "poet's" in this newspaper account is apparently a printer's error. The substitution of the word "boat's" with a change of pronouns obviously gives the correct meaning of the story.—*Editors.*

son during his lifetime, but afterwards to depend on the will of the Porte; and even this latter is only to be granted to him on the condition of his accepting these terms and delivering up the Ottoman fleet within the period of ten days. In the event of his not doing so, this pachalik is to be cut off. Egypt alone is then to be offered, with another ten days for him to deliberate on it before actual force be employed against him. The manner, however, of applying the force, should he refuse to comply with these terms—whether a simple blockade is to be established on the coast, or whether his capital is to be bombarded and his armies attacked in the Syrian provinces—is the point which still remains to be learned; *nor does a note delivered yesterday by the four ambassadors, in answer to a question put to them by the Porte, as to the plan to be adopted in such an event, throw the least light on this subject. It simply states that provision had been made, and there was no necessity for the Divan alarming itself about any contingency that might afterward arise.*"[38]

Let us analyze the foregoing quotations:

First.—The ultimatum reached Alexandria on August 11, 1840.

Second.—The letter of the correspondent of the London *Morning Chronicle* is dated August 12, 1840.

Third.—The correspondent states that the question of the Sublime Porte was put to the representatives of the four great powers, and the answer received "*yesterday*." So in his own capital, "*yesterday*" the Sublime Porte applied to the ambassadors of the four Christian powers of Europe as to what measures had been taken in reference to a circumstance vitally affecting his empire; and was told that "*provision had been made*," but he could not know what it was; and that he need not give himself any alarm "about any contingency which might arise"! From that day, "yesterday," *which was August 11, 1840*—they, the four Christian powers of Europe, and not he, would manage that.

---

[38] *Ibid.*, September 3, 1840.

On August 11, 1840, the period of three hundred ninety-one years and fifteen days, allotted to the continuance of the Ottoman power, ended; and *where was the sultan's independence?*—GONE! Who had the supremacy of the Ottoman empire in their hands?—The *four great powers;* and that empire has existed ever since only by the *sufferance* of these Christian powers. Thus was the prophecy fulfilled to the very letter.

From the first publication of the calculation of this matter in 1838, before referred to, the time set for the fulfillment of the prophecy was watched by thousands with intense interest. The exact accomplishment of the event predicted, showing, as it did, the right application of the prophecy, gave a mighty impetus to the great advent movement then beginning to attract the attention of the world.

VERSE 20 And the rest of the men which were not killed by these plagues yet repented not of the works of their hands, that they should not worship devils, and idols of gold, and silver, and brass, and stone, and of wood: which neither can see, nor hear, nor walk: 21 neither repented they of their murders, nor of their sorceries, nor of their fornication, nor of their thefts.

God designs that men shall make a note of His judgments, and receive the lessons He thereby designs to convey. But how slow they are to learn, and how blind to the indications of providence! The events that occurred under the sixth trumpet constituted the second woe, yet these judgments led to no improvement in the manners and morals of men. Those who escaped them learned nothing by their manifestation in the earth.

The hordes of Saracens and Turks were let loose as a scourge and punishment upon apostate Christendom. Men suffered the punishment, but learned no lesson from it.

 T. K. MARTIN, ARTIST

"A LITTLE BOOK OPEN"

"The voice . . . said, Go and take the little book which is open in the hand of the angel." Revelation 10: 8.

CHAPTER X

THE WORLD-WIDE PROCLAMATION OF THE SECOND ADVENT

VERSE 1 And I saw another mighty angel come down from heaven, clothed with a cloud: and a rainbow was upon his head, and his face was as it were the sun, and his feet as pillars of fire: 2 and he had in his hand a little book open: and he set his right foot upon the sea, and his left foot on the earth.

IN THIS scripture we have another instance in which the consecutive line of thought is for a time interrupted. Revelation 9 closed with the events of the sixth trumpet. The sounding of the seventh trumpet is not introduced until we reach Revelation 11: 15. All of chapter 10 and a part of chapter 11, therefore, come in parenthetically between the sixth and seventh trumpets. That which is particularly connected with the sounding of the sixth trumpet is recorded in chapter 9. The prophet has other events to introduce before the opening of another trumpet, and takes occasion to do it in the scripture which intervenes to Revelation 11: 15. Among these is the prophecy of chapter 10. Let us first look at the chronology of the message of this angel.

The Little Book.—"He had in his hand a little book *open.*" We may infer from this language that this book was at some time closed. We read in Daniel of a book which was closed and sealed to a certain time: "Thou, O Daniel, shut up the words, and seal the book, even to the time of the end: many shall run to and fro, and knowledge shall be increased." Daniel 12: 4. Since this book was closed only *until* the time of the end, it follows that *at* the time of the end the book would be opened. As this closing was mentioned in prophecy, it would be but reasonable to expect that in the predictions of events to take place at the time of the end, the *opening* of this book would also be mentioned. There is no book spoken of as closed and sealed except the book of Daniel's prophecy, and there is no account of the opening of that book unless it be here in Revelation 10. We see, furthermore, that in both places the contents ascribed to the book are the same. The book which Daniel had directions to close and seal had reference to time: "How long shall it be to the end of these wonders?" Daniel 12: 6. When the angel of this chapter comes down with the little book open, on which he bases his proclamation, he gives a message in relation to time, as will be seen in verse 6. Nothing more is required to show that both expressions refer to one book, and to prove that the little book which the angel had in his hand, open, was the book referred to in the prophecy of Daniel.

An important point is now determined in our endeavor to settle the chronology of this angel. We have seen that the prophecy, especially the prophetic periods of Daniel, were not to be opened until the time of the end. If this is the book which the angel had in his hand *open*, it follows that he proclaims his message after the time when the book should be opened, or somewhere this side of the beginning of the time of the end. All that now remains on this point is to ascertain when the time of the end began, and the book of Daniel itself furnishes data from which this can be done. In Daniel 11: 30, the papal power is brought to view. In verse 35 we read, "Some of them of understanding shall fall, to try them, and to purge, and to make them white, *even to the time of the end*." Here is the period of the supremacy of the little horn, during which time the saints, times, and laws were to be given into his hand, and from him suffer fearful persecutions. This is declared to reach to the time of the end. This period ended A. D. 1798, when the 1260 years of papal supremacy expired. There the time of the end began, and the book was opened. Since that time, many have run to and fro, and knowledge on these prophetic subjects has marvelously increased. (See comments on Daniel 12: 4.)

The chronology of the events of Revelation 10 is further ascertained from the fact that this angel appears to be identical with the first angel of Revelation 14. The points of identity between them are easily seen: They both have a special message to proclaim. They both utter their proclamation with a loud voice. They both use similar language, referring to the Creator as the maker of heaven and earth, the sea, and the things that are therein. And they both proclaim time, one swearing that time should be no more, and the other proclaiming that the hour of God's judgment has come.

But the message of Revelation 14: 6 is located this side of the beginning of the time of the end. It is a proclamation of the hour of God's judgment come, and hence must have its application in the last generation. Paul did not preach the hour of judgment come. Martin Luther and his coadjutors did not preach it. Paul reasoned of a judgment to come, indefinitely future, and Luther placed it at least three hundred years beyond his day. Moreover, Paul warns the church against preaching that the hour of God's judgment has come, until a certain time. He says: "Now we beseech you, brethren, by the coming of our Lord Jesus Christ, and by our gathering together unto Him, that ye be not soon shaken in mind, or be troubled, neither by spirit, nor by word, nor by letter as from us, as that the day of Christ is at hand. Let no man deceive you by any means: for that day shall not come, except there come a falling away first, and that *man of sin be revealed.*" 2 Thessalonians 2: 1-3. Here Paul introduces to our view the man of sin, the little horn, or the papacy, and covers with a caution the whole period of his supremacy, which, as already noticed, continued 1260 years, ending in 1798.

In 1798, therefore, the restriction against proclaiming the day of Christ at hand ceased. In 1798 the time of the end began, and the seal was taken from the little book. Since that time, therefore, the angel of Revelation 14 has gone forth proclaiming that the hour of God's judgment is come. It is since that time, too, that the angel of chapter 10 has taken his stand on sea and land, and sworn that time shall be no more. Of their identity there can now be no question. All the arguments which go to locate the one are equally effective in the case of the other.

We need not enter into any extended argument here to show that the present generation is witnessing the fulfillment of these two prophecies. In the preaching of the second advent, more especially from 1840 to 1844, began their full and circumstantial accomplishment. The position of this angel, one foot upon the sea and the other on the land, denotes the wide extent of his proclamation by sea and by land. Had this message been designed for only one country, it would have been sufficient for the angel to take his position on the land only. But he has one foot upon the sea, from which we may infer that his message would cross the ocean, and extend to the various nations and divisions of the globe. This inference is strengthened by the fact that the advent proclamation above referred to did go to every missionary station in the world. More on this will be found in comments on Revelation 14.

VERSE 3 And cried with a loud voice, as when a lion roareth: and when he had cried, seven thunders uttered their voices. 4 And when the seven thunders had uttered their voices, I was about to write: and I heard a voice from heaven saying unto me, Seal up those things which the seven thunders uttered, and write them not.

The Seven Thunders.—It would be vain to speculate upon the seven thunders, in hope of gaining a definite knowledge of what they uttered. Something evidently was uttered which it would not be well for the church to know. We must acquiesce in the directions given to John concerning them, and leave them where he left them, sealed up, unwritten, and consequently to us unknown.

VERSE 5 And the angel which I saw stand upon the sea and upon the earth lifted up his hand to heaven, 6 and sware by Him that liveth forever and ever, who created heaven, and the things that therein are, and the earth, and the things that therein are, and the sea, and the things which are therein, that there should be time no longer.

"*Time No Longer.*"—What is the meaning of this most solemn declaration? It cannot mean that with the message of this angel, time, as computed in this world, in comparison with eternity, should end. The next verse speaks of the *days* of the voice of the seventh angel, and Revelation 11: 15-19 gives us some of the events to take place under this trumpet in the present state. It cannot mean probationary time, for that does not cease until Christ closes His work as priest, which is not until after the seventh angel has begun to sound. (Revelation 11: 15, 19; 15: 5-8.) It must therefore mean prophetic time, for there is no other to which it can refer.

The word "time" in this verse is translated "delay" in the American Revised Version—a very unusual rendering of the Greek original χρόνος, *chronos*, "time," and the only one in the New Testament. Evidently the translators did not have *prophetic* time in mind, and could discern no other proper rendering of the word than "delay." Though by extension and implication this may be an admissible translation when the context seems to justify it, there is nothing in the context of verse 6 to call for such a rendering. In fact, the bitterness of the experience that follows the symbolic eating of the little book in verses 8-10 was for the very reason that the Lord's coming was to be *delayed* beyond the expectation of those who were looking for Him in 1844—and this for the very reason that their work of preaching the gospel was not yet finished, as clearly indicated in verse 11. Surely in an announcement given with so much emphasis as the one recorded in verse 6, if *delay* were meant instead of (prophetic) *time*, the regular word for "delay," ἀναβολή, *anabole*, would be used, as it is in Acts 25: 17, or ὀκνέω, *okneo*, as in Acts 9: 38. It is true that a verb derived from *chronos*, namely, χρονίζει, *chronizei*, is used in the sense of "delay," as in Matthew 24: 48 and Luke 12: 45. But *chronizei* means simply "pass time," or "letting time pass," and gains its meaning of "delay" in this way. The word *chronos*, however, denotes "time" in the absolute, and there is every reason to believe this is its meaning (in a prophetic sense) in verse 6; and that since it is used in a prediction connected with a very important prophecy, we are justified in understanding it to mean prophetic

AMERICAN BIBLE SOCIETY

THE BLESSED WORD OF GOD

Millions in all nations may now read for themselves the glad news of salvation.

time. In other words, prophetic time shall be no more—not that time should never be used in a prophetic sense, for the "days of the voice of the seventh angel" spoken of immediately after, doubtless mean the *years* of the seventh angel. It means, rather, that no prophetic period should extend beyond the time of this message. Arguments on the prophetic periods, showing that the longest ones did not extend beyond the autumn of 1844, will be found in remarks on Daniel 8: 14.

VERSE 7 But in the days of the voice of the seventh angel, when he shall begin to sound, the mystery of God should be finished, as He hath declared to His servants the prophets.

The Seventh Trumpet.—This seventh trumpet is not that which is spoken of in 1 Corinthians 15: 52 as the last trump, which wakes the sleeping dead; but it is the seventh in the series of the seven trumpets, and like the others of this series, occupies prophetic days (years) in sounding. In the days when he shall begin to sound, the mystery of God shall be finished. Not in the day when he shall begin to sound, not in the very beginning of his sounding, but in the early years of his sounding, the mystery of God shall be finished.

From the events to take place under the sounding of the seventh trumpet, its beginning may be located with sufficient definiteness at the close of the prophetic periods in 1844. Subsequent to that date the mystery of God is to be finished. The great event, whatever it is, is right upon us. Some closing and decisive work, with whatever of importance and solemnity it bears in its train, is near at hand. There is an importance connected with the finishing of any of the works of God. Such an act marks a solemn and important era. Our Saviour, when dying upon the cross, cried, "It is finished." John 19: 30. When the great work of mercy for fallen man is completed, it will be announced by a voice from the throne of God, proclaiming in tones like thunder the solemn sentence, "It is done!" Revelation 16: 17. It is therefore no uncalled-for solicitude which prompts us to inquire what bearing such events have upon our eternal hopes and interests. When we read of the finishing of the mystery of God, we ask what that mystery is, and in what its finishing consists.

"*The Mystery of God.*"—A few direct testimonies from God's word, which has been given as a lamp to our feet, will show what this mystery is. "Having made known unto us the mystery of His will, according to His good pleasure which He hath purposed in Himself: that in the dispensation of the fullness of times He might gather together in one all things in Christ, both which are in heaven, and which are on earth; even in Him." Ephesians 1: 9, 10. Here God's purpose to gather together all things in Christ is called the "mystery" of His will. This is accomplished through the gospel. "For me [Paul asks that prayers be made], that utterance may be given unto me, that I may open my mouth boldly, to make known the mystery of the gospel." Ephesians 6: 19. Here the gospel is declared plainly to be a mystery. In Colossians 4: 3, it is called the mystery of Christ. Again, "How that by revelation He made known unto me the mystery (as I wrote afore in few words), . . . that the Gentiles should be fellow heirs, and of the same body, and partakers of His promise in Christ by the gospel." Ephesians 3: 3, 6. Paul here declares that the mystery was made known to him by revelation, as he had before written. In this he refers to his Epistle to the Galatians, where he recorded what had been given him "by revelation," in these words: "I certify you, brethren, that the *gospel* which was preached of me is not after man. For I neither received it of man, neither was I taught it, but *by the revelation of Jesus Christ.*" Galatians 1: 11, 12. Here Paul tells us plainly that what he received through revelation was the gospel. In Ephesians 3: 3, he calls it the *mystery* made known to him by revelation, as he had written before. The Epistle to the Galatians was written about A. D. 54, and that to the Ephesians about A. D. 65.

In view of these testimonies, few will be disposed to deny that the mystery of God is the gospel. It is the same, then, as if the angel had declared, In the days of the voice of the seventh angel, when he shall begin to sound, the *gospel* shall be finished. But what is the finishing of the gospel? Let us first inquire for what it was given. It was given to take out from the nations a people for God's name. (Acts 15: 14.) Its finishing must, as a matter of course, be the close of this work. It will be finished when the number of God's people is made up, when mercy ceases to be offered, and probation closes.

The subject is now before us in all its magnitude. Such is the momentous work to be accomplished in the days of the voice of the seventh angel, whose trumpet notes have been reverberating through the world since the memorable epoch of 1844. God is not slack. His work is not uncertain. Are we ready for the issue?

VERSE 8 And the voice which I heard from heaven spake unto me again, and said, Go and take the little book which is open in the hand of the angel which standeth upon the sea and upon the earth. 9 And I went unto the angel, and said unto him, Give me the little book. And he said unto me, Take it, and eat it up; and it shall make thy belly bitter, but it shall be in thy mouth sweet as honey. 10 And I took the little book out of the angel's hand, and ate it up; and it was in my mouth sweet as honey: and as soon as I had eaten it, my belly was bitter.

John is here brought in to act a part as a representative of the church, probably on account of the succeeding peculiar experience of the church, which the Lord of the prophecy would cause to be put on record, but which could not well be presented under the symbol of an angel. When only a straightforward proclamation is brought to view, angels may be used as symbols to represent the religious teachers who proclaim that message, as in Revelation 14. But when some particular experience of the church is to be presented, it could most appropriately be set forth in the person of some member of the human family. Hence John is himself called upon to act a part in this symbolic representation. This being the case, the angel who here appeared to John may represent that divine messenger, who has charge of this message; or he may be introduced for the purpose of representing the nature of the message, and the source from which it comes.

The Sweet and the Bitter.—The angel of this chapter has in his hand "a little book open." In comments on verse 2 we have shown this "little book" to be the book of Daniel which was "sealed till the time of the end." Daniel 12: 9. It would be opened when the prophecies of the book were to be understood.

In comments on Daniel 8: 14 it has been shown that the work of cleansing the heavenly sanctuary began in 1844. Students of prophecy who made this discovery understood the sanctuary to mean the earth, and mistakenly regarded this prediction to mean that the Lord would come to cleanse the earth of its pollution and sin at that time.

This message of the coming of the Lord in the autumn of 1844 spread rapidly throughout America and other parts of the world. It greatly moved the hearts of men and stirred the Protestant churches of that time. Tens of thousands looked for the coming of the Lord at the close of the great prophetic period of 2300 days in 1844. (See Daniel 8: 14; 9: 25-27.) Every preparation was made to greet Him with great joy and gladness, and then came the bitterness of disappointment, for the Lord did not come. Their mistake was in their misunderstanding of the *event* to take place at the end of this prophetic period, and not in their reckoning of the *time*.

Accordingly, we read in verse 10, "The little book . . . was . . . in my mouth sweet as honey: and as soon as I had eaten it, my belly was bitter."

More Work to Be Done.—The disappointment, however, was no evidence that the Lord was not in the movement, for in this tenth chapter of Revelation He anticipates this very experience, and in the last verse points His people to a task of world-wide extent He had yet for them to perform prior to His glorious appearing, for their work had not yet been finished. This work is brought to view quite fully in the three angels' messages of the fourteenth chapter. (See similar experiences in Jeremiah 15: 16-18; Ezekiel 3: 1-3, 10.)

VERSE 11 And he said unto me, Thou must prophecy again before many peoples, and nations, and tongues, and kings.

John, standing as the representative of the church, here receives from the angel another commission. Another message joining the first and second angels' messages, is to go forth to the world. In other words, we have here a prophecy of the third angel's message, now, as we believe, in process of fulfillment. Neither will this work be done in a corner, for it is to go before "many peoples, and nations, and tongues, and kings," as will be clearly seen in our study of Revelation 14: 6-12.

S. M. HARLAN

THE BLESSED BOOK

"We have also a more sure word of prophecy; whereunto ye do well that ye take heed, as unto a light that shineth in a dark place." 2 Peter 1: 19.

CHAPTER XI

THE BATTLE BETWEEN THE BIBLE AND ATHEISM

VERSE 1 And there was given me a reed like unto a rod: and the angel stood, saying, Rise, and measure the temple of God, and the altar, and them that worship therein. 2 But the court which is without the temple leave out, and measure it not; for it is given unto the Gentiles: and the holy city shall they tread under foot forty and two months.

WE HERE have a continuation of the instruction which the angel began giving to John in the preceding chapter; hence these verses properly belong to that chapter, and should not be separated by the present division. In the last verse of Revelation 10, the angel gave a new commission to John as a representative of the church. In other words, as already shown, we have in that verse a prophecy of the third angel's message. The message is connected with the temple of God in heaven, and is designed to fit a class of people as worshipers.

The Measuring Rod.—The temple here cannot mean the church, for the church is brought to view in connection with this temple as "them that worship therein." The temple is therefore the literal temple in heaven, and the worshipers the true church on earth. But of course these worshipers are not to be measured in the sense of ascertaining the height and girth of each one in feet and inches. They are to be measured as *worshipers*, and character can be measured only by some standard of right, a law or principle of action. We are thus brought to the conclusion that the ten commandments, the standard which God has given by which to measure "the whole duty of man," are a part of the measuring rod put by the angel into the hands of John. In the fulfillment of this prophecy under the third angel's message, this very law has been put in a special way into the hands of the church. This is the standard by which the worshipers of the true God are now to be tested.

Seeing now what it is to measure those who worship in the temple, we inquire, What is meant by measuring the temple? To measure any object requires that special attention be given to that object. The call to rise and measure the temple of God is a prophetic command to the church to give the subject of the temple, or sanctuary, a special examination. But how is this to be done with a measuring rod given to the church? With the ten commandments alone we could not do it. When we take the entire message, however, we find ourselves led by it to an examination of the sanctuary on high, with the commandments of God and the ministration of Christ. Hence we conclude that the measuring rod, taken as a whole, is the special message now given to the church, which embraces the great truths peculiar to this time, including the ten commandments.

By this message, our attention has been called to the temple above, and through it the light and truth on this subject has come out. Thus we measure the temple and the altar, or the ministration connected with the temple, the work and the position of our great High Priest; and we measure the worshipers with that part of the rod which relates to character, the ten commandments.

"The court which is without the temple leave out." This must be interpreted to mean that the attention of the church is now directed to the inner temple and the service there. Matters pertaining to the court are of less consequence now. It is given to the Gentiles. That the court refers to this earth is proved thus: The court is the place where the victims were slain whose blood was to be ministered in the sanctuary. The antitypical victim must die in the antitypical court, and He died on Calvary in Judea. The Gentiles being thus introduced, the attention of the prophet is directed to the great feature of Gentile apostasy, the treading down of the holy city forty and two months during that time. Thus we are carried back into the past by an easy and natural transition, and our attention is called to a new series of events.

VERSE 3 And I will give power unto My two witnesses, and they shall prophesy a thousand two hundred and threescore days, clothed in sackcloth.

The period of "a thousand two hundred and three score days" is variously referred to in the Scriptures. It appears in three forms:

As 1260 days in this verse and Revelation 12: 6.

As 42 months in Revelation 11: 2 and 13: 5.

As 3½ times in Daniel 7: 25 and 12: 7, and Revelation 12: 14.

These all refer to the same period and can easily be calculated. A time is a year, as is evident from Daniel 11: 13, marginal reading. A year has twelve months, and a Biblical month contains thirty days. Thus we have the following:

1 year of 12 months at 30 days	- -	360 days
3½ years, or times, of 360 days	- -	1260 days
42 months of 30 days	- - -	1260 days

A year made up of 12 months will readily be conceded, but that the month has 30 days needs perhaps to be demonstrated. This can readily be seen by referring to the record of the flood in Genesis 7 and 8. There we learn the following:

1. That the flood came on the seventeenth day of the second month. (Genesis 7: 11.)

2. That the waters subsided on the seventeenth day of the seventh month. (Genesis 8: 4.)

3. That the flood continued for five months—from the second to the seventh month.

Reference to Genesis 7: 24 reveals the fact that "the waters prevailed upon the earth a hundred and fifty days." Our calculation showed five months. This text mentions 150 days; hence we have five months equaling 150 days, or 30 days to a month.

Thus we have a definite measure for calculating the prophetic periods, bearing in mind that in prophecy a day is equal to a year of ordinary time.

The Two Witnesses.—During this time of 1260 years the witnesses are in a state of sackcloth, or obscurity, and God gives them power to endure and maintain their testimony through that dark and dismal period. But who or what are these witnesses?

VERSE 4 These are the two olive trees, and the two candlesticks standing before the God of the earth.

Evident allusion is here made to Zechariah 4: 11-14, where it is implied that the two olive trees are taken to represent the word of God. David testifies, "The entrance of Thy words giveth light;" and, "Thy word is a lamp unto my feet, and a light unto my path." Psalm 119: 130, 105. Written testimony is stronger than oral. Jesus declared of the Old Testament Scriptures, "They are they which testify of Me." John 5: 39.

Says George Croly: "The 'Two Witnesses' are the Old and New Testaments. . . . The essential purpose of the Scriptures is to give *witness* to the mercy and verity of God. Our Lord commands, 'Search the Scriptures, . . . they are they which testify [bear *witness*] of Me.' This was addressed to the Jews, and described the character and office of the Old Testament. The New Testament is similarly pronounced the giver of testimony. 'This gospel of the kingdom shall be preached in all the world for a *witness* unto all nations.' (Matthew 24:14.)" [1]

These declarations and considerations are sufficient to sustain the conclusion that the Old and New Testaments are Christ's two witnesses.

VERSE 5 And if any man will hurt them, fire proceedeth out of their mouth, and devoureth their enemies: and if any man will hurt them, he must in this manner be killed.

To hurt the word of God is to oppose, corrupt, or pervert its testimony, and turn people away from it. Against those who do this work, fire proceedeth out of their mouth to devour them, that is, judgment of fire is pronounced in that word against such. It declares that they will have their punishment in the lake that burns with fire and brimstone. (Malachi 4: 1; Revelation 20: 15; 22: 18, 19.)

[1] George Croly, *The Apocalypse of St. John*, p. 164.

VERSE 6 These have power to shut heaven, that it rain not in the days of their prophecy: and have power over waters to turn them to blood, and to smite the earth with all plagues, as often as they will.

In what sense have these witnesses power to shut heaven, turn waters to blood, and bring plagues on the earth? Elijah shut heaven so that it did not rain for three years and a half, but he did it by the word of the Lord. Moses by the word of the Lord turned the waters of Egypt to blood. Just as these judgments, recorded in their testimony, have been fulfilled, so will every threatening and judgment pronounced by them against any people surely be accomplished.

"As often as they will" means that as often as judgments are recorded on their pages to take place, so often they will come to pass. An instance of this the world is yet to experience in the infliction of the seven last plagues.

VERSE 7 And when they shall have finished their testimony, the beast that ascendeth out of the bottomless pit shall make war against them, and shall overcome them, and kill them. 8 And their dead bodies shall lie in the street of the great city, which spiritually is called Sodom and Egypt, where also our Lord was crucified.

"When they shall have *finished* their testimony," that is, "in *sackcloth*." The sackcloth state ended, or as elsewhere expressed the days of persecution were shortened (Matthew 24: 22), before the period itself expired. "A 'beast' in prophecy, denotes a kingdom, or power. (See Daniel 7: 17, 23.) The question now arises, When did the sackcloth state of the witnesses close? And did such a kingdom as described make war on them at the time spoken of? If we are correct in fixing upon A. D. 538 as the time of the commencement of the sackcloth state, forty-two months being 1260 prophetic days, or years, would bring us down to A. D. 1798. About this time, then, did such a kingdom as described appear, and make war on them, etc.? Mark! this beast, or kingdom, is out of the bottomless pit—no foundation—an atheistical power— 'spiritually Egypt.' (See Exodus 5: 2: 'Pharaoh said, Who is the Lord, that I should obey His voice to let Israel go? I know not

THE GODDESS OF REASON

Throwing aside every restraint, the people of France repudiated all that pertained to God, and glorified human reason.

the Lord, neither will I let Israel go.') Here is atheism. Did any kingdom, *about* 1798 manifest the same spirit?—Yes, France; she denied the being of God in her national capacity, and made war on the 'Monarchy of heaven.' "[2]

"In the year 1793, . . . the gospel was, by a solemn act of the Legislature and the people abolished in France. The indignities offered to the actual copies of the Bible were unimportant after this; their life is in their doctrines, and the extinction of the doctrines is the extinction of the Bible. By the decree of the French Government, declaring that the nation acknowledged no God, the Old and New Testaments were *slain* throughout the limits of Republican France. But contumelies to the Sacred Books could not have been wanting, in the general plunder of every place of worship. In Lyons they were dragged at the tail of an ass in a procession through the streets. . . .

"On the 1st of November, 1793, Gobet, with the Republican priests of Paris, had thrown off the gown, and abjured Religion. On the 11th, a 'Grand Festival,' dedicated to 'Reason and Truth,' was celebrated in the Cathedral of Notre Dame, which had been desecrated, and been named 'the Temple of Reason;' a pyramid was erected in the center of the Church, surmounted by a temple, inscribed 'To philosophy.' The torch of 'Truth' was on the altar of 'Reason' spreading light, etc. The National Convention and all the authorities attended at this burlesque and insulting ceremony."[3]

Spiritual Sodom.—" 'Spiritually' this power 'is called Sodom.' What was the characteristic sin of Sodom? *Licentiousness.* Did France have this character? She did; *fornication* was established *by law* during the period spoken of. 'Spiritually' the place was 'where our Lord was crucified.' Was this true in France? It was, in more senses than one. *First*, in 1572 a plot was laid in France to destroy all the pious Huguenots;

[2] George Storrs, *Midnight Cry*, May 4, 1843, Vol. IV, Nos. 5, 6, p. 47.
[3] George Croly, *The Apocalypse of St. John*, pp. 175-177.

and in one night, *fifty thousand* of them were murdered in cold blood, and the streets of Paris literally ran with blood. Thus our Lord was 'spiritually crucified' in His members. *Again,* the watch-word and motto of the French Infidels was, 'CRUSH THE WRETCH,' meaning Christ. Thus it may be truly said, 'where our Lord was crucified.' The very spirit of the 'bottomless pit' was poured out in that wicked nation.

"But did France 'make war' on the Bible? She did; and in 1793 a decree passed the French Assembly forbidding the Bible, and under that decree the Bibles were gathered and burned, and every possible mark of contempt heaped upon them, and all the institutions of the Bible abolished; the Sabbath was blotted out, and every *tenth* day substituted for mirth and profanity. Baptism and the communion were abolished. The being of God was denied; and death pronounced to be an *eternal* sleep. The Goddess of Reason was set up, in the person of a vile woman, and publicly worshiped. Surely here is a power that exactly answers the prophecy."[4] This point will be further developed in the comments on the next verse.

VERSE 9 And they of the people and kindreds and tongues and nations shall see their dead bodies three days and a half, and shall not suffer their dead bodies to be put in graves.

"The language of this verse denotes the feelings of other nations than the one committing the outrage on the witnesses. They would see what war infidel France had made on the Bible, but would not be led nationally to engage in the wicked work, nor suffer the murdered witnesses to be *buried,* or put out of sight among themselves, though they lay dead three days and a half, that is, three years and a half, in France. No; this very attempt of France served to arouse Christians everywhere to put forth a new exertion in behalf of the Bible, as we shall presently see."[5]

---

[4] George Storrs, *Midnight Cry,* May 4, 1843, Vol. IV, Nos. 5, 6, p. 47.

[5] *Ibid.*

VERSE 10 And they that dwell upon the earth shall rejoice over them, and make merry, and shall send gifts one to another; because these two prophets tormented them that dwelt on the earth.

"This denotes the joy those felt who hated the Bible, or were tormented by it. Great was the joy of infidels everywhere for awhile. But 'the triumphing of the wicked is short;' so was it in France, for their war on the Bible and Christianity had well-nigh swallowed them all up. They set out to destroy Christ's 'two witnesses,' but they filled France with blood and horror, so that they were horror-struck at the result of their wicked deeds, and were glad to remove their impious hands from the Bible."[6]

VERSE 11 And after three days and a half the Spirit of life from God entered into them, and they stood upon their feet; and great fear fell upon them which saw them.

Witnesses Restored.—"In 1793, the decree passed the French Assembly suppressing the Bible. Just three years after, a resolution was introduced into the Assembly going to supersede the decree, and giving toleration to the Scriptures. That resolution lay on the table six months, when it was taken up, and passed without a dissenting vote. Thus, in just three years and a half, the witnesses 'stood upon their feet, and great fear fell upon them which saw them.' Nothing but the appalling results of the rejection of the Bible could have induced France to take her hands off these witnesses."[7]

"On the 17th of June, Camille Jourdan, in the 'Council of Five Hundred,' brought up the memorable report on the 'Revision of the laws relative to religious worship.' It consisted of a number of propositions, abolishing alike the Republican restrictions on Popish worship, and the Popish restrictions on Protestant.

"1. That *all* citizens might buy or hire edifices for the *free* exercise of religious worship.

---

[6] *Ibid.*

[7] *Ibid.*

"2. That *all* congregations might assemble by the sound of bells.

"3. That *no test* or *promise* of any sort unrequired from other citizens should be required of the ministers of those congregations.

"4. That any individual attempting to impede, or in any way interrupt the public worship should be fined, up to 500 livres, and not less than 50; and that if the interruption proceeded from the constituted authorities, such authorities should be fined double the sum.

"5. That entrance to assemblies for the purpose of religious worship should be free for all citizens.

"6. That all other laws concerning religious worship should be repealed.

"Those regulations, in comprehending the whole state of worship in France, were, in fact, a peculiar boon to Protestantism. Popery was already in sight of full restoration. But Protestantism, crushed under the burthen of the laws of Louis XIV, and unsupported by the popular belief, required the direct support of the state to 'stand on its feet.' The Report seems even to have had an especial view to the grievances of the Church; the old prohibitions to hold public worship, to possess places of worship, to have ingress, etc.

"From that period the Church has been free in France. . . .

"The Church and the Bible had been slain in France from November, 1793, till June, 1797. The *three years* and a *half* were expended, and the Bible, so long and so sternly repressed before, was placed in honor, and was openly the book of free Protestantism!"[8]

VERSE 12 And they heard a great voice from heaven saying unto them, Come up hither. And they ascended up to heaven in a cloud; and their enemies beheld them.

" '*Ascended up to heaven.*'—To understand this expression, see Daniel 4: 22: 'Thy greatness is grown, and *reacheth unto*

---

[8] George Croly, *The Apocalypse of St. John*, pp. 181-183.

heaven.' Here we see that the expression signifies *great exaltation.* Have the Scriptures attained to such a state of exaltation as here indicated, since France made war upon them?—They have. Shortly after, the British Bible Society was organized [1804]; then followed the American Bible Society [1816]; and these, with their almost innumerable auxiliaries, are scattering the Bible everywhere."[9] Before 1804 the Bible had been printed and circulated in fifty languages.

"Up to the end of December, 1942, the Bible in whole or in part has been translated into 1,058 languages and dialects."

No other book approaches the Bible in inexpensiveness and the number of copies circulated. The American Bible Society reported having printed and circulated, in whole or in part, 7,696,739 portions in 1940; 8,096,069, in 1941; and 6,254,642, in 1942. The British and Foreign Bible Society reported for the year ending in the middle of 1941 a circulation of 11,017,334 copies; and in 1942, 7,120,000 copies.

A conservative estimate places the number of Bibles printed annually by commercial houses at six million. Hence the annual output of Bibles and portions has reached the enormous total of from twenty-five to thirty million copies a year.

From its organization up to and including 1942, the American Bible Society had issued 321,951,266 copies; and the British and Foreign Bible Society up to March, 1942, had issued 539,664,024 copies, making a total of 861,600,000 copies put out by these two societies alone. The American Bible Society said in May, 1940: "It is estimated that nine tenths of the 2,000,000,000 people in the world might now, if they turned to the Bible, hear it read in a language they understand." The Bible is exalted as above all price, as, next to His Son, the most invaluable blessing of God to man, and as the glorious *testimony* concerning that Son. Yes; the Scriptures may truly be said to be exalted "to heaven in a cloud," a *cloud* being an emblem of heavenly elevation.

---

[9] George Storrs, *Midnight Cry,* May 4, 1843, Vol. IV, Nos. 5, 6, p. 47.

VERSE 13 And the same hour was there a great earthquake, and the tenth part of the city fell, and in the earthquake were slain of men seven thousand: and the remnant were affrighted, and gave glory to the God of heaven.

"What city? (See Revelation 17: 18: 'The *woman* which thou sawest is that *great city* which reigneth over the kings [kingdoms] of the earth.') That city is the *papal* Roman power. France is *one* of the '*ten* horns' that gave 'their power and strength unto the [*papal*] beast;' or is one of the ten kingdoms that arose out of the Western Empire of Rome, as indicated by the ten toes of Nebuchadnezzar's image, Daniel's ten-horned beast [Daniel 7: 24], and John's ten-horned dragon. [Revelation 12: 3.] France, then, was 'a tenth part of the city,' and was one of the strongest ministers of papal vengeance; but in this revolution it 'fell,' and with it fell the last *civil* messenger of papal fury. 'And in the earthquake were slain of men [margin, *names of men*] seven thousand.' France made war, in her revolution of 1798 [1789] and onward, on all titles and nobility. . . . 'And the remnant were affrighted, and gave glory to the God of heaven.' Their God-dishonoring and Heaven-defying work filled France with such scenes of blood, carnage, and horror, as made even the infidels themselves to tremble, and stand aghast; and the 'remnant' that escaped the horrors of that hour 'gave glory to God'—not willingly, but the God of heaven caused this 'wrath of man to praise Him,' by giving all the world to see that those who make war on heaven make graves for themselves; thus glory redounded to God by the very means that wicked men employed to tarnish that glory."[10]

VERSE 14 The second woe is past; and, behold, the third woe cometh quickly.

The Trumpets Resumed.—The series of seven trumpets is here again resumed. The second woe ended with the sixth trumpet, August 11, 1840, and the third woe occurs under the sounding of the seventh trumpet, which began in 1844.

---

[10] *Ibid.*, p. 48.

Then where are we? "Behold!" that is to say, mark it well, "the third woe cometh quickly." The fearful scenes of the second woe are past, and we are now under the sounding of the trumpet that brings the third and last woe. Shall we now look for peace and safety, a temporal millennium, a thousand years of righteousness and prosperity on earth? Rather let us earnestly pray the Lord to awaken a slumbering world.

Verse 15 And the seventh angel sounded; and there were great voices in heaven, saying, The kingdoms of this world are become the kingdoms of our Lord, and of His Christ; and He shall reign forever and ever. 16 And the four and twenty elders, which sat before God on their seats, fell upon their faces, and worshiped God, 17 saying, We give Thee thanks, O Lord God Almighty, which art, and wast, and art to come; because Thou hast taken to Thee Thy great power, and hast reigned.

From the fifteenth verse to the end of the chapter, we seem to be carried over the ground three distinct times from the sounding of the seventh angel to the end. In the verses here quoted, the prophet glances forward to the full establishment of the kingdom of God. Although the seventh trumpet has begun to sound, it may not yet be a fact that the great voices in heaven have proclaimed that the kingdoms of this world are become the kingdoms of our Lord and of His Christ, unless it be in anticipation of the speedy accomplishment of this event. But the seventh trumpet, like the preceding six, covers a period of time, and the transfer of the kingdoms from earthly powers to Him whose right it is to reign, is the principal event to occur in the early years of its sounding. Hence this event, to the exclusion of all else, here engages the mind of the prophet. (See remarks on verse 19.) In the next verse John goes back and takes up intervening events.

Verse 18 And the nations were angry, and Thy wrath is come, and the time of the dead, that they should be judged, and that Thou shouldst give reward unto Thy servants the prophets, and to the saints, and them that fear Thy name, small and great; and shouldst destroy them which destroy the earth.

"*The Nations Were Angry.*"—Beginning with the spontaneous outburst of revolutions in Europe in 1848, the anger of

WILLIAM HEASLIP, ARTIST

"THE NATIONS WERE ANGRY"

With unleashed fury the nations have set about to destroy one another.

nations toward one another has been constantly increasing. Jealousy and hatred among nations has been the rule rather than the exception. Particularly has this been manifested in the two world wars of the twentieth century, when it seemed that men would be willing to annihilate whole nations in the heat of their anger.

Here are the exact words of a Harvard professor:

"The twentieth century, so far, has been the bloodiest period and one of the most turbulent periods—and therefore one of the cruelest and least humanitarian—in the history of Western civilization and perhaps in the chronicles of mankind in general." [11]

"*Thy Wrath Is Come.*"—The wrath of God for the present generation is filled up in the seven last plagues (Revelation 15: 1), which consequently must here be referred to, and which are soon to be poured out upon the earth.

"*The Time of the Dead, That They Should Be Judged.*"—The great majority of the dead, that is, the wicked, are still in their graves after the visitation of the plagues, and the close of the gospel age. A work of judgment, of allotting to each one the punishment due because of his sins, is carried on by the saints in conjunction with Christ during the one thousand years following the first resurrection. (1 Corinthians 6: 2; Revelation 20: 4.) Inasmuch as this judgment of the dead follows the wrath of God, or the seven last plagues, it would seem necessary to refer it to the one thousand years of judgment upon the wicked, above mentioned; for the investigative judgment takes place *before* the plagues are poured out.

"*Thou Shouldst Give Reward Unto Thy Servants the Prophets.*"—These will enter upon their reward at the second coming of Christ, for He brings their reward with Him. (Matthew 16: 27; Revelation 22: 12.) The full reward of the saints, however, is not reached until they enter upon the possession of the new earth. (Matthew 25: 34.)

---

[11] Pitirim A. Sorokin, *Social and Cultural Dynamics*, Vol. III, p. 487.

Punishment of the Wicked.—"Shouldst destroy them which destroy the earth," refers to the time when all the wicked, who have literally devastated vast regions and wantonly destroyed human life, will be forever devoured by those purifying fires from God out of heaven. (2 Peter 3: 7; Revelation 20: 9.) Thus the seventh trumpet reaches to the end of the one thousand years. Momentous, startling, yet joyous thought! The trumpet now sounding sees the final destruction of the wicked, and the saints, clothed in a glorious immortality, safely located on the earth made new.

VERSE 19 And the temple of God was opened in heaven, and there was seen in His temple the ark of His testament: and there were lightnings, and voices, and thunderings, and an earthquake, and great hail.

The Temple Opened.—Once more the prophet carries us back to the beginning of the trumpet. After the introduction of the seventh trumpet in verse 15, the first great event that comes to the mind of the seer is the transfer of the kingdom from earthly to heavenly rule. God takes to Him His great power, and forever crushes the rebellion of this revolted earth, establishes Christ upon His own throne, and remains Himself supreme over all. We are next referred back to the state of the nations, the judgment to fall upon them, and the final destiny of both saints and sinners. (Verse 18.) After this field of vision has been scanned, our attention is called back once more in the verse now under notice, to the close of the priesthood of Christ, the last scene in the work of mercy for a guilty world.

The temple is opened, and the second apartment of the sanctuary is entered. We know it is the holy of holies that is here opened, for the ark is seen; and in that apartment alone the ark was deposited. This took place at the end of the 2300 days, when the sanctuary was to be cleansed. (Daniel 8: 14.) At that time the prophetic periods ended and the seventh angel began to sound. Since 1844, the people of God have seen by faith the open door in heaven, and the ark of God's testament within. They are endeavoring to keep every precept of the holy law written upon the tables deposited there. That the tables of the law are there, just as they were in the ark in the sanctuary erected by Moses, is evident from the terms which John uses in describing the ark. He calls it the "ark of His testament."

The ark was called the ark of the covenant, or testament, because it was made for the express purpose of containing the tables of the testimony, or ten commandments. (Exodus 25: 16; 31: 18; Deuteronomy 10: 2, 5.) It was put to no other use, and owed its name solely to the fact that it contained the tables of the law. If it did not contain the tables, it would not be the ark of God's testament, and could not truthfully be so called. Yet John, beholding the ark in heaven under the sounding of the seventh trumpet, still calls it the "ark of His testament," affording unanswerable proof that the law is still there, unaltered in one jot or tittle from the copy which for a time was committed to the care of men in the typical ark of the tabernacle during the time of Moses.

The followers of the prophetic word have also received the reed, and are measuring the temple, the altar, and those that worship therein. (Revelation 11: 1.) They are uttering their last prophecy before nations, peoples, and tongues. (Revelation 10: 11.) The drama will soon close with the lightnings, thunderings, voices, the earthquake, and great hail, which will constitute nature's last convulsion before all things are made new at the close of the thousand years. (Revelation 21: 5.) (See comments on Revelation 16: 17-21.)

VERNON NYE, ARTIST

THE CHRISTIAN CHURCH

"There appeared a great wonder in heaven; a woman clothed with the sun, and the moon under her feet, and upon her head a crown of twelve stars." Revelation 12: 1.

CHAPTER XII

THE BACKGROUND OF RELIGIOUS INTOLERANCE

VERSE 1 And there appeared a great wonder in heaven; a woman clothed with the sun, and the moon under her feet, and upon her head a crown of twelve stars: 2 and she being with child cried, travailing in birth, and pained to be delivered. 3 And there appeared another wonder in heaven; and behold a great red dragon, having seven heads and ten horns, and seven crowns upon his heads.

AN ELUCIDATION of this part of the chapter will involve little more than a mere definition of the symbols introduced. This may be given in few words.

"A woman," signifies the true church. (2 Corinthians 11: 2.) A corrupt woman is used to represent an apostate or corrupt church. (Ezekiel 23: 2-4; Revelation 17: 3-6, 15, 18.) By parity of reasoning, a pure woman, as in this instance, would represent the true church. "The sun" here signifies the light and glory of the gospel era. "The moon" is the symbol of the Mosaic period. As the moon shines with a borrowed light derived from the sun, so the former era shone with a light borrowed from the present. There they had the type and shadow; here we have the antitype and the substance. "A crown of twelve stars" appropriately symbolizes the twelve apostles. "A great red dragon" represents pagan Rome. (See comments under verses 4 and 5.) "Heaven" is the space in which this representation was seen by the apostle. We are not to suppose that the scenes here presented to John took place in heaven where God resides, for they are events which occurred upon this earth. This vision which passed before the eye of the prophet, appeared as if in the region occupied by the sun, moon, and stars, which we speak of as heaven.

Verses 1 and 2 cover a period of time beginning just previous to the opening of the Christian Era, when the church was earnestly longing for and expecting the advent of the Messiah, and extending to the full establishment of the gospel church with its crown of twelve apostles. (Luke 2: 25, 26, 38.)

No symbols more fitting and impressive could be found than are here employed. The Mosaic period shone with a light borrowed from the Christian Era, even as the moon shines with light borrowed from the sun. How appropriate, therefore, to represent the former by the moon, and the latter by the sun. The woman, the church, had the moon under her feet; that is, the Mosaic period had just ended, and the woman was clothed with the light of the gospel sun, which had just risen. By anticipation the church is represented as fully organized, with its twelve apostles, before the man child, Christ, appeared upon the scene. It was to be thus constituted immediately after Christ should begin His ministry; and He is more especially connected with this church than with that of the former period. There is no ground for misunderstanding the passage; and hence no violence is done to a correct system of interpretation by this representation.

VERSE 4 And his tail drew the third part of the stars of heaven, and did cast them to the earth: and the dragon stood before the woman which was ready to be delivered, for to devour her child as soon as it was born. 5 And she brought forth a man child, who was to rule all nations with a rod of iron: and her child was caught up unto God, and to His throne. 6 And the woman fled into the wilderness, where she hath a place prepared of God, that they should feed her there a thousand two hundred and threescore days.

"*Third Part of the Stars of Heaven.*"—The dragon drew the third part of the stars from heaven. If the twelve stars with which the woman is crowned, here used symbolically, denote the twelve apostles, then the stars thrown down by the dragon before his attempt to destroy the man child, or before the Christian Era, may denote a part of the rulers of the Jewish people. That the sun, moon, and stars are sometimes used in this symbolic sense, we have already had evidence in Revelation 8: 12. Judea became a Roman province sixty-three years before the birth of the Messiah. The Jews had three classes of rulers,—kings, priests, and the Sanhedrin. A third of these, the kings, were taken away by the Roman power. Philip Smith, after describing the siege of Jerusalem by the Romans and Herod, and its capitulation in the spring of 37 B. C., after an obstinate resistance of six months, says: "Such was the end of the Asmonean dynasty, exactly 130 years after the first victories of Judas Maccabæus, and in the seventieth year from the assumption of the diadem by Aristobulus I."[1]

This allusion to the stars undoubtedly has also a wider meaning, and is related to the truths emphasized in verses 7-9 of this chapter. As a result of the conflict there brought to view, it is evident that a third part of the angelic host, who joined with Satan in his rebellion against the Ruler of the universe, were cast out of the courts of glory.

"*The Dragon Stood Before the Woman.*"—It now becomes necessary to identify the power symbolized by the dragon, and this can be done very easily. The testimony concerning the "man child" which the dragon seeks to destroy, is applicable to only one being that has appeared in this world, and that is our Lord Jesus Christ. No other one has been caught up to God and His throne, but He has been thus exalted. (Ephesians 1: 20, 21; Hebrews 8: 1; Revelation 3: 21.) No other one has received from God the commission to rule all nations with a rod of iron, but *He* has been appointed to this work. (Psalm 2: 7-9.)

There can certainly be no doubt that the man child represents Jesus Christ. The time to which the prophecy refers is equally evident. It was the time when Christ appeared in this world as a babe in Bethlehem.

It will now be easy to find the power symbolized by the dragon, for the dragon represents some power which attempted to destroy Christ at His birth. Was any such attempt made? Who made it? No formal answer to this question need be given to anyone who has read how Herod, in a fiendish

[1] Philip Smith, *History of the World*, Vol. III, p. 181.

MARTIN FEUERSTEIN, ARTIST

THE BIRTH OF CHRIST

It was upon Christ, the Founder of the church, that Satan turned his strongest attacks.

effort to destroy the infant Jesus, sent forth and slew all the children in Bethlehem from two years old and under. But who was Herod? He was a Roman governor. From Rome Herod derived his power. Rome ruled at that time over all the world (Luke 2: 1), and was therefore the responsible actor in this event. Moreover, Rome was the only earthly government which at that time *could* be symbolized in prophecy, for the very reason that its dominion was universal. It is not, therefore, without the most conclusive reason that the Roman Empire is regarded by Protestant commentators generally to be the power indicated by the great red dragon.

It may be a fact worth mentioning that during the second, third, fourth, and fifth centuries of the Christian Era, next to the eagle the dragon was the principal standard of the Roman legions. That dragon was painted red, as if in faithful response to the picture held up by the seer of Patmos they would exclaim to the world, We are the nation which that picture represents.

Rome, as we have seen, attempted to destroy Jesus Christ through the fiendish plot of Herod. The child who was born to the waiting and watching church, was our adorable Redeemer, who is soon to rule the nations with a rod of iron. Herod could not destroy Him. The combined powers of earth and hell could not overcome Him. Though held for a time under the dominion of the grave, He rent its cruel bands, opened a way of life for mankind, and was caught up to God and His throne. He ascended to heaven in the sight of His disciples, leaving to them and us the promise that He would come again.

The church fled into the wilderness at the time the papacy was firmly established in 538, where it was nourished by the word of God and the ministration of angels during the long, dark, and bloody rule of that power for 1260 years.

VERSE 7 And there was war in heaven: Michael and His angels fought against the dragon; and the dragon fought and his angels, 8 and prevailed not; neither was their place found any more in heaven. 9 And the great dragon was cast out, that old serpent, called the devil, and Satan, which deceiveth the whole world: he was cast out into the earth, and his angels were cast out with him. 10 And I heard a loud voice saying in heaven, Now is come salvation, and strength, and the kingdom of our God, and the power of His Christ: for the accuser of our brethren is cast down, which accused them before our God day and night. 11 And they overcame him by the blood of the Lamb, and by the word of their testimony; and they loved not their lives unto the death. 12 Therefore rejoice, ye heavens, and ye that dwell in them. Woe to the inhabiters of the earth and of the sea! For the devil is come down unto you, having great wrath, because he knoweth that he hath but a short time.

War in Heaven.—The first six verses of this chapter, as has been seen, take us down to the close of the 1260 years in 1798, which marked the end of the papal supremacy. In the 7th verse it is equally plain that we are carried back into previous ages. How far?—To the time first introduced in the chapter, the days of the first advent, when with fiendish ingenuity Satan working through the power of pagan Rome sought to destroy the Saviour of men; and also back beyond that time to the very beginning of the great controversy between truth and righteousness, when in heaven itself Michael (Christ) and His angels fought against the dragon (Satan) and his angels. To prove that Michael is Christ, see Jude 9; 1 Thessalonians 4: 16; John 5: 28, 29.

"*Prevailed Not.*"—Thank God that in that early conflict the archdeceiver was defeated. As "Lucifer, son of the morning," with envy and hatred in his heart, he had presumptuously led a host of disaffected angels in rebellion against the government of God. But the Scripture says he "prevailed not," and "was cast out into the earth, and his angels were cast out with him."

Centuries later at the time of Christ's first advent, "the great dragon," "that old serpent called the devil, and Satan," put forth a supreme effort in the guise of the great red dragon, representing pagan Rome, to destroy the world's Redeemer. Satan had looked forward to Christ's mission to this earth as his last chance of success in overthrowing the plan of salvation. He came to Christ with specious temptations, in hope of overcoming Him. He tried in various ways to destroy Christ during His ministry. When he had succeeded in laying Him in the tomb, he endeavored, in malignant triumph, to hold Him there. But in every encounter the Son of God came off triumphant; and He sends back His gracious promise to His faithful followers: "To him that overcometh will I grant to sit with Me in My throne, even as *I also overcame*, and am set down with My Father in His throne." Revelation 3: 21. This shows us that Jesus while on earth waged a warfare, and obtained the victory. Satan saw his last effort fail, his last scheme miscarry. He had boasted that he would overcome the Son of God in His mission to this world, and thus render the plan of salvation an ignominious failure. Well he knew that if he was foiled in this his last desperate effort to thwart the work of God, his last hope had perished, and all was lost. In the language of verse 8, he "prevailed not," and hence the song may well be sung, "Therefore rejoice, ye heavens, and ye that dwell in them."

Their Place Found No More in Heaven.—Satan and the fallen angels had suffered a terrible defeat, which Christ describes by saying, "I beheld Satan as lightning fall from heaven" (Luke 10: 18), and Peter tells us that these fallen angels have been delivered "into chains of darkness to be reserved unto judgment" (2 Peter 2: 4).

The hope which he had long cherished of overcoming the Son of man when He took upon Himself our nature, had forever perished. His power was limited. He could no more aspire to a personal encounter with the Son of God, for Christ had vanquished him. Henceforth the church (the woman) is the object of his malice, and he resorts to all those nefarious means against her that would naturally characterize his rage.

But hereupon a song is sung in heaven, "Now *is* come salvation." How is this, if these scenes are in the past? Had salvation and strength and the kingdom of God and the power of His Christ then come? Not at all; but this song was sung prospectively. Those things were made sure. The great victory had been won by Christ which forever settled the question of their establishment.

The prophet then glances rapidly over the working of Satan from that time to the end (verses 11, 12), during which time the faithful "brethren" overcome him by the blood of the Lamb and the word of their testimony, while his wrath increases as his time grows short.

It was Satan that moved upon Herod to put the Saviour to death. But the chief agent of the archrebel in making war

MAURICE LELOIR, ARTIST

PROTESTANT FUGITIVES

They were hunted like the wild beasts of the mountains and cruelly persecuted for their faith.

upon Christ and His people during the early centuries of the Christian Era was the Roman Empire, in which paganism was the dominant religion. Thus, while the dragon primarily represents Satan, it is in a secondary sense, representative of pagan Rome.

VERSE 13 And when the dragon saw that he was cast unto the earth, he persecuted the woman which brought forth the man child. 14 And to the woman were given two wings of a great eagle, that she might fly into the wilderness, into her place, where she is nourished for a time, and times, and half a time, from the face of the serpent. 15 And the serpent cast out of his mouth water as a flood after the woman, that he might cause her to be carried away of the flood. 16 And the earth helped the woman, and the earth opened her mouth, and swallowed up the flood which the dragon cast out of his mouth. 17 And the dragon was wroth with the woman, and went to make war with the remnant of her seed, which keep the commandments of God, and have the testimony of Jesus Christ.

The Church in the Wilderness.—Here we are once more carried back to the time when Satan became fully aware that he had failed in all his attempts against the Lord of glory in His earthly mission. Seeing this, he turned with tenfold fury, as already noticed, upon the church which Christ had established. Then we have another view of the church going into that condition here spoken of as being "in the wilderness." This must denote a state of seclusion from the public gaze, and of concealment from her foes. That church which during all the Dark Ages trumpeted her lordly commands into the ears of listening Christendom, and flaunted her ostentatious banners before gaping crowds, was not the church of Christ; it was the body of the mystery of iniquity.

The "mystery of godliness" was God manifested here as a man; the "mystery of iniquity" was a man pretending to be God. This was the great apostasy produced by the union of paganism and Christianity. The true church was out of sight. In secret places they worshiped God. The caves and the hidden recesses of the valleys of the Piedmont may be taken as representative places, where the truth of the gospel was sacredly cherished from the rage of its foes. Here God watched over His church, and by His providence protected and nourished her.

The eagles' wings given her appropriately signify the haste with which the true church was obliged to seek her own safety when the man of sin was installed in power. The assistance of God was provided her to this end. The like figure is used to describe God's dealings with ancient Israel. By Moses He said to them, "Ye have seen what I did unto the Egyptians, and how I bare you on eagles' wings, and brought you unto Myself." Exodus 19: 4.

The mention of the period during which the woman is nourished in the wilderness as "a time and times and half a time," similar phraseology to that used in Daniel 7: 25, furnishes a key for the explanation of the latter passage. The same period is called in Revelation 12: 6, "a thousand two hundred and threescore days." This shows that a "time" is one year, 360 days; two "times," two years, or 720 days; and "half a time," half a year, or 180 days, making in all 1260 days. These days, being symbolic, signify 1260 literal years.

The serpent cast out of his mouth water as a flood to carry away the church. By its false doctrines the papacy had so corrupted all nations as to have absolute control of the civil power for long centuries. Through it Satan could hurl a mighty flood of persecution against the church in every direction, and this he was not slow to do. (See reference to the terrible persecutions of the church in remarks on Daniel 7: 25.) Millions of true believers were carried away by the flood, but the church was not entirely swallowed up, for the days were shortened for the elect's sake. (Matthew 24: 22.)

"The earth helped the woman" by opening its mouth and swallowing up the flood. The Protestant Reformation of the sixteenth century began its work. God raised up Martin Luther and his colaborers to expose the true character of the papacy, and break the power with which superstition had enslaved the minds of the people. Luther nailed his theses to the door of the church at Wittenberg; and the pen with which he wrote them, according to the symbolic dream of the good elector Frederick of Saxony, did indeed span the continent, and shake the triple crown on the pope's head. Princes began to espouse the cause of the Reformers. It was the dawning of religious light and liberty, and God would not suffer the darkness to swallow up its radiance.

The spell was broken. Men found that the bulls and anathemas of the pope fell harmless at their feet, just as soon as they dared exercise their God-given right to regulate their consciences by His word alone. Defenders of the true faith multiplied. Soon there was enough Protestant soil found in Europe and the New World to swallow up the flood of papal fury, and rob it of its power to harm the church. Thus the earth helped the woman, and has continued to help her to the present day, as the spirit of the Reformation and religious liberty has been fostered by the leading nations of Christendom.

War on the Remnant.—But the dragon is not yet through with his work. Verse 17 brings to view another and a final outburst of his wrath, this time against the last generation of Christians to live on the earth. We say the last generation, for the war of the dragon is directed against the *remnant* of the woman's seed, the true church, and no generation but the last can truthfully be represented by the remnant. If the view is correct that we have already reached the generation which is to witness the closing up of earthly scenes, this warfare against the truth cannot be far in the future.

This remnant is characterized by its keeping of the commandments of God, and having the testimony of Jesus Christ. This points to a Sabbath reform to be accomplished in the last days, for on the Sabbath alone as pertaining to the commandments, is there a difference of faith and practice among those who accept the decalogue as the moral law. This is more particularly brought to view in the message of Revelation 14: 9-12.

 R. M. ELDRIDGE, ARTIST

THE TEN-HORNED BEAST

John "saw a beast rise up out of the sea, having seven heads and ten horns, and upon his horns ten crowns, and upon his heads

CHAPTER XIII

THE AGELONG STRUGGLE FOR RELIGIOUS FREEDOM

VERSE 1 And I stood upon the sand of the sea, and saw a beast rise up out of the sea, having seven heads and ten horns, and upon his horns ten crowns, and upon his heads the name of blasphemy. 2 And the beast which I saw was like unto a leopard, and his feet were as the feet of a bear, and his mouth as the mouth of a lion: and the dragon gave him his power, and his seat, and great authority. 3 And I saw one of his heads as it were wounded to death; and his deadly wound was healed: and all the world wondered after the beast. 4 And they worshiped the dragon which gave power unto the beast: and they worshiped the beast, saying, Who is like unto the beast? Who is able to make war with him?

THE SEA is a symbol of "peoples, and multitudes, and nations, and tongues." Revelation 17: 15. A beast is the Bible symbol of a nation or power. It sometimes represents the civil power alone, and sometimes the ecclesiastical in connection with the civil. Whenever a beast is seen to come up out of the sea, it denotes that the power arises in a thickly populated territory. If the winds are represented as blowing upon the sea, as in Daniel 7: 2, 3, political commotion, civil strife, and revolution are indicated.

By the dragon of the previous chapter, and the beast first introduced in this, we have the Roman power as a whole brought to view in its two phases, pagan and papal; hence these two symbols have each the seven heads and ten horns. (See comments on Revelation 17: 10.)

The Leopard Beast.—The seven-headed and ten-horned beast, more briefly the leopard beast, here introduced, symbolizes a power which exercises ecclesiastical as well as civil authority. This point is of sufficient importance to justify the introduction of a few conclusive arguments which prove it.

The line of prophecy in which this symbol occurs begins with Revelation 12. The symbols of earthly governments embraced in the prophecy are the dragon of Revelation 12 and the leopard beast and the two-horned beast of Revelation 13. The same line of prophecy evidently continues into chapter 14. Beginning, therefore, with Revelation 12: 1, and ending with Revelation 14: 5, we have a line of prophecy distinct and complete in itself.

Each of the powers here introduced is represented as fiercely persecuting the church of God. The scene opens with the church under the symbol of a woman anxiously longing for the promise to be fulfilled that the seed of the woman, the Lord of glory, should appear among men. The dragon stood before the woman for the purpose of devouring her child. His evil design is thwarted, and the child is caught up to God and His throne. A period follows in which the church suffers severe oppression from this dragon power. In this part of the scene the prophet occasionally glances forward, once even down almost to the end, because all the enemies of the church were to be actuated by the spirit of the dragon. In verse 1 of Revelation 13 we are carried back to the time when the leopard beast, the successor of the dragon, begins his career. From this power the church suffers war and persecution for the long period of 1260 years. Following this period of oppression, the church has another conflict, brief but sharp and severe, with the two-horned beast. Then comes deliverance. The prophecy closes with the church brought safely through all her persecutions, and standing victorious with the Lamb on Mount Zion. Thank God for the sure promise of final victory!

The one character which ever appears the same in all these scenes, and whose history is the leading theme through all the prophecy, is the true church of God. The other characters are her persecutors, and are introduced simply because they are such. Here, as an introductory inquiry, we raise the question, Who or what is it that persecutes the true church? It is a false or apostate church. What is it that is ever warring against true religion? It is a false and counterfeit religion. Who ever heard of the mere civil power of any nation persecuting the people of God on its own initiative? Governments may war against other governments to avenge some wrong, real or imaginary, or to acquire territory and extend their power. But governments do not persecute (mark the word—do not *persecute*) people on account of their religion, unless under the control of some opposite and hostile system of religion.

Leopard Beast a Persecuting Power.—The powers introduced in this prophecy—the dragon, the leopard beast, and the two-horned beast of verses 11-17—are all *persecuting* powers. They are actuated by rage and enmity against the people and church of God. This fact is of itself sufficiently conclusive evidence that in each of these powers the ecclesiastical or religious element is the controlling power.

Take the dragon: what does it symbolize?—The undeniable answer is, Primarily Satan, as shown heretofore, and secondarily the Roman Empire. But this is not enough. No one would be satisfied with this answer and no more. It must be more definite. We therefore add, The Roman Empire in its *pagan form*, to which all must agree. But just as soon as we say *pagan*, we introduce a religious element, for paganism is one of the most gigantic systems of counterfeit religion that Satan has ever devised. The dragon, then, is so far an ecclesiastical power that the very characteristic by which it is distinguished is a false system of religion. What made the dragon persecute the church of Christ? It was because Christianity was prevailing against paganism, sweeping away its superstitions, overturning its idols, and dismantling its temples. The *religious* element of that power was touched, and persecution was the result.

We now come to the leopard beast of Revelation 13. What does that symbolize? The answer still is, The Roman Empire. But the dragon symbolized the Roman Empire, and why does not the same symbol represent it still? Ah! there has been a change in the *religious character* of the empire. This beast symbolizes Rome in its professedly Christian form. It is this *change of religion*, and this alone, which makes a change in the symbol necessary. This beast differs from the dragon only in that it presents a different *religious* aspect. Hence it would be wrong to affirm that it denotes simply the Roman civil power.

A Symbol of the Papacy.—To this beast the dragon gives his power, his seat, and great authority. By what power was pagan Rome succeeded? We all know that it was by papal Rome. It matters not to our present purpose when or by what means this change was effected. The great fact is apparent, and is acknowledged by all, that the next great phase of the Roman Empire after its pagan form was its papal. It would not be correct, therefore, to say that pagan Rome gave its power and seat to a form of government merely civil, having no religious element whatever. No stretch of the imagination can conceive of such a transaction. But two phases of empire are here recognized, and in the prophecy Rome is pagan until Rome is papal. The statement that the dragon gave to the leopard beast his power and seat, is further evidence that the dragon of Revelation 12: 3 is used as a symbol of pagan Rome. But back of both powers, and leading them on in their wicked work, is Satan himself.

But it may be said that it takes both the leopard beast and the two-horned beast to constitute the papacy, and hence it is to these that the dragon gives his power, seat, and great authority. But the prophecy does not say so. It is the leopard beast *alone* with which the dragon has to do. It is to that beast *alone* that he gives his power, seat, and great authority. It is that beast which has a head that is wounded to death, which is afterward healed; that beast after which the whole world wonders; that beast which has a mouth speaking blasphemies, and which wears out the saints for 1260 years. It does all this before the succeeding power, the two-horned beast, appears. The leopard beast alone, therefore, symbolizes the Roman Empire in its papal form, the controlling influence being ecclesiastical.

Identical With the Little Horn.—To show this more fully, we have but to draw a parallel between the little horn of Daniel

7: 8, 20, 24, 25, and this power. From this comparison it will appear that the little horn and the leopard beast symbolize the same power. The little horn is generally acknowledged to be a symbol of the papacy. There are six points by which to establish their identity:

1. The little horn was a blasphemous power. "He shall speak great words against the Most High." Daniel 7: 25. The leopard beast of Revelation 13: 6 does the same. "He opened his mouth in blasphemy against God."

2. The little horn made war with the saints, and prevailed against them. (Daniel 7: 21.) This beast also (Revelation 13: 7) makes war with the saints, and overcomes them.

3. The little horn had a mouth speaking great things. (Daniel 7: 8, 20.) Of this beast we read: "There was given unto him a mouth speaking great things and blasphemies." Revelation 13: 5.

4. The little horn arose on the cessation of the pagan form of the Roman Empire. The beast of Revelation 13: 2 arises at the same time; for the dragon, pagan Rome, gives him his power, his seat, and great authority.

5. Power was given to the little horn to continue for a time, times, and the dividing of time, or 1260 years. (Daniel 7: 25.) To this beast also power was given for forty-two months, or 1260 years. (Revelation 13: 5.)

6. At the end of that specified period of 1260 years the "saints," "times," and "laws" were to be taken out of the "hand" of the little horn. (Daniel 7: 25.) At the end of the same period, the leopard beast was himself to be led "into captivity." Revelation 13: 10. Both these specifications were fulfilled in the captivity and exile of the pope, and the temporary overthrow of the papacy by France in 1798.

These six points prove satisfactorily the identity of the little horn and the leopard beast. When we have in prophecy two symbols, as in this instance, representing powers that come upon the stage of action at the *same time*, occupy the *same territory*, maintain the *same character*, do the *same work*, exist the

 PAUL REMMEY, ARTIST

THE POPE TAKEN PRISONER IN 1798

On February 20, 1798, Pius VI was taken prisoner by Berthier, the French general.

same length of time, and meet the *same fate*, those symbols represent the *same identical power*.

Received a Deadly Wound.—The head that was wounded to death was the papal head. We are held to this conclusion by the obvious principle that whatever is spoken in prophecy of the symbol of any government, applies to that government only while it is represented by that symbol. Now Rome is represented by two symbols, the dragon and the leopard beast, because it has presented two phases, the pagan and the papal; and whatever is said of the dragon applies to Rome only in its pagan form, and whatever is said of the leopard beast applies to Rome only in its professedly Christian form. John says that it was one of the heads of this leopard beast that was wounded to death. In other words, this wound fell upon the form of government that existed in the Roman Empire after its change from paganism to Christianity. Thus it is evident that it was the papal head that was wounded to death, and whose deadly wound was healed. This wounding is the same as the going into captivity. (Revelation 13: 10.) It was inflicted when the pope was taken prisoner by Berthier, the French general, and the papal government was for a time abolished, in 1798. Stripped of his power, both civil and ecclesiastical, the captive pope, Pius VI, died in exile at Valence in France, August 29, 1799. But the deadly wound began to be healed when the papacy was re-established, though with less of its former power, by the election of a new pope, March 14, 1800.[1]

VERSE 5 And there was given unto him a mouth speaking great things and blasphemies; and power was given unto him to continue forty and two months. 6 And he opened his mouth in blasphemy against God, to blaspheme His name, and His tabernacle, and them that dwell in heaven. 7 And it was given unto him to make war with the saints, and to overcome them: and power was given him over all kindreds, and tongues, and nations. 8 And all that dwell upon the earth shall worship him, whose names are not written in the book of life of the Lamb slain from the foundation of the world. 9 If any man have an ear, let him hear. 10 He that leadeth into captivity

---

[1] See Archibald Bower, *History of the Popes*, Vol. III, pp. 409-420; George Croly, *The Apocalypse of St. John*, p. 251.

RESTORING THE POWER OF THE PAPACY

Cardinal Gasparri and Benito Mussolini signed in 1929 the concordat which restored the temporal power of the papacy.

shall go into captivity: he that killeth with the sword must be killed with the sword. Here is the patience and the faith of the saints.

Speak Blasphemies.—This beast opens his mouth "in blasphemy against God, to blaspheme His name, and His tabernacle, and them that dwell in heaven." Mention has already been made in comments on the book of Daniel as to the significance of the expression, "He shall speak great words against the Most High." Daniel 7: 25. In verse 5 in this chapter of Revelation similar words are used, for he had "a mouth speaking great things." Here, however, the word "blasphemy" is added, and this evidently points to the fact that the great words will be blasphemous enunciations against the God of heaven.

In the Gospels we find two indications of what constitutes blasphemy. In John 10: 33 we read that the Jews falsely charged Jesus with blasphemy because, said they, "Thou, being a man, makest Thyself God." This in the case of the Saviour was untrue, because He *was* the Son of God. He was "Immanuel, God With Us." But for man to assume the prerogatives of God and to take the titles of deity—this is blasphemy.

Again, in Luke 5: 21 we see the Pharisees endeavoring to catch Jesus in His words. "Who is this which speaketh blasphemies?" said they. "Who can forgive sins, but God alone?" Jesus could pardon transgressions, for He was the divine Saviour. But for man, mortal man, to claim such authority is blasphemy indeed.

We might ask if the power represented by this symbol has fulfilled this part of the prophecy. In comments on Daniel 7: 25 we saw clearly from the evidence submitted that he had spoken "great words" against the God of heaven. Now observe what is said regarding the claim of the priesthood to forgive sins:

"The priest holds the place of the Saviour Himself, when, by saying, 'Ego te absolvo' [I thee absolve], he absolves from sin. . . . To pardon a single sin requires all the omnipotence of God. . . . But what only God can do by His omnipotence, the priest can also do by saying 'Ego te absolvo a peccatis tuis.' . . . Innocent III has written: 'Indeed, it is not too much to say that in view of the sublimity of their offices the priests are so many gods.' "[2]

Note still further the blasphemous utterances of this power:

"But our wonder should be far greater when we find that in obedience to the words of His priests—HOC EST CORPUS MEUM [This is My body]—God Himself descends on the altar, that He comes wherever they call Him, and as often as they call Him, and places Himself in their hands, even though they should be His enemies. And after having come, He remains, entirely at their disposal; they move Him as they please, from one place to another; they may, if they wish, shut Him up in the tabernacle, or expose Him on the altar, or carry Him outside the church; they may, if they choose, eat His flesh, and give Him for the food of others. 'Oh, how very great is their power,' says St. Laurence Justinian, speaking of priests. 'A word falls from their lips and the body of Christ is there substantially formed from the matter of bread, and the Incarnate Word descended from heaven, is found really present on the table of the altar!' "[3]

"Thus the priest may, in a certain manner, be called the creator of his Creator. . . . 'The power of the priest,' says St. Bernardine of Sienna, 'is the power of the divine person; for the transubstantiation of the bread requires as much power as the creation of the world.' "[4]

Thus this beast power blasphemes the temple in heaven by turning the attention of his subjects to his own throne and palace instead of to the tabernacle of God; by diverting their attention from the sacrifice of the Son of God to the sacrifice of the mass.

---

[2] Alphonsus de Liguori, *Dignity and Duties of the Priest*, pp. 34-36.

[3] *Ibid.*, pp. 26, 27.

[4] *Ibid.*, pp. 32, 33.

He blasphemes them that dwell in heaven by assuming to exercise the power of forgiving sins, and so turns away the minds of men from the mediatorial work of Christ and His heavenly assistants in the sanctuary above.

By verse 10 we are again referred to the events of 1798, when that power that had for 1260 years led the saints of God into captivity, was itself led into captivity.

VERSE 11 And I beheld another beast coming up out of the earth; and he had two horns like a lamb, and he spake as a dragon.

Two-Horned Beast.—This verse brings to view the third great symbol in the line of prophecy we are examining, usually denominated the two-horned beast. We inquire for its application. The dragon, pagan Rome, and the leopard beast, papal Rome, present before us great organizations standing as the representatives of two great systems of false religion. Analogy would seem to require that the remaining symbol, the two-horned beast, have a similar application, and find its fulfillment in some nation which is the representative of still another great system of religion. The only remaining system which is exercising a controlling influence in the world today is Protestantism. Abstractly considered, paganism embraces all heathen lands, containing more than half the population of the globe. Catholicism, which may perhaps be considered as including the religion of the Greek Orthodox Church, so nearly identical with it, belongs to nations which compose a large part of Christendom. A clear portrayal of Mohammedanism and its influence has been given in other prophecies. (See comments on Daniel 11 and Revelation 9.) But Protestantism is the religion of nations which constitute the vanguard of the world in liberty, enlightenment, progress, and power.

A Symbol of America.—If, then, Protestantism is the religion to which we are to look, to what nation as the representative of that religion does the prophecy have application? There are notable Protestant nations in Europe, but for reasons which will hereafter appear, the symbol cannot apply to any of these. A careful investigation has led to the conclusion that it does apply to Protestant America, or the United States of America. The reason for such an application and the evidence by which it is supported we will carefully consider.

Are there any reasons why we should expect that the United States would be mentioned in prophecy? On what conditions have other nations found a place in the prophetic record? First, that they have acted a prominent part in the world's history; and second, and above all, that they have had jurisdiction over, or maintained important relations with, the people of God. In the records of the Bible and of secular history, we find data from which to deduce this rule respecting the prophetic mention of earthly governments: A nation enters prophecy when the work and destiny of God's people are definitely linked with it. All these conditions are certainly fulfilled in the United States. The conviction has fastened itself upon many minds that the rise and progress of this nation has been of such a nature that Providence saw fit to forecast it in prophecy.

Governor Pownal, an English statesman, predicted in 1780, while the American Revolution was in progress, that this country would become independent; that a civilizing activity, beyond what Europe could ever know, would animate it; and that its commercial and naval power would be found in every quarter of the globe. He then speaks of the probable establishment of this country as a free and sovereign power as " 'a revolution that has stranger marks of *divine interposition*, superseding the ordinary course of human affairs, than any other event which this world has experienced.' "[5]

George Alfred Townsend, speaking of the misfortunes that have attended the other governments in the Western Hemisphere says:

---

[5] Quoted by Hon. Charles Sumner, "Prophetic Voices About America," *Atlantic Monthly*, September, 1867, p. 290.

"The history of the United States was separated by a beneficent Providence far from this wild and cruel history of the rest of the continent."[6]

Such considerations as these are calculated to arouse in every mind a strong expectation that this nation will be found to have some part to act in the carrying out of God's providential purposes in this world, and that somewhere it will be spoken of in the prophetic word.

Chronology of This Power.—At what period in this world's history is the rise of this power placed in the prophecy? On this point, the foundation for the conclusions at which we must arrive is already laid in the facts set forth regarding the leopard beast. It was at the time when this beast went into captivity, or was killed with the sword (verse 10), or had one of its heads wounded to death (verse 3), that John saw the two-horned beast coming up. If the leopard beast, as we have conclusively proved, signifies the papacy, and the going into captivity met its fulfillment in the temporary overthrow of the papacy by the French in 1798, then we have the time definitely specified when we are to look for the rise of this power. The expression "coming up" must signify that the power to which it applies was but newly organized, and was then just rising into prominence and influence.

Can anyone doubt what nation was actually "coming up" in 1798? Certainly it must be admitted that the United States of America is the *only* power that meets the specifications of the prophecy on this point of chronology.

The struggle of the American colonies for independence began in 1775. In 1776, they declared themselves a free and independent nation. In 1777, delegates from the thirteen original States—New Hampshire, Massachusetts, Rhode Island, Connecticut, New York, New Jersey, Pennsylvania, Delaware, Maryland, Virginia, North Carolina, South Carolina, and Georgia—in Congress assembled, adopted Articles

[6] George Alfred Townsend, *The New World Compared With the Old*, p. 635.

of Confederation. In 1783, the War of the Revolution closed with a treaty of peace with Great Britain, whereby the independence of the United States was acknowledged, and territory ceded to the extent of 815,615 square miles. In 1787, the Constitution was framed, and by July 26, 1788, it was ratified by eleven of the thirteen original States; and on the 1st of March, 1789, it went into effect. The United States thus began with less than one million square miles of territory, and less than four million citizens. Thus we come to the year 1798, when this nation is introduced into prophecy.

John Wesley, in his notes on Revelation 13, written in 1754, says of the two-horned beast:

"He has not yet come, though he cannot be far off. For he is to appear at the end of the forty-two months of the first beast." [7]

Age of This Power.—There is good evidence in the prophecy to show that the government symbolized by the two-horned beast is introduced in the early part of its career; that is, while a *youthful* power. John's words are, "I beheld another beast coming up out of the earth; and he had two horns *like a lamb*." Why does not John simply say, "He had two horns"? Why does he add "like a lamb"? It must be for the purpose of denoting the character of this beast, showing that it is not only of an innocent and harmless demeanor, but also that it is a *youthful power;* for the horns of a lamb are horns that have barely begun to grow.

Bear in mind that by the preceding argument on chronology, our gaze is fixed on the year 1798, when the power symbolized was then youthful. What notable power was at that time coming into prominence, but still in its youth? England was not, nor was France, nor Russia, nor any European power. For a young and rising power at that epoch, we are obliged to turn our eyes to the *New World*. But as soon as we turn them in that direction, they rest inevitably upon the

[7] John Wesley, *Explanatory Notes Upon the New Testament*, p. 735, comment on Revelation 13: 11.

United States as the power in question. No other power west of the Atlantic Ocean fits the description.

Location of the Two-Horned Beast.—A single declaration of the prophecy is sufficient to guide us to important and correct conclusions on this point. John calls it "another beast." It therefore is no part of the first beast; and the power symbolized by it is likewise no part of that which is intended by that beast. This is fatal to the claim of those who avoid the application of this symbol to the United States by saying that it denotes some phase of the papacy; for in such a case it would be a part of the preceding, or leopard, beast.

Since this is "another" beast, "coming up out of the earth," it must be found in some territory not covered by any other symbols. Babylon and Medo-Persia covered all the civilized part of Asia. Greece covered Eastern Europe, including Russia. Rome, with the ten kingdoms into which it was divided, as represented by the ten toes of the image of Daniel 2, the ten horns of the fourth beast of Daniel 7, the ten horns of the dragon of Revelation 12, and the ten horns of the leopard beast of Revelation 13, covered all Western Europe. In other words, all the Eastern Hemisphere known to history and civilization is covered by prophetic symbols respecting the application of which there is scarcely any room for doubt.

But there is a mighty nation in the Western Hemisphere, worthy, as we have seen, of being mentioned in prophecy, which is not yet brought in. There is one symbol remaining whose application has not yet been made. All the symbols but one are applied, and all the available areas of the Eastern Hemisphere are covered by the applications. Of all the symbols mentioned, one alone, the two-horned beast of Revelation 13, is left. Of all the countries of the earth respecting which any reason exists why they should be mentioned in prophecy, one alone, the United States of America, remains. Does the two-horned beast represent the United States? If it does, then all the symbols find an application, and all the ground is covered. If it does not, it follows that the United

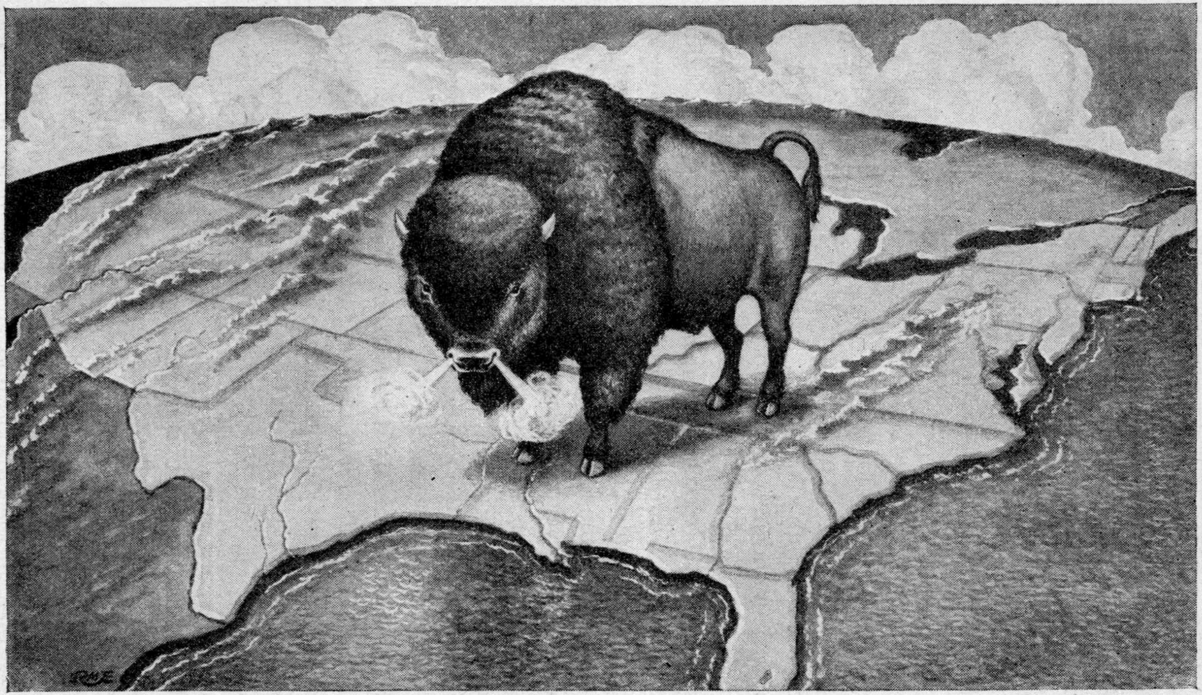

 R. M. ELDRIDGE, ARTIST

THE BEAST WITH LAMBLIKE HORNS

"I beheld another beast coming up out of the earth; and he had two horns like a lamb, and he spake as a dragon."

Revelation 13: 11

States is not represented in prophecy, and the symbol of the two-horned beast is left without a nation to which it can apply. But the first of these suppositions is not probable, and the second is not possible.

Another consideration pointing to the location of this power is drawn from the fact that John saw it arising from the earth. If the sea, from which the leopard beast arose (Revelation 13: 1) denotes peoples, nations, and multitudes (Revelation 17: 15), the earth would suggest, by contrast, a new and previously unoccupied territory. By exclusion from Eastern continents, and by looking to territory not previously known to civilization, we turn of necessity to the Western Hemisphere.

Manner of Its Rise.—The manner in which the two-horned beast was seen coming up shows, equally with its location, age, and chronology, that it is a symbol of the United States. John saw the beast coming up "out of the earth." This expression must have been designedly used to point out the contrast between the rise of this beast and that of other national prophetic symbols. The four beasts of Daniel 7 and the leopard beast of Revelation 13 all arose out of the sea. New nations generally rise by overthrowing other nations, and taking their place. But no other nation was overturned in order to make room for the United States, and the attainment of its independence was already fifteen years in the past when it came into the field of prophecy. The prophet saw only peace.

The word which is used in verse 11 to describe the manner in which this beast comes up, is very expressive. It is ἀναβαῖνον, *anabainon*, one of the prominent definitions of which is, "to grow or spring up as a plant." It is a remarkable fact that this same figure has been chosen by political writers, without any reference to the prophecy, as the one conveying the best idea of the manner in which the United States has arisen. George Alfred Townsend says:

"In this web of islands, the West Indies, began the life of both [North and South] Americas. There Columbus saw land; there Spain began her baneful and brilliant Western empire; thence Cortez departed for Mexico, De Soto for the Mississippi, Balboa for the Pacific, and Pizarro for Peru. The history of the United States was separated by a beneficent Providence far from this wild and cruel history of the rest of the continent, and *like a silent seed we grew into empire;* while empire itself, beginning in the South, was swept by so interminable hurricane that what of its history we can ascertain is read by the very lightnings that devastated it. The growth of English America may be likened to a series of lyrics sung by separate singers, which, coalescing, at last make a vigorous chorus, and this, attracting many from afar, swells and is prolonged, until presently it assumes the dignity and proportions of epic song."[8]

A writer in the Dublin *Nation* spoke of the United States as a wonderful empire which was "*emerging*," and "*amid the silence of the earth* daily adding to its power and pride."

Edward Everett, in an oration on the English exiles who founded this government, said:

"Did they look for a retired spot, inoffensive for its obscurity, and safe in its remoteness, where the little church of Leyden might enjoy the freedom of conscience? Behold the mighty regions over which, in *peaceful conquest—victoria sine clade* [victory without strife]—they have borne the banners of the cross."[9]

Will the reader now look at these expressions side by side—"coming up out of the earth," "emerging amid the silence of the earth," "like a silent seed we grew into empire," "mighty regions" secured by "peaceful conquest." The first is from the prophet, stating what *would be* when the two-horned beast should arise; the others are from political writers, telling what *has been* in the history of the United States of America. Can anyone fail to see that the last three are exactly synonymous

---

[8] George Alfred Townsend, *The New World Compared With the Old*, p. 635.

[9] Edward Everett, "Oration Delivered at Plymouth, December 22, 1824," *Orations and Speeches*, p. 42.

with the first, and that they record a complete accomplishment of the prediction?

Another inquiry naturally follows: Has the United States "come up" in a manner to meet the specifications of the prophecy? Let us see. A short time before the great Reformation in the days of Martin Luther, more than four hundred years ago, this Western Hemisphere was discovered. The Reformation awoke the nations that were fettered in the galling bonds of superstition and oppression, to the great truth that it is the heaven-born right of every man to worship God according to the dictates of his own conscience. But rulers are loath to lose their power, and religious intolerance continued to oppress the people. Under these circumstances, a body of religious heroes at length determined to seek in the wilds of America that measure of civil and religious freedom which they so much desired. In pursuance of their noble purpose, one hundred of these voluntary exiles landed from the "Mayflower" on the coast of New England, December 21, 1620. "There," says Martyn, "New England was born," and this was "its first baby cry, a prayer and a thanksgiving to the Lord."[10]

Another permanent English settlement had been made at Jamestown, Virginia, in 1607. In process of time, other settlements were made and colonies organized, which were all subject to the English crown till the Declaration of Independence, July 4, 1776.

The population of these colonies amounted in 1701 to 262,000; in 1749, to 1,046,000; in 1775, to 2,803,000.[11] Then came the struggle for independence, the establishment of a united constitutional government, and the proclamation to the world that here all could find an asylum from oppression and intolerance. From the Old World came immigrants by the thousand, adding by peaceful means to the population and

[10] W. Carlos Martyn, *The Pilgrim Fathers*, p. 89.

[11] "The People and Progress of the United States," *The United States Magazine*, Vol. II, August, 1855, p. 71.

prosperity of the new nation. Large territories were purchased or acquired by treaty to make room for all who came to settle. Now, passing over more than 150 years, to the second quarter of the twentieth century, the territory of the United States has expanded to more than three and a half million square miles, and its population has increased to over 135,000,000 people.

The growth of the United States in material prosperity and enlightened development is an astonishment to the world, and furnishes an ample basis for the application of the prophecy.

Character of Its Government Symbolized.—Under this division of the subject we find still further evidence that the symbol represents the United States. In describing this power, John says that it had "two horns like a lamb." The horns of a lamb indicate youthfulness, innocence, and gentleness. As a power which has but recently arisen, the United States answers to the symbol admirably in respect to age, while no other power can be found to do this. Considered as an index of power and character, it can be decided what constitutes the two horns of the government, if it can be ascertained what is the secret of its power, and what reveals its character, or constitutes its outward profession. The Hon. J. A. Bingham gives us the clue to the whole matter when he states that the object of those who first sought these shores was to found "what the world had not seen for ages; viz., a church without a pope, and a state without a king." Expressed in other words, this would be a government in which the ecclesiastical should be separate from the civil power, and civil and religious liberty would be characteristic.

It needs no argument to show that this is precisely the profession of the American government. Article IV., sec. 4, of the Constitution of the United States, reads in part: "The United States shall guarantee to every State in this Union a republican form of government." Article VI: "No religious test shall ever be required as a qualification to any office or public trust under the United States." The First Amendment to the Constitution begins as follows: "Congress shall make no law respecting an establishment of religion, or prohibiting the free exercise thereof." These articles profess the amplest guaranty of *civil* and *religious* liberty, the entire and perpetual separation of church and state. What better symbols of them could be given than "two horns like a lamb"? In what other country can be found a condition of things which would represent so completely this feature of the symbol?

Republican in Form.—The two-horned beast, with a noticeable absence of crowns upon its horns, symbolizes a nation with a republican form of government. A crown is an appropriate symbol of a kingly or dictatorial form of government, and the absence of crowns, as in this case, would suggest a government in which the power is not vested in any such ruling member, but is lodged in the hands of the people.

But this is not the most conclusive proof that the nation here symbolized is republican in its form of government. From verse 14 we learn that appeal is made to the people when any national action is to be performed: "Saying to them that dwell on the earth, that *they* should make an image to the beast." This is emphatically the case in the United States. The Constitution on which it was founded guarantees "a republican form of government," as shown above. This constitutes another link in the chain of evidence that this symbol applies to the United States of America. There is no other government to which anyone could reasonably think of applying this symbol.

A Protestant Nation.—The two-horned beast symbolizes a nation which cannot be Catholic in religion. The papacy is a religion that is fundamentally a union of church and state. The Constitution of the United States of America (Article VI) declares that "no religious test shall ever be required as a qualification to any office or public trust," and thereby establishes a perpetual separation of church and state. Civil and religious liberty is a fundamental principle of Protestantism. The founders of this great land, living close to all of the events that resulted from a union of church and state, were jealous of the liberties that they claimed as the rights of all, and were quick to denounce anything that savored of a union of church and state. From the religious standpoint, therefore, the United States is a Protestant nation, and meets the requirement of the prophecy admirably in this respect. Thus again the prophecy points directly to this nation.

Before entering upon a discussion of another aspect of this prophetic symbol, let us review the points already established:

The power symbolized by the two-horned beast must be some nation distinct from the powers of the Old World, whether civil or ecclesiastical.

It must arise in the Western Hemisphere.

It must be seen assuming a position of prominence and influence about the year 1798.

It must rise in a peaceful and quiet manner, not augmenting its power and expanding its territory, as other nations have done, by aggressive wars and successful conquests.

Its progress must be so evident as to strike the beholder with as much wonder as would the perceptible growth of an animal before his eyes.

It must be republican in its form of government.

It must be Protestant in its religion.

It must exhibit before the world, as an index of its character and the elements of its government, two great principles which are in themselves perfectly just, innocent, and lamblike.

It must perform its work after 1798.

We have seen that of all these specifications, it can be said that they are conclusively met in the history of the United States thus far; and that they are not met in the history of any other nation. It is therefore impossible to apply the symbol of Revelation 13: 11 to any other nation than the United States of America.

To Speak as a Dragon.—Now that we have identified the United States of America as the power symbolized by the two-horned beast, we can follow through without fear or prejudice the course that that nation takes as marked out clearly in the prophecy itself. In doing so, let us observe once more that the dragon as the first of the three beasts in the chain of prophecy under consideration, was a relentless persecutor of the church of God. The leopard beast that followed was likewise a persecuting power, destroying the lives of millions of Christians during a period of 1260 years. As we come to the third beast, with two horns like a lamb, it is declared that he "spake as a dragon." This can only mean that at some time his nature changes from that of a lamb to that of a dragon, that he speaks as a dragon, and that he does the same kind of work as the dragon before him.

Permit us to say at this juncture that it is with much pain that we contemplate a nation arising so peaceably and devoted to such noble principles of government, taking on the nature of the beasts that preceded it, and in doing so descending to the role of persecutor of God's people. We have no other choice, however, but to be guided in our study by the divinely inspired outline so plainly given us in the prophecy. Since the United States is the power denoted by the symbol that speaks as a dragon, it follows that it will enact unjust and oppressive laws against the religious belief and practice of its citizens so that it may be justly called a persecuting power.

VERSE 12 And he exerciseth all the power of the first beast before him, and causeth the earth and them which dwell therein to worship the first beast, whose deadly wound was healed.

To Exercise Persecuting Power.—Not only does this nation speak as a dragon, but it is declared that he also "exerciseth all the power of the first beast before him." Looking back a little, we find that the first beast before him is the leopard, a symbol of the papacy. The only conclusion that can be drawn is that a so-called Protestant nation will exercise the persecuting power of the papacy, and thereby become pseudo-Protestant, that is, the "false prophet" mentioned in Revelation 19: 20, and explained under the next topic.

The exercise of this power takes the form of causing the people in his jurisdiction "to worship the first beast," the papacy. The Greek word for "worship" used here is a very significant one. It is from the simple verb κυνέω, *kuneo*, "I kiss," compounded with a preposition to indicate that the kiss is directed toward someone—in this case the papacy, or its titular head the pope. It is ordinarily translated "do obeisance to, bow down to," and is used by the Septuagint in Nebuchadnezzar's decree to all "people, nations, and languages" to "fall down and *worship* the golden image" he had set up in the plain of Dura. Daniel 3: 4, 5. Such "worship" must mean to submit to the authority and decree of the one to whom obeisance is made. This is the picture given in the prophecy of the "worship" given to the papacy by a so-called Protestant people.

VERSE 13 And he doeth great wonders, so that he maketh fire come down from heaven on the earth in the sight of men, 14 and deceiveth them that dwell on the earth, by the means of those miracles which he had power to do in the sight of the beast; saying to them that dwell on the earth, that they should make an image to the beast, which had the wound by a sword, and did live.

"*He Doeth Great Wonders.*"—In that part of the prediction which sets forth the work of the two-horned beast we read that "he doeth great wonders, so that he maketh fire come down from heaven on the earth in the sight of men." In this specification we have still further proof that the United States is the power represented by the two-horned beast. That we are living in an age of wonders, none will deny. We would refer the reader to our remarks on Daniel 12: 4 concerning the wonderful achievements of the present age, and for some illustrations of the leading triumphs of scientific and inventive skill.

But the prophecy is not fulfilled in the great advancement in knowledge, in discoveries, and in inventions so notable at the present time. For the wonders to which the prophet had reference are evidently wrought for the purpose of deceiving the people, as we read in verse 14: "Deceiveth them that dwell on the earth by the means of those miracles which he had power to do in the sight of the beast."

We should now ascertain by what means the miracles in question are wrought, for Revelation 16: 13, 14 refers to "the spirits of devils working miracles, which go forth unto the kings of the earth and of the whole world."

In predicting events to occur just before His second coming, the Saviour says: "There shall arise false christs, and false prophets, and shall show great signs and wonders; insomuch that, if it were possible, they shall deceive the very elect." Matthew 24: 24. Here again are wonders foretold, wrought for the purpose of deception, so powerful that were it possible even the very elect would be deceived by them.

Thus we have a prophecy (and there are many others) setting forth the development in the last days of a wonder-working power, manifested to a startling and unprecedented degree to propagate falsehood and error. The "spirits of devils" were to go forth to "the whole world," but the nation with which this development is especially connected in Revelation 13, is that represented by the two-horned beast, or false prophet. We must therefore conclude that the prophecy calls for such a work as this in America. Do we find anything like it at the present time?

There is a widespread belief and teaching current among all classes of society, that when a man dies and his body is laid away in the grave, an immortal "spirit" or "soul" within him does not really die, but soars away to its place of reward or punishment. This belief naturally leads one to ask, "If disembodied spirits are alive, why may they not communicate with us?" There are thousands who believe that they can and do, and who claim to have communication with departed friends.

But the Bible, in the most explicit terms, assures us that the dead are wholly inactive and unconscious until the resurrection; that the dead know not anything (Ecclesiastes 9: 5); that every operation of the mind has ceased (Psalm 146: 4); that

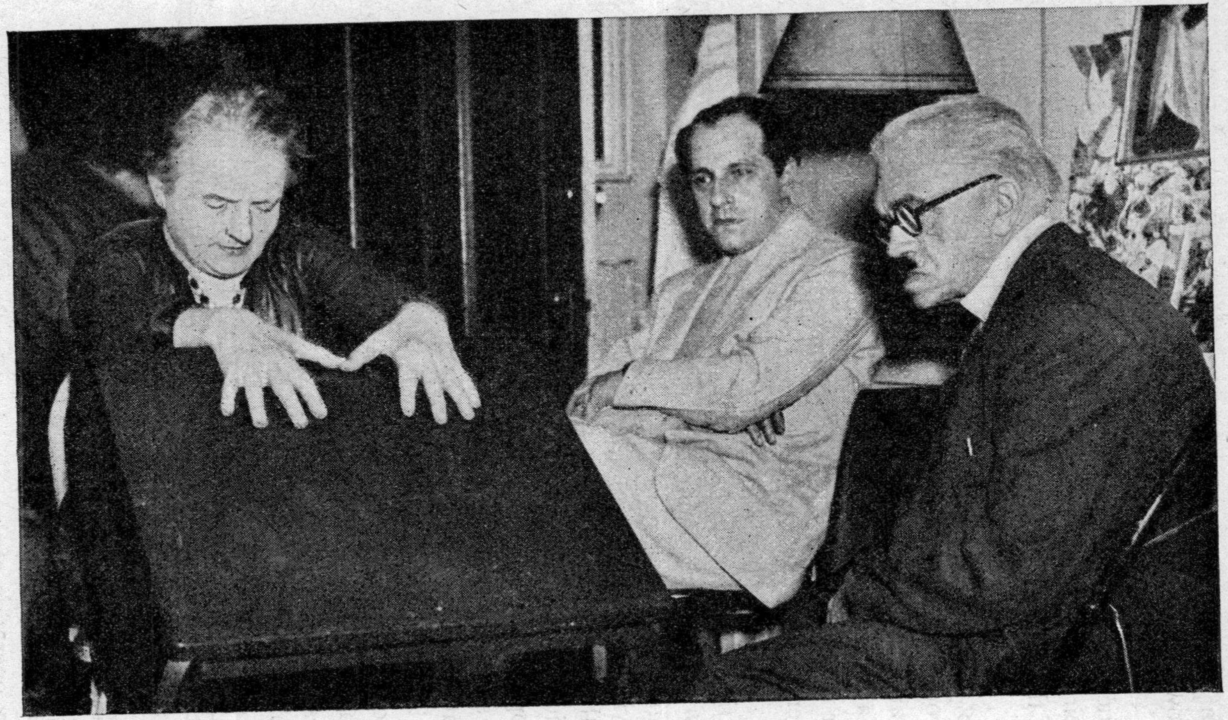

A MODERN SPIRITISTIC DEMONSTRATION

A modern spiritistic demonstration, with a woman medium officiating, shows what sometimes is seen in a modern seance.

every emotion of the heart is suspended (Ecclesiastes 9: 6); and that there is neither work, nor device, nor knowledge, nor wisdom in the grave, where they lie (Ecclesiastes 9: 10). Whatever intelligence, therefore, comes to us professing to be one of our dead friends, comes claiming to be what from the word of God we know he is not. That our dead friends do not return to us is shown in 2 Samuel 12: 23, where David says of his dead child, "Now he is dead, . . . I shall go to him, but he shall not return to me." Any such intelligence that comes to us cannot be a good angel, for angels of God do not lie. Spirits of devils do lie, and this has been their work ever since the first lie about dying was told by their leader in Eden, "Ye shall not surely die," when the Lord had said plainly to Adam, "Thou shalt surely die." Genesis 3: 4; 2: 17.

Birthplace of Spiritism.—Modern spiritism also answers to the prophecy in that it had its origin in the United States, thus connecting its wonders with the work of the two-horned beast. Beginning in Hydesville, New York, in the family of John D. Fox in the latter part of March, 1848, it spread with incredible rapidity through all the world.

Much excitement was caused by these supposed revelations, and some rather prominent persons undertook to investigate the "rapping delusion," as it was commonly called. From that time onward, spiritism has remained a force in the modern world; and it is a force which has steadily grown. It is difficult to determine the number of its adherents, because so many who believe and practice its teachings regard themselves as belonging to no denomination at all; yet on the other hand many retain their membership in a non-spiritist denominational group while nevertheless attempting communication with the dead. It has been estimated that there are 16,000,000 spiritists in North America; and in the world—including those heathen religions in which spiritism plays so prominent a part—doubtless hundreds of millions.

As Sir Arthur Conan Doyle remarked some years ago: "The lowly manifestations of Hydesville have ripened into results which have engaged the finest group of intellects in this country during the last twenty years, and which are destined, in my opinion, to bring about far the greatest development of human experience which the world has ever seen."[12] "If such a view of Christianity were generally accepted, and if it were enforced by assurance and demonstration from the New Revelation which is, as I believe, coming to us from the other side, then I think we should have a creed which might unite the churches, which might be reconciled to science, which might defy all attacks, and which might carry the Christian faith on for an indefinite period."[13]

Teachings of Spiritism.—But the doctrines which spiritists teach are certainly not in harmony with the word of God. As to their attitude toward the Bible, notice the following paragraph:

"We have no desire to hide the plain fact that there is much in some parts of the Bible which does not amalgamate with our teaching, being, indeed, the admixture of human error which came through the mind of the chosen medium."[14] "In no case are the books as they now stand the work of their reputed author. They are the compilation of Ezra and his scribes, and do but embody the conceptions and legends of the period. . . . We mention this to avoid at once the necessity of replying to any texts from these books which may be quoted as an argument."[15]

As to the relation of spiritists to Christ and His atoning work, observe the following significant remark:

"They [the spirits] also testify that Jesus Christ has nothing to do with the question of life and death, and they know nothing about the 'mediation of our Saviour Jesus Christ.' "[16]

---

[12] Sir Arthur Conan Doyle, "The New Revelation," *Metropolitan*, January, 1918, p. 69.

[13] *Ibid.*, p. 75.

[14] William Stainton Moses, *Spirit Teachings*, p. 74.

[15] *Ibid.*, p. 189.

[16] James A. Findlay, in *The Rock of Truth*, p. 288.

Believers in spiritism have no place, either, for the second advent of our Lord and Saviour Jesus Christ:

"Jesus Christ is now arranging His plans for the gathering of His people, for the further revelation of the truth, as well as for the purging away of the erroneous beliefs which have accumulated in the past. I have heard something of this from other sources. Is this then the return of Christ? It is the spiritual return. There will be no such physical return as man has dreamed of. This will be the return to His people, by the voice of His messengers speaking to those whose ears are open."[17]

Phenomena of Spiritism.—How significant are these words! Centuries ago the seer of Patmos declared that in this country would arise a power that "doeth great wonders," and, lo, spiritism appears claiming to do these very things.

Spiritism answers accurately to the prophecy in the exhibition of great signs and wonders. Among its achievements the following may be noted: Various articles have been transported from place to place by spirits. Beautiful music has been produced independent of human agency, with and without the aid of visible instruments. Many well-attested cases of healing have been presented. Persons have been carried through the air by spirits in the presence of spectators. Tables have been suspended in the air with several persons upon them. Spirits also have presented themselves in bodily form and talked with audible voices.

The power represented in this prophecy is to make "fire come down from heaven on the earth in the sight of men." But this as well as other manifestations of its power are for the purpose of deceiving "them that dwell on the earth." The miracles that are wrought are by "the spirits of devils." Revelation 16: 14. And many are the warnings in the word of God against making contact with evil spirits. In the days of the early church solemn warnings were given to the church

---

[17] William Stainton Moses, *Spirit Teachings*, pp. 150, 151.

of God: "Now the Spirit speaketh expressly, that in the latter times some shall depart from the faith, giving heed to seducing spirits, and doctrines of devils." 1 Timothy 4: 1. God's counsel to His people in these last days is, "When they shall say unto you, Seek unto them that have familiar spirits, and unto wizards that peep, and that mutter: should not a people seek unto their God? For the living to the dead? To the law and to the testimony: if they speak not according to this word, it is because there is no light in them." Isaiah 8: 19, 20.

VERSE 15 And he had power to give life unto the image of the beast, that the image of the beast should both speak, and cause that as many as would not worship the image of the beast should be killed. 16 And he causeth all, both small and great, rich and poor, free and bond, to receive a mark in their right hand, or in their foreheads: 17 and that no man might buy or sell, save he that had the mark, or the name of the beast, or the number of his name.

Makes an Image to the Beast.—Closely associated with this working of miracles is the erection of an image to the beast. The prophet thus connects the two in verse 14: "And deceiveth them that dwell on the earth by the means of those miracles which he had power to do in the sight of the beast; saying to them that dwell on the earth, that they should make an image to the beast which had the wound by a sword, and did live." The deception accomplished by the working of the miracles prepares the way for compliance with this demand for the formation of an image to the beast.

To understand what would constitute an image of the papal beast, we must first gain some definite idea of what constitutes the papacy itself. The full development of the beast, or the establishment of papal supremacy, dates from the famous letter of Justinian, which was made effective in A. D. 538, constituting the pope the head of the church and the corrector of heretics. The papacy was a church clothed with civil power—an ecclesiastical body having authority to punish all dissenters with confiscation of goods, imprisonment, torture, and death. What would be an image of the papacy?—Another ecclesiastical establishment clothed with civil power, in other words, a union of church and state. How could such an image be formed in the United States? Let the Protestant churches be clothed with power to define and punish heresy, to enforce their dogmas under the pains and penalties of the civil law, and should we not have an exact representation of the papacy during the days of its supremacy?

To be sure we would. But is such an eventuality possible in a country whose foundation stones are civil and religious liberty, and where every man's right to "life, liberty, and the pursuit of happiness" has gone unchallenged throughout the years? Let us examine the evidence.

Nation Founded on Liberty.—The hand of God wrought with the noble and God-fearing men who laid so well the foundations of the new nation. Said the Hon. Henry D. Estabrook, speaking before the Connecticut Bar Association: "On this great continent, which God had kept hidden in a little world—here, with a new heaven and a new earth, where former things had passed away, the people of many nations, of various needs and creeds, but united in heart and soul and mind for the single purpose, builded an altar to Liberty, the first ever built or that ever could be built, and called it—The Constitution of the United States."[18]

This was in the year 1787. The prophet saw the lamblike beast coming up out of the earth about 1798—surely this is no mere coincidence. George Washington, the first President of the United States, in his inaugural address said:

"No people can be bound to acknowledge and adore the Invisible Hand which conducts the affairs of men more than the people of the United States. Every step by which they have advanced to the character of an independent nation, seems to have been distinguished by some token of providential agency."[19]

---

[18] State Bar Association of Connecticut, *Annual Report, 1916*, p. 73.

[19] *Annals of Congress*, Vol. I, p. 28.

In their reply to this notable address the Senate declared: "When we contemplate the coincidence of circumstances, and wonderful combination of causes, which gradually prepared the people of this country for independence; when we contemplate the rise, progress, and termination of the late war, which gave them a name among the nations of the earth; we are, with you, unavoidably led to acknowledge and adore the great Arbiter of the universe, by whom empires rise and fall."[20]

Struggle Against Religious Tyranny.—These were not only godly men, but they were wise and farseeing men. When certain religious groups made appeal that "explicit acknowledgment of the only true God and Jesus Christ" be made in the Constitution, their request was denied. In writing of this incident, Thomas Jefferson said: "The insertion was rejected by a great majority, in proof that they meant to comprehend within the mantle of its protection the Jew and the Gentile, the Christian and Mahometan, the Hindoo, and Infidel of every denomination."[21]

The House Judiciary Committee, February 18, 1874, in reply to a similar petition, reported: "As this country, the foundation of whose government they were then laying, was to be the home of the oppressed of all nations of the earth, whether Christian or pagan, and in full realization of the dangers which the union between church and state had imposed upon so many nations of the Old World, with great unanimity [they agreed] that it was inexpedient to put anything into the Constitution or frame of government which might be construed to be a reference to any religious creed or doctrine."[22]

History attests the fact that these great men who laid the foundation stones upon which the United States was erected looked forward with almost prophetic vision to the dangers to

---

[20] *Ibid.*, p. 32.
[21] *The Writings of Thomas Jefferson*, Vol. I, p. 45.
[22] *U. S. House Reports*, 43d Congress, 1st Session, No. 143.

personal liberty which some day would confront the country. Their fears were well expressed by Thomas Jefferson: "The spirit of the times may alter, will alter. Our rulers will become corrupt, our people careless. A single zealot may commence persecution, and better men be his victims. It can never be too often repeated, that the time for fixing every essential right on a legal basis, is while our rulers are honest and ourselves united. From the conclusion of this war we shall be going downhill. It will not then be necessary to resort every moment to the people for support. They will be forgotten, therefore, and their rights disregarded. They will forget themselves, but in the sole faculty of making money, and will never think of uniting to effect a due respect for their rights. The shackles, therefore, which shall not be knocked off at the conclusion of this war, will remain on us long, will be made heavier and heavier, till our rights shall revive or expire in a convulsion."[23]

On the Fourth of July, 1788, an address was delivered by Justice James Wilson, in which he pointed out how the enemies of liberty were already working. He said: "The enemies of liberty are artful and insidious. A counterfeit steals her dress, imitates her manner, forges her signature, assumes her name. But the real name of the deceiver is licentiousness. Such is her effrontery, that she will charge liberty to her face with imposture; and she will, with shameless front, insist that herself alone is the genuine character, and that herself alone is entitled to the respect which the genuine character deserves. With the giddy and undiscerning, on whom a deeper impression is made by dauntless impudence than by modest merit, her pretentions are often successful. She receives the honors of liberty, and liberty herself is treated as a traitor and a usurper. Generally, however, this bold impostor acts only a secondary part. Though she alone appear upon the stage, her motions are regulated by dark ambition, who sits concealed

[23] "Notes on Virginia," Query 17, *The Writings of Thomas Jefferson*, Vol. VIII, p. 402.

behind the curtain, and who knows that despotism, his other favorite, can always follow the success of licentiousness. Against these enemies of liberty, who act in concert, though they appear on opposite sides, the patriot citizen will keep a watchful guard."[24]

Threatened With Ecclesiastical Domination.—Let it be noted that in the panorama of coming events which passed before the prophet John, he witnessed this same amazing change in the nature of the two-horned beast. It eventually began to speak "as a dragon" and to control the worship of its people, "saying to them that dwell upon the earth, that they should make an image to the beast."

The beast "which had the wound by a sword, and did live," is the papacy. This was a church dominating the civil power. In other words, it was a union of church and state, and enforced its religious dogmas by the civil power, under pain of confiscation of goods, imprisonment, and death. An image to this beast would be another ecclesiastical organization clothed with civil power—another union of church and state—to enforce religious dogmas by law.

Evidence that such an image will be formed is seen in the fact that already large and influential organizations, such as the National Reform Association, the International Reform Bureau, the Lord's Day Alliance of the United States, and the Federal Council of the Churches of Christ in America, have been formed, by professed Protestants, and for years have been persistently working to the end of establishing and enforcing religious standards by law. Also Roman Catholic societies in the United States, in harmony with their tradition for centuries, are looking to a like end. Ultimately these two forces are destined to join hands in a common effort.

The avowed object of the National Reform Association is "to secure such an amendment to the Constitution of the United States as will . . . indicate that this is a Christian

---

[24] *The Works of the Honourable James Wilson*, Vol. III, p. 307.

nation, and place all the Christian laws, institutions, and usages of our government on an undeniably legal basis in the fundamental law of the land."[25]

Upon the question of making this a "Christian nation," Bishop Earl Cranston, D. D., of the Methodist Episcopal Church, in an address delivered in Foundry Methodist Church, Washington, D. C., March 13, 1910, made the following observation:

"Suppose this were to be declared a Christian nation by a Constitutional interpretation to that effect. What would that mean? Which of the two contending definitions of Christianity would the word 'Christian' indicate?—The Protestant idea, of course, for under our system majorities rule, and the majority of Americans are Protestants. Very well. But suppose that by the addition of certain contiguous territory with twelve or more millions of Roman Catholics, the annexation of a few more islands with half as many more, and the same rate of immigration as now, the majority some years hence should be Roman Catholics,—who doubts for a moment that the reigning Pope would assume control of legislation and government? He would say, with all confidence and consistency, 'This is a Christian nation. It was so claimed from the beginning and so declared many years ago. A majority defined then what Christianity was, the majority will define now what Christianity now is and is to be.' That 'majority' would be the Pope."[26]

This association, organized for so-called "National Reform" has no compunctions about uniting with the papacy to bring about its design to establish a national religion. It declares: "We cordially, gladly, recognize the fact that in the South American Republics, and in France and other European countries, the Roman Catholics are the recognized advocates of national Christianity, and stand opposed to all the

---

[25] David McAllister, *The National Reform Movement, Its History and Principles*, p. 16; Constitution of the National Reform Association, Art. II.

[26] "*The Church and the Government*," p. 7.

C. DUMARESQ. ARTIST

A NEW NATION AROSE
The signing of the Declaration of Independence adopted on July 4, 1776.

proposals of secularism. . . . Whenever they are willing to co-operate in resisting the progress of political atheism, we will gladly join hands with them. In a world's conference for the promotion of national Christianity—which ought to be held at no distant day—many countries could be represented only by Roman Catholics."[27]

Shall we now notice the avowed objective of the other organizations?

In a *History of the International Reform Bureau* the society in a self-appraisal declares, "The Reform Bureau is the first 'Christian lobby' established at our National Capital to speak to government in behalf of all denominations."[28]

On pages 61 and 65 of the foregoing work it is stated that the securing of compulsory Sunday legislation is one of the chief objects of this and other like organizations.

Speaking before the United States Senate Judiciary Committee against the Supreme Court bill, Professor Theodore Graebner, of Concordia College, St. Louis, made this interesting observation:

"Some 50 years ago the National Reform Association sought . . . to make all public education Christian and thereby make Jesus Christ the King of the nation. . . . The movement persists to the present day, and is issuing an enormous amount of literature all directed to the end of adopting a Christian amendment."[29]

The actual objective of this organization is to force religion upon the people by legal enactment—to secure a Sunday blue law, and to standardize the Christianity of the people.

From a leaflet published by the Lord's Day Alliance of the United States we learn that their objective is:

"(1) To preserve the Lord's day [Sunday] for America; (2) to secure an active Alliance in every State not yet organ-

---

[27] *Christian Statesman*, December 11, 1884, p. 2.

[28] *History of the International Reform Bureau*, p. 2.

[29] U. S. Senate Judiciary Committee Hearings, *Reorganization of the Federal Judiciary*, Part 3, p. 681.

ized: (3) to induce the general government as far as possible to set the example of Sabbath observance."

By all this is meant the securing, as far as possible, of compulsory state and national Sunday legislation—the very means by which the church gained control of the state and by which church and state were united in the fourth and fifth centuries of the Christian Era.

The Federal Council of Churches of Christ in America, which is by far the most powerful and representative combination of Protestant churches in the nation, claiming at its beginning to represent eighteen organizations and 50,000,000 communicants, in stating its reasons for existence declared:

"That the great Christian bodies of our country should stand together . . . [in dealing with] questions like those of marriage and divorce, Sabbath desecration, social evils," etc.[30]

In defining how they purpose to deal with Sabbath desecration, the Federal Council declared:

"That all encroachments upon the claims and the sanctities of the Lord's day should be stoutly resisted through the press, the Lord's day associations and alliances, and by such legislation as may be secured to protect and preserve this bulwark of our American Christianity."[31]

Thus it will be seen that the securing of laws for the enforcement of Sunday observance is a prominent feature in all these organizations in their efforts to "Christianize" the nation. In doing this many fail to see that they are repudiating the principles of Christianity, of Protestantism, and of the United States Government, and playing directly into the hand of that power which originated the Sunday sabbath, and gained control of the civil power through Sunday legislation—the papacy.

This danger was clearly discerned by the lawmakers of the United States more than a century ago. In 1830, certain

---

[30] Federal Council of the Churches of Christ in America, *Report of the First Meeting of the Federal Council, Philadelphia, 1908*, pp. 5, 6.

[31] *Ibid.*, p. 103.

memorials for prohibiting the transportation of the mails and the opening of post offices on Sunday, which had been referred to the Congressional Committee on Post Offices and Post Roads, came up for consideration. The committee reported unfavorably to the petition of the memorialists. Its report was adopted, and printed by order of the Senate of the United States, and the committee was discharged from any further consideration of the subject. Of the Constitution it said:

"The committee look in vain to that instrument for a delegation of power authorizing this body to inquire and determine what part of time, or whether any, has been set apart by the Almighty for religious exercises. . . .

"The Constitution regards the conscience of the Jew as sacred as that of the Christian; and gives no more authority to adopt a measure affecting the conscience of a solitary individual, than that of a whole community. That representative who would violate this principle, would lose his delegated character, and forfeit the confidence of his constituents. If Congress shall declare the first day of the week holy, it will not convince the Jew nor the Sabbatarian. It will dissatisfy both, and consequently convert neither. . . . If a solemn act of legislation shall in *one* point define the law of God, or point out to the citizen one religious duty, it may with equal propriety proceed to define *every* part of divine revelation; and enforce *every* religious obligation, even to the forms and ceremonies of worship, the endowment of the church, and the support of the clergy.

"The framers of the Constitution recognized the eternal principle that man's relation with his God is above human legislation, and his rights of conscience inalienable."[32]

Seeking to Establish Righteousness by Law.—A thousand pities that the religious leaders in these days are not equally sensitive to the dangers which lurk beneath their program to make the people good by legal enactment of religious dogmas.

---

[32] "Sunday Mail," *U. S. House Reports*, Vol. II, No. 271, pp. 1-4.

We are not unmindful of the noble service the Protestant churches have rendered to humanity and to the world by introducing and defending the great principles of Protestantism, by propagating the gospel, and by championing the cause of freedom.

Let no one think that we wish to reflect in any way upon the character of the men engaged in this enterprise. They are men of the highest moral standing, sincerely solicitous for the welfare of the nation, and honestly trying to check and remove the evils which are rampant in society. That their efforts will in many ways be productive of good, no one can doubt. We wish them all possible success in their work for the promotion of temperance, the elimination of war, the safeguarding of youth, and other like noble purposes. For these things all Christians are bound to work and pray.

Why then are these good men misled into doing something against which the Bible utters a solemn warning? The reason is that they have turned aside from the counsel of God given them in His word, and are going about to establish righteousness and the kingdom of God in the earth in their own way. They have slighted the prophetic portions of the Bible, by which one may know what stage of the conflict between the kingdom of Christ and that of Satan has been reached in his day, and how he can co-operate with the providence of God for the times in which he is living. They have lost touch with their divine Leader and with the means He is using today to advance His kingdom in the earth. They have a mistaken conception of the kingdom which is to come, and are looking for a kingdom mixed with earthly elements, to be set up by earthly agencies, such as the ballot, legislation, and education.

Under such circumstances it is not surprising that they should be working at cross-purposes with the providence of God. The mistake of failing to heed and be guided by the instruction of God's word, is a fatal one. The more zeal a church has when it is off the track and pursuing a wrong course, the greater will be the damage which it will do.

The apostle Paul points to a time when men would have "a form of godliness," but would deny "the power thereof."

We greatly regret to see the Protestant church active in the fulfillment of this prophetic picture. While the power of God is lacking, the outward services of true Christian worship are maintained. With the loss of the power of God the churches are turning more and more to the state to supply what they lack. It is the testimony of all history that just in proportion as any popular and extensive ecclesiastical organization loses the spirit and power of God, it clamors for the support of the civil arm and finally religion becomes a part of the state. Thus it will be in the formation of the image of the beast, for the prophecy declares: "He had power to give life unto the image of the beast, that the image of the beast should both speak, and cause that as many as would not worship the image of the beast should be killed." Revelation 13: 15.

Let now an ecclesiastical organization be formed, let the government legalize such an organization and give it power to enforce upon the people the dogmas which the different denominations can all adopt as the basis of union, and what do we have? Exactly what the prophecy represents—an image to the papal beast endowed with life by the two-horned beast, to speak and act with power.

The Mark of the Beast.—The two-horned beast enforces upon its subjects the mark of the first beast. We have now in the prophecy three agents introduced, which we must carefully distinguish from one another to avoid confusion.

The papal beast is the power designated as "the beast," "the first beast," "the beast which had the wound by a sword, and did live," and "the beast whose deadly wound was healed." These expressions all refer to the same power, and wherever they occur in this prophecy, they have exclusive reference to the papacy.

The two-horned beast is the power introduced in Revelation 13: 11, and is represented through the remainder of the prophecy by the pronoun "he." Wherever this pronoun occurs, down to the seventeenth verse (with possibly the exception of the sixteenth verse, which perhaps may refer to the image), it refers invariably to the two-horned beast.

The image of the beast is usually called in the following chapters of Revelation, "the image;" so there is no danger of confusing this with any other agent. The acts ascribed to the image are speaking as a dragon and enforcing the worship of itself under the penalty of death. This is the only enactment which the prophecy mentions as enforced under the death penalty.

The mark of the beast is enforced by the two-horned beast, either directly or through the image. The penalty attached to a refusal to receive this mark is a forfeiture of all social privileges, a deprivation of the right to buy and sell. The mark is the mark of the papal beast. Against this worship of the beast and his image, and the receiving of his mark, the third angel's message of Revelation 14: 9-12 is a most solemn and thrilling warning.

This, then, is the issue which according to this prophecy we are soon to be called upon to meet. Human organizations, controlled and inspired by the spirit of the dragon, are to command men to do those acts which are in reality the worshiping of an apostate religious power and the receiving of his mark. If they refuse to do this, they lose the rights of citizenship, and become outlaws in the land. They must do that which constitutes the worship of the image of the beast, or forfeit their lives. On the other hand, God sends forth a message a little before this fearful crisis comes upon the people, as we shall see in remarks on Revelation 14: 9-12, declaring that all who do any of these things "shall drink of the wine of the wrath of God, which is poured out without mixture into the cup of His indignation." He who refuses to comply with these demands of earthly powers exposes himself to the severest penalties which human beings can inflict. He who *does* comply, exposes himself to the most terrible threatenings of divine wrath to be found in the word of God. The question whether they will obey God or man is to be decided by the people of the present age under the heaviest pressure, from both sides, that has ever been brought to bear upon any generation.

The worship of the beast and his image and the receiving of his mark must be something that involves the greatest offense that can be committed against God, to call down so severe a denunciation of wrath against it. This is a work, as has already been shown, which takes place in the last days. As God has given us in His word most abundant evidence to show when we are in the last days, that no one need be overtaken by the day of the Lord as by a thief, so likewise He has given us the evidence whereby we may determine what it means to receive the mark of the beast, that we may avoid the fearful penalty so sure to follow its reception. God does not so trifle with human hopes and human destinies as to pronounce a most fearful doom against a certain sin, and then place it out of our power to understand what that sin is, so that we have no means of guarding against it.

We therefore now call attention to the important inquiry, What constitutes the mark of the beast? The figure of a mark is borrowed from an ancient custom. Thomas Newton says:

"It was customary among the ancients for servants to receive the mark of their master, and soldiers of their general, and those who were devoted to any particular deity, of the particular deity to whom they were devoted. These marks were usually impressed on their right hand or on their forehead, and consisted of some hieroglyphic characters, or of the name expressed in vulgar letters, or of the name disguised in numerical letters, according to the fancy of the imposer."[33]

Prideaux[34] says that Ptolemy Philopater ordered all the Jews who applied to be enrolled as citizens of Alexandria to have the form of an ivy leaf (the badge of his god, Bacchus) impressed upon them with a hot iron, under pain of death.

---

[33] Thomas Newton, *Dissertations on the Prophecies*, Vol. II, p. 296.

[34] Humphrey Prideaux, *The Old and New Testament Connected in the History of the Jews*, Vol. II, pp. 78, 79.

The word used for mark in this prophecy is χάραγμα, *charagma*, and is defined to mean, "a graving, sculpture; a mark cut in or stamped." It occurs nine times in the New Testament, and with the single exception of Acts 17: 29, refers every time to the mark of the beast. Of course, we are not to understand in this symbolic prophecy that a literal mark is intended, but the giving of the literal mark, as practiced in ancient times is used as a figure to illustrate certain acts that will be performed in the fulfillment of this prophecy. From the literal mark as formerly employed, we learn something of its meaning as used in the prophecy, for between the symbol and the thing symbolized there must be some resemblance. The mark as literally used, signified that the person receiving it was the servant of the person whose mark he bore, acknowledged his authority, and professed allegiance to him. So the mark of the beast, or of the papacy, must be some act or profession by which the authority of that power is acknowledged. What is it?

Characteristics of Papal Power.—It would naturally be looked for in some of the special characteristics of the papal power. Describing that power under the symbol of a little horn, Daniel speaks of it as waging a special warfare against God, wearing out the saints of the Most High, and thinking to change times and laws. The prophet expressly specifies on this point: "He shall . . . *think* to change times and laws." Daniel 7: 25. These laws must certainly be the laws of the Most High. To apply the expression to human laws, and make the prophecy read, He shall speak great words against the Most High, and shall wear out the saints of the Most High, and think to change human laws, would be doing evident violence to the language of the prophet. But apply it to the laws of God, and let it read, He shall speak great words against the Most High, and shall wear out the saints of the Most High, and shall think to change the times and laws of the Most High, and all is consistent and forcible. For the word "law" the Hebrew has דָּת, *dath*, and the Septuagint reads, νόμος, *nomos*, in the singular, "law," which more directly suggests the law of God. The papacy has been able to do more than merely "think" to change human laws. It has changed *them* at pleasure. It has annulled the decrees of kings and emperors, and absolved subjects from allegiance to their rightful sovereigns. It has thrust its long arm into the affairs of nations, and brought rulers to its feet in the most abject humility. But the prophet beholds greater acts of presumption than these. He sees it endeavor to do what it was not able to do, but could only think to do. He sees it attempt an act which no man, nor any combination of men, can ever accomplish, to change the law of the Most High. Bear this in mind while we look at the testimony of another sacred writer on this very point.

The apostle Paul speaks of the same power in 2 Thessalonians 2. He describes it, in the person of the pope, as "that man of sin" "sitting as God in the temple of God" (that is, the church), and exalting himself "above all that is called God, or that is worshiped." According to this, the pope sets himself up as the one for all the church to look to for authority, in the place of God.

We ask the reader to ponder carefully the question how he can exalt himself *above* God. Search through the whole range of human devices, go to the extent of human effort, and by what plan, by what move, by what claim, could this usurper exalt himself above God? He might institute any number of ceremonies, he might prescribe any form of worship, he might exhibit any degree of power; but as long as God had requirements which the people felt bound to regard in preference to his, so long he would not be *above* God. He might enact a law, and teach the people that they were under as great obligations to that as to the law of God; then he would only make himself *equal* with God.

But he is to do more than this; he is to attempt to raise himself *above* Him. Then he must promulgate a law which *conflicts* with the law of God, and demand obedience to his own law in preference to God's law. The most effective way in which he could place himself in the position assigned in the prophecy would be for him to change the law of God. If he can cause this change to be adopted by the people in the place of the original enactment, then he, the law changer, puts himself above God, the lawmaker. This is the very work that Daniel said the power represented by the little horn would think to do.

Such a work as this the papacy will accomplish according to the prophecy, and the prophecy cannot fail. When this is done, what do the people of the world have? They have two laws demanding obedience—one the law of God as originally enacted by Him, an embodiment of His will, and expressing His claims upon His creatures; the other, a revised edition of that law, emanating from the pope of Rome, and expressing his will. How is it to be determined which of these powers the people honor and worship?—It is determined by the law which they keep. If they keep the law of God as given by Him, they worship and obey God. If they keep the law as changed by the papacy, they worship that power.

But further, the prophecy does not say that the little horn, the papacy, should set aside the law of God, and give one entirely different. This would not be to change the law, but simply to give a new one. He was only to attempt a *change*, so that the law that comes from God and the law that comes from the papacy are precisely alike, excepting the change which the papacy has made. The two laws have many points in common. But none of the precepts which they contain in common can distinguish a person as the worshiper of either power in preference to the other. If God's law says, "Thou shalt not kill," and the law as given by the papacy says the same, no one can tell by a person's observance of that precept whether he designs to obey God rather than the pope, or the pope rather than God. But when a precept that has been changed is the subject of action, then whoever observes that precept as originally given by God, is thereby distinguished as a worshiper of God; and he who keeps it as changed is thereby marked as a follower of the power that made the change. In no other way can the two classes of worshipers be distinguished.

From this conclusion, no candid mind can dissent, but in this conclusion we have a general answer to the question, "What constitutes the mark of the beast?" The answer is simply this: The *mark* of the beast is the *change* which the beast has attempted to make in the law of God.

Change in the Law of God.—We now inquire what that change is. By the law of God, we mean the moral law, the only law in the universe of immutable and perpetual obligation. Defining the term "law" according to the sense in which it is almost universally used in Christendom, Webster says, "The moral law is summarily contained in the decalogue, written by the finger of God on two tables of stone, and delivered to Moses on Mount Sinai."

In our comment on Daniel 7: 25, in regard to the prediction of the prophet that the papacy would "think to change times and laws," we produced evidence from the *Roman Catechism* based on the unquestioned authority of the Council of Trent, and published by order of Pope Pius V by the Vatican press in Rome, that the church changed the *day* of the Sabbath from the seventh to the first day of the week. While that catechism records the full wording of the fourth commandment as it reads in the Bible, and while it is retained in full in the official Catholic Bible in Latin, the Vulgate, and in its official translation into English, the Douay Bible; yet the teaching catechisms provided for Roman Catholic priests and teachers in modern times omit all that commandment but the first sentence, "Remember that thou keep holy the Sabbath day," and add extended testimony that the change of the Sabbath day from Saturday to Sunday was made on "the authority of the Catholic Church and apostolic tradition." Whatever may be said on the text of the *Catechism of the Council of Trent* and that of the Roman Catholic Bible about retaining the entire commandment as it reads in the Scripture, nevertheless the *practice* of the prelates and priests is to teach only observance of a Sabbath *institution*, but locate it on the *first* day of the week instead of the seventh, by the authority of the church.

Let it be borne in mind, that, according to the prophecy, he was to *think* to change times and laws. This plainly conveys the idea of *intention* and *design*, and makes these qualities essential to the change in question. But respecting the omission of the second commandment, Catholics argue that it is included in the first, and hence should not be numbered as a separate commandment; and on the tenth they claim that there is so plain a distinction of ideas as to require two commandments; so they make the coveting of a neighbor's wife the ninth command, and the coveting of his goods the tenth.

In all this they claim that they are giving the commandments exactly as God intended to have them understood; so, while we may regard them as errors in their interpretation of the commandments, we cannot set them down as professedly *intentional changes*. Not so, however, with the fourth commandment. Respecting this commandment, they do not claim that their version is like that given by God. They expressly claim a change here, and also that the change has been made by the church. How these later catechisms, with their ecclesiastical imprimatur, read, is illustrated herewith.

Some of the simpler catechisms make no mention of a change of religious days, but state categorically that the *Sabbath* commandment teaches *Sunday* observance:

"Q. Say the Third Commandment.

"A. Remember that thou keep holy the Sabbath day.

"Q. What is commanded by the Third Commandment?

"A. To sanctify the Sunday."[35]

Others say that the Catholic Church changed the day of worship. In *A New Catechism of Christian Doctrine and Practice*, we find the following under the subject of the third commandment:

---

[35] *James Butler's Catechism*, p. 34.

"What day was the Sabbath?

"The seventh day, our Saturday.

"Do you keep the Sabbath?

"No: we keep the Lord's Day.

"Which is that?

"The first day: Sunday.

"Who changed it?

"The Catholic Church."[36]

In the well-known Baltimore catechism, we find this explanation:

"Q. What is the third Commandment?

"A. The third Commandment is: Remember thou keep holy the Sabbath day.

"Q. What are we commanded by the third Commandment?

"A. By the third Commandment we are commanded to keep holy the Lord's day. . . .

"Q. Are the Sabbath day and the Sunday the same?

"A. The Sabbath day and the Sunday are not the same. The Sabbath day is the seventh day of the week, and is the day which was kept holy in the old law; the Sunday is the first day of the week, and is the day which is kept holy in the new law.

"Q. Why does the Church command us to keep the Sunday holy instead of the Sabbath?

"A. The Church commands us to keep the Sunday holy instead of the Sabbath because on Sunday Christ rose from the dead, and on Sunday He sent the Holy Ghost upon the Apostles."[37]

In *The Catholic Christian Instructed* we read:

"*Q.*—What warrant have you for keeping the Sunday preferably to the ancient Sabbath, which was the Saturday?

"*A.*—We have for it the authority of the Catholic Church, and apostolical tradition.

---

[36] James Bellord, *A New Catechism of Christian Doctrine and Practice*, pp. 86, 87.

[37] *A Catechism of Christian Doctrine*, No. 2, Prepared and Enjoined by Order of the Third Plenary Council of Baltimore, p. 65.

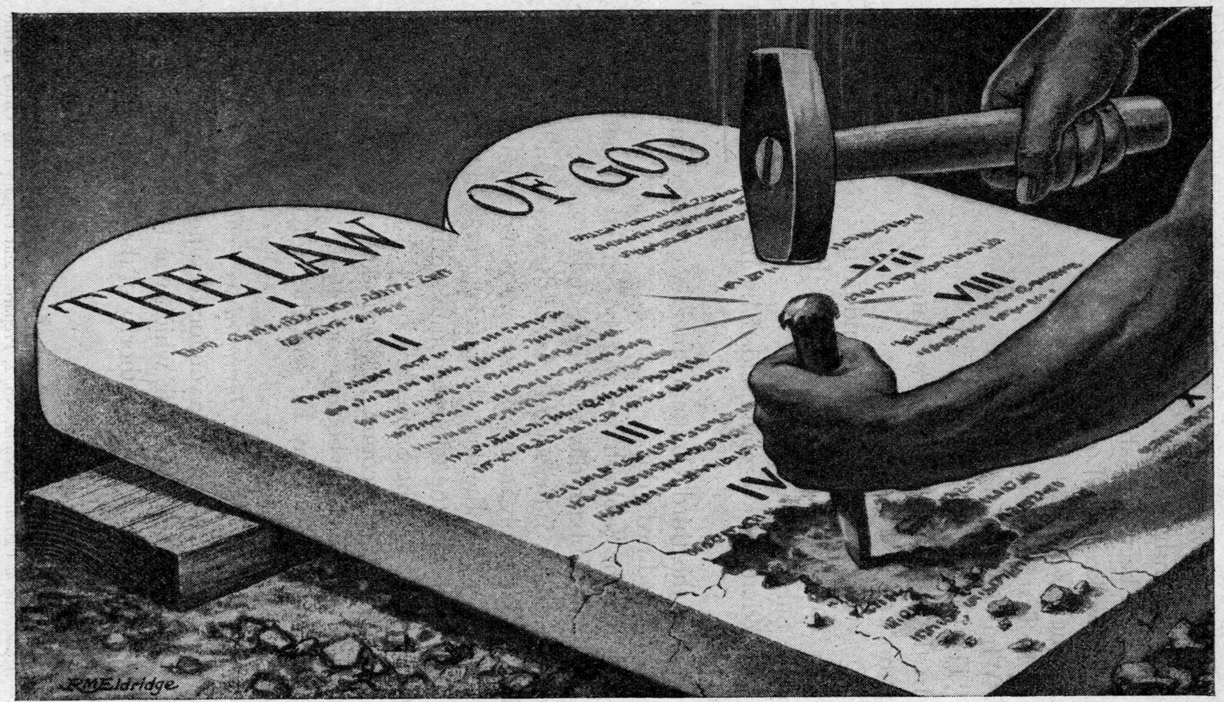

R. M. ELDRIDGE, ARTIST

THE ATTEMPT TO CHANGE GOD'S LAW

A distinguishing feature of the great apostate power brought to light in the prophecies is its attempt to change the law of God.

"*Q.*—Does the Scripture anywhere command the Sunday to be kept for the Sabbath?

"*A.*—The Scripture commands us to hear the church (Matt. 18: 17; Luke 10: 16), and to hold fast the traditions of the apostles (2 Thess. 2: 15), but the Scriptures do not in particular mention this change of the Sabbath."[38]

In *A Doctrinal Catechism* we find further testimony to the same point:

"*Ques.*—Have you any other way of proving that the church has power to institute festivals of precept?

"*Ans.*—Had she not such power, she could not have done that in which all modern religionists agree with her—she could not have substituted the observance of Sunday, the first day of the week, for the observance of Saturday, the seventh day, a change for which there is no Scriptural authority."[39]

In *An Abridgment of the Christian Doctrine* we find this testimony:

"*Q.*—How prove you that the church hath power to command feasts and holy days?

"*A.*—By the very act of changing the Sabbath into Sunday, which Protestants allow of; and therefore they fondly contradict themselves by keeping Sunday strictly, and breaking most other feasts commanded by the same church.

"*Q.*—How prove you that?

"*A.*—Because by keeping Sunday they acknowledge the church's power to ordain feasts, and to command them under sin."[40]

In *The Catechism Simply Explained*, are these questions and answers:

"What is the third commandment?

"The third commandment is, 'Remember that thou keep holy the Sabbath day.'

"What are we commanded by the third commandment?

---

[38] Richard Challoner, *The Catholic Christian Instructed*, p. 202.

[39] Stephen Keenan, *A Doctrinal Catechism*, p. 174.

[40] Henry Tuberville, *An Abridgment of the Christian Doctrine*, p. 58.

"By the third commandment we are commanded to keep the Sunday holy.

"The Jews' Sabbath Day was the Saturday; we Christians keep the Sunday holy. The Church, by the power our Lord gave her, changed the observance of the Saturday to the Sunday."[41]

This is what the papal power claims to have done respecting the fourth commandment. Catholics plainly acknowledge that there is no Scriptural authority for the change they have made, but that it rests wholly upon the authority of the church. They claim as a token, or mark, of the authority of that church the "*very act of changing the Sabbath into Sunday*," and set it forth as proof of its power in this respect.

"But," says one, "I supposed that Christ changed the Sabbath." A great many suppose so, for they have been so taught. We would remind such persons, however, that according to the prophecy the only change ever to be made in the law of God, was to be made by the little horn of Daniel 7, the man of sin of 2 Thessalonians 2; and that the only change that has been made in it is the change of the Sabbath. Now, if Christ made this change, He filled the office of the blasphemous power spoken of by both Daniel and Paul—a conclusion that is repulsive to any Christian.

Why should anyone labor to prove that Christ changed the Sabbath? Whoever does this is performing a thankless task. The pope will not thank him; for if it is proved that Christ wrought this change, then the pope is robbed of his badge of authority and power. No truly enlightened Protestant will thank him; for if he succeeds, he only shows that the papacy has not done the work which it was predicted it should do, that the prophecy has failed, and that the Scriptures are unreliable. The matter would better stand as the prophecy has it, and the claim which the pope unwittingly puts forth would better be granted.

---

[41] H. Canon Cafferata, *The Catechism Simply Explained*, p. 89.

When a person is charged with any work, and that person steps forth and confesses that he has done the work, that is usually considered sufficient to settle the matter. So, when the prophecy affirms that a certain power shall change the law of God, and in due time that very power arises, does the work foretold, and then openly claims that he has done it, what need have we of further evidence? The world should not forget that the great apostasy foretold by Paul has taken place; that the man of sin for long ages held almost a monopoly of Christian teaching in the world; that the mystery of iniquity has cast the darkness of its shadow and the errors of its doctrines over almost all Christendom; and that out of this era of error and darkness and corruption, the theology of our day has come. Would it, then, be strange if there were yet some relics of popery to be discarded before the Reformation will be complete? Alexander Campbell, founder of the Disciples of Christ Church, speaking of the different Protestant sects, says:

"All of them retain in their bosom, in their ecclesiastical organizations, worship, doctrines, and observances, various relics of popery. They are at best a reformation of popery, and only reformations in part. The doctrines and traditions of men yet impair the power and progress of the gospel in their hands."[42]

The nature of the change which the little horn has attempted to effect in the law of God is worthy of notice. True to his purpose to exalt himself above God, he undertakes to change that commandment which, among them all, is the fundamental commandment of the law, the one which makes known who the lawgiver is, and contains his signature of royalty. The fourth commandment does this; no other one does. Four others, it is true, contain the word *God*, and three of them the word *Lord*, also. But who is this Lord God of whom they speak? Without the fourth commandment it is impossible to tell, for idolaters of every grade apply these terms to the

---

[42] Alexander Campbell, *Christian Baptism*, p. 15.

multitudinous objects of their adoration. With the fourth commandment to point out the Author of the decalogue, the claims of every false god are annulled at one stroke. The God who here demands our worship is not any created being, but the One who created all things. The Maker of the earth and the sea, the sun and the moon, and all the starry host, the Upholder and Governor of the universe, is the One who claims, and who from His position has a right to claim, our supreme regard in preference to every other object. The commandment which makes known these facts is therefore the very one we might suppose that power which designed to exalt itself above God would undertake to change. God gave the Sabbath as a weekly reminder of Himself, and as a memorial of His work in creating the heavens and the earth, a great barrier against heathenism and idolatry. It is the signature and seal against atheism and idolatry. It is the signature and seal of the law. This the papacy in its teaching and practice has removed from its place, and has substituted another institution, which the church sets forth as the sign of its authority.

Issue Is Between Sabbath and Sunday.—This change of the fourth commandment must therefore be the change to which the prophecy points, and the Sunday sabbath must be the mark of the beast! Some who have long been taught to regard this institution with reverence will perhaps start back with little less than feelings of horror at this conclusion. We have not space, nor is this perhaps the place, to enter into an extended argument on the Sabbath question, and an exposition of the origin and nature of the observance of the first day of the week. Let us submit this one proposition: If the seventh day is still the Sabbath enjoined in the fourth commandment; if the observance of the first day of the week has no foundation whatever in the Scriptures; if this observance has been brought in as a Christian institution, and designedly put in place of the Sabbath of the decalogue by that power which is symbolized by the beast, and placed there as a badge and token of its power to legislate for the church—is not the change from Sabbath to Sunday inevitably the mark of the beast? The answer must be in the affirmative. The hypotheses just set forth are all certainties.

Who Receives the Mark of the Beast?—It will be said again, Then all Sundaykeepers have the mark of the beast; then all the good of past ages who kept this day had the mark of the beast; then Luther, Whitefield, the Wesleys, and all who have done a good and noble work of reformation, had the mark of the beast; then all the blessings that have been poured upon the reformed churches have been poured upon those who had the mark of the beast; and all Christians of the present day who are keeping Sunday as the Sabbath, have the mark of the beast. We answer, Not so! We are sorry to say that some professedly religious teachers, though many times corrected, persist in misrepresenting us on this point. We have never so held; we have never so taught. Our premises lead to no such conclusions.

Please give close attention. The mark and worship of the beast are enforced by the two-horned beast. The receiving of the mark of the beast is a specific act which the two-horned beast is to cause to be done. The third angel's message of Revelation 14 is a warning mercifully sent out in advance to prepare the people for the coming danger. There can therefore be no worship of the beast, nor receiving of his mark such as the prophecy contemplates, until it is *enforced* by the two-horned beast, and knowingly accepted by the individual. We have seen that *intention* was essential to the change which the papacy has made in the law of God, to constitute it the mark of that power; so *intention* is necessary in the adoption of that change by the individual, to constitute it the receiving of that mark. In other words, a person must adopt the change knowing it to be the work of the beast, and receive it on the authority of that power in opposition to the requirement of God, before it can be said that he has received the mark of the beast.

But how is it with those mentioned above, who have kept Sunday in the past, and the majority of those who are keeping it today? Do they keep it as an institution of the papacy?—No. Have they decided between this and the Sabbath of our Lord, understanding the claims of each?—No. On what ground have they kept it, and on what do they still keep it?—They suppose they are keeping a commandment of God. Have such the mark of the beast?—By no means. Their course is attributable to an error unwittingly received from the Church of Rome, not to an act of worship intentionally rendered to it.

But how is it to be in the future? The church which is to be prepared for the second coming of Christ must be entirely free from papal errors and corruptions. A reform must hence be made on the Sabbath question. The third angel of Revelation 14 proclaims the commandments of God, leading men to the true Sabbath in the place of the counterfeit. The dragon is stirred, and so controls the wicked governments of the earth that all the authority of human power shall be exerted to enforce the claims of the man of sin. Then the issue is fairly before the people. They are required by the law of God to keep the true Sabbath; they are required by the law of the Catholic Church, of the pseudo-Protestant church, and of the land to keep the counterfeit sabbath. For refusing to keep the true, the message threatens the unmingled wrath of God; for refusing the false, earthly governments threaten them with persecution and death. With this issue before the people, what does he do who yields to the human requirement? He virtually says to God, I know your claims, but I will not heed them. I know that the power I am required to worship is unchristian, but I yield to it to save my life. I renounce your allegiance, and bow to the usurper. The beast is henceforth the object of my adoration; under his banner, in opposition to your authority, I henceforth array myself; to him, in defiance of your claims, I henceforth yield the obedience of my heart and life.

Such is the spirit which will actuate the hearts of the beast worshipers—a spirit which insults the God of the universe to His face, and is prevented only by lack of power from overthrowing His government and annihilating His throne. Is it any wonder that Jehovah pronounces against so Heaven-daring a course the most terrible threatening that His word contains?

The Closing Work.—We have now seen what would properly constitute an image to the beast, such as the two-horned beast is to make, and also the prospect that such an image will sometime be set up in the United States of America. We have also learned what constitutes the mark of the beast, which is to be enforced upon all the people. An ecclesiastical organization composed of different sects in the land, in coalition with Roman Catholicism, by the promulgation and enforcement of a civil Sunday-sabbath law, would fulfill what the prophecy sets forth in reference to the image and the mark of the beast. These movements, or their exact equivalent, are called for by the prophecy. The line of evidence leading to these conclusions is so direct and well defined that there is no avoiding them. They are a clear and logical sequence from the premises given us.

When the application of Revelation 13: 11-17 to America was first made, as early as the year 1850, these positions were taken respecting a union of the churches and a Sunday-law movement. At that time no sign appeared that such an issue would ever arise. But there was the prophecy. The United States had given abundant evidence by its location, the time of its rise, the manner of its rise, and its apparent character, that it was the power symbolized by the two-horned beast. There could be no mistake in the conclusion that it was the very nation intended by that symbol. But here were predictions indicating a union of church and state, and the enforcement of the papal sabbath as a mark of the beast. It was no small act of faith to take the position at that time that the United States would pursue such a policy without any apparent probability it would do so.

The founders of the American Republic, in drafting its organic laws, never intended that any trouble should arise over a question of conscience. The Federal Constitution and most of the State constitutions have provisions guaranteeing the fullest religious liberty. But the development of the Sunday-law movement since 1850 amply demonstrates that the prophecy can be fulfilled in spite of the safeguards against intolerance erected by the founding fathers.

Just how the tyranny over the souls and bodies of men is to be developed is not specified in the prophecy. It may come by one man or a set of men—political, religious, or otherwise. But it controls all—small and great. It governs finances, for rich and poor feel its grip. It rules economics, for no one can buy or sell without its permission and mark. It dictates religion, for it forces all, under penalty of death, to worship according to its laws.

It is naturally repugnant to the American mind to think that religious persecution might mar the fair record of the nation founded on liberty to all. But during the entire history of the country, from its very founding, farseeing statesmen have recognized that the tendency to enforce religious dogmas by civil law is all too common with mankind, and is liable to break out in active persecution in unexpected places.

To the honor of the nation, it should be said that throughout its history noble statesmen have largely held in check the tendency which the founders foresaw working in the body politic. But no American can shut his eyes to the fact that paralleling these noble efforts, zealous but misguided religious leaders have attempted the civil enforcement of religious usages.

The prophecy predicts that a period of persecution will come. The two-horned beast causes all to receive a mark, and all who will not worship the image to be killed; that is, he wills, purposes, and endeavors to do this. He makes such an enactment, passes such a law. But it does not follow that all, and we do not think even many, will be put to death. God will interpose in behalf of His people. Those who have kept the word of Christ's patience will be kept from falling in this hour of temptation. (Revelation 3: 10.) Those who have made God their refuge will be kept from all evil. (Psalm 91: 9, 10.) All who are found written in the book will be delivered. (Daniel 12: 1.) As victors over the beast and his image, they will be redeemed from among men, and raise a song of triumph before the throne of God. (Revelation 14: 2-4.)

VERSE 18 Here is wisdom. Let him that hath understanding count the number of the beast: for it is the number of a man; and his number is Six hundred threescore and six.

The Number of His Name.—The number of the beast, says the prophecy, "is the number of a man." If it is to be derived from a name or title, the natural conclusion would be that it must be the name or title of some particular or representative man. The most plausible expression we have seen suggested as containing the number of the beast, is one of the titles applied to the pope of Rome. That title is this: *Vicarius Filii Dei*, "Vicegerent of the Son of God." It is worthy of note that the Douay Version of the Bible has the following comment on Revelation 13: 18: "The numeral letters of his name shall make up this number." Taking the letters out of this title which are used as Roman numerals, we have V, 5; I, 1; C, 100; I, 1; U (formerly the same as V), 5; I, 1; L, 50; I, 1; I, 1; D, 500; I, 1. Adding these numbers together, we have 666.

It has been argued that the title of the popes should be reckoned according to the Greek gematria, since John wrote in Greek, but since the title appears in Latin, and Latin is the official language of the Church of Rome and the language of its adopted Bible, the Vulgate, such a procedure would destroy the numerical value of that title in its own language. It would seem reasonable that a Latin title should exhibit its Latin numerical values rather than Greek letter values.

As to the practice of representing names by numbers we read: "It was a method practiced among the ancients, to denote names by numbers."[43]

---

[43] Matthew Henry, *Commentary*, Vol. III, p. 1065, note on Revelation 13: 18.

"Representing numbers by letters of the alphabet gave rise to a practice among the ancients of representing names also by numbers. Examples of this kind abound in the writings of heathens, Jews, and Christians."[44]

"It was a method practiced among the ancients, to denote names by numbers: as the name of *Thouth* or the Egyptian Mercury was signified by the number 1218. . . . It hath been the usual method in all God's dispensations, for the Holy Spirit to accommodate His expressions to the customs, fashions, and manners of the several ages. Since then this art and mystery of numbers was so much used among the ancients, it is less wonderful that the beast also should have his number, and his number is 666."[45]

This title, *Vicarius Filii Dei*, or some equivalent form of it, has appeared so frequently in Roman Catholic literature and rituals for centuries, that it scarcely seems necessary to add other proof of its validity and importance. Some of the variations of the title are: Vicar of Christ, Vicar of Jesus Christ, Vicar of God. A quotation from the noted Cardinal Manning illustrates these various forms of the same title:

"So in like manner they say now, 'See this Catholic Church, this Church of God, feeble and weak, rejected even by the very nations called Catholic. There is Catholic France, and Catholic Germany, and Catholic Italy, giving up this exploded figment of the temporal power of the *Vicar of Jesus Christ*.' And so, because the Church seems weak, and the *Vicar of the Son of God* is renewing the Passion of his Master upon earth, therefore we are scandalized, therefore we turn our faces from him."[46] (Italics ours.)

Several other variations of this title are used elsewhere in this same book.

On the importance of the pope's position as indicated by the title under consideration, or its equivalents, we quote from

---

[44] Adam Clarke, *Commentary on the New Testament*, Vol. II, p. 1025, note on Revelation 13: 18.

[45] Thomas Newton, *Dissertations on the Prophecies*, Vol. II, pp. 298, 299.

[46] Cardinal Manning, *The Temporal Power of the Vicar of Jesus Christ*, pp. 140, 141.

J. A. Wylie, in his comment on the Apology of Ennodius written in defense of Pope Symmachus:

"We find the council [of Rome, A. D. 502 or 503] convoked by Theodoric demurring to investigate the charges alleged against Pope Symmachus, on the grounds set forth by his apologist Ennodius, which were, 'that the Pope, as God's Vicar, was the judge of all, and could himself be judged by no one.' 'In this apology,' remarks Mosheim, 'the reader will perceive that the foundations of that enormous power which the popes of Rome afterwards acquired were now laid.' "[47]

In recent years, the validity of this title has been questioned, but historical evidence remains that this arrogated title has served to support the authority of the popes in building up their vast temporal supremacy during the heyday of Romanism in medieval times, and in maintaining their spiritual authority to this day.

The particular title *Vicarius Filii Dei* appeared as early as 752-774 in a document historically known as the "Donation of Constantine." Though this document was later proved to have been written by someone else and signed with the name of Constantine the Great to give it the weight of his authority —a practice not uncommon in medieval times—yet this so-called Donation of Constantine was used as valid by at least nine of the popes over a period of seven centuries or more in establishing the spiritual and temporal supremacy of the bishops of Rome.

The title itself was obviously an invention to designate the office of Peter as the first pope in harmony with the widely known claim of the Roman Catholic Church that the words of Jesus in Matthew 16: 18, 19, conferred upon Peter the first bishopric of the church—a view which Protestants have never allowed—and that this bishopric descended to his successors in the papal seat, as stated in the Donation of Constantine and maintained by the church to this day.[48]

---

[47] J. A. Wylie, *The Papacy*, pp. 35, 36.

[48] See Christopher Coleman, *Constantine the Great and Christianity*, p. 178.

The document employing the title was confirmed by a church council, says Binius, a high Roman Catholic dignitary of Cologne, quoted by Labbe and Cossart.[49] It was incorporated in Roman Catholic canon law by Gratian, and when this last-named work was revised and published, with endorsement by Pope Gregory XIII, the title was retained.[50] When Lucius Ferraris wrote his elaborate theological work about 1755, he gave under the article "Papa" the title Vicarius Filii Dei, and cited the revised canon law as his authority. Again when Ferraris's work was revised and enlarged, and published in Rome in 1890, the document and title were still retained.[51]

Of Ferraris's theological work just cited, the *Catholic Encyclopedia* says that it "will ever remain a precious mine of information."[52]

We quote herewith from the Latin of the Donation of Constantine, confirmed by a church council, incorporated in Roman Catholic canon law, and cited by Ferraris:

"Ut sicut Beatus Petrus in terris Vicarius Filii Dei fuit constitutus, ita et Pontifices eius successores in terris principatus potestatem amplius, quam terrenae imperialis nostrae serenitatis mansuetudo habere videtur."[53]

Cristopher Coleman translates this paragraph from the Canon law of Gratian as follows:

"As the blessed Peter is seen to have been constituted Vicar of the Son of God on the earth, so the pontiffs who are the representatives of that same chief of the apostles, should obtain from us and our empire the power of a supremacy greater than the clemency of our earthly imperial serenity."[54]

A freer translation by Edwin Lee Johnson, professor of Latin and Greek, Vanderbilt University, reads: "Just as the

---

49 P. Labbe and G. Cossart, *Sacrosancta Concilia*, Vol. 1, col. 1539-1541.

50 *Corpus Juris Canonici*, Lyons, 1622.

51 Lucius Ferraris, *Prompta Bibliotheca* (Rome, 1890), Vol. VI, p. 43, col. 2.

52 *Catholic Encyclopedia* (1913), Vol. VI, p. 48, art., "Ferraris."

53 Lucius Ferraris, *Prompta Bibliotheca*, (edition of 1890), art., "Papa," II, Vol. VI, p. 43.

54 Christopher B. Coleman, *The Treatise of Lorenzo Valla on the Donation of Constantine*, p. 13.

Blessed Peter was appointed on earth vicar of the Son of God, so also it seems that the Pontiffs, his successors, hold on earth the power of the chief rule rather than (that) His Excellency, His Imperial Serene Highness on earth, (should hold it)."

Thus closes Revelation 13, leaving the people of God with the powers of earth in deadly array against them and the decrees of death and banishment from society upon them for their adherence to the commandments of God. Spiritism will be, at the time specified, performing its most imposing wonders, deceiving all the world except the elect. (Matthew 24: 24; 2 Thessalonians 2: 8-12.) This will be the "hour of temptation," or trial, which is to come, as the closing test, upon all the world, to try them that dwell upon the earth, as mentioned in Revelation 3: 10. What is the issue of this conflict? This important inquiry is not left unanswered. The first five verses of the following chapter complete the chain of this prophecy, and reveal the glorious triumph of the champions of the truth.

 FRANKLIN BOOTH, ARTIST

THE THREE ANGEL HERALDS

Bearing the warning of God's judgment hour, three angels speed forth to every nation, kindred, tongue, and people.

CHAPTER XIV

GOD'S FINAL WARNING TO A WICKED WORLD

VERSE 1 And I looked, and, lo, a Lamb stood on the Mount Sion, and with Him an hundred forty and four thousand, having His Father's name written in their foreheads. 2 And I heard a voice from heaven, as the voice of many waters, and as the voice of a great thunder: and I heard the voice of harpers harping with their harps: 3 and they sung as it were a new song before the throne, and before the four beasts, and the elders: and no man could learn that song but the hundred and forty and four thousand, which were redeemed from the earth. 4 These are they which were not defiled with women; for they are virgins. These are they which follow the Lamb whithersoever He goeth. These were redeemed from among men, being the first fruits unto God and to the Lamb. 5 And in their mouth was found no guile: for they are without fault before the throne of God.

A WONDERFUL feature of the prophetic word is that the people of God are never brought into positions of trial and difficulty, and there abandoned. After taking them into scenes of danger, the voice of prophecy does not leave them there to guess their fate, in doubt, perhaps despair, as to the final result. Rather, it takes them through to the end, and reveals the final triumph of the faithful.

The first five verses of Revelation 14 are an example of this. The thirteenth chapter closed with a view of the people of God, a small and apparently weak and defenseless company, in deadly conflict with the mightiest powers of earth which the dragon is able to muster to his service. A decree is passed, backed up by the supreme power of the land, that they shall worship the image and receive the mark, under pain of death if they refuse to comply. What can the people of God do in such a conflict and in such an extremity? What will become of them? Glance forward with the apostle to the very next scene in the unfolding drama, and what do we behold?—The same company standing on Mount Zion with the Lamb, a victorious company, playing on symphonic harps in the court of heaven. Thus are we assured that when the time of our conflict with the powers of darkness comes, deliverance is not only certain, but will immediately be brought to the people of God.

The 144,000.—We believe that the 144,000 here seen on Mount Zion are the saints who were in Revelation 13 brought to view as objects of the wrath of the beast and his image.

They are identical with those sealed, as described in Revelation 7, who have already been shown to be the righteous who are alive at the second coming of Christ.

They are "redeemed from among men" (verse 4), an expression which can be applicable only to those who are translated from among the living. Paul labored, if by any means he might attain to the resurrection from among the dead. (Philippians 3: 11.) This is the hope of those who sleep in Jesus—a resurrection from the dead. A redemption from among men, from among the living, must mean a different thing, and can mean only one thing, and that is translation. Hence the 144,000 are living saints, who will be translated at the second coming of Christ. (See comment on verse 13.)

On what Mount Zion does John see this company standing?—The Mount Zion above; for the song of harpers, which no doubt is uttered by these very ones, is heard from heaven. This is the same Zion from which the Lord utters His voice when He speaks to His people in close connection with the coming of the Son of man. (Joel 3: 16; Hebrews 12: 25-28; Revelation 16: 17.) An acceptance of the fact that there is a Mount Zion in heaven, and a Jerusalem above, would be a powerful antidote for the false doctrine of a second probation and a millennium of peace on earth.

Only a few more particulars respecting the 144,000, in addition to those given in Revelation 7, will claim our attention:

They have the name of the Lamb's Father written in their foreheads. In Revelation 7, they are said to have the seal of

God in their foreheads. An important key to an understanding of the seal of God is thus furnished, for we at once perceive that the Father regards His name as His seal. That commandment of the law which contains God's name is therefore the seal of the law. The Sabbath commandment is the only one that contains the descriptive title which distinguishes the true God from all false gods. Wherever this was placed, there the Father's name was said to be. (Deuteronomy 12: 5, 14, 18, 21; 14: 23; 16: 2, 6; etc.) Therefore whoever truly keeps this commandment has the seal of the living God.

They sing a new song which no other company is able to learn. In Revelation 15: 3, it is called the song of Moses and the song of the Lamb. The song of Moses, as may be seen by reference to Exodus 15, was a song of experience and deliverance. Therefore the song of the 144,000 is the song of their deliverance. No others can join in it, for no other company will have had an experience like theirs.

They "were not defiled with women." A woman is in Scripture the symbol of a church, a virtuous woman representing a pure church, a corrupt woman, an apostate church. It is, then, a characteristic of this company that at the time of their deliverance they are not defiled with the fallen churches of the land, nor do they have any connection with them. Yet we are not to understand that they never had any connection with these churches, for it is only at a certain time that people become defiled by them. In Revelation 18: 4 we find a call issued to the people of God while they are in Babylon, to come out *lest* they become partakers of her sins. Heeding that call, and leaving her connection, they escape the defilement of her sins. So of the 144,000: though some of them may have once had a connection with corrupt churches, they sever that connection when it would become sin to retain it longer.

They follow the Lamb whithersoever He goeth. We understand that this is spoken of them in their redeemed state. They are the special companions of their glorified Lord in the kingdom. Of the same company and the same time, we read,

"The Lamb which is in the midst of the throne shall feed them, and *shall lead* them unto living fountains of waters." Revelation 7: 17.

They are "first fruits unto God and to the Lamb." This term appears to be applied to different ones to denote special conditions. Christ is the first fruits as the antitype of the wave-sheaf. The first receivers of the gospel are called by James a kind of first fruits. (James 1: 18.) So the 144,000, being prepared for the heavenly garner here on earth during the troublous scenes of the last days, being translated to heaven without seeing death, and occupying a pre-eminent position, are in this sense called first fruits unto God and the Lamb. With this description of the 144,000 triumphant, the line of prophecy which began with Revelation 12 comes to a close.

VERSE 6 And I saw another angel fly in the midst of heaven, having the everlasting gospel to preach unto them that dwell on the earth, and to every nation, and kindred, and tongue, and people, 7 saying with a loud voice, Fear God, and give glory to Him; for the hour of His judgment is come: and worship Him that made heaven, and earth, and the sea, and the fountains of waters.

The First Angel's Message.—Another scene and another chain of prophetic events is introduced in these verses. We know that this is so, because the preceding verses of this chapter describe a company of the redeemed in the immortal state —a scene which constitutes a part of the prophetic chain beginning with the first verse of Revelation 12, and with which that chain of events closes, for no prophecy goes beyond the immortal state. Whenever we are brought in a line of prophecy to the end of the world, we know that that line ends there, and that what is introduced subsequently belongs to a new series of events. The book of Revelation in particular is composed of these independent prophetic chains, as has already been set forth in a number of examples.

The message described in these two verses is the first of what are known as "the three angels' messages of Revelation 14." We are justified by the prophecy itself in designating them the first, second, and third. In the verses that follow, the last one is distinctly called "the *third* angel," from which we infer that the one preceding was the *second* angel; and the one before that, the *first* angel.

These angels are evidently symbolic, for the work assigned them is that of preaching the everlasting gospel to the people. But the preaching of the gospel has not been entrusted to literal angels; it has been committed to men, who are responsible for this sacred trust placed in their hands. Each of these three angels, therefore, symbolizes those who are commissioned to make known to their fellow men the special truths which constitute the burden of these messages.

Literal angels are intensely interested in the work of grace among men, being sent forth to minister to those who shall be heirs of salvation. As there is order in all the movements and appointments of the heavenly world, it may not be fanciful to suppose that a literal angel has charge and oversight of the work of each message. (Hebrews 1: 14; Revelation 1: 1; 22: 16.)

In these symbols we see the sharp contrast the Bible draws between earthly and heavenly things. Wherever earthly governments are to be represented, even the best of them, the most appropriate symbol that can be found is a wild beast. But when the work of God is to be sent forth, an angel clad in beauty and girt with power is used to symbolize it.

The importance of the work set forth in Revelation 14: 6-12 will be apparent to anyone who attentively studies it. Whenever these messages are to be proclaimed, they must from the very nature of the case constitute the great theme of interest for that generation. We do not mean that the great mass of mankind then living will give them attention, for in every age of the world the present truth for that time has been too often overlooked. But they constitute the theme to which the people will pay most earnest regard if they are awake to what concerns their highest interests.

When God commissions His ministers to announce to the world that the hour of His judgment is come, that Babylon has fallen, and that whoever worships the beast and his image must drink of His wrath poured out unmingled into the cup of His indignation—a threat more terrible than any other that can be found in the Scriptures—no man, except at the peril of his soul, can treat these warnings as nonessential, or pass them by with neglect and disregard. Hence the necessity in every age for the most earnest endeavor to understand the work of the Lord, lest we lose the benefit of the present truth. This is especially true today, when so many evidences betoken the soon coming of earth's final crisis.

This angel of Revelation 14: 6 is called "another angel," from the fact that John had previously seen an angel flying through heaven in a similar manner, as described in Revelation 8: 13, proclaiming that the last three of the series of seven trumpets were woe trumpets. (See comments on Revelation 8: 13.)

The Time of the Message.—The first point to be determined is the time when this message is to be given. When may the proclamation, "The hour of His judgment is come," be expected? The possibility that it may be in our own day makes it essential for us to examine this question with serious attention. But more positive proof that this is so will appear as we proceed. It should set every pulse bounding, and every heart beating high with a sense of the sublime importance of this hour in which we live.

Only three positions are possible on this question of the time of this prophecy. These positions are that this message has been given in the past, as in the days of the apostles, or in the days of the Reformers; that it is to be given in a future age; or that it belongs to the present generation.

We inquire first respecting the past. The very nature of the message forbids the idea that it could have been given in the days of the apostles. They did not proclaim that the hour of God's judgment had come. If they had, it would not have been true, and their message would have been stamped with the infamy of falsehood. They *did* have something to say respecting the judgment, but they pointed to an indefinite future for its accomplishment. In Christ's own words, the final judgment of Sodom and Gomorrah, Tyre, Sidon, Chorazin, and Capernaum, was located indefinitely in the future from that day. (Matthew 10: 15; 11: 21-24.) Paul declared to the superstitious Athenians that God had appointed a day in which He would judge the world. (Acts 17: 31.) He reasoned before Felix "of righteousness, temperance, and judgment to come." Acts 24: 25. To the Romans he wrote concerning a day when God should judge the secrets of men by Jesus Christ. (Romans 2: 16.) He pointed the Corinthians forward to a time when "we must all appear before the judgment seat of Christ." 2 Corinthians 5: 10. James wrote to the brethren scattered abroad that they were at some time in the future to be judged by the law of liberty. (James 2: 12.) Both Peter and Jude speak of the first rebel angels as reserved unto the judgment of the great day, still in the future at that time, to which the ungodly in this world are also reserved. (2 Peter 2: 4, 9; Jude 6.) How different is all this from ringing out upon the world the startling declaration that "the hour of His judgment *is* come!"—a sound which must be heard when the solemn message before us is given.

From the days of the apostles nothing has taken place which anyone could construe as the fulfillment of this first message, until we come to the Reformation of the sixteenth century. Some claim that Luther and his colaborers gave the first message, and that the two following messages have been given since his day. This is a question to be decided by historical fact rather than by argument. Hence we inquire for the evidence that the Reformers made any such proclamation. Their teaching has been fully recorded, and their writings preserved. When and where did they arouse the world with the proclamation that the hour of God's judgment had come? We find no record that such was the burden of their preaching.

"The above passage [Revelation 14: 6-11] is by some interpreters supposed to relate to the period of the Reformation, and to have been fulfilled in the preaching of Luther and the other eminent persons who were raised up at that time to proclaim the errors of the Romish Church. . . . But it appears to me that there are insuperable objections to these interpretations. The first angel is instrumental in preaching the gospel much more extensively than the Reformers could do. So far were they from preaching to all the inhabitants of the earth that they did not even preach through the whole of Christian Europe. The Reformation was not permitted to enter into some of the most extensive kingdoms of the Romish jurisdiction. It was entirely excluded from Spain, Portugal, and Italy. Neither could it be said, in consistence with truth, at the time of the Reformation that 'the hour of God's judgment is come.' . . . The hour of God's judgment is a time well known and exactly defined in the chronological prophecies of Daniel and John."[1]

"I hope," said Luther, "the last day of judgment is not far, I persuade myself verily it will not be absent full three hundred years longer; for God's word will decrease and be darkened for want of true shepherds and servants of God. The voice will sound and be heard erelong: 'Behold the Bridegroom cometh.' God neither will nor can suffer this wicked world much longer, He must strike in with the dreadful day, and punish the contemning of His word."[2]

Such records ought to be decisive, as far as the Reformers are concerned.

The foregoing considerations being sufficient to forbid the application of the judgment message to the past, we now turn to the view that locates it in a future age, beyond the second advent. The reason urged for locating the message in that time is the fact that John saw the angel flying through heaven immediately after he had seen the Lamb standing on Mount Zion with the 144,000, which is a future event. If the book of Revelation were one consecutive prophecy, there would be

---

[1] William Cuninghame, *A Dissertation on the Seals and Trumpets of the Apocalypse*, p. 255.
[2] Martin Luther, *Familiar Discourses*, pp. 7, 8.

force in this reasoning; but as it consists of a series of independent lines of prophecy, and as it has already been shown that one such chain ends with verse 5 of this chapter, and a new one begins with verse 6, the foregoing view cannot be sustained. To show that the message cannot have its fulfillment in an age beyond the second advent it will be sufficient to give a few reasons.

The apostolic commission extended only to the "harvest," which is the end of the world. (Matthew 13: 39.) If therefore this angel with "the everlasting gospel" comes after that event, he preaches another gospel, and subjects himself to the anathema of Paul in Galatians 1: 8.

The second message cannot of course be given before the first, but the second message announces the fall of Babylon, and a voice is heard from heaven after that, saying, "Come out of her, My people." How absurd to locate this after the second advent of Christ, seeing that all God's people, both living and dead, are at that time caught up to meet the Lord in the air, to be thenceforth forever with Him. (1 Thessalonians 4: 17.) They cannot be called out of Babylon after this. Christ does not take them to Babylon, but to the Father's house, where there are many mansions. (John 14: 2, 3.)

A glance at the third angel's message, which must be fulfilled in a future age if the first one is, will still further show the difficulty of this view. This message warns against the worship of the beast, which refers, beyond question, to the papal beast. But the papal beast is destroyed and given to the burning flame when Christ comes. (Daniel 7: 11; 2 Thessalonians 2: 8.) He goes into the lake of fire at that time, to disturb the saints of the Most High no more. (Revelation 19: 20.) Why should we involve ourselves in the inconsistency of locating a message against the worship of the beast at a time when the beast has ceased to exist, and his worship is impossible?

In Revelation 14: 13 a blessing is pronounced upon the dead which die in the Lord "from henceforth," that is, from the time the threefold message begins to be given. This is a complete demonstration of the fact that the message must be given prior to the first resurrection, for after that event all who have a part therein can die no more. We therefore dismiss this view concerning the future age as unscriptural and impossible.

The Judgment Hour a Distinctive Note.—We are now prepared to examine the third view, that the message belongs to the present generation. The argument on the two preceding points has done much to establish the present proposition. If the message has not been given in the past, and cannot be given in the future after Christ comes, where else can we locate it but in the present generation, since we are obviously in the last days just preceding Christ's second coming? Indeed, the very nature of the message itself confines it to the last generation of men. It proclaims that the hour of God's judgment has come. The judgment pertains to the closing of the work of salvation for the world, and the proclamation announcing its approach can therefore be made only as we come near the end. It is further shown that the message belongs to the present time when it is proved that this angel is identical with the angel of Revelation 10, who utters his message in this generation. That the first angel of Revelation 14 and the angel of Revelation 10 are identical, see presentation in chapter 10.

The apostle Paul who before Felix the Roman governor reasoned of "judgment to come," proclaimed to his hearers on Mars' Hill that God "hath appointed a day in the which He will judge the world in righteousness by that Man whom He hath ordained." Acts 17: 31.

The prophecy of the 2300 days of Daniel 8 and 9 pointed unmistakably to this judgment hour. This longest time prophecy in the Scriptures reaches from 457 B. C. to A. D. 1844. Then, as we have seen in the study of Daniel's prophecy, the sanctuary was to be cleansed. This cleansing, according to the type in Leviticus 16, was the final work of atonement. That the work of the last day of the year in the typical service was none other than the day of judgment in type, will be seen from the following quotations:

"The great Day of Atonement, with its services so peculiar and impressive, fell on the tenth day of the seventh month. . . . It was a day wherein every man was called to fast and afflict his soul; to mournfully and penitently reflect upon his sinful ways and transgressions. . . . He who thus failed to mourn was threatened with the penalty of death, as *a direct visitation* of judgment from the hand of Jehovah."[3] "Let us note well the actual Day of Atonement. It was on the tenth day of the seventh month. The Jubilee also commenced on the same day and was ushered in by the blowing of the solemn trumpet; emblem of a *God coming near* in judgment."[4]

"It was supposed that on New Year Day (Tishri 1) the divine decrees were written down, and that on the Day of Atonement (Tishri 10) they are sealed, so that the decade is known by the name of 'Terrible Days' and the 'Ten Penitential Days.' So awful was the Day of Atonement that we are told in a Jewish book of ritual that the very angels run to and fro in fear and trembling, saying, '*Lo, the Day of Judgment has come!*' "[5]

" 'God, seated on His throne to judge the world . . . openeth the Book of Records; it is read, every man's signature being found therein. The great trumpet is sounded; a still small voice is heard; the angels shudder, saying, "*This is the day of judgment.*" . . . On New Year's Day the decree is written; on the Day of Atonement it is sealed who shall live and who are to die.' "[6]

One might ask if such a message has been given to the world. Again, Is a message of this character being proclaimed to the world today? We believe that the great second advent movement of the past century answers exactly to the prophecy.

Second Advent of Christ Another Distinctive Note.—As early as 1831, William Miller, of Low Hampton, New York, by an

---

[3] Albert Whalley, *The Red Letter Days of Israel*, p. 101.
[4] *Ibid.*, p. 116.
[5] F. W. Farrar, *The Early Days of Christianity*, pp. 237, 238.
[6] *Jewish Encyclopedia*, Vol. II, p. 286.

earnest and consistent study of the prophecies, was led to the conclusion that the gospel age was near its close. He placed the termination, which he thought would occur at the end of the prophetic periods, about the year 1843. This date was afterward extended to the autumn of 1844. We call his investigations a consistent study of the prophecies, because he adopted a sound rule of interpretation. This lies at the base of every religious reformation, and of every advance movement in prophetic knowledge. This rule is to take all the language of the Scriptures, just as we would that of any other book, to be literal, unless the context or the laws of language require it to be understood figuratively; and to let scripture interpret scripture. True, on a vital point he made a mistake, as will be explained hereafter; but in principle, and in a great number of particulars, he was correct. He was on the right road, and made an immense advance over every theological system of his day. When he began to promulgate his views, they met with general favor, and were followed by great religious awakenings in different parts of the land.

Soon a multitude of colaborers gathered around his standard, among whom may be mentioned such men as F. G. Brown, Charles Fitch, Josiah Litch, J. V. Himes, and others, who were then eminent for piety, and men of influence in the religious world. The period marked by the years 1840-1844 was one of intense activity and great progress in this work. A message was proclaimed to the world which bore every characteristic of a fulfillment of the proclamation of Revelation 14: 6, 7. It was indeed that gospel of the kingdom which Christ declared should be preached in all the world for a witness unto all nations, and then the end should come. (Matthew 24: 14.) The fulfillment of either of these scriptures involves the preaching of the nearness of the end. The gospel could not be preached to all nations as a *sign* of the end, unless it was understood to be such, and the proximity of the end was at least one of its leading themes. The *Advent Herald* well expressed the truth on this point in the following language:

"As an indication of the approach of the end, there was, however, to be seen 'another angel flying through the midst of heaven, having the everlasting gospel to preach unto them that dwell on the earth, and to every nation, and kindred, and tongue, and people.' Revelation 14: 6. The burden of this angel was to be the *same* gospel which had been before proclaimed; but connected with it was the additional motive of the *proximity* of the kingdom—'saying with a loud voice, Fear God, and give glory to Him; for the hour of His judgment is come: and worship Him that made heaven, and earth, and the sea, and the fountains of waters.' Verse 7. No mere preaching of the gospel, without announcing its *proximity*, could fulfill this message."[7]

The persons who were engaged in this movement supposed it to be a fulfillment of prophecy, and claimed that they were giving the message of Revelation 14: 6, 7.

"I would now say to you this night, 'Fear God and give glory to Him for the hour of His judgment is come,' in a strict and literal sense. We are now at the close of that last day concerning which the apostle says: 'Hereby we know that it is the last time.' . . . We are just at the evening of that day—we are at the last hour of that day; and it is very nigh, very nigh, even at the door. My dear hearers, I beseech you to consider that it is near at hand, at the very door, according to all who have studied this matter and have sought the teaching of God; . . . that they are all of one mind; that . . . the reign of Christ—is just at hand."[8]

"Revelation 14 represents the angel flying into the midst of heaven, having the everlasting gospel to preach to them that dwell upon the earth, and to every nation, and kindred, and tongue, and people. When the event takes place which is signified by this symbol, the day of the Lord's judgment is actually at hand, for the angel cries unto all men, 'Fear God,

---

[7] Editorial, in *The Advent Herald*, Dec. 14, 1850, p. 364.
[8] J. M. Campbell, *The Everlasting Gospel.*

and give glory to Him; for the hour of His judgment *is come.*' "[9]

"It is the duty of all to call upon those to 'fear God and give glory to Him, for the hour of His judgment is come,' but more especially is it the duty of God's ministers."[10]

But the general movement respecting the second advent of Christ, and the proclamation that "the hour of His judgment is come," was not confined to the Western Hemisphere. It was world-wide. It fulfilled in this respect the proclamation of the angel "to every nation, and kindred, and tongue, and people." Mourant Brock, an Anglican clergyman, and a strong leader in the advent movement in the British Isles, tells us:

"It is not merely in Great Britain that the expectation of the near return of the Redeemer is entertained, and the voice of warning raised, but also in America, India, and on the Continent of Europe. I was lately told by one of our German missionaries that in Wirtemburgh there is a Christian colony of several hundreds, one of the chief features of which is the looking for the Second Advent. And a Christian minister from near the shores of the Caspian Sea has told me, that there is the same daily expectation among his nation. They constantly speak of it as 'the day of consolation.' In a little publication, entitled 'The Millennium,' the writer says that he understands in America about 300 ministers of the Word are thus preaching 'the Gospel of the kingdom,' whilst in this country, he adds, about 700 of the Church of England are raising the same cry."[11]

Dr. Joseph Wolff traveled in Arabia, through the region inhabited by the descendants of Hobab, Moses' brother-in-law. He speaks as follows of a book which he saw in Yemen:

"The Arabs of this place have a book called 'Seera,' which treats of the *second coming of Christ, and His reign in glory!*" "In Yemen . . . I spent six days with the children of Rechabites.

---

[9] John Bayford, *The Messiah's Kingdom*, p. 283.
[10] J. W. Brooks, *Elements of Prophetical Interpretation*, pp. 166, 167.
[11] Mourant Brock, *Glorification*, pp. 10, 11, footnote.

. . . They drink no wine, plant no vineyards, sow no seed, live in tents, and remember the word of Jonadab the son of Rechab. With them were children of Israel of the tribe of Dan, who reside near Yerim in Hatramawt [sic], *who expected, in common with the children of Rechab, the speedy arrival of the Messiah in the clouds of heaven.*"[12]

D. T. Taylor speaks as follows concerning the wide diffusion of the advent hope:

"In Wurtemberg, there is a Christian colony numbering hundreds, who look for the speedy advent of Christ; also another of like belief on the shores of the Caspian; the Molokaners, a large body of Dissenters from the Russian Greek Church, residing on the shores of the Baltic—a very pious people, of whom it is said, 'Taking the Bible alone for their creed, the *norm* of their faith is simply the Holy Scriptures'—are characterized by the 'expectation of Christ's immediate and visible reign upon earth.' In Russia, the doctrine of Christ's coming and reign is preached to some extent, and received by many of the lower class. It has been extensively agitated in Germany, particularly in the south part among the Moravians. In Norway, charts and books on the advent have been circulated extensively, and the doctrine has been received by many. Among the Tartars in Tartary, there prevails an expectation of Christ's advent about this time. English and American publications on this doctrine have been sent to Holland, Germany, India, Ireland, Constantinople, Rome, and to nearly every missionary station on the globe. . . .

"Joseph Wolff, D. D., according to his journals, between the years 1821 and 1845, proclaimed the Lord's speedy advent in Palestine, Egypt, on the shores of the Red Sea, Mesopotamia, the Crimea, Persia, Georgia, throughout the Ottoman Empire, in Greece, Arabia, Turkistan, Bokhara, Afghanistan, Cashmere, Hindustan, Thibet, in Holland, Scotland, and Ireland, at Constantinople, Jerusalem, St. Helena, also on

[12] Joseph Wolff, *Narrative of a Mission to Bokhara*, pp. 40, 42.

shipboard in the Mediterranean, and at New York City to all denominations. He declares he has preached among Jews, Turks, Mohammedans, Parsees, Hindus, Chaldeans, Yeseedes, Syrians, Sabeans, to pashas, sheiks, shahs, the kings of Organtsh and Bokhara, the queen of Greece, etc.; and of his extraordinary labors the *Investigator* says, 'No individual has, perhaps, given greater publicity to the doctrine of the second coming of the Lord Jesus Christ than has this well-known missionary to the world. Wherever he goes, he proclaims the approaching advent of the Messiah in glory.' "[13]

Another prominent writer in the great second advent movement writes:

"But that the Lord's warning was in reality heard and that the voice did at that very time go forth in the church as to the nearness of the advent, is undeniable. It may be safely affirmed that from the year 1828 to 1833 . . . a greater number of tracts and works on the subject of the advent and declaring its nearness went forth to the public and were advertised in the leading religious journals of the day than had previously appeared in any whole century, in the whole period that had elapsed from the age of the apostles; yea, probably than in the whole of the centuries from that age."[14]

That the mistake made by Adventists in 1844 was *not* in the *time*, has been shown by the argument on the seventy weeks and the 2300 days in Daniel 9. It *was* in the *nature of the event* to occur at the end of those days, as has been shown in the argument on the sanctuary in Daniel 8. Supposing the earth to be the sanctuary, with its cleansing to be accomplished by fire at the revelation of the Lord from heaven, they naturally looked for the appearing of Christ at the end of the days.

Through their misapprehension on this point, they met with a crushing disappointment, predicted in the Scripture itself, though everything which the prophecy declared, and everything which they were warranted to expect, took place

---

[13] D. T. Taylor, *The Voice of the Church*, pp. 343, 344.

[14] William Cuninghame. *A Dissertation on the Seals and Trumpets of the Apocalypse*, p. 443.

with absolute accuracy at that time. There the cleansing of the sanctuary began; but this did not bring Christ to this earth, for the earth is not the sanctuary; and its cleansing does not involve the destruction of the earth, for cleansing is accomplished with the blood of a sacrificial offering, not with fire. Here was the bitterness of the little book to the church. (Revelation 10: 10.) Here was the coming of one like the Son of man, not to this earth, but to the Ancient of days. (Daniel 7: 13, 14.) Here was the coming of the Bridegroom to the marriage, as set forth in the parable of the ten virgins in Matthew 25.

The foolish virgins then said to the wise, "Give us of your oil; for our lamps are gone ["going" margin,] out." The wise answered, "Go and buy for yourselves." "While they went to buy, the Bridegroom came." This is not the coming of Christ to this earth, for it is a coming which precedes the marriage; but the marriage, that is, the reception of the kingdom (see comments on Revelation 21), must precede His coming to this earth to receive to Himself His people, who are to be the guests at the marriage supper. (Luke 19: 12; Revelation 19: 7-9.) This coming in the parable must therefore be the same as the coming to the Ancient of days spoken of in Daniel 7: 13, 14.

"And they that were ready went in with Him to the marriage: and the door was shut." After the Bridegroom comes to the marriage, there is an examination of guests to see who are ready to participate in the ceremony, according to the parable of Matthew 22: 1-13. As the last thing before the marriage, the King comes in to see the guests, to ascertain if all are properly arrayed in the wedding garment; and whoever, after due examination, is found with the garment on, and is accepted by the King, never after loses that garment, but is sure of immortality. But this question of fitness for the kingdom can be determined only by the investigative judgment of the sanctuary.

This closing work in the sanctuary, which is the cleansing of the sanctuary and the atonement, is therefore nothing else than the examination of the guests to see who have on the wedding garment. Consequently until this work is finished, it is not determined who are "ready" to go in to the marriage. "They that were *ready* went in with Him to the marriage." By this short expression we are carried from the time when the Bridegroom comes to the marriage, entirely through the period of the cleansing of the sanctuary, or the examination of the guests. When this is concluded, probation will end, and the door will be shut.

The connection of the parable with the message under examination is now apparent. It brings to view a period of making ready the guests for the marriage of the Lamb, which is the work of judgment to which the message brings us when it declares, "The hour of His judgment is come." This message was to be proclaimed with a loud voice. It went forth with the power thus indicated between the years 1840-44, more especially in the autumn of the latter year, bringing us to the end of the 2300 days, when the work of judgment started as Christ began the work of cleansing the sanctuary.

As has been already shown, this work did not bring us to the close of probation but rather to the beginning of the investigative judgment. In this judgment hour we are now living. Today, as in the period to which reference has been made, the judgment message is being heralded to all the earth. Today the solemn judgment proclamation is sounding "to every nation, and kindred, and tongue, and people, saying with a loud voice, Fear God, and give glory to Him; for the hour of His judgment is come." Revelation 14: 6, 7.

Before passing on to the consideration of the second angel's message, let us contemplate for a moment the importance and sublime significance of the wonderful truth here so clearly revealed. We are standing on the very threshold of the eternal world. God's last message of mercy is now going to every nation and kindred and tongue and people. The final scenes in the great plan of salvation are even now being enacted in the sanctuary above. Think of it! The hour of God's judgment *is come.* The investigative judgment that concerns every soul and that immediately precedes the coming of Jesus, is now going forward in heaven. A wedding garment—the spotless robe of Christ's own righteousness—has at infinite cost been provided for all who will accept it. "How will it fare with thee and me when the King comes in?" "My little children, these things write I unto you, that ye sin not. And if any man sin, we have an advocate with the Father, Jesus Christ the righteous." 1 John 2: 1.

VERSE 8 And there followed another angel, saying, Babylon is fallen, is fallen, that great city, because she made all nations drink of the wine of the wrath of her fornication.

The Second Angel's Message.—The time of this message is determined to a great extent by that of the first message. The first cannot but precede the second; but the first is confined to the last days. Yet the second must be given before the end, for no move of the kind described is possible after that event. It is therefore a part of that religious movement which takes place in the last days with special reference to the coming of Christ.

The inquiries therefore follow: What is meant by the term "Babylon"? What is her fall? How does it take place? As to the meaning of the word, we learn something from the marginal readings of Genesis 10: 10 and 11: 9. The beginning of Nimrod's kingdom was Babel, or Babylon. The place was called Babylon, meaning "confusion," because God there confounded the language of the builders of the tower. The name is here used figuratively to designate the great symbolic city of the book of Revelation, probably with special reference to the significance of the term and the circumstances from which it originated. It applies to something on which, as specifying its chief characteristics, may be written the word "confusion."

There are but three possible things to which the word can be applied. These are the apostate religious world in general, the papal church in particular, and the city of Rome. In examining these terms, we shall first show what Babylon is not.

Babylon is not confined to the Roman Catholic Church. That this church is a very prominent component part of great Babylon, is not denied. The descriptions in Revelation 17 seem to apply particularly to that church. But the name which she bears on her forehead, "Mystery, Babylon the Great, the Mother of Harlots and Abominations of the Earth," reveals other family connections. If this church is the mother, who are the daughters? The fact that these daughters are spoken of, shows that there are other religious bodies besides the Roman Catholic Church which come under this designation. Again, there is to be a call made in connection with this message, "Come out of her, My people." Revelation 18: 1-4. As this message is located in the present generation, it follows, if no other church but the Roman Catholic is included in Babylon, that the people of God are now found in the communion of that church, and are to be called out. But this conclusion, no Protestant at least will be willing to allow.

Babylon is not the city of Rome. The argument relied upon to show that the city of Rome is the Babylon of the Apocalypse runs thus: The angel told John that the woman which he had seen was the great city which reigned over the kings of the earth, and that the seven heads of the beast are seven mountains upon which the woman sits. Then, by taking the city and the mountains to be literal, and finding Rome built upon seven hills, the application is made at once to literal Rome.

The principle upon which this interpretation rests is the assumption that the explanation of a symbol must always be literal. It falls to the ground the moment it can be shown that symbols are sometimes explained by substituting for them other symbols, and then explaining the latter. This can easily be done. In Revelation 11: 3, the symbol of the two witnesses is introduced. The next verse reads: "These are the two olive trees and the two candlesticks standing before the God of the earth." In this case the first symbol is said to be the same as another symbol which is elsewhere clearly explained. So in the case before us. "The seven heads are seven mountains," and "The woman is that great city;" and it will not be difficult to show that the mountains and the city are used symbolically. The reader's attention is directed to the following:

We are informed in Revelation 13 that one of the seven heads was wounded to death. This head therefore cannot be a literal mountain, for it would be folly to speak of wounding a mountain to death.

Each of the seven heads has a crown upon it. But who ever saw a literal mountain with a crown upon it?

The seven heads are evidently successive in order of time, for we read, "Five are fallen, and one is, and the other is not yet come." Revelation 17: 10. But the seven hills on which Rome is built are not successive, and it would be absurd to apply such language to them.

According to Daniel 7: 6, compared with Daniel 8: 8, 22, heads denote governments, and according to Daniel 2: 35, 44, and Jeremiah 51: 25, mountains denote kingdoms. According to these facts, a literal translation of Revelation 17: 9, 10 removes all obscurity: "The seven heads are seven mountains on which the woman sitteth, and are seven kings." It will thus be seen that the angel represents the heads as mountains, and then explains the mountains to be seven successive kings. The meaning is transferred from one symbol to another, and then an explanation is given of the second symbol.

From the foregoing argument, it follows that the "woman" cannot represent a literal city, for the mountains upon which the woman sits being symbolic, a literal city cannot sit upon symbolic mountains. Again, Rome was the seat of the dragon of Revelation 12, and the dragon transferred it to the beast. (Revelation 13: 2.) Thus it became the seat of the beast; but it would be a singular mixture of figures to make the seat, which is sat upon by the beast, and a woman sitting upon the beast refer to the same thing.

Were the city of Rome the Babylon of the Apocalypse, what nonsense should we have in Revelation 18: 1-4, for in this case the fall of Babylon would be the overthrow and destruction of the city, in fact, its utter consumption by fire, according to verse 8. But mark what takes place after the fall. Babylon becomes "the habitation of devils, and the hold of every foul spirit, and a cage of every unclean and hateful bird." How can this happen to a city after that city is destroyed, even being utterly burned with fire? Again, after this a voice is heard, saying, "Come out of her, My people." Are God's people all in Rome?—Not to any great extent. How many can we suppose to be there to be called out after the city is burned with fire? It is not necessary to say more to show that Babylon cannot be the city of Rome.

What Does Babylon Signify?—Babylon signifies the universal worldly church. After seeing it cannot be either of the other two possible things to which it could be applied, it must mean this. But we are not left to this kind of reasoning on this subject. Babylon is called "a woman." A woman, used as a symbol, signifies a church. The woman of Revelation 12 was interpreted to mean a church. The woman of Revelation 17 should undoubtedly be interpreted as also signifying a church. The character of the woman determines the character of the church represented, a chaste woman standing for a pure church, a vile woman for an impure, or apostate, church. The woman Babylon is herself a harlot, and the mother of daughters like herself. This circumstance, as well as the name itself, shows that Babylon is not limited to any single ecclesiastical body, but must be composed of many. It must take in all of a like nature, and represent the entire corrupt, or apostate, church of the earth. This will perhaps explain the language of Revelation 18: 24, which represents that when God makes requisition upon great Babylon for the blood of His martyrs, in her will be found "the blood of prophets, and of saints, and of all" that have been slain upon the earth.

Through the centuries practically every country of Europe has had its state church, and the most of these countries to the present day have their established religions, and zealously oppose dissenters. Babylon has made all nations drunken with the wine of her fornication, that is, her false doctrines. It can therefore symbolize nothing less than the universal worldly church.

The great city Babylon is composed of three divisions. So the great religions of the world may be arranged under three heads. The first, oldest, and most widespread is paganism, separately symbolized under the form of a dragon. The second is the great papal apostasy, symbolized by the beast. The third is the daughters, or descendants from that church, symbolized by the two-horned beast, though that does not embrace them all. War, oppression, conformity to the world, religious formalism, the worship of mammon, pursuit of pleasure, and the maintenance of very many errors of the Roman Catholic Church, identify with sad and faithful accuracy the great body of the Protestant churches as an important constituent part of this great Babylon.

A glance at some of the ways in which the Protestant church has deported herself will still further show this. When Rome had the power, she destroyed vast multitudes of those whom she adjudged heretics. The Protestant church has shown the same spirit. Witness the burning of Michael Servetus by the Protestants of Geneva with John Calvin at their head. Witness the long-continued oppression of dissenters by the Church of England. Witness the hanging of Quakers and the whipping of Baptists even by the Puritan fathers of New England, themselves fugitives from like oppression by the Church of England. But these, some may say, are things of the past. True, yet they show that when persons governed by strong religious prejudice have the power to coerce dissenters, they cannot forbear to use it—a state of things which we look for in this country under a further fulfillment of the closing prophecy of Revelation 13.

It was the will of Christ that His church should be one. He prayed that His disciples might be one, as He and the Father were one; for this would give power to His gospel, and cause the world to believe in Him. Instead of this, look at the confusion that exists in the Protestant world, the many sectional walls that divide it into a network of societies, and the many creeds, discordant as the languages of those who were dispersed at the tower of Babel. God is not the author of all these. It is this state of things which the word "Babylon," as a descriptive term, appropriately designates. It is evidently used for this purpose, and not as a term of reproach. Instead of being stirred with feelings of resentment when this term is mentioned, people should rather examine their position, to see if in faith or practice they are guilty of any connection with this great city of confusion. If so, they should separate at once therefrom.

The true church is a chaste virgin. (2 Corinthians 11: 2.) The church that is joined with the world in friendship, is a harlot. It is this unlawful connection with the kings of the earth that constitutes her the great harlot of the Apocalypse. (Revelation 17.) Thus the Jewish Church, at first espoused to the Lord (Jeremiah 2: 3; 31: 32), became a harlot (Ezekiel 16). When this church apostatized from God, it was called Sodom (Isaiah 1), just as "the great city" (Babylon) is so called in Revelation 11. The unlawful union with the world of which Babylon is guilty, is positive proof that it is not the civil power. That the people of God are in her midst immediately before her overthrow is proof that she is professedly a religious body. For these reasons, it is very evident that the Babylon of the Apocalypse is the *professed church united with the world.*

"*Babylon Is Fallen.*"—The fall of Babylon will next claim attention. After learning what constitutes Babylon, it will not be difficult to decide what is meant by the declaration that Babylon is fallen. As Babylon is not a literal city, the fall cannot be a literal overthrow. We have already seen what an absurdity this would involve. Besides, the clearest distinction is maintained by the prophecy itself between the fall and the destruction of Babylon. Babylon "falls" before it is with violence "thrown down," as a millstone cast into the sea, and "utterly burned with fire." The fall is therefore a spiritual fall, for after the fall the voice is addressed to the people of God who are still in her connection, "Come out of her, My people." The reason is immediately given, "that ye be not partakers of her sins, and that ye receive not of her plagues." Babylon therefore still exists in sin and her plagues are still future after the fall.

Those who make Babylon apply exclusively to the papacy, claim that the fall of Babylon is the loss of civil power by the papal church. Because of the fall of Babylon, she becomes the hold of foul spirits and hateful birds; but such is not at all the result to Rome of the loss of civil power.

The people of God are called out of Babylon on account of her increasing sinfulness resulting from the fall, but the loss of the temporal power of the papacy constitutes no additional reason why the people of God should leave that church.

Babylon meets with this spiritual fall "because she made all nations drink of the wine of the wrath [not anger, but intense passion] of her fornication." There is but one thing to which this can refer, and that is false doctrines. She has corrupted the pure truths of God's word, and made the nations drunken with pleasing fables.

In the form of the papacy she has supplanted the gospel by substituting for it a false system of salvation:

Through the doctrine of the Immaculate Conception she denies that God in Christ dwelt in human flesh.

She has sought to set aside the mediation of Christ and has put another system of mediation in its place.

She has attempted to take away the priesthood of Jesus and substitute an earthly priesthood.

She has made salvation dependent upon confession to mortal man and thus has separated the sinner from Jesus, the only one through whom his sins can be forgiven.

She condemns the way of salvation through faith as "damnable heresy," and substitutes the doctrine of salvation by works.

Her crowning blasphemy is the doctrine of transubstantiation, or the idolatrous sacrifice of the mass, which is declared to be "one and the same as that of the cross" and which, in "some senses," is said to have "the advantage over Calvary," for by it "the work of our redemption is carried out."

Among doctrines she teaches contrary to the word of God, may be mentioned the following:

The substitution of tradition and the voice of the church as an infallible guide in the place of the Bible.

The change of the Sabbath of the fourth commandment, the seventh day, into the festival of Sunday as the rest day of the Lord and a memorial of His resurrection, a memorial which has never been commanded, and can by no possible means appropriately commemorate that event. Fathered by heathenism as "the wild solar holiday of all pagan times," Sunday was led to the font by the pope, and christened as an institution of the gospel church. Thus an attempt was made to destroy a memorial which the great God had set up to commemorate His own magnificent creative work, and erect another in its stead to commemorate the resurrection of Christ, for which there was no occasion, as the Lord Himself had already provided a memorial for that purpose in baptism by immersion.

The doctrine of the natural immortality of the soul. This also was derived from the pagan world, and the "Fathers of the church" became the foster-fathers of this pernicious doctrine as a part of divine truth. This error nullifies the two great Scripture doctrines of the resurrection and the general judgment, and furnishes an open door to modern spiritism. From it have sprung such other evil doctrines as the conscious state of the dead, saint worship, mariology, purgatory, reward at death, prayers and baptisms for the dead, eternal torment, and universal salvation.

The doctrine that the saints, as disembodied spirits, find their eternal inheritance in faraway, indefinable regions, "beyond the bounds of time and space." Thus multitudes have been turned away from the Scriptural view that this present earth is to be destroyed by fire at the day of judgment and perdition of ungodly men, and that from its ashes the voice of Omnipotence will evoke a new earth, which will be the future everlasting kingdom of glory, and which the saints will possess as their eternal inheritance.

Sprinkling instead of immersion, the latter being the only Scriptural mode of baptism, and a fitting memorial of the burial and resurrection of our Lord, for which purpose it was designed. By the corruption of this ordinance and its destruction as a memorial of the resurrection of Christ, the way was prepared for the substitution of something else for this purpose —the Sunday rest day.

That the coming of Christ is a spiritual, not a literal event, and was fulfilled at the destruction of Jerusalem, or is fulfilled in conversion, at death, or in spiritism. How many minds have by such teaching been forever closed against the Scriptural view that the second coming of Christ is a future definite event, literal, personal, visible, resulting in destruction of all His foes, and everlasting life to all his people!

The doctrine of a temporal millennium, or a thousand years of peace and prosperity and righteousness all over the earth before the second coming of Christ. This doctrine is especially calculated to shut the ears of the people against the evidences of the second advent near, and will probably lull as many souls into a state of carnal security leading to their final ruin, as any heresy which has ever been devised by the great enemy of truth.

Application of the Fall of Babylon.—To come now more particularly to the application of the prophecy concerning the fall of Babylon, let us see how the religious world stood with reference to the possibility of such a change when the time came for the proclamation of this second message in connection with the first about the year 1844. Paganism was only apostasy and corruption in the beginning, and is so still. No spiritual fall is possible there. Roman Catholicism had been in a fallen con-

 T. K. MARTIN, ARTIST

GOD'S CALL TO SERVICE

A mighty movement, born of God, responds to the challenge of the present hour.

dition for many centuries. But the Protestant churches had begun the great work of reformation from papal corruption and had done noble work. They were, in a word, in such a position that with them a spiritual fall was possible. The conclusion is therefore inevitable that the message announcing the fall had reference almost wholly to the Protestant churches.

The question may then be asked why this announcement was not made sooner, if so large a part of Babylon had been so long fallen. The answer is at hand: Babylon as a whole could not be said to be fallen so long as one division of it remained unfallen. It could not be announced, therefore, until a change for the worse came over the Protestant world, and the truth through which alone the path of progress lay, had been compromised. When this took place, and a spiritual fall was experienced in this last branch, then the announcement concerning Babylon as a whole could be made, as it could not have been made before—"Babylon is fallen."

It may be proper to inquire further how the reason assigned for the fall of Babylon—that she made all nations drink of the wine of the wrath of her fornication—would apply to the Protestant churches at the time in question. The answer is, It would apply most pertinently. The fault with Babylon lies in her confusion of the truth and her consequent false doctrines. Because she industriously propagates these, clinging to them when light and truth which would correct them is offered, she is in a fallen state.

With the Protestant churches, the time had come for an advance to higher religious ground. They could accept the proffered light and truth, and reach the higher attainment, or they could reject it, and lose their spirituality and favor with God, or, in other words, experience a spiritual fall.

The truth which God saw fit to use as an instrument in this work was the first angel's message. The hour of God's judgment come, and with it the imminent second advent of Christ, was the doctrine preached. After listening long enough to see the blessing that attended the doctrine, and the good results that accrued from it, the churches as a whole rejected it with scorn and scoffing. They were thereby tested, for they then plainly betrayed the fact that their hearts were with the world, not with the Lord, and that they preferred to have it so.

But the message would have healed the evils then existing in the religious world. The prophet exclaims, perhaps with reference to this time, "We would have healed Babylon, but she is not healed." Jeremiah 51: 9. Do you ask how we know this would have been the effect of receiving the message? We answer, Because this was the effect with all who did receive it. They came from different denominations, and their denominational barriers were leveled to the ground; conflicting creeds were shivered to atoms; the unscriptural hope of a temporal millennium was abandoned; false views of the second advent were corrected; pride and conformity to the world were swept away; wrongs were made right; hearts were united in the sweetest fellowship; and love and joy reigned supreme. If the doctrine did this for the few who did receive it, *it would have done the same for all if all had received it*, but the message was rejected.

Everywhere throughout the land the cry was raised, "Babylon is fallen," and, in anticipation of the movement brought to view in Revelation 18: 1-4, those proclaiming the message added, "Come out of her, My people." Thousands severed their connection with the various denominations as the result.

A marked change then came over the churches in respect to their spiritual condition. When a person refuses the light, he necessarily puts himself in darkness; when he rejects truth, he inevitably forges the shackles of error about his own limbs. Loss of spirituality—a spiritual fall—must follow. This the churches experienced. They chose to adhere to old errors, and still promulgate their false doctrines among the people. The light of truth therefore left them.

Some of them felt and deplored the change. A few testimonies from their writers describe their condition at that time.

The *Christian Palladium*, in 1844, spoke in the following mournful strain: "In every direction we hear the dolorous sound, wafted upon every breeze of heaven, chilling as the blast from the icebergs of the north, settling like an incubus on the breasts of the timid, and drinking up the energies of the weak, that lukewarmness, division, anarchy, and desolation are distressing the borders of Zion."[15]

In 1844 the *Religious Telescope* used the following language: "We have never witnessed such a general declension of religion as at the present. . . . When we call to mind how 'few and far between' cases of true conversion are, and the almost unparalleled impenitence and hardness of sinners, we almost involuntarily exclaim, 'Has God forgotten to be gracious? or is the door of mercy closed?' "[16]

About that time, proclamations of fasts and seasons of prayer for the return of the Holy Spirit were sent out in the religious papers. Even the Philadelphia *Sun* in November, 1844, had the following: "The undersigned, ministers and members of various denominations in Philadelphia and vicinity, solemnly believing that the present 'signs of the times'—the spiritual dearth of our *churches generally* and the extreme evils in the world around us—seem to call loudly on all Christians for *a special season of prayer*, do therefore hereby agree, by divine permission, to unite in *a week of special prayer to Almighty God*, for the outpouring of His Holy Spirit on our city, our country, and the world."[17]

Charles G. Finney, well-known evangelist, said in February, 1844: "We have had the facts before our minds, that, in general, the Protestant churches of our country, as such, were either apathetic or hostile to nearly all the moral reforms of the age. There are partial exceptions, yet not enough to render the fact otherwise than general. We have also another corroborative fact—the almost universal absence of revival

[15] "The Remedy," *Christian Palladium*, May 15, 1844, p. 409.
[16] "Great Spiritual Dearth," *Religious Telegraph*, December 4, 1844, p. 76.
[17] *Philadelphia Sun*, November 11, 1844.

influence in the churches. The spiritual apathy is almost all-pervading, and is fearfully deep; so the religious press of the whole land testifies. . . . *The churches generally are becoming sadly degenerate.* They have gone very far from the Lord, and He has withdrawn Himself from them."

In November, 1844, the *Oberlin Evangelist* remarked editorially:

"Some of our religious journals deplore, and all attest the fact that revivals have almost ceased in our churches. It is long since a period of so general dearth has been known. There is a great revival of political spirit, and of zeal in all the departments of business operations: but alas! decline and death sit like an incubus on the bosom of Christian activity and of holy love for God as for souls. The external forms of religion are sustained, the routine of Sabbath duties goes on: but those seasons of 'refreshing from the presence of the Lord,' in which fearfulness surprises the hypocrite, conviction fastens on the sinner, and humble hearts cleave to the promises and wrestle mightily for the conversion of souls—those seasons are known only as they [are] held in sweet remembrance—days that were, but are no longer."[18]

Not only did the churches suffer a distinct loss of spirituality in 1844, but the decline since then has been marked and continuous.

The *Congregationalist* said in November, 1858: "The revived piety of our churches is not such that one can confidently infer, from its mere existence, its legitimate, practical fruits. It ought, for example, to be as certain, after such a shower of grace, that the treasuries of our benevolent societies would be filled, as it is after a plentiful rain that the streams will swell in their channels. But the managers of our societies are bewailing the feebleness of the sympathy and aid of the churches.

"There is another and sadder illustration of the same general truth. The *Watchman and Reflector* recently stated that

[18] "Revivals," *Oberlin Evangelist,* November 20, 1844, p. 189.

there had never been among the Baptists so lamentable a spread of church dissension as prevails at present. . . . Even a glance at the weekly journals of our own denomination will evince that the evil is by no means confined to the Baptists."[19]

The leading Methodist paper, the New York *Christian Advocate*, in 1883 contained an article from which we copy these statements:

"1. Disguise it as you like, the church, in a general sense, is spiritually in a rapid decline. While it grows in number and money it is becoming extremely feeble and limited in its spirituality, both in the pulpit and pew. It is assuming the shape and character of the church at Laodicea.

"2. . . . There are thousands of ministers, local and conference, and many thousands of the laity, who are dead and worthless as barren fig-trees. They contribute nothing of a temporal or spiritual nature to the progress and triumphs of the gospel throughout the earth. If all these dry bones in our church and its congregations could be resurrected and brought into requisition by faithful, active service, what new and glorious manifestations of divine power would break forth!"[20]

The editor of the *Western Christian Advocate* in 1893 wrote the following of his church:

"To the Church of Methodists, Write, The great trouble with us today is, that the rescue of imperiled souls is our last and least consideration. Many of our congregations are conducted on the basis of social clubs. They are made centers of social influence. Membership is sought in order to advance one's prospects in society, business, or politics. Preachers are called who know how to

> " 'Smooth down the rugged text to ears polite,
> And snugly keep damnation out of sight.'

"The Sunday services are made the occasion of displaying the elegancies of apparel in the latest fashions. Even the little

---

[19] "Breadth of Christian Culture," *Congregationalist*, November 19, 1858. p. 186.
[20] "The Greatest of Questions," New York *Christian Advocate*, August 30, 1883, p. 549.

ones are tricked out as though they were the acolytes of pride. If the 'Rules' are read, it is to comply with the letter of a law whose spirit has long since fled. The class-books are filled with names of unconverted men and women. Official members may be found in box, dress-circle, and parquet of opera and theater. Communicants take in the races, and give and attend cardparties and dances. The distinction between inside and outside is so obscure that men smile when asked to unite with the Church, and sometimes tell us that they find the best men outside.

"When we go to the masses, it is too often with such ostentatious condescension that self-respect drives them from us.

"And yet we have so spread out, under the inflation of the rich and ungodly, that they are a necessity to us. The enforcement of the unmistakable letter of the Discipline for a single year would cut our membership in half, bankrupt our Missionary Society, close our fashionable churches, paralyze our connectional interests, and leave our pastors and bishops unpaid and in distress. But the fact remains, that one of two things must happen—the Discipline must purge the church, or God's Holy Spirit will seek other organized agencies. The ax is laid at the root of the tree. The call is to repentance. God's work must be done. If we are in the way, He will remove us."[21]

The New York *Independent* of December 3, 1896, contained an article from D. L. Moody, from which the following is an extract:

"In a recent issue of your paper I saw an article from a contributor which stated that there were over three thousand churches in the Congregational and Presbyterian bodies of this country that did not report a single member added by profession of faith last year. Can this be true? The thought has taken such hold of me that I can't get it out of my mind. It

[21] *Western Christian Advocate*, July 19, 1893, p. 456.

is enough almost to send a thrill of horror through the soul of every true Christian.

"If this is the case with these two large denominations, what must be the condition of the others also? Are we all going to sit still and let this thing continue? Shall our religious newspapers and our pulpits keep their mouths closed like 'dumb dogs that cannot bark' to warn people of approaching danger? Should we not all lift up our voice like a trumpet about this matter? What must the Son of God think of such a result of our labor as this? What must an unbelieving world think about a Christianity that can't bring forth any more fruit? And have we no care for the multitudes of souls going down to perdition every year while we all sit and look on? And this country of ours, where will it be in the next ten years, if we don't awake out of sleep?"[22]

The state of spiritual declension into which the churches generally had "fallen" as a result of their rejection of the first angel's message led to their acceptance of erroneous and corrupt doctrines. In the latter part of the nineteenth century a marked change was to be seen in the attitude of both leaders and people of the Protestant churches toward the basic doctrines of the Scriptures of truth. Having rejected the true, they accepted the false. The theory of evolution accepted by many church leaders in the words of one great religious writer "turned the Creator out of doors." A religious apologist for the theory declared that "prayer is communion with my inner racial self."

The effects of the evolution theory on the faith of the churches is so apparent that public comments upon the situation are commonplace. A professor of philosophy in a great university remarks:

"Today it seems that the great Hebrew-Christian moral tradition, the most ancient part of our heritage, is crumbling to pieces before our very eyes. . . . The faith in science has

[22] Dwight L. Moody, "Those Three Thousand Churches," New York *Independent*, December 3, 1896, p. 1.

grown so strong, so self-sufficient, so deeply rooted in the processes of our society, that many of those who feel it have lost all desire to combine it with any other. . . . The man who trusts a physical science to describe the world finds no conceivable place into which to fit a deity. . . . The philosophies that express their [men's] basic interests today are no longer concerned, as they were in the nineteenth century, with vindicating a belief in God and immortality. Those ideas have simply dropped out of any serious attempt to reach an understanding of the world. . . . The present conflict of religious faith with science is no longer with a scientific explanation of the world, but with a scientific explanation of religion. The really revolutionary effect of the scientific faith on religion today is not its new view of the universe, but its new view of religion."[23]

What that new view of religion is, is frankly stated by a spokesman of modern liberalism:

"Liberal Protestants have abandoned belief in the verbal infallibility of the Bible."[24] "We believe that Jesus was a human being, not a supernatural being different from all other men in quality. We believe that he was born in the normal way, and that he faced the problems and the difficulties of life with no secret reinforcements of miraculous power. . . . To us Jesus' death is, in essence, no different from the death of other heroes."[25] "Today the ancient belief that Jesus will reappear in the sky, inaugurate a dramatic world judgment, sentence Satan and the demons to hell, and lead the angels and the Christians into paradise, has dwindled from a universally accepted and enormously influential Christian conviction to the esoteric doctrine of a minority. Once a modern man accepts what historians tell him about the age of the universe, and once he accepts what scientists tell him about

---

[23] John Herman Randall, "The Forces That Are Destroying Traditional Beliefs," *Current History*, June, 1929, pp. 359-361.

[24] James Gordon Gilkey, *A Faith to Affirm*, p. 3. By permission of the Macmillan Company, publishers.

[25] *Ibid.*, pp. 9, 10.

the nature of the evolutionary process, he cannot believe that there will ever be any such spectacular wind-up of the world's affairs as the one which the early Christians believed would presently take place."[26] "We propose to take from the Christianity of the past the elements which seem of abiding value, combine with them the religious convictions and the ethical insights which have emerged during recent times, and from this composite material shape a new formulation of the Christian message. We frankly admit that our gospel is not the 'old gospel,' or even the modified version of the old gospel which is now proclaimed in conservative pulpits. Ours is, we confess, a 'new gospel.' "[27]

The acceptance by Protestantism of the first angel's message would have enabled the church to become a light to "all nations." But betraying her trust by her rejection of the message, she left the nations without the witness of *present truth* that they might have had, to grope in the darkness of error and superstition resulting from the intoxicating and stupefying influences of the system of false doctrines she had built up and refused to relinquish.

Robert M. Hutchins, president of the University of Chicago, in speaking of our spiritual condition, said: "We do not know where we are going, or why, and we have almost given up the attempt to find out. We are in despair because the keys which were to open the gates of heaven have let us into a larger but more oppressive prison house. We think [thought] those keys were science and the free intelligence of man. They have failed us. We have long since cast off God. To what can we now appeal?"[28]

In its issue of May 24, 1941, the Philadelphia *Inquirer* editorially attempts to analyze our condition: "We appear to have reached one of those portentous periods in history when

---

[26] *Ibid.*, p. 24.

[27] *Ibid.*, p. 26.

[28] Robert M. Hutchins, quoted in "The Revolt Against Science," *The Christian Century*, January 24, 1934. Dr. Hutchins says he meant "thought" instead of "think."

civilization halts and stands aghast in the presence of forces too complex and too terrible in their potentialities accurately to be appraised. Confronted by problems that can be disregarded by none but lighthearted children and lightheaded fools, we have reached the crossroads where every signpost points to bafflement. For years there have been increasingly bitter assaults upon religion. We have felt it was not our concern if 'the old faiths loosen and fall.' It would seem that in this, as in past civilizations when they were nearing their inevitable end, we—and by 'we' is meant mankind in general—have grown too cocksure of ourselves. . . .

"We have watched, many of us with scant misgivings, the growth of queer cults and the recrudescence of pagan philosophies. Unperturbed, we have witnessed the rise of modern Humanism, with its denial of a power greater than our own; its exalting of man to equality with his Maker. Now, when civilization may be dying on its feet, the barrage balloons of our self-sufficiency are in process of being blasted out of the sky. Human creatures at last are beginning to discover that they are not little gods—but only little men."[29]

But as the popular churches depart farther and farther from God, they at length reach such a condition that true Christians can no longer maintain a connection with them; and then they will be called out. This we look for in the future, in fulfillment of Revelation 18: 1-4. We believe it will come, when, in addition to their corruptions, the churches begin to raise against the saints the hand of oppression. (See comments on Revelation 18.)

VERSE 9 And the third angel followed them, saying with a loud voice, If any man worship the beast and his image, and receive his mark in his forehead, or in his hand, 10 the same shall drink of the wine of the wrath of God, which is poured out without mixture into the cup of His indignation; and he shall be tormented with fire and brimstone in the presence of the holy angels, and in the presence of the Lamb: 11 and the smoke of their torment ascendeth up forever and ever: and they have no rest day nor night, who worship the beast and his image, and whosoever receiveth the mark of

[29] "Will They Turn to Religion?" Philadelphia *Inquirer*, May 24, 1941, p. 10.

his name. 12 Here is the patience of the saints: here are they that keep the commandments of God, and the faith of Jesus.

The Third Angel's Message.—This is a message of most fearful import. No more severe threatening of divine wrath can be found in all the Bible. The sin against which it warns must be a terrible sin, and it must be one so plainly defined that all who will may understand it, and thus know how to avoid the judgments pronounced against it.

It will be noticed that these messages are cumulative, that is, one does not cease when another is introduced. Thus, for a time the first message was the only one going forth. The second message was introduced, but that did not put an end to the first. From that time there were two messages. The third followed them, not to supersede them, but only to join with them, so that we now have three messages going forth simultaneously, or, rather, a *threefold* message, embracing the truths of all three, the last one of course being the culminating proclamation. Until the work is done, it will never cease to be true that the hour of God's judgment has come, nor that Babylon has fallen. These facts still continue to be proclaimed in connection with the truths introduced by the third message.

There will also be noticed a logical connection between the messages themselves. Viewing the situation immediately before the first message was introduced, we see the Protestant religious world sadly in need of reformation. Divisions and confusion existed in the churches. They were still clinging to many papal errors and superstitions. The power of the gospel was impaired in their hands. To correct these evils, the doctrine of the second coming of Christ was introduced, and proclaimed with power. They should have received it and been quickened by it into new life, as they would have been had they received it. Instead of this, they rejected it, and suffered the consequences spiritually. Then followed the second message, announcing the result of that rejection, and declaring what was not only a fact in itself, but a judicial verdict of God upon them for their recreancy in this respect;

namely, that God had departed from them, and they had met with a spiritual fall.

This did not have the effect to arouse them and lead them to correct their errors, as it was sufficient to do had they been willing to be admonished and corrected. What follows? The way is open for a still further retrograde movement, for wider apostasy and still greater evils. The powers of darkness will press forward their work, and if the churches still persist in this course of shunning light and rejecting truth, they will soon find themselves worshiping the beast and receiving his mark. This will be the logical sequence of that course of action which began with the rejection of the first message.

Now another proclamation is sent forth, announcing in solemn tones that if any man shall do this, he shall drink of the wine of the wrath of God, which is poured out without mixture into the cup of His indignation. That is to say, you rejected the first message, and met with a spiritual fall. If you continue to reject truth and disregard the warnings sent out, you will exhaust God's last means of grace, and finally meet with a literal destruction for which there will be no remedy. This is as severe a threatening as God can make to be inflicted in this life, and it is the last. A few will heed it and be saved, but the multitude will pass on and perish.

The proclamation of the third angel's message is the last special religious movement to be made before the Lord appears, for immediately following this, John beholds one like the Son of man coming upon a great white cloud to reap the harvest of the earth. This can represent nothing else than the second coming of Christ. If therefore the coming of Christ is at the door, the time has come for the proclamation of this message. There are many who with voice and pen are earnestly teaching that we are in the last days of time, and that the coming of Christ is at the door; but when we remind them of this prophecy, they are suddenly at sea, without anchor, chart, or compass. They do not know what to do with it. They can see as well as we that if what they are teaching respecting the coming of Christ is true, and the Lord is at hand, somewhere—yes, all over the land—should be heard the warning notes of this third angel's message.

The arguments on the two preceding messages fix the time of the third, and show that it belongs to the present day. But the best evidence that the message is now going to the world, is found in the events that demonstrate its fulfillment. We have identified the first message as a leading proclamation in the great Advent movement of 1840-1844. We have seen the fulfillment of the second message in connection with that movement in the latter year. Let us now look at what has taken place since that time.

When Christ did not come in 1844, the entire Adventist body was thrown into more or less confusion. Many gave up the movement entirely. More concluded that the argument on the time was wrong, and immediately endeavored to re-adjust the prophetic periods, and set a new time for the Lord to come—a work which they have continued more or less to the present time, fixing a new date as each one passed. A few searched closely and candidly for the cause of the mistake, and were confirmed in their views of the providential character of the advent movement, and in the correctness of the argument on the *time*, but saw that a mistake had been made in their understanding of the sanctuary, by which error the disappointment could be explained. They learned that the sanctuary in Daniel 8: 14 was not this earth, as had been supposed, that the cleansing was not to be by fire, and that the prophecy on this point did not involve the coming of the Lord at all. They found in the Scriptures clear evidence that the sanctuary referred to was the temple in heaven, which Paul calls "the sanctuary," the "true tabernacle, which the Lord pitched and not man." They saw further that its cleansing, according to the type, would consist of the final ministration of the priest in the second apartment, or most holy place. They then understood that the time had come for the fulfillment of Revelation 11: 19: "The temple of God was opened in heaven, and there was seen in His temple the ark of His testament."

Having their attention thus called to the ark, they were naturally led to an examination of the law contained in the ark. That the ark contained the law was evident from the very name applied to it. It was called "the ark of His testament," but it would not have been the ark of His "testament," and it could not have been so called, had it not contained the law. Here then was the ark in heaven, the great antitype of the ark which, during typical times, existed here on earth. The law which this heavenly ark contained must consequently be the great original of which the law on the tables in the earthly ark was but a transcript, or copy. Both these laws must read precisely alike, word for word, jot for jot, tittle for tittle. To suppose otherwise would involve only falsehood.

That law, then, is still the law of God's government, and its fourth precept now as in the beginning demands the observance of the seventh day of the week as the Sabbath. No one who admits the argument on the sanctuary disputes this point.

Thus the Sabbath reform was brought to view; and it was seen that whatever had been done in opposition to this law, especially in the introduction of a day of rest and worship which destroyed the Sabbath of Jehovah, must be the work of the papal beast, that power which was to oppose God, to attempt to change His laws and try to exalt himself above God. But this is the exact work in reference to which the third angel utters his warning. Hence it began to be seen by the believers of 1844 that the period of the third angel's message synchronizes with the period of the cleansing of the sanctuary, which began with the ending of the 2300 days in 1844, and that the proclamation is based on the great truths developed by this subject.

Thus the light of the third angel's message dawned upon the church. They saw at once that the world would have a right to demand of those who professed to be giving that message, an explanation of all the symbols which it contains—

the beast, the image, the worship, and the mark. Hence these points were made subjects of special study. The testimony of the Scriptures was found to be clear and abundant, and it did not take long to formulate from the truths revealed, definite statements and proofs in explanation of all these points.

A Message of Warning.—The argument showing what constitutes the beast, the image, and the mark, has already been given in comments on Revelation 13; and it has been shown that the two-horned beast, which erects the image and enforces the mark, is the United States of America. It is this work, and these agents, against which the third angel's message utters its warning, which is further proof that this message is now in order, and shows the most conclusive harmony in all these prophecies. The arguments we need not here repeat; it will be sufficient to recapitulate the points established.

The "beast" is the Roman Catholic power.

The "mark of the beast" is that institution which this power sets forth as proof of its authority to legislate for the church, and command the consciences of men under sin. It consists in a change of the law of God, by which the signature of royalty is taken from the law. The seventh-day Sabbath, the great memorial of Jehovah's creative work, is torn from its place in the decalogue, and a false and counterfeit sabbath, the first day of the week, is set up in its stead.

The "image of the beast" is some ecclesiastical combination which will resemble the beast in being clothed with power to enforce its decrees with the pains and penalties of the civil law.

The "two-horned beast," by which the image, is given power to speak and act, represents the United States of America, which is moving toward the formation of the image of the beast.

The two-horned beast enforces the mark of the beast, that is, it establishes by law the observance of the first day of the week, or the Sunday rest day. What is being done in this direction has already been noticed. The movement is urged on by individuals and by organized groups which mix agitation for religious laws with their better aims.

But the people are not to be left in the dark in this matter. The third angel's message utters a solemn protest against all this evil. It exposes the work of the beast, shows the nature of its opposition to the law of God, warns the people against compliance with its demands, and points the way of truth to all. This naturally excites opposition, and the church is led so much the more to seek the aid of human power in behalf of its dogmas as they are shown to be sadly lacking in divine authority.

What has this message accomplished, and what showing does it make in the world today? In answer to this query, some striking facts may be presented. The first publication in its interests was issued in 1849. Today this message is proclaimed by books, tracts, and periodicals in 200 different languages, and maintains 83 publishing houses scattered throughout both hemispheres, in which are published 313 periodicals. The value of its literature sold during 1942 amounted to $5,467,664.99. Its evangelistic work is carried forward in 413 countries, and preached in more than 810 languages.

Such a movement is at least a phenomenon to be explained. We have found movements which fulfill most strikingly and accurately the first and second angels' messages. Here is another which now challenges the attention of the world as a fulfillment of the third. It *claims* to be a fulfillment, and asks the world to examine the credentials on which it bases its right to such a claim. Let us look at them.

"The third angel followed them." So this movement follows the two previously mentioned. It takes up and continues the promulgation of the truths they uttered, and adds to them what the third angel's message involves besides.

The third message is characterized as a warning against the beast. So this movement holds prominent among its themes an explanation of this symbol, telling the people what it is, and exposing its blasphemous claims and works.

The third message warns all against worshiping the beast. So this movement explains how this beast-power has brought into Christendom certain institutions which antagonize the requirements of the Most High, and shows that if we yield to these, we worship this power, "Know ye not," says Paul, "that to whom ye yield yourselves servants to obey, his servants ye are to whom ye obey?" Romans 6: 16.

The third message warns all against receiving the mark of the beast. So this movement makes it the burden of its work to show what the mark of the beast is, and to warn against its reception. It is the more solicitous to do this, because this unchristian power has worked so cunningly that the majority are deceived into making unconscious concessions to its authority. It is shown that the mark of the beast is an institution which has been arrayed in Christian garb, and insidiously introduced into the Christian church in such a way as to nullify the authority of Jehovah and enthrone that of the beast. Stripped of all disguises, it is simply setting up a counterfeit sabbath of its own on the first day of the week, in place of the Sabbath of the Lord on the seventh day—a usurpation which the great God cannot tolerate, and from which the remnant church must fully clear itself before it will be prepared for the coming of Christ. Hence the urgent warning, Let no man worship the beast or receive his mark.

The third message has something to say against the worship of the image of the beast. So this movement speaks of this subject also, telling what the image will be, or at least explaining the prophecy of the two-horned beast. It reveals where the image is to be formed. The prophecy concerns this generation; and is evidently on the verge of fulfillment.

There is no religious enterprise extant today except that of the Seventh-day Adventists which claims to be a fulfillment of the third angel's message—no other which holds forth as its prominent themes the very subjects of which this book is composed. What shall we do with these things? Is this the fulfillment? It must so stand, unless its claims can be disproved;

PAUL REMMEY, ARTIST

A COMMANDMENT-KEEPING PEOPLE

"Here are they that keep the commandments of God, and the faith of Jesus." Revelation 14: 12.

unless it can be shown that the first and second angels' messages have not been heard; that the positions taken in reference to the beast, the image, the mark, and the worship are not correct; and that all the prophecies, and signs, and evidences which show that the coming of Christ is near, and consequently that this message is due, can be wholly set aside. This the intelligent Bible student will hardly undertake.

The result of the proclamation as declared in verse 12, still further proves the correctness of the positions here taken. It brings out a company of whom it can be said, "Here are they that keep the commandments of God and the faith of Jesus." In the very heart of Christendom this work is being done, and those who receive the message are rendered peculiar by their practice in reference to the commandments of God. What difference is there in practice, and what only difference among Christians in this respect?—Only this: some think that the fourth commandment is kept by devoting the first day of the week to rest and worship. Others claim that the seventh day is the one set apart to such duties, and spend its hours accordingly, resuming on the first day their ordinary labor. No plainer line of demarcation could be drawn between two classes. The time which one class regards as sacred and devotes to religious uses, the other looks upon as only secular and devotes to ordinary labor. One class is devoutly resting, the other zealously laboring. One class, pursuing its worldly vocations, finds the other class withdrawn from all such pursuits, and the avenue of commercial intercourse between them abruptly closed. Thus for two days in the week these two classes are kept apart by difference of doctrine and practice in regard to the fourth commandment. On no other commandment could there be so marked a difference.

The Sabbath Made Prominent in the Message.—The third angel's message brings its adherents to the observance of the seventh day, for in this way only are they made peculiar, inasmuch as an observance of the first day would not distinguish a person from the masses who were already observing that day when the message was introduced. In this we find still further evidence that Sundaykeeping is the mark of the beast, for the message, presenting as its chief burden a warning against receiving the mark of the beast, will of course bring its adherents to discard that practice which constitutes the mark, and to adopt the opposite course. It does lead them to discard the observance of the first day of the week, and adopt that of the seventh day. In view of this, it is at once seen that there is here more than an inference that Sundaykeeping is the mark of the beast against which it warns us, and that the observance of the seventh day is its opposite.

This is in harmony with the argument on the seal of God, as given in the remarks on Revelation 7. It was there shown that sign, seal, mark, and token are synonymous terms, and that God takes His Sabbath to be His sign, or seal in reference to His people. Thus God has a seal, which is His Sabbath. The beast has a mark, which is a counterfeit sabbath. One is the seventh day, the other is the first day. Christendom will at last be divided into just two classes: those who are sealed with the seal of the living God—that is, have His sign, or keep His Sabbath; and those who receive the mark of the beast—that is, have his sign, or keep his counterfeit sabbath. In reference to this issue, the third angel's message both enlightens and warns us.

As so much importance attaches to the seventh-day Sabbath, it will be proper to present here the leading facts connected with the Sabbath institution.

The Sabbath was instituted in the beginning, at the conclusion of the first week of time. (Genesis 2: 1-3.)

It was the seventh day of that week, and was based on facts which are inseparably connected with its very name and existence—facts which can never be changed. God's resting on the seventh day made it His rest day, or the Sabbath (rest) of the Lord; and it can never cease to be His rest day, as that fact never can be changed. He sanctified, or set apart, the day then and there, the record states; and that sanctification can never cease, unless it is removed by an act on the part of Jehovah as direct and explicit as that by which He placed it upon the day in the beginning. No one claims that this has ever been done, and one could not prove it if he did so claim.

The Sabbath has nothing in it of a typical or ceremonial nature, for it was instituted before man sinned, and hence belongs to a time when in the very nature of things a type or shadow could not exist.

The laws and institutions which existed before man's fall were primary in their nature. They grew out of the relation between God and man, and man and man, and were such as would always have remained if man never had sinned, and were not affected by his sin. In other words, they were in the nature of things immutable and eternal. Ceremonial and typical laws owed their origin to the fact that man had sinned. These were from dispensation to dispensation subject to change; and these, and these only, were abolished at the cross. The Sabbath law was a primary law, and therefore immutable and eternal.

The sanctification of the Sabbath in Eden assures its existence from creation to Sinai. Here it was placed in the very bosom of the decalogue as God spoke it with an audible voice, and wrote it with His finger on tables of stone—circumstances which forever separate it from ceremonial laws, and place it among the moral and eternal.

The Sabbath is not indefinite, any seventh day after six of labor. The law from Sinai (Exodus 20: 8-11) makes it as definite as language can make it. The events that gave it birth (Genesis 2: 1-3) confine it to the definite seventh day. The 6,240 Sabbath miracles in the wilderness, three each week for forty years—a double supply of manna on the sixth day, the preservation of the sixth-day manna on the seventh day, and none on the seventh day (Exodus 16)—show that it is one particular day, and not simply a proportion of time. To claim otherwise would be like claiming that Washington's Birthday or Independence Day was only a 365th part of a year, and might be celebrated on any other day as well as the day upon which it occurred.

The Sabbath is a part of that law which our Lord openly declared that He came not to destroy. On the other hand, He most solemnly affirmed that it should endure in every jot and tittle while the earth should continue. (Matthew 5: 17-20.)

It is a part of that law which Paul declares is *not* made void but established by faith in Christ. (Romans 3: 31.) On the contrary the ceremonial or typical law, which pointed to Christ and ceased at the cross, *is* made void, or superseded, by faith in Him. (Ephesians 2: 15.)

It is a part of that royal law, a law pertaining to the King Jehovah, which James declares is a law of liberty, and which shall judge us at the last day. God does not have different standards of judgment for different ages of the world. (James 2: 11, 12.)

It is the "Lord's day" of Revelation 1: 10. (See comments on that verse.)

It appears as the institution in reference to which a great reform is predicted in the last days. (Isaiah 56: 1, 2 compared with 1 Peter 1: 5.) Under this head would also come the message under consideration.

In the new creation, the Sabbath, true to its origin and nature, again appears, and will thenceforward shed its blessings upon God's people through all eternity. (Isaiah 66: 22, 23.)

Such is a brief synopsis of some of the arguments to show that the Sabbath law has been in no wise relaxed, and the institution in no way changed; and that a person cannot be said to keep the commandments of God unless he keeps His day. To have to do with such an institution is a high honor. To pay heed to its claims will prove an infinite blessing.

Punishment of Beast Worshipers.—These shall be tormented with fire and brimstone in the presence of the holy angels and of the Lamb. When is this torment inflicted? Revelation 19: 20 shows that at the second coming of Christ there is a manifestation of fiery judgments which may be called a lake of fire and brimstone, into which the beast and the false prophet are cast *alive*. This can refer only to the destruction visited upon them at the beginning, not at the end, of the thousand years.

There is a remarkable passage in Isaiah to which we are obliged to refer in explanation of the phraseology of the threatening of the third angel, and which unquestionably describes scenes to take place here at the second advent and in the desolate state of the earth during the thousand years following. That the language in the Revelation was borrowed from this prophecy can hardly fail to be seen. After describing the Lord's anger upon the nations, the great slaughter of their armies, and the departing of the heavens as a scroll, the prophet says: "It is the day of the Lord's vengeance, and the year of recompenses for the controversy of Zion. And the streams thereof shall be turned into pitch, and the dust thereof into brimstone, and the land thereof shall become burning pitch. It shall not be quenched night nor day; the smoke thereof shall go up forever: from generation to generation it shall lie waste; none shall pass through it forever and ever." Isaiah 34: 8-10. Since it is expressly revealed that there is to be a lake of fire in which all sinners perish at the end of the thousand years, we can only conclude that the destruction of the living wicked at the beginning of this period, and the final doom of all the ungodly at its close, are similar.

The expression "forever and ever" cannot here denote eternity. This is evident from the fact that this punishment is inflicted on this earth, where time is measured by day and night. This is further shown from the passage in Isaiah already referred to, if that is, as above suggested, the language from which this is borrowed, and applies to the same time. That language is spoken of the land of Idumea; but whether it be taken to mean literally the land of Edom, south and east of Judea, or to represent, as it doubtless does, this whole earth at the time when the Lord Jesus shall be revealed from heaven in flaming fire, and the year of recompenses for the controversy of Zion comes, in either case the scene must eventually terminate. This earth is finally to be made new, cleansed of every stain of sin, every vestige of suffering and decay, and to become the habitation of righteousness and joy throughout eternal ages. The word αἰών, *aion*, here translated "forever," is defined thus by G. Abbott-Smith in *A Manual Greek Lexicon of the New Testament:* "*A space of time*, as, a lifetime, generation, period of history, an indefinitely long period." So without doing violence to the accepted meaning of the Greek word, we may here interpret it in harmony with other plain statements of Scripture.

The period of the third angel's message is a time of patience with the people of God. Paul and James both give us instruction on this point. (Hebrews 10: 36; James 5: 7, 8.) Meanwhile this waiting company are keeping the commandments of God—the ten commandments—and the faith of Jesus, that is, all the teachings of Christ and His apostles as contained in the New Testament. The true Sabbath as given in the decalogue is thus brought out in vivid contrast with the counterfeit sabbath, the mark of the beast, which finally distinguishes those who reject the third angel's message.

VERSE 13 And I heard a voice from heaven saying unto me, Write, Blessed are the dead which die in the Lord from henceforth: Yea, saith the Spirit, that they may rest from their labors; and their works do follow them. 14 And I looked, and behold a white cloud, and upon the cloud one sat like unto the Son of man, having on His head a golden crown, and in His hand a sharp sickle. 15 And another angel came out of the temple, crying with a loud voice to Him that sat on the cloud, Thrust in Thy sickle, and reap: for the time is come for Thee to reap; for the harvest of the earth is ripe. 16 And He that sat on the cloud thrust in His sickle on the earth; and the earth was reaped.

A Solemn Crisis.—Events grow solemn as we near the end. It is this fact which gives to the third angel's message, now going forth, its unusual degree of solemnity and importance. It is the last warning to go forth prior to the coming of the Son of man, here represented as seated upon a white cloud, a crown upon His head, and a sickle in His hand, to reap the harvest of the earth.

We are fast passing over a line of prophecy which culminates in the revelation of the Lord Jesus from heaven in flaming fire, to take vengeance on His foes, and to reward His saints. Not only so, but we have come so near its accomplishment that the next link in the chain is this crowning and momentous event. Time never rolls backward. As the river does not falter as it approaches the precipice, but bears all floating bodies over with resistless power; and as the seasons never reverse their course, but summer follows in the path of the budding fig-tree, and winter treads close upon the falling leaf; so we are borne onward and onward, whether we will or not, whether prepared or not, to the unavoidable and irreversible crisis. Ah, how little do the proud professor of religion and the careless sinner dream of the doom that is impending! How hard, even for those who know and profess the truth, to realize it as it is!

A Blessing Promised.—John is commanded by a voice from heaven to write, "Blessed are the dead which die in the Lord from henceforth;" and the response of the Spirit is, "Yea, . . . that they may rest from their labors; and their works do follow them." "From henceforth" must signify from some particular point of time. What point?—Evidently from the beginning of the message in connection with which this is spoken. But why are those who die after this point of time blessed? There must be some special reason for pronouncing this benediction upon them. Is it not because they escape the time of fearful peril which the saints are to encounter as they close their pilgrimage? While they are thus blessed in common with all the righteous dead, they have an advantage over them in being doubtless that company who are raised to everlasting life in the special resurrection in Daniel 12: 2.

It will be noticed that in this line of prophecy three angels precede the Son of man on the white cloud, and three are introduced after that symbol. The opinion has already been expressed that literal angels are engaged in the scenes here described. The first three have charge of the three special messages. The message of the fourth angel is evidently to be uttered after the Son of man finishes His priestly work, and takes His seat upon the white cloud, but before He appears in the clouds of heaven. As the language is addressed to Him who is seated upon the white cloud, having in His hand a sharp sickle ready to reap, it must denote a message of prayer on the part of the church, after their work for the world is done, probation has ceased, and nothing remains but for the Lord to appear and take His people to Himself. It is doubtless the day-and-night cry spoken of by our Lord in Luke 18: 7, 8, in connection with the coming of the Son of man. This prayer will be answered; the elect will be avenged; for does not the parable read, "Shall not God avenge His own elect, which cry day and night unto Him?" He that is seated upon the cloud will thrust in His sickle, and the saints, under the figure of the wheat of the earth, will be gathered into the heavenly garner.

The Wheat Garnered.—"He that sat on the cloud," says the prophecy, "thrust in His sickle on the earth; and the earth was reaped." By this language we are carried past the second advent, with its accompanying scenes of destruction to the wicked and salvation to the righteous. Beyond these scenes we must therefore look for the application of the following verses.

VERSE 17 And another angel came out of the temple which is in heaven, he also having a sharp sickle. 18 And another angel came out from the altar, which had power over fire; and cried with a loud cry to him that had the sharp sickle, saying, Thrust in thy sharp sickle, and gather the clusters of the vine of the earth; for her grapes are fully ripe. 19 And the angel thrust in his sickle into the earth, and gathered the vine of the earth, and cast it into the great winepress of the wrath of God. 20 And the winepress was trodden without the city, and blood came out of the winepress, even unto the horse bridles, by the space of a thousand and six hundred furlongs.

The Winepress of God's Wrath.—The last two angels have to do with the wicked, who are most fitly represented by the purple clusters of the vine of the earth. May it not be that the closing doom of that class at the end of the thousand years is here presented, the prophecy thus making a final disposition of both the righteous and the wicked—the righteous clothed with immortality, and safely established in the kingdom, the wicked perishing outside the city?

This can hardly be applied at the time of the second advent, for events are here given in chronological order, and the destruction of the wicked would be contemporaneous with the gathering of the righteous. Again, the living wicked at Christ's coming drink of the "cup" of His indignation. But this passage brings to view the time when they perish in the "winepress" of His wrath, which is said to be trodden "without the city," answering completely to the description of Revelation 20: 9, this latter expression more naturally denoting their complete and final destruction.

The angel comes out of the temple, where the records are kept and the punishment is determined. The other angel has power over fire. This may have some connection with the fact that fire is the agent by which the wicked are at last to be destroyed, although, to carry out the figure, the wicked are likened to the clusters of the vine of the earth, and are said to be cast into the great winepress which is trodden without the city. Blood comes out of the winepress, even to the horses' bridles. We know that the wicked are doomed to be swallowed up at last in a flood of all-devouring flame descending from God out of heaven, but what preceding slaughter may take place among the doomed host, we do not know. It is not improbable that this language will be literally fulfilled. As the first four angels of this series denoted a marked movement on the part of the people of God, the last two may denote the same; for the saints are to have some part to act in meting out and executing the final punishment of the wicked. (1 Corinthians 6: 2; Psalm 149: 9.)

The Saints Triumphant.—This prophecy closes as others do, with the triumph of God, Christ, and the redeemed.

 R. M. ELDRIDGE, ARTIST

"IT IS FINISHED!"

"The temple was filled with smoke from the glory of God, and from His power; and no man was able to enter into the temple." Revelation 15: 8.

CHAPTER XV

PREPARING THE VIALS OF DIVINE WRATH

THIS chapter introduces the seven last plagues, a manifestation of Heaven's unmingled wrath, in its full measure upon the last generation of the wicked. The work of mercy is then forever past.

VERSE 1 And I saw another sign in heaven, great and marvelous, seven angels having the seven last plagues; for in them is filled up the wrath of God. 2 And I saw as it were a sea of glass mingled with fire: and them that had gotten the victory over the beast, and over his image, and over his mark, and over the number of his name, stand on the sea of glass, having the harps of God. 3 And they sing the song of Moses the servant of God, and the song of the Lamb, saying, Great and marvelous are Thy works, Lord God Almighty; just and true are Thy ways, Thou King of saints. 4 Who shall not fear Thee, O Lord, and glorify Thy name? For Thou only art holy: for all nations shall come and worship before Thee; for Thy judgments are made manifest. 5 And after that I looked, and, behold, the temple of the tabernacle of the testimony in heaven was opened: 6 and the seven angels came out of the temple, having the seven plagues, clothed in pure and white linen, and having their breasts girded with golden girdles. 7 And one of the four beasts gave unto the seven angels seven golden vials full of the wrath of God, who liveth forever and ever. 8 And the temple was filled with smoke from the glory of God, and from His power; and no man was able to enter into the temple, till the seven plagues of the seven angels were fulfilled.

A Preparatory Scene.—Thus reads the fifteenth chapter. By it we are carried back to a new series of events. The whole chapter is but an introduction to the most terrible judgments of the Almighty ever to be visited upon this earth—the seven last plagues. What we behold here is a solemn preparation for the outpouring of these unmixed vials. Verse 5 shows that these plagues fall after the close of the ministration in the sanctuary, for the temple is opened before they are poured out. They are given to seven angels clothed in linen pure and white, a fit emblem of the purity of God's righteousness and justice in the infliction of these judgments. They receive these vials from one of the four beasts, or living creatures. These living beings were shown in comments on Revelation 4 to be a class of Christ's assistants in His sanctuary work. How appropriate then that they should be the ones to deliver to the ministers of vengeance the vials of the wrath to be poured upon those who have slighted Christ's mercy, abused His long-suffering, heaped contumely upon His name, and crucified Him afresh in the persecution of His followers! While the seven angels are performing their fearful mission, the temple is filled with the glory of God, and no man—οὐδεἰς, *oudeis*, "no one, no being"—can enter there. This shows that the work of mercy is closed, since there is no ministration in the sanctuary during the infliction of the plagues. Hence they are manifestations of the wrath of God without any mixture of mercy.

God's People Remembered.—In this scene the people of God are not forgotten. The prophet is permitted to anticipate somewhat in verses 2-4, and behold them as victors upon the sea which had the appearance of glass mingled with fire. They sing the song of Moses and the Lamb as they stand upon that sparkling expanse of glory. The sea of glass upon which these victors stand, is the same as that brought to view in Revelation 4: 6, which was before the throne in heaven. As we have no evidence that it has yet changed its location, and the saints are seen upon it, we have here indubitable proof in connection with Revelation 14: 1-5 that the saints are taken to heaven to receive a part of their reward. Thus, as if the bright sun should burst through the midnight cloud, some scene is presented or some promise given to the humble followers of the Lamb in every hour of temptation, to assure and reassure them of God's love and care for them, and of the certainty of their final reward. "Say ye to the righteous," wrote Isaiah of old, "that it shall be well with him;" but, "Woe unto the wicked! It shall be ill with him." Isaiah 3: 10, 11.

The song the victors sing, the song of Moses and the Lamb, is given here in epitome: "Great and marvelous are thy works,

Lord God Almighty; just and true are thy ways, thou King of saints." It is a song of infinite grandeur. How comprehensive in its terms! How sublime in its theme! It appeals to the works of God which are a manifestation of His glory. With immortal vision the saints will be able to comprehend them as they cannot in the present state, even though astronomy reveals enough to fill all hearts with admiration. From our little world we pass out to our sun ninety-three million miles away; on to its nearest neighboring sun, twenty-five million million miles away; on to the great double polestar, from which it takes light four hundred years to reach our world; on past systems, groups, constellations, till we reach the great star Rigel, in Orion, shining with the power of fifteen thousand suns like ours! What then must be the grand center around which these myriads of shining orbs revolve! Well may the song be sung, "Great and marvelous are Thy works." But the song covers another field also, the field of God's providence and grace: "Just and true are Thy ways, Thou King of saints." All the dealings of God with all His creatures in the eyes of the redeemed and the sight of all worlds will be forever vindicated. After all our blindness, all our perplexities, all our trials, we shall be able to exclaim at last in the exuberance of satisfied joy, "Just and true are Thy ways, Thou King of saints."

 FRANKLIN BOOTH, ARTIST

WHEN THE SEVENTH PLAGUE STRIKES

Struck by a mighty earthquake and a destroying hail, the lost will blaspheme as they perish.

CHAPTER XVI

SEVEN PLAGUES DEVASTATE THE EARTH

VERSE 1 And I heard a great voice out of the temple saying to the seven angels, Go your ways, and pour out the vials of the wrath of God upon the earth. 2 And the first went, and poured out his vial upon the earth; and there fell a noisome and grievous sore upon the men which had the mark of the beast, and upon them which worshiped his image.

THIS chapter is a description of the seven vials of the unmingled wrath of God, and the effects that follow as they are poured upon the earth. Our first inquiries are, What is the true position on these points? Are they symbolical, and mostly fulfilled in the past? Or are they literal, and all future?

Time of the Plagues.—The description of the first plague clearly reveals at once the time when it shall fall upon the earth, for it is poured out upon those who have the mark of the beast, and who worship his image—the very work against which the third angel warns us. This is conclusive proof that these judgments are not poured out until after this angel closes his work, and that the class who hear his warning and reject it, are the ones to receive the first drops from the overflowing vials of God's indignation. If these plagues are in the past, the image of the beast and his worship are in the past. If these are past, the two-horned beast, which makes this image, and all his work, are in the past. If these are past, then the third angel's message, which warns us in reference to this work, is in the past; and if this is ages in the past, then the first and second messages which precede it were also ages in the past. Then the prophetic periods, on which the messages are based, especially the 2300 days, ended ages ago. If this is so, the seventy weeks of Daniel 9 are thrown wholly into the Jewish period, and the great proof of the Messiahship of Christ is destroyed. But it has been shown in remarks on Revelation 7, 13, 14, that the first and second messages have been given in our own day; that the third is now in process of accomplishment; that the two-horned beast has come upon the stage of action, and is preparing to do the work assigned him; and that the formation of the image and the enforcement of the worship are just in the future. Unless all these positions can be overthrown, the seven last plagues must also be assigned wholly to the future.

But there are other reasons for locating them in the future and not in the past.

Under the fifth plague, men blaspheme God because of their *sores*, the same sores, of course, caused by the outpouring of the first plague. This shows that these plagues all fall upon one and the *same generation* of men, some being, no doubt, swept off by each one, yet some surviving through the terrible scenes of them all.

These plagues are the wine of God's wrath without mixture, threatened by the third angel. (Revelation 14: 10; 15: 1.) Such language cannot be applied to any judgments visited upon the earth while Christ pleads with His Father in behalf of our fallen race. Therefore we must locate them in the future, when probation shall have closed.

Another and more definite testimony on the beginning and duration of these plagues is found in these words: "The temple was filled with smoke from the glory of God, and from His power; and no man was able to enter into the temple, till the seven plagues of the seven angels were fulfilled." Revelation 15: 8. The temple here introduced is evidently that which is mentioned in Revelation 11: 19: "The temple of God was opened in heaven, and there was seen in His temple the ark of His testament." In other words, we have before us the heavenly sanctuary. When the seven angels with the seven golden vials receive their commission, the temple is filled with smoke from the glory of God, and no being can enter into the temple, or sanctuary, until the angels have fulfilled their work. There will therefore be no ministration in the sanctuary during this time. Consequently, these vials are not poured out until the close of the ministration in the tabernacle above, but immediately follow that event. Christ is then no longer a mediator. Mercy, which has long stayed the hand of vengeance, pleads no more. The servants of God are all sealed. What could then be expected but that the storm of vengeance should fall, and earth be swept with the besom of destruction?

Since the time of these judgments places them in the very near future, treasured up against the day of wrath, we proceed to inquire into their nature, and the result when the solemn and fearful mandate goes forth from the temple to the seven angels, saying, "Go your ways, and pour out the vials of the wrath of God upon the earth." Here we are called to look into the "armory" of the Lord, and behold the "weapons of His indignation." Jeremiah 50: 25. Here are brought forth the treasures of hail, which have been reserved against the time of trouble, against the day of battle and war. (Job 38: 22, 23.)

The First Plague.—"The first went, and poured out his vial upon the earth; and there fell a noisome and grievous sore upon the men which had the mark of the beast, and upon them which worshiped his image." (See also Zechariah 14: 12.)

There is no apparent reason why this should not be regarded as strictly literal. These plagues are almost identical with those which God inflicted upon the Egyptians as He was about to deliver His people from the yoke of bondage, the reality of which is seldom, if ever, called in question. God is now about to reward His people with their final deliverance and redemption, and His judgments will be manifested in a manner no less literal and terrible. What the sore here threatened is, we are not informed. Perhaps it may be similar to the parallel plague which fell upon Egypt. (Exodus 9: 8-11.)

VERSE 3 And the second angel poured out his vial upon the sea; and it became as the blood of a dead man: and every living soul died in the sea.

UNDERWOOD & UNDERWOOD

THE EUPHRATES RIVER

The River Euphrates, symbol of the nation so long holding dominion over its waters, affords no real barrier to a modern army.

The Second Plague.—A more infectious and deadly substance can scarcely be conceived of than the blood of a dead man; and the thought that the great bodies of water on the earth, which are doubtless meant by the term *sea*, will be changed to such a state under this plague, presents a fearful picture. We have here the remarkable fact that the term *living soul* is applied to irrational animals, the fish and living creatures of the sea. This is, we believe, the only instance of such an application in the Authorized Version. In the original languages, however, it occurs frequently, showing that the term as applied to man in the beginning (Genesis 2: 7) cannot be taken as furnishing any evidence that he is endowed with an immaterial and immortal essence called the soul.

VERSE 4 And the third angel poured out his vial upon the rivers and fountains of waters; and they became blood. 5 And I heard the angel of the waters say, Thou art righteous, O Lord, which art, and wast, and shalt be, because Thou hast judged thus. 6 For they have shed the blood of saints and prophets, and Thou hast given them blood to drink; for they are worthy. 7 And I heard another out of the altar say, Even so, Lord God Almighty, true and righteous are Thy judgments.

The Third Plague.—Such is the description of the terrible retribution for the "blood of saints" shed by violent hands, visited upon those who have done, or wish to do, such deeds. Though the horrors of that hour when the fountains and rivers of water shall be like blood, cannot now be realized, the justice of God will stand vindicated, and His judgments approved. Even the angels are heard exclaiming, "Thou art righteous, O Lord, . . . because Thou hast judged thus. For they have shed the blood of saints and prophets. . . . Even so, Lord God Almighty, true and righteous are Thy judgments."

It may be asked how the last generation of the wicked can be said to have shed the blood of saints and prophets, since the last generation of saints are not to be slain. Reference to Matthew 23: 34, 35; 1 John 3: 15, will explain. These scriptures show that guilt attaches to motive no less than to action.

No generation ever formed a more determined purpose to devote the saints to indiscriminate slaughter than the present generation will, not far in the future. (See comments on Revelation 12: 17; 13: 15.) In motive and purpose, they do shed the blood of saints and prophets, and are every whit as guilty as if they were able to carry out their wicked intentions.

It would seem that none of the human family could long survive a continuance of a plague so terrible as this. It must therefore be limited in its duration, as was the similar one on Egypt. (Exodus 7: 17-21, 25.)

VERSE 8 And the fourth angel poured out his vial upon the sun; and power was given unto him to scorch men with fire. 9 And men were scorched with great heat, and blasphemed the name of God, which hath power over these plagues: and they repented not to give Him glory.

The Fourth Plague.—It is worthy of notice that every succeeding plague tends to augment the calamity of the previous ones and to heighten the anguish of the guilty sufferers. We have now a noisome and grievous sore preying upon men, inflaming their blood, and pouring its feverish influence through their veins. In addition to this, they have only blood to allay their burning thirst. As if to crown all, power is given unto the sun, and it pours upon them a flood of fire, and they are scorched with great heat. Here, as the record runs, their woe first seeks utterance in fearful blasphemy.

VERSE 10 And the fifth angel poured out his vial upon the seat of the beast; and his kingdom was full of darkness; and they gnawed their tongues for pain, 11 and blasphemed the God of heaven because of their pains and their sores, and repented not of their deeds.

The Fifth Plague.—An important fact is established by this testimony. The plagues do not at once destroy all their victims, for some who were at first smitten with sores, are still living under the fifth vial, and gnawing their tongues for pain. An illustration of this vial will be found in Exodus 10: 21-23. It is poured upon the seat of the beast, the papacy. The seat of the beast is wherever the papal see is located, which has been thus far, and without doubt will continue to be, the city of Rome. "His kingdom" probably embraces all those who are ecclesiastical subjects of the pope wherever they may be.

As those who place the plagues in the past have the first five already wholly accomplished, we here pause a moment to inquire where in past ages the judgments here threatened have been fulfilled. Can judgments so terrible be inflicted, and noboby know it? If not, where is the history of the fulfillment? When did a noisome and grievous sore fall upon a specified and extensive part of mankind? When did the sea become as the blood of a dead man, and every living soul die in it? When did the fountains and rivers become blood, and people have blood to drink? When did the sun so scorch men with fire as to extort from them curses and blasphemy? When did the subjects of the beast gnaw their tongues for pain, and at the same time blaspheme God on account of their sores? In these plagues, says Inspiration, is *filled up* the wrath of God, but if they can be fulfilled and nobody know it, who shall henceforth consider His wrath so terrible a thing, or shrink from His judgments when they are threatened?

VERSE 12 And the sixth angel poured out his vial upon the great river Euphrates; and the water thereof was dried up, that the way of the kings of the east might be prepared. 13 And I saw three unclean spirits like frogs come out of the mouth of the dragon, and out of the mouth of the beast, and out of the mouth of the false prophet. 14 For they are the spirits of devils, working miracles, which go forth unto the kings of the earth and of the whole world, to gather them to the battle of that great day of God Almighty. 15 Behold, I come as a thief. Blessed is he that watcheth, and keepeth his garments, lest he walk naked, and they see his shame. 16 And he gathered them together into a place called in the Hebrew tongue Armageddon.

The Sixth Plague.—What is the great River Euphrates, upon which this vial is poured out? One view is that it is the literal River Euphrates in Asia. Another is that it is a symbol of the nation occupying the territory through which that river flows. The latter opinion is preferable for many reasons.

It would be difficult to see what end would be gained by the drying up of the literal river, as that would not offer an obstruction at all serious to the progress of an advancing army. It should be noticed that the drying up takes place to prepare the way of the *kings* of the East, that is, regular military organizations, and not a promiscuous and unequipped crowd of men, women, and children, like the children of Israel at the Red Sea or at the Jordan River. The Euphrates is only about 1,400 miles in length, about one third the size of the Mississippi. Without difficulty, Cyrus turned the whole river from its channel at his siege of Babylon. Notwithstanding the numerous wars that have been carried on along its banks, and the mighty hosts that have crossed and recrossed its streams, it never yet had to be dried up to let them pass.

It would be as necessary to dry up the River Tigris as the Euphrates, for that is nearly as large as the latter. Its source is only fifteen miles from that of the Euphrates in the mountains of Armenia, and it runs nearly parallel with it and but a short distance from it throughout its whole course. Yet the prophecy says nothing of the Tigris.

The *literal* drying up of the rivers takes place under the fourth vial, when power is given to the sun to scorch men with fire. Under this plague occur beyond question the scenes of drouth and famine so graphically described by Joel, and as one result of these it is expressly stated that "*the rivers of waters are dried up*." (See Joel 1: 14-20.) The Euphrates can hardly be an exception to this visitation of drouth; hence not much would remain to be literally dried up under the sixth vial.

These plagues, from the very nature of the case, must be manifestations of wrath and judgments upon men; but if the drying up of the literal Euphrates is all that is brought to view, this plague is not of such a nature, and turns out to be no serious affair, after all.

With these objections existing against considering the Euphrates a literal river, it must be understood figuratively as symbolizing the power holding possession of the territory watered by that river when it is observed as beginning to dry up. All agree that that power was Turkey. Hence we may look for the fulfillment of the specifications of this prophecy to affect definitely the Turkish nation.

It is so used in other places in the Scriptures. (See Isaiah 8: 7; Revelation 9: 14.) In this latter text, all must concede that the Euphrates symbolizes the Turkish power; and being the first and only other occurrence of the word in the Revelation, it may well be considered as governing its use in this book.

The drying up of the river in this sense would be the diminution of the Turkish nation, the gradual shrinking of its borders. This is what has actually happened.

At its height the Ottoman Empire extended on the east to the Tigris and the Caspian Sea; on the south to Aden, including Arabia, Palestine, Egypt, Algiers; on the north, the kingdom of Hungary, the Balkan States, the Crimea. Turkey waged war again and again with the mightiest armies of Europe, with Germany, Russia, and others. She carried her conquests deep into Asia, and received appeals for assistance from India. But this mighty scourge of Christendom did not pass her bounds. In the events leading up to 1840 she all but collapsed, and since then has rapidly declined. Let us consider some of her losses.

Turkey lost the kingdom of Hungary in 1718; the Crimea in 1774; Greece, 1832; Rumania, Montenegro, and Bulgaria, 1878; Tripoli, 1912; Egypt was lost in 1914; Mesopotamia was taken by Britain in 1917; Palestine, 1917; Syria, 1918; the Hejaz about the same time. At the close of World War I, the straits and Constantinople were made international, and the Turkish capital was removed to Ankara. Turkey recovered western Anatolia, including Smyrna, from the Greeks; she regained the western portion of Armenia, the headwaters of the Euphrates; she recovered her ancient capital Constantinople in Europe, with a portion of Thrace; but little territory was left to this one-time mighty empire. Her dominion has been reduced province by province, until she retains but a shadow of her former possessions. Surely the nation symbolized by the Euphrates *is* drying up.

But it may be objected that while contending for the literality of the plagues, we nevertheless make one of them a symbol. We answer, No. A power is introduced, it is true, under the sixth vial, in its symbolic form, just as it is under the fifth, where we read of the seat of the beast, which is a well-known symbol; or as we read again in the first plague of the mark of the beast, his image, and its worship, which are also symbols. All that is here insisted upon, is the literality of the *judgments* that result from each vial, which are literal in this case as in all the others, though the organizations which suffer these judgments may be brought to view in their symbolic form.

The Battle of Armageddon.—It may be asked how the way of the kings of the East will be prepared by the drying up, or consumption, of the Ottoman power? The answer is obvious. For what is the way of these kings to be prepared? Is it not that they may come up to the battle of the great day of God Almighty? Where is the battle to be fought? The answer of the prophet is that those who fight this battle will be gathered together "into a place called in the Hebrew tongue Armageddon." This name is drawn from the ancient valley of Megiddo, where so many fierce and decisive battles were fought in Old Testament times. Concerning the name "Armageddon," Lyman Abbott, in *A Dictionary of Religious Knowledge* says:

"This name is given to the great plain of central Palestine which extends from the Mediterranean to the Jordan, separating the mountain ranges of Carmel and Samaria from those of Galilee. . . . It is the ancient plain of Megiddo, the Armageddon of Revelation 16: 16."[1]

On the importance of this battlefield, George Cormack says:

"Megiddo was the military key of Syria. It commanded at once the highway northward to Phœnicia and Cœle-Syria

[1] Lyman Abbott and T. J. Conant, *A Dictionary of Religious Knowledge*, pp. 326, 327, art. "Esdraelon."

and the road across Galilee to Damascus and the valley of the Euphrates. . . . The vale of Kishon and the region of Megiddo were inevitable battlefields. Through all history they retained that qualification; there many of the great contests of southwestern Asia have been decided."[2]

Admitting that "Megiddo was the military key of Syria" and that it commanded the highways of the Near East, the reader may still be interested to know why, aside from the direct prophetic statement that the final battle will there be fought, this region should be chosen by the nations of earth as the scene of the last great conflict. To answer this logical question we submit the conclusions of others whose years of investigation of social, economic, and political reasons which lead nations to fight, entitle them to consideration.

"With the fall of Ottoman sovereignty . . . there will arise once more the Eternal Question of the position of Asia Minor. That land is the corridor between Europe and Asia, along which have passed most of the European conquerors—the Russians alone excepted—who have invaded Asia, and most of the Asiatic conquerors who have invaded Europe."[3]

Mark this opinion long held concerning Constantinople and its environs by H. Huntington Powers: "Constantinople with its tributary straits is the most strategic site in the world. . . . When Napoleon and the Czar Alexander sat down at Tilsit to divide the world between them, Alexander is said to have pled with Napoleon: 'Give or take what you will, but give us Constantinople. For Constantinople my people are prepared to make any sacrifice.' Napoleon bent long over the map, and then straightening up with sudden resolution replied: 'Constantinople? Never! That means the rule of the world.' . . . Merchant and strategist alike still rank Constantinople as the most valuable of territorial possessions."[4]

---

[2] George Cormack, *Egypt in Asia*, p. 83.

[3] J. B. Firth, "The Partition of Asia," *The Fortnightly Review*, May, 1915, p. 795.

[4] H. Huntington Powers, *The Things Men Fight For*, pp. 74, 77.

 WILLIAM HEASLIP, ARTIST

THE BATTLE OF ARMAGEDDON

Again we read concerning the shift of interest from Constantinople to Asiatic Turkey:

"The problem of Constantinople has perplexed and distressed the world during many centuries. Numerous wars have been waged and innumerable lives have been sacrificed by the nations desiring to possess or control that glorious city and the wonderful Narrows which separate Europe from Asia and which connect the Black Sea and the Mediterranean, the East and the West, the Slavonic and the Latin-Germanic world. Hitherto it was generally believed that an attempt to settle the question of Constantinople would inevitably lead to a world war among the claimant States, that their agreement was impossible. Hence diplomats thought with dread of the question of Constantinople, which seemed insoluble. . . . However, while we may rejoice that the ever-threatening problem of Constantinople has at last been eliminated, it seems possible that another, a far greater and a far more dangerous one, may almost immediately arise in its place. The question of Asiatic Turkey is forcing itself to the front." [5]

Because the territory so long held by Turkey has dominated the great trade routes of three continents it has never ceased to be coveted by those who would rise to world domination. The discovery of vast reservoirs of oil in the Near East has greatly increased the desire of nations to possess Asia Minor and the region drained by the Euphrates River. Indeed the discovery that the words of Job 29: 6, "the rock poured me out rivers of oil," was not hyperbole but literal truth, has led every first-class nation to recognize that oil deposits said to be equal to those of the Western Hemisphere constitute an invaluable possession in the hands of those who would dominate the commercial and military world.

But why should the kings of the East be interested in this question which definitely affects the Near East? Let it not be forgotten that there have been in the past three invasions of

---

[5] J. Ellis Barker, *The Great Problems of British Statesmanship*, p. 55.

the Near East by Oriental conquerors—which invasions have richly rewarded the invaders. With the entire East "in the throes of rebirth" it is not unnatural that they should covet the liquid gold of the Euphrates Valley.

In an interview given by the noted British general, Sir Ian Hamilton to Kingsbury Smith, staff correspondent of the International News Service, as General Hamilton spoke of the menace to Western European civilization of Asiatic penetration, he predicted that "the spot where Europe may attempt to halt Asiatic penetration will become the last battlefield of all time and mark the end of civilization." He said further, "I have looked carefully at the map and the best spot for Europe to meet and throw back Asia is called Megiddo, or, in some maps, Armageddon."[6]

From the language of these writers it would seem obvious that if such mighty armies as would be made up of "the kings of the earth and of the whole world" should gather together anywhere from the ancient valley of Megiddo through the vast stretches of the Euphrates valley and Asia Minor, to fight the "battle of that great day of God Almighty," what is comprehended territorially by the term "Armageddon" in the prophecy would be fully met.

For centuries the territories of Palestine and the Euphrates valley have been under the control of Mohammedan rulers, who were amenable to the Turkish nation. Logically, then, the Turk will come to his end before the kings of the earth debouch their armies in that territory. The end of the Turk opens the way for the battle of Armageddon.

The Three Unclean Spirits.—An event to be noticed under this plague is the issuing forth of the three unclean spirits to gather the nations to the great battle. The agency now already abroad in the world known as modern spiritism, is in every way a fitting means to be employed in this work. But it may be asked how a work which is already going on can be

[6] New York *Journal and American,* January 17, 1938, p. 2.

designated by that expression, when the spirits are not introduced into the prophecy until the pouring out of the sixth plague, which is still future. We answer that in this, as in many other movements, the agencies which Heaven designs to employ in the accomplishment of certain ends, go through a process of preliminary preparation for the part which they are to act. Thus, before the spirits can have such absolute authority over the race as to gather them to battle against the King of kings and Lord of lords, they must first win their way among the nations of the earth, and cause their teaching to be received as of divine authority and their word as law. This work they are now doing, and when they shall have once gained full influence over the nations in question, what fitter instrument could be employed to gather them to so rash and hopeless an enterprise?

To many it may seem incredible that the nations should be willing to engage in such an unequal warfare as to go up to battle against the Lord of hosts; but it is one province of these spirits of devils to deceive, for they go forth working miracles, and thereby deceive the kings of the earth, that they should believe a lie.

That great statesmen recognize the influence of spiritism, or the spirits of devils, in influencing nations to go to war, is seen in the following statement by Sir Edward Grey, when speaking to the House of Commons. In describing the workings of these forces, the British Foreign Secretary accurately said: "It is really as if in the atmosphere of the world there were some mischievous influence at work, which troubles and excites every part of it." [7]

Ramsay MacDonald, twice Prime Minister of Britain, said,

"It would seem as if they were all bewitched, or laboring under some doom imposed upon them by devils. . . . People were beginning to feel that there was something devilish in the

[7] Sir Edward Grey, London *Times*, November 28, 1911, p. 13.

operations now going on to increase armies, navies, and air forces."[8]

The sources from which these spirits issue, denote that they will work among three great religious divisions of mankind, represented by the dragon, the beast, and the false prophet, or paganism, Roman Catholicism, and apostate Protestantism.

But what is the force of the caution thrown out in verse 15? Probation must have closed, and Christ have left His mediatorial position, before the plagues begin to fall. Is there danger of falling after that? It will be noticed that this warning is spoken in connection with the working of the spirits. The inference therefore is that it is retroactive, applying from the time these spirits begin to work to the close of probation, and that by a use of tenses sometimes occurring in the Greek language, the present tense is put for the past, as if it had read, Blessed is he that hath watched and kept his garments, as the shame and nakedness of all who have not done this will at this time especially appear.

"He gathered them." Who are the ones here spoken of as "gathered," and what agency is to be used in gathering them? If the word "them" refers to the kings of verse 14 it is certain that no good agency would be made use of to gather them; and if the spirits are referred to by the word "he," why is it in the singular number? The peculiarity of this construction has led some to read the passage thus: "And he [Christ] gathered them [the saints] into a place called in the Hebrew tongue Armageddon [the illustrious city, or New Jerusalem]." But this position is untenable.

Let us notice how the text really reads. The word for "spirits" is πνεύματα, *pneumata*, a noun in the plural number. According to an established law of Greek language, when a plural noun is in the neuter gender, as *pneumata* is, it requires the verb to be in the singular. Accordingly, in verse 14, the verb "go forth" with "spirits" as its subject, is in

[8] Ramsay MacDonald, quoted in "Disarmament Labour Party's Motion," London *Times*, July 24, 1923, p. 7.

the singular number in the Greek original. Likewise, also, as the narrative is resumed following the parenthetical exhortation in verse 15, the verb "gathered" is also in the singular in the Greek to co-ordinate with "go forth" in verse 14, since these two verbs have the same subject "which," that should not be printed as a supplied word, and that stands for "spirits." There is therefore every sound reason for translating verse 16, "They [the spirits] gathered them [the kings] together into a place called in the Hebrew tongue Armageddon." This interpretation is supported by other versions.

"They gathered them together into the place which is called in Hebrew Har-Magedon," says the American Revised Version. "They did bring them together to the place that is called in Hebrew Armageddon," reads Young's Literal Translation of the Bible. Hence it is logical to conclude that the persons gathered are the minions of Satan, not the saints; that it is the work of the spirits, not of Christ; and that the place of assemblage is not in the New Jerusalem at the marriage supper of the Lamb, but at Armageddon (or Mount Megiddo), at "the battle of that great day of God Almighty."

VERSE 17 And the seventh angel poured out his vial into the air; and there came a great voice out of the temple of heaven, from the throne, saying, It is done. 18 And there were voices, and thunders, and lightnings; and there was a great earthquake; such as was not since men were upon the earth, so mighty an earthquake, and so great. 19 And the great city was divided into three parts, and the cities of the nations fell: and great Babylon came in remembrance before God, to give unto her the cup of the wine of the fierceness of His wrath. 20 And every island fled away, and the mountains were not found. 21 And there fell upon men a great hail out of heaven, every stone about the weight of a talent: and men blasphemed God because of the plague of the hail; for the plague thereof was exceeding great.

The Seventh Plague.—Thus has Inspiration described the last judgment which is to be inflicted in the present state of the earth upon those who are incorrigibly rebellious against God. Some of the plagues are local in their application, but this one is poured out into the air. The atmosphere envelops the whole earth, and it follows that this plague will envelop equally the habitable globe. It will be universal. The very air will be deadly.

The gathering of the nations has taken place under the sixth vial, and the battle remains to be fought under the seventh. Here are brought to view the instrumentalities with which God will slay the wicked. At this time it may be said, "The Lord hath opened His armory, and hath brought forth the weapons of His indignation." Jeremiah 50: 25.

The Scripture declares, "There were voices." Above all will be heard the voice of God. "The Lord also shall roar out of Zion, and utter His voice from Jerusalem, and the heavens and the earth shall shake; but the Lord will be the hope of His people, and the strength of the children of Israel." Joel 3: 16. (See also Jeremiah 25: 30; Hebrews 12: 26.) The voice of God will cause the great earthquake, such as was not since men were upon the earth.

"Thunders, and lightnings"—another allusion to the judgments of Egypt. (See Exodus 9: 23.) The great city is divided into three parts; that is, the three grand divisions of the false and apostate religions of the world (the great city), paganism, Roman Catholicism, and apostate Protestantism, seem to be set apart each to receive its appropriate doom. The cities of the nations fall; universal desolation spreads over the earth; every island flees away, and the mountains are not found. Thus great Babylon comes in remembrance before God. Read her judgments, as more fully described in Revelation 18.

"A great hail out of heaven, falling upon men," is the last instrumentality used in the infliction of punishment upon the wicked—the bitter dregs of the seventh vial. God has solemnly addressed the wicked, saying, "Judgment also will I lay to the line, and righteousness to the plummet: and the hail shall sweep away the refuge of lies, and the waters shall overflow the hiding place." Isaiah 28: 17. (See also Isaiah 30: 30.) The Lord asks Job if he has seen the treasures of the hail, which He has "reserved against the time of trouble, against the day of battle and war." Job 38: 22, 23.

Every hailstone is said to be "about the weight of a talent." According to various authorities, a talent as a weight is about fifty-seven pounds avoirdupois. What could withstand the force of stones of such an enormous weight falling from heaven? But mankind, at this time, will have no shelter. The cities have fallen in a mighty earthquake, the islands have fled away, and the mountains are not found. Again the wicked give vent to their woe in blasphemy, for the plague of the hail is "exceeding great."

Some faint idea of the terrible effect of such a disaster as is here predicted, may be inferred from the following sketch of a hailstorm on the Bosphorus, by Commodore Porter:

"We had got perhaps a mile and a half on our way, when a cloud rising in the west gave indications of an approaching rain. In a few minutes we discovered something falling from the heavens with a heavy splash, and of a whitish appearance. I could not conceive what it was, but observing some gulls near, I supposed it to be them darting for fish, but soon after discovered that they were large balls of ice falling. Immediately we heard a sound like rumbling thunder, or ten thousand carriages rolling furiously over the pavement. The whole Bosphorus was in a foam, as though heaven's artillery had been discharged upon us and our frail machine. Our fate seemed inevitable; our umbrellas were raised to protect us, but the lumps of ice stripped them into ribbons. We fortunately had a bullock's hide in the boat, under which we crawled, and saved ourselves from further injury. One man of the three oarsmen had his hand literally smashed; another was much injured in the shoulder; Mr. H. received a severe blow in the leg; my right hand was somewhat disabled, and all more or less injured. . . .

"It was the most awful and terrific scene that I ever witnessed, and God forbid that I should be ever exposed to such another! Balls of ice as large as my two fists fell into the boat, some of them came with such violence as certainly to have broken an arm or leg had they struck us in those parts. One of them struck the blade of an oar, and split it. The scene lasted, maybe five minutes; but it was five minutes of the most awful feeling that I ever experienced. When it passed over, we found the surrounding hills covered with masses of ice, I cannot call it hail, the trees stripped of their leaves and limbs, and everything looking desolate. . . . .

"The scene was awful beyond all description. I have witnessed repeated earthquakes; the lightning has played, as it were, about my head; and wind roared, and the waves have at one moment thrown me to the sky, and the next have sunk me into the deep abyss. I have been in action, and have seen death and destruction around me in every shape of horror; but I never before had the feeling of awe which seized upon me on this occasion, and still haunts, and I fear will ever haunt me. . . . My porter, the boldest of my family, who had ventured an instant from the door, had been knocked down by a hailstone, and had they not dragged him in by the heels, would have been battered to death. . . . Two boatmen were killed in the upper part of the village, and I have heard of broken bones in abundance. . . . Imagine to yourself, however, the heavens suddenly frozen over, and as suddenly broken to pieces in irregular masses, of from half a pound to a pound weight, and precipitated to the earth."[9]

Reader, if such were the desolating effects of a hailstorm of ice, which discharged stones double the size of a man's fist, weighing at most a pound or so, who can depict the consequences of that coming storm in which "*every stone*" will be more than fifty pounds in weight? As surely as God's word is truth, He is thus soon to punish a guilty world. May it be ours, according to the promise, to have "sure dwellings" and "quiet resting places" in that terrific hour. Isaiah 32: 18, 19.

"There came a great voice out of the temple of heaven, from the throne, saying, It is done!" Thus all is finished. The cup of human guilt has been filled up. The last soul has availed

---

[9] David Porter, *Constantinople and Its Environs,* Vol. I, pp. 44-47.

itself of the plan of salvation. The books are closed. The number of the saved is completed. The final period is placed to this world's history. The vials of God's wrath are poured out upon a corrupt generation. The wicked have drunk them to the dregs, and sunk into the realm of death for a thousand years. Reader, where do you wish to be found after that great decision?

But what is the condition of the saints while the "overflowing scourge" is passing over? They are the special subjects of God's protection, without whose notice not a sparrow falls to the ground. Many are the promises which come crowding in to afford them comfort, summarily contained in the beautiful and expressive language of the psalmist:

"I will say of the Lord, He is my refuge and my fortress; my God; in Him will I trust. Surely He shall deliver thee from the snare of the fowler, and from the noisome pestilence. He shall cover thee with His feathers, and under His wings shalt thou trust: His truth shall be thy shield and buckler. Thou shalt not be afraid for the terror by night; nor for the arrow that flieth by day; nor for the pestilence that walketh in darkness; nor for the destruction that wasteth at noonday. A thousand shall fall at thy side, and ten thousand at thy right hand; but it shall not come nigh thee. Only with thine eyes shalt thou behold and see the reward of the wicked. Because thou hast made the Lord, which is my refuge, even the Most High, thy habitation; there shall no evil befall thee, neither shall any plague come nigh thy dwelling." Psalm 91: 2-10.

THE WOMAN ON THE SCARLET BEAST

"Upon her forehead was a name written, MYSTERY, BABYLON THE GREAT, THE MOTHER OF HARLOTS AND ABOMINATIONS OF THE

CHAPTER XVII

A WORLD UNION OF CHURCH AND STATE

VERSE 1 And there came one of the seven angels which had the seven vials, and talked with me, saying unto me, Come hither; I will show unto thee the judgment of the great whore that sitteth upon many waters: 2 with whom the kings of the earth have committed fornication, and the inhabitants of the earth have been made drunk with the wine of her fornication. 3 So he carried me away in the spirit into the wilderness: and I saw a woman sit upon a scarlet colored beast, full of names of blasphemy, having seven heads and ten horns. 4 And the woman was arrayed in purple and scarlet color, and decked with gold and precious stones and pearls, having a golden cup in her hand full of abominations and filthiness of her fornication: 5 and upon her forehead was a name written, MYSTERY, BABYLON THE GREAT, THE MOTHER OF HARLOTS AND ABOMINATIONS OF THE EARTH.

IN VERSE 19 of the preceding chapter, we were informed that "great Babylon came in remembrance before God, to give unto her the cup of the wine of the fierceness of His wrath." The prophet now takes up more particularly the subject of this great Babylon. In order to give a full presentation of it, he goes back to recount some of the facts of her history. That this apostate woman as presented in this chapter is a symbol of the Roman Catholic Church, is generally believed by Protestants. Between this church and the kings of the earth there has been illicit connection. With the wine of her fornication, her false doctrines, the inhabitants of the earth have been made drunk.

Church and State.—This prophecy is more definite than others applicable to the Roman power in that it distinguishes between church and state. We here have the woman, the church, seated upon a scarlet-colored beast, the civil power, by which she is upheld, and which she controls and guides to her own ends, as a rider controls the animal upon which he is seated.

The vesture and decorations of this woman, as brought to view in verse 4, are in striking harmony with the application made of this symbol. Purple and scarlet are the chief colors in the robes of popes and cardinals. Among the myriads of precious stones which adorn her service, according to eyewitnesses, silver is scarcely known, and gold itself is less noticeable than are costly gems. From the golden cup in her hand—symbol of purity of doctrine and profession, which should have contained only that which is unadulterated and pure, or, only that which is in full accordance with truth—there came forth only abominations, and the wine of her fornication, fit symbol of her abominable doctrines and still more abominable practices.

The symbol of a woman with a cup in her hand is said to have been used at a papal jubilee.

"In 1825, on the occasion of the jubilee, Pope Leo XII struck a medal, bearing on the one side his own image, and on the other, that of the Church of Rome symbolized as a 'Woman,' holding in her left hand a cross and in her right a *cup*, with the legend around her, *Sedet super universum*, 'The whole world is her seat.'"[1]

This woman is explicitly called Babylon. Is Rome, then, Babylon, to the exclusion of all other religious bodies?—No, she cannot be, from the fact that she is called the *mother* of harlots, as already noticed, which shows that there are other independent religious organizations that constitute the apostate daughters, and belong to the same great family.

VERSE 6 And I saw the woman drunken with the blood of the saints, and with the blood of the martyrs of Jesus: and when I saw her, I wondered with great admiration. 7 And the angel said unto me, Wherefore didst thou marvel? I will tell thee the mystery of the woman, and of the beast that carrieth her, which hath the seven heads and ten horns.

A Cause of Wonder.—Why should John "wonder with great wonder," as it reads in the original, when he saw the woman drunken with the blood of saints? Was persecution of the

[1] Alexander Hislop, *The Two Babylons*, p. 6.

people of God any strange thing in his day? Had he not seen Rome launch its most fiery anathemas against the church, himself being in banishment under its cruel power at the time he wrote? Why, then, should he be astonished, as he looked forward, and saw Rome still persecuting the saints? The secret of his wonder was this: All the persecution he had witnessed had been from pagan Rome, the open enemy of Christ. It was not strange that pagans should persecute Christ's followers. But when he looked forward and saw a church professedly *Christian* persecuting the followers of the Lamb, and drunk with their blood, he could but wonder with great amazement.

VERSE 8 The beast that thou sawest was, and is not; and shall ascend out of the bottomless pit, and go into perdition: and they that dwell on the earth shall wonder, whose names were not written in the book of life from the foundation of the world, when they behold the beast that was, and is not, and yet is. 9 And here is the mind which hath wisdom. The seven heads are seven mountains, on which the woman sitteth. 10 And there are seven kings: five are fallen, and one is, and the other is not yet come; and when he cometh, he must continue a short space. 11 And the beast that was, and is not, even he is the eighth, and is of the seven, and goeth into perdition.

Rome in Three Phases.—The beast of which the angel here speaks is evidently the scarlet-colored beast. A wild beast, like the one thus introduced, is the symbol of an oppressive and persecuting power. While the Roman power as a nation had a long, uninterrupted existence, it passed through certain phases during which this symbol would not be applicable to it, and during which time the beast, in such prophecies as the present might be said not to be, or not to exist. Thus Rome in its pagan form was a persecuting power in its relation to the people of God, during which time it constituted the beast that was. But when the empire was nominally converted to Christianity, there was a transition from paganism to another phase of religion falsely called Christian. During a brief period, while this transition was going on, it lost its ferocious and persecuting character, and then it could be said of the beast that it was not. As time passed, it developed into the papacy, and

G. DORE. ARTIST

THE TRIUMPH OF THE CROSS

"The Lamb shall overcome them: for He is Lord of lords and King of kings." Revelation 17: 14.

again assumed its bloodthirsty and oppressive character.

The Seven Heads.—The seven heads are explained to be, first, seven mountains, and then seven kings. The expression in verse 10, "and there are seven kings," reads in the original, "and are seven kings." This makes the sentence read: "The seven heads are seven mountains . . . and are seven kings," thus identifying heads, mountains, and kings.

The angel says further, "five [kings] are fallen," or passed away. Again he says, "one [king] is"—the sixth was then reigning. "The other is not yet come; and when he cometh he must continue a short space." Last of all, "the beast that was, and is not, even he is the eighth, and is of the seven."

From this account of the seven kings, we understand that when the one that had "not yet come" at the time of which John was writing, appears on the scene, he is here called an eighth, though he is really "of the seven," in the sense that he absorbed and exercised their power. It is this one whose career we are interested to follow. Of this one it is said that his destiny was to go "into perdition," that is, to perish utterly. This repeats the affirmation made in verse 8 concerning "the beast that thou sawest," which in turn is the "scarlet colored beast," on which the woman sat. We have shown that this beast symbolizes civil power, which according to the narrative before us, passes through seven phases represented also in the leopard beast of Revelation 13, until an eighth appears and continues to the end. Since we have already shown that papal Rome grew out of and succeeded pagan Rome, we must conclude that the eighth head, which was of the seven and ultimately exercised their power, represents the papacy, with all its mixture of so-called Christian doctrines with pagan superstitions and observances.

VERSE 12 And the ten horns which thou sawest are ten kings, which have received no kingdom as yet; but receive power as kings one hour with the beast. 13 These have one mind, and shall give their power and strength unto the beast. 14 These shall make war with the Lamb, and the Lamb shall overcome them: for He is Lord of lords, and King of kings: and they that are with Him are called, and chosen, and faithful.

The Ten Horns.—On this subject see remarks on Daniel 7: 7, where the ten horns are shown to represent the ten kingdoms that rose out of the Roman Empire. They receive power one hour (ὥρα, *hora*, an indefinite space of time) with the beast. That is, they reign a length of time *contemporaneously* with the beast, during which time they give to it their power and strength.

Croly offers this comment on verse 12: "The prediction defines the epoch of the papacy by the formation of the ten kingdoms of the Western Empire. 'They shall receive power *one hour* with the beast.' The translation should be, 'in the same era' (μίαν ὥραν, [*mian horan*]). The ten kingdoms shall be *contemporaneous*, in contradistinction to the 'seven heads,' which were *successive*."[2]

This language doubtless refers to the past, when the kingdoms of Europe were unanimous in giving their support to the papacy. The treatment which these kingdoms are finally to give the papacy is expressed in verse 16, where it is said that they shall hate the harlot, make her desolate and naked, eat her flesh, and burn her with fire. A part of this work the nations of Europe have been doing for years. The completion of it, burning her with fire, will be accomplished when Revelation 18: 8 is fulfilled.

"These shall make war with the Lamb." Verse 14. Here we are carried into the future, to the time of the great and final battle, for at this time the Lamb bears the title of King of kings and Lord of lords, a title which He assumes when He ceases His intercessory priesthood at the close of probation. (Revelation 19: 11-16.)

VERSE 15 And he saith unto me, The waters which thou sawest, where the whore sitteth, are peoples, and multitudes, and nations, and tongues. 16 And the ten horns which thou sawest upon the beast, these shall hate the whore, and shall make her desolate and naked, and shall eat her flesh, and burn her with fire. 17 For God hath put in their hearts to fulfill His will, and to agree, and give their kingdom unto the beast, until the words of God

[2] George Croly, *The Apocalypse of St. John*, pp. 264, 265.

shall be fulfilled. 18 And the woman which thou sawest is that great city, which reigneth over the kings of the earth.

Destiny of the Harlot.—In verse 15 we have a plain definition of the Scripture symbol of waters; they denote peoples, multitudes, nations, and tongues. The angel told John, while calling his attention to this subject, that he would show him the judgment of this great harlot. In verse 16 that judgment is specified. This chapter has naturally more especial reference to the mother, or Catholic Babylon. The next chapter, if we mistake not, deals with the character and destiny of another great branch of Babylon, the harlot daughters.

 R. M. ELDRIDGE, ARTIST

A CALL FROM HEAVEN

"Come out of her, My people, that ye be not partakers of her sins, and that ye receive not of her plagues." Revelation 18: 4.

CHAPTER XVIII

THE DOOM OF MODERN BABYLON

VERSE 1 And after these things I saw another angel come down from heaven, having great power; and the earth was lightened with his glory. 2 And he cried mightily with a strong voice, saying, Babylon the great is fallen, is fallen, and is become the habitation of devils, and the hold of every foul spirit, and a cage of every unclean and hateful bird. 3 For all nations have drunk of the wine of the wrath of her fornication, and the kings of the earth have committed fornication with her, and the merchants of the earth are waxed rich through the abundance of her delicacies.

SOME movement of mighty power is symbolized in these verses. (See comments on verse 4 of this chapter.) The consideration of a few facts will guide us unmistakably to the application. In Revelation 14 we had a message announcing the fall of Babylon. "Babylon" is a term which embraces not only paganism and the Roman Catholic Church, but religious bodies which have withdrawn from that church, but bringing many of her errors and traditions with them.

A Spiritual Fall.—The fall of Babylon here spoken of cannot be literal destruction, for there are events to take place in Babylon after her fall which utterly forbid this idea. For instance, the people of God are there after her fall, and are called out in order that they may not receive of her plagues, which include her literal destruction. The fall is therefore a spiritual one, for the result of it is that Babylon becomes the habitation of devils, and the hold of every foul spirit, and a cage of every unclean and hateful bird. These are terrible descriptions of apostasy, showing that, as a consequence of her fall, she piles up an accumulation of sins even to the heavens, and becomes subject to the judgments of God, which can no longer be delayed.

Since the fall here introduced is a spiritual one, it must apply to some branch of Babylon outside of the pagan or papal divisions; for from the beginning of their history paganism has been a false religion, and the papacy an apostate one. Further, as this fall is said to occur but a short period before Babylon's final destruction, certainly this side of the rise and predicted triumph of the papal church, this testimony cannot apply to any religious organizations but such as have sprung from that church. These started out on reform. They ran well for a season, and had the approbation of God; but bringing some of her erroneous doctrines with them, and fencing themselves about with creeds of their own, they have failed to keep pace with the advancing light of prophetic truth. This has left them where they will finally develop a character as odious in the sight of God as that of the church from which they withdrew.

Alexander Campbell, founder of the Disciples of Christ Church, says: "A reformation of popery was attempted in Europe full three centuries ago. It ended in a Protestant hierarchy, and swarms of dissenters. Protestantism has been reformed into Presbyterianism, that into Congregationalism, and that into Baptistism, etc., etc. Methodism has attempted to reform all, but has reformed itself into many forms of Wesleyism. . . . All of them retain in their bosom—in their ecclesiastical organizations, worship, doctrines, and observances—various relics of popery. They are at best a reformation of popery, and only reformations in part. The doctrines and traditions of men yet impair the power and progress of the gospel in their hands." [1]

Abundant testimony might be produced from persons in high standing in these various denominations, written, not for the purpose of being captious and finding fault, but from a vivid sense of the fearful condition to which these churches have fallen. The term Babylon, as applied to them, is not a term of reproach, but is simply expressive of the confusion and diversity of sentiment that exists among them. Babylon need not have fallen. She might have been healed (Jeremiah 51: 9) by receiving the truth, but she rejected it.

---

[1] Alexander Campbell, *Christian Baptism*, p. 15.

In not accepting the truth of the second coming of Christ and in rejecting the first angel's message, the churches failed to walk in the advanced light shining on their pathway from the throne of God. As a result, confusion and dissension reign within their borders. Worldliness and pride are fast choking every plant of heavenly growth.

But in this chapter we have the fall of Babylon mentioned again. In the previous reference it followed the sounding of the first angel's message, and the divine declaration then was, "There followed another angel, saying, Babylon is fallen, is fallen." Now the later pronouncement from heaven is, "He cried mightily with a strong voice, saying, Babylon the great is fallen, is fallen, and is become the habitation of devils." Here is a further step in the development of apostasy, and the next few pages will reveal the extent of this final phase of the fall of Babylon.

Time of This Fall.—At what time do these verses have their application? When may this movement be looked for? If the position here taken is correct, that these churches, this branch of Babylon, experienced a spiritual fall by the rejection of the first angel's message of Revelation 14, the announcement in the chapter now under consideration could not have gone forth previous to that time. It is, then, either simultaneous with the message of the fall of Babylon in Revelation 14, or it is given at a later period than that. It cannot be at the same time with that, for that merely announces the fall of Babylon, while this adds several particulars which at that time were neither fulfilled nor in process of fulfillment. We are therefore to look this side of 1844, when the previous message went forth, for the announcement brought to view in this chapter. We therefore inquire, Has any such message been given from that time to the present? The answer is, Yes. We are now hearing the third angel's message, which is the last to be given before the coming of the Son of man. As declension has increased in the religious world, that message has been augmented by the warning of Revelation 18: 1-4, which thus constitutes a feature of the third angel's message which is now being proclaimed with power and lighting the world with its glory.

The Work of Spiritism.—The latter phase of the work brought to view in verse 2 is in process of accomplishment, and will soon be completed, by the work of spiritism. What are called in Revelation 16: 14 "spirits of devils, working miracles," are secretly but rapidly working their way into the religious denominations above referred to. Their creeds have been formulated under the influence of the wine (errors) of Babylon, one of which is that the spirits of our dead friends, conscious, intelligent, and active, are all about us.

A significant feature in the work of spiritism just now, is the religious garb it is assuming. Keeping in the background its grosser principles, which it has heretofore carried so largely in the front, it now assumes to appear as respectably religious as any other denomination in the land. It talks of sin, repentance, the atonement, salvation through Christ, in almost as orthodox language as do genuine Christians. Under the guise of this profession, what is to hinder it from entrenching itself in almost every denomination in Christendom? We have shown that the basis of spiritism, the immortality of the soul, is a fundamental dogma in the creeds of almost all the churches. What, then, can save Christendom from its seductive influence?

Herein is seen another sad result of rejecting the truths offered to the world by the messages of Revelation 14. Had the churches received these messages, they would have been shielded against this delusion; for among the great truths developed by the religious movement in the time of the great advent awakening, is the important doctrine that the soul of man is not naturally immortal; that eternal life is the gift of Jesus Christ, and can be obtained only through Him; that the dead are unconscious; and that the rewards and punishments of the future world lie beyond the resurrection and the day of judgment.

These truths strike a deathblow to the first and vital claim of spiritism. What foothold can that doctrine secure in any mind fortified by such truth? The spirit comes, and claims to be the disembodied soul, or spirit, of a dead man. It is met with the fact that that is not the kind of soul, or spirit, which man possesses; that the "dead know not anything;" that this, its first pretension, is a lie, and that the credentials it offers, show it to belong to the synagogue of Satan. Thus it is at once rejected, and the evil it would do is effectually prevented. But the great mass of religionists stand opposed to the truth which would thus shield them, and they thereby expose themselves to this last manifestation of satanic cunning.

Modern Liberalism.—While spiritism is thus working, startling changes are manifesting themselves in high places in some of the denominations. The infidelity of the present age, under the seductive names of "science," "higher criticism," "evolution," and "modern liberalism," has permeated most of the theological colleges of the land, and to a large extent has made serious incursions into the Protestant churches.

Public attention was forcibly called to this situation by a writer, Mr. Harold Bolce, in the *Cosmopolitan Magazine* for May, 1909. After making an investigation into the character of the teaching that was being imparted in some of the leading universities of this country, he reported the results in the *Cosmopolitan*, which drew forth this comment from the editor:

"What Mr. Bolce sets down here is of the most astounding character. Out of the curricula of American colleges, a dynamic movement is upheaving ancient foundations, and promising a way for revolutionary thought and life. Those who are not in close touch with the great colleges of the country will be astonished to learn the creeds being fostered by the faculties of our great universities. In hundreds of classrooms it is being taught daily that the decalogue is no more sacred than a syllabus; that the home as an institution is doomed; that there are no absolute evils; that immorality is simply an act in contravention of society's accepted standards. . . . These are some of the revolutionary and sensational teachings submitted with academic warrant to the minds of hundreds of thousands of students in the United States."[2]

The results of modern liberalism have been all too apparent in the work of the Protestant churches. Writers in the various communions have freely pointed out the lack of interest in the preaching of the gospel and the decline of missions in particular. One writer states the situation in this way:

"Too largely I suspect our churches have become weak, uncertain as to their purpose, lifeless, characterized by a deadly respectability and lacking a sense of mission. The average congregation is primarily concerned with raising enough money to pay the pastor and to keep the property in good repair. There is little deep-seated conviction any longer that 'we have a story to tell to the nations.' The gospel of salvation and evangelism as respects the whole world has been diluted into a satisfactory and responsible ethic and the church is a society of good people who want the blessings of religion to attend them during their moments of exaltation or grief, but are quite content to absent themselves from the church and its divine mission so long as they can clothe themselves in the aura of respectability which attaches to church membership. Is this too caustic an indictment of the church?"[3]

Another writer states the attitude of the churches toward missions:

"Coupled with the fact that only a minority of church members give conscientiously is the change in belief about missions. Missionary boards may persuade themselves that the falling off in their receipts is due to high taxes and lowered incomes, but pastors who are in touch with donors recognize a definite increase of resistance to making donations designed for extension of the gospel beyond our borders. The number of otherwise loyal parishioners who doggedly announce that

---

[2] *Cosmopolitan Magazine*, May, 1909, p. 665.

[3] Dale D. Welch, "Real Issues and Great Choices," *The Presbyterian*, January 9, 1941, p. 3.

they 'don't believe in missions' is mounting. The caliber of these opponents gives pause. . . .

"The average annual per capita giving in twenty-two non-Roman communions now shows $11.28 for congregational expenses, against $2.19 for all non-local work. . . .

"The average of gifts beyond self-support coasts from 29.69 per cent of the total income with the United Presbyterian Church to 11.14, 12.30, and 10.02 per cent with the last-named trio. Small wonder we are being urged to 're-think missions.' "[4]

Such results as these are declared to follow:

"While missionary zeal was waning, the situation was further complicated by the revelation that other than evangelical missionaries were being commissioned and sent to the foreign fields. These were the 'adventurers' of a 'new civilization,' the 'creators of a new world,' and were mainly filled with a social passion. . . .

"World evangelization was again given a cruel blow in the critical findings of the Laymen's Foreign Missions Inquiry Report. Although the object of this enterprise, which began in 1930 and continued to 1933, was 'to aid laymen to determine their attitude toward foreign missions by reconsidering the functions of such missions in the world of today,' with undoubtedly the aim not only to remodel missions but to increase financial receipts, the result was only more controversy and decreased giving."[5]

Results of Apostasy.—From the standpoint of such a lamentable outlook, and under the leadership of such men, how long before Babylon will become full of spirits that are foul, and birds that are hateful and unclean? What progress has already been made in this direction! How would the godly fathers and mothers of the generation that lived just before the first angel's message was given, could they hear the teaching and behold

---

[4] Phillips Endecott Osgood, "How Much Do You Help the Church?" *The Atlantic Monthly*, January, 1940, p. 56, footnote.

[5] "Is It a Lost Cause?" editorial in *The Watchman-Examiner*, February 1, 1940, p. 105.

INTERNATIONAL

THE VATICAN AND ST. PETER'S

Modern Protestantism still holds to many of the doctrines of Rome. The call is to come out of her.

the practices of the religious world, stand aghast at the fearful contrast between their time and ours, and deplore the sad degeneracy! But Heaven is not to let all this pass in silence. A mighty proclamation is being made, calling the attention of all the world to the fearful counts in the indictment against unfaithful religious bodies, that the justice of the judgments that follow may plainly appear.

Verse 3 shows the wide extent of the influence of Babylon, and the evil that has resulted and will result from her course, and hence the justness of her punishment. The merchants of the earth are waxed rich through the *abundance* of her delicacies. Who take the lead in all the extravagances of the age? Who load their tables with the richest and choicest viands? Who are foremost in extravagance in dress and all costly attire? Who are the personification of pride and arrogance? Are not church members in the very forefront of those who seek after the material and prideful things of life?

But there is a redeeming feature in this picture. Degenerate as Babylon has become as a body, there are exceptions to the general rule; for God has still a people there, and she must be entitled to some regard on their account until all who will answer are called from her communion. Nor will it be necessary to wait long for this consummation. Soon Babylon will become so thoroughly leavened with the influence of these evil agents that her condition will be fully manifest to all the honest in heart, and the way will be prepared for the work which the apostle now introduces.

VERSE 4 And I heard another voice from heaven, saying, Come out of her, My people, that ye be not partakers of her sins, and that ye receive not of her plagues. 5 For her sins have reached unto heaven, and God hath remembered her iniquities. 6 Reward her even as she rewarded you, and double unto her double according to her works: in the cup which she hath filled fill to her double. 7 How much she hath glorified herself, and lived deliciously, so much torment and sorrow give her: for she saith in her heart, I sit a queen, and am no widow, and shall see no sorrow. 8 Therefore shall her plagues come in one day, death, and mourning, and famine; and she shall be utterly burned with fire: for strong is the Lord God who judgeth her.

The voice coming from heaven denotes that it is a message of power attended with heavenly glory. How marked becomes the interposition of Heaven, and how the agents for the accomplishment of God's work multiply, as the great crisis approaches! This voice from heaven is called "another" voice, showing that a new agency is here introduced. We now have five celestial messengers expressly mentioned as engaged in this last religious reformation. These are the first, second, and third angels of Revelation 14; fourth, the angel of verse 1 of this chapter; and fifth, the agency indicated by the "voice" of verse 4, now before us. Three of these are already in operation. The second angel has joined the first, and the third has joined them. The first and second have not ceased. All three are now united in proclaiming a threefold message. The angel of verse 1 here enters upon his mission, as conditions call for his work. The divine call from heaven to come out of Babylon takes place in connection with his work.

"*Come Out of Her, My People.*"—Proof has already been offered to show that the message of verses 1 and 2 of this chapter is given in connection with the now current threefold message. An idea of its extent and power may be gathered from the description of the angel there given. The first angel's message is said to go with a "loud voice." The same is also said of the third message, but this angel, instead of simply flying "in the midst of heaven" like the others, is said to "*come down* from heaven." He comes with a message more pointed and direct. He has "great power," and the earth is "lightened with his glory." No such description of a message from heaven to man is elsewhere to be found in all the Bible. This is the last, and as is meet, it comes with surpassing glory and unwonted power. It is an awful hour when a world's destiny is to be decided—a most solemn crisis when an entire contemporaneous generation of the human family is to pass the bounds of probation, as the last note of mercy is sounded.

In such a time, the world must not be left without warning. So amply must the great facts be heralded that none can plead a reasonable ignorance of the impending doom. Every excuse must be taken away. The justice and long-suffering and forbearance of God in delaying threatened vengeance until all have had an opportunity to receive a knowledge of His will, and time to repent, must be vindicated. An angel is sent forth panoplied with heavenly power. The light that encircles the throne enshrouds him. He comes to the earth. None but the spiritually dead—yea, "twice dead, and plucked up by the roots"—would fail to realize his presence. Light flashes everywhere. The dark places are lighted up. While his presence dispels the shadows, his voice in thunder tones utters a warning. He cries "mightily." It is no parlor announcement, but a *cry*, a *mighty* cry, a cry with a *strong voice.*

The fatal defects in the profession of a worldly church are again pointed out. Their errors are once more, and for the last time, exposed. The inadequacy of the present standard of godliness to meet the final crisis is emphasized beyond all mistaking. The inevitable connection between their cherished errors and everlasting and irretrievable destruction is heralded until the earth resounds with the cry. Meanwhile, great Babylon's sins mount up to the heavens, and the remembrance of her iniquities comes up before God. The storm of vengeance gathers. Soon it will burst upon the great city of confusion, and proud Babylon will go down as a millstone sinks into the depths of the sea.

Suddenly another voice rings out from heaven, "Come out of her, My people!" The humble, sincere, devoted children of God, of whom there are some still left, and who sigh and cry over the abominations done in the land, heed the voice, wash their hands of her sins, separate from her communion, escape, and are saved, while Babylon becomes the victim of the just judgments of God. These are stirring times for the church. Let us be ready for the crisis.

The fact that God's people are called out so as not to be partakers of her sins, shows that it is not until a certain time that people become guilty by being connected with Babylon.

Verses 6 and 7 are a prophetic declaration that she will be rewarded or punished according to her works. Bear in mind that this testimony applies to that part of Babylon which is subject to a spiritual fall. As already pointed out, it must apply especially to the "daughters," the denominations who persist in clinging to the personal traits of the "mother," and keeping up the family resemblance. These, as pointed out previously, are to attempt a sweeping persecution against the truth and the people of God. By these the "image to the beast" is to be formed. These are to have what will be to them a new experience—the use of the civil arm to enforce their dogmas.

It is doubtless this first intoxication of power that leads this branch of Babylon to cherish in her heart the boast, "I sit a queen, and am no widow;" that is, I am no longer χήρα, *chera*, "one bereaved," or destitute of power, as I have been. She declares, Now I rule like a queen, and I shall see no sorrow. With blasphemy she boasts God is in the Constitution, the church is enthroned, and will henceforth bear sway. The expression, "Reward her even as she rewarded you," seems to show that the time for this message to reach its climax, and for the saints to be finally called out, will be when she begins to raise against them the arm of oppression. As she fills up the cup of persecution to the saints, so the angel of the Lord will persecute her. (Psalm 35: 6.) Judgments from on high will bring upon her in a twofold degree ("double unto her double"), the evil which she thought to bring upon the humble servants of the Lord.

The day in which her plagues come, mentioned in verse 8, must be a prophetic day, or at least cannot be a literal day, for it would be impossible for famine to come in that length of time. The plagues of Babylon are without doubt the seven last plagues, which have already been examined. The plain inference from the language of this verse in connection with Isaiah 34: 8, is that a year will be occupied in that terrible visitation.

VERSE 9 And the kings of the earth, who have committed fornication and lived deliciously with her, shall bewail her, and lament for her, when they shall see the smoke of her burning, 10 standing afar off for the fear of her torment, saying, Alas, alas that great city Babylon, that mighty city! For in one hour is thy judgment come. 11 And the merchants of the earth shall weep and mourn over her; for no man buyeth their merchandise any more.

A Fitting Retribution.—The infliction of the first plague must result in a complete suspension of traffic in those articles of luxury for which Babylon is noted. When the merchants of these things, who are to a great extent citizens of this symbolic city, and who have been made rich by their traffic in these things, suddenly find themselves and their neighbors smitten with putrefying sores, their traffic suspended, and vast stores of merchandise on hand, but none to buy them, they lift up their voices in lamentation for the fate of this great city. If there is anything which will draw from the men of this generation a *sincere* cry of distress, it is that which touches their treasures. There is a fitness in this retribution. They who but a short time before had issued a decree that the saints of God should neither buy nor sell, now find themselves put under the same restriction in a far more effectual way.

The question may arise how persons involved in the same calamity can stand *afar off* and lament. It must be remembered that this desolation is brought to view under a figure, and the figure is that of a city visited with destruction. Should calamity come upon a literal city, it would be natural for its inhabitants to flee from that city if they had opportunity, and standing afar off, lament its fall. Just in proportion to their terror and amazement at the evil impending, would be the distance at which they would stand from their devoted city. The figure the apostle uses would not be complete without a feature of this kind, and he uses it, not to imply that people would literally flee from the symbolic city, which would be impossible, but to denote their *terror* and *amazement* at the descending judgments.

VERSE 12 The merchandise of gold, and silver, and precious stones, and of pearls, and fine linen, and purple, and silk, and scarlet, and all thyine wood, and all manner vessels of ivory, and all manner vessels of most precious wood, and of brass, and iron, and marble, 13 and cinnamon, and odors, and ointments, and frankincense, and wine, and oil, and fine flour, and wheat, and beasts, and sheep, and horses, and chariots, and slaves, and souls of men.

Babylon's Merchandise.—In these verses we have an enumeration of great Babylon's merchandise, which includes everything pertaining to luxurious living, pomp, and worldly display. All kinds of mercantile traffic are brought to view. The declaration concerning "slaves and souls of men" may pertain more particularly to the spiritual domain, and have reference to slavery of conscience by the creeds of these bodies, which in some cases is more oppressive than physical bondage.

VERSE 14 And the fruits that thy soul lusted after are departed from thee, and all things which were dainty and goodly are departed from thee, and thou shalt find them no more at all.

Gluttony Rebuked.—The fruits here mentioned are, according to the original, "autumnal fruits." In this we find a prophecy that the "delicacies of the season," upon which the gourmand so sets his pampered appetite, will be suddenly cut off. This, of course, is the work of the famine, which is the result of the fourth vial. Revelation 16: 8.

VERSE 15 The merchants of these things, which were made rich by her, shall stand afar off for the fear of her torment, weeping and wailing, 16 and saying, Alas, alas that great city, that was clothed in fine linen, and purple, and scarlet, and decked with gold, and precious stones, and pearls! 17 For in one hour so great riches is come to nought. And every shipmaster, and all the company in ships, and sailors, and as many as trade by sea, stood afar off, 18 and cried when they saw the smoke of her burning, saying, What city is like unto this great city! 19 And they cast dust on their heads, and cried, weeping and wailing, saying, Alas, alas that great city, wherein were made rich all that had ships in the sea by reason of her costliness! For in one hour is she made desolate.

Emotions of the Wicked.—The reader can readily imagine the cause of this universal voice of mourning, lamentation, and woe. Imagine the plague of sores preying upon men, the rivers turned to blood, the sea like the blood of a dead man, the sun scorching men with fire, the traders' traffic gone, and their silver and gold unable to deliver them, and we need not wonder at their exclamations of distress, nor that shipmasters and sailors join in the general wail. Very different is the emotion of the saints, as the following testimony shows:

VERSE 20 Rejoice over her, thou heaven, and ye holy apostles and prophets; for God hath avenged you on her. 21 And a mighty angel took up a stone like a great millstone, and cast it into the sea, saying, Thus with violence shall that great city Babylon be thrown down, and shall be found no more at all. 22 And the voice of harpers, and musicians, and of pipers, and trumpeters, shall be heard no more at all in thee; and no craftsman, of whatsoever craft he be, shall be found any more in thee; and the sound of a millstone shall be heard no more at all in thee; 23 and the light of a candle shall shine no more at all in thee; and the voice of the bridegroom and of the bride shall be heard no more at all in thee: for thy merchants were the great men of the earth; for by thy sorceries were all nations deceived. 24 And in her was found the blood of prophets, and of saints, and of all that were slain upon the earth.

Emotions of the Righteous.—The apostles and prophets are here called upon to rejoice over great Babylon in her destruction, as it is in close connection with this destruction that they will be delivered from the power of death and the grave by the first resurrection.

Like a great millstone dropped into the sea, Babylon sinks to rise no more. The various arts and crafts that have been employed in her midst, and have ministered to her desires, shall be practiced no more. The pompous music that has been heard in her imposing but formal and lifeless service, dies away forever. The scenes of festivity and gladness, when the bridegroom and the bride have been led before her altars, shall be witnessed no more.

Her sorceries constitute her leading crime, and sorcery is a practice which is involved in the spiritism of today. "In her was found the blood" of "all that were slain upon the earth." From this it is evident that ever since the introduction of a false religion into the world, Babylon has existed. In her has been found, all along, opposition to the work of God, and persecution of His people. In reference to the guilt of the last generation, see comments on Revelation 16: 6.

THE ARMIES OF HEAVEN

Riding from their celestial abode, the cavalry of heaven will follow their divine Commander to punish the nations of earth.

CHAPTER XIX

KING OF KINGS AND LORD OF LORDS

VERSE 1 And after these things I heard a great voice of much people in heaven, saying, Alleluia; Salvation, and glory, and honor, and power, unto the Lord our God: 2 for true and righteous are His judgments: for He hath judged the great whore, which did corrupt the earth with her fornication, and hath avenged the blood of His servants at her hand. 3 And again they said, Alleluia. And her smoke rose up forever and ever.

CONTINUING the subject of Revelation 18, the apostle here introduces the song of triumph which the redeemed saints strike up on their harps when they behold the complete destruction of the system of great Babylon, which is in opposition to God and His true worship. This destruction takes place and this song is sung in connection with the second coming of Christ at the beginning of the thousand years.

Forever and Ever.—There can but one query arise on this scripture: How can it be said that her smoke rose up forever and ever? Does not this language imply eternity of suffering? Let it be remembered that this expression is taken from the Old Testament, and to gain a correct understanding of it, we must go back to its first introduction, and consider its import as there used. In Isaiah 34 will be found the language from which, in all probability, such expressions as these are drawn. Under the figure of Idumea, a certain destruction is brought to view. It is said of that land that its streams should be turned into pitch, its dust into brimstone, that it should become burning pitch, and not be quenched night nor day, but that its smoke should go up forever. This language is spoken, as all must concede, of one of two things, either of the particular country called Idumea, or of the whole earth under that name. In either case it is evident that this phrase, "forever and ever," must be limited in its application. Probably the whole earth is meant, from the fact that the chapter opens with an address to the earth "and all that is therein; the world, and all that come forth of it;" and "the indignation of the Lord" is declared to be upon all nations.

Whether this refers to the depopulation and desolation of the earth at the second advent, or to the purifying fires that shall purge it of the effects of the curse at the end of the thousand years, the expression must still be limited; for after all this, a renovated earth is to come forth, to be the abode of the nations of the saved throughout eternity. Three times in the Bible smoke is spoken of as going up forever: once here in Isaiah 34, of the land of Idumea as a figure of the earth; in Revelation 14 (which see), of the worshipers of the beast and his image; and again in the chapter we are now considering, in regard to the destruction of great Babylon. All these apply to the very same time, and describe the same scenes, namely, the destruction visited upon this earth, the worshipers of the beast, and all the pomp of great Babylon, at the second advent of our Lord and Saviour.

VERSE 4 And the four and twenty elders and the four beasts fell down and worshiped God that sat on the throne, saying, Amen; Alleluia. 5 And a voice came out of the throne, saying, Praise our God, all ye His servants, and ye that fear Him, both small and great. 6 And I heard as it were the voice of a great multitude, and as the voice of many waters, and as the voice of mighty thunderings, saying, Alleluia: for the Lord God omnipotent reigneth. 7 Let us be glad and rejoice, and give honor to Him: for the marriage of the Lamb is come, and His wife hath made herself ready. 8 And to her was granted that she should be arrayed in fine linen, clean and white: for the fine linen is the righteousness of saints.

A Song of Triumph.—"The Lord God omnipotent reigneth," is the language of this song. He reigns at the present time, and has ever reigned in reality, though sentence against an evil work has not been executed speedily. Now He reigns by the open manifestation of His power in the subjugation of all His foes.

"Rejoice, . . . for the marriage of the Lamb is come, and His wife hath made herself ready." Who is "the bride, the Lamb's wife," and what is the marriage? The Lamb's wife is the New Jerusalem which is above. This will be noticed more fully in Revelation 21. The marriage of the Lamb is His reception of this city. When He receives this city, He receives it as the glory and metropolis of His kingdom; hence with it He receives His kingdom, and the throne of His father David. This may well be the event designated by the marriage of the Lamb.

That the marriage relation is often taken to illustrate the union between Christ and His people, is granted, but the marriage of the Lamb here spoken of is a definite event to take place at a definite time. If the declaration that Christ is the head of the church as the husband is the head of the wife (Ephesians 5: 23), proves that the church is now the Lamb's wife, then the marriage of the Lamb took place long ago. But that cannot be, according to this scripture, which locates it in the future. Paul told his Corinthian converts that he had espoused them to one husband, even Christ. This is true of all converts. But while this figure is used to denote the relation that they then assumed to Christ, was it a fact that the marriage of the Lamb took place in Corinth in Paul's day, and that it has been going on for the past nineteen hundred years? Further remarks on this point are deferred to a consideration of Revelation 21.

But if the city is the bride, it may be asked how it can be said that she made *herself* ready. We answer, By the figure of personification, which attributes life and action to inanimate objects. (See a notable example in Psalm 114.) Again, the query may arise on verse 8 how a city can be arrayed in the righteousness of the saints, but if we consider that a city without inhabitants would be but a dreary and cheerless place, we see at once how this is. Reference is had to the countless number of its glorified inhabitants in their shining apparel. The raiment was *granted* to her. What is granted to her? Isaiah 54 and Galatians 4: 21-31 will explain. To the new-covenant city are granted many more children than to the old. These are her glory and rejoicing. The goodly apparel of this city, so to speak, consists of the hosts of the redeemed and immortal ones who walk its golden streets.

VERSE 9 And he saith unto me, Write, Blessed are they which are called unto the marriage supper of the Lamb. And he saith unto me, These are the true sayings of God. 10 And I fell at his feet to worship him. And he said unto me, See thou do it not: I am thy fellow servant, and of thy brethren that have the testimony of Jesus: worship God: for the testimony of Jesus is the Spirit of prophecy.

The Marriage Supper.—Many are the allusions to this marriage supper in the New Testament. It is referred to in the parable of the marriage of the king's son (Matthew 22: 1-14), and again in Luke 14: 16-24. It is the time when we shall eat bread in the kingdom of God when we are recompensed at the resurrection of the just. (Luke 14: 12-15.) It is the time when we shall drink of the fruit of the vine with our Redeemer in His heavenly kingdom. (Matthew 26: 29; Mark 14: 25; Luke 22: 18.) It is the time when we shall sit at His table in the kingdom (Luke 22: 30), and He will gird Himself, and come forth and serve us (Luke 12: 37). Blessed indeed are they who have the privilege of partaking of this glorious feast.

John's Fellow Servant.—A word on verse 10, in reference to those who think they find here an argument for consciousness in death. The mistake which such persons make on this scripture is in supposing that the angel declares to John that he is one of the old prophets come back to communicate with him. The person employed in giving the Revelation to John is called an angel, and angels are not the departed spirits of the dead. Whoever takes the position that they are, is to all intents a spiritist, for this is the very foundation stone of their theory. But the angel says no such thing. He simply says that he is the fellow servant of John, as he had been the fellow servant of his brethren the prophets. The term "fellow servant" implies that they were all on a common footing as servants of the great God; hence he was not a proper object for John to worship. Calling the prophets "thy brethren," signifies that they all belong to the same class in the service of God. (See comment on Revelation 1: 1, "His Angel.")

VERSE 11 And I saw heaven opened, and behold a white horse; and He that sat upon him was called Faithful and True, and in righteousness He doth judge and make war. 12 His eyes were as a flame of fire, and on His head were many crowns; and He had a name written, that no man knew, but He Himself. 13 And He was clothed with a vesture dipped in blood: and His name is called The Word of God. 14 And the armies which were in heaven followed Him upon white horses, clothed in fine linen, white and clean. 15 And out of His mouth goeth a sharp sword, that with it He should smite the nations: and He shall rule them with a rod of iron: and He treadeth the winepress of the fierceness and wrath of Almighty God. 16 And He hath on His vesture and on His thigh a name written, KING OF KINGS, AND LORD OF LORDS. 17 And I saw an angel standing in the sun; and he cried with a loud voice, saying to all the fowls that fly in the midst of heaven, Come and gather yourselves together unto the supper of the great God; 18 that ye may eat the flesh of kings, and the flesh of captains, and the flesh of mighty men, and the flesh of horses, and of them that sit on them, and the flesh of all men, both free and bond, both small and great. 19 And I saw the beast, and the kings of the earth, and their armies, gathered together to make war against Him that sat on the horse, and against His army. 20 And the beast was taken, and with him the false prophet that wrought miracles before him, with which he deceived them that had received the mark of the beast, and them that worshiped his image. These both were cast alive into a lake of fire burning with brimstone. 21 And the remnant were slain with the sword of Him that sat upon the horse, which sword proceeded out of His mouth: and all the fowls were filled with their flesh.

Christ's Second Coming.—With verse 11 a new scene is introduced. We are here carried back to the second coming of Christ, this time under the symbol of a warrior riding forth to battle. Why is He represented thus?—Because He is going forth to war, to meet "the kings of the earth and their armies," and this would be the only proper character in which to represent Him on such a mission. His vesture is dipped in blood. (See a description of the same scene in Isaiah 63:1-4.) The armies of heaven, the angels of God, follow Him. Verse 15 shows how He rules the nations with a rod of iron when they are given Him for an inheritance, as recorded in the second Psalm, which popular theology interprets to mean the conversion of the world.

But would not such an expression as "treadeth the winepress of the fierceness and wrath of Almighty God," be a very singular description of a work of grace upon the hearts of the heathen for their conversion? The great and final display of the "winepress of God's wrath," and also of "the lake of fire," occurs at the end of the thousand years, as described in Revelation 20; and to that it would seem that the full and formal description of Revelation 14: 18-20 must apply. But the destruction of the living wicked at the second coming of Christ, at the beginning of the thousand years, furnishes a scene on a smaller scale, similar in both these respects to what takes place at the close of that period. Hence in the verses before us we have this mention of both the winepress of wrath and the lake of fire.

Christ has at this time closed His mediatorial work, and laid off His priestly robes for kingly attire; for He has on His vesture and on His thigh a name written, King of kings and Lord of lords. This is in harmony with the character in which He here appears, for it was the custom of warriors anciently to have some kind of title inscribed upon their vesture. (Verse 16.)

What is to be understood by the angel standing in the sun? In Revelation 16: 17 we read of the seventh vial being poured out into the air, from which it was inferred that as the air envelops the whole earth, that plague would be universal. May not the same principle of interpretation apply here, and show that the angel standing in the sun, and issuing his call from there to the fowls of heaven to come to the supper of the great God, denotes that this proclamation will go wherever the sun's rays fall upon this earth? The fowls will be obedient to the call, and fill themselves with the flesh of horses, kings, captains, and mighty men. Thus, while the saints are partaking of the marriage supper of the Lamb, the wicked in their own persons furnish a great supper for the fowls of the heavens.

The beast and the false prophet are taken. The false prophet is the one that works miracles before the beast and is identical with the two-horned beast of Revelation 13, to whom the same work, for the same purpose, is there attributed. The fact that these are cast *alive* into the lake of fire, shows that these powers will not pass away and be succeeded by others, but will be living powers at the second advent of Christ.

The papacy has long been in the field, and has come to the closing scenes in its career. Its overthrow is emphatically predicted in other prophecies than the one now before us, notably in Daniel 7: 11, in which the prophet says that he beheld until the beast was slain, and his body destroyed and given to the burning flame. This power must be very near the close of its existence. But it does not perish until Christ appears, for it then goes alive into the lake of fire.

The other power associated with it, the two-horned beast, we see fast approaching the climax of the work it has to do before it also goes alive into the lake of fire. How impressive is the thought that we see before us two great prophetic agencies which are by all the evidences near the close of their history, which yet are not to cease until the Lord shall appear in all His glory.

It appears from verse 21 that there is a remnant not numbered with the beast or the false prophet. These are slain by the sword of Him that sits upon the horse, which sword proceeds out of His mouth. This sword is doubtless what is spoken of elsewhere as "the spirit of His mouth" and "the breath of His lips," with which the Lord shall slay the wicked at His appearing and kingdom. (2 Thessalonians 2: 8; Isaiah 11: 4.)

 FRANKLIN BOOTH, ARTIST

THE RESURRECTION

In response to the voice of their Redeemer, the righteous of all ages will come forth to everlasting life.

CHAPTER XX

THE WORLD'S MILLENNIAL NIGHT

VERSE 1 And I saw an angel come down from heaven, having the key of the bottomless pit and a great chain in his hand. 2 And he laid hold on the dragon, that old serpent, which is the devil, and Satan, and bound him a thousand years, 3 and cast him into the bottomless pit, and shut him up, and set a seal upon him, that he should deceive the nations no more, till the thousand years should be fulfilled: and after that he must be loosed a little season.

THE EVENT with which this chapter opens seems to follow the events of the preceding chapter in chronological order. The inquiries that here arise are, Who is the angel that comes down from heaven? What are the key and the chain which he has in his hand? What is the bottomless pit? What is meant by binding Satan a thousand years?

Is this angel Christ, as some suppose? Evidently not. A bright ray of light is thrown from the old typical service directly upon this passage.

Satan is the Scapegoat.—Christ is the great High Priest of the gospel age. On the Day of Atonement anciently two goats were taken by the priest, and lots were cast upon them, one for the Lord, and the other for the scapegoat. The goat upon which the Lord's lot fell, was then slain, and his blood carried into the sanctuary to make an atonement for the children of Israel. After this the sins of the people were confessed upon the head of the other, or scapegoat, and he was sent away by the hand of a fit man into the wilderness, a place not inhabited. As Christ is the priest of the gospel age, a few arguments will show Satan to be the antitypical scapegoat.

The Hebrew word for scapegoat, as given in the margin of Leviticus 16: 8, is "Azazel." On this verse, William Jenks remarks: "Scapegoat. See diff. opin. in Bochart. Spencer, after the oldest opinions of the Hebrews and Christians, thinks *Azazel is the name of the devil;* and so Rosenm., whom see. The

Syr. has *Azzail,* the 'angel (strong one) who revolted.' "[1] The devil is here evidently pointed out. Thus we have the definition of the Scripture term in two ancient languages, with the oldest opinion of the Christians, in favor of the view that the scapegoat is a type of Satan.

Charles Beecher says: "What goes to confirm this is that the most ancient paraphrases and translations treat Azazel as a proper name. The Chaldee paraphrase and the targums of Onkelos and Jonathan would certainly have translated it if it was not a proper name, but they do not. The Septuagint, or oldest Greek version, renders it by ἀποπομπαῖος, *apopompaios,* a word applied by the Greeks to a malign deity sometimes appeased by sacrifices. Another confirmation is found in the book of Enoch, where the name Azalzel, evidently a corruption of Azazel, is given to one of the fallen angels, thus plainly showing what was the prevalent understanding of the Jews at that day. Still another evidence is found in the Arabic, where Azazel is employed as the name of the evil spirit."[2]

Here is the Jewish interpretation:

"Far from involving the recognition of Azazel as a deity, the sending of the goat was, as stated by Naḥmanides, a symbolic expression of the idea that the people's sins and their evil consequences were to be sent back to the spirit of desolation and ruin, the source of all impurity."[3]

In a striking manner these views harmonize with the events to take place in connection with the cleansing of the heavenly sanctuary, as revealed to us in the Scriptures of truth.

In the type we see the sin of the transgressor transferred to the victim. We see that sin borne by the ministration of the priest and the blood of the offering into the sanctuary. On the tenth day of the seventh month we see the priest, with the blood of the sin offering for the people, remove all their sins from the sanctuary, and lay them upon the head of the scape-

---

[1] William Jenks, *The Comprehensive Commentary,* Vol. I, p. 410, note on Leviticus 16: 8.

[2] Charles Beecher, *Redeemer and Redeemed,* pp. 67, 68.

[3] *Jewish Encyclopedia,* Vol. II, p. 366, art. "Azazel."

goat. And we see the goat bear them away into a land not inhabited. (Leviticus 1: 1-4; 4: 3-6; 16: 5-10, 15, 16, 20-22.)

Answering to these events in the type, we behold in the antitype, the great offering for the world made on Calvary. The sins of all those who avail themselves of the merits of Christ's shed blood by faith in Him, are borne by the ministration of Christ into the new-covenant sanctuary. After Christ, the minister of the true tabernacle (Hebrews 8: 2), has finished His ministration, He will remove the sins of His people from the sanctuary, and lay them upon the head of their author, the antitypical scapegoat, the devil. The devil will be sent away, bearing them into a land not inhabited.

"Let us contemplate that scene at Christ's return to earth. The Church has been judged; Israel has been judged; the Gentile nations have been also judged. . . . Now it is Satan's turn to be judged also; and our High Priest is seen 'putting' the moral blame to where it rightly belongs; judging the great corruptor and banishing him to a place of separation from the affairs of men." [4]

"Satan is not here, as some allege against this opinion, put on an equality with God; for the two goats were both brought 'to Jehovah,' and were His; while the very casting of lots, which was in itself a solemn appeal to God, shows that Jehovah claimed the power of disposal. Neither can it be objected that this was in any sense a sacrifice to Satan, for the animal was not slain to him; it was only sent to him in disgrace. Bearing upon it sins which God had already forgiven, it was sent to Azazel in the wilderness.

"The phrase 'scape-goat,' by which the strange term Azazel is rendered in our version, came from the '*hircus emissarius*' [goat emissary], of the Vulgate. The term Azazel may mean the 'apostate one'—a name which Satan merits, and which he seems to have borne among the Jews. It was Satan that brought sin into the world; and this seduction of

---

[4] Albert Whalley, *The Red Letter Days of Israel*, p. 125.

man adds to his guilt, and consequently to his punishment. Sin is now pardoned in God's mercy. The one goat was sacrificed as a sin offering; its blood was carried into the holy place, and the mercyseat was sprinkled with it. Guilt was therefore canceled; by this shedding of blood there was remission. But sin, though pardoned, is yet hateful to God, and it cannot dwell in His sight: it is removed away to a 'land not inhabited' —severed from God's people, and sent away to man's first seducer. The sins of a believing world are taken off them, and rolled back on Satan, their prime author and instigator. Though the penalty is remitted to believers, it is not remitted to him who brought them into apostasy and ruin. The tempted are restored, but the whole punishment is seen to fall on the archtempter. Hell is 'prepared for the devil and his angels.' "[5]

This we believe to be the very event described in the verses under notice. At the time here specified, the sanctuary service is closed. Christ lays upon the head of the devil the sins which have been transferred to the sanctuary, and which are imputed to the saints no more. The devil is sent away, *not* by the hand of the High Priest, but by the hand of another person, according to the type, into a place here called the bottomless pit.

The Key and the Chain.—It cannot be supposed that the key and the chain are literal; they are rather used merely as symbols of the power and authority with which this angel is clothed on this occasion for the accomplishment of his mission.

The Bottomless Pit.—The original word signifies an abyss, bottomless, deep, profound. Its use seems to be such as to show that the word denotes any place of darkness, desolation, and death. Thus in Revelation 9: 1, 2, it is applied to the barren wastes of the Arabian desert, and in Romans 10: 7, to the grave. But the use which specially throws light upon the meaning of the word here is found in Genesis 1: 2, where we

[5] John Eadie, *Biblical Cyclopædia*, p. 577, art. "Scape-Goat."

read that "darkness was upon the face of the *deep*." The word there rendered "deep" is the same word that is here rendered "bottomless pit," and the text might have been translated, "Darkness was upon the face of the abyss, or bottomless pit." We all know that the word "deep" as there used is applied to the earth in its chaotic state. Precisely this it must mean in this third verse of Revelation 20. Let it be borne in mind that at the time the angel does this work, the earth is a vast charnel house of desolation and death. The voice of God has shaken it to its foundations; the islands and mountains have been moved out of their places; the great earthquake has leveled to the earth the mightiest works of man; the seven last plagues have left their all-desolating trail over the earth; the burning glory attending the coming of the Son of man has borne its part in accomplishing the general desolation; the wicked have been given to the slaughter, and their putrefying flesh and bleaching bones lie unburied, ungathered, and unlamented from one end of the earth to the other.

Thus is the earth made empty and waste, and turned upside down. (Isaiah 24: 1.) Thus is it brought back again, partly at least, to its original state of confusion and chaos. (See Jeremiah 4: 19-26, especially verse 23.) What better term could be used to describe the earth thus rolling on in its course of darkness and desolation for a thousand years than that of abyss, or bottomless pit? Here Satan will be confined during this time, amid the ruins which indirectly his own hands have wrought, unable to flee from his habitation of woe, or to repair in the least degree its hideous ruin.

Binding of Satan.—We well know that Satan, in order to work, must have subjects upon whom to work. Without these, he can do nothing. But during the thousand years of his confinement to this earth, all the saints are in heaven beyond the power of his temptations, and all the wicked are in their graves beyond his power to deceive. His sphere of action is circumscribed, and thus is he bound, being condemned throughout this period to a state of hopeless inactivity. To a

Events Marking the Beginning of the Millennium
SEVEN LAST PLAGUES
CHRIST'S SECOND COMING
THE WICKED PERISH
RIGHTEOUS DEAD RAISED
THE RIGHTEOUS ASCEND TO HEAVEN
GOD'S
LAW
Events Marking the Close of the Millennium
CHRIST and SAINTS DESCEND
HOLY CITY DESCENDS
WICKED DEAD RAISED
SATAN LOOSED
THE WICKED DESTROYED

THE MILLENNIUM

During the millennium Satan will be bound (confined) to the desolate earth, while the saints in heaven engage in judgment.

mind that has been as busy as his has been for the past six thousand years in deceiving the inhabitants of the world from generation to generation, this must be a punishment of the most intense severity.

According to this exposition, the "binding" of Satan means simply placing beyond his reach the subjects upon whom he works. His being "loosed" means their being brought again by a resurrection to a position where he can again exercise his power upon them. On this exposition some say that we have mistaken the personnel, and have the wicked bound, instead of the devil. Yet how often do we hear, in the daily transactions of life, such expressions as these: My way was completely hedged up. My hands were completely tied. But when persons use such expressions, do we imagine that some insurmountable obstacle was literally thrown across the path they were traveling, or that their hands were literally confined with ropes or cords?—No; we understand that a combination of circumstances rendered it impossible for them to act. Even so here. Why will not people grant to the Bible the same liberty of speech that they give without question to their fellow men?

More than this, there is here a great limitation of Satan's power, which may well be called a "binding." He no longer has the power of traversing space and visiting other worlds, but like man he is confined to this earth, which he nevermore leaves. The place of the ruin he has wrought now becomes his gloomy prison house until he is led out to execution at the end of the thousand years.

VERSE 4 And I saw thrones, and they sat upon them, and judgment was given unto them: and I saw the souls of them that were beheaded for the witness of Jesus, and for the word of God, and which had not worshiped the beast, neither his image, neither had received his mark upon their foreheads, or in their hands; and they lived and reigned with Christ a thousand years. 5 But the rest of the dead lived not again until the thousand years were finished. This is the first resurrection. 6 Blessed and holy is he that hath part in the first resurrection: on such the second death hath no power, but they shall be priests of God and of Christ, and shall reign with Him a thousand years.

Exaltation of the Saints.—From the devil in his gloomy confinement, John now directs our attention to the saints in victory and glory, the saints reigning with Christ. Their employment is to assign to the wicked dead the punishment due their evil deeds. From that general assembly John then selects two classes as worthy of especial attention: the martyrs who had been beheaded for the witness of Jesus, and those who had not worshiped the beast and his image. The latter class, those who refuse the mark of the beast and his image, are of course the ones who hear and obey the third angel's message of Revelation 14. But these are not the ones who are beheaded for the witness of Jesus, as some who claim that the last generation of saints are all to be slain, would have us believe. The word rendered "which," in the expression, "which had not worshiped the beast," shows that there is another class introduced. The word is the compound relative, ὅστις, *hostis*, "whoever," not merely the simple relative ὅς, *hos*, "who," and is defined by Liddell and Scott, "Whosoever, whichsoever, *any one who*, anything which." As one class, John saw the martyrs, and as another he saw *those who* had not worshiped the beast and his image.

It is true that ὅστις, *hostis*, is sometimes used as a simple relative, as in 2 Corinthians 3: 14; Ephesians 1: 23, but never in such constructions as this, where it is preceded by the conjunction καί, *kai*, "and."

Lest anyone should say that if we render the passage "and whosoever had not worshiped the beast," we thereby include millions of heathen and sinners who have not worshiped the beast, and promise them a reign of a thousand years with Christ, we would call attention to the fact that the preceding chapter states that the wicked had all been slain, and the seal of death had been set upon them for a thousand years. John is here viewing only the righteous company who have part in the first resurrection.

To avoid the doctrine of two resurrections, some claim that the passage, "The rest of the dead lived not again until the thousand years were finished," is an interpolation, not found in the original, and hence not genuine. Even if this were so, it would not disprove the main proposition that the righteous dead are raised by themselves in a "first resurrection," and that there is a second resurrection a thousand years later, in which all the wicked are brought from their graves.

But the criticism is not true, for all scholarship is against it. The English Revised Version makes no reference to this text as being "not found" in ancient manuscripts. The American Revised Version does not give the slightest hint that a part of the text is omitted. Rotherham's translation, though noting elsewhere "doubtful" renderings, says nothing about this text being spurious. It is found in Tischendorf's eight editions of the Greek New Testament, and in the Greek text of Westcott and Hort. The sentence occurs also in all the Greek New Testaments issued by the world-renowned critics, Griesbach, Wordsworth, Lachmann, Tregelles, and Alford. Three or four Greek manuscripts do not have this sentence; sixteen hundred and ninety-seven of them do contain it if they have the Revelation at all.

Two Resurrections.—"The rest of the dead lived not again until the thousand years were finished." Whatever may be said to the contrary, no language could more plainly prove two resurrections. The first is a resurrection of the righteous at the beginning of the thousand years. The second is that of the wicked at the end of the millennium. On such as have part in the first resurrection, the second death will have no power. They can pass unharmed through the elements which destroy the wicked like chaff. They will be able to dwell with devouring fire and everlasting burnings. (Isaiah 33: 14, 15.) They will be able to go forth and look upon the carcasses of the men who have transgressed against the Lord, as the quenchless fire and undying worm are preying upon them. (Isaiah 66: 24.) The difference between the righteous and the wicked in this respect is seen again in the fact that while God is to the latter a consuming fire, He is to His people both a sun and a shield.

Wicked Raised to Life.—The wicked who are raised at the end of the thousand years actually live again as they have once lived on the earth. To deny this is to do violence to this scripture. In what physical condition they will be raised, we are not informed. It is usual to say on this point that what we have lost unconditionally in Adam, is restored unconditionally in Christ. With respect to physical condition, this should not perhaps be taken in an unlimited sense, for the race has lost greatly in stature and vital force, which need not be restored to the wicked. If they are brought back to the average mental and physical condition which they possessed during life or the period of their probation, that would certainly be sufficient to enable them to receive understandingly the last judgment due them for all their deeds done while living here upon this earth.

VERSE 7 And when the thousand years are expired, Satan shall be loosed out of his prison, 8 and shall go out to deceive the nations which are in the four quarters of the earth, Gog and Magog, to gather them together to battle: the number of whom is as the sand of the sea. 9 And they went up on the breadth of the earth, and compassed the camp of the saints about, and the beloved city: and fire came down from God out of heaven, and devoured them. 10 And the devil that deceived them was cast into the lake of fire and brimstone, where the beast and the false prophet are, and shall be tormented day and night forever and ever.

Perdition of Ungodly Men.—At the end of the one thousand years, the holy city New Jerusalem, in which the saints have dwelt in heaven during that period, comes down and is located upon the earth. It then becomes the camp of the saints, around which the risen wicked gather, numberless as the sand of the sea. The devil deceives them, and thus brings them to this battle. They are induced to undertake an impious warfare upon the Holy City, in prospect of some advantage to be gained by fighting against the saints. Satan doubtless persuades them that they can overcome the saints, dispossess them of their city, and still hold possession of the earth. But fire comes down from God out of heaven, and devours them. The word here rendered "devoured," Moses Stuart admits is "intensive," and signifies "to eat up, devour, so that it denotes utter excision." [6]

This is the time of the perdition of ungodly men,—the time when "the elements shall melt with fervent heat, the earth also," and when the works that are in the earth shall be burned up. (2 Peter 3: 7, 10.) In the light of these scriptures, we can see how the wicked are to receive their recompense in the earth. (Proverbs 11: 31.) We can see also that this recompense is not eternal life in misery, but an "utter excision," entire and complete destruction.

The Wicked Never Tread the New Earth.—Two views deserve a passing notice at this point. The first is that the earth is renewed at the second coming of Christ, and is the habitation of the saints during the thousand years. The other is that when Christ appears the second time, He sets up His kingdom in Palestine, and performs in connection with His saints a work of conquest over the nations left on the earth during the thousand years, and subdues them to Himself.

One among many objections to the first view is that it makes the wicked come up in their resurrection, and with the devil at their head, tread with their unhallowed feet upon the purified and holy earth, while the saints, who have held possession for a thousand years, are obliged to yield the ground, and flee into the city. We cannot believe that the saints' inheritance will ever be thus marred, or that the fair plains of the earth made new will ever be soiled with the polluting tread of the resuscitated wicked. Besides outraging all ideas of propriety, there is no scripture from which even an inference can be drawn to support this position.

As to the second view, one among many of its absurdities is that although Christ and His saints have conquered the earth during the thousand years, at the end of this period the wicked get the upper hand, they lose their territory, the work of a thousand years is undone, and they are compelled to beat an

[6] Moses Stuart, *A Commentary on the Apocalypse*, Vol. II, p. 369.

ignominious retreat into the city for shelter, leaving the earth to the undisputed sway of their foes.

A Thousand Years in Heaven.—In contrast with these theories, there is harmony in the view herein presented. The saints are with Christ in heaven during the thousand years while the earth lies desolate. The saints and the city come down, and the wicked dead are raised and come up against it. There the latter receive their judgment. From the purifying fires which destroy them come forth the new heavens and the new earth, to be the abode of the righteous throughout endless ages.

The Subjects of Torment.—From verse 10, some have argued that the devil alone was to be tormented day and night, but the testimony of this verse includes more than that. The verb phrase "shall be tormented" is in the plural, and makes affirmation concerning the beast and the false prophet, whereas it would be in the singular number if it referred to the devil alone. It will be noticed in the expression, "where the beast and the false prophet are," that "are" is a supplied word. It would be more proper to supply the words "were cast," co-ordinating with what was spoken of the devil just before. A more exact translation, too, supplies the word "also" after "where." The sentence would then read, "The devil was cast into the lake of fire, where *also* the beast and the false prophet *were cast.*" The beast and the false prophet were cast into the lake of fire and destroyed, at the beginning of the thousand years. (Revelation 19: 20.) The individuals of whom their organizations were then composed, now come up in the second resurrection, and a similar and final destruction is visited upon them under the names Gog and Magog.

The Lake of Fire.—Some reader may be inclined to ask for a definition of the lake of fire. As a comprehensive definition, may it not be called a symbol of the agencies which God employs to close up His controversy with the living wicked at the beginning of the thousand years, and with all the hosts of the ungodly at the end of that period? Literal fire will of course be largely employed in this work. We can better describe its effects than the thing itself. At the second coming of Christ, it is the flaming fire in which the Lord Jesus is revealed, the spirit of His mouth and brightness of His coming by which the man of sin is to be consumed, the fire in which great Babylon shall be utterly burned. (Revelation 18: 8.) At the end of the thousand years, it is the day that shall burn as an oven (Malachi 4: 1); it is the fervent heat that shall melt the elements and the earth, and burn up the works that are in it; it is the fire of Tophet prepared for the king (the devil and his angels, Matthew 25: 41), the pile whereof is deep and large, and which "the breath of the Lord, like a stream of brimstone, doth kindle" (Isaiah 30: 33). In short, it is the fire that comes down from God out of heaven. (On the expression, "tormented day and night forever and ever," see comments on Revelation 14: 11.)

VERSE 11 And I saw a great white throne, and Him that sat on it, from whose face the earth and the heaven fled away; and there was found no place for them. 12 And I saw the dead, small and great, stand before God; and the books were opened: and another book was opened, which is the book of life: and the dead were judged out of those things which were written in the books, according to their works. 13 And the sea gave up the dead which were in it; and death and hell delivered up the dead which were in them: and they were judged every man according to their works. 14 And death and hell were cast into the lake of fire. This is the second death. 15 And whosoever was not found written in the book of life was cast into the lake of fire.

A Throne of Judgment.—With verse 11, John introduces another scene in connection with the final doom of the ungodly. It is the great white throne of judgment, before which they are assembled to receive their awful sentence of condemnation and death. Before this throne the heavens and the earth flee away, so that no place is found for them. A moment's reflection on the changes which must then take place in the earth will bring out the great force of this language. The scene is that of Peter's burning day, which is the "perdition of ungodly men," and in which even the "elements" melt with fervent heat. (2 Peter 3: 7-13.)

Fire comes down from God out of heaven. The works that are in the world are burned up, and the wicked are destroyed. This is the fire of Gehenna, which contains all the elements necessary to consume utterly every mortal being that comes under its power. (Mark 9: 43-48.) Then will be fulfilled Isaiah 66: 24: "They [the righteous] shall go forth, and look upon the carcasses of the men that have transgressed against Me: for their worm shall not die, neither shall their fire be quenched; and they shall be an abhorring unto all flesh."

Then also will be fulfilled Isaiah 33: 14: "Who among us shall dwell with the devouring fire? Who among us shall dwell with everlasting burnings?" The answer in the following verses shows it to be the righteous. This must be the time to which Isaiah's questions and answers apply.

In all this conflagration the elements are not destroyed. They are only melted and purged from the taint of sin and every token of the curse. The almighty fiat then goes forth, "Behold, I make all things new. . . . It is done." Revelation 21: 5, 6. At the first creation, "the morning stars sang together, and all the sons of God shouted for joy." Job 38: 7. At this new creation, that song and shout will be augmented by the glad voices of the redeemed. So will this earth, wrenched for a time by sin from its intended orbit of joy and peace, be brought back renewed into harmony with a loyal universe, to be the everlasting home of the saved.

The Books of Record.—Men are judged out of the things written in the books, from which we learn the solemn fact that a record of all our deeds is kept on high. A faithful and unerring record is made by the angelic secretaries. The wicked cannot conceal from them any of their deeds of darkness. They cannot bribe them to pass over in the record their unlawful acts. They must meet them again, and be judged accordingly.

Execution of the Sentence.—The wicked are to be punished according to their works. The Scriptures declare that they shall be rewarded according to their deeds. That the degree of suffering which each one is to endure is taken into the account as a part of the punishment for his sins, is evident: "That servant, which knew his lord's will, and prepared not himself, neither did according to his will, shall be beaten with many stripes. But he that knew not, and did commit things worthy of stripes, shall be beaten with few stripes. For unto whomsoever much is given, of him shall be much required." Luke 12: 47, 48.

The Book of Life.—Why, it may be asked, is the book of life brought forth on this occasion, when all who have part in the second resurrection, beyond which this scene is located, are already forejudged to the second death? At least one apparent reason is, that all may see that none of the names of all the multitude who die the second death are in the book of life, and why they are not there; and if the names have ever been there, why they were not retained. Thus all the intelligences of the universe may see that God acts with justice and impartiality.

It is stated also that "death and hell were cast into the lake of fire. This is the second death." Here is the final epitaph of all the forces from first to last that have risen up to oppose the will and work of the Lord. Satan originated and led out in this nefarious work. A part of heaven's angels joined him in his false position and murderous work, and for him and them the everlasting fire was prepared. (Matthew 25: 41.) Men become involved only because they join him in his rebellion. But here the controversy closes. The fire is to them everlasting because it allows of no escape, and of no cessation until they are consumed. The second death is their punishment, and it is "everlasting punishment" (Matthew 25: 46) because they never find release from its dread embrace. "The wages of sin is *death*," not punishing forever. Romans 6: 23.

To sum up the argument, "Whosoever was not found written in the book of life was cast into the lake of fire." Reader, is your name written in the book of life? Are you striving to avert in your own case the fearful doom that awaits the ungodly? Rest not until you have reason to believe that your name is among those who are to share at last in eternal life.

C. MENTE. ARTIST

THE HOLY CITY

"I John saw the holy city, new Jerusalem, coming down from God out of heaven, prepared as a bride adorned for her husband." Revelation 21: 2.

CHAPTER XXI

A NEW HEAVEN AND A NEW EARTH

THE SUBJECT of this chapter, beginning with verse 2, is the New Jerusalem, but before that is introduced, John tells us how the present heaven and earth and sea are to be disposed of:

VERSE 1 And I saw a new heaven and a new earth: for the first heaven and the first earth were passed away; and there was no more sea.

New Heaven and New Earth.—By the first heaven and first earth, John unquestionably means the present heaven and earth, "the heavens and the earth which are now." 2 Peter 3: 7. Some have supposed that when the Bible speaks of the third heaven, in which are Paradise and the tree of life (2 Corinthians 12: 2 and Revelation 2: 7), it refers to the heaven which is yet future, and does not prove that there is a Paradise and a tree of life literally in existence in heaven at the present time. They base their view on the fact that Peter speaks of three heavens and earths: those before the flood, the ones which now are, and the ones which are to come. But that theory is completely overturned by the first verse of Revelation 21; for John here reckons but two heavens and earths. The ones which now are he calls the *first*, so that the future new heavens would, according to this count, be the *second*, and not the *third*, as Peter is supposed to reckon. Hence it is certain that Peter did not design to establish a numerical order, in accordance with which we should speak of one as the first, another as the second, and the last as the third. The object of his reasoning was simply to show that as a literal heaven and earth succeeded to the destruction of the earth by the flood, so a literal heaven and earth would result from the renovation of the present system by fire. There is no proof, therefore, that when the Bible speaks of the third heaven, it refers simply to the third state of the present heavens and earth, for then all the Bible writers would uniformly have so reckoned it. Thus the arguments of those who endeavor to disprove a literal Paradise and tree of life in existence now, fall to the ground.

The Bible certainly recognizes three heavens in the present constitution of things, namely, the first, or atmospheric heaven, which the fowls of the air inhabit; the second, the planetary heaven, the region of the sun, moon, and stars; and the third, high above the others, where Paradise and the tree of life are found (Revelation 2: 7), where God has His residence and His throne (Revelation 22: 1, 2), to which Paul was caught up in heavenly vision (2 Corinthians 12: 2), to which Christ ascended when He left the earth (Revelation 12: 5), where He now, as Priest-King, sits upon the throne with His Father (Zechariah 6: 13), and where the glorious city stands, awaiting the saints when they enter into life (Revelation 21: 2). Blessed be God that from that bright land intelligence has been brought to this far-off world of ours! Thanks be to His holy name that a way has been opened, which leads like a straight and shining path of light up to those blest abodes!

The Sea No More.—Because John says, "There was no more sea," the question is sometimes asked, Is there, then, to be no sea in the new earth? It does not certainly follow from this text that there will be none; for John is speaking only of the present heaven and earth and sea. It might be translated thus: For the first heaven and the first earth were passed away, and the sea [οὐκ ἔστιν ἔτι, *ouk estin eti*, is no more] also passed away; that is, the old sea no longer appeared, any more than the old heaven and the old earth. Yet there may be a new sea as there is a new earth.

Adam Clarke says on this passage: "The *sea* no more appeared than did the first *heaven* and *earth*. All was made *new;* and probably the new sea occupied a different position, and was differently distributed, from that of the old sea."[1]

[1] Adam Clarke, *Commentary on the New Testament*, Vol. II, p. 1058, note on Revelation 21: 1.

The river of life, of which we read in the following chapter, proceeds from the throne of God, and flows through the broad street of the city. It must find some place into which to discharge its waters, and what could that be but the new-earth sea? That there will be a sea, or seas, in the new earth, may be inferred from the prophecy which speaks of Christ's future reign as follows: "His dominion shall be from sea even to sea, and from the river even to the ends of the earth." Zechariah 9: 10. But that three quarters of the globe will then, as now, be abandoned to a waste of waters, can hardly be expected. The new world, where God's faithful people are to dwell, will have everything which will contribute to proportion, utility, and beauty.

VERSE 2 And I John saw the holy city, New Jerusalem, coming down from God out of heaven, prepared as a bride adorned for her husband. 3 And I heard a great voice out of heaven saying, Behold, the tabernacle of God is with men, and He will dwell with them, and they shall be His people, and God Himself shall be with them, and be their God. 4 And God shall wipe away all tears from their eyes; and there shall be no more death, neither sorrow, nor crying, neither shall there be any more pain: for the former things are passed away.

The Father's House.—In connection with the view which John has of the holy city coming down from God out of heaven, a voice is heard, saying, "The tabernacle of God is with men, and He will dwell with them." The great God takes up His abode on this earth, but we do not suppose that God is confined to this, or any other one of the worlds of His creation. He here has a throne, and the earth enjoys so much of His presence that it may be said that He dwells among men and dwells there in a different sense from ever before. Why should this be thought a strange thing? God's only-begotten Son is here as ruler of His special kingdom. The holy city will be here. The heavenly hosts take an interest in this world probably above what they feel in any other; yea, reasoning from one of the Saviour's parables, there will be more joy in heaven over one world redeemed than over ninety and nine which have needed no redemption.

 FRANKLIN BOOTH, ARTIST

REUNION IN HEAVEN

Home at last. Families and friends will be united. There will be no partings, no heartaches, sickness, or sorrow in the heavenly abode.

No Cause for Tears.—"God shall wipe away all tears from their eyes." He does not literally wipe away tears from the eyes of His people, for there will be no tears in that kingdom to be wiped away. He wipes away tears by removing all causes of tears.

VERSE 5 And He that sat upon the throne said, Behold, I make all things new. And He said unto me, Write: for these words are true and faithful. 6 And He said unto me, It is done. I am Alpha and Omega, the beginning and the end. I will give unto him that is athirst of the fountain of the water of life freely.

The New Creation.—He that sits upon the throne is the same being that is mentioned in verses 11, 12 of the preceding chapter. He says, "I make all things new;" not, I make all new things. The earth is not destroyed, annihilated, and a new one created, but all things are made over new. Let us rejoice that these words are true. When this is accomplished, all will be ready for the utterance of that sublime sentence, "It is done." The dark shadow of sin has then forever vanished. The wicked, root and branch (Malachi 4: 1), are destroyed out of the land of the living, and the universal anthem of praise and thanksgiving (Revelation 5: 13) goes up from a redeemed world and a clean universe to a covenant-keeping God.

VERSE 7 He that overcometh shall inherit all things; and I will be his God, and he shall be My son. 8 But the fearful, and unbelieving, and the abominable, and murderers, and whoremongers, and sorcerers, and idolaters, and all liars, shall have their part in the lake which burneth with fire and brimstone: which is the second death.

The Great Inheritance.—The overcomers are "Abraham's seed, and heirs according to the promise." Galatians 3: 29. The promise embraces the world (Romans 4: 13); and the saints will go forth upon the new earth, not as servants or aliens, but as lawful heirs to the heavenly estate and proprietors of the soil.

Fear That Hath Torment.—But the fearful and unbelieving have their part in the lake that burneth with fire and brimstone. The word "fearful" has been a trouble to some conscientious ones, who have had fears more or less in all their Christian experience. It may be well, therefore, to inquire what kind of fear is here meant. It is not fear of our own weakness, or of the power of the tempter. It is not fear of sinning, or of falling out by the way, or of coming short at last. Such fear drives us to the Lord for help. But the fear mentioned here is connected with unbelief, a fear of the ridicule and opposition of the world, a fear to trust God and venture out upon His promises, a fear that He will not fulfill what He has declared, and that consequently one will be left to shame and loss for believing on Him. Cherishing such fear, one can be only half-hearted in His service. This is most dishonoring to God. This is the fear which we are commanded not to have. (Isaiah 51: 7.) This is the fear which brings into condemnation here, and will finally bring all who are controlled by it into the lake of fire, which is the second death.

VERSE 9 And there came unto me one of the seven angels which had the seven vials full of the seven last plagues, and talked with me, saying, Come hither, I will show thee the bride, the Lamb's wife. 10 And he carried me away in the spirit to a great and high mountain, and showed me that great city, the holy Jerusalem, descending out of heaven from God, 11 having the glory of God: and her light was like unto a stone most precious, even like a jasper stone, clear as crystal; 12 and had a wall great and high, and had twelve gates, and at the gates twelve angels, and names written thereon, which are the names of the twelve tribes of the children of Israel: 13 on the east three gates; on the north three gates; on the south three gates; and on the west three gates. 14 And the wall of the city had twelve foundations, and in them the names of the twelve apostles of the Lamb.

The Bride the Lamb's Wife.—This testimony is positive that the New Jerusalem is the bride, the Lamb's wife. The angel told John distinctly that he would show him the bride, the Lamb's wife. We may be sure that he did not deceive him, but fulfilled his promise to the very letter. All that he did show him was the New Jerusalem, which must therefore be the Lamb's wife. It would be unnecessary to offer a word of proof that this city is not the church, were it not that popular theology has so mystified the Scriptures as to give it this application. This city cannot be the church, because it would be absurd to talk of the church as lying foursquare, and having a north side, a south side, an east side, and a west side. It would be incongruous to speak of the church as having a wall great and high, and having twelve gates, three on each side toward the four points of the compass. Indeed, the whole description of the city which is given in this chapter would be more or less obscure if applied to the church.

In writing to the Galatians, Paul speaks of the same city and says that it is the *mother of us all*, referring to the church. The church, then, is not the city itself, but the children of the city. Verse 24 of the chapter under comment, speaks of the nations of the saved, who walk in the light of this city. These nations who are the saved, and on earth constitute the church, are distinct from the city, in the light of which they walk. It follows that the city is a literal city, built of all the precious materials here described.

But how can it then be the bride, the Lamb's wife? Inspiration has seen fit to speak of it under this figure, and with every believer in the Bible that should be sufficient. The figure is first introduced in Isaiah 54. The new-covenant city is there brought to view. It is represented as being desolate while the old covenant was in force, and the Jews and old Jerusalem were the special objects of God's care. It is said to her that "the children of the desolate" shall be many more than "the children of the married wife." It is further said to her, "Thy Maker is thine husband," and the closing promise of the Lord to this city contains a description similar to the one which we have here in Revelation, namely, "I will lay thy stones with fair colors, and lay thy foundations with sapphires; and I will make thy windows of agates, and thy gates of carbuncles, and all thy borders of pleasant stones. And all thy children shall be taught of the Lord." Isaiah 54: 11-13.

It is this very promise to which Paul refers, and upon which he comments in his epistle to the Galatians, when he says, "But Jerusalem which is above is free, which is the mother of us all" (Galatians 4: 26), for he in the next verse quotes this very prophecy from the book of Isaiah to sustain his declaration. Here then Paul makes an inspired application of Isaiah's prophecy which cannot be mistaken, and in this he shows that under the figure of a "woman," a "wife" whose "children" were to be multiplied, the Lord by the prophet speaks of the New Jerusalem, the city above, as contrasted with the earthly Jerusalem in the land of Palestine. Of that city the Lord calls Himself the "husband." In addition to this, we have positive testimony to the same facts in Revelation 21.

With this view, all is harmony. Christ is called the Father of His people (Isaiah 9: 6), the Jerusalem above is called our mother, and we are called the children. Carrying out the figure of marriage, Christ is represented as the Bridegroom, the city as the bride, and we, the church, as the guests. There is not confusion of personalities here. But the popular view, which makes the city the church, and the church the bride, makes the church at the same time both mother and children, both bride and guests.

The view that the marriage of the Lamb is the inauguration of Christ as King upon the throne of David, and that the parables of Matthew 22: 1-14; 25: 1-13; Luke 12: 35-37; 19: 12-27, apply to that event, is further confirmed by a well-known ancient custom. It is said that when a person took his position as ruler over the people, and was invested with that power, it was called a marriage, and the usually accompanying feast was called a marriage supper. Adam Clarke, in his note on Matthew 22: 2, thus speaks of it:

"*A Marriage for His Son.—A marriage feast*, so the word γάμους [*gamous*] properly means. Or a feast of inauguration, when his son was put in possession of the government, and thus he and his new subjects became married together. (See 1 Kings 1: 5-9, 19, 25, etc., where such a feast is mentioned.)" [2] Many eminent critics understand this parable as indicating

[2] Adam Clarke, *Commentary on the New Testament*, Vol. I, p. 209, note on Matthew 22: 2.

the Father's induction of His Son into His Messianic kingdom.

A Christian City.—The names of the twelve apostles in the foundations of the city, show it to be a Christian and not a Jewish city. The names of the twelve tribes on the gates, show that all the saved from all ages, are reckoned as belonging to some one of the twelve tribes, for all must enter the city through some one of these twelve gates. This explains those instances in which Christians are called Israel, and are addressed as the twelve tribes, as in Romans 2: 28, 29; 9: 6-8; Galatians 3: 29; Ephesians 2: 12, 13; James 1: 1; Revelation 7: 4.

VERSE 15 And he that talked with me had a golden reed to measure the city, and the gates thereof, and the wall thereof. 16 And the city lieth foursquare, and the length is as large as the breadth: and he measured the city with the reed, twelve thousand furlongs. The length and the breadth and the height of it are equal. 17 And he measured the wall thereof, an hundred and forty and four cubits, according to the measure of a man, that is, of the angel. 18 And the building of the wall of it was of jasper: and the city was pure gold, like unto clear glass.

The City's Dimensions.—According to this testimony the city is laid out in a perfect square, measuring equally on all sides. The measure of the city, John declares, was twelve thousand furlongs. Twelve thousand furlongs, eight furlongs to the mile, equal fifteen hundred miles. It may be understood that this measure is the measure of the whole circumference of the city, not merely of one side. This appears, from Kitto, to have been the ancient method of measuring cities. The whole circumference was taken, and that was said to be the measure of the city. According to this rule, the New Jerusalem will be three hundred and seventy-five miles in length on each side. The length, breadth, and height of it are equal. From this language, the question has arisen whether the city shown to John was as high as it was long and broad. The word rendered "equal" is ἴσος, *isos*. From the definitions given by Liddell and Scott, we learn that it may be used to convey the idea of proportion: the height was proportionate to the length and breadth. Greenfield, in defining one of its cognate words, *ἰσώτης*, *isotes*, gives to it the sense of "equal proportion," and refers to 2 Corinthians 8: 13, 14, as an example where this definition is quite admissible. And this idea is strengthened by the fact that the wall was only a hundred and forty-four cubits high. Taking the cubit at about twenty-two inches, the length which is most commonly assigned to the ancient cubit, it would give only two hundred and sixty-four feet as the height of the wall. Now if the city is just as high as it is long and broad, that is, three hundred and seventy-five miles, this wall of less than three hundred feet would be in comparison a most insignificant affair. Probably therefore the height of the buildings of the city is to be judged by the height of the wall, which is distinctly given.

The building of the wall was of jasper. This precious stone is usually described as of "a beautiful bright green color, sometimes clouded with white or spotted with yellow." This we understand to be the material of the main body of the wall built upon the twelve foundations hereafter described. Let it be remembered that this jasper wall was "clear as crystal" (verse 11), revealing all the glories within.

VERSE 19 And the foundations of the wall of the city were garnished with all manner of precious stones. The first foundation was jasper; the second, sapphire; the third, a chalcedony; the fourth, an emerald; 20 the fifth, sardonyx; the sixth, sardius; the seventh, chrysolite; the eighth, beryl; the ninth, a topaz; the tenth, a chrysoprasus; the eleventh, a jacinth; the twelfth, an amethyst.

A Literal City.—If we consider this description exclusively metaphorical, as is done by many who profess to be Bible teachers, and spiritualize away this city into ethereal nothingness, how unmeaning do these minute descriptions appear! But if we take it in its natural and obvious signification, and look upon the city as the prophet evidently intended, as a literal and tangible abode, our glorious inheritance, the beauties of which we are to look upon with our own eyes, how the glory of the scene is enhanced!

Though it is not for mortal man of himself to conceive of the grandeur of the things which God has prepared for those who love Him, yet viewed as a literality, men may delight to contemplate the glories of their future abode. We love to dwell upon those descriptions which convey to our minds an idea of the loveliness and beauty which will characterize our eternal home. As we become absorbed in the contemplation of an inheritance tangible and sure, courage springs up anew, hope revives, faith plumes her wings. With feelings of thanksgiving to God that He has placed it within our power to gain an entrance to the mansions of the redeemed, we resolve anew, despite the world and all its obstacles, that we will be among the sharers in the proffered joy. Let us, then, look at the precious foundation stones of that great city, through whose gates of pearl God's people may hope soon to enter. While many gemmologists assert that it is difficult to identify the precious stones of the Bible, the following interesting tabulation by Moses Stuart will give some idea of the beauty and variety of colors in the foundation.

The Glorious Foundation.—"The word *adorned* [garnished], may raise a doubt here whether the writer means to say that into the various courses of the foundation ornamental precious stones were only here and there inserted. But taking the whole description together, I do not apprehend this to have been his meaning.

"*Jasper*, as we have seen above, is usually a stone of green, transparent color, with red veins. But there are many varieties.

"*Sapphire* is of a beautiful azure, or sky-blue, color, almost as transparent and glittering as a diamond.

"*Chalcedony* seems to be a species of agate, or more properly the onyx. The onyx of the ancients was probably of a bluish white, and semipellucid.

"The *emerald* was of a vivid green, and next to the ruby in hardness.

"*Sardonyx* is a mixture of chalcedony and cornelian, which last is of a flesh-color.

"*Sardius* is probably the cornelian. Sometimes, however, the red is quite vivid.

"*Chrysolithe*, as its name imports, is of a yellow or gold color, and is pellucid. From this was probably taken the conception of the pellucid gold which constitutes the material of the city.

"*Beryl* is of a sea-green color.

"The *topaz* of the present day seems to be reckoned as yellow; but that of the ancients appears to have been pale green. . . .

"*Chrysopras*, of a pale yellow and greenish color, like a scallion; sometimes it is classed at the present day under topaz.

"*Hyacinth* [jacinth] of a deep red or violet color.

"*Amethyst*, a gem of great hardness and brilliancy, of a violet color, and usually found in India.

"In looking over these various classes, we find the first four to be of a green or bluish cast; the fifth and sixth, of a red or scarlet; the seventh, yellow; the eighth, ninth, and tenth, of different shades of the lighter green; the eleventh and twelfth of a scarlet or splendid red. There is a classification, therefore, in this arrangement; a mixture not dissimilar to the arrangement in the rainbow, with the exception that it is more complex."[3]

VERSE 21 And the twelve gates were twelve pearls; every several gate was of one pearl: and the street of the city was pure gold, as it were transparent glass.

Gates of Pearl.—The beautiful city of God, built of materials most precious here on earth, is very appropriately described as having gates of pearl. But more than that, the scripture says that each gate is of a single pearl. Irridescent and glowing with the beautiful colors reflected from the foundations, these portals swing wide to welcome the redeemed to their eternal home.

Streets of Burnished Gold.—In this verse, as also in verse 18, the city is spoken of as built of gold, pure, like clear glass, that is, transparent glass. Think for a moment what the appearance of a street so paved would be. The gorgeous palaces on

---

[3] Moses Stuart, *A Commentary on the Apocalypse*, Vol. II, pp. 383, 384.

either side would be reflected beneath, and the boundless expanse of the heavens above would also appear below; so that to the person walking those golden streets it would appear that both he himself and the city were suspended between the infinite heights above and the unfathomable depths below, while the mansions on either side of the street, having also powers of reflection, would marvelously multiply both palaces and people, and would render the whole scene novel, pleasing, beautiful, and grand beyond conception.

VERSE 22 And I saw no temple therein: for the Lord God Almighty and the Lamb are the temple of it.

The Living Temple.—With a temple is naturally associated the idea of sacrifices and mediatorial work, but when the city is located upon the new earth, there will be no such work to be performed. Sacrifices and offerings, and all mediatorial work based on them, will be forever past. Hence there will be no need of the outward symbol of such work. But the temple in old Jerusalem, besides being a place for sacrificial worship, was the beauty and glory of the place. As if to anticipate the question that might arise as to what would constitute the ornament and glory of the new city if there is to be no temple therein, the prophet answers, "The Lord God Almighty and the Lamb are the temple of it."

VERSE 23 And the city had no need of the sun, neither of the moon, to shine in it: for the glory of God did lighten it, and the Lamb is the light thereof. 24 And the nations of them which are saved shall walk in the light of it: and the kings of the earth do bring their glory and honor into it. 25 And the gates of it shall not be shut at all by day: for there shall be no night there. 26 And they shall bring the glory and honor of the nations into it. 27 And there shall in no wise enter into it anything that defileth, neither whatsoever worketh abomination, or maketh a lie: but they which are written in the Lamb's book of life.

No Night There.—It is in the city alone, probably, that there is no night. There will of course be days and nights in the new earth, but they will be days and nights of surpassing glory. In speaking of this time, the prophet says, "Moreover, the light of the moon shall be as the light of the sun, and the light of the sun shall be sevenfold, as the light of seven days, in the day that the Lord bindeth up the breach of His people, and healeth the stroke of their wound." Isaiah 30: 26. But if the light of the moon in that state is as the light of the sun, how can there be said to be night there? The light of the sun will be sevenfold, so that although the night is to be as our day, the day will be sevenfold brighter, making the contrast between day and night there as marked, perhaps, as at the present time. Both will be surpassingly glorious.

Verse 24 speaks of nations and kings. The nations are the nations of the saved, and in the new-earth state we are all kings in a certain sense. We possess a "kingdom," and are to "reign" forever and ever.

But it appears from some of our Saviour's parables, as in Matthew 25: 21, 23, that some will occupy in a special sense the position of rulers, and may thus be spoken of as kings of the earth in connection with the nations of the saved. These bring their glory and honor into the city, when on the Sabbaths and new moons they there come up to worship before God. (Isaiah 66: 23.)

Reader, do you want a part in the eternal glories of this heavenly city? See to it, then, that your name is written in the Lamb's book of life; for those only whose names are on that heavenly "roll of honor" can enter there.

THE HOME OF THE SAVED

Hail Earth renewed! Celestial Paradise!
Fit dwelling place, with all thy loveliness,
Thy long reproach for ever wiped away,
And fairer now than when at first thy God
Pronounced thee good—fit dwelling place, so pure,
So beauteous, so adorned with smiling peace,
For all the saints, all the redeemed of men;
Who through thy gates, immortal City fair,
Thy gates of pearl, will freely enter in,
Where violence and riot never come,
And walk thy bright and dazzling streets of gold;
And to the stream of life, the crystal stream
Fast by the throne of God, have access free;
And from the tree of life, high arching o'er,
Pluck the eternal fruit and eat and live;
And in Thy glad'ning smiles, O King of saints!
Glory unspeakable possess; for in
Thy presence bright, there fullness is of joy,
At Thy right hand, pleasures for ever more.

From the poem "The Warning Voice of Time and Prophecy," by Uriah Smith.)

 FRANKLIN BOOTH, ARTIST

"THEY SHALL SEE HIS FACE"

Truly the greatest joy that will come to the redeemed will be to look upon the blessed face of their beloved Redeemer.

CHAPTER XXII

PEACE AT LAST

VERSE 1 And he showed me a pure river of water of life, clear as crystal, proceeding out of the throne of God and of the Lamb. 2 In the midst of the street of it, and on either side of the river, was there the tree of life, which bare twelve manner of fruits, and yielded her fruit every month: and the leaves of the tree were for the healing of the nations.

THE ANGEL continues to show John the wonderful things of the city of God. In the midst of the street of the city was the tree of life.

The Broad Street.—Although the word "street" is here used in the singular number with the definite article "the" before it, it is not supposed that there is but one street in the city, for there are twelve gates, and there must of course be a street leading to each gate. But the street here spoken of is *the* street by way of distinction, the main street, or, as the original word signifies, the broad way, the great avenue.

The River of Life.—The tree of life is in the midst of this street, but is on either side of the river of life. Therefore the river of life is also in the midst of the street of the city. This river proceeds from the throne of God. The picture thus presented before the mind is this: The glorious throne of God at the head of this broad way, or avenue; out of that throne the river of life, flowing lengthwise through the center of the street; and the tree of life growing on either side, forming a high and magnificent arch over that majestic stream, and spreading its life-bearing branches far away on either side. How wide this broad street is, we have no means of determining, but it will be at once perceived that a city three hundred seventy-five miles square, would have an ample space for its great avenue.

The Tree of Life.—But how can the tree of life be but one tree, and still be on either side of the river? It is evident that there is but one tree of life. From Genesis to the Revelation it is spoken of as but one—*the* tree of life. To be at once on both sides of the river, it must have more than one trunk, in which case it would be united above in order to form but one tree. John, caught away in the Spirit, and presented with a minute view of this wonderful object, says that it was on either side of the river.

The tree of life bears twelve kinds of fruit, and yields its fruit every month. This fact throws light upon the declaration in Isaiah 66: 23, that all flesh shall come up "from one new moon to another" to worship before the Lord of hosts. The Greek phrase in the verse before us is κατὰ μῆνα ἕκαστον, *kata mena hekaston*, "each month."

The Septuagint has here μὴν ἐκ μηνός, *men ek menos*, "from month to month." The redeemed come up to the holy city from month to month to partake of the fruit of the tree of life. Its leaves are for the healing of the nations,—literally, the *service* of the nations. This cannot be understood as implying that any will enter the city in a diseased or deformed condition to need healing; for then the conclusion would follow that there will always be persons there in that condition, as we have no reason to understand that the service of the leaves, whatever it is, will not be perpetual, like the use of the fruit. But the idea of disease and deformity in the immortal state is contrary to the express declarations of Scripture. "The inhabitant shall not say, I am sick." Isaiah 33: 24.

VERSE 3 And there shall be no more curse: but the throne of God and of the Lamb shall be in it; and His servants shall serve Him.

This language proves that the great God, the Father, is referred to, as well as the Son. The marks of the curse, the deadly miasma, and the ghastly scenes of desolation and decay, will no more be seen on the earth. Every breeze will be balmy and life-giving, every scene beauty, and every sound music.

VERSE 4 And they shall see His face; and His name shall be in their foreheads.

The word "His," in the sentence, "They shall see His face," refers to the Father; for He is the one whose name is in their foreheads. That it is the Father, we learn from Revelation 14: 1. This will be a fulfillment of the promise in Matthew 5: 8, "Blessed are the pure in heart: for they shall see God."

VERSE 5 And there shall be no night there; and they need no candle, neither light of the sun; for the Lord God giveth them light: and they shall reign forever and ever. 6 And he said unto me, These sayings are faithful and true: and the Lord God of the holy prophets sent His angel to show unto His servants the things which must shortly be done. 7 Behold, I come quickly: blessed is he that keepeth the sayings of the prophecy of this book.

Here, again, we have the declaration that there shall be no night in the city, for the Lord God will be the light of the place. Christ Himself, through whom all these revelations have come, repeats the promise which has been the hope of men through the ages, "Behold, I come quickly." To keep the sayings of the prophecy of this book is to obey the injunctions connected with the prophecy, as, for instance, in Revelation 14: 9-12.

VERSE 8 And I John saw these things, and heard them. And when I had heard and seen, I fell down to worship before the feet of the angel which showed me these things. 9 Then saith he unto me, See thou do it not: for I am thy fellow servant, and of thy brethren the prophets, and of them which keep the sayings of this book: worship God. 10 And he saith unto me, Seal not the sayings of the prophecy of this book: for the time is at hand. 11 He that is unjust, let him be unjust still: and he which is filthy, let him be filthy still: and he that is righteous, let him be righteous still: and he that is holy, let him be holy still. 12 And, behold, I come quickly; and My reward is with Me, to give every man according as his work shall be.

For remarks on verses 8 and 9, see comments on Revelation 19: 10. In verse 10 John is told not to seal the sayings of the prophecy of this book. The popular theology of our day says that the book is sealed. One of two things follows from this: either John disobeyed his instructions, or the theology above referred to is viewing the matter with closed eyes, in "the spirit of deep sleep." (Read Isaiah 29: 10-14.) Verse 11 proves that probation closes and the cases of all are unalterably fixed before the coming of Christ; for in the next verse

© SOUTHERN PUBLISHING ASSN. FRANKLIN BOOTH, ARTIST

THE TREE AND THE RIVER OF LIFE

"Eye hath not seen, nor ear heard, neither have entered into the heart of man, the things which God hath prepared for them that love Him." 1 Corinthians 2:9.

Christ says, "Behold, I come quickly." What presumption, then, to claim, as some do, that there will be probation even after that event! Christ's reward is with Him, to give every man as his work shall be. This is another conclusive proof that there can be no probation after that event. All the living wicked, those "that know not God," the heathen, and those "that obey not the gospel of our Lord Jesus Christ," the sinners of Christian lands (2 Thessalonians 1: 8), will be visited with swift destruction from Him who then comes in flaming fire to take vengeance on His foes.

The declaration of verse 11 marks the close of probation, which is the close of Christ's work as mediator. But we are taught by the subject of the sanctuary that this work closes with the examination of the cases of the living in the investigative judgment. When this is accomplished, the irrevocable fiat can be pronounced.

VERSE 13 I am Alpha and Omega, the beginning and the end, the first and the last. 14 Blessed are they that do His commandments, that they may have right to the tree of life, and may enter in through the gates into the city.

Christ here gives to Himself the appellation of Alpha and Omega, the beginning and the end, the first and the last. Verse 14, as before noticed, is the language of Christ. The commandments of which He speaks are His Father's.

Keeping His Commandments.—Reference here must be to the ten commandments as delivered on Mt. Sinai. He pronounces a blessing upon those who keep them. Thus in the closing chapter of the word of God, and near the very close of the last testimony which the faithful and true Witness there left for His people, He solemnly pronounces a blessing upon those who keep the commandments of God. Let those who believe in the abolition of the law, candidly consider the decisive bearing of this important fact.

Instead of the reading, "Blessed are they that do His commandments," some translations, including the Revised Version, have, "Blessed are they that wash their robes." On this point Alford has this note: "The difference in the readings is curious, being in the original that between *poiountes tas entolas autou*, and *plunontes tas stolas auton*, either of which might easily be mistaken for the other."[1] In view of the fact that the words and letters in these two phrases are so strikingly alike, it is not surprising that this difference of reading is found. But there seems to be good evidence that the first is the original, from which the latter is a variation by the error of transcribers. Thus the Syriac New Testament, one of the very earliest translations from the original Greek, reads according to the Authorized Version. And Cyprian, whose writings antedate any extant Greek manuscript, quotes the text as reading, "Blessed are they that do His commandments."[2] We may therefore safely consider this as the genuine reading.

VERSE 15 For without are dogs, and sorcerers, and whoremongers, and murderers, and idolaters, and whosoever loveth and maketh a lie.

Dog is the Bible symbol of a shameless and impudent man. Who would wish to be left in the company of those whose lot is outside the city of God? Yet how many will stand condemned as idolaters, how many as those who make lies, and how many more as those who love them, and love to circulate them after they are made!

VERSE 16 I Jesus have sent Mine angel to testify unto you these things in the churches. I am the root and the offspring of David, and the bright and morning star.

Jesus testifies these things in the churches, showing that the entire book of Revelation is given to the seven churches, which is another incidental proof that the seven churches are representatives of the church through the entire gospel age. Christ is the offspring of David, in that He appeared on earth in the line of David's descendants. He is the root of David, inasmuch as He is the great prototype of David, and the maker and upholder of all things.

---

[1] Henry Alford, *The New Testament for English Readers*, note on Revelation 22: 14, Vol. II, part II, p. 1100.

[2] "The Treatises of Cyprian," XII, *The Ante-Nicene Fathers*, Vol. V, p. 525.

VERSE 17 And the Spirit and the bride say, Come. And let him that neareth say, Come. And let him that is athirst come. And whosoever will, let him take the water of life freely.

The Invitation to Come.—Thus are all invited to come. The Lord's love for mankind would not be satisfied in merely preparing the blessings of eternal life, opening the way to them, and announcing that all might come who would; but He sends out an earnest invitation to come. He sets it forth as a favor done to Himself if those invited will come and partake of the infinite blessings provided by His infinite love. His invitation, how gracious, how full, how free! None of those who are finally lost will ever have occasion to complain that the provisions made for their salvation were not sufficiently ample. They can never reasonably object that the light given to show them the way of life was not sufficiently clear. They can never excuse themselves on the ground that the invitations and entreaties that Mercy has given them to turn and live, were not sufficiently full and free. From the very beginning, there has been a power exerted as strong as could be exerted and still leave man his own free agent,—a power to draw him heavenward, and raise him from the abyss into which he has fallen. "Come!" has been the entreaty of the Spirit from the lips of God Himself, from the lips of His prophets, from the lips of His apostles, and from the lips of His Son, even while, in His infinite compassion and humility, He was paying the debt of our transgression.

The last message of mercy as it is now going forth, is another and final utterance of divine long-suffering and compassion. Come, is the invitation it gives. Come, for all things are ready. The last sound that will fall from Mercy's lips on the ear of the sinner before the thunders of vengeance burst upon him, will be the heavenly invitation, Come. So great is the loving-kindness of a merciful God to rebellious man.

Yet they will not come. Acting independently and deliberately, they refuse to come. So when they shall see Abraham, Isaac, and Jacob in the kingdom of God, and themselves thrust out, they will have no one to accuse, no one to blame, but themselves. They will be brought to feel this in all its bitterness, for the time will come when Robert Pollok's thrilling description of the condemnation of the lost will be true to the letter:

"And evermore the thunders, murmuring, spoke
From out the darkness, uttering loud these words,
Which every guilty conscience echoed back:
'Ye knew your duty, but ye did it not.'
Dread words! that barred excuse, and threw the weight
Of every man's perdition on himself,
Directly home. . . .
'Ye knew your duty, but ye did it not!' "[3]

The bride also says, Come. But the bride is the city, and how does it say, Come? If we could be strengthened to behold the living glories of that city and live, and should be permitted to gaze upon its dazzling beauty, and be assured that we had a perfect right to enter therein, and revel in its glory forever and ever, would it not then say to us, Come, with a persuasion which no power could resist? Who of us, in view of this, could turn away, and say, I have no desire for an inheritance there?

But though we cannot now look upon that city, the unfailing word of God has promised it, and that is sufficient to inspire us with implicit and living faith. Through the channel of that faith it says to us, Come. Come, if you would inherit mansions where sickness, sorrow, pain, and death can never enter; if you would have a right to the tree of life, and pluck its immortal fruit, and eat and live; if you would drink of the water of the river of life, that flows from the throne of God, clear as crystal. Come, if you would obtain through those glittering gates of pearl an abundant entrance into the eternal city; if you would walk its streets of transparent gold; if you would behold its glowing foundation stones; if you would see the King in His beauty on His throne. Come, if you would sing the jubilee song of millions, and share their joy. Come, if

[3] Robert Pollok, *The Course of Time*, book IX.

you would join the anthems of the redeemed with their melodious harps, and know that your exile is forever over, and this is your eternal home. Come, if you would receive a palm of victory, and know that you are forever free. Come, if you would exchange the furrows of your care-worn brow for a jeweled crown. Come, if you would see the salvation of the ransomed myriads, the glorified throng which no man can number. Come, if you would drink from the pure fountain of celestial bliss, if you would shine as the stars forever in the firmament of glory, if you would share in the unutterable rapture that fills the triumphant hosts as they behold before them unending ages of glory ever brightening and joys ever new.

The bride *does* say, Come. Who of us can resist the invitation? The word of truth is pledged to us that if we keep the commandments of God and the faith of Jesus, we *shall* have right to the tree of life, we *shall* enter in through the gates into the city. We shall feel that we are at home in our Father's house, the very mansions prepared for us, and realize the full truth of the cheering words, "Blessed are they which are called unto the marriage supper of the Lamb." Revelation 19: 9.

"Let him that heareth say, Come." We have heard of the glory, of the beauty, of the blessings, of that goodly land, and we say, Come. We have heard of the river with its verdant banks, of the tree with its healing leaves, of the bowers that bloom in the Paradise of God, and we say, Come. Whosoever will, let him come, and take of the water of life freely.

VERSE 18 For I testify unto every man that heareth the words of the prophecy of this book, If any man shall add unto these things, God shall add unto him the plagues that are written in this book: 19 and if any man shall take away from the words of the book of this prophecy, God shall take away his part out of the book of life, and out of the holy city, and from the things which are written in this book.

What is it to add to, or take from, the book of this prophecy? Let it be borne in mind that it is the book of this prophecy, or the Revelation, which is the subject of remark; hence the words in regard to adding to or taking from have exclusive

 FRANKLIN BOOTH, ARTIST

THE BLESSED INVITATION

Heaven's invitation is today, just as it was in Galilee, Come unto Me. Come, dear reader, come now.

reference to this book. Nothing can be called an addition except something added to it with the intention of having it considered as a genuine part of the book of Revelation. To take from the book would be to suppress some part of it. As the book of Revelation could not be called an addition to the book of Daniel, so if God should see fit to make further revelations to us by His Spirit, it would be no addition to the book of Revelation unless it should claim to be a part of that book.

VERSE 20 He which testifieth these things saith, Surely I come quickly. Amen. Even so, come, Lord Jesus. 21 The grace of our Lord Jesus Christ be with you all. Amen.

The word of God is given to instruct us in reference to the plan of salvation. The second coming of Christ is to be the climax and completion of that great plan. It is most appropriate, therefore, that the book should close with the solemn announcement, "Surely I come quickly." Be it ours to join with fervent hearts in the response of the apostle, "Amen. Even so, come, Lord Jesus."

Thus closes the volume of inspiration—closes with that which constitutes the best of all promises, and the substance of the Christian's hope, the return of Christ. Then shall the elect be gathered, and bid a long farewell to all the ills of this mortal life. How rich in all that is precious to the Christian is this promise! Wandering an exile in this evil world, separated from the few of like precious faith, he longs for the companionship of the righteous, the communion of saints. Here he shall obtain it, for all the good shall be gathered, not from one land only, but from all lands; not from one age only, but from all ages—the great harvest of all the good, coming up in long and glorious procession, while angels shout the harvest home, and the timbrels of heaven sound forth in joyous concert. A song before unheard, unknown, in the universe, the song of the redeemed, shall add its thrilling notes of rapture and melody to the universal jubilee. So shall the saints be gathered, to be joyful in one another's presence forever and ever—

"While the glory of God, like a molten sea,
Bathes the immortal company."

This gathering has nothing in it but that which is desirable. The saints can but sigh and pray for it. Like Job, they cry out for the presence of God. Like David, they cannot be satisfied till they awake in His likeness. In this mortal condition we groan, being burdened, not for that we would be "unclothed, but clothed upon." We can but be "upon tiptoe" for the adoption, to wit, the redemption of the body. Our eyes are open for its visions, our ears are waiting to catch the sounds of the heavenly music, and our hearts are beating in anticipation of its infinite joy. Our appetites are growing sharp for the marriage supper. We cry out for the living God, and long to come into His presence. Come, Lord Jesus, come quickly. No tidings more welcome than the announcement that the command has gone forth from the Lord to His angels, "Gather together unto Me My elect from the four winds of heaven."

The place of gathering has nothing but attraction. Jesus, the fairest among ten thousand, is there. The throne of God and of the Lamb, in the glory of which the sun disappears as the stars vanish in the light of day, is there. The city of jasper and gold, whose builder and maker is God, is there. The river of life, sparkling with the glory of God and flowing from His throne in infinite purity and peace, is there. The tree of life, with its healing leaves and life-giving fruit, is there. Abraham, Isaac, and Jacob, Noah, Job, and Daniel, prophets, apostles, and martyrs, the perfection of heavenly society, will be there. Visions of beauty are there; fields of living green, flowers that never fade, streams that never dry, products in variety that never ends, fruits that never decay, crowns that never dim, harps that know no discord, and all else of which a taste purified from sin and raised to the plane of immortality, can form any conception or think desirable, all these will be there.

Benediction.—We must be there. We must bask in the forgiving smiles of God, to whom we have become reconciled, and sin no more. We must have access to that exhaustless fount of vitality, the fruit of the tree of life, and never die. We must repose under the shadow of its leaves, which are for the service of the nations, and never again grow weary. We must drink from the life-giving fountain, and thirst nevermore; we must bathe in its silvery spray, and be refreshed; we must walk on its golden sands, and feel that we are no longer exiles. We must exchange the cross for the crown, and feel that the days of our humiliation are ended. We must lay down the staff and take the palm branch, and feel that the journey is done. We must put off the garments of our warfare for the white robes of triumph, and feel that the conflict is ended and the victory gained. We must exchange the toilworn, dusty raiment of our pilgrimage for the glorious vesture of immortality, and feel that sin and the curse can nevermore pollute us. O day of rest and triumph, and every good, delay not thy dawning. Let the angels be quickly sent to gather the elect. Let the promise be fulfilled which bears in its train these matchless glories.

EVEN SO, COME, LORD JESUS.

"The prophecy came not in old time by the will of man: but holy men of God spake as they were moved by the Holy Ghost."
2 Peter 1: 21.

BIBLIOGRAPHY

BOOKS

Abbott, Lyman, and Conant, T. J., eds. *A Dictionary of Religious Knowledge.* New York: Harper and Bros., 1902.

Abbott-Smith, G. *A Manual Greek Lexicon of the New Testament.* New York: Charles Scribner's Sons, 1922.

Adams, George Burton. *Civilization During the Middle Ages.* New York: Charles Scribner's Sons, 1898.

Alford, Henry. *The New Testament for English Readers.* New edition. Boston: Lee and Shepard, 1875.

Alison, Sir Archibald. *History of Europe from the Commencement of the French Revolution in 1789 to the Restoration of the Bourbons in 1815.* Ninth edition. London: William Blackwood and Sons, 1854.

The American Tract Society. "Some Memorials of Edward Lee." Tract No. 379. *The Publications of the American Tract Society.* Vol. XI. New York: The American Tract Society, [n.d.]

Andrews, Samuel J. *Life of Our Lord upon the Earth.* New York: Charles Scribner, 1862.

Annals of Congress. See U. S. Congress.

The Ante-Nicene Fathers. Edited by Alexander Roberts and James Donaldson. Revised by A. Cleveland Coxe. Authorized edition. New York: Charles Scribner's Sons, 1899.

Arnold, Edwin. *Poetical Works.* Boston: Roberts Bros., 1889.

Barber, John W., *Connecticut Historical Collections.* Second edition. New Haven: Durrie & Peck and J. W. Barber, 1836.

Barker, J. Ellis. *The Great Problems of British Statesmanship.* London: John Murray, 1917.

Barker, William B. *Lares and Penates.* London: Ingram, Cooke and Co., 1853.

Barnes, Albert. *Notes: Critical, Illustrative, and Practical, on the Book of Daniel.* New York: Leavitt and Allen, 1859.

Notes, Explanatory and Practical, on the Book of Revelation. Carefully revised and corrected. London: George Routledge and Co., 1852.

Baudrillart, Alfred. *The Catholic Church, the Renaissance, and Protestantism.* London: Kegan Paul, Trench, Trubner and Co., 1908.

Bayford, John. *Messiah's Kingdom,* or a Brief Inquiry concerning what is revealed in Scripture relative to the fact, the time, the signs, and the circumstances of the second advent of the Lord Jesus Christ. London: Printed for the Author, 1820.

BEECHER, CHARLES. *Redeemer and Redeemed, an Investigation of the Atonement and of Eternal Judgment.* Boston: Lee and Shepard, 1864.

BELLORD, JAMES. *A New Catechism of Christian Doctrine and Practice*, American Edition, Authorized. Notre Dame, Indiana: The Ave Maria, 1907.

BENSON, JOSEPH. *The New Testament of Our Lord and Saviour Jesus Christ . . . With Critical, Explanatory, and Practical Notes.* New York: T. Carlton and J. Porter. [n.d.]

BLISS, S. *Analysis of Sacred Chronology.* Revised, with notes. Oakland, California: Pacific Press Publishing House, 1887.

BLOOMFIELD, S. T. *The Greek Testament With English Notes, Critical, Philological, and Exegetical.* First American from the second London edition. Boston: Perkins and Marvin, 1837.

BLUNT, HENRY. *A Practical Exposition of the Epistles to the Seven Churches of Asia.* Fifth edition. London: J. Hatchard & Son, Hamilton, Adams, and Co., 1845.

BOWER, ARCHIBALD. *The History of the Popes From the Foundation of the See of Rome to A. D. 1758;* With an Introduction and a Continuation to the Present Time, by Samuel Hanson Cox. Philadelphia: Griffith and Simon, 1847.

BROCK, MOURANT. *Glorification.* London: James Nisbet and Co., 1845.

BROOKS, J. W. *Elements of Prophetical Interpretation.* Philadelphia: Orrin Rogers, 1841.

BURR, ENOCH FITCH. *Ecce Coelum*, or Parish Astronomy. Twenty-first edition. New York: American Tract Society, 1867.

BUTLER, JAMES. *The Most Rev. Dr. James Butler's Catechism.* New York: P. J. Kennedy, 1887.

BURRITT, ELIJAH H. *The Geography of the Heavens.* A new edition, revised and illustrated by Hiram Mattison. New York: F. J. Huntington, 1853.

CAFFERATA, H. CANON. *The Catechism Simply Explained.* St. Louis, Mo.: B. Herder Book Co., 1932.

Cambridge Ancient History. New York: The Macmillan Co., 1929.

Cambridge Bible for Schools and Colleges. The Book of Daniel, With Introduction and Notes by S. R. Driver. Edited for the Syndics of the University Press by A. F. Kirkpatrick. Cambridge: University Press, 1900.

Cambridge Medieval History. New York: The Macmillan Co., 1936.

Cambridge Modern History. New York: The Macmillan Co., 1936.

CAMPBELL, ALEXANDER. *Christian Baptism With Its Antecedents and Consequences.* Bethany, Va.: Alexander Campbell, 1853.

CAMPBELL, J. M. *The Everlasting Gospel.* Greenoch: R. K. Lush, 1830.

Catechism of Christian Doctrine, No. 2, Prepared and Enjoined by Order of the Third Plenary Council of Baltimore. New York: The Paulist Press, 1929.

Catechism of the Council of Trent. Translated by J. Donovan. Dublin: James Duffy, Sons and Co. [pref. 1829.]

Catholic Encyclopedia. New York: Robert Appleton Co., 1909.

CHALLONER, RICHARD. *The Catholic Christian Instructed*. Baltimore: Metropolitan Press, 1844.

CHURCH, RICHARD W. *The Beginning of the Middle Ages*. New York: Charles Scribner's Sons, 1887.

CLARKE, ADAM. *The Holy Bible, With a Commentary and Critical Notes. The Old Testament*. New York: Lane and Scott, 1850.

The New Testament of Our Lord and Saviour Jesus Christ, With a Commentary and Critical Notes. A new edition. New York: George Lane and Levi Scott, 1851.

CLEMENT, CLARA ERSKINE. *Egypt*. Boston: D. Lothrop & Co., 1880.

Codex Justiniani, lib. 1, tit. 1; translation as given in *The Petrine Claims*, R. F. Littledale, p. 293. London: Society for Promoting Christian Knowledge, 1889.

COLEMAN, CHRISTOPHER B. *Constantine the Great and Christianity*. New York: The Columbia University Press, 1914.

The Treatise of Lorenzo Valla on the Donation of Constantine. New Haven: Yale University Press, 1922.

COOK, F. C. *The Bible Commentary. New Testament*. New York: Charles Scribner's Sons, 1890.

CORMACK, GEORGE. *Egypt in Asia, a Plain Account of Pre-Biblical Syria and Palestine*. London: Adam and Charles Black, 1908.

CORMENIN, LOUIS MARIE DE. *The Public and Private History of the Popes of Rome*. Translated from the French. Philadelphia: James M. Campbell, 1847.

Corpus Juris Canonici. Lyones, 1622.

Cottage Bible and Family Expositor; Containing the Old and New Testaments, With Practical Expositions and Explanatory Notes by Thomas Williams. . . . Edited by William Patton. Hartford: Case, Tiffany and Co., 1853.

CRANSTON, EARL. *The Church and the Government*. Washington, D. C., 1910.

CROLY, GEORGE. *The Apocalypse of St. John*. Second edition, revised. London: C. and J. Rivington, 1828.

CRUDEN, ALEXANDER. *A Complete Concordance to the Holy Scriptures*. New edition. New York: Fleming H. Revell Co. [n.d.]

CUNINGHAME, WILLIAM. *A Dissertation on the Seals and Trumpets of the Apocalypse and the Prophetical Period of 1260 Years*. Fourth edition, corrected and enlarged. London: Thomas Cadell, et al., 1843.

CUSA, NICHOLAS KREBS VON. *Conjectures of Cardinal Nicholas von Cusa Concerning the Last Days.*

D'AUBIGNE, See MERLE D'AUBIGNE, JEAN HENRI.

DAVIDSON, BENJAMIN. *The Analytical Hebrew and Chaldee Lexicon.* London: Samuel Bagster and Sons. [n.d.]

Dialogues on Prophecy. London: James Nisbet, 1828.

DODDRIDGE, PHILIP. *The Family Expositor: or a Paraphrase and Version of the New Testament, With Critical Notes.* Seventh edition. London: T. Longman, *et al.*, 1792.

DOWLING, JOHN. *The History of Romanism, From the Earliest Corruptions of Christianity.* A new edition. New York: Edward Walker, 1871.

DUNKIN, EDWIN. *The Heavens and the Earth.*

DUPIN, LOUIS ELLIES. *Bibliotheca Patrum: or, A New History of Ecclesiastical Writers.* London: Abel Swal and Tim. Childe, 1693.

DURUY, VICTOR. *The History of the Middle Ages.* Translated from the twelfth edition by E. H. and M. D. Whitney, with notes and revisions by George Burton Adams. New York: Henry Holt and Co., 1891.

EADIE, JOHN. *Biblical Cyclopædia.* New edition, revised. London: Charles Griffin and Co. [pref. 1901.]

ELLIOTT, EDWARD B. *Horæ Apocalypticæ.* Second edition, carefully revised. London: Seeley, Burnside, and Seeley, 1846.

EMERTON, EPHRAIM. *Introduction to the Study of the Middle Ages* (375-814). New York: Ginn and Co., 1916.

Encyclopædia Americana. Philadelphia: Lea and Blanchard, 1849.

Encyclopædia Britannica. Eleventh edition. New York: The Encyclopædia Britannica Co., 1910.

EVERETT, EDWARD. "Oration Delivered at Plymouth, December 22, 1824." *Orations and Speeches on Various Occasions.* Boston: American Stationer's Co., 1836.

FARRAR, F. W. *The Early Days of Christianity.* Author's edition. New York: Cassell, Petter, Galpin and Co. [pref. 1882.]

Federal Council of the Churches of Christ in America. *Report of the First Meeting of the Federal Council, Philadelphia, 1908.* Edited by Elias B. Sanford. New York: The Revell Press, 1909.

FERRARIS, LUCIUS. *Prompta Bibliotheca.* Venice: Gaspar Storti, 1772.
Prompta Bibliotheca. Rome, 1890.

FINDLAY, JAMES ARTHUR. *The Rock of Truth, or Spiritualism, the Coming World Religion.* Philadelphia: David McKay Co., 1933.

FOGG, WALTER. *One Thousand Sayings of History.* Boston: The Beacon Press, Inc., 1929.

Geddes, Michael. "A View of the Court of Inquisition in Portugal." *Miscellaneous Tracts*. Third edition. Vol. I. London: B. Barker, *et al.*, 1730.

Gesenius, William. *A Hebrew and English Lexicon of the Old Testament*, including the Biblical Chaldee. Translated by Edward Robinson. Twentieth edition. Boston: Crocker and Brewster. [n.d.]

Gibbon, Edward. *The History of the Decline and Fall of the Roman Empire*. Edited by H. H. Milman. A new edition. New York: Harper and Bros. [pref. 1845.]

The Student's Gibbon. Abridged by William Smith. New York: Harper and Bros., 1884.

Gilkey, James Gordon. *A Faith to Affirm*. New York: The Macmillan Co., 1940.

Greenfield, William. *The Polymicrian Greek Lexicon to the New Testament*. Philadelphia: Henry Perkins, 1848. (Bound with his Novum Testamentum, Greek.)

Hales, William. *A New Analysis of Chronology and Geography, History and Prophecy*. Second edition, corrected and improved. London: C. J. G. and F. Rivington, 1830.

Harduin, P. Joannis. *Acta Conciliorum*. Paris: Typographia Regia, 1714.

Henry, Matthew. *A Commentary on the Old and New Testaments*. New and illustrated edition. Louisville, Kentucky: Baptist Book Concern. [pref. 1710.]

Herodotus. Translated by Henry Cary. London: G. Bell and Sons, 1917.

Hislop, Alexander. *The Two Babylons*. Popular edition. London: S. W. Partridge and Co., 1907.

History of the International Reform Bureau. See International Reform Bureau.

Hodgkin, Thomas. *Theodoric the Goth, the Barbaric Champion of Civilization*. New York: G. P. Putnam's Sons, 1891.

International Reform Bureau. *Patriotic Studies of a Quarter Century of Moral Legislation in Congress . . . 1888-1911*. Edited by Wilbur F. Crafts. Washington, D. C.: International Reform Bureau, 1911.

Jeans, James H. *The Stars in Their Courses*. New York: The Macmillan Co., 1931.

Jefferson, Thomas. *The Writings of Thomas Jefferson*. Edited by H. A. Washington. New York: H. W. Derby, 1861.

Jenks, William, ed. *The Comprehensive Commentary on the Holy Bible*. Brattleboro: Brattleboro Typographic Co., 1838.

Jewish Encyclopedia. New York: Funk and Wagnalls Co., 1903.

Joachim of Floris. *Concordantia*. Edition of 1519.

Josephus, Flavius. "Antiquities of the Jews." *The Works of Flavius Josephus*. Translated by William Whiston. Standard edition. Philadelphia: The John C. Winston Co. [n.d.]

Keenan, Stephen. *A Doctrinal Catechism*. New York: Edward Dunigan and Bro., 1851.

Keith, Alexander. *The Signs of the Times*. Third edition. Edinburgh: William Whyte and Co., 1833.

Kenyon, Sir Frederick. *The Bible and Archaeology*. New York and London: Harper and Bros., 1940.

Kitto, John. *Cyclopædia of Biblical Literature*. London: Adam and Charles Black. [n.d.]

Kurtz, John Henry. *Manual of Sacred History*. Translated from the sixth German edition by Charles F. Schaeffer. Sixth edition. Philadelphia: Lindsay and Blakiston, 1860.

Labbe, P. and Cossart, G. *Sacrosancta Concilia*. Paris: Typographical Society, 1671.

Latourette, Kenneth Scott. *A History of the Expansion of Christianity*. New York: Harper and Bros., 1937.

Lecky, William Edward Hartpole. *History of the Rise and Influence of the Spirit of Rationalism in Europe*. London: Longman, Green, Longman, Roberts, and Green, 1865.

Lepicier, Alexius M. *The Stability and Progress of Dogma*. Rome, 1910.

Liddell, Henry G., and Scott, Robert. *A Greek-English Lexicon* . . . with corrections and additions by Henry Drisler. New York: Harper and Bros., 1860.

Liguori, Alphonsus de. *Dignity and Duties of the Priest*. Edited by Eugene Grimm. Brooklyn: Redemptorist Fathers, 1927.

Limborch, Philip. *The History of the Inquisition*. Translated into English by Samuel Chandler. London: J. Gray, 1731.

Litch, Josiah. *Prophetic Expositions*. Boston: Joshua V. Himes, 1842.

The Probability of the Second Coming of Christ About A. D. 1843. Boston: David H. Ela, 1838.

Lockhart, John Gibson. *The History of Napoleon Buonaparte*. New York: J. and J. Harper, 1833.

Luther, Martin. *The Familiar Discourses of Dr. Martin Luther*. Translated by Henry Bell. A new edition revised and corrected by Joseph Kerby. London: Baldwin, Craddock, and Joy, 1818.

McAllister, David. *The National Reform Movement, Its History and Principles*. Allegheny: Christian Statesman Co., 1898.

MACHIAVELLI, NICCOLO. *The History of Florence*. A new translation. London: Henry G. Bohn, 1854.

MADDEN, RICHARD ROBERT. *Travels in Turkey, Egypt, Nubia, and Palestine*. London: Henry Colburn, 1829.

MADELIN, LOUIS. *The French Revolution*. New York: Putnam's Sons, 1916.

MANNING, HENRY EDWARD CARDINAL. *The Temporal Power of the Vicar of Jesus Christ*. Second edition. London: Burns and Lambert, 1862.

MARTYN, W. CARLOS. *The Pilgrim Fathers of New England*. New York: The American Tract Society, 1867.

MERLE D'AUBIGNE, JEAN HENRI. *History of the Reformation of the Sixteenth Century*. Translated by H. White, and carefully revised. New York: Worthington Co. [pref. 1885.]

MILLER, WILLIAM. *Evidence From Scripture and History of the Second Coming of Christ About the Year 1843*. Second edition. Troy, N. Y.: Elias Gates, 1838.

MILMAN, HENRY HART. *History of Latin Christianity, Including That of the Popes to the Pontificate of Nicholas V*. Fourth edition. London: John Murray, 1883.

MOSES, WILLIAM STAINTON. *Spirit Teachings*. Seventh edition. London: London Spiritualist Alliance, 1912.

MOSHEIM, JOHN LAWRENCE. *An Ecclesiastical History, Ancient and Modern*. Translated by Archibald Maclaine. London: R. Baynes, 1819.

New International Encyclopedia. Second edition. New York: Dodd, Mead and Co., 1923.

NEWTON, SIR ISAAC. *Observations Upon the Prophecies of Daniel*. A new edition by P. Borthwick. London: James Nisbet, 1831.

NEWTON, THOMAS. *Dissertations on the Prophecies*. Tenth edition. London: F. C. and J. Rivington, et al., 1804.

NEWTON, WILLIAM. *Lectures on the First Two Visions of the Book of Daniel*. Philadelphia: William S. and Alfred Martien, 1859.

OMAN, CHARLES. *The Dark Ages, 476-918. Period I*. Third edition. London: Rivingtons, 1898.

OLMSTED, DENISON. *The Mechanism of the Heavens*. London: T. Nelson and Sons, 1853.

PERRY, WALTER C. *The Franks From Their First Appearance in History to the Death of King Pepin*. London: Longman, Brown, Green, Longmans, and Roberts, 1857.

PFLUGK-HARTTUNG, JULIUS VON. *A History of All Nations. The Early Middle Ages*. Translated under the supervision of John Henry Wright. Philadelphia: Lea Bros. and Co., 1902.

Pollok, Robert. *The Course of Time.* Boston: Phillips, Sampson, and Co., 1858.

Porter, David. *Constantinople and Its Environs.* New York: Harper and Bros., 1835.

Possinus, Petrus. *Observationum Pachymerianarum ad Historiam Rerum Michaelis Palæologi* in *Corpus Scriptorum Historiæ Byzantinæ,* "Georgius Pachymeres," Volumen Alternum. Bonnae: Impensis Ed. Weberi, 1835.

Powers, Harry Huntington. *The Things Men Fight For.* New York: The Macmillan Co., 1917.

Prideaux, Humphrey. *The Old and New Testament Connected in the History of the Jews and Neighboring Nations.* Fifteenth American, from the twentieth London edition. New York: Harper and Bros., 1842.

Ranke, Leopold. *The History of the Popes.* Translated by E. Foster. London: George Bell and Sons, 1889.

Rawlinson, George. *The Seven Great Monarchies of the Ancient Eastern World.* New York: John B. Alden, 1885.

Robinson, Nugent, comp. *A History of the World.* New York: P. F. Collier, 1887.

Rollin, Charles. *The Ancient History of the Egyptians, Carthaginians, Assyrians, Babylonians, Medes and Persians, Macedonians, and Grecians.* Translated from the French. Fifteenth edition. London: C. and J. Rivington, 1828.

Schaff, Philip. *History of the Christian Church.* Third revision. New York: Charles Scribner's Sons, 1903.

Scott, Thomas. *The New Testament of Our Lord and Saviour Jesus Christ . . . With Explanatory Notes.* Stereotype edition, carefully revised. Hartford: S. Andrus and Son, 1855.

Scott, Sir Walter. *The Life of Napoleon Buonaparte, Emperor of the French.* Philadelphia: Carey, Lea and Carey, 1827.

Sears, Robert. *Wonders of the World.* New York: Robert Sears, J. S. Redfield, Clinton Hall, 1843.

Seiss, Joseph A. *Lectures on the Apocalypse.* Twelfth edition. Philadelphia: Philadelphia School of the Bible. [n.d.]

Smith, Philip. *A History of the World From the Creation to the Fall of the Western Roman Empire.* New York: D. Appleton and Co., 1883.

Sorokin, Pitirim A. *Social and Cultural Dynamics.* New York: American Book Co., 1937.

Spofford, Ainsworth R., and Gibbon, Charles, eds. *The Library of Choice Literature.* Philadelphia: Gebbie and Co., 1882.

Stanley, Arthur Penrhyn. *Lectures on the History of the Eastern Church.* New York: Charles Scribner, 1862.

State Bar Association of Connecticut. *Annual Report, 1916.*

Strong, James. *A Concise Dictionary of the Words in the Greek Testament.* New York: Eaton and Mains, 1890. (Bound with Strong's *Exhaustive Concordance.*)

Stuart, Moses. *A Commentary on the Apocalypse.* New York: M. H. Newman, 1845.

Hints on the Interpretation of Prophecy. Andover: Allen, Morrill and Wardwell, 1842.

Taylor, D. T. *The Voice of the Church on the Coming Kingdom of the Redeemer* Revised and edited by H. L. Hastings. Seventh edition. Boston: H. L. Hastings, 1864.

Tenney, Samuel. In *Collections of Massachusetts Historical Society for the Year 1792.* Vol. I. Boston: 1792.

Thayer, Joseph Henry. *Greek-English Lexicon.* New York: Harper and Bros., 1894.

Theodoret and Evagrius. *A History of the Church, from A. D. 322 . . . to A. D. 427 by Theodoret, and from A. D. 431 to A. D. 594 by Evagrius.* Translated from the Greek. London: Henry G. Bohn, 1854. (Bohn's Ecclesiastical Library.)

Thompson, Augustus Charles. *Morning Hours in Patmos.* Boston: Gould and Lincoln, 1860.

Townsend, George Alfred. *The New World Compared With the Old.* Hartford, Conn.: S. M. Betts and Co., 1870.

Tregelles, S. P. *Remarks on the Prophetic Visions in the Book of Daniel.* Sixth edition. London: Samuel Bagster and Sons, 1883.

Tuberville, Henry. *An Abridgment of the Christian Doctrine.* New York: Edward Dunigan and Bros. [approved 1883.]

U. S. Congress. *The Debates and Proceedings in the Congress of the United States.* Washington: Gales and Seaton, 1834. (Annals of the Congress of the United States.)

U. S. Congress. Senate. Committee on the Judiciary. *Reorganization of the Federal Judiciary.* Hearings before the Committee on the Judiciary, U. S. Senate, Seventy-fifth Congress, First session, on S. 1392, A Bill to reorganize the Judicial branch of the Government. Part 3, March 22 to March 25, 1937. Washington: U. S. Government Printing Office, 1937.

U. S. House. "Sunday Mail." *U. S. House Reports.* Vol. II, No. 271.

U. S. House Reports, 43rd Congress, First Session, No. 143.

Watson, Richard. *A Biblical and Theological Dictionary.* Revised by the American editors. New York: B. Waugh and T. Mason, 1832.

Webster, Noah. "Vocabulary of the Names of Noted . . . Persons and Places." *An American Dictionary of the English Language.* Springfield, Mass.: G. and C. Merriam, 1882.

Wesley, John. *Explanatory Notes Upon the New Testament.* 1754.

Whalley, Albert. *The Red Letter Days of Israel.* London: Marshall Bros., 1926.

White, James. *History of France.* New York: D. Appleton and Co., 1870.

Whittier, John Greenleaf. *The Complete Works of John Greenleaf Whittier.* Cambridge edition. Boston: Houghton, Mifflin Co., 1894.

Wiesler, Karl. *A Chronological Synopsis of the Four Gospels.* Translated by Edmund Venables. Second edition, revised. London: George Bell and Sons, 1877. (Bohn's Theological Library.)

Williams, Samuel. In *Memoirs of the American Academy of Arts and Sciences.* Vol. I. Boston: Adams and Nourse, 1785.

Wilson, James. *The Works of the Honourable James Wilson.* Philadelphia: Bronson and Chauncey, 1804.

Wolff, Joseph. *Narrative of a Mission to Bokhara in the Years 1843-1845.* Fourth edition. London: John W. Parker, 1846.

Wylie, J. A. *The Papacy; Its History, Dogmas, Genius, and Prospects.* Edinburgh: Johnstone and Hunter, 1851.

MAGAZINES AND NEWSPAPERS

Cosmopolitan Magazine. May, 1909, Editor's note to p. 665.

Doyle, Sir Arthur Conan. "The New Revelation," *Metropolitan,* January, 1918, pp. 69, 75.

Firth, J. B. "The Partition of Asia," London *Fortnightly Review,* May, 1915.

Grey, Sir Edward. "Speech in the House of Commons," London *Times,* November 28, 1911.

Hutchins, Robert M. Quoted in "The Revolt Against Science," *The Christian Century,* January 24, 1934.

Moody, Dwight L. "Those Three Thousand Churches," New York *Independent,* December 3, 1896, p. 1.

Osgood, Phillips Endecott. "How Much Do You Help the Church?" *The Atlantic Monthly,* January, 1940, p. 56.

Randall, John Herman, Jr. "Effects of Science and Industry on Religion." *Current History,* June, 1929.

SMITH, KINGSBURY. New York *Journal and American*, Monday, January 17, 1938, p. 2.

STORRS, GEORGE. "Exposition of Revelation 22." *Midnight Cry*, May 4, 1843. Vol. IV, Nos. 5 and 6, p. 47.

SUMNER, CHARLES. Quoted in "Prophetic Voices About America," *The Atlantic Monthly*, September, 1867, p. 290.

WELCH, DALE D. "Real Issues and Great Choices." *The Presbyterian*, January 9, 1941, p. 3.

———. *Advent Herald*, December 14, 1850, p. 364.

———. Boston *Gazette*, May 29, 1780.

———. "Breadth of Christian Culture." *Congregationalist*, November 18, 1858, p. 186.

———. *Christian Statesman*, December 11, 1884, p. 2.

———. "Disarmament Labour Party's Motion," London *Times*, July 24, 1923, p. 7.

———. "Is It a Lost Cause?" *The Watchman-Examiner*, February 1, 1940, p. 105.

———. New York *Journal of Commerce*, November 14, 1833, Vol. VIII, No. 534, p. 2.

———. Philadelphia *Sun*, November 11, 1844.

———. "The Greatest of Questions." New York *Christian Advocate*, Thursday, August 30, 1883, p. 549.

———. "The People and Progress of the United States." *The United States Magazine of Science, Art, Manufactures, Agriculture, Commerce, and Trade*, Vol. II, August, 1855, p. 71.

———. "The Remedy." *Christian Palladium*, May 15, 1844, p. 409.

———. "To the Church of Methodists, Write!" Western *Christian Advocate*, July 18, 1893, p. 456.

———. "Turkey." London *Morning Chronicle*, September 3, 1840.

———. "Turkey." London *Morning Chronicle*, September 18, 1840.

———. "Great Spiritual Dearth," *Religious Telescope*, December 4, 1844, p. 76.

———. "Revivals." *Oberlin Evangelist*, November 20, 1844, p. 189.

———. "Will They Turn to Religion?" Philadelphia *Inquirer*, May 24, 1941, p. 10.

"Surely the Lord God will do nothing, but He revealeth His secret unto His servants the prophets."
Amos 3: 7.

SCRIPTURE INDEX

JOEL

HABAKKUK

ZECHARIAH

MALACHI

MATTHEW

"Believe in the Lord your God, so shall ye be established: believe His prophets, so shall ye prosper."
2 Chronicles 20: 20.

TOPICAL INDEX